D0802011

Baseball America
2021 ALMANAC

Editor
Chris Hilburn-Trenkle

Contributing Editors
Ben Badler, Teddy Cahill, Carlos Collazo, J.J. Cooper,
Matt Eddy, Josh Norris

Contributing Writers
Scott Miller, Harvey Sahker

Database and Application Development
Brent Lewis

Design & Production
CREATIVE DIRECTOR: James Alworth
GRAPHIC DESIGNER: Leah Tyner

Programming & Technical Development
Brent Lewis

Translation Assistance
Kelly Wong

Cover Photos
MAIN PHOTO: Mookie Betts.
PHOTO BY: Ronald Martinez/Getty Images

For additional copies, visit our Website at
BaseballAmerica.com or call 1-800-845-2726 to order.
US $22.95 / CAN $30.95, plus shipping and handling
per order. Expedited shipping available.
Distributed by Simon & Schuster.
ISBN-13: 978-1-7355482-0-3
Statistics provided by Major League Baseball Advanced Media
and Compiled by Baseball America.

EDITOR'S NOTE: Major league statistics are based on final, unofficial 2020 averages.

» The organization statistics, which begin on page 45, include all players who participated in at least one game during the 2020 season.

» Pitchers' batting statistics are not included, nor are the pitching statistics of field players who pitched in less than two games.

» For players who played with more than one team in the same league, the player's cumulative statistics appear on the line immediately after the player's statistics with each team.

TABLE OF CONTENTS

Mookie Betts

RONALD MARTINEZ/GETTY IMAGES

MAJOR LEAGUES

A Year Like No Other

BY SCOTT MILLER

Never before in 150 summers of professional baseball was there a season like 2020. And unless you were 102 years of age or older, you've never lived through a year like the one the world endured.

Oh, spring training started like it always does in February, with the Washington Nationals reporting to Florida as the defending World Series champions and 29 other clubs dreaming of taking their place. The sun was warm and optimism was high, everywhere. For those who inclined to keep up with the news as pitchers and catchers reported to Florida and Arizona, there was some distant chatter of something called the novel coronavirus that was rampaging through China, and world health experts were worriedly tracking it as it crossed borders, seas and air spaces.

Still, casual early-spring workouts moved into exhibition preparation and then into Cactus and Grapefruit League games. Even as things became more dire elsewhere, there was little thought that the United States was about to be swallowed whole by the first pandemic since the Spanish Flu raged across the country in 1918. Even then, in a 16-team league, everyone played somewhere between 123 and 131 games. Babe Ruth earned two victories on the mound while leading the Boston Red Sox to a World Series win over the Chicago Cubs. Yes, Boston's final title until the 2004 team finally smashed the legendary Curse of Babe Ruth.

Then came March 11, 2020: College basketball conference tournaments in full swing, a full slate of exhibition games, life moving ahead both as orderly and chaotic as usual when, just minutes before tipoff of an NBA game between Utah and Oklahoma City that night, league officials postponed the game when the Jazz's Rudy Gobert tested positive for the novel coronavirus.

Word crackled around the country like lightning, including into the Sloan Park press box of the Cubs, who were just about to begin a Cactus League game that evening against a San Diego Padres split-squad team. The game went on, but it was a sobering evening on which the clock suddenly began to move in slow motion. Within a couple of hours that evening, actor Tom Hanks tweeted from Australia that he and his wife, Rita, had contracted the virus.

Forget a buzz sweeping through the room,

Athletics manager Bob Melvin on March 12 addressed reporters regarding COVID-19.

CHRISTIAN PETERSEN/GETTY IMAGES

that evening a buzz swept through the world. On March 12, the college conference basketball tournaments began toppling like dominoes. And though Grapefruit and Cactus League games went on, overnight a feeling of inevitability had swept through the game that something was dramatically changing.

That morning, the Oakland A's stayed in their clubhouse for meetings rather than take the field for their workout. Manager Bob Melvin, addressing the looming thought that baseball, like the NBA, which immediately suspended its season indefinitely, soon would be facing an interruption in play said, "It's probably the prudent thing to do. I mean, this thing seems to be spreading and getting worse by the day. And, you know, something severe, you're probably better off taking care of it sooner than later."

In Arizona, the weather foretold what was coming on that Thursday. It was gray, cold, gloomy and rainy. The Cubs' game with the Dodgers was postponed, and shortly afterward came news that everything else would follow.

"We just all need to take precautions and be safe," Cubs' third baseman and union player representative Kris Bryant said. "I have a lot of family members who are older, too, and I'd love to keep them safe, and our fans and everyone around the game. It just shows that there are things bigger than baseball, and these are things we need to take very seriously."

Then on that cold, spring afternoon, Bryant was asked a question about what seemed like a far, far away worst-case scenario: What about the prospect of playing some games early in the season in empty stadiums with no fans in attendance?

"I keep saying it's people's safety and health that is the most important thing," Bryant said. "If we can find a way to not put people in jeopardy, that's what I'm all for.

"People's live mean more to me than baseball."

By that evening, commissioner Rob Manfred had ordered spring training suspended and the start of the regular season delayed by at least two weeks. Initially, players intended to stay put and work out in spring camps until this passed. As is often the case when life tosses a curveball, the thought was that sports could serve as a shelter in the storm.

But even in the digital age, what we would soon come to know as COVID-19 was moving too quickly for even the Internet. By the weekend, baseball ordered its spring facilities closed and players and club personnel scattered for what many figured would be just a couple of weeks.

It turned out to be more than four months.

Not until early July did 30 major league teams reconvene for the 2020 season. And when they did, it was a wholly different world, one in which we quickly learned who truly were the essential workers, how unimportant sports could suddenly feel in the midst of a world health crisis … and yet, how valuable baseball and the rest remained as an entertainment outlet.

When the game finally did return after four long months of virus-induced, world uncertainty and lockdown and hard negotiations between the players and owners, it was with a wholly different look that couldn't have been predicted even in the season's first iteration of spring training.

Clubs reconvened around the Fourth of July holiday for Spring Training 2.0, preparing for an abbreviated 60-game season. It would be the shortest MLB season ever played, and the quietest: With the pandemic raging across the country, federal and state health officials advised MLB that while the season could go on, it was not safe enough to allow in-stadium fans.

For those who perhaps still weren't inclined to take the virus seriously, there already were some prominent examples and learning opportunities. Atlanta star and BA Player of the Year Freddie Freeman was down with COVID-19 for nearly two weeks, reporting late to camp and nearly going to the hospital on July 3 with a fever of 104.5.

"That was the scariest night for me," Freeman told reporters upon his return. "… I said a little prayer that night, because I've never been that hot before. My body was really, really hot so I said, 'Please don't take me.' I wasn't ready."

The schedule was torn up and re-drawn as the first significant step in MLB working overtime to dodge the virus. Instead of the usual national travel, clubs instead were kept in their own geographic pods so as to eliminate long plane flights and minimize travel as much as possible while attempting to keep players and staff safe and healthy. Teams played only other clubs in their division for a total of 40 games. The other 20 games were interleague play scheduled against teams of the corresponding division in the other league. AL East teams played NL East teams, the Central played the Central and the West played the West.

Aside from the schedule, some rules were changed significantly, too, including more than the one rule that already had been implemented and caused a stir, a three-batter minimum for relief pitchers: Rosters were increased to 28, with each team maintaining a 30-man "taxi squad" that worked out and stayed ready in its home city since the minor league season was to be canceled entirely. For the first time ever the DH rule was implemented in the National League. For games that stretched beyond nine innings, all extra innings would begin with a runner on second base.

Manfred once had floated that last idea as a possible way to increase the pace of extra-inning games, but now it became more than simply a thought and carried with it a totally different reason: Nobody wanted one of those 18-inning games that went late into the night, chewed through a pitching staff and resulted in those overnight calls to summon pitching reinforcements to catch crack-of-dawn flights the next day and scramble to meet the team. One of the keys to playing through the virus was to keep players out of public airports and other public spaces as much as possible.

The biggest key to playing the season to completion, however, we soon learned, was for the game to stay more flexible and more fluid, even once the season started, than ever before.

This started on Opening Night, when, as a delicious pitching matchup between the Yankees' new marquee free agent Gerrit Cole (nine years, $324 million) and the defending world cham-

Commissioner Rob Manfred canceled spring training on March 12 due to the pandemic.

pion Nationals' Max Scherzer played out, MLB announced a late agreement with the players to expand the postseason to 16 teams from 10.

Part of this was designed as a way to incorporate more games including more teams in a season that was sure to be ending just when it had the feeling it was still beginning. Most of it, of course, was for the purpose of generating millions more dollars in postseason television money, a way to recoup some of the billions the owners and players were losing in a summer that saw the nation's unemployment rates balloon to the largest numbers since the Great Depression.

Baseball's adjusting-on-the-fly by necessity wouldn't stop by simply changing the postseason format even after the first pitch of the season. Despite mandating health protocols to cope with the coronavirus from the outset—significant COVID-19 testing so as to isolate those carrying the virus, players wearing masks in the clubhouse and in the dugouts, no spitting on the field, personnel divided into Tiers 1, 2 and 3 and extremely limited access to Tier 1 members (players), no media (Tier 3) in the clubhouse or even on the field—the game's worst fear came to fruition during the first weekend of the season when a COVID-19 outbreak struck the Miami Marlins.

Knowing it already was going to be a significant challenge to squeeze 60 games into a 63-day span

even under the best of circumstances, baseball quickly announced after the Marlins' outbreak that all doubleheaders would consist of two seven-inning games, rather than the traditional nine. Mostly, officials recognized, a schedule loaded with makeup doubleheaders could decimate a pitching staff. Also, looking for every possible angle to dodge the virus, officials wanted to limit time at the stadiums for all personnel.

The Marlins, who eventually had a total of 20 players and staff members test positive, quarantined in Philadelphia for several days and made flurries of roster moves while MLB moved some games around like checkers on a board. With the Phillies' season paused because of possible exposure to the virus by playing the Marlins, MLB re-directed the Yankees—who had not been exposed—from a scheduled series in Philadelphia to a series with Baltimore instead. And when the Marlins resumed play, a series with the Orioles was moved from Miami to Baltimore because the virus numbers in the Miami-area were blowing up.

Then the virus found the St. Louis Cardinals and embedded deeply enough into their clubhouse that the Cardinals' were on ice 16 days with 18 positive tests among players and staff members. When they finally emerged and their schedule was re-drawn, the Cardinals were to play 11 doubleheaders and an exhausting total of 53 games in 44 days—starting with a trip to Chicago, for which the Cards rented 41 vehicles and everyone drove individually, as if back in American Legion days.

Even at that, one doubleheader against Detroit that had been postponed was left in limbo as it was decided that one would only be played if it had a direct bearing on either team's playoff situation (it didn't, it wasn't played and the Cardinals finished at 58 games).

The Cards' run of games wasn't unprecedented, but it was close: According to the Elias Sports Bureau, the last team to endure a similar schedule was the 1975 Minnesota Twins, who played 54 games over 48 days, including 11 doubleheaders.

The outbreaks, especially within the first 10 days of the schedule, immediately caused concern that the 2020 season would be over for baseball practically before it had started. They also created an atmosphere of distrust: Were the players on those teams following health protocols as rigorously as expected? As more questions were asked, those under fire lashed back.

"I think it's incredible how people are just, like, looking to find this answer, as if to create this

CONTINUED ON PAGE 11

ALEX TRAUTWIG/GETTY IMAGES

PLAYER OF THE YEAR

Mr. Consistent Bags His Best Year To Date

BY GABE BURNS

The biggest home run Freddie Freeman hit this season came July 17, one week before Opening Day. When the Braves held their first team workouts on July 3, they did so without their all-star first baseman and franchise pillar. Freeman had tested positive for COVID-19, adding further uncertainty to a season that many in the industry, including Braves manager Brian Snitker, were skeptical would finish.Hours before Snitker informed reporters of Freeman's status on July 4, Freeman was laying in his bed, drenched in sweat and praying for his life. His fever peaked at 104.5 degrees."I said a little prayer that night," Freeman recalled. "I've never been that hot before. My body was really, really hot. So I said, 'Please don't take me.' I wasn't ready. It got a little worrisome that night."That evening was the worst of Freeman's COVID-19 experience. His fever dropped when he woke the next morning. He was finally fever-free on July 6, though he didn't regain a sense of taste or smell until days later. July 9 was Freeman's final day feeling symptoms. Being symptom-free didn't clear him to rejoin the team, however. He still needed consecutive negative tests to return.

The Braves readied to start without their best player. On July 16, Snitker said they would "need to make a decision soon."

The next morning around 9:15 a.m., Braves trainer George Poulis called Freeman. "You hit a home run," he said.

Freeman had registered the back-to-back

Freddie Freeman led the majors in doubles (23) and runs (51) en route to his first MVP.

negatives needed to rejoin the team. Around 2 p.m., Freeman was at Truist Park working out. The rest of the Braves were off that day, but some of the coaches were available to assist him. Freeman admitted he felt sore after hitting, running and fielding, but he was euphoric to be back with the team.

Exactly two weeks after fearing for his life, he was preparing to face reigning Cy Young Award winner Jacob deGrom and the Mets.

"You forget sometimes how much you love this game when it gets taken away from you," Freeman said. "I really did truly miss it."

Always Mr. Consistent, Freeman reached the best level of his career. He hit .341/.462/.640 with 13 home runs, 53 RBIs and 51 runs while playing 60 games. He led the National League with 23 doubles. He added his usual Gold Glove-caliber defense at first base.

Most importantly, as he would tell you: The Braves went 35-25, earning their third consecutive NL East division title.Freeman capped his MVP candidacy on Sept. 25, when his 11th-inning, walk-off homer clinched the No. 2 playoff seed for the Braves. He had entered the game as a pinch-hitter.

For what he overcame and for what he achieved in 2020, he is truly deserving of the distinction Major League Player of The Year.

PREVIOUS POY WINNERS

2010: Roy Halladay, RHP, Phillies
2011: Matt Kemp, OF, Dodgers
2012: Mike Trout, OF, Angels
2013: Mike Trout, OF, Angels
2014: Clayton Kershaw, LHP, Dodgers
2015: Bryce Harper, OF, Nationals
2016: Mike Trout, OF, Angels
2017: Jose Altuve, 2B, Astros
2018: Mike Trout, OF, Angels
2019: Justin Verlander, RHP, Astros

Full list: BaseballAmerica.com/awards

blame game," John Mozeliak, the Cardinals' president of baseball operations, said on a videoconference call during his team's shutdown. "And so I find that rather sickening and annoying.

"We're in the pandemic, the likelihood of where someone could have gotten this could be anywhere from a grocery store, to a bar, and everywhere in between. But trying to determine that I don't think is very helpful. And even if I knew, I probably would not say publicly. I wouldn't want somebody brandished with that label."

Baseball investigated both the Marlins' and Cardinals' outbreaks not for the purpose of punishment, but to learn where the health protocols might be failing. Some things were tightened immediately, such as a team-designated "compliance officer" traveling with the club to ensure that rules were being followed and ensure that while traveling, players would not leave the road hotel property without a valid excuse. Meals were prepared for players at the hotel and either picked up at a designated area and taken back to a players' room for consumption or simply delivered to the players' room. Even once-innocent morning trips to get coffee became verboten.

Remarkably, once baseball navigated past the Marlins' and Cardinals' outbreaks, the game was able to successfully dodge the virus in enough places to conclude the 60-game season on schedule, in late September.

It was an enormous credit to all involved: The game's owners and officials, who were responsible for salvaging what they could of the season and creating this giant labyrinth of paths and health protocols, and the players, who exhibited perhaps more self-discipline and respect for the game than perhaps they even realized.

By mid-October, during the ALCS and NLCS, MLB announced that for the season, out of 169,143 tests, just 91 had come back as new positives. Of those, 57 were players and 34 were staff members. In all, nine of the 30 clubs went the entire season without a positive test.

In the end, in many ways it was a far more difficult season than any other despite the fact that barely more than one-third of a normal season's schedule was played.

"The year's been difficult, I'm not going to sugarcoat it," Houston pitcher Lance McCullers Jr. said during the playoffs. "With the COVID, all of the protocols, the ups and downs of the season … it was a difficult year."

And even that may have been a giant understatement as everyone looked toward 2021 in fervent hope that some normalcy would return.

New Era of Moneyball

Looming in the background even before the pandemic struck was the fact that the current Basic Agreement between the players and owners, which has guaranteed a run of 25 years' worth of labor peace, was set to expire following the 2021 season.

Yet one of the byproducts of the coronavirus was to place an unintended spotlight on a rift between the two sides that has been expanding since the last Basic Agreement was locked in and, in the players'

CONTINUED ON PAGE 13

AMERICAN LEAGUE STANDINGS

East	W	L	PCT	GB	Manager	General Manager	Finish	Last Penn.
Tampa Bay Rays	40	20	.667	---	Kevin Cash	Erik Neander	1st	2020
New York Yankees	33	27	.550	7	Aaron Boone	Brian Cashman	6th	2009
Toronto Blue Jays	32	28	.533	8	Charlie Montoyo	Ross Atkins	7th	1993
Baltimore Orioles	25	35	.417	15	Brandon Hyde	Mike Elias	12th	1983
Boston Red Sox	24	36	.400	16	Ron Roenicke	Brian O'Halloran	13th	2018

Central	W	L	PCT	GB	Manager	General Manager	Finish	Last Penn.
Minnesota Twins	36	24	.600	---	Rocco Baldelli	Thad Levine	2nd	1991
Cleveland Indians	35	25	.583	1	Terry Francona	Mike Chernoff	4th	2016
Chicago White Sox	35	25	.583	1	Rick Renteria	Rick Hahn	4th	2005
Kansas City Royals	26	34	.433	10	Mike Matheny	Dayton Moore	10th	2015
Detroit Tigers	23	35	.397	12	Ron Gardenhire	Al Avila	14th	2012

West	W	L	PCT	GB	Manager	General Manager	Finish	Last Penn.
Oakland Athletics	36	24	.600	---	Bob Melvin	David Forst	2nd	1990
Houston Astros	29	31	.483	7	Dusty Baker	James Click	8th	2019
Seattle Mariners	27	33	.450	9	Scott Servais	Jerry Dipoto	9th	Never
Los Angeles Angels	26	34	.433	10	Joe Maddon	Billy Eppler	10th	2002
Texas Rangers	22	38	.367	14	Chris Woodward	Jon Daniels	15th	2011

Wild Card Series: Rays defeated Blue Jays 2-0, Yankees defeated Indians 2-0, Astros defeated Twins 2-0 and Athletics defeated White Sox 2-1 in best-of-three series. **Division Series:** Rays defeated Yankees 3-2 and Astros defeated Athletics 3-1 in best-of-five series. **Championship Series:** Rays defeated Astros 4-3 in a best-of-seven series.

ROOKIE OF THE YEAR

Gonsolin Edges Out Strong Field

BY J.J. COOPER

Baseball America has never had a tougher time picking its Rookie of the Year. That's not to say picking the top rookie is ever easy.

We choose one overall major league winner across both leagues, so the field is often crowded. We struggle each year to compare the value of pitchers with hitters, and we debate the merits of quick bursts of production versus larger samples of playing time.

The final weight we apply to our award is future value. We want our winner to appear wise in the decades to come. The 2009 rookie class is instructive. Chris Coghlan won the baseball writers' National League award, while BA selected Andrew McCutchen as its Rookie of the Year. Both players had seasons of equivalent value, but nobody would disagree that McCutchen had more long-term value.

Because of the 60-game season in 2020, the degree of difficulty for balancing rookie performance with future value was amplified. BA has never chosen a position player as its Rookie of the Year who played 60 games or fewer—or a pitcher on the basis of just two months of work. If 2020 were a normal season, every one of our ROY candidates would have received an "incomplete." Sample size matters, especially for rookies, because a month or two is not long enough to get a full reading on a player. Is a great month a hot streak? Is a bad month a sign of a long-term issue or just a dip before an adjustment?

In the end, we chose Dodgers righthander Tony Gonsolin as our Rookie of the Year. His combination of present performance and future outlook separated him from the field, if barely. Gonsolin was late to summer camp in July after testing positive for COVID-19. The setback meant he got a late start and began the season at the Dodgers' alternate training site. He thinks the test might have been a false positive. Regardless, he was out of rhythm when Opening Day arrived. From Gonsolin's first start on July 31 to the end of the season, he reeled off a string of solid outings.

Tony Gonsolin posted a 2.31 ERA and 0.84 WHIP in nine appearances (eight starts).

He tallied 16.2 scoreless innings to start the season. Among all pitchers with at least 40 innings, rookies and veterans alike, he ranked 11th in ERA (2.31), fourth in WHIP (0.84), eighth in home run rate (0.39 per nine innings) and ninth in both walk rate (1.4 per nine) and strikeout-to-walk ratio (6.57).

Opponents hit just .193/.229/.289. Gonsolin keeps hitters from getting comfortable with his plus command and control and his ability to attack different quadrants of the strike zone. He can both elevate and work down in the zone with his mid-90s fastball, while his split-changeup and slider are effective down in the zone as swing-and-miss pitches.

Given what he has shown in the big leagues, he should be a rotation stalwart for the Dodgers for years to come.

Gonsolin earned Rookie of the Year honors, even if we wish we had gotten to watch him pitch for a few more months.

PREVIOUS ROY WINNERS

2010: Jason Heyward, OF, Braves
2011: Jeremy Hellickson, RHP, Rays
2012: Mike Trout, OF, Angels
2013: Jose Fernandez, RHP, Marlins
2014: Jose Abreu, 1B, White Sox
2015: Kris Bryant, 3B, Cubs
2016: Corey Seager, SS, Dodgers
2017: Aaron Judge, OF, Yankees
2018: Shohei Ohtani, RHP/DH, Angels
2019: Pete Alonso, 1B, Mets

Full list: BaseballAmerica.com/awards

view, the free-agent market has become chillier.

The four months' of negotiating it took to get there, unscheduled and unexpected talks fraught with leaks from both sides, became an ugly spectacle that was tone-deaf and unnecessarily risked alienating a significant portion of the game's fans, many of whom already were dealing with illness, job loss, depression and anxiety.

Initially, the players and owners worked out the early logistics of suspending spring training and how to re-start the season without too much difficulty. One of the key early items: Owners agreed to grant players full service time for the year no matter how fractional the season became. This would be based on 2019: All players who played a full season then would be credited for a full year in '20 no matter how many games were lost to the virus. Others qualifying who didn't play a full year in '19 would accrue an equivalent amount of service time from that year in '20 depending whether they stuck in the majors.

Significantly, the owners also agreed in late March to a $170 million salary advance to the players.

The problem came when negotiations picked back up later in the spring and early summer to re-start the season when it became apparent that the virus and the calendar would not allow for a 162-game schedule and owners, claiming billions of dollars in lost revenue, wanted the players to accept deeper salary cuts.

Based on the first agreement, the players would be paid 100% of their salary prorated based on a per-game basis. If 80 games were played, for example, then the players would be paid their full per-game salary for 80 games.

But the owners and players couldn't agree on what they purportedly first agreed on: The owners said it was understood they would go back in and negotiate further once the virus cleared enough that they could read the landscape; the players said no dice.

As 2018 AL Cy Young winner Blake Snell said on his Twitch channel: "For me to take a pay cut is not happening, because the risk is through the roof. It's a shorter season, less pay. No, I gotta get my money. I'm not playing unless I get mine, OK? And that's just the way it is for me. Like, I'm sorry you guys think differently, but the risk is way the hell higher and the amount of money I'm making is way lower. Why would I think about doing that?"

Snell was scheduled to make $7 million in 2020, and he stood as an example as to how the sliding-scale salary structure would affect players.

Neither side would budge, so eventually it came down to how many games would be played: Fewer games, the owners could dole out less salary. The players wanted more games so they could earn more. Even this became dicey: One of the owners' proposals that included a suggestion on how to divide up salaries was based on the low-end of the structure. Because of the $170 million salary advance awarded earlier, owners were aware of the fact that the younger, low-salaried players who were due to make around the MLB minimum of $563,500 would have already been paid and would essentially be playing the short season without any

NATIONAL LEAGUE STANDINGS

East	W	L	PCT	GB	Manager	General Manager	Finish	Last Penn.
Atlanta Braves	35	25	.583	---	Brian Snitker	Alex Anthopoulos	3rd	1999
Miami Marlins	31	29	.517	4	Don Mattingly	Michael Hill	5th	2003
Philadelphia Phillies	28	32	.467	7	Joe Girardi	Matt Klentak	10th	2009
New York Mets	26	34	.433	9	Luis Rojas	Brodie Van Wagenen	11th	2015
Washington Nationals	26	34	.433	9	Dave Martinez	Mike Rizzo	11th	2019

Central	W	L	PCT	GB	Manager	General Manager	Finish	Last Penn.
Chicago Cubs	34	26	.567	---	David Ross	Jed Hoyer	4th	2016
St. Louis Cardinals	30	28	.517	3	Mike Shildt	Mike Girsch	5th	2013
Cincinnati Reds	31	29	.517	3	David Bell	Nick Krall	5th	1990
Milwaukee Brewers	29	31	.483	5	Craig Counsell	David Stearns	8th	1982 (AL)
Pittsburgh Pirates	19	41	.317	15	Derek Shelton	Ben Cherington	15th	1979

West	W	L	PCT	GB	Manager	General Manager	Finish	Last Penn.
Los Angeles Dodgers	43	17	.717	---	Dave Roberts	Andrew Friedman	1st	2020
San Diego Padres	37	23	.617	6	Jayce Tingler	A.J. Preller	2nd	1998
San Francisco Giants	29	31	.483	14	Gabe Kapler	Scott Harris	8th	2014
Colorado Rockies	26	34	.433	17	Bud Black	Jeff Bridich	11th	2007
Arizona Diamondbacks	25	35	.417	18	Torey Lovullo	Mike Hazen	14th	2001

Wild Card Series: Dodgers defeated Brewers 2-0, Padres defeated Cardinals 2-1, Marlins defeated Cubs 2-0 and Braves defeated Reds 2-0 in best-of-three series. **Division Series:** Dodgers defeated Padres 3-0 and Braves defeated Marlins 3-0 in best-of-five series. **Championship Series:** Dodgers defeated Braves 4-3 in a best-of-seven series.

paychecks.

By mid-June, the bickering was thick enough that the players cut off negotiations. Players' Union director Tony Clark concluded a statement with the memorable line, "Unfortunately, [it] appears that further dialogue with the league would be futile. It's time to get back to work. Tell us when and where."

That became the players' battle cry, , with several hashtagging it on social media: "#WhenAnd Where." Ending negotiations and forcing Manfred to unilaterally implement a season allowed the Union to retain its right to file a grievance in the future alleging the owners did not bargain in good faith.

Manfred did implement a season, and finally the game could get back to focusing on the stuff between the baselines instead of in the tiresome contract proposals.

"It was disappointing. It was embarrassing at times. ... There is no trust [between MLB and the MLB Players' Association] ... is the best way to put it," Miami CEO Derek Jeter said during a video appearance for Marlins' fans. "Hopefully things will change moving forward. It was pretty sad to see the back and forth being played out publicly at a time like now. So many people filing for unemployment throughout the country—over 30 million people, 40 million people with no jobs. They really don't want to hear owners and players going back and forth about how much money they deserve and how much money they need.

"I get it. I was a player. I feel as though players should fight for everything that they feel as though they should have. I'll always support them in that sense. But in this particular case, I think something should have been done behind the scenes."

Meanwhile, the business of baseball appeared to be booming despite the pandemic on one front: The league reached a seven-year extension with Turner Sports worth approximately $3.75 billion, according to Sports Businenss Daily. The deal starts in 2022 and runs through 2028 with the annual amount working out to some $535 million. All told, a 65 percent increase over the current eight-year, $2.6 billion Turner Sports deal.

For some clubs, money remained no object. On July 22, the eve of their season opener, the Los Angeles Dodgers announced they had reached a long-term extension with star outfielder Mookie Betts. The deal, for 12 years and $365 million, cements the future of the core player for the Dodgers over the next decade or more.

It was the fitting conclusion of a blockbuster trade with Boston for the 2018 AL Most Valuable

The Astros faced scrutiny and questions regarding their 2017 sign-stealing scandal.

MICHAEL REAVES/GETTY IMAGES

Player.

The Red Sox had been unable to sign Betts to a long-term, franchise-player deal and he had just one more season left before free agency. Using their financial capital, the Dodgers packaged outfielder Alex Verdugo along with infield prospect Jeter Downs and catching prospect Connor Wong to acquire Betts along with lefthanded starter David Price, absorbing $48 of the $93 million still owed to Price on the final two years of his deal.

Tarnished Astros

One thing the pandemic did was quickly divert attention away from the Houston Astros, who were the focal point for all the wrong reasons.

Long suspected by many in the game of perfecting some form of digital cheating, the Astros' cover was blown wide open by an investigation published by The Athletic in November 2019, the ramifications of which bled all the way into the start of 2020.

Whistleblower, veteran pitcher and ex-Astro Mike Fiers detailed an elaborate sign-stealing scheme during Houston's World Series championship season of 2017 in which a strategically placed camera in center field at Minute Maid Park was trained on the opposing catcher. The live footage was then relayed in real time to a television just off the dugout behind the Astros' dugout.

Team employees were stationed to watch the television and decode signs. As they did, they would bang on a trash can, usually to signal an offspeed pitch. If there were no bangs, in most

ALL-ROOKIE TEAM 2020

Pos	Player, Team	Age	AB	AVG	OBP	SLG	2B	HR	RBI	SB	Rundown
C	Sean Murphy, Athletics	25	116	.233	.364	.457	5	7	14	0	Led all rookie catchers with 7 HRs and 14 RBIs
1B	Jared Walsh, Angels	26	99	.293	.324	.646	4	9	26	0	Ranked second among qualified rookies in OPS (.970)
2B	Jake Cronenworth, Padres	26	172	.285	.354	.477	15	4	20	3	Led all rookies in extra-base hits (22), sixth in OPS (.831)
3B	Alec Bohm, Phillies	23	160	.338	.400	.481	11	4	23	1	Ranked top five among rookies in hits (54), doubles (11)
SS	Willi Castro, Tigers	23	129	.349	.381	.550	4	6	24	0	Had more multi-hit games (13) than hitless games (8)
OF	Kyle Lewis, Mariners	25	206	.262	.364	.437	3	11	28	5	Led all rookies in runs (37), tied for first in HRs (11)
OF	Luis Robert, White Sox	22	202	.233	.302	.436	8	11	31	9	Led all rookies in stolen bases (9), tied for first in HRs (11)
OF	Ryan Mountcastle, Orioles	23	126	.333	.386	.492	5	5	23	0	Ranked top 10 among rookies in hits (42) and HRs (5)
DH	Ke'Bryan Hayes, Pirates	23	85	.376	.442	.682	7	5	11	1	Finished tied for sixth among 3B in defensive runs saved

Pos	Pitcher, Team	Age	W	L	SV	ERA	IP	SO	BB	Rundown
SP	Dustin May, Dodgers	22	3	1	0	2.57	56	44	16	2.57 ERA ranked first among rookies who pitched 50 innings
SP	David Peterson, Mets	24	6	2	0	3.44	50	40	24	Ranked first among rookie starting pitchers in WAR (1.5)
SP	Tony Gonsolin, Dodgers	26	2	2	0	2.31	47	46	7	Led qualified rookies in WHIP (0.84), third in ERA (2.31)
SP	Cristian Javier, Astros	23	5	2	0	3.48	54	54	18	Ranked third among qualified rookies in WHIP (0.99)
SP	Brady Singer, Royals	23	4	5	0	4.06	64	61	23	Led all rookies in strikeouts (61), innings pitched (64.1)
RP	Devin Williams, Brewers	25	4	1	0	0.33	27	53	9	Ranked first among qualified pitchers in strikeout rate (53%)

cases the Houston hitter could load up expecting a fastball.

A subsequent MLB investigation revealed the Astros cheated all the way through the 2017 season, including the postseason, and also in 2018. Astros' general manager Jeff Luhnow and manager A.J. Hinch each was suspended for a year, the Astros were stripped of their first- and second-round picks in both the 2020 and 2021 amateur drafts and the organization was fined $5 million, the maximum allowable. Owner Jim Crane, whom the MLB report claimed was unaware of the cheating, fired both Luhnow and Hinch shortly after the report was made public.

Outrage gripped the game, especially in Los Angeles, where the Dodgers and their fans immediately said this essentially meant that they would have, and should have, been world champions in '17 but for Houston's cheating.

Meanwhile, players throughout the game were enraged that none of the Astros players was punished. As part of the investigation and while attempting to learn how pervasive electronic thievery is throughout the game in an age in which every team even has MLB-issued iPads in the dugout during games, Manfred granted the Houston players full immunity from punishment in a bid to learn the unvarnished truth.

Consequently, as players throughout the game poured into spring training in February, many of them lined up to whack the Astros like a piñata at a birthday party.

"Everyone knows they stole the ring from us," Dodgers outfielder Cody Bellinger, the 2019 NL MVP, told reporters in Arizona.

"I feel like every single guy over there needs a beating," Atlanta outfielder Nick Markakis said. "It's wrong. They're messing with people's careers."

The Astros didn't curry any public sympathy throughout the trashing because they offered either no apologies or half-hearted ones. Crane ducked responsibility, saying he didn't think he should be held accountable, on the day the Commissioner's Report came out and then denied the cheating impacted the '17 World Series during a news conference on the first day the Astros' full-squad worked out at their spring training site in West Palm Beach, Fla.

That, and the fact that the national media mob was camped out with the Astros, just a few hundred yards away from the Nationals' side of their shared complex, did not sit well with the defending champions' general manager, Mike Rizzo.

"The Commissioner did an investigation and found that they cheated in 2017 and 2018," Rizzo told reporters. "Somebody has got to say the word over there: Cheated. That's important to me."

Aside from criticism over not punishing the Astros players, Manfred also was put on the defensive by those who demanded that he strip the franchise of the World Series title in '17, or questioned why he hadn't. And at a spring training press conference in Arizona, he only turned up the heat when he said, "the idea of an asterisk or asking for a piece of metal back seems futile."

The Dodgers became even more livid, with Justin Turner shooting back, "For him to devalue it the way he did yesterday just tells me how out of touch he is with the players in this game. At this point the only thing devaluing that trophy is that it says 'Commissioner' on it."

Because the Astros were not scheduled for any interleague games in Dodger Stadium, a couple of hundred Dodgers fans purchased tickets to go boo them in Anaheim when they played their first series of the season there in early April. Of course, that series and everything else in April, May and June was wiped out because of the coronavirus.

And when baseball did re-emerge in July, the irony was that the only silver lining in playing in empty ballparks came for the game's biggest villains: The Astros would not have to listen to the jeers and catcalls of the haters all summer long.

Already having lost Cole to the Yankees via free agency, the Astros absorbed another blow after ace Justin Verlander made just one start and headed to the injured list, lost for the season to Tommy John surgery.

At one point using nine rookie pitchers on their staff, the Astros suffered the ignominy of finishing 29-31 and becoming the first American League team to qualify for the playoffs with a sub-.500 record. However, they dispatched Minnesota, Oakland and then stormed back from a three-game deficit and forced No. 1 seed Tampa Bay to a Game 7 before losing while playing in their fourth consecutive ALCS.

The fallout from their cheating scandal also rippled into Boston, where the Red Sox fired manager Alex Cora just before spring training for his involvement in the scheme, and New York, where the Mets axed their new manager Carlos Beltran, who was a veteran player on the '17 team who was fingered as one of the instigators.

As for the Astros, with Cole gone and Verlander injured, it sure seems like you can see the end of their run from here: George Springer, Michael Brantley and Josh Reddick all were eligible for free agency following the '20 season, while Lance McCullers Jr., Carlos Correa, Aledmys Diaz and closer Roberto Osuna all were eligible for arbitration.

Demanding Justice

High emotions continued to crest through the turbulent summer, and they went far beyond the Houston cheating scandal and the tortured negotiations between the owners and the players.

Protests raged in cities all across the country following the killing of George Floyd by Minneapolis police on May 25 after his arrest for allegedly using a counterfeit bill, and in the continuing aftermath of the death of Breonna Taylor, who was killed when plainclothes Louisville police officers stormed her apartment in a raid gone wrong in March. On June 14 a young Black man was shot to death by Atlanta police in a fast food parking lot, and then came the police shooting of Jacob Blake in Kenosha, Wis., in late August.

Following the death of Blake, a shortened baseball season already delayed at the start paused again

The fallout from the Astros sign-stealing scandal led to Alex Cora's one-year ouster.

MADDIE MEYER/GETTY IMAGES

when multiple games were postponed on Aug. 26, when players balked at playing. In Los Angeles, Mookie Betts first made the decision to sit out and his Dodgers' teammates quickly rallied around him and voted not to play.

When more players decided to sit out, seven more MLB games were postponed the next day, including Colorado-Arizona, Oakland-Texas, Minnesota-Detroit, Boston-Toronto, Tampa Bay-Baltimore, Philadelphia-Washington and New York Mets-Miami.

At Citi Field, following a 42-second moment of silence before the Mets-Marlins game in deference to Jackie Robinson Day, which was to be celebrated on Friday, the teams walked off the field after the moment and, as he left, Miami outfielder Lewis Brinson covered home plate with a Black Lives Matter T-shirt.

In Buffalo, where the Red Sox game with the Blue Jays was postponed, Boston manager Ron Roenicke was especially emotional in putting his team's protest—and, really, the two days' worth—into words.

"If you're a kid and you turn on the TV tonight and you don't see that we're playing, and you asked your parents, 'Why aren't the Red Sox playing?' I hope the parents have a serious discussion with their kids and tell them what's going on, or explain what's going on," Roenicke said. "Because we need to discuss these things more, we need to listen more. And that's the only way that we're going to change."

Until these protests, former Oakland catcher Bruce Maxwell had been the only MLB player ever to protest social injustices and police brutality publicly, when, Colin Kaepernick-like, he took a knee during the national anthem on Sept. 23, 2017.

"Even my mother called and said it's amazing seeing all these people message you and sharing your photo and who want you to talk here and there, and three years ago nobody was to be found," said Maxwell, who started the summer playing professionally in Mexico before signing a minor league deal with the Mets.

In a statement issued on July 3, the Cleveland organization publicly announced that it is considering changing its nickname and going away from "Indians", a move that now is widely expected within the next couple of years. Atlanta appears intent on keeping the name "Braves."

Meanwhile, the Baseball Writers' Association of America announced that 89% of its members voted to remove the name of Judge Kenesaw Mountain Landis from its Most Valuable Player awards after more than 75 years. Landis never had a Black player in the majors during his long reign as commissioner.

Generation Next

Compared to the normal 162-game schedule, the 60-game sprint seemed to finish in the blink of an eye. But one enormous recent trend continued: The all-or-nothing approach of today's hitters and the power games of today's pitchers.

The per-team rate of clubbing 1.28 home runs per game was the second-highest in history, trailing only that of 2019. In fact, five of the six highest per-game totals have been posted within the past six years. Launch angles continue to rule as players flock to their private hitting instructors during the winter and show up in the spring ready to mash.

Meanwhile, the strikeout rate reached another all-time high, for the first time averaging more than one an inning at 9.1.

Overall, 36% of all plate appearances ended with a strikeout, walk or home run. In turn, singles, triples, sacrifice hits, sacrifice flies and intentional walks all dipped to all-time per-game lows. And as on-base percentage has usurped batting average as the go-to indicator, batting average continues to recede as yesterday's news: This year's .245 mark was the lowest batting average since the DH first was introduced in 1973. The last time it was below .245? Try 1972, when MLB hitters batted .244.

Meantime, the emphasis of launch angle combined with the ongoing proliferation of defensive shifts helped sabotage batting average on balls in play as well, which, at .292, registered at its lowest since 1992.

As the years progress, 200 should also be known for the exciting breakouts of the San Diego Padres and Chicago White Sox, two of the game's most exciting young teams who appear to be at the very beginning of a good run of success.

The Padres, who made the playoffs for the first time since 2006 and finished with a winning record, 37-23, for the first time since 2010, saw years of rebuilding and stockpiling young talent pay off with the continued emergence of budding superstar Fernando Tatis Jr., the dominance of starter Dinelson Lamet, the re-emergence of Manny Machado, Eric Hosmer and Wil Myers and smart trades for Jake Cronenworth, Tommy Pham, Trent Grisham and Mike Clevinger.

The White Sox were buoyed by an MVP-caliber season from Jose Abreu, the steady excellence of Tim Anderson, the electricity of Luis Robert, Eloy Jimenez and Yoan Moncada, Nick Madrigal and the arms of Lucas Giolito, who fired a no-hitter, and up-and-coming youngsters Dylan Cease and Dane Dunning.

The Sox's Robert and the Padres' Cronenworth led a pack of talented rookies who flashed enough excitement to leave us wanting more—more than at any time in the past few generations. With only a 60-game season, not only did their talents flash meteorically across the horizon, but they also will enter 2021 naturally needing to prove that they've got the stamina to keep playing like they did over a full schedule.

Seattle center fielder Kyle Lewis was marvelous on both sides of the ball (he led all rookies with 90 total bases and was a defensive gem), Milwaukee's Devin Williams was like the second coming of Josh Hader given his off-the-charts strikeout rate (he fanned 53 of 100 batters faced), righthanders Dustin May and Tony Gonsolin were key parts of the Dodgers' changing of the guard, Pirates third baseman Ke'Bryan Hayes didn't say hello until Sept. 1 yet still ranked second in total bases among all rookie third basemen, Phillies third sacker Alec Bohm was second in on-base percentage among all qualified rookies and Braves righthander Ian Anderson stepped up when Atlanta suffered key rotation injuries to Mike Soroka and Cole Hamels throughout the season.

CONTINUED ON PAGE 19

ORGANIZATION OF THE YEAR

Dodgers Are Game's Model Franchise

BY BILL PLUNKETT

It's good to be rich. Always has been.

As one of baseball's blue-chip franchises, the Dodgers have never been short on resources. The club plays in 58-year-old Dodger Stadium, one of baseball's crown jewels that fills with nearly four million fans a year and cashes a fat check annually from one of the richest TV deals in professional sports.

But to be rich and smart, that's when special things can happen. That combination produces things like three National League pennants in four years, a World Series title and a second Organization of the Year award from Baseball America in that four-year span.

"Organization of the Year is an incredible honor," Dodgers team president and CEO Stan Kasten said of his franchise winning the honor for 2020. "To do that in a year when we won the World Series, to do that in a year when we are also the ESPN Humanitarian Team of the Year, to do that in a year when we are also hosting the largest Covid testing site in America (in the parking lots outside Dodger Stadium), to do that in a year when we opened up the stadium to a massive voting center—these are things that make me very, very proud of our organization."

Kasten is justifiably proud of the way the Dodgers met the challenges of an unprecedented season.

On the field, no team was better. Their 43-17 record in the shortened regular season translates to 116 wins in the standard 162-game season. In the postseason, they went 13-5, dispatching the Rays, Padres and Braves, the teams that had the second-, third- and fourth-best

Stan Kasten presided over the Dodgers' first World Series title in 32 years.

ALEX TRAUTWIG/MLB PHOTOS VIA GETTY IMAGES

records in baseball along the way to their first World Series title in 32 years.

The Dodgers defeated the Rays in six games in the World Series with a roster that featured more homegrown players than any other team in the postseason.

NLCS and World Series MVP Corey Seager was the Dodgers' first-rounder in 2012. Pitching hero Julio Urias was signed out of Mexico that same summer. So was Victor Gonzalez, one of four rookies in the Dodgers' postseason bullpen. The five pitchers who started their 18 postseason games—Walker Buehler, Tony Gonsolin, Clayton Kershaw, Dustin May and Urias—and four of the five who were credited with postseason wins have never thrown a pitch for another organization.

The team's ability, headed by president of baseball operations Andrew Friedman, to find value where others missed it is yet another separator, as is the team's impressive player development staff.

And on the eve of spring training, the Dodgers took one last big swing to land Mookie Betts from the Red Sox, setting them up for a historic season that ended with a World Series and being named Organization of the Year.

PREVIOUS WINNERS

2010: San Francisco Giants
2011: St. Louis Cardinals
2012: Cincinnati Reds
2013: St. Louis Cardinals
2014: Kansas City Royals
2015: Pittsburgh Pirates
2016: Chicago Cubs
2017: Los Angeles Dodgers
2018: Milwaukee Brewers
2019: Tampa Bay Rays

Full list: BaseballAmerica.com/awards

Baseball At Its Best

While any discussion of the game's best all-around player continues to begin with Mike Trout, not only does the Los Angeles Angels' superstar have some growing competition, but it's right in his backyard in Southern California.

By season's end, new Dodgers' acquisition Mookie Betts was among the favorites to win the NL Most Valuable Player award, which would bookend the AL MVP award he won in 2018. Meanwhile, down the I-5 freeway, the Padres' Tatis Jr. was nearly by unanimous consent the game's most exciting player.

With Trout having signed a 12-year extension two springs ago, Betts having inked a 12-year deal in July and Tatis Jr. still years from free agency, (and the Padres, as you can imagine, are moving to prioritize signing him long term) baseball fans in Southern California are spoiled by their riches. The only thing missing continues to be the Angels making the playoffs: They haven't been since 2014, and Tatis Jr. now already has doubled Trout's total postseason games played, 6-3.

Betts was extraordinary, but Atlanta's Freddie Freeman finished the season as the NL MVP. He led the NL in runs (51), doubles (23) and fWAR (3.4) while hitting .341 with 13 homers and a 1.102 OPS. His Braves' teammate, Marcell Ozuna, produced a stellar season as well. Ozuna led the NL in homers (18), RBIs (56), total bases (145) and was third in batting average (.338), on-base percentage (.431) and slugging percentage (.636).

Cleveland's pitching factory continued to churn out aces, with Shane Bieber following Corey Kluber as the No. 1 starter nobody wanted to face. Bieber didn't allow an earned run in six of his 12 starts and led the majors in ERA (1.63), wins (8), strikeouts (122), strikeouts per nine innings (14.2), FIP (2.07) and ERA+ (281). Ohio also was home to Cincinnati's Trevor Bauer, who won the NL Cy Young.

Bauer led the NL in ERA (1.73), WHIP (0.795) and fanned 100 hitters over 73 innings. He also led the majors in complete games at two, a number that not only exhibited dominance but also carried with it the novelty of '20: Both of Bauer's complete games came in seven-inning doubleheaders.

The New York Yankees' season was sidetracked by injuries, demoting them into a wild-card entrant for the postseason, but D.J. LeMahieu won the AL batting title (.364) and led the league in on-base percentage (.421) and OPS (1.011) while Luke Voit led the AL in homers (22) and ranked second in RBIs (52) and slugging percentage (.610). Cleveland's Jose Ramirez got hot late and helped push the Indians into the postseason, ranking second in OPS (.993) and third in slugging percentage (.607).

Though the Washington Nationals went from World Series champions all the way to missing a postseason slot, young slugger Juan Soto made a singular case as perhaps the most dominant and feared slugger of all. Soto led the NL in batting average (.351), on-base percentage (.490), slugging percentage (.695) and OPS (1.185).

Standing in the Hall of Fame

Even bucolic Cooperstown didn't escape the difficulty of 2020 when the Hall of Fame announced that, because of the pandemic, it was canceling ceremonies for the first time since 1960, when no players were elected.

A record crowd of more than 70,000 was expected for the induction of Derek Jeter, Larry Walker, Ted Simmons and the late Marvin Miller, who as the first leader of the Players' Union transformed the sport in a seismic way.

Instead, the Hall plans to induct the class of 2020 along with the class of 2021 next summer. When that happens, however, it sadly will be missing a small handful of its members. As if this year weren't difficult enough, the sadness and weight of 2020 was driven home with the deaths of six Hall of Famers: Al Kaline, Tom Seaver, Lou Brock, Bob Gibson, Whitey Ford and Joe Morgan.

"It's been a heck of a year," Houston manager Dusty Baker said in October, invoking the names of some other players who passed away in '20 as well.

"From Claudell Washington to Al Kaline to Tom Seaver to Lou Brock to Bob Gibson to Jimmy Wynn, all of my partners are leaving. Boy, they've got a heck of a pitching staff and heck of an outfield in heaven. I was just thinking, 'Who is the Lord going to start for his rotation? Is he going to start Whitey Ford first? Gibson? Seaver?' Boy, it just sort of puts things in perspective."

Managerial Musical Chairs

A full one-third of the 30 clubs opened 2020 with new managers: Boston (Ron Roenicke), Kansas City (Mike Matheny), Houston (Dusty Baker), the Los Angeles Angels (Joe Maddon), Philadelphia (Joe Girardi), the New York Mets (Luis Rojas), the Chicago Cubs (David Ross), Pittsburgh (Derek Shelton), San Diego (Jayce

CONTINUED ON PAGE 21

MAJOR LEAGUES

MAJOR LEAGUE *ALL-STARS*

At 21 years old, Juan Soto became the youngest MLB batting champion (.351).

Shane Bieber won the Triple Crown with an 8-1, 1.63 mark and 122 strikeouts.

FIRST TEAM

Pos.	Player, Team	AVG	OBP	SLG	AB	R	H	2B	3B	HR	RBI	BB	SO	SB	CS
C	Travis d'Arnaud, Braves	.321	.386	.533	165	19	53	8	0	9	34	16	50	1	0
1B	Freddie Freeman, Braves	.341	.462	.640	214	51	73	23	1	13	53	45	37	2	0
2B	D.J. LeMahieu, Yankees	.364	.421	.590	195	41	71	10	2	10	27	18	21	3	0
3B	Jose Ramirez, Indians	.292	.386	.607	219	45	64	16	1	17	46	31	43	10	3
SS	Fernando Tatis Jr., Padres	.277	.366	.571	224	50	62	11	2	17	45	27	61	11	3
OF	Mookie Betts, Dodgers	.292	.366	.562	219	47	64	9	1	16	39	24	38	10	2
OF	Juan Soto, Nationals	.351	.490	.695	154	39	54	14	0	13	37	41	28	6	2
OF	Mike Trout, Angels	.281	.390	.603	199	41	56	9	2	17	46	35	56	1	1
DH	Jose Abreu, White Sox	.317	.370	.617	240	43	76	15	0	19	60	18	59	0	0

Pos.	Player, Team	W	L	ERA	G	GS	SV	IP	H	R	ER	HR	BB	SO	WHIP
SP	Trevor Bauer, Reds	5	4	1.73	11	11	0	73	41	17	14	9	17	100	0.79
SP	Shane Bieber, Indians	8	1	1.63	12	12	0	77	46	15	14	7	21	122	0.87
SP	Yu Darvish, Cubs	8	3	2.01	12	12	0	76	59	18	17	5	14	93	0.96
SP	Jacob deGrom, Mets	4	2	2.38	12	12	0	68	47	21	18	7	18	104	0.96
SP	Dinelson Lamet, Padres	3	1	2.09	12	12	0	69	39	18	16	5	20	93	0.86
RP	Devin Williams, Brewers	4	1	0.33	22	0	0	27	8	4	1	1	9	53	0.63

SECOND TEAM

Pos.	Player, Team	AVG	OBP	SLG	AB	R	H	2B	3B	HR	RBI	BB	SO	SB	CS
C	J.T. Realmuto, Phillies	.266	.349	.491	173	33	46	6	0	11	32	16	48	4	1
1B	Luke Voit, Yankees	.277	.338	.610	213	41	59	5	0	22	52	17	54	0	0
2B	Brandon Lowe, Rays	.269	.362	.554	193	36	52	9	2	14	37	25	58	3	0
3B	Manny Machado, Padres	.304	.370	.580	224	44	68	12	1	16	47	26	37	6	3
SS	Trea Turner, Nationals	.335	.394	.588	233	46	78	15	4	12	41	22	36	12	4
OF	Marcell Ozuna, Braves	.338	.431	.636	228	38	77	14	0	18	56	38	60	0	0
OF	Dominic Smith, Mets	.316	.377	.616	177	27	56	21	1	10	42	14	45	0	0
OF	Mike Yastrzemski, Giants	.297	.400	.568	192	39	57	14	4	10	35	30	55	2	1
DH	Nelson Cruz, Twins	.303	.397	.595	185	33	56	6	0	16	33	25	58	0	0

Pos.	Player, Team	W	L	ERA	G	GS	SV	IP	H	R	ER	HR	BB	SO	WHIP
SP	Corbin Burnes, Brewers	4	1	2.11	12	9	0	60	37	15	14	2	24	88	1.02
SP	Gerrit Cole, Yankees	7	3	2.84	12	12	0	73	53	27	23	14	17	94	0.96
SP	Dallas Keuchel, White Sox	6	2	1.99	11	11	0	63	52	15	14	2	17	42	1.09
SP	Kenta Maeda, Twins	6	1	2.70	11	11	0	67	40	20	20	9	10	80	0.75
SP	Hyun-Jin Ryu, Blue Jays	5	2	2.69	12	12	0	67	60	22	20	6	17	72	1.15
RP	Liam Hendriks, Athletics	3	1	1.78	24	0	14	25	14	6	5	1	3	37	0.67

EXECUTIVE OF THE YEAR

Andrew Friedman

JAYNE KAMIN-ONCEA/GETTY IMAGES

The Dodgers got to the World Series based on the many of the tenets and principles Andrew Friedman believes strongly in, including a deep roster with positional versatility, a pitching staff with flexible roles, a focus on run prevention, a strong and positive clubhouse culture and a manager who embraces data and is willing to make bold decisions with buy-in from his players.

Friedman, after transforming the Rays into a contender during his years in Tampa Bay, built the Dodgers up in his six years in Los Angeles. The team annually has one of the top farm systems in baseball and one of the most formidable rosters in the major leagues.

And now, Friedman and the Dodgers have a World Series title, the franchise's first since 1988.

PREVIOUS WINNERS

2010: Jon Daniels, Rangers
2011: Doug Melvin, Brewers
2012: Billy Beane, Athletics
2013: Dan Duquette, Orioles
2014: Dan Duquette, Orioles
2015: Sandy Alderson, Mets
2016: Chris Antonetti, Indians
2017: Brian Cashman, Yankees
2018: Dave Dombrowski, Red Sox
2019: Mike Rizzo, Nationals

Full list: BaseballAmerica.com/awards

MANAGER OF THE YEAR

Brian Snitker

SCOTT AUDETTE/MLB PHOTOS

Brian Snitker, 65, has spent more than four decades with the Braves. After a career coaching in the minors and serving on MLB staffs, he took over as the Braves' interim manager in May 2016 when Fredi Gonzalez was fired after a dreadful start.

He guided that team to a 12-2 finish to the season, then reached the postseason in back-to-back years in 2018 and 2019, but he saved his best work for the 2020 season.

Snitker expertly navigated the Braves to a third straight division title despite myriad pitching injuries and an atypical 60-game season.

The Braves won their first playoff series since 2001 and Snitker led them all the way to within one game of a World Series bid, proving himself as our Manager of the Year.

PREVIOUS WINNERS

2010: Bobby Cox, Braves
2011: Joe Maddon, Rays
2012: Buck Showalter, Orioles
2013: Clint Hurdle, Pirates
2014: Buck Showalter, Orioles
2015: Joe Maddon, Cubs
2016: Terry Francona, Indians
2017: A.J. Hinch, Astros
2018: Bob Melvin, Athletics
2019: Craig Counsell, Brewers

Full list: BaseballAmerica.com/awards

CONTINUED FROM PAGE 19

Tingler) and San Francisco (Gabe Kapler).

At season's end, the White Sox fired Rick Renteria despite making the playoffs, which gave Renteria the distinction of having been let go by both Chicago clubs. Boston let Roenicke go and in Detroit, veteran skipper Ron Gardenhire retired with a week left in the season, citing health and family reasons.

In the executive suites, the Angels fired general manager Billy Eppler and the Phillies reassigned GM Matt Klentak as those two clubs' search for a path to the playoffs continued with frustrating results. A total of 27 of baseball's 30 teams have made the playoffs in the past six years—all except the Phillies, Angels and Mariners.

On-Field Ongoings

The season itself was unusual in that each team played in its own geographic pods because of the coronavirus and didn't stray into other parts of the country.

That produced as many mysteries as results. For example, in dominating the National League with a 43-17 record but while only playing two teams that would finish with winning records (San Diego and Oakland), how good, really, were the Los Angeles Dodgers? It was left to October to answer that question.

For the Dodgers, it was their eighth consecutive NL West title, a run of dominance not seen since the Atlanta Braves of the 1990s and early 2000s. For the Padres, it was their first winning record since 2010.

Oakland won the AL West to unseat the Houston Astros but lost third baseman Matt Chapman to a hip injury late in the season. Part of the reason for the Astros' decline was that they lost ace Justin Verlander, who only made one start, to Tommy John surgery.

In the Central, the Minnesota Twins weren't quite the "Bomba Squad" from the year before, but they bopped enough to win the division for a second consecutive season. The additions of free agents Kenta Maeda and Josh Donaldson helped.

Cleveland's second-place finish came replete with significant questions surrounding the future of superstar shortstop Francisco Lindor, who is eligible for free agency following the 2021 season. The White Sox had control of the division as late as Sept. 22 but a rough trip to Ohio in which they lost two of three in Cincinnati and then four straight to Cleveland doomed them to third place.

The Chicago Cubs, under new skipper David Ross, bounced back to win the NL Central after failing to make the playoffs in 2019. In all, four clubs from the division qualified for the expanded playoffs this year, with St. Louis, Cincinnati and Milwaukee joining the Cubs.

Tampa Bay (40-20) posted the best record in the AL to win the East and shock the Yankees, dumping them into second place. For a second consecutive season, the Yanks were hit hard by injuries with Giancarlo Stanton and Aaron Judge again spending time on the Injured List. When DJ LeMahieu, Judge, Aaron Hicks, Luke Voit, Stanton, Gio Urshela and Gleyber Torres lined up as the first seven hitters for Game 1 of the Division Series against the Rays, it was just the fourth time in the past two seasons those men played for the Yanks on the same day over the past two years, according to research from The Athletic's Jayson Stark.

Somehow, despite losing starter Mike Soroka early in the season and with free agent veteran starter Cole Hamels failing to launch because of a sore shoulder, Atlanta nevertheless won its third straight NL East title. Freddie Freeman, Ronald Acuna Jr. and Marcell Ozuna had splendid seasons offensively, Max Fried and Anderson stepped up in the rotation and Brian Snitker continues to prove he is one of the adept managers in any dugout.

Milestones & More

The brevity of the season limited the opportunity for many historical moments, but the Angels' Albert Pujols nevertheless added a couple more to his well-decorated career. An RBI single against Houston on Aug. 25 pushed him into sole pos-

Albert Pujols hit two home runs on Sept. 18, passing Willie Mays (660) in fifth place.

JAYNE KAMIN-ONCEA/GETTY IMAGES

session of third place on baseball's all-time RBIs list, moving him past Alex Rodriguez and behind only Hall of Famers Hank Aaron (2,297) and Babe Ruth (2,214). Pujols finished the season at 2,100. Or, if you look at it another way, Pujols might be second instead of third on the historical RBIs list: RBIs did not become an official statistic until 1920 and, as such, the Elias Sports Bureau, baseball's official statistician, recognizes neither Babe Ruth nor Cap Anson as members of the 2,000-RBI club.

Three weeks later, Pujols moved into fifth place on the all-time home run list when he passed Willie Mays' 660 by smashing not one, but two homers in a game with the Texas Rangers to push him to 662. Pujols elicited chuckles when he told reporters that when he tied Mays at 660 on Sept. 13, he received a teasing e-mail from Mays reading, "What took you so long?"

The moment highlighted the weirdness of the season, of course, when Pujols passed the Hall of Famer Mays in a quiet ballpark with no fans.

Pujols' teammate Mike Trout celebrated Labor Day weekend by setting an Angels' franchise record with his 300th career home run, edging past Tim Salmon's 299.

Two days before Trout's 300th, also in Southern California, Clayton Kershaw become the third-youngest pitcher to strike out 2,500 hitters. Only Hall of Famers Nolan Ryan (31 years, 101 days) and Walter Johnson (31 years, 197 days) hit that

EZRA SHAW/GETTY IMAGES

Mike Trout hit his 300th career home run this season, setting a new franchise record in the process.

mark at an age younger than Kershaw (32 years, 168 days).

On the final Thursday of the season, St. Louis' Yadier Molina collected his 2,000th career hit, making him only the 12th man whose primary position was catcher to ever achieve that mark.

Meanwhile, the shortened season prolonged Detroit's Miguel Cabrera in his chase for 500 home runs: He hit 10 to finish the year at 487. Five hundred should be inevitable for Cabrera, who, at 37, still has three years left on his contract.

The Future?

Say one thing for the bruising negotiations between the players and the owners that got the game back on the field in the middle of a worldwide pandemic in 2020: Perhaps the silver lining is that the process will help jump-start negotiations for the next Collective Bargaining Agreement. The current one expires after the 2021 season and, based on tension between the sides, the game's unprecedented (in the time of the players' union) 25-year streak of labor peace could be in jeopardy.

However it turns out, the next several months are expected to be turbulent, at the very least. And aside from the usual assortment of items with huge financial ramifications (free agency and arbitration issues and finer points, luxury tax, revenue sharing) will be some issues that 2020 introduced.

For one thing, the National League adopted the DH for the first time ever in '20. While it is widely expected that the NL will eventually use the DH like everyone else, the timing was expected to coincide with the start of the new labor deal in 2022. If the DH to the NL is inevitable, will baseball revert back for possibly only one year in 2021 to NL pitchers hitting? It doesn't seem likely, but stay tuned.

Expanded playoffs likely are here to stay, but perhaps not the 16-team tournament that we watched in 2020. Speaking to the Associated Press on the eve of the World Series, commissioner Rob Manfred suggested settling at 12 or 14 teams—which would be up from 10 of the past several years but down from this year's record participation.

One thing to remember: This is an issue that must be negotiated with the players, it is not one in which Manfred can unilaterally make a decision.

The commissioner also voiced support for continuing the 2020 experiment of starting all extra innings with a runner on second base. That would be a significant break in the game's tradition and while Manfred said the players seem to like it and it seemed to have some support on social media, many in the game's old guard blanch at the idea.

One other thing to keep an eye on: Manfred said that the 30 clubs combined for $3 billion in

Miguel Cabrera leads all active players with a .313 batting average in 18 seasons.

operating losses this year because of the pandemic, which caused all regular-season games to be played in empty parks. It may be worth listening to the chatter regarding expansion.

Dave Dombrowski, the former top baseball executive in Montreal, Miami, Detroit and Boston, now is part of a group looking to bring an expansion baseball team to Nashville. Worth noting is that shortly after baseball's last enormous financial calamity, the 1994-1995 players' strike, MLB awarded expansion franchises to Arizona and Tampa Bay and raked in a $130 million entry fee for each organization.

Current estimates are that today's expansion fees could be as high as $1.6 billion or more. Nashville, Portland, Montreal and Charlotte, N.C., are the four cities that keep popping up in the rumor mill. But first, baseball must solve glaring stadium issues that have been going on for years in Oakland and Tampa Bay, as well as attendance issues in Miami.

Because as we head into the winter of 2020-2021, the only certainty about the future was the uncertainty, for both the game and the world. Without a vaccine for the coronavirus, normalcy still seems a long way off.

And most pressing in that regard in the baseball world is, what will spring training and the regular season of '21 even look like? Will fans be allowed to attend games again? How many? And will baseball be able to play a regular, intersectional schedule again?

Our fingers are crossed.

ACTIVE LEADERS

Career leaders among players who played in a game in 2020. Batters require 3,000 plate appearances and pitchers 1,000 innings to qualify for percentage titles.

BATTERS			PITCHERS		
AVG	Miguel Cabrera	.313	ERA	Clayton Kershaw	2.43
OBP	Joey Votto	.419	SO/9	Yu Darvish	11.12
SLG	Mike Trout	.582	BB/9	Josh Tomlin	1.31
OPS	Mike Trout	1.000	HR/9	Clayton Kershaw	0.70
R	Albert Pujols	1,843	W	Justin Verlander	226
H	Albert Pujols	3,236	L	Felix Hernandez	136
2B	Albert Pujols	669	SV	Craig Kimbrel	348
3B	Dexter Fowler	82	IP	Justin Verlander	2,988
HR	Albert Pujols	662	SO	Justin Verlander	3,013
RBI	Albert Pujols	2,100	BB	Justin Verlander	851
BB	Albert Pujols	1,331	AVG	Clayton Kershaw	.208
SO	Chris Davis	1,852	G	Joe Smith	782
XBH	Albert Pujols	1,347	GS	Zack Greinke	459
SB	Dee Gordon	333	HR	Cole Hamels	310

ARIZONA DIAMONDBACKS
Taylor Widener ..... July 25
Daulton Varsho ..... July 30
Andy Young .... Aug. 1
Jeremy Beasley .... Aug. 11
Riley Smith .... Aug. 26
Wyatt Mathisen .... Sept. 7
Pavin Smith .... Sept. 12

ATLANTA BRAVES
William Contreras . July 24
Cristian Pache ...... Aug. 21
Ian Anderson .... Aug. 26
Patrick Weigel .... Sept. 4
Tucker Davidson .. Sept. 26

BALTIMORE ORIOLES
Keegan Akin ...... Aug. 14
Ramon Urias .... Aug. 20
Ryan Mountcastle Aug. 21
Dean Kremer .... Sept. 6
Bruce
Zimmermann ..... Sept. 17

BOSTON RED SOX
Jonathan Arauz .... July 24
Kyle Hart .... Aug. 13
Bobby Dalbec ...... Aug. 30
Robinson Leyer .... Aug. 31
Domingo Tapia ... Sept. 11
Tanner Houck Sept.15

CHICAGO CUBS
Tyson Miller .... Aug. 17
Brailyn Marquez . Sept. 27

CHICAGO WHITE SOX
Codi Heuer .... July 24
Luis Robert .... July 24
Jimmy Lambert .... July 25
Nick Madrigal ...... July 31
Matt Foster .... Aug. 1
Yermin Mercedes .. Aug. 2
Zack Burdi .... Aug. 8
Luis Gonzalez ...... Aug. 18
Dane Dunning ..... Aug. 19
Bernardo Flores Jr. Sept. 3
Jonathan Stiever Sept. 13
Garrett Crochet .. Sept. 18

CINCINNATI REDS
Shogo Akiyama .... July 24
Tejay Antone .... July 27
Tyler Stephenson .. July 27
Mark Payton .... Aug. 22
Jose Garcia .... Aug. 27

CLEVELAND INDIANS
Daniel Johnson ..... July 25
Cam Hill .... July 26
Triston McKenzie . Aug. 22
Kyle Nelson .... Sept. 10

COLORADO ROCKIES
Ryan Castellani .... Aug. 8
Ashton Goudeau .. Aug. 19
Antonio Santos ... Sept. 1
Jose Mujica .... Sept. 8
Tommy Doyle ..... Sept. 23

DETROIT TIGERS
Beau Burrows ...... July 27
Anthony Castro .... July 27
Kyle Funkhouser ... July 27
Rony Garcia .... July 28
Isaac Paredes ..... Aug. 17
Tarik Skubal .... Aug. 18
Casey Mize .... Aug. 19
Derek Hill .... Sept. 4
Sergio Alcantara ... Sept. 6
Daz Cameron .... Sept. 9

HOUSTON ASTROS
Enoli Paredes ...... July 24
Blake Taylor .... July 24
Cristian Javier ...... July 25
Brandon Bailey .... July 26
Taylor Jones .... July 26
Brandon Bielak .... July 27
Nivaldo Rodriguez July 28
Andre Scrubb ...... July 28
Humberto
Castellanos .... Aug. 4
Carlos Sanabria ... Aug. 5
Luis Garcia .... Sept. 4

KANSAS CITY ROYALS
Tyler Zuber .... July 24
Edward Olivares ... July 25
Brady Singer .... July 25
Foster Griffin .... July 27
Nick Heath .... July 30
Kris Bubic .... July 31
Carlos Hernandez ... Sept. 1
Scott Blewett .... Sept. 18

LOS ANGELES ANGELS
Jo Adell .... Aug. 4
Jahmai Jones .... Aug. 4
Elliot Soto .... Sept. 25

LOS ANGELES DODGERS
Victor Gonzalez ... July 31
Keibert Ruiz .... Aug. 16
Mitch White .... Aug. 28
Zach McKinstry ... Sept. 16

MIAMI MARLINS
Nick Neidert .... July 25
Alex Vesia .... July 25
Jordan Holloway ... July 26
Monte Harrison ..... Aug. 4
Eddy Alvarez .... Aug. 5
Sterling Sharp ...... Aug. 5
Jorge Guzman ...... Aug. 6
Humberto Mejia .... Aug. 7

Daniel Castano ...... Aug. 8
Lewin Diaz .... Aug. 15
Jesus Sanchez ...... Aug. 21
Sixto Sanchez ...... Aug. 22
Brandon Leibrandt Aug. 23
Brian Navarreto ... Aug. 23
Trevor Rogers ...... Aug. 25
Jazz Chisholm ..... Sept. 1
Johan Quezada ... Sept. 12
Braxton Garrett .. Sept. 13

MILWAUKEE BREWERS
J.P. Feyereisen ...... July 24
Mark Mathias .... Aug. 4
Angel Perdomo ... Aug. 18
Drew Rasmussen . Aug. 19
Phil Bickford .... Sept. 1
Justin Topa .... Sept. 1

MINNESOTA TWINS
Aaron Whitefield .. July 25
Ryan Jeffers .... Aug. 20
Brent Rooker .... Sept. 4
Travis Blankenhorn Sept. 15
Edwar Colina ...... Sept. 25

NEW YORK METS
Andres Gimenez ... July 24
David Peterson ..... July 28
Franklyn Kilome ... Aug. 1
Ali Sanchez .... Aug. 10

NEW YORK YANKEES
Brooks Kriske .... July 29
Nick Nelson .... Aug. 1
Albert Abreu .... Aug. 8
Estevan Florial ..... Aug. 28
Deivi Garcia .... Aug. 30
Miguel Yajure ...... Aug. 31
Clarke Schmidt .... Sept. 4

OAKLAND ATHLETICS
Vimael Machin ..... July 26
Jordan Weems ..... July 28
James Kaprielian . Aug. 16
Jonah Heim .... Aug. 25
Daulton Jefferies Sept. 12

PHILADELPHIA PHILLIES
Ramon Rosso .... July 24
Spencer Howard .... Aug. 9
Alec Bohm .... Aug. 13
Connor Brogdon .. Aug. 13
JoJo Romero .... Aug. 21
Mauricio Llovera ... Sept. 6
Rafael Marchan .. Sept. 14
Mickey Moniak ... Sept. 16
Garrett Cleavinger Sept. 17
Adonis Medina ... Sept. 20

PITTSBURGH PIRATES
JT Brubaker .... July 26
Cody Ponce .... Aug. 2

Nick Mears .... Aug. 8
Brandon Waddell . Aug. 14
Will Craig .... Aug. 27
Ke'Bryan Hayes ..... Sept. 1
Blake Cederlind .. Sept. 15
Jared Oliva .... Sept. 21

ST. LOUIS CARDINALS
Kwang Hyun Kim .. July 24
Kodi Whitley .... July 26
Dylan Carlson ...... Aug. 15
Max Schrock .... Aug. 15
Jake Woodford ..... Aug. 15
Seth Elledge .... Aug. 16
Rob Kaminsky ...... Aug. 16
John Nogowski .... Aug. 16
Roel Ramirez .... Aug. 16
Nabil Crismatt ..... Aug. 17
Ricardo Sanchez .. Aug. 17
Jesus Cruz .... Aug. 18
Johan Oviedo Aug.19

SAN DIEGO PADRES
Edward Olivares .... July 25
Jake Cronenworth July 26
Luis Patino .... Aug. 5
Jorge Mateo .... Aug. 13
Luis Campusano ... Sept. 4
Jorge Ona .... Sept. 7

SAN FRANCISCO GIANTS
Dany Jimenez .... July 23
Joe McCarthy .... July 23
Caleb Baragar ..... July 25
Chadwick Tromp .. July 29
Joey Bart .... Aug. 20
Luis
Alexander Basabe Aug. 27

SEATTLE MARINERS
Jose Marmolejos... July 24
Anthony Misiewicz July 24
Yohan Ramirez ..... July 24
Evan White .... July 24
Joseph Odom........ July 28
Joey Gerber .... Aug. 4
Ljay Newsome ..... Aug. 20
Aaron Fletcher ..... Aug. 22

TAMPA BAY RAYS
Ryan Thompson .... July 24
Yoshi Tsutsugo ..... July 24
Josh Fleming .... Aug. 23

TEXAS RANGERS
Leody Taveras .... July 24
Anderson Tejeda ... Aug. 6
Wes Benjamin ...... Aug. 16
Kyle Cody .... Aug. 21
Eli White .... Sept. 1
John King .... Sept. 4
Sam Huff .... Sept. 11
Sherten Apostel .. Sept. 12
Demarcus Evans . Sept. 18

TORONTO BLUE JAYS
Santiago Espinal ... July 25
Thomas Hatch ...... July 26
Shun Yamaguchi ... July 26
Nate Pearson .... July 29
Julian
Merryweather ..... Aug. 20
Alejandro Kirk..... Sept. 12
Hector Perez .... Sept. 16
Patrick Murphy ... Sept. 18

WASHINGTON NATIONALS
Kyle Finnegan .... July 25
Dakota Bacus .... Aug. 9
Seth Romero .... Aug. 13
Luis Garcia .... Aug. 14
Wil Crowe .... Aug. 22
Ben Braymer .... Aug. 28
Yadiel Hernandez Sept. 10

CLUB BATTING

	AVG	G	AB	R	H	2B	3B	HR	RBI	BB	SO	SB	OBP	SLG
Boston	.265	60	2083	292	552	118	7	81	278	187	545	31	.330	.445
Chicago	.261	60	2047	306	534	94	6	96	294	179	571	20	.326	.453
Baltimore	.258	60	2026	274	523	102	7	77	264	164	514	19	.321	.429
Toronto	.255	60	2023	302	516	104	4	88	288	203	508	33	.325	.441
Los Angeles	.248	60	2020	294	501	97	8	85	285	239	490	21	.332	.430
New York	.247	60	1915	315	473	87	7	94	301	251	480	27	.342	.447
Detroit	.245	58	1893	249	463	78	12	62	242	147	567	19	.303	.397
Kansas City	.244	60	1988	248	485	97	7	68	237	172	527	49	.309	.402
Minnesota	.242	60	1937	269	468	81	3	91	258	186	528	14	.315	.427
Houston	.240	60	1992	279	478	103	12	69	268	192	440	22	.312	.408
Tampa Bay	.238	60	1975	289	470	105	12	80	274	243	608	48	.328	.425
Cleveland	.228	60	1959	248	446	96	5	59	234	239	517	25	.317	.372
Seattle	.226	60	1929	254	435	88	5	60	244	207	545	50	.309	.370
Oakland	.225	60	1908	274	430	91	11	71	264	238	524	26	.322	.396
Texas	.217	60	1936	224	420	80	9	62	204	167	548	49	.285	.364

CLUB PITCHING

	ERA	G	CG	SHO	SV	IP	H	R	ER	HR	BB	SO	AVG
Cleveland	3.29	60	1	7	20	536	440	209	196	68	157	621	.223
Tampa Bay	3.56	60	0	4	23	527.2	475	229	209	70	168	552	.238
Minnesota	3.58	60	0	4	17	513.1	448	215	204	62	170	535	.232
Oakland	3.77	60	1	5	17	515.1	471	232	216	69	165	506	.240
Chicago	3.81	60	1	6	13	527	448	246	223	71	217	523	.226
Kansas City	4.30	60	1	4	19	517	500	272	247	76	211	517	.254
Houston	4.31	60	0	0	16	524	472	275	251	70	217	526	.239
New York	4.35	60	2	2	14	500.2	455	270	242	83	168	528	.236
Baltimore	4.51	60	0	1	11	518.2	489	294	260	79	192	487	.246
Toronto	4.60	60	0	1	17	524.2	517	312	268	81	250	519	.255
Texas	5.02	60	2	3	10	516.2	479	312	288	81	236	489	.242
Seattle	5.03	60	1	0	15	516.2	482	303	289	79	230	469	.245
Los Angeles	5.09	60	1	2	12	525.1	492	321	297	82	199	523	.246
Boston	5.58	60	0	2	14	524	587	351	325	98	252	537	.281
Detroit	5.63	58	1	1	11	492.1	511	318	308	91	192	444	.265

CLUB FIELDING

	PCT	PO	A	E	DP		PCT	PO	A	E	DP
Houston	.991	1572	546	20	48	Los Angeles	.983	1576	485	36	36
Minnesota	.990	1540	459	20	39	Toronto	.982	1574	530	38	47
Seattle	.989	1550	502	23	48	Chicago	.982	1581	517	38	48
Oakland	.987	1546	489	26	33	Texas	.981	1550	467	40	40
Detroit	.987	1477	502	27	46	Baltimore	.980	1556	511	43	42
Cleveland	.986	1608	500	30	46	Boston	.979	1572	522	45	59
Kansas City	.985	1551	503	31	62	New York	.976	1502	472	48	37
Tampa Bay	.985	1583	541	33	52						

INDIVIDUAL BATTING LEADERS

	AVG	G	AB	R	H	2B	3B	HR	RBI	BB	SO	SB
DJ LeMahieu, New York	.364	50	195	41	71	10	2	10	27	18	21	3
Tim Anderson, Chicago	.322	49	208	45	67	11	1	10	21	10	50	5
David Fletcher, Los Angeles	.319	49	207	31	66	13	0	3	18	20	25	2
Jose Abreu, Chicago	.317	60	240	43	76	15	0	19	60	18	59	0
Alex Verdugo, Boston	.308	53	201	36	62	16	0	6	15	17	45	4
Lourdes Gurriel Jr., Toronto	.308	57	208	28	64	14	0	11	33	14	48	3
Nelson Cruz, Minnesota	.303	53	185	33	56	6	0	16	33	25	58	0
Xander Bogaerts, Boston	.300	56	203	36	61	8	0	11	28	21	41	8
Michael Brantley, Houston	.300	46	170	24	51	15	0	5	22	17	28	2
Jeimer Candelario, Detroit	.297	52	185	30	55	11	3	7	29	20	49	1

INDIVIDUAL PITCHING LEADERS

	W	L	ERA	G	GS	CG	SV	IP	H	R	ER	BB	SO
Shane Bieber, Cleveland	8	1	1.63	12	12	0	0	77.1	46	15	14	21	122
Dallas Keuchel, Chicago	6	2	1.99	11	11	0	0	63.1	52	15	14	17	42
Chris Bassitt, Oakland	5	2	2.29	11	11	0	0	63	56	18	16	17	55
Hyun-Jin Ryu, Toronto	5	2	2.69	12	12	0	0	67	60	22	20	17	72
Kenta Maeda, Minnesota	6	1	2.7	11	11	0	0	66.2	40	20	20	10	80
Gerrit Cole, New York	7	3	2.84	12	12	2	0	73	53	27	23	17	94
Carlos Carrasco, Cleveland	3	4	2.91	12	12	0	0	68	55	22	22	27	82
Marco Gonzales, Seattle	7	2	3.1	11	11	1	0	69.2	59	27	24	7	64
Dylan Bundy, Los Angeles	6	3	3.29	11	11	1	0	65.2	51	27	24	17	72
Lance Lynn, Texas	6	3	3.32	13	13	1	0	84	64	34	31	25	89

AWARD WINNERS

Selected by Baseball Writers Association of America

MOST VALUABLE PLAYER

Player	1st	2nd	3rd	Total
Jose Abreu, White Sox	21	8	1	374
Jose Ramirez, Indians	8	17	3	303
D.J. LeMahieu, Yankees	1	5	15	230
Shane Bieber, Indians			4	173
Mike Trout, Angels			4	172
Nelson Cruz, Twins			1	128
Tim Anderson, White Sox			1	125
Brandon Lowe, Rays				104
Luke Voit, Yankees				85
Anthony Rendon, Angels			1	42
Teoscar Hernandez, Blue Jays				8
Alex Verdugo, Red Sox				6
Liam Hendriks, Athletics				4
Hyun Jin Ryu, Blue Jays				4
George Springer, Astros				4
Byron Buxton, Twins				2
Xander Bogaerts, Red Sox				1
David Fletcher, Angels				1
Dallas Keuchel, White Sox				1
Kyle Lewis, Mariners				1
Salvador Perez, Royals				1
Eddie Rosario, Twins				1

CY YOUNG AWARD

Player	1st	2nd	3rd	Total
Shane Bieber, Indians	30			210
Kenta Maeda, Twins		18	4	92
Hyun Jin Ryu, Blue Jays		4	7	51
Gerrit Cole, Yankees		2	6	50
Dallas Keuchel, White Sox		5	4	46
Lance Lynn, Rangers		1	3	22
Lucas Giolito, White Sox			3	18
Chris Bassitt, Athletics			2	10

ROOKIE OF THE YEAR

Player	1st	2nd	3rd	Total
Kyle Lewis, Mariners	30			150
Luis Robert, White Sox		27	2	83
Cristian Javier, Astros		11		11
Sean Murphy, Athletics		1	4	7
Willi Castro, Tigers		1	4	7
James Karinchak, Indians			5	5
Jared Walsh, Angels		1	1	4
Ryan Mountcastle, Orioles			1	1

MANAGER OF THE YEAR

Manager	1st	2nd	3rd	Total
Kevin Cash, Rays	22	5	1	126
Rick Renteria, White Sox	5	9	9	61
Charlie Montoyo, Blue Jays	2	10	7	47
Bob Melvin, Athletics	1	3	8	22
Rocco Baldelli, Twins		3	4	13
Dusty Baker, Astros			1	1

GOLD GLOVE WINNERS

Selected by AL Managers

P—Griffin Canning, Angels. C—Roberto Perez, Indians. 1B—Evan White, Mariners. 2B—Cesar Hernandez, Indians. 3B—Isiah Kiner-Falefa, Rangers. SS—J.P. Crawford, Mariners. LF—Alex Gordon, Royals. CF—Luis Robert, White Sox. RF—Joey Gallo, Rangers.

BATTING

GAMES

Jose Abreu, Chicago	60
Maikel Franco, Kansas City	60
Vladimir Guerrero Jr., Toronto	60
Francisco Lindor, Cleveland	60
4 others	60

AT-BATS

Whit Merrifield, Kansas City	248
Jose Abreu, Chicago	240
Francisco Lindor, Cleveland	236
Cesar Hernandez, Cleveland	233
Rafael Devers, Boston	232

PLATE APPEARANCES

Francisco Lindor, Cleveland	266
Cavan Biggio, Toronto	265
Whit Merrifield, Kansas City	265
Jose Abreu, Chicago	262
Cesar Hernandez, Cleveland	261

RUNS

Tim Anderson, Chicago	45
Jose Ramirez, Cleveland	45
Jose Abreu, Chicago	43
Cavan Biggio, Toronto	41
3 others	41

HITS

Jose Abreu, Chicago	76
DJ LeMahieu, New York	71
Whit Merrifield, Kansas City	70
Tim Anderson, Chicago	67
2 others	66

TOTAL BASES

Jose Abreu, Chicago	148
Jose Ramirez, Cleveland	133
Luke Voit, New York	130
Mike Trout, Los Angeles	120
Eloy Jimenez, Chicago	119

DOUBLES

Cesar Hernandez, Cleveland	20
Jose Iglesias, Baltimore	17
Cavan Biggio, Toronto	16
Rafael Devers, Boston	16
4 others	16

TRIPLES

Kyle Tucker, Houston	6
Jeimer Candelario, Detroit	3
Kevin Kiermaier, Tampa Bay	3
Isiah Kiner-Falefa, Texas	3
3 others	3

EXTRA-BASE HITS

Jose Abreu, Chicago	34
Jose Ramirez, Cleveland	34
Rafael Devers, Boston	28
Eloy Jimenez, Chicago	28
Mike Trout, Los Angeles	28

HOME RUNS

Luke Voit, New York	22
Jose Abreu, Chicago	19
Jose Ramirez, Cleveland	17
Mike Trout, Los Angeles	17
2 others	16

RUNS BATTED IN

Jose Abreu, Chicago	60
Luke Voit, New York	52
Jose Ramirez, Cleveland	46
Mike Trout, Los Angeles	46
Rafael Devers, Boston	43

Jose Abreu

SACRIFICES

Delino DeShields, Cleveland	4
Reese McGuire, Toronto	4
Cedric Mullins, Baltimore	4
Andrew Velazquez, Baltimore	4
2 others	3

SACRIFICE FLIES

Kyle Seager, Seattle	6
Mark Canha, Oakland	5
Yuli Gurriel, Houston	5
Franmil Reyes, Cleveland	5
5 others	4

HIT BY PITCHES

Ramon Laureano, Oakland	12
Mark Canha, Oakland	10
Dylan Moore, Seattle	8
Kyle Seager, Seattle	7
2 others	7

WALKS

Carlos Santana, Cleveland	47
Cavan Biggio, Toronto	41
Aaron Hicks, New York	41
Anthony Rendon, Los Angeles	38

Mark Canha, Oakland	37

STOLEN BASES

Adalberto Mondesi, Kansas City	24
Manuel Margot, Tampa Bay	12
Whit Merrifield, Kansas City	12
Dylan Moore, Seattle	12
Jose Ramirez, Cleveland	10

STOLEN BASE PERCENTAGE

Cavan Biggio, Toronto	1.000
Xander Bogaerts, Boston	1.000
Mike Tauchman, New York	1.000
Leody Taveras, Texas	1.000
Jonathan Villar, Toronto	1.000

STRIKEOUTS

Miguel Sano, Minnesota	90
Evan White, Seattle	84
Joey Gallo, Texas	79
Matt Olson, Oakland	77
Willy Adames, Tampa Bay	74

AT-BATS PER STRIKEOUT

Tommy La Stella, LA/Oakland	16.3
DJ LeMahieu, New York	9.3
David Fletcher, Los Angeles	8.3

Yuli Gurriel, Houston	7.8
Whit Merrifield, Kansas City	7.5

DOUBLE PLAYS

Jose Abreu, Chicago	10
Anthony Rendon, Los Angeles	10
Nelson Cruz, Minnesota	8
Rafael Devers, Boston	8
Francisco Lindor, Cleveland	8
Jonathan Schoop, Detroit	8

MULTI-HIT GAMES

Jose Abreu, Chicago	21
Eloy Jimenez, Chicago	21
Whit Merrifield, Kansas City	21
Jose Ramirez, Cleveland	21
Tim Anderson, Chicago	20

ON-BASE PERCENTAGE

DJ LeMahieu, New York	.421
Anthony Rendon, Los Angeles	.418
Nelson Cruz, Minnesota	.397
Mike Trout, Los Angeles	.390
Mark Canha, Oakland	.387

ON-BASE PLUS SLUGGING

DJ LeMahieu, New York	1.011
Jose Ramirez	.993
Mike Trout, Los Angeles	.993
Nelson Cruz, Minnesota	.992
Jose Abreu, Chicago	.987

PITCHING

WINS

Shane Bieber, Cleveland	8
Gerrit Cole, New York	7
Marco Gonzales, Seattle	7
Dylan Bundy, Los Angeles	6
Randy Dobnak, Minnesota	6
6 others	6

LOSSES

Matthew Boyd, Detroit	7
Kolby Allard, Texas	6
Kris Bubic, Kansas City	6
Aaron Civale, Cleveland	6
Kyle Gibson, Texas	6
2 others	6

GAMES

Scott Barlow, Kansas City	32
Jimmy Cordero, Chicago	30
Jose Cisnero, Detroit	29
Mike Mayers, Los Angeles	29
Greg Holland, Kansas City	28

GAMES STARTED

Lance Lynn, Texas	13
Jose Berrios, Minnesota	12
Shane Bieber, Cleveland	12
Matthew Boyd, Detroit	12
11 others	12

GAMES FINISHED

Brad Hand, Cleveland	21
Liam Hendriks, Oakland	20
Alex Colome, Chicago	18
Rafael Montero, Texas	16
Taylor Rogers, Minnesota	16

COMPLETE GAMES

Gerrit Cole, New York	2
Matthew Boyd, Detroit	1
Dylan Bundy, Los Angeles	1
Aaron Civale, Cleveland	1
6 others	1

Lance Lynn

JONATHAN DANIEL/GETTY IMAGES; DENIS POROY/GETTY IMAGES

SHUTOUTS

Gerrit Cole, New York	1
Kyle Gibson, Texas	1
Lucas Giolito, Chicago	1
Brad Keller, Kansas City	1
Mike Minor, Texas/Oakland	1

SAVES

Brad Hand, Cleveland	16
Liam Hendriks, Oakland	14
Alex Colome, Chicago	12
Ryan Pressly, Houston	12
Matt Barnes, Boston	9
Taylor Rogers, Minnesota	9

INNINGS PITCHED

Lance Lynn, Texas	84
Shane Bieber, Cleveland	77.1
Aaron Civale, Cleveland	74
Gerrit Cole, New York	73
Lucas Giolito, Chicago	72.1

HITS ALLOWED

Aaron Civale, Cleveland	82
Kyle Gibson, Texas	73
Matthew Boyd, Detroit	67
Zack Greinke, Houston	67
Jordan Lyles, Texas	67

RUNS ALLOWED

Jordan Lyles, Texas	49
Matthew Boyd, Detroit	46
Kyle Gibson, Texas	44
Aaron Civale, Cleveland	39
Tanner Roark, Toronto	39

HOME RUNS ALLOWED

Matthew Boyd, Detroit	14
Gerrit Cole, New York	14
Tanner Roark, Toronto	14
Lance Lynn, Texas	13
5 others	12

WALKS ALLOWED

Dylan Cease, Chicago	34
Justin Dunn, Seattle	31
Kyle Gibson, Texas	30
Spencer Turnbull, Detroit	29
2 others	28

Brad Hand

LOWEST WALKS PER NINE

Marco Gonzales, Seattle	0.9
Zack Greinke, Houston	1.21
Kenta Maeda, Minnesota	1.35
Aaron Civale, Cleveland	1.95
Framber Valdez, Houston	2.04

HIT BATTERS

Ryan Yarbrough, Tampa Bay	7
Kyle Gibson, Texas	6
Lance Lynn, Texas	6
Matthew Boyd, Detroit	5
6 others	5

STRIKEOUTS

Shane Bieber, Cleveland	122
Lucas Giolito, Chicago	97
Gerrit Cole, New York	94
Tyler Glasnow, Tampa Bay	91
Lance Lynn, Texas	89

STRIKEOUTS PER NINE

Shane Bieber, Cleveland	14.2
Lucas Giolito, Chicago	12.1
Gerrit Cole, New York	11.6
Carlos Carrasco, Cleveland	10.9
Kenta Maeda, Minnesota	10.8

STRIKEOUTS PER NINE

(Relievers)

Mike Mayers, Los Angeles	12.9
Scott Barlow, Kansas City	11.7
Jose Cisnero, Detroit	10.5
Gio Gonzalez, Chicago	9.8
Matt Andriese, Los Angeles	9.3

DOUBLE PLAYS

Dylan Cease, Chicago	10
Martin Perez, Boston	10
Randy Dobnak, Minnesota	9
Brad Keller, Kansas City	9
Framber Valdez, Houston	9

PICKOFFS

Tyler Alexander, Detroit	2
Jose Berrios, Minnesota	2
Griffin Canning, Los Angeles	2
Ross Detwiler, Chicago	2
Mike Fiers, Oakland	2
3 others	2

WILD PITCHES

Tyler Glasnow, Tampa Bay	7
Blake Snell, Tampa Bay	7
Carlos Carrasco, Cleveland	6
Pete Fairbanks, Tampa Bay	6
Framber Valdez, Houston	6
Taylor Williams, Seattle	6

WALKS PLUS HITS PER INNING

Kenta Maeda, Minnesota	0.75
Shane Bieber, Cleveland	0.87
Marco Gonzales, Seattle	0.95
Gerrit Cole, New York	0.96
Dylan Bundy, Los Angeles	1.04

OPPONENT AVERAGE

Shane Bieber, Cleveland	.167
Kenta Maeda, Minnesota	.168
Lucas Giolito, Chicago	.184
Gerrit Cole, New York	.197
Lance Lynn, Texas	.206

WORST ERA

Matthew Boyd, Detroit	6.71
Kyle Gibson, Texas	5.35
Aaron Civale, Cleveland	4.74
Martin Perez, Boston	4.50
Andrew Heaney, Los Angeles	4.46

FIELDING

PITCHER

PCT	12 players	1.000
PO	Lance McCullers Jr., Houston	11
A	Kenta Maeda, Minnesota	11
DP	Zack Greinke, Houston	3
	2 others	3
E	Jordan Montgomery, New York	3

CATCHER

PCT	Roberto Perez, Cleveland	1.000
	2 others	1.000
PO	Martin Maldonado, Houston	375
A	Michael Perez, Tampa Bay	25
DP	Christian Vazquez, Boston	3
E	Gary Sanchez, New York	6
CS	Roberto Perez, Cleveland	10
PB	Gary Sanchez, New York	5

FIRST BASE

PCT	Yuli Gurriel, Houston	.998
	2 others	.998
PO	Jose Abreu, Chicago	430
A	Yuli Gurriel, Houston	50
DP	Carlos Santana, Cleveland	44
E	Jose Abreu, Chicago	5

SECOND BASE

PCT	Jonathan Schoop, Detroit	.994
PO	Hanser Alberto, Baltimore	84
A	Cesar Hernandez, Cleveland	139
DP	Jose Altuve, Houston	36
E	Jose Altuve, Houston	4
	4 others	4

THIRD BASE

PCT	Gio Urshela, New York	.992
PO	Anthony Rendon, Los Angeles	48
A	Kyle Seager, Seattle	115
DP	Maikel Franco, Kansas City	17
	Yoan Moncada, Chicago	17
E	Rafael Devers, Boston	14

SHORTSTOP

PCT	Carlos Correa, Houston	.995
	Francisco Lindor, Cleveland	.995
PO	Adalberto Mondesi, Kansas City	85
A	Marcus Semien, Oakland	147
DP	Adalberto Mondesi, Kansas City	37
E	Willy Adames, Tampa Bay	9
	Gleyber Torres, New York	9

OUTFIELD

PCT	12 players	1.000
PO	Luis Robert, Chicago	151
A	Teoscar Hernandez, Toronto	7
	Alex Verdugo, Boston	7
DP	Teoscar Hernandez, Toronto	2
	2 others	2
E	Alex Verdugo, Boston	4

2020 STATISTICS

CLUB BATTING

	AVG	G	AB	R	H	2B	3B	HR	RBI	BB	SO	SB	OBP	SLG
New York	.272	60	2023	286	551	106	7	86	278	197	498	20	.348	.459
Atlanta	.268	60	2074	348	556	130	3	103	338	239	573	23	.349	.483
Washington	.264	60	1968	293	519	112	12	66	279	192	451	33	.336	.433
San Francisco	.263	60	2019	299	532	107	14	81	290	195	499	19	.335	.451
Colorado	.257	60	2057	275	528	84	16	63	264	161	543	42	.311	.405
Philadelphia	.257	60	1948	306	500	90	10	82	289	229	480	35	.342	.439
San Diego	.257	60	1972	325	506	103	12	95	312	204	479	55	.333	.466
Los Angeles	.256	60	2042	349	523	97	6	118	327	228	471	29	.338	.483
Miami	.244	60	1935	263	472	82	5	60	247	191	537	51	.319	.384
Arizona	.241	60	1997	269	482	101	12	58	255	181	461	23	.312	.391
St. Louis	.234	58	1752	240	410	73	7	51	231	205	477	18	.323	.371
Milwaukee	.223	60	1920	247	429	83	5	75	238	221	582	15	.313	.389
Chicago	.220	60	1918	265	422	82	8	74	248	229	568	24	.318	.387
Pittsburgh	.220	60	1932	219	425	76	6	59	210	167	521	16	.284	.357
Cincinnati	.212	60	1842	243	390	76	3	90	237	239	534	29	.312	.403

CLUB PITCHING

	ERA	G	CG	SHO	SV	IP	H	R	ER	HR	BB	SO	AVG
Los Angeles	3.02	60	0	5	15	538.2	424	213	181	66	145	517	.213
Cincinnati	3.84	60	3	5	9	504	401	243	215	67	213	615	.215
San Diego	3.86	60	1	5	13	520.1	456	241	223	70	170	565	.234
St. Louis	3.90	58	2	2	13	473	376	229	205	69	204	464	.216
Chicago	3.99	60	2	8	16	518.1	451	240	230	74	182	523	.233
Milwaukee	4.16	60	1	8	14	517.1	446	264	239	67	189	614	.229
Atlanta	4.41	60	0	4	13	524.1	494	288	257	69	220	506	.247
San Francisco	4.64	60	1	0	13	517.2	474	297	267	69	210	488	.241
Pittsburgh	4.68	60	1	3	6	513	451	298	267	80	249	536	.235
Arizona	4.84	162	0	7	50	1459	1364	766	713	225	570	1497	.253
Miami	4.86	162	3	7	36	1454	1452	794	731	258	546	1392	.261
New York	4.98	162	0	6	47	1432	1394	789	732	215	463	1475	.255
Washington	5.09	162	2	8	27	1444	1340	808	760	236	615	1378	.271
Philadelphia	5.14	162	1	6	31	1440	1511	911	829	241	584	1443	.279
Colorado	5.59	162	1	5	28	1449	1576	958	895	270	589	1264	.280

CLUB FIELDING

	PCT	PO	A	E	DP		PCT	PO	A	E	DP
Cincinnati	0.986	1512	442	27	36	St. Louis	.983	1419	489	33	46
Chicago	0.986	1555	559	30	46	Los Angeles	.982	1616	544	40	46
San Diego	0.985	1561	502	32	46	Miami	.981	1512	549	39	60
Atlanta	0.985	1573	533	33	52	Colorado	.981	1579	633	42	78
New York	0.985	1540	494	32	39	Washington	.981	1511	462	39	48
Milwaukee	0.984	1552	494	34	45	San Francisco	.980	1553	491	41	43
Arizona	0.983	1555	474	35	54	Pittsburgh	978	1539	511	47	53
Philadelphia	.983	1491	536	35	57						

INDIVIDUAL BATTING LEADERS

	AVG	G	AB	R	H	2B	3B	HR	RBI	BB	SO	SB
Juan Soto, Washington	.351	48	154	39	54	14	0	13	37	41	28	6
Freddie Freeman, Atlanta	.341	60	214	51	73	23	1	13	53	45	37	2
Marcell Ozuna, Atlanta	.338	60	228	38	77	14	0	18	56	38	60	0
Trea Turner, Washington	.335	59	233	46	78	15	4	12	51	22	36	12
Donovan Solano, San Francisco	.326	54	190	22	62	15	1	3	29	10	39	0
Michael Conforto, New York	.322	54	202	40	65	12	0	9	31	24	57	3
Raimel Tapia, Colorado	.321	51	184	26	59	8	2	1	17	14	38	8
Dominic Smith, New York	.316	50	177	27	56	21	1	10	42	14	45	0
Jeff McNeil, New York	.311	52	183	19	57	14	0	4	23	20	24	0
Corey Seager, Los Angeles	.307	52	212	38	65	12	1	15	41	17	37	1

INDIVIDUAL PITCHING LEADERS

	W	L	ERA	G	GS	CG	SV	IP	H	R	ER	BB	SO
Trevor Bauer, Cincinnati	5	4	1.73	11	11	2	0	73	41	17	14	17	100
Yu Darvish, Chicago	8	3	2.01	12	12	0	0	76	59	18	17	14	93
Dinelson Lamet, San Diego	3	1	2.09	12	12	0	0	69	39	18	16	20	93
Jacob deGrom, New York	4	2	2.38	12	12	0	0	68	47	21	18	18	104
Zach Davies, San Diego	7	4	2.73	12	12	0	0	69.1	55	26	21	19	63
Zac Gallen, Arizona	3	2	2.75	12	12	0	0	72	55	24	22	25	82
Kyle Hendricks, Chicago	6	5	2.88	12	12	1	0	81.1	73	26	26	8	64
Zack Wheeler, Phillies	4	2	2.92	11	11	0	0	71	67	26	23	16	53
Brandon Woodruff, Milwaukee	3	5	3.05	13	13	1	0	73.2	55	26	25	18	91
Adam Wainwright, St. Louis	5	3	3.15	10	10	2	0	65.2	54	25	23	15	54

AWARD WINNERS

Selected by Baseball Writers Association of America

MOST VALUABLE PLAYER

Player	1st	2nd	3rd	Total
Freddie Freeman, Braves	28	2		410
Mookie Betts, Dodgers	2	21	5	268
Manny Machado, Padres		2	16	221
Fernando Tatis Jr., Padres		2	5	201
Juan Soto, Nationals		3	2	172
Marcell Ozuna, Braves			2	167
Trea Turner, Nationals				83
Mike Yastrzemski, Giants				81
Corey Seager, Dodgers				43
Trevor Bauer, Reds				32
Trevor Story, Rockies				23
Ronald Acuna Jr., Braves				21
Dominic Smith, Mets				16
Yu Darvish, Cubs				14
Paul Goldschmidt, Cardinals				9
Brandon Belt, Giants				2
Wil Myers, Padres				2
Max Fried, Braves				1
Ian Happ, Cubs				1
Dansby Swanson, Braves				1
Ryan Tepera, Cubs				1
Devin Williams, Brewers				1

CY YOUNG AWARD

Player	1st	2nd	3rd	Total
Trevor Bauer, Reds	27	3		201
Yu Darvish, Cubs	3	24	2	123
Jacob deGrom, Mets		3	23	89
Dinelson Lamet, Padres			5	57
Max Fried, Braves				15
Corbin Burnes, Brewers				12
Aaron Nola, Phillies				3
Devin Williams, Brewers				3
Kyle Hendricks, Cubs				2
Zac Gallen, Diamondbacks				2
Clayton Kershaw, Dodgers				2

ROOKIE OF THE YEAR

Player	1st	2nd	3rd	Total
Devin Williams, Brewers	14	6	7	95
Alec Bohm, Phillies	9	8	5	74
Jake Cronenworth, Padres	6	12	8	74
Tony Gonsolin, Dodgers	1	1	3	11
Dustin May, Dodgers		2	2	8
Ke'Bryan Hayes, Pirates		1	2	5

MANAGER OF THE YEAR

Manager	1st	2nd	3rd	Total
Don Mattingly, Marlins	20	8		124
Jayce Tingler, Padres	6	13	2	71
David Ross, Cubs	1	2	14	25
Brian Snitker, Braves	1	2	5	16
Dave Roberts, Dodgers	1	2	2	13
Mike Shildt, Cardinals		3	1	10

GOLD GLOVE WINNERS

Selected by NL Managers

P—Max Fried, Braves. C—Tucker Barnhart, Reds. 1B—Anthony Rizzo, Cubs. 2B—Kolten Wong, Cardinals. 3B—Nolan Arenado, Rockies. SS—Javier Baez, Cubs. LF—Tyler O'Neill, Cardinals. CF—Trent Grisham, Padres. RF—Mookie Betts, Dodgers.

BATTING

GAMES
Starling Marte, Miami	61
Nick Castellanos, Cincinnati	60
Freddie Freeman, Atlanta	60
Didi Gregorius, Philadelphia	60
3 others	60

AT-BATS
Dansby Swanson, Atlanta	237
Trevor Story, Colorado	235
Trea Turner, Washington	233
Starling Marte, Miami	228
Marcell Ozuna, Atlanta	228

PLATE APPEARANCES
Marcell Ozuna, Atlanta	267
Dansby Swanson, Atlanta	264
Freddie Freeman, Atlanta	262
Trevor Story, Colorado	259
Trea Turner, Washington	259

RUNS
Freddie Freeman, Atlanta	51
Fernando Tatis Jr., San Diego	50
Dansby Swanson, Atlanta	49
Mookie Betts, Los Angeles	47
2 others	46

HITS
Trea Turner, Washington	78
Marcell Ozuna, Atlanta	77
Freddie Freeman, Atlanta	73
Manny Machado, San Diego	68
Trevor Story, Colorado	68

TOTAL BASES
Marcell Ozuna, Atlanta	145
Freddie Freeman, Atlanta	137
Trea Turner, Washington	137
Manny Machado, San Diego	130
Fernando Tatis Jr., San Diego	128

DOUBLES
Freddie Freeman, Atlanta	23
Dominic Smith, New York	21
Christan Walker, Arizona	18
Jake Cronenworth, San Diego	15
4 others	15

TRIPLES
Mike Yastrzemski, San Francisco	4
Asdrubal Cabrera, Washington	3
Jake Cronenworth, San Diego	3
Eduardo Escobar, Arizona	3
3 others	3

EXTRA-BASE HITS
Freddie Freeman, Atlanta	37
Marcell Ozuna, Atlanta	32
Dominic Smith, New York	32
Wil Myers, San Diego	31
Trea Turner, Washington	31

HOME RUNS
Marcell Ozuna, Atlanta	18
Fernando Tatis Jr., San Diego	17
Pete Alonso, New York	16
Mookie Betts, Los Angeles	16
4 others	16

RUNS BATTED IN
Marcell Ozuna, Atlanta	56
Freddie Freeman, Atlanta	53
Manny Machado, San Diego	47
Fernando Tatis Jr., San Diego	45
2 others	42

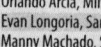

Marcell Ozuna

SACRIFICES
Austin Hedges, San Diego	5
Adam Eaton, Washington	4
Greg Garcia, San Diego	3
Garrett Hampson, Colorado	3
Adam Haseley, Philadelphia	3

SACRIFICE FLIES
Charlie Blackmon, Colorado	5
Jesus Aguilar, Miami	4
Nolan Arenado, Colorado	4
Josh Bell, Pittsburgh	4
4 others	4

HIT BY PITCHES
Willson Contreras, Chicago	14
Keston Hiura, Milwaukee	11
Anthony Rizzo, Chicago	10
Starling Marte, Miami	9
Victor Robles, Washington	9

WALKS
Bryce Harper, Philadelphia	49
Christian Yelich, Milwaukee	46
Freddie Freeman, Atlanta	45
Juan Soto, Washington	41
Max Muncy, Los Angeles	39

STOLEN BASES
Trevor Story, Colorado	15
Roman Quinn, Philadelphia	12
Trea Turner, Washington	12
Fernando Tatis Jr., San Diego	11
3 others	10

STOLEN BASE PERCENTAGE
Monte Harrison, Miami	1.000
Tommy Pham, San Diego	1.000
Roman Quinn, Philadelphia	1.000
Trent Grisham, San Diego	.909
3 others	.889

STRIKEOUTS
Keston Hiura, Milwaukee	85
Christian Yelich, Milwaukee	76
Javier Baez, Chicago	75
Dansby Swanson, Atlanta	71
Nick Castellanos, Cincinnati	69

AT-BATS PER STRIKEOUT
Nolan Arenado, Colorado	9.1
Starling Marte, Arizona	8.6
Didi Gregorius, Philadelphia	7.7
Jeff McNeil, New York	7.6
Trea Turner, Washington	6.5

Trea Turner

DOUBLE PLAYS
Orlando Arcia, Milwaukee	10
Evan Longoria, San Francisco	10
Manny Machado, San Diego	9
Colin Moran, Pittsburgh	9
4 others	8

MULTI-HIT GAMES
Corey Seager, Los Angeles	22
Trea Turner, Washington	22
Charlie Blackmon, Colorado	21
Freddie Freeman, Atlanta	21
Manny Machado, San Diego	21

ON-BASE PERCENTAGE
Juan Soto, Washington	.490
Freddie Freeman, Atlanta	.462
Marcell Ozuna, Atlanta	.431
Bryce Harper, Philadelphia	.420
Paul Goldschmidt, St. Louis	.417

ON-BASE PLUS SLUGGING
Juan Soto, Washington	1.185
Freddie Freeman, Atlanta	1.102
Marcell Ozuna, Atlanta	1.067
Dominic Smith, New York	.993
Ronald Acuna Jr., Atlanta	.987

PITCHING

WINS
Yu Darvish, Chicago	8
Zach Davies, San Diego	7
Max Fried, Atlanta	7
Kyle Hendricks, Chicago	6
3 others	6

LOSSES
Luke Weaver, Arizona	9
Trevor Williams, Pittsburgh	8
Patrick Corbin, Washington	7
Rick Porcello, New York	7
3 others	6

GAMES
Tyler Rogers, San Francisco	29
Shane Greene, Atlanta	28
Kenley Jansen, Los Angeles	27
Chris Stratton, Pittsburgh	27
Blake Treinen, Los Angeles	27

GAMES STARTED
Kyle Freeland, Colorado	13
German Marquez, Colorado	13
Brandon Woodruff, Milwaukee	13
Luis Castillo, Cincinnati	12
14 others	12

GAMES FINISHED
Kenley Jansen, Los Angeles	24
Brandon Kintzler, Miami	21
Edwin Diaz, New York	19
Mark Melancon, Atlanta	19
2 others	17

COMPLETE GAMES
Trevor Bauer, Cincinnati	2
Aaron Nola, Philadelphia	2
Adam Wainwright, St. Louis	2
Tyler Anderson, San Francisco	1
11 others	1

SHUTOUTS
Trevor Bauer, Cincinnati	2
Mike Clevinger, San Diego	1
Zach Eflin, Philadelphia	1
Kyle Hendricks, Chicago	1
Alec Mills, Chicago	1

Aaron Nola, Philadelphia 1

SAVES
Josh Hader, Milwaukee 13
Brandon Kintzler, Miami 12
Kenley Jansen, Los Angeles 11
Mark Melancon, Atlanta 11
Daniel Hudson, Washington 10

INNINGS PITCHED
German Marquez, Colorado 81.2
Kyle Hendricks, Chicago 81.1
Yu Darvish, Chicago 76
B. Woodruff, Milwaukee 73.2
Antonio Senzatela, Colorado 73.1

HITS ALLOWED
Patrick Corbin, Washington 85
German Marquez, Colorado 78
Kyle Freeland, Colorado 77
Rick Porcello, New York 74
Kyle Hendricks, Chicago 73

RUNS ALLOWED
Trevor Williams, Pittsburgh 42
Johnny Cueto, San Francisco 41
Adrian Houser, Milwaukee 41
German Marquez, Colorado 41
Rick Porcello, New York 41

HOME RUNS ALLOWED
Trevor Williams, Pittsburgh 15
Steven Matz, New York 14
Chris Paddack, San Diego 14
Austin Voth, Washington 14
2 others 13

WALKS ALLOWED
Robbie Ray, Arizona 31
Chad Kuhl, Pittsburgh 28
Ryan Castellani, Colorado 26
Johnny Cueto, San Francisco 26
Sonny Gray, Cincinnati 25

LOWEST WALKS PER NINE
Kyle Hendricks, Chicago 0.89
Yu Darvish, Chicago 1.66
Zack Wheeler, Philadelphia 2.03
Adam Wainwright, St. Louis 2.06
Trevor Bauer, Cincinnati 2.1

HIT BATTERS
Logan Webb, San Francisco 7
Zack Wheeler, Philadelphia 7

Madison Bumgarner, Arizona 6
Steven Brault, Pittsburgh 5
5 others 5

STRIKEOUTS
Jacob deGrom, New York 104
Trevor Bauer, Cincinnati 100
Aaron Nola, Philadelphia 96
Yu Darvish, Chicago 93
Dinelson Lamet, San Diego 93

STRIKEOUTS PER NINE
Jacob deGrom, New York 13.8
Trevor Bauer, Cincinnati 12.3
Max Scherzer, Washington 12.3
Dinelson Lamet, San Diego 12.1
Aaron Nola, Philadelphia 12.1

STRIKEOUTS PER NINE
(Relievers)
Chris Stratton, Pittsburgh 11.7
Seth Lugo, New York 11.7
Tejay Antone, Cincinnati 11.5

Jacob deGrom

Brent Suter, Milwaukee 11.0
Derek Holland, Pittsburgh 10.1

DOUBLE PLAYS
Kyle Freeland, Colorado 14
Zack Wheeler, Philadelphia 13
Jake Arrieta, Philadelphia 9
Zac Gallen, Arizona 9
Antonio Senzatela, Colorado 9

PICKOFFS
Tyler Anderson, San Francisco 4
Max Fried, Atlanta 4
Wandy Peralta, San Francisco 3
Vince Velasquez, Philadelphia 3
4 others 2

WILD PITCHES
Sonny Gray, Cincinnati 7
Robbie Ray, Arizona 6
Max Scherzer, Washington 6
Corbin Burnes, Milwaukee 5
13 others 4

**WALKS PLUS HITS
PER INNING**
Trevor Bauer, Cincinnati 0.79
Dinelson Lamet, San Diego 0.86
Jacob DeGrom, New York 0.96
Yu Darvish, Chicago 0.96
B. Woodruff, Milwaukee 0.99

OPPONENT AVERAGE
Trevor Bauer, Cincinnati .159
Dinelson Lamet, San Diego .161
Jacob DeGrom, New York .190
B. Woodruff, Milwaukee .204
Aaron Nola, Philadelphia .205

WORST ERA
Johnny Cueto, San Francisco 5.40
Jon Lester, Chicago 5.16
Patrick Corbin, Washington 4.66
Alec Mills, Chicago 4.48
Kyle Freeland, Colorado 4.33

FIELDING

PITCHER
PCT	13 players	1.000
PO	Pablo Lopez, Miami	11
A	Max Fried, Atlanta	15
DP	Antonio Senzatela, Colorado	4
E	German Marquez, Colorado	3

CATCHER
PCT	3 players	1.000
PO	Wilson Ramos, New York	396
A	Jacob Stallings, Pittsburgh	22
DP	4 players	3
E	Yadier Molina, St. Louis	5
CS	Jacob Stallings, Pittsburgh	9
CS	Willson Contreras, Chicago	9
PB	Travis d'Arnaud, Atlanta	5

FIRST BASE
PCT	3 players	.998
PO	Freddie Freeman, Atlanta	427
A	Anthony Rizzo, Chicago	44
DP	Freddie Freeman, Atlanta	44
E	2 players	5

SECOND BASE
PCT	2 players	.994
PO	Keston Hiura, Milwaukee	66
A	Kolten Wong, St. Louis	129
DP	Kolten Wong, St. Louis	29
E	2 players	7

THIRD BASE
PCT	Manny Machado, San Diego	.987
PO	Eugenio Suarez, Cincinnati	47
A	Brian Anderson, Miami	119
DP	Nolan Arenado, Colorado	19
E	Brian Anderson, Miami	9

SHORTSTOP
PCT	Dansby Swanson, Atlanta	.991
PO	Trevor Story, Colorado	88
A	Trevor Story, Colorado	161
DP	Trevor Story, Colorado	49
E	Trevor Story, Colorado	10

OUTFIELD
PCT	13 players	1.000
PO	Trent Grisham, San Diego	134
A	Michael Conforto, New York	6
DP	Charlie Blackmon, Colorado	2
DP	Dylan Carlson, St. Louis	2
E	Mookie Betts, Los Angeles	4

TODD KIRKLAND/GETTY IMAGES

2020 POSTSEASON

SEAN M HAFFEY/GETTY IMAGES

The Dodgers posted the best record in baseball and beat the Rays in the World Series in six games.

Dodgers Cement Their Legacy, Earn First Title In 32 Years

BY SCOTT MILLER

Winning the last game of the season cements—and changes—reputations. For 32 years, every single player who passed through Los Angeles wearing Dodgers blue has been overshadowed by Kirk Gibson's home run, Orel Hershiser's dominance, Tommy Lasorda's triumph and never-ending scoreboard highlights of the rest of the 1988 Dodgers that shocked Oakland to become World Series champions.

The 2020 Dodgers dragged the added weight of eight NL West titles and two NL pennants (2017, 2018) with no rings to show.

That all changed, finally, on a glorious yet strange night in Arlington, Texas at the first neutral-site World Series in baseball history when the Dodgers took down the Tampa Bay Rays in Game 6 to claim their first title since the days of Gibson and Hershiser.

So, too, did the reputation of ace Clayton Kershaw: The future Hall of Famer who had become the target of so many slings and arrows for his October failures earned two victories and, now, will forever be known as a World Series champion.

So, too, will manager Dave Roberts, who never wavered in the face of harsh criticism in previous Octobers for some of his managerial decisions.

Roberts never had a doubt that this was going to be the Dodgers' year and, looking backward, the signs were everywhere.

The Dodgers steamrolled to the best record in baseball during the COVID-19-shortened season at 43-17. They finished six games ahead of the

San Diego Padres, dominated at home (21-9) and blasted their way to an MLB-best +136 run differential, a whopping 52 runs better than the second-place Padres (+84).

The Dodgers paced the majors with 118 homers in those 60 games, and their per-game average of 1.97 was the best in MLB history. Mookie Betts and A.J. Pollock led the power display with 16 each and three other Dodgers reached double-digits. Then, in the World Series, the Dodgers became the first team ever to have nine different players hit at least one home run.

Not to mention the Dodgers led the majors in team ERA (3.02), opponent batting average (.213) and WHIP (1.06).

Roberts became the first manager ever to lead a team to a division title in each of his first five seasons managing. Under Roberts, the Dodgers have produced the game's best record since 2016.

Meanwhile, the Dodgers are 528-343 (.606) since Andrew Friedman became president of baseball operations, including posting the most wins in franchise history in 2019 (106).

But it wasn't until this October that they won a World Series, when reputations were changed and cemented.

The Road to the World Series

It was the most unusual October in MLB history. For one thing, because the playoffs were expanded to 16 teams, it was the most challenging path ever simply to get to the World Series. And because of the coronavirus, only the Wild Card Series was played in the hosts' home stadiums.

The Division Series, League Championship Series and World Series were at neutral sites: The American League Division Series was played in San Diego's Petco Park and Dodger Stadium. The NL Division Series' were played at Globe Life Field in Arlington and Houston's Minute Maid Park.

The expanded playoffs included the top two finishers in each division plus two more wild-card teams, resulting in the first time that sub.-500 clubs played in an MLB postseason—the Brewers and Astros each finished 29-31. The Brewers were swept by the Dodgers and the Astros swept the Twins, adding to Minnesota's postseason misery.

Another oddity: Because the virus-induced change to the regular-season schedule kept teams in their own geographical pods, it wasn't until October that intersectional matchups occurred. Those did not go well for the AL and NL Central divisions. Seven total teams from the Central qualified for the playoffs, and they combined to go 2-14. Of the eight teams eliminated in the first

Shortstop Corey Seager took home the NLCS MVP and the World Series MVP.

KELLY GAVIN/MLB PHOTOS VIA GETTY IMAGES

round, seven came from the Central divisions. And they went meekly: Central teams were shut out in five of their eight first-round losses.

In happier stories, the most inspirational may have been the Marlins regrouping after a COVID-19 outbreak the first weekend of the season to claim their first postseason spot since 2003. Then, in an interesting parallel to '03, the Marlins beat the Cubs in a Wild Card Series before losing to Atlanta in the Division Series. Gone, though, was the game's second-longest playoff drought after the Seattle Mariners (2001).

Meanwhile, the Padres, playing in their first postseason since 2006, dropped the first game to St. Louis before storming back to win the next two and advance to the Division Series, where they were beaten by the Dodgers.

As things turned out, the Dodgers' closest call of the fall came in the NLCS, where they fell behind Atlanta three games to one and then trailed the Braves 2-0 and 3-2 in Game 7 before picking up a run in the sixth and another in the seventh to upend Atlanta. Corey Seager was named NLCS MVP after going 9 for 29 with five homers and 11 RBIs. His seven extra-base hits tied Atlanta's Javy Lopez (1996) for the all-time NLCS record.

In the AL, the good news for the Yankees was that they finally had a healthy Aaron Judge and Giancarlo Stanton when the postseason started, and when they blasted Tampa Bay 9-3 in Game

1 of their Division Series in a four-homer power display, including longballs from both Judge and Stanton, it looked like maybe they were going to exact vengeance on the AL East winner. The Rays, however, pushed the Yankees to Game 5 and then pinch-hitter Mike Brosseau shocked everybody by walloping a go-ahead homer in the bottom of the eighth against closer Aroldis Chapman.

It was an indelible moment, especially given the bad blood between the Yankees and Rays over the past few years. The Yankees were positioned where they wanted to be up to that point, with $324-million man Gerrit Cole starting Game 5. But then Chapman was felled by an undrafted free agent from Northwest Indiana who played college ball at tiny Oakland University in Rochester, Mich.

So the Rays moved on to the ALCS where they again were extended as far as the series would go, this time by an Astros team with a core aiming for what would be its third World Series in four years. Houston was just gaining its footing after posting a losing record in the regular season and remained steady despite falling behind three games to one thanks in no small part to a dizzing array of sensational Rays defensive plays.

The Rays, though, won Game 7, 4-2, thanks to a memorable start from Charlie Morton and stellar work from relief aces Nick Anderson and Pete Fairbanks.

October's breakout star Randy Arozarena was named as the ALCS MVP, the first rookie ever to

be honored as such. Acquired in a deal with St. Louis during the offseason, Arozarena smashed four homers, went 9 for 28, scored six runs and collected six RBIs against the Astros.

Dodger Blue Finish

A Tampa Bay-Los Angeles World Series was incredibly appropriate for two reasons. Like the Dodgers, the Rays (40-20) finished with the best record in their league. It was the fourth time in the wild card era that No. 1 seeds from the AL and NL advanced to the Fall Classic. Also, it matched the Rays, a heavily analytics-based team, against the Dodgers and Friedman, the former Tampa Bay GM who laid the foundation for the Rays' only other World Series appearance in 2008.

The Dodgers dominated Game 1 behind an ace-like performance from Kershaw. Tampa Bay evened the Series in Game 2, notable for the Dodgers using an "opener"—Tony Gonsolin— thus, ahem, borrowing a strategy invented by the Rays a couple of years ago.

The Dodgers dominated Game 3 and appeared late in Game 4 to be on their way to seizing a commanding Series lead when, suddenly, the game took one of the most bizarre turns in World Series history when the Rays scored two runs on a wild play in the bottom of the ninth to steal an 8-7 win and even the World Series at two games apiece.

Hyperbole? Not at all. Arozarena scored the winning run with two outs in the bottom of the

AMERICAN LEAGUE CHAMPIONS, 1996–2020

American League postseason results in Wild Card Era, 1996-present, where (*) denotes wild card playoff entrant.

YEAR	CHAMPIONSHIP SERIES	ALCS MVP	DIVISION SERIES	DIVISION SERIES
2020	Tampa Bay 4, Houston 3	Randy Arozarena, OF, Tampa Bay	Tampa Bay 3, New York 2	Houston 3, Oakland 1
2019	Houston 4, New York 2	José Altuve, 2B, Houston	Houston 3, Tampa Bay* 2	New York 3, Minnesota 0
2018	Boston 4, Houston 1	Jackie Bradley Jr., OF, Boston	Boston 3, New York* 1	Houston 3, Cleveland 0
2017	Houston 4, New York 3	Justin Verlander, RHP, Houston	New York* 3, Cleveland 2	Houston 3, Boston 1
2016	Cleveland 4, Toronto 1	Andrew Miller, LHP, Cleveland	Toronto* 3, Texas 0	Cleveland 3, Boston 0
2015	Kansas City 4, Toronto 2	Alcides Escobar, SS, Kansas City	Kansas City 3, Houston* 2	Baltimore 3, Texas 2
2014	Kansas City 4, Baltimore 0	Lorenzo Cain, OF, Kansas City	Kansas City 3, Los Angeles 0	Baltimore 3, Detroit 0
2013	Boston 4, Detroit 2	Koji Uehara, RHP, Boston	Boston 3, Tampa Bay* 1	Detroit, 3, Oakland 2
2012	Detroit 4, New York 0	Delmon Young, OF, Detroit	New York 3, Baltimore* 2	Detroit 3, Oakland 2
2011	Texas 4, Detroit 2	Nelson Cruz, OF, Texas	Detroit 3, New York 2	Texas 3, Tampa Bay* 1
2010	Texas 4, New York 2	Josh Hamilton, OF, Texas	Texas 3, Tampa Bay 2	New York* 3, Minnesota 0
2009	New York 4, Los Angeles 2	C.C. Sabathia, LHP, New York	New York 3, Minnesota 0	Los Angeles 3, Boston* 0
2008	Tampa Bay 4, Boston 3	Matt Garza, RHP, Tampa Bay	Boston* 3, Los Angeles 1	Tampa Bay 3, Chicago 1
2007	Boston 4, Cleveland 3	Josh Beckett, RHP, Boston	Boston 3, Los Angeles 0	Cleveland 3, New York* 1
2006	Detroit 4, Oakland 0	Placido Polanco, 2B, Detroit	Detroit* 3, New York 1	Oakland 3, Minnesota 0
2005	Chicago 4, Los Angeles 1	Paul Konerko, 1B, Chicago	Chicago 3, Boston* 0	Los Angeles 3, New York 2
2004	Boston 4, New York 3	David Ortiz, DH, Boston	Boston* 3, Anaheim 0	New York 3, Minnesota 1
2003	New York 4, Boston 3	Mariano Rivera, RHP, New York	New York 3, Minnesota 1	Boston* 3, Oakland 2
2002	Anaheim 4, Minnesota 1	Adam Kennedy, 2B, Anaheim	Anaheim* 3, New York 1	Minnesota 3, Oakland 2
2001	New York 4, Seattle 1	Andy Pettitte, LHP, New York	Seattle 3, Cleveland 2	New York 3, Oakland* 2
2000	New York 4, Seattle 2	David Justice, OF, New York	New York 3, Oakland 2	Seattle* 3, Chicago 0
1999	New York 4, Boston 1	Orlando Hernandez, RHP, New York	Boston* 3, Cleveland 2	New York 3, Texas 0
1998	New York 4, Cleveland 2	David Wells, LHP, New York	Cleveland 3, Boston* 1	New York 3, Texas 0
1997	Cleveland 4, Baltimore 2	Marquis Grissom, OF, Cleveland	Cleveland 3, New York* 2	Baltimore 3, Seattle 1
1996	New York 4, Baltimore 1	Bernie Williams, OF, New York	Baltimore* 3, Cleveland 1	New York 3, Texas 1

ninth on a play on which the Dodgers committed two fielding errors—center fielder Chris Taylor bobbled pinch-hitter Brett Phillips' single up the middle, and then catcher Will Smith whiffed on catching a relay throw to the plate. Kiermaeier scored the tying run from second—with two outs, he was running on the pitch and was going to tie the game regardless of Taylor's bobble.

But utter wackiness set in when Arozarena, sprinting all the way from first, stumbled rounding third base and ultimately fell halfway between third and home. He looked like an easy out and extra innings appeared imminent. Except, when Smith missed the catch while trying to rush a sweep tag, Arozarena, who had started back to third base, U-turned and dashed home as the ball bounced to the backstop. Closer Kenley Jansen failed to back up the plate and Arozarena scored the winning run. Phillips, meanwhile, was a utilityman who hadn't had a hit since Sept. 25 and wasn't even on the Rays' ALCS roster. After the Dodgers winning, this play will be the most-remembered thing about the 2020 World Series.

Kershaw made sure the Dodgers regained their balance in Game 5, including emerging from trouble in a fifth inning that turned out to be the Rays' last gasp. With the Rays trailing 3-2 with two on and runners at the corners, Margot broke from third on an attempted straight steal of home. Kershaw, a lefty whose back was to third base, calmly stepped off the rubber and threw home.

Margot was out by inches, ending the inning. The Dodgers then wrapped up the World Series with a 4-2 win in Game 5 and a 3-1 triumph in Game 6, which became notable when a dominant Blake Snell, working on a two-hit shutout, was hooked by manager Kevin Cash with one out in the sixth and a 1-0 lead. He had faced Mookie Betts, Corey Seager and Justin Turner six times combined with six strikeouts. Yet, with Betts due up a third time, Cash summoned Nick Anderson, and six pitches later the Rays' lead was gone.

Capping off an incredible fall, Seager added a World Series MVP to his NLCS MVP. And while MLB was able to navigate its way through a world-wide pandemic to successfully finish its abbreviated season as a model to people everywhere of what can be accomplished by doing things the right way, an ugly reminder of just how perilous things remained came in the eighth inning.

The Dodgers were forced to remove the heart of their team, Justin Turner, because a positive COVID-19 test came back during the game. Turner immediately was sent into self-isolation, but he returned to the field during the Dodgers' celebration and eventually removed his mask for pictures.

The incident ricocheted around the country and MLB announced an investigation a day later.

In a way, there couldn't have been a more fitting ending to a 2020 season that was never a sure thing to begin.

NATIONAL LEAGUE CHAMPIONS, 1996–2020

National League postseason results in Wild Card Era, 1996-present, where (*) denotes wild card playoff entrant.

YEAR	CHAMPIONSHIP SERIES	NLCS MVP	DIVISION SERIES	DIVISION SERIES
2020	Los Angeles 4, Atlanta 3	Corey Seager, SS, Los Angeles	Los Angeles 3, San Diego 0	Atlanta 3, Miami 0
2019	Washington 4, St. Louis 0	Howie Kendrick, 2B, Washington	Washington* 3, Los Angeles 2	St. Louis 3, Atlanta 2
2018	Los Angeles 4, Milwaukee 3	Cody Bellinger, 1B/OF, Los Angeles	Los Angeles 3, Atlanta 1	Milwaukee 3, Colorado 0*
2017	Los Angeles 4, Chicago 1	Justin Turner, 3B/Chris Taylor, CF, L.A.	Los Angeles 3, Arizona* 0	Chicago 3, Washington 2
2016	Chicago 4, Los Angeles 2	Javier Baez, 2B/Jon Lester, LHP, Chicago	Chicago 3, San Francisco* 1	Los Angeles 3, Washington 2
2015	New York 4, Chicago 0	Daniel Murphy, 2B, New York	New York 3, Los Angeles 2	Chicago* 3, St. Louis 1
2014	San Francisco 4, St. Louis 1	Madison Bumgarner, LHP, San Francisco	San Francisco 3, Washington 1	St. Louis 3, Los Angeles 1
2013	St. Louis 4, Los Angeles 2	Michael Wacha, RHP, St. Louis	St. Louis 3, Pittsburgh* 2	Los Angeles 3, Atlanta 1
2012	San Francisco 4, St. Louis 3	Marco Scutaro, 2B, San Francisco	St. Louis* 3, Washington 2	San Francisco 3, Cincinnati 2
2011	St. Louis 4, Milwaukee 2	David Freese, 3B, St. Louis	St. Louis* 3, Philadelphia 2	Milwaukee 3, Arizona 2
2010	San Francisco 4, Philadelphia 2	Cody Ross, OF, San Francisco	Philadelphia 3, Cincinnati 0	San Francisco 3, Atlanta* 1
2009	Philadelphia 4, Los Angeles 1	Ryan Howard, 1B, Philadelphia	Los Angeles 3, St. Louis 0	Philadelphia 3, Colorado* 1
2008	Philadelphia 4, Los Angeles 1	Cole Hamels, LHP, Philadelphia	Los Angeles 3, Chicago 0	Philadelphia 3, Milwaukee* 1
2007	Colorado 4, Arizona 0	Matt Holliday, OF, Colorado	Arizona 3, Chicago 0	Colorado* 3, Philadelphia 0
2006	St. Louis 4, New York 3	Jeff Suppan, RHP, St. Louis	New York 3, Los Angeles* 0	St. Louis 3, San Diego 1
2005	Houston 4, St. Louis 2	Roy Oswalt, RHP, Houston	St. Louis 3, San Diego 0	Houston* 3, Atlanta 1
2004	St. Louis 4, Houston 3	Albert Pujols, 1B, St. Louis	St. Louis 3, Los Angeles 1	Houston* 3, Atlanta 2
2003	Florida 4, Chicago 3	Ivan Rodriguez, C, Florida	Florida* 3, San Francisco 1	Chicago 3, Atlanta 2
2002	San Francisco 4, St. Louis 1	Benito Santiago, C, San Francisco	San Francisco* 3, Atlanta 2	St. Louis 3, Arizona 0
2001	Arizona 4, Atlanta 1	Craig Counsell, SS, Arizona	Atlanta 3, Houston 0	Arizona 3, St. Louis* 2
2000	New York 4, St. Louis 1	Mike Hampton, LHP, New York	St. Louis 3, Atlanta 0	New York* 3, San Francisco 1
1999	Atlanta 4, New York 2	Eddie Perez, C, Atlanta	Atlanta 3, Houston 1	New York* 3, Arizona 1
1998	San Diego 4, Atlanta 2	Sterling Hitchcock, LHP, San Diego	Atlanta 3, Chicago* 0	San Diego 3, Houston 1
1997	Florida 4, Atlanta 2	Livan Hernandez, RHP, Florida	Florida* 3, San Francisco 0	Atlanta 3, Houston 0
1996	Atlanta 4, St. Louis 3	Javy Lopez, C, Atlanta	St. Louis 3, San Diego 0	Atlanta 3, Los Angeles* 0

MAJOR LEAGUES

Year	Winner	Loser	Result
1904	NO SERIES		
1905	New York (NL)	Philadelphia (AL)	4-1
1906	Chicago (AL)	Chicago (NL)	4-2
1907	Chicago (NL)	Detroit (AL)	4-0
1908	Chicago (NL)	Detroit (AL)	4-1
1909	Pittsburgh (NL)	Detroit (AL)	4-3
1910	Philadelphia (AL)	Chicago (NL)	4-1
1911	Philadelphia (AL)	New York (NL)	4-2
1912	Boston (AL)	New York (NL)	4-3-1
1913	Philadelphia (AL)	New York (NL)	4-1
1914	Boston (NL)	Philadelphia (AL)	4-0
1915	Boston (AL)	Philadelphia (NL)	4-1
1916	Boston (AL)	Brooklyn (NL)	4-1
1917	Chicago (AL)	New York (NL)	4-2
1918	Boston (AL)	Chicago (NL)	4-2
1919	Cincinnati (NL)	Chicago (AL)	5-3
1920	Cleveland (AL)	Brooklyn (NL)	5-2
1921	New York (NL)	New York (AL)	5-3
1922	New York (NL)	New York (AL)	4-0
1923	New York (AL)	New York (NL)	4-2
1924	Washington (AL)	New York (NL)	4-3
1925	Pittsburgh (NL)	Washington (AL)	4-3
1926	St. Louis (NL)	New York (AL)	4-3
1927	New York (AL)	Pittsburgh (NL)	4-0
1928	New York (AL)	St. Louis (NL)	4-0
1929	Philadelphia (AL)	Chicago (NL)	4-1
1930	Philadelphia (AL)	St. Louis (NL)	4-2
1931	St. Louis (NL)	Philadelphia (AL)	4-3
1932	New York (AL)	Chicago (NL)	4-0
1933	New York (NL)	Washington (AL)	4-1
1934	St. Louis (NL)	Detroit (AL)	4-3
1935	Detroit (AL)	Chicago (NL)	4-2
1936	New York (AL)	New York (NL)	4-2
1937	New York (AL)	New York (NL)	4-1
1938	New York (AL)	Chicago (NL)	4-0
1939	New York (AL)	Cincinnati (NL)	4-0
1940	Cincinnati (NL)	Detroit (AL)	4-3
1941	New York (AL)	Brooklyn (NL)	4-1
1942	St. Louis (NL)	New York (AL)	4-1
1943	New York (AL)	St. Louis (NL)	4-1
1944	St. Louis (NL)	St. Louis (AL)	4-2
1945	Detroit (AL)	Chicago (NL)	4-3
1946	St. Louis (NL)	Boston (AL)	4-3
1947	New York (AL)	Brooklyn (NL)	4-3
1948	Cleveland (AL)	Boston (NL)	4-2
1949	New York (AL)	Brooklyn (NL)	4-1
1950	New York (AL)	Philadelphia (NL)	4-0
1951	New York (AL)	New York (NL)	4-2
1952	New York (AL)	Brooklyn (NL)	4-3
1953	New York (AL)	Brooklyn (NL)	4-2
1954	New York (NL)	Cleveland (AL)	4-0
1955	Brooklyn (NL)	New York (AL)	4-3
1956	New York (AL)	Brooklyn (NL)	4-3
1957	Milwaukee (NL)	New York (AL)	4-3
1958	New York (AL)	Milwaukee (NL)	4-3
1959	Los Angeles (NL)	Chicago (AL)	4-2
1960	Pittsburgh (NL)	New York (AL)	4-3
1961	New York (AL)	Cincinnati (NL)	4-1
1962	New York (AL)	San Francisco (NL)	4-3
1963	Los Angeles (NL)	New York (AL)	4-0
1964	St. Louis (NL)	New York (AL)	4-3
1965	Los Angeles (NL)	Minnesota (AL)	4-3
1966	Baltimore (AL)	Los Angeles (NL)	4-0
1967	St. Louis (NL)	Boston (AL)	4-3
1968	Detroit (AL)	St. Louis (NL)	4-3
1969	New York (NL)	Baltimore (AL)	4-1
1970	Baltimore (AL)	Cincinnati (NL)	4-1

Clayton Kershaw

Year	Winner	Loser	Result
1971	Pittsburgh (NL)	Baltimore (AL)	4-3
1972	Oakland (AL)	Cincinnati (NL)	4-3
1973	Oakland (AL)	New York (NL)	4-3
1974	Oakland (AL)	Los Angeles (NL)	4-1
1975	Cincinnati (NL)	Boston (AL)	4-3
1976	Cincinnati (NL)	New York (AL)	4-0
1977	New York (AL)	Los Angeles (NL)	4-2
1978	New York (AL)	Los Angeles (NL)	4-2
1979	Pittsburgh (NL)	Baltimore (AL)	4-3
1980	Philadelphia (NL)	Kansas City (AL)	4-2
1981	Los Angeles (NL)	New York (AL)	4-2
1982	St. Louis (NL)	Milwaukee (AL)	4-3
1983	Baltimore (AL)	Philadelphia (NL)	4-1
1984	Detroit (AL)	San Diego (NL)	4-1
1985	Kansas City (AL)	St. Louis (NL)	4-3
1986	New York (NL)	Boston (AL)	4-3
1987	Minnesota (AL)	St. Louis (NL)	4-3
1988	Los Angeles (NL)	Oakland (AL)	4-1
1989	Oakland (AL)	San Francisco (NL)	4-0
1990	Cincinnati (NL)	Oakland (AL)	4-0
1991	Minnesota (AL)	Atlanta (NL)	4-3
1992	Toronto (AL)	Atlanta (NL)	4-2
1993	Toronto (AL)	Philadelphia (NL)	4-2
1994	NO SERIES		
1995	Atlanta (NL)	Cleveland (AL)	4-2
1996	New York (AL)	Atlanta (NL)	4-2
1997	Florida (NL)	Cleveland (AL)	4-3
1998	New York (AL)	San Diego (NL)	4-0
1999	New York (AL)	Atlanta (NL)	4-0
2000	New York (AL)	New York (NL)	4-1
2001	Arizona (NL)	New York (AL)	4-3
2002	Anaheim (AL)	San Francisco (NL)	4-3
2003	Florida (NL)	New York (AL)	4-2
2004	Boston (AL)	St. Louis (NL)	4-0
2005	Chicago (AL)	Houston (NL)	4-0
2006	St. Louis (NL)	Detroit (AL)	4-1
2007	Boston (AL)	Colorado (NL)	4-0
2008	Philadelphia (NL)	Tampa Bay (AL)	4-1
2009	New York (AL)	Philadelphia (NL)	4-2
2010	San Francisco (NL)	Texas (AL)	4-1
2011	St. Louis (NL)	Texas (AL)	4-3
2012	San Francisco (NL)	Detroit (AL)	4-0
2013	Boston (AL)	St. Louis (NL)	4-2
2014	San Francisco (NL)	Kansas City (AL)	4-3
2015	Kansas City (AL)	New York (NL)	4-1
2016	Chicago (NL)	Cleveland (AL)	4-3
2017	Houston (AL)	Los Angeles (NL)	4-3
2018	Boston (AL)	Los Angeles (NL)	4-1
2019	Washington (NL)	Houston (AL)	4-3
2020	Los Angeles (NL)	Tampa Bay (AL)	4-2

RONALD MARTINEZ/GETTY IMAGES

WORLD SERIES BOX SCORES

GAME ONE October 20, 2020

LOS ANGELES DODGERS 8, TAMPA BAY RAYS 3

	1	2	3	4	5	6	7	8	9	R	H	E
TAMPA BAY	0	0	0	0	1	0	2	0	0	3	6	0
LOS ANGELES	0	0	0	2	4	2	0	0	X	8	10	0

TAMPA BAY	AB	R	H	RBI	BB	SO	LOB	AVG
Díaz, Y, 1B	4	0	1	0	0	0	0	.250
Lowe, B, 2B	4	0	0	0	0	1	1	.000
Arozarena, DH	3	0	0	0	1	1	0	.000
Renfroe, RF	2	0	0	0	0	1	2	.000
a-Meadows, PH-RF	2	0	0	0	0	1	0	.000
Margot, LF	4	1	1	0	0	2	2	.250
Wendle, 3B-SS	4	1	1	0	0	0	0	.250
Adames, SS	2	0	0	0	0	2	0	.000
Choi, PH	0	0	0	0	0	0	0	.000
b-Brosseau, PH-3B	1	0	1	1	0	0	0	1.000
Kiermaier, CF	3	1	2	2	0	0	0	.667
Zunino, C	3	0	0	0	0	2	2	.000
TOTALS	32	3	6	3	1	10	7	.188

a-Struck out for Renfroe in the 7th. b-Singled for Choi in the 7th. 2B: Wendle (1, Floro). HR: Kiermaier (1, 5th inning off Kershaw, 0 on, 2 out). TB: Brosseau; Díaz, Y; Kiermaier 5; Margot; Wendle 2. RBI: Brosseau (1); Kiermaier 2 (2).

LOS ANGELES	AB	R	H	RBI	BB	SO	LOB	AVG
Betts, RF	4	2	2	1	1	1	0	.500
Seager, C, SS	2	1	0	0	3	0	1	.000
Turner, 3B	4	1	1	0	1	2	4	.250
Muncy, 1B	4	2	2	2	1	0	2	.500
Smith, W, DH	5	1	1	1	0	2	4	.200
Bellinger, CF	4	1	1	2	0	1	3	.250
Taylor, Ch, 2B-LF	3	0	2	1	1	1	0	.667
Pederson, LF	2	0	0	0	0	2	2	.000
a-Hernández, K, PH-2B	2	0	1	1	0	0	0	.500
Barnes, A, C	4	0	0	0	0	2	3	.000
TOTALS	34	8	10	8	7	11	19	.294

a-singled for Pederson in the 5th. 2B: Turner (1, Fleming); Muncy (1, Fleming). HR: Bellinger (1, 4th inning off Glasnow, 1 on, 1 out); Betts (1, 6th inning off Fleming, 0 on, 0 out). TB: Bellinger 4; Betts 5; Hernández, K; Muncy 3; Smith, W; Taylor, Ch 2; Turner 2. RBI: Bellinger 2 (2); Betts (1); Hernández, K (1); Muncy 2 (2); Smith, W (1); Taylor, Ch (1).

TAMPA BAY	IP	H	R	ER	BB	SO	HR	ERA
Glasnow (L, 0-1)	4.1	3	6	6	6	8	1	12.46
Yarbrough	0.2	2	0	0	0	0	0	0.00
Fleming	2.2	5	2	2	1	2	1	6.75
Curtiss	0.1	0	0	0	0	1	0	0.00
TOTALS	8.0	10	8	8	7	11	2	9.00

LOS ANGELES	IP	H	R	ER	BB	SO	HR	ERA
Kershaw (W, 1-0)	6.0	2	1	1	1	8	1	1.50
Floro	0.1	2	2	2	0	1	0	54.00
González, V	0.2	2	0	0	0	0	0	0.00
Báez, P	1.0	0	0	0	0	0	0	0.00
Kelly	1.0	0	0	0	0	1	0	0.00
TOTALS	9.0	6	3	3	1	10	1	5.00

WP: Glasnow. Pitches-strikes: Glasnow 112-58; Yarbrough 19-13; Fleming 40-25; Curtiss 3-3; Kershaw 78-53; Floro 15-8; Gonzalez, V 14-7; Baez, P 11-7; Kelly 10-5.

GAME TWO October 21, 2020

TAMPA BAY RAYS 6, LOS ANGELES DODGERS 4

	1	2	3	4	5	6	7	8	9	R	H	E
TAMPA BAY	1	0	0	2	2	1	0	0	0	6	10	0
LOS ANGELES	0	0	0	0	2	1	0	1	0	4	5	1

TAMPA BAY	AB	R	H	RBI	BB	SO	LOB	AVG
Meadows, DH	3	1	1	0	0	0	0	.200
a-Díaz, Y, PH-DH	1	0	1	0	1	0	0	.400
1-Renfroe, PR-DH	0	0	0	0	0	0	0	.000
Lowe, B, 2B	5	2	2	3	0	1	2	.222
Arozarena, LF	3	0	1	0	2	0	0	.167
2-Phillips, PR-LF	0	0	0	0	0	0	0	.000
Choi, 1B	3	2	1	0	0	1	1	.333
b-Brosseau, PH-1B	2	0	0	0	1	4	.333
Margot, RF	3	1	2	1	1	0	0	.429
Wendle, 3B	3	0	1	3	0	0	1	.286
Adames, SS	4	0	1	0	0	1	3	.167
Kiermaier, CF	4	0	0	0	0	2	2	.286
Zunino, C	4	0	0	0	0	0	0	.000
TOTALS	35	6	10	6	4	7	13	.239

a-Singled for Meadows in the 7th. b-Struck out for Choi in the 7th. 1-Ran for Díaz, Y in the 9th. 2-Ran for Arozarena in the 9th. 2B: Wendle (2, May); Adames (1, Wood, A). HR: Lowe, B 2 (2, 1st inning off Gonsolin, 0 on, 1 out, 5th inning off May, 1 on, 2 out). TB: Adames 2; Arozarena; Choi; Díaz, Y; Lowe, B 8; Margot 2; Meadows; Wendle 2. RBI: Lowe, B 3 (3); Wendle 3 (3).

LOS ANGELES	AB	R	H	RBI	BB	SO	LOB	AVG
Betts, RF	3	0	0	0	1	1	0	.286
Seager, C, SS	4	1	2	1	0	1	0	.333
Turner, 3B	4	0	1	0	0	2	2	.250
Muncy, 1B	3	0	0	0	1	1	1	.286
Smith, W, C	4	1	1	1	0	2	2	.222
Bellinger, CF	3	0	0	0	1	1	1	.143
Pollock, DH	2	0	0	0	0	1	2	.000
a-Rios, PH-DH	2	0	0	0	0	2	0	.000
Hernández, K, 2B	1	1	0	0	1	1	0	.333
b-Pederson, PH-LF	1	0	0	0	0	0	0	.000
c-Barnes, A, PH	1	0	0	0	0	0	0	.000
Taylor, Ch, LF-2B	4	1	1	2	0	3	0	.429
TOTALS	32	4	5	4	4	15	10	.227

a-Struck out for Pollock in the 6th. b-Flied out for Hernández, K in the 7th. c-Flied out for Pederson in the 9th. 2B: Turner (2, Fairbanks). HR: Taylor, Ch (1, 5th inning off Snell, 1 on, 2 out); Smith, W (1, 6th inning off Anderson, N, 0 on, 1 out); Seager, C (1, 8th inning off Fairbanks, 0 on, 0 out). TB: Seager, C 5; Smith, W 4; Taylor, Ch 4; Turner. RBI: Seager, C (1); Smith, W (2); Taylor, Ch 2 (3).

TAMPA BAY	IP	H	R	ER	BB	SO	HR	ERA
Snell	4.2	2	2	2	4	9	1	3.86
Anderson, N (W, 1-0)	1.1	1	1	1	0	2	1	6.75
Fairbanks (H, 1)	1.2	2	1	1	0	1	1	5.40
Loup (H, 1)	1.0	0	0	0	0	2	0	0.00
Castillo, D (S, 1)	0.1	0	0	0	0	1	0	0.00
TOTALS	9.0	5	4	4	4	15	3	6.35

LOS ANGELES	IP	H	R	ER	BB	SO	HR	ERA
Gonsolin (L, 0-1)	1.1	1	1	1	1	1	1	6.75
Floro	1.1	0	0	0	0	0	0	10.80
González, V	1.0	0	1	1	1	0	0	5.40
May	1.1	4	3	3	0	1	1	20.25
Kelly	1.0	2	1	1	0	2	0	4.50
Wood, A	2.0	2	0	0	1	2	0	0.00
McGee	1.0	1	0	0	1	1	0	0.00
TOTALS	9.0	10	6	6	4	7	2	4.50

IBB: Arozarena (by Wood, A). Pitches-strikes: Snell 88-49; Anderson, N 19-12; Fairbanks 23-16; Loup 11-9; Castillo, D 3-3; Gonsolin 29-16; Floro 19-10; González, V 10-6; May 25-19; Kelly 16-13; Wood, A 26-24; McGee 16-9.

GAME 3 October 23, 2020

LOS ANGELES DODGERS 6, TAMPA BAY RAYS 2

	1	2	3	4	5	6	7	8	9	R	H	E
LOS ANGELES	1	0	2	2	0	1	0	0	0	6	10	0
TAMPA BAY	0	0	0	1	0	0	0	1	2	4	0	

LOS ANGELES	AB	R	H	RBI	BB	SO	LOB	AVG
Betts, RF	5	0	2	1	0	1	0	.333
Seager, C, SS	3	1	1	0	1	0	1	.333
Turner, 3B	5	2	2	1	0	1	3	.308
Muncy, 1B	4	0	2	1	1	1	1	.364
Smith, W, DH	4	0	0	0	1	1	4	.154
Bellinger, CF	4	1	1	0	0	1	2	.182
Taylor, Ch, 2B-LF	4	0	0	0	0	3	2	.273
Pederson, LF	3	1	1	0	0	0	0	.167
a-Hernández, K, PH-2B	1	0	0	0	0	1	0	.250
Barnes, A, C	3	1	1	2	0	1	0	.125
TOTALS	36	6	10	6	3	10	13	.245

a-Struck out for Pederson in the 8th. 2B: Turner (3, Morton). HR: Turner (1, 1st inning off Morton, 0 on, 2 out); Barnes, A (1, 6th inning off Curtiss, 0 on, 2 out). TB: Barnes, A 4; Bellinger; Betts 2; Muncy 2; Pederson; Seager, C; Turner 6. RBI: Barnes, A 2 (2); Betts (2); Muncy 2 (4); Turner (1).

TAMPA BAY	AB	R	H	RBI	BB	SO	LOB	AVG
Meadows, DH	4	0	1	0	0	1	0	.222
Lowe, B, 2B	4	0	0	0	0	3	1	.154
Arozarena, LF	4	1	1	1	0	2	1	.200
Choi, 1B	4	0	0	0	0	2	0	.143
Margot, RF	3	1	1	0	0	2	0	.400
Wendle, 3B	3	0	0	0	0	1	2	.200
Adames, SS	3	0	1	0	0	0	0	.222
Kiermaier, CF	2	0	0	0	1	0	1	.222
Zunino, C	2	0	0	0	1	1	1	.000

	AB	R	H	RBI	BB	SO	LOB	AVG
a-Tsutsugo, PH	1	0	0	0	0	0	0	.000
Perez, M, C	0	0	0	0	0	0	0	.000
TOTALS	30	2	4	2	1	13	5	.206

a-Grounded out for Zunino in the 8th. 2B: Margot (1, Buehler); Adames (2, Buehler). HR: Arozarena (1, 9th inning off Jansen, K, 0 on, 2 out). TB: Adames 2; Arozarena 4; Margot 2; Meadows. RBI: Adames (1); Arozarena (1).

LOS ANGELES	IP	H	R	ER	BB	SO	HR	ERA
Buehler (W, 1-0)	6.0	3	1	1	1	10	0	1.50
Treinen	1.0	0	0	0	0	2	0	0.00
Graterol, B	1.0	0	0	0	0	0	0	0.00
Jansen, K	1.0	1	1	1	0	1	1	9.00
TOTALS	9.0	4	2	2	1	13	1	3.67

TAMPA BAY	IP	H	R	ER	BB	SO	HR	ERA
Morton (L, 0-1)	4.1	7	5	5	1	6	1	10.38
Curtiss	1.2	2	1	1	1	2	1	4.50
Sherriff	1.0	0	0	0	1	1	0	0.00
Thompson	1.0	0	0	0	0	1	0	0.00
McClanahan	1.0	1	0	0	0	0	0	0.00
TOTALS	9.0	10	6	6	3	10	2	6.23

HBP: Seager, C (by Morton). Pitches-strikes: Buehler 93-67; Treinen 14-9; Graterol, B 7-5; Jansen, K 15-11; Morton 91-58; Curtiss 30-22; Sherriff 17-10; Thompson 6-5; McClanahan 26-17.

GAME 4 *October 24, 2020*

TAMPA BAY RAYS 8, LOS ANGELES DODGERS 7

	1	2	3	4	5	6	7	8	9	R	H	E
LOS ANGELES	1	0	1	0	1	1	2	1	0	7	15	2
TAMPA BAY	0	0	0	1	1	3	1	0	2	8	10	0

LOS ANGELES	AB	R	H	RBI	BB	SO	LOB	AVG
Betts, RF	5	0	0	0	0	1	3	.235
Seager, C, SS	5	3	4	2	0	0	0	.500
Turner, 3B	5	2	4	1	0	0	1	.444
Muncy, 1B	4	0	1	1	1	1	4	.333
Smith, W, C	4	1	1	0	1	1	4	.176
Bellinger, DH	4	0	0	0	0	1	2	.133
Pollock, CF	2	0	1	0	1	0	1	.250
a-Pederson, PH-LF	2	0	2	2	0	0	0	.375
Taylor, Ch, LF-CF	5	1	1	0	0	2	5	.250
Hernández, K, 2B	4	0	1	1	0	0	2	.250
TOTALS	40	7	15	7	4	6	22	.282

a-Singled for Pollock in the 7th. 2B: Pollock (1, Yarbrough); Hernández, K (1, Castillo, D); Turner (4, Loup); Taylor, Ch (1, Anderson, N). HR: Turner (2, 1st inning off Yarbrough, 0 on, 2 out); Seager, C (2, 3rd inning off Yarbrough, 0 on, 2 out). TB: Hernández, K 2; Muncy; Pederson 2; Pollock 2; Seager, C 7; Smith, W; Taylor, Ch 2; Turner. RBI: Hernández, K (2); Muncy (5); Pederson 2 (2); Seager, C 2 (3); Turner (2).

TAMPA BAY	AB	R	H	RBI	BB	SO	LOB	AVG
Díaz, Y, 1B-3B	3	0	0	0	1	2	1	.250
1-Wendle, PR-3B	1	0	0	0	0	0	0	.182
Arozarena, DH	4	3	3	1	1	0	1	.357
Brosseau, 3B	2	0	1	0	0	1	1	.400
a-Choi, PH-1B	0	1	0	0	2	0	0	.143
2-Phillips, PR-RF	1	0	1	1	0	0	0	1.000
Margot, LF	2	0	0	0	0	2	1	.333
b-Meadows, PH-LF	2	0	0	0	0	1	3	.182
Lowe, B, 2B	4	1	1	3	0	2	2	.176
Adames, SS	4	0	1	0	0	0	1	.231
Renfroe, RF-1B	4	1	1	1	0	1	2	.167
Zunino, C	2	0	0	0	1	2	0	.000
c-Tsutsugo, PH	1	0	0	0	1	0	0	.000
Kiermaier, CF	4	2	2	1	0	2	1	.308
TOTALS	34	8	10	7	5	14	14	.229

a-Walked for Brosseau in the 6th. b-Struck out for Margot in the 6th. c-Struck out for Zunino in the 9th. 1-Ran for Díaz, Y in the 7th. 2-Ran for Choi in the 8th. HR: Arozarena (2, 4th inning off Urías, 0 on, 0 out); Renfroe (1, 5th inning off Urías, 0 on, 0 out); Lowe, B (3, 6th inning off Báez, P, 2 on, 1 out); Kiermaier (2, 7th inning off Báez, P, 0 on, 1 out). TB: Adames; Arozarena; Brosseau; Kiermaier 5; Lowe, B 4; Phillips; Renfroe 4. RBI: Arozarena (2); Kiermaier (3); Lowe, B 3 (6); Phillips (1); Renfroe (1).

LOS ANGELES	IP	H	R	ER	BB	SO	HR	ERA
Urías	4.2	4	2	2	1	9	2	3.86
Treinen	0.2	1	2	2	1	1	0	10.80
Báez, P (BS, 1)	1.2	2	2	2	1	2	2	6.75
Kolarek (H, 1)	0.2	0	0	0	1	1	0	0.00
Graterol, B (H, 1)	0.1	1	0	0	0	0	0	0.00
Jansen, K (L, 0-1)(BS, 1)	0.2	2	2	1	1	1	0	10.80
TOTALS	8.2	10	8	7	5	14	4	4.54

TAMPA BAY	IP	H	R	ER	BB	SO	HR	ERA
Yarbrough	3.1	5	2	2	1	1	2	4.50
Thompson	0.2	0	0	0	0	1	0	0.00
Fairbanks	1.0	2	1	1	0	1	0	6.75
Castillo, D	1.0	1	1	1	2	1	0	6.75
Loup (H, 2)	0.1	2	2	2	0	1	0	13.50
Anderson, N (BS, 1)	1.1	3	1	1	1	1	0	6.75
Curtiss (W, 1-0)	1.1	2	0	0	0	0	0	2.70
TOTALS	9.0	15	7	7	4	6	2	6.43

WP: Urías; Fairbanks. IBB: Bellinger (by Anderson, N). Pitches-strikes: Urías 80-56; Treinen 16-10; Báez, P 26-15; Kolarek 9-5; Graterol, B 7-3; Jansen, K 21-12; Yarbrough 69-40; Thompson 5-4; Fairbanks 12-8; Castillo, D 26-13; Loup 11-9; Anderson, N 23-15; Curtiss 14-10.

GAME 5 *October 25, 2020*

LOS ANGELES DODGERS 4, TAMPA BAY RAYS 2

	1	2	3	4	5	6	7	8	9	R	H	E
LOS ANGELES	2	1	0	0	1	0	0	0	0	4	6	1
TAMPA BAY	0	0	2	0	0	0	0	0	0	2	7	0

LOS ANGELES	AB	R	H	RBI	BB	SO	LOB	AVG
Betts, RF	5	1	1	0	0	1	2	.227
Seager, C, SS	3	1	1	1	1	1	0	.471
Turner, 3B	4	0	0	0	0	1	2	.364
Muncy, 1B	3	1	2	1	1	0	0	.389
Smith, W, DH	4	0	0	0	0	3	3	.143
Bellinger, CF	4	0	1	1	0	1	1	.158
Taylor, Ch, 2B-LF	4	0	0	0	0	1	3	.200
Pederson, LF	2	1	1	1	0	0	0	.400
Hernández, K, 2B	1	0	0	0	0	0	0	.222
Barnes, A, C	2	0	0	0	2	0	1	.100
TOTALS	32	4	6	4	5	8	12	.264

2B: Betts (1, Glasnow). 3B: Pederson (1, 2nd inning off Glasnow, 0 on, 0 out); Muncy (1, 5th inning off Glasnow, 0 on, 2 out). TB: Bellinger; Betts 2; Muncy 5; Pederson 4; Seager, C. RBI: Bellinger (3); Muncy (6); Pederson (3); Seager, C (4).

TAMPA BAY	AB	R	H	RBI	BB	SO	LOB	AVG
Díaz, Y, 1B	3	1	2	1	0	0	0	.364
Choi, PH	0	0	0	0	0	0	0	.143
c-Brosseau, PH-1B	0	0	0	0	1	0	0	.400
Arozarena, DH	4	0	1	1	0	0	3	.333
Lowe, B, 2B	4	0	0	0	0	3	3	.143
Margot, LF	3	0	2	0	1	1	0	.400
Renfroe, RF	1	0	0	0	0	1	1	.143
a-Meadows, PH-RF	2	0	0	0	0	1	1	.154
Wendle, 3B	4	0	0	0	0	1	4	.133
Adames, SS	3	0	1	0	0	2	4	.176
Kiermaier, CF	3	1	2	0	0	1	0	.375
Zunino, C	2	0	0	0	0	2	1	.000
b-Tsutsugo, PH	1	0	0	0	0	0	1	.000
Perez, M, C	0	0	0	0	0	0	0	.000
TOTALS	31	2	7	2	3	10	18	.228

a-Struck out for Renfroe in the 7th. b-Flied out for Zunino in the 8th. c-Walked for Choi in the 8th. 3B: Díaz, Y (1, Kershaw). TB: Arozarena; Díaz, Y 4; Kiermaier 2; Margot 2. RBI: Arozarena (3); Díaz, Y (1).

LOS ANGELES	IP	H	R	ER	BB	SO	HR	ERA
Kershaw (W, 2-0)	5.2	5	2	2	2	6	0	2.31
May (H, 1)	1.2	1	0	0	0	2	0	9.00
González, V (H, 1)	0.2	0	0	0	1	0	0	3.86
Treinen (S, 1)	1.0	1	0	0	0	2	0	6.75
TOTALS	9.0	7	2	2	3	10	0	4.03

TAMPA BAY	IP	H	R	ER	BB	SO	HR	ERA
Glasnow (L, 0-2)	5.0	6	4	4	3	7	2	9.64
Loup	0.2	0	0	0	1	0	0	9.00
Castillo, D	1.1	0	0	0	0	0	0	3.38
Sherriff	1.0	0	0	0	0	1	0	0.00
Thompson	1.0	0	0	0	1	1	0	0.00
TOTALS	9.0	6	4	4	5	8	2	5.93

WP: González, V; Glasnow 3. Pitches-strikes: Kershaw 85-56; May 30-22; González, V 12-8; Treinen 12-9; Glasnow 102-61; Loup 12-6; Castillo, D 8-6; Sherriff 16-10; Thompson 15-9.

GAME 6 *October 27, 2020*

LOS ANGELES DODGERS 3, TAMPA BAY RAYS 1

	1	2	3	4	5	6	7	8	9	R	H	E
TAMPA BAY	1	0	0	0	0	0	0	0	0	1	5	0
LOS ANGELES	0	0	0	0	2	0	1	X	3	5	0

TAMPA BAY	AB	R	H	RBI	BB	SO	LOB	AVG
Choi, 1B	2	0	0	0	1	1	0	.111
a-Díaz, Y, PH-1B	1	0	0	0	0	1	1	.333
Arozarena, LF	4	1	2	1	0	1	2	.364
Meadows, DH	3	0	1	0	0	1	1	.188
b-Renfroe, PH-DH	1	0	0	0	0	0	0	.125
Lowe, B, 2B	3	0	0	0	1	2	0	.125
Margot, RF	4	0	0	0	0	1	2	.316
Wendle, 3B	3	0	0	0	0	2	1	.111
c-Brosseau, PH	1	0	0	0	0	1	0	.333
Adames, SS	4	0	0	0	0	3	0	.143
Kiermaier, CF	3	0	1	0	0	1	0	.368
Zunino, C	3	0	1	0	0	2	1	.063
1-Phillips, PR	0	0	0	0	0	0	0	1.000
Perez, M, C	0	0	0	0	0	0	0	.000
TOTALS	32	1	5	1	2	16	9	.216

a-Struck out for Choi in the 7th. b-Grounded out for Meadows in the 8th. c-Struck out for Wendle in the 9th. 1-Ran for Zunino in the 7th. 2B: Kiermaier (1, Gonsolin). HR: Arozarena (3, 1st inning off Gonsolin, 0 on, 1 out). TB: Arozarena 5; Kiermaier 2; Meadows; Zunino. RBI: Arozarena (4).

LOS ANGELES	AB	R	H	RBI	BB	SO	LOB	AVG
Betts, RF	4	2	2	1	0	2	1	.269
Seager, C, SS	3	0	0	1	1	2	0	.400
Turner, 3B	3	0	0	0	0	2	1	.320
Hernández, K, 2B	1	0	0	0	0	1	1	.200
Muncy, 1B	4	0	0	0	0	1	2	.318
Smith, W, DH	3	0	1	0	0	0	1	.167
Bellinger, CF	3	0	0	0	0	1	1	.136
Taylor, Ch, 2B-LF	3	0	1	0	0	1	1	.217
Pollock, LF	2	0	0	0	0	0	1	.167
a-Pederson, PH	0	0	0	0	1	0	0	.400
Rios, 3B	0	0	0	0	0	0	0	.000
Barnes, A, C	3	1	1	0	0	1	1	.154
TOTALS	29	3	5	2	2	11	11	.251

a-Intentionally walked for Pollock in the 7th. 2B: Betts (2, Anderson, N); Smith, W (1, Fairbanks). HR: Betts (2, 8th inning off Fairbanks, 0 on, 0 out). TB: Barnes, A; Betts 6; Smith, W 2; Taylor, Ch. RBI: Betts (3); Seager, C (5).

TAMPA BAY	IP	H	R	ER	BB	SO	HR	ERA
Snell	5.1	2	1	1	0	9	0	2.70
Anderson, N (L, 1-1)(BS, 2)	0.1	1	1	1	0	0	0	9.00
Loup	0.1	0	0	0	0	0	0	7.71
Fairbanks	1.1	2	1	1	2	2	1	6.75
Yarbrough	0.2	0	0	0	0	0	0	3.86
TOTALS	8.0	5	3	3	2	11	1	5.54

LOS ANGELES	IP	H	R	ER	BB	SO	HR	ERA
Gonsolin	1.2	3	1	1	2	4	1	6.00
Floro	0.1	0	0	0	0	1	0	9.00
Wood, A	2.0	0	0	0	0	3	0	0.00
Báez, P	0.2	1	0	0	0	0	0	5.40
González, V (W, 1-0)	1.1	0	0	0	0	3	0	2.45
Graterol, B (H, 2)	0.2	1	0	0	0	0	0	0.00
Urías (S, 1)	2.1	0	0	0	0	4	0	2.57
TOTALS	9.0	5	1	1	2	16	1	3.52

WP: Anderson, N. IBB: Pederson (by Fairbanks). Pitches-strikes: Snell 73-48; Anderson, N 10-5; Loup 6-3; Fairbanks 34-20; Yarbrough 2-1; Gonsolin 48-30; Floro 3-3; Wood, A 20-16; Báez, P 10-7; González, V 18-12; Graterol, B 8-5; Urías 27-19.

AMERICAN LEAGUE WILD CARD SERIES
TAMPA BAY RAYS VS. TORONTO BLUE JAYS

TORONTO	AVG	G	AB	R	H	2B	3B	HR	RBI	BB	SO	SB
Bo Bichette, SS	.000	2	6	0	0	0	0	0	0	1	1	0
Cavan Biggio, 3B	.125	2	8	0	1	1	0	0	0	0	6	0
Randal Grichuk, CF	.143	2	7	0	1	0	0	0	0	1	5	0
Vlad Guerrero Jr., 1B	.143	2	7	0	1	0	0	0	0	4	0	0
Lourdes Gurriel Jr., LF	.250	2	8	0	2	1	0	0	0	0	1	0
Teoscar Hernandez, RF	.143	2	7	1	0	0	0	0	1	0	4	0
Danny Jansen, C	.400	2	5	2	2	0	0	2	2	0	0	0
Alejandro Kirk, DH	.333	1	3	0	1	0	0	0	0	0	0	0
Reese McGuire, C	-	1	0	0	0	0	0	0	0	0	0	0
Joe Panik, 2B	.167	2	6	0	1	0	0	0	0	0	1	0
Travis Shaw, 1B	.250	1	4	0	1	0	0	0	0	0	1	0
Rowdy Tellez, PH	1.000	1	1	1	1	0	0	0	0	0	0	0
Jonathan Villar, 2B	.000	1	2	0	0	0	0	0	0	0	1	0
Totals	.188	2	64	3	12	2	0	2	3	3	23	0

TORONTO	W	L	ERA	G	GS	SV	IP	H	R	ER	BB	SO

		AVG	G	AB	R	H	2B	3B	HR	RBI	BB	SO	SB
Anthony Bass		0	0	0.00	1	0	0	1.0	0	0	0	2	1
Ryan Borucki		0	0	0.00	1	0	0	0.2	0	0	0	0	1
A.J. Cole		0	0	54.00	1	0	0	0.1	1	2	2	1	1
Rafael Dolis		0	0	0.00	1	0	0	1.0	1	0	0	0	0
Thomas Hatch		0	0	0.00	2	0	0	2.0	0	0	0	0	3
Nate Pearson		0	0	00.0	0	1	0	2.0	0	0	0	0	5
Robbie Ray		0	1	3.00	1	0	0	3.0	1	1	1	5	5
Hyun Jin Ryu		0	1	16.20	1	1	0	1.2	8	7	3	1	3
Matt Shoemaker		0	0	0.00	1	1	0	3.0	2	0	0	0	2
Ross Stripling		0	0	6.75	1	0	0	1.1	3	1	1	0	1
Totals		0	2	3.94	2	2	0	16.0	16	11	7	5	20

TAMPA BAY	AVG	G	AB	R	H	2B	3B	HR	RBI	BB	SO	SB
Willy Adames, SS	.167	2	6	0	1	0	0	0	0	1	3	1
Randy Arozarena, LF	.500	2	8	3	4	2	1	0	1	1	1	0
Mike Brosseau, 1B	.667	1	3	1	2	0	0	0	0	0	0	0
Ji-Man Choi, 1B	.000	2	3	0	0	0	0	0	0	0	1	0
Yandy Diaz, 3B	.000	1	2	1	0	0	0	0	0	2	1	0
Kevin Kiermaier, CF	.143	2	7	1	1	0	0	0	0	0	3	0
Brandon Lowe, 2B	.250	2	8	0	2	0	0	0	0	1	4	0
Nate Lowe, 1B	.000	1	3	0	0	0	0	0	0	0	2	0
Manuel Margot, LF	.429	2	7	2	3	0	1	0	3	0	1	0
Brett Phillips, LF	-	1	0	0	0	0	0	0	0	0	0	0
Hunter Renfroe, RF	.200	2	5	1	1	0	0	1	4	0	3	0
Yoshi Tsutsugo, DH	.000	1	2	0	0	0	0	0	0	1	0	0
Joey Wendle, 3B	.000	2	2	1	0	0	0	0	0	1	1	0
Mike Zunino, C	.286	2	7	1	2	0	0	2	4	0	4	0
Totals	.254	2	63	11	16	2	1	3	10	5	20	1

TAMPA BAY	W	L	ERA	G	GS	SV	IP	H	R	ER	BB	SO
Nick Anderson	0	0	3.38	2	0	0	2.2	2	1	1	0	0
Diego Castillo	0	0	0.00	1	0	0	0.2	1	0	0	0	1
Pete Fairbanks	0	0	0.00	1	0	1	1.0	1	0	0	0	2
Tyler Glasnow	1	0	3.00	1	1	0	6.0	6	2	2	1	8
Aaron Loup	0	0	0.00	1	0	0	0.2	1	0	0	0	1
Blake Snell	1	0	0.00	1	1	0	5.2	1	0	0	2	9
Ryan Thompson	0	0	0.00	1	0	0	1.1	0	0	0	0	2
Totals	2	0	1.50	2	2	1	18.0	12	3	3	3	23

SCORE BY INNINGS

TORONTO	0	0	1	0	1	0	0	1	0			3
TAMPA BAY	1	6	1	1	0	0	2	0	0			11

OAKLAND ATHLETICS VS. CHICAGO WHITE SOX

CHICAGO	AVG	G	AB	R	H	2B	3B	HR	RBI	BB	SO	SB
Jose Abreu, 1B	.286	3	14	1	4	1	0	1	2	0	1	0
Tim Anderson, SS	.643	3	14	2	9	2	0	0	0	0	0	0
Zack Collins, PH	.000	1	1	0	0	0	0	0	0	0	1	0
Jarrod Dyson, LF	.000	2	1	0	0	0	0	0	0	0	1	0
Edwin Encarnacion, DH	.000	1	2	0	0	0	0	0	0	0	2	0
Adam Engel, RF	.250	3	12	1	3	1	0	1	1	0	5	0
Leury Garcia, LF	.000	2	6	0	0	0	0	0	0	0	3	0
Yasmani Grandal, C	.200	3	10	2	2	0	0	0	2	4	4	0
Eloy Jimenez, DH	.500	1	2	0	1	0	0	0	0	0	0	0
Nick Madrigal, 2B	.250	3	12	1	3	0	0	0	0	0	0	0
Nomar Mazara, RF	.500	2	6	0	3	1	0	0	1	0	2	0
James McCann, C	.167	2	6	1	1	0	0	0	0	0	3	0
Yoan Moncada, 3B	.077	3	13	1	1	0	0	0	1	4	1	0
Luis Robert, CF	.308	3	13	2	4	0	0	1	2	0	4	0
Yolmer Sanchez, PR	-	1	0	0	0	0	0	0	0	0	0	0
Totals	.277	3	112	11	31	6	0	5	11	6	29	1

CHICAGO	W	L	ERA	G	GS	SV	IP	H	R	ER	BB	SO
Aaron Bummer	0	0	0.00	2	0	0	1.1	1	0	0	1	1
Dylan Cease	0	0	0.00	1	0	0	1.0	0	0	0	0	0
Alex Colome	0	0	0.00	2	0	1	2.0	0	0	0	1	1
Jimmy Cordero	0	0	0.00	2	0	0	3.2	1	0	0	1	2
Garrett Crochet	0	0	0.00	1	0	0	0.2	0	0	0	0	2
Dane Dunning	0	0	0.00	1	0	0	0.2	2	0	0	0	0
Matt Foster	0	0	0.00	1	0	0	0.1	0	0	0	2	0
Lucas Giolito	1	0	1.29	1	1	0	7.0	2	1	1	1	8
Codi Heuer	0	0	7.71	2	0	0	2.1	2	2	2	1	2
Dallas Keuchel	0	1	8.10	1	1	0	3.1	6	5	3	0	4
Evan Marshall	0	1	3.38	2	0	0	2.2	3	2	1	2	2
Carlos Rodon	0	0	*.**	1	0	0	0.1	1	2	2	2	0
Totals	1	2	3.24	3	3	1	25.0	18	12	9	11	22

OAKLAND	AVG	G	AB	R	H	2B	3B	HR	RBI	BB	SO	SB
Mark Canha, RF	.100	3	10	1	1	0	0	0	1	2	1	0
Khris Davis, DH	.250	2	8	1	2	0	0	1	1	0	2	0

	AVG	G	AB	R	H	2B	3B	HR	RBI	BB	SO	SB
Robbie Grossman, LF	.000	2	7	1	0	0	0	0	0	1	2	0
Tommy La Stella, 2B	.273	3	11	3	3	0	0	0	0	1	2	0
Jake Lamb, 3B	.200	3	5	0	1	0	0	0	0	0	0	0
Ramon Laureano, CF	.182	3	11	1	2	0	0	0	1	0	4	0
Sean Murphy, C	.375	3	8	3	3	0	0	1	2	2	1	0
Matt Olson, 1B	.000	3	9	0	0	0	0	0	1	3	6	0
Nate Orf, 2B	-	1	0	0	0	0	0	0	0	0	0	0
Chad Pinder, 3B	.333	3	9	3	0	0	0	0	2	1	2	0
Stephen Piscotty, RF	.000	1	3	0	0	0	0	0	0	0	1	0
Marcus Semien, SS	.250	3	12	2	3	1	0	1	2	1	1	0
Totals	**.194**	**3**	**93**	**12**	**18**	**1**	**0**	**3**	**10**	**11**	**22**	**0**
OAKLAND	W	L	ERA	G	GS	SV	IP	H	R	ER	BB	SO
Chris Bassitt	1	0	1.29	1	1	0	7.0	6	1	1	1	5
Jake Diekman	0	0	0.00	3	0	1	1.2	0	0	0	2	1
Mike Fiers	0	0	5.40	1	1	0	1.2	5	1	1	1	2
Liam Hendriks	0	0	6.75	2	0	1	2.2	5	2	2	1	8
Jesus Luzardo	0	1	8.10	1	1	0	3.1	6	3	3	0	5
Frankie Montas	1	0	4.50	1	0	0	2.0	2	1	1	0	2
Yusmeiro Petit	0	0	7.71	2	0	0	2.1	4	2	2	0	2
Joakim Soria	0	0	4.50	2	0	0	2.0	2	1	1	1	1
Lou Trivino	0	0	0.00	1	0	0	0.2	0	0	0	0	0
J.B. Wendelken	0	0	0.00	2	0	0	3.2	1	0	0	0	3
Totals	**2**	**1**	**3.67**	**3**	**3**	**2**	**27.0**	**31**	**11**	**11**	**6**	**29**

SCORE BY INNINGS

CHICAGO	0	2	4	0	1	0	0	3	1	11
OAKLAND	2	2	0	5	2	0	0	1	0	12

MINNESOTA TWINS VS. HOUSTON ASTROS

HOUSTON	AVG	G	AB	R	H	2B	3B	HR	RBI	BB	SO	SB
Jose Altuve, 2B	.000	2	7	0	0	0	0	0	1	2	0	0
Michael Brantley, DH	.286	2	7	2	2	1	0	0	2	2	2	0
Alex Bregman, 3B	.143	2	7	0	1	0	0	0	0	2	0	0
Carlos Correa, SS	.500	2	6	2	3	0	0	1	1	2	1	0
Yuli Gurriel, 1B	.125	2	8	1	1	0	0	0	0	1	0	0
Martin Maldonado, C	.143	2	7	0	1	0	0	0	0	3	3	0
Josh Reddick, RF	.125	2	8	1	1	0	0	0	0	0	4	0
George Springer, CF	.111	2	9	1	1	0	0	0	1	0	1	0
Myles Straw, CF	-	1	0	0	0	0	0	0	0	0	0	0
Kyle Tucker, LF	.375	2	8	0	3	0	0	0	2	0	1	0
Totals	**.194**	**2**	**67**	**7**	**13**	**1**	**0**	**1**	**7**	**8**	**13**	**0**
HOUSTON	W	L	ERA	G	GS	SV	IP	H	R	ER	BB	SO
Zack Greinke	0	0	2.25	1	1	0	4.0	2	1	1	3	1
Cristian Javier	1	0	0.00	1	0	0	3.0	0	0	0	0	2
Ryan Pressly	0	0	0.00	1	0	1	1.0	0	0	0	0	2
Brooks Raley	0	0	0.00	1	0	0	0.2	1	0	0	1	1
Jose Urquidy	0	0	2.08	1	1	0	4.1	2	1	1	2	3
Framber Valdez	1	0	0.00	1	1	0	5.0	2	0	0	2	5
Totals	**2**	**0**	**1.00**	**2**	**2**	**1**	**18.0**	**7**	**2**	**2**	**10**	**14**
MINNESOTA	AVG	G	AB	R	H	2B	3B	HR	RBI	BB	SO	SB
Luis Arraez, 2B	.000	2	6	0	0	0	0	0	0	2	1	0
Willians Astudillo, PH	.000	1	1	0	0	0	0	0	0	0	0	0
Alex Avila, C	-	1	0	0	0	0	0	0	0	0	0	0
Byron Buxton, CF	.250	2	4	0	1	0	0	0	0	0	3	1
Jake Cave, LF	.000	1	1	0	0	0	0	0	0	0	1	0
Nelson Cruz, DH	.333	2	6	0	2	2	0	0	2	2	1	0
Mitch Garver, PH	.000	1	1	0	0	0	0	0	0	0	0	0
Marwin Gonzalez, 3B	.200	2	5	1	1	0	0	0	0	1	0	0
Ryan Jeffers, C	.000	2	5	0	0	0	0	0	0	0	2	0
Max Kepler, RF	.000	2	5	1	0	0	0	0	0	3	1	0
Alex Kirilloff, RF	.250	1	4	0	1	0	0	0	0	0	1	0
Jorge Polanco, SS	.143	2	7	0	1	0	0	0	0	1	2	0
Eddie Rosario, LF	.000	2	7	0	0	0	0	0	0	1	1	0
Miguel Sano, 1B	.143	2	7	0	1	0	0	0	0	2	1	0
Totals	**.119**	**2**	**59**	**2**	**7**	**2**	**0**	**0**	**2**	**10**	**14**	**1**
MINNESOTA	W	L	ERA	G	GS	SV	IP	H	R	ER	BB	SO
Jose Berrios	0	0	1.80	1	1	0	5.0	2	1	1	2	4
Tyler Duffey	0	0	4.50	2	0	0	2.0	3	1	1	1	2
Kenta Maeda	0	0	0.00	1	1	0	5.0	2	0	0	3	5
Trevor May	0	0	0.00	2	0	0	2.0	0	0	0	0	0
Taylor Rogers	0	0	9.00	2	0	0	1.0	2	1	1	1	1
Sergio Romo	0	1	0.00	1	0	0	0.2	2	3	0	1	0
Cody Stashak	0	1	4.50	1	0	0	2.0	1	1	1	0	1
Caleb Thielbar	0	0	0.00	1	0	0	0.1	1	0	0	0	0
Totals	**0**	**2**	**2.00**	**2**	**2**	**0**	**18.0**	**13**	**7**	**4**	**8**	**13**

SCORE BY INNINGS

HOUSTON	0	0	0	1	0	0	2	0	4	7
MINNESOTA	0	0	1	0	1	0	0	0	0	2

CLEVELAND INDIANS VS. NEW YORK YANKEES

NEW YORK	AVG	G	AB	R	H	2B	3B	HR	RBI	BB	SO	SB
Mike Ford, 1B	-	1	0	0	0	0	0	0	0	0	0	0
Clint Frazier, PH	.000	1	1	0	0	0	0	0	0	0	1	0
Brett Gardner, LF	.375	2	8	3	3	1	0	1	3	2	4	0
Aaron Hicks, CF	.125	2	8	4	1	0	1	0	0	3	4	0
Kyle Higashioka, C	.200	1	5	0	1	0	0	0	0	0	1	0
Aaron Judge, RF	.111	2	9	1	1	0	0	1	2	2	4	0
DJ LeMahieu, 2B	.300	2	10	1	3	0	0	0	2	1	1	0
Gary Sanchez, C	.250	1	4	1	1	0	0	1	3	0	1	0
Giancarlo Stanton, DH	.286	2	7	3	2	0	0	2	3	2	3	0
Mike Tauchman, DH	-	1	0	0	0	0	0	0	0	0	0	0
Gleyber Torres, SS	.714	2	7	3	5	0	0	1	3	3	0	0
Gio Urshela, 3B	.333	2	9	3	3	0	0	1	5	0	3	0
Luke Voit, 1B	.429	2	7	2	3	2	0	0	1	2	1	0
Tyler Wade, 2B	-	2	0	0	0	0	0	0	0	0	0	0
Totals	**.307**	**2**	**75**	**22**	**23**	**3**	**1**	**7**	**22**	**15**	**23**	**0**
NEW YORK	W	L	ERA	G	GS	SV	IP	H	R	ER	BB	SO
Zack Britton	0	0	13.50	1	0	0	1.1	0	2	2	2	1
Luis Cessa	0	0	4.50	1	0	0	2.0	2	1	1	1	2
Aroldis Chapman	1	0	0.00	1	0	0	2.0	1	0	0	0	4
Gerrit Cole	1	0	2.57	1	1	0	7.0	6	2	2	0	13
Chad Green	0	0	0.00	1	0	0	1.1	3	0	0	0	3
Jonathan Loaisiga	0	0	27.00	1	0	0	0.1	1	1	1	2	0
Masahiro Tanaka	0	2	13.50	1	1	0	4.0	5	6	6	3	3
Totals	**2**	**0**	**6.00**	**2**	**2**	**0**	**18.0**	**18**	**12**	**12**	**8**	**25**
CLEVELAND	AVG	G	AB	R	H	2B	3B	HR	RBI	BB	SO	SB
Delino DeShields, CF	.286	2	7	2	2	0	0	0	1	2	0	0
Austin Hedges, PH	.000	1	1	0	0	0	0	0	0	0	0	0
Cesar Hernandez, 2B	.375	2	8	2	3	1	0	0	1	1	3	0
Sandy Leon, C	.000	2	1	0	0	0	0	0	0	0	0	0
Francisco Lindor, SS	.125	2	8	1	1	1	0	0	0	1	0	0
Jordan Luplow, LF	.500	1	2	0	1	1	0	0	2	0	0	0
Oscar Mercado, RF	.000	1	1	0	0	0	0	0	0	0	1	0
Tyler Naquin, RF	.125	2	8	0	1	0	0	0	1	0	4	0
Josh Naylor, LF	.714	2	7	3	5	3	0	1	3	0	0	0
Roberto Perez, C	.333	2	6	0	2	0	0	0	1	0	2	0
Jose Ramirez, 3B	.429	2	7	1	3	0	0	0	4	2	1	0
Franmil Reyes, DH	.000	2	7	2	0	0	0	0	0	2	5	0
Carlos Santana, 1B	.000	2	8	1	0	0	0	0	0	3	2	0
Totals	**.254**	**2**	**71**	**12**	**18**	**9**	**0**	**1**	**12**	**8**	**25**	**0**
CLEVELAND	W	L	ERA	G	GS	SV	IP	H	R	ER	BB	SO
Shane Bieber	0	1	13.50	1	1	0	4.2	9	7	7	2	7
Carlos Carrasco	0	0	12.00	1	1	0	3.0	2	4	4	3	6
Adam Cimber	0	0	40.50	1	0	0	0.2	2	3	3	1	0
Brad Hand	0	1	27.00	1	0	0	0.2	3	2	2	1	1
Cam Hill	0	0	9.00	1	0	0	2.0	3	2	2	0	2
James Karinchak	0	0	*.**	1	0	0	0.0	1	1	1	2	0
Phil Maton	0	0	2.70	2	0	0	3.1	1	1	1	1	1
Triston McKenzie	0	0	10.80	1	0	0	1.2	1	2	2	2	1
Oliver Perez	0	0	0.00	1	0	0	0.1	1	0	0	0	0
Cal Quantrill	0	0	0.00	1	0	0	0.1	0	0	0	1	1
Nick Wittgren	0	0	0.00	1	0	0	1.1	0	0	0	2	3
Totals	**0**	**2**	**11.00**	**2**	**2**	**0**	**18.0**	**23**	**22**	**22**	**15**	**23**

SCORE BY INNINGS

NEW YORK	2	1	1	6	3	2	4	0	3	22
CLEVELAND	4	0	1	1	2	0	2	1	1	12

AMERICAN LEAGUE DIVISION SERIES

TAMPA BAY RAYS VS. NEW YORK YANKEES

NEW YORK	AVG	G	AB	R	H	2B	3B	HR	RBI	BB	SO	SB
Mike Ford, PH	.000	2	2	0	0	0	0	0	0	0	1	0
Clint Frazier, LF	.333	3	6	1	2	0	0	1	1	0	4	0
Brett Gardner, LF	.364	4	11	3	4	0	0	0	2	0	6	0
Aaron Hicks, CF	.389	5	18	2	7	1	0	0	3	3	1	0
Kyle Higashioka, C	.308	4	13	2	4	0	0	1	2	1	2	0
Aaron Judge, RF	.143	5	21	2	3	0	0	2	3	2	6	0
DJ LeMahieu, 2B	.273	5	22	3	6	0	0	0	2	2	3	0
Gary Sanchez, C	.000	2	4	0	0	0	0	0	0	0	3	0
Giancarlo Stanton, DH	.316	5	19	4	6	1	0	4	10	2	7	0
Gleyber Torres, SS	.313	5	16	2	5	0	0	1	2	4	6	2
Gio Urshela, 3B	.105	5	19	1	2	0	0	0	0	2	4	0

	AVG	G	AB	R	H	2B	3B	HR	RBI	BB	SO	SB
Luke Voit, 1B	.111	5	18	3	2	1	0	1	1	2	6	0
Tyler Wade, 2B	-	2	0	1	0	0	0	0	0	1	0	0
Totals	.243	5	169	24	41	3	0	10	24	21	49	2

NEW YORK	W	L	ERA	G	GS	SV	IP	H	R	ER	BB	SO
Zack Britton	0	0	0.00	3	0	0	4.0	1	0	0	2	6
Luis Cessa	0	0	4.50	2	0	0	2.0	1	1	1	2	2
Aroldis Chapman	0	1	3.38	2	0	0	2.2	1	1	1	1	4
Gerrit Cole	1	0	3.18	2	2	0	11.1	7	4	4	4	17
Deivi Garcia	0	0	9.00	1	1	0	1.0	1	1	1	0	4
Chad Green	1	0	4.50	3	0	0	4.0	3	2	2	1	5
J.A. Happ	0	1	13.50	1	0	0	2.2	5	4	4	3	2
Jonathan Holder	0	0	0.00	1	0	0	1.0	0	0	0	0	1
Michael King	0	0	0.00	1	0	0	2.0	0	0	0	0	1
Jonathan Loaisiga	0	0	5.40	1	0	0	1.2	2	1	1	0	1
Jordan Montgomery	0	0	2.25	1	1	0	4.0	3	1	1	3	4
Nick Nelson	0	0	0.00	2	0	0	2.0	1	0	0	0	2
Adam Ottavino	0	0	13.50	1	0	0	0.2	0	1	1	1	0
Masahiro Tanaka	0	1	11.25	1	1	0	4.0	8	5	5	1	4
Totals	2	3	4.40	5	5	1	43.0	33	21	21	18	49

TAMPA BAY	AVG	G	AB	R	H	2B	3B	HR	RBI	BB	SO	SB
Willy Adames, SS	.133	5	15	2	2	0	0	0	0	3	6	0
Randy Arozarena, LF	.421	5	19	5	8	0	0	3	3	1	4	0
Mike Brosseau, 3B	.400	3	5	1	2	0	0	1	0	2	0	0
Ji-Man Choi, 1B	.267	5	15	2	4	1	0	1	3	3	0	0
Yandy Diaz, DH	.111	3	9	0	1	0	0	0	0	4	2	0
Kevin Kiermaier, CF	.235	5	17	2	4	2	0	1	4	0	5	0
Brandon Lowe, 2B	.000	5	18	0	0	0	0	0	1	4	7	0
Manuel Margot, RF	.111	4	9	1	1	0	0	1	2	1	1	0
Austin Meadows, RF	.154	4	13	2	2	0	0	2	2	1	6	0
Michael Perez, C	.400	3	5	1	2	0	0	1	3	0	0	0
Brett Phillips, RF	.000	3	2	0	0	0	0	0	0	0	1	0
Hunter Renfroe, RF	.000	1	1	0	0	0	0	0	0	0	0	0
Yoshi Tsutsugo, DH	.000	2	6	0	0	0	0	0	0	0	1	0
Joey Wendle, 3B	.353	5	17	4	6	0	0	0	0	1	6	1
Mike Zunino, C	.083	4	12	1	1	0	0	1	2	0	8	0
Totals	.202	5	163	21	33	3	0	11	21	18	49	1

TAMPA BAY	W	L	ERA	G	GS	SV	IP	H	R	ER	BB	SO
Jose Berrios	0	0	1.80	1	1	0	5.0	2	1	1	2	4
Tyler Duffey	0	0	4.50	2	0	0	2.0	3	1	1	1	2
Kenta Maeda	0	0	0.00	1	1	0	5.0	2	0	0	3	5
Trevor May	0	0	0.00	2	0	0	2.0	0	0	0	0	1
Taylor Rogers	0	0	9.00	1	0	0	1.0	2	1	1	1	1
Sergio Romo	0	1	0.00	1	0	0	0.2	2	3	0	1	0
Cody Stashak	0	1	4.50	1	0	0	2.0	1	1	1	0	1
Caleb Thielbar	0	0	0.00	1	0	0	0.1	1	0	0	0	0
Totals	0	2	2.00	2	2	0	18.0	13	7	4	8	13

SCORE BY INNINGS

										R
NEW YORK	1	3	2	4	3	2	0	3	6	24
TAMPA BAY	2	3	5	3	5	3	4	0	1	0	21

OAKLAND ATHLETICS VS. HOUSTON ASTROS

HOUSTON	AVG	G	AB	R	H	2B	3B	HR	RBI	BB	SO	SB
Jose Altuve, 2B	.400	4	15	5	6	0	0	2	5	3	3	0
Michael Brantley, LF	.368	4	19	6	7	1	0	2	5	0	2	0
Alex Bregman, 3B	.400	4	15	6	6	1	0	1	2	2	1	0
Carlos Correa, SS	.500	4	14	3	7	0	0	3	11	4	3	0
Aledmys Diaz, DH	.200	2	5	1	1	0	0	1	2	0	2	0
Dustin Garneau, C	-	1	0	0	0	0	0	0	0	0	0	0
Yuli Gurriel, 1B	.067	4	15	1	1	0	0	0	1	1	0	0
Martin Maldonado, C	.143	4	14	3	2	0	0	1	1	0	8	0
Josh Reddick, RF	.182	4	11	2	2	0	0	0	0	1	2	0
George Springer, CF	.389	4	18	4	7	1	0	2	4	0	7	0
Myles Straw, CF	-	1	0	0	0	0	0	0	0	0	0	0
Kyle Tucker, RF	.412	4	17	3	7	0	0	0	2	0	3	0
Totals	.322	4	143	33	46	3	0	12	33	11	28	0

HOUSTON	W	L	ERA	G	GS	SV	IP	H	R	ER	BB	SO
Zack Greinke	0	0	7.71	1	1	0	4.2	5	4	4	1	4
Josh James	0	0	27.00	1	0	0	1.0	3	3	3	1	0
Cristian Javier	1	0	0.00	2	0	0	3.1	3	0	0	1	6
Lance McCullers Jr.	0	0	9.00	1	0	0	4.0	8	5	4	1	5
Enoli Paredes	0	0	0.00	3	0	0	3.2	0	0	0	0	4
Ryan Pressly	0	0	6.00	3	0	1	3.0	4	2	2	1	2
Brooks Raley	0	1	9.00	1	0	0	2.0	1	2	2	2	2
Andre Scrubb	0	0	0.00	1	0	0	1.0	1	0	0	0	2
Blake Taylor	1	0	0.00	3	0	0	2.0	1	0	0	2	0
Jose Urquidy	0	0	8.31	1	1	0	4.1	5	4	4	1	3
Framber Valdez	1	0	2.57	1	1	0	7.0	5	2	2	1	4
Totals	3	1	5.25	4	4	1	36.0	36	22	21	11	32

OAKLAND	AVG	G	AB	R	H	2B	3B	HR	RBI	BB	SO	SB
Mark Canha, RF	.200	4	15	2	3	0	0	1	2	0	6	0
Khris Davis, DH	.250	4	16	2	4	0	0	2	3	0	8	0
Robbie Grossman, LF	.300	4	10	2	3	2	0	0	0	2	2	0
Tommy La Stella, 2B	.313	4	16	2	5	1	0	1	2	1	1	0
Jake Lamb, 3B	.000	1	2	0	0	0	0	0	0	0	1	0
Ramon Laureano, CF	.200	4	15	3	3	1	0	2	4	1	3	0
Sean Murphy, C	.143	4	14	1	2	0	0	1	2	0	3	0
Matt Olson, 1B	.214	4	14	4	3	0	0	2	2	2	4	0
Nate Orf, 2B	-	1	0	0	0	0	0	0	0	0	0	0
Chad Pinder, 3B	.308	4	13	2	4	1	0	2	5	2	4	0
Stephen Piscotty, RF	.250	2	4	0	1	0	0	0	0	0	0	0
Marcus Semien, SS	.533	4	15	4	8	0	0	1	2	3	0	0
Totals	.269	4	134	22	36	5	0	12	22	11	32	0

OAKLAND	W	L	ERA	G	GS	SV	IP	H	R	ER	BB	SO
Chris Bassitt	0	0	6.75	1	1	0	4.0	9	3	3	0	4
Jake Diekman	0	0	6.00	3	0	0	3.0	3	2	2	0	4
Liam Hendriks	1	0	0.00	1	0	0	3.0	1	0	0	0	4
Jesus Luzardo	0	0	8.31	1	1	0	4.1	5	4	4	2	2
Sean Manaea	0	1	8.31	1	1	0	4.1	5	4	4	1	2
T.J. McFarland	0	0	0.00	2	0	0	2.0	0	0	0	1	2
Mike Minor	0	0	0.00	3	0	0	3.2	2	0	0	1	2
Frankie Montas	0	1	12.27	1	1	0	3.2	7	5	5	1	3
Yusmeiro Petit	0	0	18.00	3	0	0	2.0	4	4	4	1	2
Joakim Soria	0	0	9.00	2	0	0	2.0	3	2	2	1	0
Lou Trivino	0	0	4.50	3	0	0	2.0	1	1	1	2	2
Jordan Weems	0	0	*.**	1	0	0	0.0	2	2	2	1	0
J.B. Wendelken	0	1	18.00	2	0	0	1.0	4	6	2	1	1
Totals	1	3	7.46	4	4	0	35.0	46	33	29	11	28

SCORE BY INNINGS

										R
HOUSTON	2	0	2	9	9	6	3	0	2	33
OAKLAND	1	7	1	3	3	0	3	2	2	22

AMERICAN LEAGUE CHAMPIONSHIP SERIES

TAMPA BAY RAYS VS. HOUSTON ASTROS

HOUSTON	AVG	G	AB	R	H	2B	3B	HR	RBI	BB	SO	SB
Jose Altuve, 2B	.462	7	26	6	12	2	0	3	5	6	5	0
Michael Brantley, DH	.346	7	26	2	9	0	0	1	4	4	5	1
Alex Bregman, 3B	.143	7	28	4	4	0	0	0	1	5	0	0
Carlos Correa, SS	.259	7	27	2	7	1	0	2	5	2	7	0
Aledmys Diaz, 3B	.417	6	12	2	5	0	0	0	0	1	3	0
Dustin Garneau, C	.000	1	2	0	0	0	0	0	0	0	2	0
Yuli Gurriel, 1B	.143	7	21	3	3	0	0	0	0	5	2	0
Martin Maldonado, C	.214	7	14	3	3	2	0	0	4	7	0	0
Josh Reddick, RF	.235	7	17	1	4	0	0	0	0	1	5	0
George Springer, CF	.233	7	30	3	7	0	0	2	5	2	6	0
Myles Straw, CF	-	4	0	0	0	0	0	0	0	0	0	0
Garrett Stubbs, C	-	1	0	0	0	0	0	0	0	0	0	0
Abraham Toro, PH	-	1	0	0	0	0	0	0	0	0	1	0
Kyle Tucker, LF	.208	7	24	1	5	0	0	1	2	2	7	0
Totals	.260	7	227	22	59	5	0	9	21	29	54	1

HOUSTON	W	L	ERA	G	GS	SV	IP	H	R	ER	BB	SO
Luis Garcia	0	0	0.00	1	1	0	2.0	0	0	0	2	1
Zack Greinke	1	0	3.00	1	1	0	6.0	5	2	2	1	7
Josh James	0	0	3.00	2	0	0	3.0	2	1	1	0	3
Cristian Javier	0	0	9.00	2	0	0	3.0	2	3	3	2	5
Lance McCullers Jr.	0	2	3.38	2	2	0	10.2	8	7	4	1	18
Enoli Paredes	0	0	10.80	4	0	0	3.1	3	4	4	4	5
Ryan Pressly	1	0	0.00	3	0	2	3.1	3	0	0	0	4
Brooks Raley	0	0	0.00	4	0	0	3.0	2	0	0	2	6
Andre Scrubb	0	0	3.00	3	0	0	3.0	3	1	1	2	5
Blake Taylor	0	0	2.45	5	0	0	3.2	4	1	1	0	4
Jose Urquidy	0	1	2.57	2	1	0	7.0	5	3	2	3	7
Framber Valdez	1	1	2.25	2	2	0	12.0	7	3	3	7	17
Totals	3	4	3.15	7	7	2	60.0	44	25	21	24	81

TAMPA BAY	AVG	G	AB	R	H	2B	3B	HR	RBI	BB	SO	SB
Willy Adames, SS	.118	7	17	1	2	2	0	0	3	9	8	0
Randy Arozarena, LF	.321	7	28	6	9	1	0	4	6	2	10	0
Mike Brosseau, 2B	.000	5	10	0	0	0	0	0	0	1	6	0
Ji-Man Choi, 1B	.385	5	13	3	5	0	0	1	1	4	6	0
Yandy Diaz, 1B	.154	4	13	1	2	0	0	0	0	3	4	0

	AVG	G	AB	R	H	2B	3B	HR	RBI	BB	SO	SB
Kevin Kiermaier, CF	.167	5	12	1	2	2	0	0	0	0	6	0
Brandon Lowe, 2B	.154	7	26	4	4	0	0	1	1	1	10	0
Manuel Margot, CF	.261	7	23	4	6	0	0	3	6	2	8	0
Austin Meadows, RF	.091	6	22	1	2	0	0	0	0	1	6	0
Michael Perez, C	.000	2	2	0	0	0	0	0	0	0	2	0
Hunter Renfroe, RF	.222	4	9	0	2	1	0	0	2	0	6	0
Yoshi Tsutsugo, DH	.400	2	5	0	2	0	0	0	0	0	0	0
Joey Wendle, 3B	.143	7	21	2	3	0	0	0	2	1	4	0
Mike Zunino, C	.278	7	18	2	5	0	0	2	4	0	6	0
Totals	**.201**	**7**	**219**	**25**	**44**	**6**	**0**	**11**	**25**	**24**	**81**	**0**

TAMPA BAY	W	L	ERA	G	GS	SV	IP	H	R	ER	BB	SO
Jose Alvarado	0	0	0.00	1	0	0	1.2	1	0	0	3	4
Nick Anderson	0	1	8.31	3	0	1	4.1	7	4	4	3	0
Diego Castillo	0	0	2.45	3	0	2	3.2	4	2	1	3	3
John Curtiss	0	0	2.08	4	1	0	4.1	4	1	1	2	4
Pete Fairbanks	0	0	2.08	3	0	1	4.1	3	1	1	1	6
Josh Fleming	0	0	6.00	1	0	0	3.0	3	2	2	1	1
Tyler Glasnow	0	1	6.00	1	1	0	6.0	8	4	4	2	5
Aaron Loup	0	0	0.00	4	0	0	2.1	2	0	0	1	3
Shane McClanahan	0	0	16.20	1	0	0	1.2	5	3	3	1	2
Charlie Morton	2	0	0.00	2	2	0	10.2	7	0	0	2	11
Aaron Slegers	0	0	0.00	2	0	0	3.2	1	0	0	2	0
Blake Snell	1	1	3.00	2	2	0	9.0	9	3	3	6	6
Ryan Thompson	0	0	0.00	3	0	0	1.2	2	0	0	0	2
Ryan Yarbrough	1	0	3.60	1	1	0	5.0	3	2	2	2	5
Totals	**4**	**3**	**3.08**	**7**	**7**	**4**	**61.1**	**59**	**22**	**21**	**29**	**54**

SCORE BY INNINGS

HOUSTON	4	0	3	0	6	3	2	2	2	22
TAMPA BAY	5	2	1	3	2	6	2	3	1	25

NATIONAL LEAGUE WILD CARD SERIES

LOS ANGELES DODGERS VS. MILWAUKEE BREWERS

MILWAUKEE	AVG	G	AB	R	H	2B	3B	HR	RBI	BB	SO	SB
Orlando Arcia, SS	.143	2	7	1	1	0	0	1	2	0	4	0
Ryan Braun, RF	.000	1	2	0	0	0	0	0	0	0	2	0
David Freitas, C	.000	1	1	0	0	0	0	0	0	0	1	0
Ben Gamel, PH	.000	1	1	0	0	0	0	0	0	0	1	0
Avisail Garcia, CF	.500	2	8	0	4	0	0	0	0	0	3	0
Jedd Gyorko, 1B	.143	2	7	0	1	0	0	0	0	0	3	0
Ryon Healy, DH	.000	1	3	0	0	0	0	0	0	0	1	0
Keston Hiura, 2B	.167	2	6	0	1	0	0	0	1	0	2	0
Omar Narvaez, C	.000	2	1	0	0	0	0	0	0	0	1	0
Jacob Nottingham, C	.000	2	4	0	0	0	0	0	0	0	3	0
Jace Peterson, PH	-	1	0	0	0	0	0	0	0	0	0	0
Eric Sogard, 3B	.000	1	3	0	0	0	0	0	0	1	0	0
Tyrone Taylor, RF	.000	2	5	0	0	0	0	0	0	0	3	0
Luis Urias, 3B	.500	1	2	0	1	0	0	0	0	0	0	0
Daniel Vogelbach, DH	.200	2	5	1	1	0	0	0	0	0	2	0
Christian Yelich, LF	.222	2	9	0	2	1	0	0	0	0	4	0
Totals	**.172**	**2**	**64**	**2**	**11**	**2**	**0**	**1**	**2**	**4**	**28**	**0**

MILWAUKEE	W	L	ERA	G	GS	SV	IP	H	R	ER	BB	SO
Josh Hader	0	0	0.00	1	0	0	1.1	0	0	0	0	2
Adrian Houser	0	0	0.00	1	0	0	2.0	1	0	0	1	0
Freddy Peralta	0	0	9.00	1	0	0	1.0	1	1	1	0	1
Drew Rasmussen	0	0	0.00	1	0	0	1.0	1	0	0	0	2
Brent Suter	0	1	16.20	1	1	0	1.2	3	3	3	5	0
Justin Topa	0	0	0.00	1	0	0	2.0	1	0	0	1	0
Brandon Woodruff	0	1	5.79	1	1	0	4.2	5	3	3	0	9
Eric Yardley	0	0	0.00	1	0	0	2.1	0	0	0	0	1
Totals	**0**	**2**	**3.94**	**2**	**2**	**0**	**16.0**	**12**	**7**	**7**	**7**	**17**

LOS ANGELES	AVG	G	AB	R	H	2B	3B	HR	RBI	BB	SO	SB
Austin Barnes, C	.667	1	3	1	2	0	0	0	1	0	0	0
Cody Bellinger, CF	.286	2	7	0	2	0	0	0	0	1	3	0
Mookie Betts, RF	.429	2	7	1	3	3	0	0	3	1	3	0
Enrique Hernandez, 2B	-	2	0	0	0	0	0	0	0	0	0	0
Max Muncy, 1B	.000	2	5	0	0	0	0	0	0	2	4	0
Joc Pederson, PH	.000	1	1	0	0	0	0	0	0	0	0	0
AJ Pollock, LF	.200	2	5	1	1	1	0	0	1	1	1	0
Edwin Rios, DH	.000	1	3	0	0	0	0	0	0	0	1	0
Corey Seager, SS	.143	2	7	2	1	0	0	1	1	1	2	0
Will Smith, C	.000	2	6	0	0	0	0	0	0	1	2	0
Chris Taylor, 2B	.500	2	6	2	3	1	0	0	0	1	1	0
Justin Turner, 3B	.000	2	8	0	0	0	0	0	0	0	1	0
Totals	**.207**	**2**	**58**	**7**	**12**	**5**	**0**	**1**	**7**	**7**	**17**	**0**

LOS ANGELES	W	L	ERA	G	GS	SV	IP	H	R	ER	BB	SO
Walker Buehler	0	0	4.50	1	1	0	4.0	3	2	2	2	8
Brusdar Graterol	0	0	0.00	1	0	1	1.0	1	0	0	0	0
Kenley Jansen	0	0	0.00	1	0	0	1.0	0	0	0	1	1
Clayton Kershaw	1	0	0.00	1	1	0	8.0	3	0	0	1	13
Blake Treinen	0	0	0.00	1	0	0	1.0	1	0	0	0	1
Julio Urias	1	0	0.00	1	0	0	3.0	3	0	0	0	5
Totals	**2**	**0**	**1.00**	**2**	**2**	**2**	**18.0**	**11**	**2**	**2**	**4**	**28**

SCORE BY INNINGS

MILWAUKEE	0	0	0	2	0	0	0	0	0	2
LOS ANGELES	2	1	0	0	3	0	1	0	0	7

ATLANTA BRAVES VS. CINCINNATI REDS

CINCINNATI	AVG	G	AB	R	H	2B	3B	HR	RBI	BB	SO	SB
Shogo Akiyama, LF	.000	2	5	0	0	0	0	0	0	0	2	0
Aristides Aquino, LF	.333	1	6	0	2	0	0	0	0	0	2	0
Tucker Barnhart, C	.000	2	5	0	0	0	0	0	0	0	3	0
Curt Casali, C	.000	2	2	0	0	0	0	0	0	0	1	0
Nick Castellanos, RF	.300	2	10	0	3	1	0	0	0	0	4	0
Matt Davidson, PH	-	1	0	0	0	0	0	0	0	0	0	0
Kyle Farmer, SS	.000	1	5	0	0	0	0	0	0	0	2	0
Freddy Galvis, SS	.333	2	3	0	1	0	0	0	0	1	1	0
Jose Garcia, PH	.000	1	1	0	0	0	0	0	0	0	0	0
Brian Goodwin, CF	.000	2	1	0	0	0	0	0	0	0	1	0
Travis Jankowski, DH	-	1	0	0	0	0	0	0	0	0	0	0
Mike Moustakas, 2B	.000	2	8	0	0	0	0	0	0	1	2	0
Nick Senzel, CF	.286	2	7	0	2	0	0	0	0	0	2	0
Eugenio Suarez, 3B	.222	2	9	0	2	0	0	0	0	1	4	0
Joey Votto, 1B	.222	2	9	0	2	0	0	0	0	1	3	0
Jesse Winker, DH	.167	2	6	0	1	0	0	0	0	1	2	0
Totals	**.169**	**2**	**77**	**0**	**13**	**1**	**0**	**0**	**0**	**5**	**28**	**1**

CINCINNATI	W	L	ERA	G	GS	SV	IP	H	R	ER	BB	SO
Trevor Bauer	0	0	0.00	1	1	0	7.2	2	0	0	0	12
Archie Bradley	0	1	27.00	1	0	0	0.1	2	1	1	0	0
Luis Castillo	0	1	1.69	1	1	0	5.1	6	1	1	1	7
Amir Garrett	0	0	-	1	0	0	0.0	1	0	0	0	0
Raisel Iglesias	0	0	16.20	2	0	0	1.2	2	4	3	3	5
Michael Lorenzen	0	0	0.00	2	0	0	2.2	2	0	0	0	6
Lucas Sims	0	0	0.00	2	0	0	2.0	2	0	0	1	5
Totals	**0**	**2**	**2.21**	**2**	**2**	**0**	**20.1**	**15**	**6**	**5**	**5**	**35**

ATLANTA	AVG	G	AB	R	H	2B	3B	HR	RBI	BB	SO	SB
Ronald Acuna Jr., CF	.364	2	11	0	4	2	0	0	1	0	4	1
Ozzie Albies, 2B	.250	2	8	1	2	0	0	0	0	1	1	1
Charlie Culberson, PR	-	1	0	0	0	0	0	0	0	0	0	0
Travis d'Arnaud, C	.222	2	9	2	2	0	0	0	0	0	4	0
Adam Duvall, LF	.125	2	8	1	1	0	0	1	2	1	6	0
Tyler Flowers, C	-	1	0	0	0	0	0	0	0	0	0	0
Freddie Freeman, 1B	.167	2	6	1	1	0	0	0	1	3	1	0
Nick Markakis, RF	.222	2	9	0	2	0	0	0	0	0	4	0
Marcell Ozuna, DH	.111	2	9	1	1	0	0	1	2	0	5	0
Cristian Pache, RF	-	2	0	0	0	0	0	0	0	0	0	0
Austin Riley, 3B	.125	2	8	1	1	0	0	0	0	0	5	0
Dansby Swanson, SS	.111	2	9	0	1	0	0	0	0	0	5	0
Totals	**.195**	**2**	**77**	**6**	**15**	**2**	**0**	**2**	**6**	**5**	**35**	**2**

ATLANTA	W	L	ERA	G	GS	SV	IP	H	R	ER	BB	SO
Ian Anderson	1	0	0.00	1	1	0	6.0	2	0	0	2	9
Max Fried	0	0	0.00	1	1	0	7.0	6	0	0	0	5
Shane Greene	0	0	0.00	1	0	0	0.1	2	0	0	0	1
Chris Martin	0	0	0.00	2	0	0	2.0	0	0	0	0	4
Tyler Matzek	0	0	0.00	1	0	0	1.1	2	0	0	0	4
Mark Melancon	0	0	0.00	2	0	0	2.0	0	0	0	0	1
A.J. Minter	1	0	0.00	1	0	0	0.2	0	0	0	1	1
Darren O'Day	0	0	0.00	1	0	0	0.1	1	0	0	2	1
Will Smith	0	0	0.00	2	0	0	2.0	1	0	0	0	5
Totals	**2**	**0**	**0.00**	**2**	**2**	**0**	**22.0**	**13**	**0**	**0**	**5**	**28**

SCORE BY INNINGS

CINCINNATI	0	0	0	0	0	0	0	0	0	0	0	0	0
ATLANTA	0	0	0	1	0	0	4	0	0	0	0	1	6

CHICAGO CUBS VS. MIAMI MARLINS

MIAMI	AVG	G	AB	R	H	2B	3B	HR	RBI	BB	SO	SB
Jesus Aguilar, DH	.250	2	8	1	2	1	0	1	2	0	2	0
Brian Anderson, 3B	.000	2	9	0	0	0	0	0	0	0	4	0
Jon Berti, 2B	.200	2	5	0	1	0	0	0	0	2	0	2
Lewis Brinson, RF	.000	2	1	1	0	0	0	0	0	0	0	0
Garrett Cooper, 1B	.250	2	8	1	2	0	0	1	1	1	3	0

	AVG	G	AB	R	H	2B	3B	HR	RBI	BB	SO	SB
Corey Dickerson, LF	.143	2	7	1	1	0	0	1	3	2	2	0
Monte Harrison, CF	-	2	0	0	0	0	0	0	0	0	0	1
Matt Joyce, RF	.200	2	5	0	1	1	0	0	0	2	1	0
Starling Marte, CF	.500	1	4	1	2	1	0	0	0	0	0	0
Miguel Rojas, SS	.286	2	7	1	2	0	0	0	0	1	0	0
Magneuris Sierra, CF	.333	2	3	0	1	0	0	0	1	0	1	0
Chad Wallach, C	.143	2	7	1	1	0	0	0	0	3	7	0
Totals	**.203**	**2**	**64**	**7**	**13**	**3**	**0**	**3**	**7**	**8**	**17**	**3**

MIAMI	W	L	ERA	G	GS	SV	IP	H	R	ER	BB	SO
Sandy Alcantara	1	0	1.35	1	1	0	6.2	3	1	1	3	4
Richard Bleier	0	0	0.00	2	0	0	1.0	0	0	0	0	0
Brad Boxberger	1	0	0.00	1	0	0	1.1	0	0	0	0	0
Yimi Garcia	0	0	0.00	2	0	0	2.0	0	0	0	0	4
Brandon Kintzler	0	0	0.00	2	0	1	2.0	2	0	0	0	4
Sixto Sanchez	0	0	0.00	1	1	0	5.0	4	0	0	2	6
Totals	**2**	**0**	**0.50**	**2**	**2**	**1**	**18.0**	**9**	**1**	**1**	**5**	**16**

CHICAGO	AVG	G	AB	R	H	2B	3B	HR	RBI	BB	SO	SB
Javier Baez, SS	.125	2	8	0	1	0	0	0	0	0	3	0
David Bote, 2B	.000	1	4	0	0	0	0	0	0	0	2	0
Kris Bryant, 3B	.000	2	8	0	0	0	0	0	0	0	2	0
Victor Caratini, C	.167	2	6	0	1	0	0	0	0	0	1	0
Willson Contreras, C	.250	2	4	0	1	0	0	0	0	1	0	0
Billy Hamilton, CF	-	1	0	0	0	0	0	0	0	0	0	0
Ian Happ, CF	.500	2	8	1	4	0	0	1	1	0	1	0
Jason Heyward, RF	.286	2	7	0	2	1	0	0	0	0	1	0
Jason Kipnis, 2B	.000	2	3	0	0	0	0	0	0	1	1	0
Cameron Maybin, LF	.000	2	2	0	0	0	0	0	0	0	0	0
Anthony Rizzo, 1B	.000	2	8	0	0	0	0	0	0	0	3	0
Kyle Schwarber, LF	.000	2	4	0	0	0	0	0	0	0	3	1
Totals	**.145**	**2**	**62**	**1**	**9**	**2**	**0**	**1**	**1**	**5**	**16**	**0**

CHICAGO	W	L	ERA	G	GS	SV	IP	H	R	ER	BB	SO
Andrew Chafin	0	0	0.00	1	0	0	0.1	0	0	0	0	0
Yu Darvish	0	1	2.70	1	1	0	6.2	5	2	2	2	6
Kyle Hendricks	0	1	4.26	1	1	0	6.1	5	3	3	3	3
Jeremy Jeffress	0	0	10.80	2	0	0	1.2	3	2	2	0	2
Craig Kimbrel	0	0	0.00	1	0	0	1.1	0	0	0	2	2
Ryan Tepera	0	0	0.00	1	0	0	0.2	0	0	0	1	2
Dan Winkler	0	0	0.00	1	0	0	1.0	0	0	0	0	2
Totals	**0**	**2**	**3.50**	**2**	**2**	**0**	**18.0**	**13**	**7**	**7**	**8**	**17**

SCORE BY INNINGS

MIAMI	0	0	0	0	0	0	7	0	0	7
CHICAGO	0	0	0	0	0	0	0	0	0	0

SAN DIEGO PADRES VS. ST. LOUIS CARDINALS

ST. LOUIS	AVG	G	AB	R	H	2B	3B	HR	RBI	BB	SO	SB
Harrison Bader, CF	.111	3	9	1	1	0	0	0	2	0	7	0
Dylan Carlson, LF	.333	3	9	2	3	1	0	0	0	4	3	1
Matt Carpenter, DH	.222	3	9	3	2	1	0	0	2	3	4	0
Austin Dean, PH	.000	1	1	0	0	0	0	0	0	0	1	0
Paul DeJong, SS	.200	3	10	2	2	1	0	0	1	3	2	0
Tommy Edman, 3B	.214	3	14	2	3	0	0	0	0	0	3	0
Dexter Fowler, RF	.286	3	14	1	4	1	0	0	2	0	4	0
Paul Goldschmidt, 1B	.231	3	13	2	3	1	0	2	3	1	2	0
Brad Miller, PH	.000	1	1	0	0	0	0	0	0	0	0	0
Yadier Molina, C	.462	3	13	2	6	2	0	0	2	1	1	0
Tyler O'Neill, LF	-	3	0	0	0	0	0	0	0	0	0	0
Kolten Wong, 2B	.214	3	14	1	3	1	0	0	1	4	0	0
Totals	**.252**	**3**	**107**	**16**	**27**	**8**	**0**	**3**	**16**	**12**	**27**	**1**

ST. LOUIS	W	L	ERA	G	GS	SV	IP	H	R	ER	BB	SO
Genesis Cabrera	0	0	18.00	2	0	0	1.0	1	2	2	3	1
Jack Flaherty	0	1	1.50	1	1	0	6.0	6	1	1	2	8
Giovanny Gallegos	1	0	9.00	2	0	0	2.0	3	2	2	1	3
Austin Gomber	0	0	0.00	1	0	0	1.1	2	0	0	1	2
Ryan Helsley	0	0	5.40	2	0	0	1.2	1	1	1	0	2
Kwang Hyun Kim	0	0	7.36	1	1	0	3.2	5	3	3	2	2
Andrew Miller	0	0	0.00	1	0	0	0.2	1	0	0	0	0
Daniel Ponce de Leon	0	1	27.00	1	0	0	1.0	2	3	3	1	2
Alex Reyes	0	0	2.70	2	0	1	3.1	2	3	1	2	3
Adam Wainwright	0	0	5.40	1	1	0	3.1	6	2	2	2	3
Tyler Webb	0	0	13.50	1	0	0	0.2	1	1	1	0	0
Kodi Whitley	0	0	27.00	1	0	0	0.1	1	1	1	0	0
Totals	**1**	**2**	**6.12**	**3**	**3**	**1**	**25.0**	**31**	**19**	**17**	**14**	**26**

SAN DIEGO	AVG	G	AB	R	H	2B	3B	HR	RBI	BB	SO	SB
Jake Cronenworth, 2B	.625	3	8	4	5	0	1	1	2	2	1	0
Trent Grisham, CF	.000	3	11	1	0	0	0	0	0	3	6	0
Eric Hosmer, 1B	.167	3	12	1	2	1	0	0	3	1	2	0
Manny Machado, 3B	.143	3	14	1	2	0	0	1	2	0	2	0
Mitch Moreland, DH	.500	2	6	1	3	0	0	0	0	0	2	0
Wil Myers, RF	.333	3	12	2	4	0	0	2	4	2	3	0
Austin Nola, C	.000	3	8	2	0	0	0	0	2	3	5	0
Tommy Pham, LF	.462	3	13	1	6	2	0	0	1	0	1	2
Jurickson Profar, LF	.571	3	7	1	4	0	0	0	0	1	0	0
Fernando Tatis Jr., SS	.455	3	11	5	5	1	0	2	5	3	3	0
Totals	**.304**	**3**	**102**	**19**	**31**	**4**	**1**	**6**	**19**	**14**	**26**	**3**

SAN DIEGO	W	L	ERA	G	GS	SV	IP	H	R	ER	BB	SO
Austin Adams	1	0	9.00	2	0	0	1.0	0	1	1	1	1
Zach Davies	0	0	18.00	1	1	0	2.0	5	4	4	1	3
Tim Hill	0	0	0.00	1	0	0	1.0	0	0	0	0	1
Pierce Johnson	0	0	0.00	3	0	0	2.1	2	0	0	1	5
Adrian Morejon	0	0	0.00	2	0	0	3.0	1	0	0	0	2
Chris Paddack	0	1	23.14	1	1	0	2.1	8	6	6	0	1
Emilio Pagan	1	0	0.00	3	0	0	3.0	2	0	0	2	2
Luis Patino	0	0	0.00	1	0	0	1.0	1	0	0	1	0
Drew Pomeranz	0	0	0.00	3	0	0	3.0	1	2	0	1	2
Garrett Richards	0	0	0.00	2	0	0	1.1	0	0	0	0	1
Trevor Rosenthal	0	0	6.00	3	0	1	3.0	3	2	2	3	5
Craig Stammen	0	0	0.00	2	1	0	2.2	2	0	0	1	2
Matt Strahm	0	0	6.75	2	0	0	1.1	2	1	1	1	2
Totals	**2**	**1**	**4.67**	**3**	**3**	**1**	**27.0**	**27**	**16**	**14**	**12**	**27**

SCORE BY INNINGS

ST. LOUIS	5	3	2	0	0	2	0	2	2	16
SAN DIEGO	1	1	1	2	1	5	5	3	0	19

NATIONAL LEAGUE DIVISION SERIES

LOS ANGELES DODGERS VS. SAN DIEGO PADRES

SAN DIEGO	AVG	G	AB	R	H	2B	3B	HR	RBI	BB	SO	SB
Greg Allen, LF	-	1	0	0	0	0	0	0	0	0	0	0
Luis Campusano, PH	.000	1	1	0	0	0	0	0	0	0	1	0
Jason Castro, C	.000	1	1	0	0	0	0	0	0	0	0	0
Jake Cronenworth, 2B	.200	3	10	1	2	0	0	0	1	2	4	0
Trent Grisham, CF	.273	3	11	0	3	1	0	0	2	1	5	0
Eric Hosmer, 1B	.154	3	13	2	2	0	0	1	1	0	3	0
Manny Machado, 3B	.167	3	12	2	2	0	0	1	1	1	2	0
Mitch Moreland, DH	.500	2	2	1	1	1	0	0	1	0	0	0
Wil Myers, RF	.100	3	10	1	1	0	0	1	2	5	1	0
Austin Nola, C	.222	3	9	0	2	0	0	0	1	1	2	0
Tommy Pham, DH	.273	3	11	3	0	0	0	0	1	4	1	0
Jurickson Profar, LF	.000	3	8	0	0	0	0	0	0	0	1	0
Fernando Tatis Jr., SS	.182	3	11	0	2	1	0	0	0	2	4	1
Totals	**.182**	**3**	**99**	**9**	**18**	**4**	**0**	**2**	**8**	**10**	**31**	**3**

SAN DIEGO	W	L	ERA	G	GS	SV	IP	H	R	ER	BB	SO
Austin Adams	0	0	0.00	2	0	0	0.2	0	0	0	3	1
Dan Altavilla	0	0	4.50	2	0	0	2.0	2	1	1	1	2
Mike Clevinger	0	0	0.00	1	1	0	1.0	0	0	0	3	1
Zach Davies	0	1	7.20	1	1	0	5.0	9	4	4	0	3
Tim Hill	0	0	0.00	2	0	0	1.1	1	1	0	1	2
Pierce Johnson	0	0	10.80	2	0	0	1.2	1	2	2	1	2
Adrian Morejon	0	1	13.50	1	1	0	2.0	2	3	3	2	2
Emilio Pagan	0	0	0.00	2	0	0	2.0	0	0	0	0	1
Luis Patino	0	0	5.40	2	0	0	1.2	1	1	1	1	0
Drew Pomeranz	0	0	0.00	2	0	0	1.0	2	0	0	2	2
Garrett Richards	0	1	13.50	2	0	0	1.1	1	2	2	2	3
Trevor Rosenthal	0	0	36.00	1	0	0	1.0	2	4	4	2	1
Craig Stammen	0	0	13.50	2	0	0	2.0	3	3	3	1	2
Matt Strahm	0	0	18.00	2	0	0	1.0	5	2	2	1	0
Ryan Weathers	0	0	0.00	1	0	0	1.1	0	0	0	2	1
Totals	**0**	**3**	**7.92**	**3**	**3**	**0**	**25.0**	**29**	**23**	**22**	**20**	**22**

LOS ANGELES	AVG	G	AB	R	H	2B	3B	HR	RBI	BB	SO	SB
Austin Barnes, C	1.000	1	2	1	2	0	0	0	0	0	0	0
Cody Bellinger, CF	.333	3	12	2	4	0	1	1	5	2	3	0
Mookie Betts, RF	.333	3	12	5	4	2	0	0	1	2	2	1
Enrique Hernandez, 2B	.000	3	5	0	0	0	0	0	0	0	3	0
Gavin Lux, PH	.000	1	1	0	0	0	0	0	0	0	1	0
Max Muncy, 1B	.273	3	11	3	3	1	0	0	2	4	2	0
Joc Pederson, DH	.400	3	5	2	2	0	0	0	1	0	1	0
AJ Pollock, LF	.300	3	10	3	3	0	0	0	1	0	1	1
Corey Seager, SS	.364	3	11	3	4	2	0	0	3	3	0	1
Will Smith, C	.455	3	11	5	5	2	0	0	3	3	2	0
Chris Taylor, 2B	.000	3	11	1	0	0	0	0	0	2	4	0
Justin Turner, 3B	.200	3	10	4	2	0	0	0	0	3	3	2
Totals	**.287**	**3**	**101**	**23**	**29**	**7**	**1**	**1**	**20**	**20**	**22**	**3**

LOS ANGELES	W	L	ERA	G	GS	SV	IP	H	R	ER	BB	SO
Pedro Baez	0	0	0.00	1	0	0	1.0	0	0	0	0	2
Walker Buehler	0	0	2.25	1	1	0	4.0	2	1	1	4	8
Dylan Floro	0	0	0.00	1	0	0	1.0	1	0	0	0	0
Victor Gonzalez	0	0	0.00	1	0	0	1.0	1	0	0	0	0
Brusdar Graterol	0	0	0.00	1	0	0	1.1	0	0	0	0	0
Kenley Jansen	0	0	13.50	2	0	0	1.1	3	2	2	0	2
Joe Kelly	0	0	0.00	1	0	1	0.1	0	0	0	2	0
Clayton Kershaw	1	0	4.50	1	1	0	6.0	6	3	3	0	6
Adam Kolarek	0	0	27.00	1	0	0	0.2	3	2	2	2	0
Dustin May	1	0	0.00	2	1	0	3.0	0	0	0	1	4
Blake Treinen	0	0	0.00	3	0	0	2.1	1	0	0	0	2
Julio Urias	1	0	0.00	1	0	0	5.0	1	0	1	0	6
Totals	3	0	2.67	3	3	1	27.0	18	9	8	10	31

SCORE BY INNINGS

SAN DIEGO	0	3	0	1	0	3	0	0	2	9
LOS ANGELES	0	1	8	2	2	4	2	0	4	23

ATLANTA BRAVES VS. MIAMI MARLINS

MIAMI	AVG	G	AB	R	H	2B	3B	HR	RBI	BB	SO	SB
Jesus Aguilar, DH	.154	3	13	0	2	0	0	0	0	0	5	0
Jorge Alfaro, C	.000	2	3	0	0	0	0	0	0	0	0	0
Brian Anderson, 3B	.400	3	10	1	4	1	0	0	1	1	3	0
Jon Berti, 2B	.167	3	12	1	2	0	0	0	0	0	5	0
Lewis Brinson, RF	.000	3	5	0	0	0	0	0	0	0	2	0
Jazz Chisholm, 2B	.333	1	3	0	1	0	0	0	0	1	0	0
Garrett Cooper, 1B	.100	3	10	1	1	1	0	0	2	2	2	0
Corey Dickerson, LF	.250	3	12	0	3	0	0	0	0	0	3	0
Matt Joyce, RF	.167	3	6	0	1	0	0	0	1	0	2	0
Miguel Rojas, SS	.091	3	11	1	1	0	0	0	1	0	2	0
Magneuris Sierra, CF	.250	3	8	1	2	1	0	0	0	0	3	0
Chad Wallach, C	.000	3	7	0	0	0	0	0	0	0	3	0
Totals	.170	3	100	5	17	4	0	1	5	4	31	0

MIAMI	W	L	ERA	G	GS	SV	IP	H	R	ER	BB	SO
Sandy Alcantara	0	1	7.50	1	1	0	6.0	8	5	5	1	8
Richard Bleier	0	0	0.00	1	0	0	1.0	0	0	0	0	0
Brad Boxberger	0	0	0.00	2	0	0	2.0	0	0	0	2	2
Yimi Garcia	0	0	20.25	2	0	0	1.1	4	3	3	1	1
James Hoyt	0	0	9.00	2	0	0	1.0	1	1	1	0	1
Brandon Kintzler	0	0	0.00	1	0	0	1.0	1	0	0	0	1
Pablo Lopez	0	1	3.60	1	1	0	5.0	3	2	2	0	7
Trevor Rogers	0	0	10.80	1	0	0	1.2	4	3	2	1	2
Sixto Sanchez	0	1	12.00	1	1	0	3.0	4	4	4	3	2
Ryne Stanek	0	0	0.00	2	0	0	2.0	0	0	0	3	3
Nick Vincent	0	0	0.00	1	0	0	1.0	1	0	0	0	1
Totals	0	3	6.12	3	3	0	25.0	26	18	17	11	28

ATLANTA	AVG	G	AB	R	H	2B	3B	HR	RBI	BB	SO	SB
Ronald Acuna Jr., CF	.182	3	11	4	2	0	0	1	1	2	7	1
Ozzie Albies, 2B	.167	3	12	2	2	1	0	0	0	1	2	0
Travis d'Arnaud, C	.600	3	10	3	6	2	0	2	7	3	1	0
Adam Duvall, LF	.083	3	12	0	1	1	0	0	1	0	5	0
Freddie Freeman, 1B	.167	3	12	2	2	0	0	0	0	2	0	0
Nick Markakis, RF	.167	3	12	0	2	1	0	0	0	0	3	0
Marcell Ozuna, DH	.308	3	13	3	4	1	0	0	3	0	5	0
Cristian Pache, RF	-	3	0	0	0	0	0	0	0	0	0	0
Austin Riley, 3B	.333	3	9	1	3	0	0	0	0	2	5	0
Dansby Swanson, SS	.400	3	10	3	4	0	1	2	5	1	2	0
Totals	.287	3	101	23	29	7	1	1	20	20	22	3

ATLANTA	W	L	ERA	G	GS	SV	IP	H	R	ER	BB	SO
Ian Anderson	1	0	0.00	1	1	0	5.2	3	0	0	1	8
Max Fried	0	0	9.00	1	1	0	4.0	6	4	4	0	4
Shane Greene	0	0	0.00	1	0	0	1.0	1	0	0	0	0
Chris Martin	0	0	9.00	1	0	0	1.0	2	1	1	0	1
Tyler Matzek	0	0	0.00	2	0	0	2.0	0	0	0	0	4
Mark Melancon	0	0	0.00	2	0	1	2.0	0	0	0	0	3
A.J. Minter	0	0	0.00	1	0	0	1.0	0	0	0	0	1
Darren O'Day	0	0	0.00	2	0	0	1.1	1	0	0	0	1
Will Smith	1	0	0.00	2	0	0	2.0	1	0	0	0	1
Jacob Webb	0	0	0.00	1	0	0	1.0	1	0	0	0	1
Kyle Wright	1	0	0.00	1	0	0	6.0	3	0	0	2	7
Totals	3	0	1.67	3	3	1	27.0	17	5	5	4	31

SCORE BY INNINGS

MIAMI	0	1	3	0	0	0	0	1	0	5
ATLANTA	1	1	6	2	2	0	6	0	0	18

NATIONAL LEAGUE CHAMPIONSHIP SERIES
LOS ANGELES DODGERS VS. ATLANTA BRAVES

ATLANTA	AVG	G	AB	R	H	2B	3B	HR	RBI	BB	SO	SB
Ronald Acuna Jr., RF	.167	7	24	6	4	2	0	0	1	5	6	1
Ozzie Albies, 2B	.333	7	27	5	9	1	0	2	4	2	6	1
Johan Camargo, 3B	.250	4	8	0	2	1	0	0	1	2	3	0
Charlie Culberson, RF	.667	2	3	0	2	0	0	0	0	0	1	0
Travis d'Arnaud, C	.174	7	23	1	4	0	0	0	3	4	7	0
Adam Duvall, LF	-	1	0	0	0	0	0	0	0	0	0	0
Tyler Flowers, C	.333	1	3	1	1	0	0	0	0	0	0	0
Freddie Freeman, 1B	.360	7	25	6	9	3	0	2	6	3	5	0
Nick Markakis, LF	.250	6	16	2	4	1	0	0	0	1	6	0
Marcell Ozuna, DH	.276	7	29	4	8	2	0	2	6	2	4	0
Cristian Pache, CF	.182	7	22	3	4	1	0	1	4	3	4	0
Austin Riley, 3B	.143	7	28	2	4	0	0	1	4	1	10	0
Pablo Sandoval, 1B	.000	3	3	0	0	0	0	0	0	0	2	0
Dansby Swanson, SS	.269	7	26	3	7	2	0	1	4	4	12	0
Totals	.245	7	237	33	58	13	1	9	33	27	64	4

ATLANTA	W	L	ERA	G	GS	SV	IP	H	R	ER	BB	SO
Ian Anderson	0	0	2.57	2	2	0	7.0	6	2	2	7	7
Grant Dayton	0	0	36.00	1	0	0	2.0	8	8	8	1	2
Max Fried	0	1	2.84	2	2	0	12.2	12	4	4	6	14
Shane Greene	0	0	1.93	4	0	0	4.2	3	1	1	1	5
Chris Martin	0	1	1.80	5	0	0	5.0	3	1	1	2	5
Tyler Matzek	1	0	1.69	4	0	0	5.1	4	1	1	3	6
Mark Melancon	0	0	0.00	3	0	0	2.1	2	1	0	0	0
A.J. Minter	0	0	4.15	3	1	0	4.1	4	2	2	0	8
Darren O'Day	0	0	27.00	2	0	0	0.2	2	2	2	0	1
Will Smith	1	1	16.20	3	0	0	1.2	2	3	3	3	1
Josh Tomlin	0	0	10.13	2	0	0	2.2	4	3	3	0	4
Jacob Webb	0	0	13.50	2	0	0	2.0	4	3	3	1	5
Bryse Wilson	1	0	1.50	1	1	0	6.0	1	1	1	1	5
Kyle Wright	0	1	94.50	1	1	0	0.2	5	7	7	2	0
Huascar Ynoa	0	0	0.00	1	0	0	4.0	1	0	0	4	4
Totals	3	4	5.61	7	7	1	61.0	61	39	38	31	67

LOS ANGELES	AVG	G	AB	R	H	2B	3B	HR	RBI	BB	SO	SB
Austin Barnes, C	.286	3	7	0	2	0	0	0	0	0	2	0
Matt Beaty, LF	-	2	0	0	0	0	0	0	0	1	0	0
Cody Bellinger, CF	.200	7	25	3	5	0	1	2	5	6	9	1
Mookie Betts, RF	.269	7	26	4	7	1	0	0	1	5	4	1
Enrique Hernandez, 2B	.308	6	13	2	4	0	0	2	2	1	2	0
Max Muncy, 1B	.227	7	22	6	5	2	0	2	6	9	11	0
Joc Pederson, LF	.389	6	18	2	7	0	0	1	3	1	2	0
AJ Pollock, LF	.200	6	20	0	4	0	0	0	0	0	3	0
Edwin Rios, 3B	.222	4	9	2	2	0	0	2	3	2	5	0
Corey Seager, SS	.310	7	29	8	9	2	0	5	11	1	6	0
Will Smith, C	.357	7	28	3	5	1	0	1	7	0	10	0
Chris Taylor, 2B	.222	5	18	3	4	2	0	0	0	2	8	0
Justin Turner, 3B	.280	7	25	6	7	2	0	1	1	3	4	0
Totals	.254	7	240	39	61	10	1	16	39	31	67	2

LOS ANGELES	W	L	ERA	G	GS	SV	IP	H	R	ER	BB	SO
Pedro Baez	0	0	2.70	4	0	0	3.1	2	1	1	2	5
Walker Buehler	1	0	0.82	2	2	0	11.0	10	1	1	5	13
Dylan Floro	0	0	3.86	2	0	0	2.1	2	3	1	1	4
Tony Gonsolin	0	1	9.95	2	1	0	6.1	5	7	7	6	8
Victor Gonzalez	0	0	4.50	3	0	0	2.0	2	1	1	2	2
Brusdar Graterol	0	0	8.10	4	0	0	3.1	3	3	3	1	4
Kenley Jansen	0	0	0.00	3	0	1	3.0	0	0	0	0	3
Joe Kelly	0	0	0.00	2	0	0	1.1	2	0	0	0	0
Clayton Kershaw	0	1	7.20	1	1	0	5.0	7	4	4	1	4
Adam Kolarek	0	0	13.50	2	0	0	0.2	6	3	3	0	2
Dustin May	0	0	3.86	3	2	0	4.2	5	3	2	5	6
Jake McGee	0	0	5.40	3	0	0	1.2	3	1	1	0	3
Blake Treinen	1	1	6.75	4	0	0	5.1	5	4	4	0	2
Julio Urias	2	0	1.13	2	1	0	8.0	3	1	1	2	5
Alex Wood	0	0	3.38	2	0	0	2.2	3	1	1	2	3
Totals	4	3	4.35	7	7	1	62.0	58	33	30	27	64

SCORE BY INNINGS

ATLANTA	3	2	1	4	4	6	3	3	7	33
LOS ANGELES	14	1	6	1	1	4	8	0	4	39

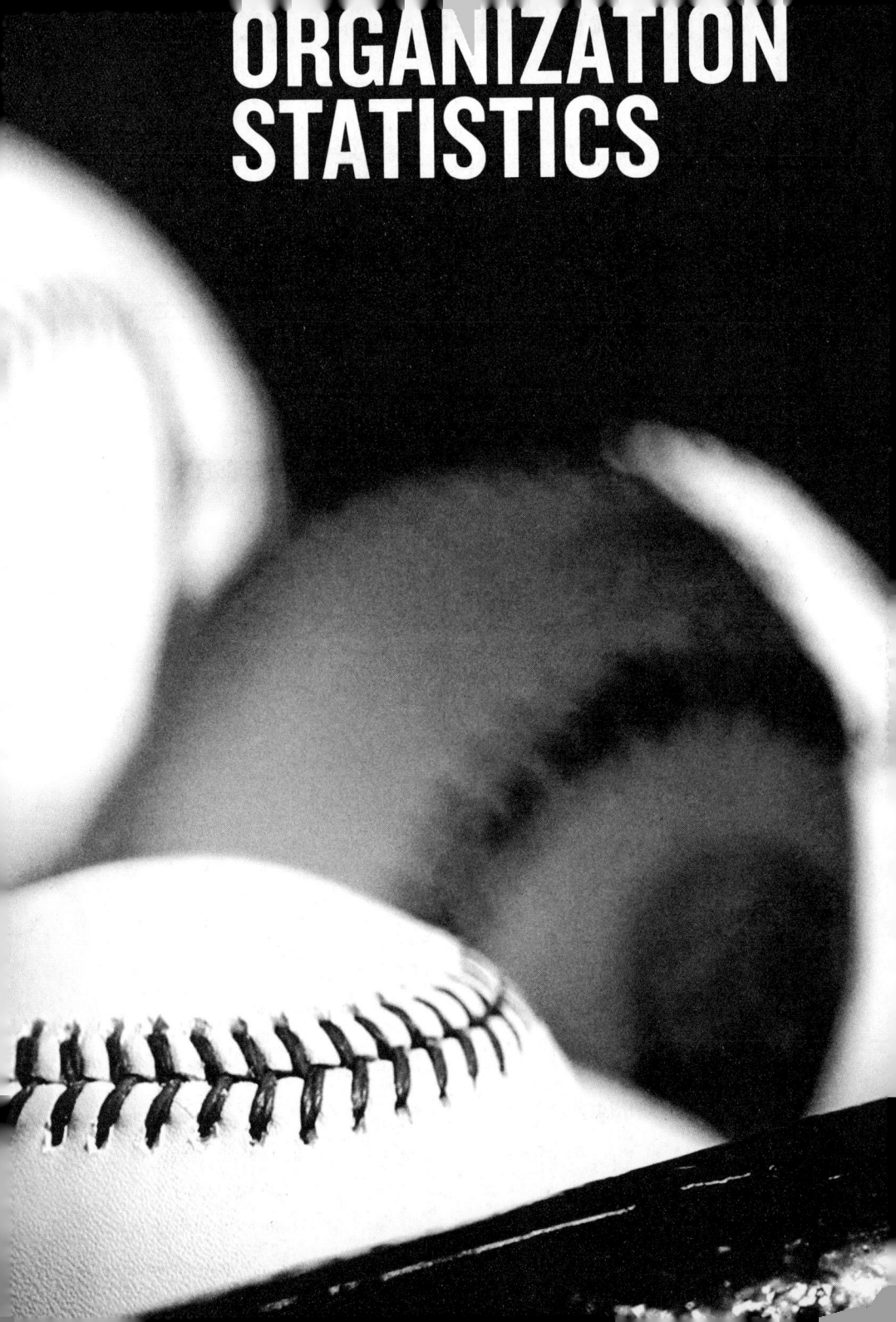

ORGANIZATION
STATISTICS

Arizona Diamondbacks

SEASON IN A SENTENCE: The D-backs added Madison Bumgarner, Starling Marte and Kole Calhoun in the offseason and expected to contend for the playoffs in 2020, but instead they went 25-35 and finished the year as baseball's most disappointing team.

HIGH POINT: Righthander Zac Gallen made history Aug. 28 when he pitched seven innings with one run allowed against the Giants. With the outing, Gallen held opponents to three earned runs or less in each of his first 22 career starts, a major league record for a player to begin his career. Gallen would extend his record to 23 starts the following week against the Dodgers.

LOW POINT: The D-backs rebounded from a slow start to put themselves back in playoff contention by mid-August, but their postseason dreams ended with a miserable 2-18 stretch that lasted from Aug. 19-Sept. 9. The offense hit an anemic .192/.272/.322 during the stretch and averaged barely three runs per game.

NOTABLE ROOKIES: Catcher/outfielder Daulton Varsho received his first callup with the team out of playoff contention and hit .188/.287/.366 in 37 games. First baseman Pavin Smith and second baseman Andy Young also got into 12 games at the end of the season and each hit their first career home run. Righthanders Keury Mella (2-0, 1.80), Riley Smith (2-0, 1.47) and Taylor Widener (0-1, 4.50) stepped up to help fortify the pitching staff out of the bullpen.

KEY TRANSACTIONS: The D-backs signed Bumgarner to a five-year, $70 million contract, Calhoun to a two-year, $16 million contract and acquired Marte in a trade with the Pirates in the offseason. Bumgarner went 1-4, 6.48 and saw his velocity decline substantially, Calhoun hit a team-high 16 home runs but also batted .226 and Marte was traded to the Marlins in August. Righthander Archie Bradley (Reds) and lefthanders Robbie Ray (Blue Jays) and Andrew Chafin (Cubs) were all shipped away at the deadline, as well, as the team pivoted toward a rebuild. The D-backs acquisitions made it clear that Arizona's focus is more in the intermediate term than the long term. They received young pitchers Caleb Smith and Humberto Mejia, both of whom had major league experience, for Marte. They also acquired infielder Josh VanMeter in the Bradley trade and lefthander Travis Bergen in the Ray trade, who each had major league time, as well.

OPENING DAY PAYROLL: $64,201,669 (14th)

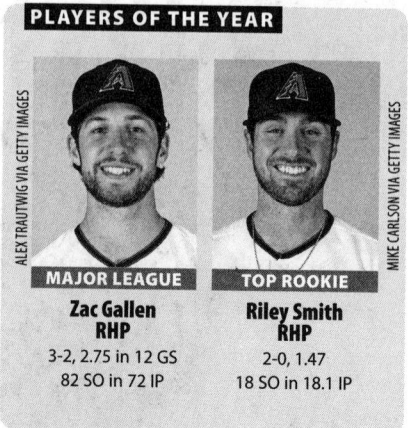

PLAYERS OF THE YEAR

MAJOR LEAGUE
Zac Gallen
RHP
3-2, 2.75 in 12 GS
82 SO in 72 IP

TOP ROOKIE
Riley Smith
RHP
2-0, 1.47
18 SO in 18.1 IP

ORGANIZATION LEADERS

Batting		*Minimum 100 AB
MAJORS		
* AVG	Starling Marte	.311
* OPS	Kole Calhoun	.864
HR	Kole Calhoun	16
RBI	Kole Calhoun	40

Pitching		#Minimum 30 IP
MAJORS		
W	Taylor Clarke	3
W	Merrill Kelly	3
W	Zac Gallen	3
# ERA	Zac Gallen	2.75
SO	Zac Gallen	82
SV	Archie Bradley	6

ORGANIZATION STATISTICS

ARIZONA DIAMONDBACKS
NATIONAL LEAGUE

Batting	B-T	HT	WT	DOB	AVG	vLH	vRH	G	AB	R	H	2B	3B	HR	RBI	BB	HBP	SH	SF	SO	SB	CS	SLG	OBP
Ahmed, Nick	R-R	6-2	200	3-15-90	.266	.274	.263	57	199	29	53	10	1	5	29	18	0	0	0	46	4	0	.402	.327
Calhoun, Kole	L-L	5-10	210	10-14-87	.226	.229	.225	54	190	35	43	9	0	16	40	28	6	0	4	50	1	1	.526	.338
Cron, Kevin	R-R	6-5	255	2-17-93	.000	.000	.000	8	17	0	0	0	0	0	0	1	2	0	0	7	0	0	.000	.150
Escobar, Eduardo	B-R	5-10	210	1-5-89	.212	.213	.211	54	203	22	43	7	3	4	20	15	2	0	2	41	1	0	.335	.270

Batting	B-T	HT	WT	DOB	AVG	vLH	vRH	G	AB	R	H	2B	3B	HR	RBI	BB	HBP	SH	SF	SO	SB	CS	SLG	OBP
Jay, Jon	L-L	5-11	200	3-15-85	.160	.000	.182	18	50	5	8	1	0	1	4	3	1	0	3	12	0	0	.240	.211
Kelly, Carson	R-R	6-2	210	7-14-94	.221	.130	.276	39	122	11	27	5	0	5	19	6	1	0	0	29	0	0	.385	.264
Lamb, Jake	L-R	6-3	215	10-9-90	.116	.000	.119	18	43	2	5	1	0	0	1	6	1	0	0	17	0	1	.140	.240
Locastro, Tim	R-R	6-1	195	7-14-92	.290	.224	.450	33	69	15	20	4	1	2	7	8	4	1	0	14	4	0	.464	.395
Marte, Ketel	B-R	6-1	210	10-12-93	.287	.423	.233	45	181	19	52	14	1	2	17	7	4	0	3	21	1	0	.409	.323
Marte, Starling	R-R	6-1	195	10-9-88	.311	.379	.290	33	122	23	38	8	1	2	14	10	5	0	1	19	5	2	.443	.384
2-team total (28 Miami Marlins)					.281	.290	.277	61	228	36	64	14	1	6	27	12	9	0	1	41	10	2	.430	.340
Mathisen, Wyatt	R-R	6-0	210	12-30-93	.222	.333	.083	9	27	5	6	0	0	2	5	5	1	0	0	12	0	0	.444	.364
Peralta, David	L-L	6-1	220	8-14-87	.300	.261	.312	54	203	19	61	10	1	5	34	13	0	0	2	45	1	0	.433	.339
Rojas, Josh	L-R	6-1	200	6-30-94	.180	.222	.147	17	61	9	11	0	0	0	2	7	0	0	2	16	1	1	.180	.257
Smith, Pavin	L-L	6-2	210	2-6-96	.270	.429	.233	12	37	7	10	0	1	1	4	5	0	0	2	8	1	0	.405	.341
VanMeter, Josh	L-R	5-11	190	3-10-95	.194	.250	.179	12	36	6	7	2	0	1	5	4	1	0	0	8	0	0	.333	.293
2-team total (14 Cincinnati Reds)					.129	.182	.119	26	70	9	9	3	0	2	6	7	2	0	0	24	1	0	.257	.228
Vargas, Ildemaro	B-R	6-0	180	7-16-91	.150	.091	.222	8	20	2	3	0	0	0	1	0	0	0	0	5	0	0	.150	.190
2-team total (6 Chicago Cubs)					.172	.133	.214	14	29	3	5	0	0	1	1	1	0	0	0	8	0	0	.276	.200
Varsho, Daulton	L-R	5-10	205	7-2-96	.188	.143	.212	37	101	16	19	5	2	3	9	12	2	0	0	33	3	1	.366	.287
Vogt, Stephen	L-R	6-0	211	11-1-84	.167	.111	.175	26	72	6	12	5	0	1	7	8	0	0	1	18	0	0	.278	.247
Walker, Christian	R-R	6-0	210	3-28-91	.271	.232	.284	57	218	35	59	18	1	7	34	19	3	0	3	50	1	1	.459	.333
Young, Andy	R-R	6-0	200	5-10-94	.192	.111	.375	12	26	3	5	2	0	1	4	5	3	0	0	10	0	0	.385	.382

Pitching	B-T	HT	WT	DOB	W	L	ERA	G	GS	CG	SV	IP	H	R	ER	HR	BB	SO	AVG	vLH	vRH	K/9	BB/9
Beasley, Jeremy	R-R	6-3	245	11-20-95	0	0	0.00	1	0	0	0	2	0	0	0	0	0	1	.667	1.000	.500	27.00	0.00
Bergen, Travis	L-L	6-1	215	10-8-93	1	0	4.05	7	0	0	1	7	4	3	3	1	8	8	.182	.167	.200	10.80	10.80
Bracho, Silvino	R-R	5-10	190	7-17-92	0	0	18.00	1	0	0	0	1	2	2	2	1	0	1	.400	.500	.333	9.00	0.00
Bradley, Archie	R-R	6-4	215	8-10-92	1	0	4.22	10	0	0	6	11	13	5	5	0	3	12	.317	.286	.350	10.13	2.53
2-team total (6 Cincinnati Reds)					2	0	2.95	16	0	0	6	18	17	6	6	1	3	18	.246	.176	.314	8.84	1.47
Bumgarner, Madison	R-L	6-4	255	8-1-89	1	4	6.48	9	9	0	0	42	47	31	30	13	13	30	.276	.255	.285	6.48	2.81
Chafin, Andrew	L-L	6-2	235	6-17-90	1	1	8.10	11	0	0	0	7	9	6	6	1	4	10	.310	.294	.333	13.50	5.40
2-team total (4 Chicago Cubs)					1	2	6.52	15	0	0	1	10	11	7	7	2	5	13	.275	.273	.278	12.10	4.66
Clarke, Taylor	R-R	6-4	220	5-13-93	3	0	4.36	12	5	0	0	43	35	23	21	8	21	40	.217	.185	.240	8.31	4.36
Crichton, Stefan	R-R	6-3	205	2-29-92	2	2	2.42	26	0	0	5	26	22	7	7	1	9	23	.229	.185	.246	7.96	3.12
Gallen, Zac	R-R	6-2	198	8-3-95	3	2	2.75	12	12	0	0	72	55	24	22	9	25	82	.210	.213	.207	10.25	3.13
Ginkel, Kevin	L-R	6-4	235	3-24-94	0	2	6.75	19	0	0	1	16	21	13	12	3	13	18	.318	.241	.378	10.13	7.31
Grace, Matt	L-L	6-4	215	12-14-88	0	1	54.00	3	0	0	0	1	5	6	6	1	2	2	.625	.500	.667	18.00	18.00
Guerra, Junior	R-R	6-0	235	1-16-85	1	2	3.04	25	0	0	0	24	17	10	8	1	15	21	.205	.219	.196	7.99	5.70
Kelly, Carson	R-R	6-2	210	7-14-94	0	0	0.00	1	0	0	0	1	1	0	0	0	0	0	.250	.500	.000	0.00	0.00
Kelly, Merrill	R-R	6-2	210	10-14-88	3	2	2.59	5	5	0	0	31	26	9	9	5	5	29	.218	.173	.254	8.33	1.44
Lewicki, Artie	R-R	6-3	195	4-8-92	0	0	5.40	2	0	0	0	3	7	2	2	0	1	5	.412	.500	.385	13.50	2.70
Lopez, Yoan	R-R	6-3	205	1-2-93	0	1	5.95	20	0	0	0	20	21	15	13	4	9	16	.269	.355	.213	7.32	4.12
Mantiply, Joe	R-L	6-4	215	3-1-91	0	0	15.43	4	0	0	0	2	3	4	4	0	4	2	.273	.286	.250	7.71	15.43
Mella, Keury	R-R	6-2	230	8-2-93	2	0	1.80	11	0	0	0	10	10	3	2	1	3	10	.263	.200	.286	9.00	2.70
Payamps, Joel	R-R	6-2	225	4-7-94	0	0	3.00	2	0	0	0	3	2	1	1	0	0	2	.000	.000	.333	6.00	9.00
Ray, Robbie	L-L	6-2	215	10-1-91	1	4	7.84	7	7	0	0	31	31	27	27	9	31	43	.258	.229	.271	12.48	9.00
Rondon, Hector	R-R	6-3	225	2-26-88	1	0	7.65	23	0	0	0	20	25	18	17	6	11	23	.298	.281	.308	10.35	4.95
Smith, Caleb	R-L	6-0	206	7-28-91	0	0	2.45	4	3	0	0	11	5	3	3	2	6	12	.128	.091	.143	9.82	4.91
2-team total (1 Miami Marlins)					0	0	2.57	5	4	0	0	14	6	4	4	3	12	15	.125	.143	.118	9.64	7.71
Smith, Riley	R-R	6-1	175	1-15-95	2	0	1.47	6	0	0	0	18	15	3	3	1	5	18	.234	.143	.279	8.84	2.45
Weaver, Luke	R-R	6-2	185	8-21-93	1	9	6.58	12	12	0	0	52	63	39	38	10	18	55	.292	.320	.265	9.52	3.12
Widener, Taylor	L-R	6-0	230	10-24-94	0	1	4.50	12	0	0	0	20	14	10	10	5	12	22	.192	.265	.128	9.90	5.40
Young, Alex	L-L	6-3	220	9-9-93	2	4	5.44	15	7	0	0	46	51	30	28	11	14	39	.277	.241	.292	7.58	2.72

Fielding

Catcher	PCT	G	PO	A	E	DP	PB
Kelly	.993	38	291	13	2	1	3
Varsho	1.000	10	52	3	0	0	1
Vogt	1.000	23	184	7	0	1	0

First Base	PCT	G	PO	A	E	DP
Cron	1.000	1	1	0	0	0
Lamb	1.000	12	63	7	0	7
Smith	1.000	5	40	2	0	4
Vargas	.952	5	19	1	1	2
Vogt	1.000	1	5	0	0	0
Walker	.990	43	268	28	3	40

Second Base	PCT	G	PO	A	E	DP
Escobar	1.000	3	6	7	0	2
Marte	.994	41	65	90	1	22
Rojas	1.000	8	9	18	0	2
VanMeter	1.000	10	14	17	0	9
Vargas	1.000	3	0	4	0	1
Young	1.000	4	5	5	0	3

Third Base	PCT	G	PO	A	E	DP
Escobar	.934	47	26	87	8	13
Lamb	1.000	3	1	3	0	0
Mathisen	.905	7	6	13	2	4
VanMeter	.833	2	1	4	1	0
Vargas	1.000	1	0	1	0	0
Young	.000	3	0	0	3	0

Shortstop	PCT	G	PO	A	E	DP
Ahmed	.963	57	61	121	7	33
Marte	.875	2	4	3	1	0
Rojas	1.000	2	2	2	0	1

Outfield	PCT	G	PO	A	E	DP
Calhoun	.990	48	102	1	1	1
Jay	1.000	17	32	0	0	0
Locastro	.981	25	51	0	1	0
Marte	1.000	3	5	0	0	0
Marte	1.000	33	71	2	0	0
Peralta	1.000	45	86	1	0	1
Rojas	1.000	1	1	0	0	0
Smith	1.000	5	5	0	0	0
Varsho	1.000	19	47	1	0	0
Young	--	1	0	0	0	0

Atlanta Braves

SEASON IN A SENTENCE: After winning a third consecutive National League East title, the Braves took the next step in the playoffs, making the NLCS and coming within a win of making the World Series after going up 3-1 against the eventual champion Dodgers.

HIGH POINT: Beating the Reds in a three-game series in the Wild Card Series gave the team its first playoff round victory since 2001, and the Braves added to the playoff sweetness by blitzing the division-rival Marlins 3-0 in the National League Division Series. While the Braves had seen regular season success at various points this century, they had largely swung and missed entirely in the postseason. That changed in 2020. The Braves pitching in both of those series was exceptional. The Braves shut out their opponents in four of their five playoff wins in the first two rounds of the National League playoffs.

LOW POINT: The Braves overcame plenty of injuries to their starting rotation over the course of the season, but the biggest blow undoubtedly came when 22-year-old staff ace Mike Soroka suffered a torn achilles in just his third start of the season. Soroka had a 1.59 ERA through his first two starts and was the foundation of the team's pitching staff. He missed the rest of the season, adding significantly more uncertainty for the team's rotation the rest of the way.

NOTABLE ROOKIES: Atlanta called on plenty of rookie arms in 2020, but no one was more impressive than righthander Ian Anderson, who posted a 1.95 ERA over six starts and was one of the better rookie pitchers in baseball. Righthander Kyle Wright continued to show flashes and exhausted his rookie status, while righthanders Bryse Wilson and Huascar Ynoa both had big moments for Atlanta in the postseason. Outfielder Cristian Pache made the postseason roster.

KEY TRANSACTIONS: The Braves were second in baseball in runs and home runs in 2020 and signing outfielder/designated hitter Marcell Ozuna

to a one-year deal on Jan. 21 is a big reason why. It's the second straight year GM Alex Anthopoulos has successfully brought in a veteran on a one-year deal to solidify the middle of the lineup, after making a similar move for third baseman Josh Donaldson in 2019. The signings of veteran arms Cole Hamels and Felix Hernandez didn't help the team's pitching staff—Hamels was hurt much of the season and Hernandez opted out of the campaign.

OPENING DAY PAYROLL: $66,275,488 (13th)

PLAYERS OF THE YEAR

SCOTT AUDETTE VIA GETTY IMAGES

MIKE CARLSON VIA GETTY IMAGES

MAJOR LEAGUE	TOP ROOKIE
Freddie Freeman	**Ian Anderson**
1B	**RHP**
.341/.462/.640	3-2, 1.95,
13 HR, 53 RBIs	41 SO in 32.1 IP
MLB-best 23 doubles	

ORGANIZATION LEADERS

Batting		*Minimum 100 AB
MAJORS		
*AVG	Freddie Freeman	.341
*OPS	Freddie Freeman	1.102
HR	Marcell Ozuna	18
RBI	Marcell Ozuna	56

Pitching		#Minimum 30 IP
MAJORS		
W	Max Fried	7
# ERA	Max Fried	2.25
SO	Max Fried	50
SV	Mark Melancon	11

ORGANIZATION STATISTICS

ATLANTA BRAVES
NATIONAL LEAGUE

Batting	B-T	HT	WT	DOB	AVG	vLH	vRH	G	AB	R	H	2B	3B	HR	RBI	BB	HBP	SH	SF	SO	SB	CS	SLG	OBP
Acuna Jr., Ronald	R-R	6-0	205	12-18-97	.250	.226	.256	46	160	46	40	11	0	14	29	38	4	0	0	60	8	1	.581	.406
Adams, Matt	L-R	6-3	245	8-31-88	.184	.667	.152	16	49	4	9	2	0	2	9	2	0	0	0	18	0	0	.347	.216
Albies, Ozzie	B-R	5-8	165	1-7-97	.271	.214	.289	29	118	21	32	5	0	6	19	5	1	0	0	30	3	1	.466	.306
Camargo, Johan	B-R	6-0	195	12-13-93	.200	.233	.189	35	120	16	24	8	0	4	9	6	1	0	0	35	0	0	.367	.244

Batting

Batting	B-T	HT	WT	DOB	AVG	vLH	vRH	G	AB	R	H	2B	3B	HR	RBI	BB	HBP	SH	SF	SO	SB	CS	SLG	OBP
Contreras, William	R-R	6-0	180	12-24-97	.400	.000	.500	4	10	0	4	1	0	0	1	0	0	0	0	4	0	0	.500	.400
Culberson, Charlie	R-R	6-1	200	4-10-89	.143	.000	.333	9	7	2	1	1	0	0	1	0	0	0	0	4	0	0	.286	.143
d'Arnaud, Travis	R-R	6-2	210	2-10-89	.321	.235	.344	44	165	19	53	8	0	9	34	16	2	0	1	50	1	0	.533	.386
Duvall, Adam	R-R	6-1	215	9-4-88	.237	.277	.224	57	190	34	45	8	0	16	33	15	3	0	1	54	0	0	.532	.301
Flowers, Tyler	R-R	6-4	260	1-24-86	.217	.118	.250	22	69	5	15	6	0	1	5	8	3	0	0	34	0	0	.348	.325
Freeman, Freddie	L-R	6-5	220	9-12-89	.341	.245	.373	60	214	51	73	23	1	13	53	45	3	0	0	37	2	0	.640	.462
Hechavarria, Adeiny	R-R	6-0	195	4-15-89	.254	.273	.250	27	59	7	15	3	0	0	2	4	0	0	0	12	0	0	.305	.302
Inciarte, Ender	L-L	5-11	190	10-29-90	.190	.217	.183	46	116	17	22	2	1	1	10	12	0	1	2	25	4	1	.250	.262
Jackson, Alex	R-R	6-2	215	12-25-95	.286	.000	.400	5	7	0	2	1	0	0	0	0	0	0	0	4	0	0	.429	.286
Markakis, Nick	L-L	6-1	210	11-17-83	.254	.375	.237	37	130	15	33	15	0	1	15	10	1	0	0	23	0	1	.392	.312
Ozuna, Marcell	R-R	6-1	225	11-12-90	.338	.356	.333	60	228	38	77	14	0	18	56	38	0	0	1	60	0	0	.636	.431
Pache, Cristian	R-R	6-2	215	11-19-98	.250	1.000	.000	2	4	0	1	0	0	0	0	0	0	0	0	2	0	0	.250	.250
Riley, Austin	R-R	6-3	240	4-2-97	.239	.244	.238	51	188	24	45	7	1	8	27	16	1	0	1	49	0	0	.415	.301
Sandoval, Pablo	B-R	5-10	268	8-11-86	.000	--	.000	1	2	0	0	0	0	0	0	2	0	0	0	1	0	0	.000	.500
2-team total (33 San Francisco Giants)					.214	.300	.203	34	84	5	18	1	0	1	6	8	1	0	1	19	0	0	.262	.287
Schebler, Scott	L-R	6-1	228	10-6-90	.000	--	.000	1	1	0	0	0	0	0	0	0	0	0	0	0	0	0	.000	.000
Swanson, Dansby	R-R	6-1	190	2-11-94	.274	.186	.294	60	237	49	65	15	0	10	35	22	4	0	1	71	5	0	.464	.345

Pitching

Pitching	B-T	HT	WT	DOB	W	L	ERA	G	GS	CG	SV	IP	H	R	ER	HR	BB	SO	AVG	vLH	vRH	K/9	BB/9
Anderson, Ian	R-R	6-3	170	5-2-98	3	2	1.95	6	6	0	0	32	21	11	7	1	14	41	.172	.145	.200	11.41	3.90
Chacin, Jhoulys	R-R	6-3	215	1-7-88	1	0	7.20	2	0	0	0	5	6	4	4	1	3	3	.286	.250	.308	5.40	5.40
Culberson, Charlie	R-R	6-1	200	4-10-89	0	0	0.00	1	0	0	0	1	0	0	0	0	0	0	.000	--	.000	0.00	0.00
Davidson, Tucker	L-L	6-2	215	3-25-96	0	1	10.80	1	1	0	0	2	3	7	2	1	4	2	.333	.000	.500	10.80	21.60
Dayton, Grant	L-L	6-2	210	11-25-87	2	1	2.30	18	0	0	0	27	22	9	7	4	11	32	.214	.121	.257	10.54	3.62
Erlin, Robbie	R-L	5-11	200	10-8-90	0	0	8.49	7	5	0	0	23	28	22	22	8	6	21	.289	.444	.229	8.10	2.31
2-team total (2 Pittsburgh Pirates)					0	0	8.10	9	5	0	0	27	33	24	24	8	7	25	.295	.424	.241	8.44	2.36
Foltynewicz, Mike	R-R	6-4	195	10-7-91	0	1	16.20	1	1	0	0	3	4	6	6	3	4	3	.333	.143	.600	8.10	10.80
Fried, Max	L-L	6-4	190	1-18-94	7	0	2.25	11	11	0	0	56	42	14	14	2	19	50	.211	.220	.209	8.04	3.05
Greene, Shane	R-R	6-4	200	11-17-88	1	0	2.60	28	0	0	0	28	22	9	8	2	9	21	.229	.286	.185	6.83	2.93
Hamels, Cole	L-L	6-4	205	12-27-83	0	1	8.10	1	1	0	0	3	3	3	3	0	1	2	.250	.000	.273	5.40	2.70
Jackson, Luke	R-R	6-2	210	8-24-91	2	0	6.84	19	0	0	0	26	39	23	20	2	13	20	.345	.375	.323	6.84	4.44
Martin, Chris	R-R	6-8	225	6-2-86	1	1	1.00	19	0	0	1	18	8	3	2	1	3	20	.129	.107	.147	10.00	1.50
Matzek, Tyler	L-L	6-3	230	10-19-90	4	3	2.79	21	0	0	0	29	23	9	9	1	10	43	.211	.190	.224	13.34	3.10
Melancon, Mark	R-R	6-1	215	3-28-85	2	1	2.78	23	0	0	11	23	22	8	7	1	7	14	.262	.333	.208	5.56	2.78
Milone, Tommy	L-L	6-0	215	2-16-87	0	0	14.90	3	3	0	0	10	22	16	16	4	2	9	.449	.500	.439	8.38	1.86
Minter, A.J.	L-L	6-0	215	9-2-93	1	1	0.83	22	0	0	0	22	15	3	2	1	9	24	.200	.250	.176	9.97	3.74
Newcomb, Sean	L-L	6-5	255	6-12-93	0	2	11.20	4	4	0	0	14	20	17	17	4	6	10	.333	.381	.308	6.59	3.95
O'Day, Darren	R-R	6-4	220	10-22-82	4	0	1.10	19	0	0	0	16	8	3	2	1	5	22	.136	.100	.143	12.12	2.76
Rusin, Chris	L-L	6-2	200	10-22-86	0	0	8.10	1	0	0	0	3	6	3	3	1	3	3	.429	.375	.500	8.10	8.10
Smith, Will	R-L	6-5	255	7-10-89	2	2	4.50	18	0	0	0	16	11	8	8	7	4	18	.190	.200	.184	10.13	2.25
Sobotka, Chad	R-R	6-7	225	7-10-93	0	0	12.27	4	0	0	0	6	5	5	5	0	2	2	.333	.500	.250	4.91	4.91
Soroka, Mike	R-R	6-5	225	8-4-97	0	1	3.95	3	3	0	0	14	11	7	6	0	7	8	.224	.308	.130	5.27	4.61
Tomlin, Josh	R-R	6-1	190	10-19-84	2	2	4.76	17	5	0	0	40	40	22	21	6	8	36	.263	.231	.287	8.17	1.82
Toussaint, Touki	R-R	6-3	215	6-20-96	0	2	8.88	7	5	0	0	24	27	28	24	7	16	30	.276	.255	.294	11.10	5.92
Webb, Jacob	R-R	6-2	210	8-15-93	0	0	0.00	8	0	0	0	10	7	2	0	0	5	10	.200	.000	.280	9.00	4.50
Weigel, Patrick	R-R	6-6	240	7-8-94	0	0	27.00	1	0	0	0	1	2	2	2	0	3	0	.667	1.000	.500	0.00	40.50
Wilson, Bryse	R-R	6-2	220	12-20-97	1	0	4.02	6	2	0	1	16	18	7	7	2	9	15	.286	.429	.214	8.62	5.17
Wright, Kyle	R-R	6-4	215	10-2-95	2	4	5.21	8	8	0	0	38	35	23	22	7	24	30	.243	.288	.197	7.11	5.68
Ynoa, Huascar	R-R	6-2	220	5-28-98	0	0	5.82	9	5	0	0	22	23	14	14	2	13	17	.277	.226	.308	7.06	5.40

Fielding

Catchr	PCT	G	PO	A	E	DP	PB
Contreras	1.000	4	21	1	0	0	0
d'Arnaud	.990	35	289	4	3	1	5
Flowers	.995	22	181	5	1	0	1
Jackson	1.000	4	24	0	0	0	0

First Base	PCT	G	PO	A	E	DP
Adams	1.000	2	15	0	0	2
Culberson	1.000	4	8	0	0	2
Freeman	.998	58	427	32	1	44
Riley	.944	4	14	3	1	1

Second Base	PCT	G	PO	A	E	DP
Albies	.982	29	43	65	2	13
Camargo	.988	21	38	41	1	15
Culberson	1.000	1	3	0	0	1
Hechavarria	1.000	12	16	23	0	7

Third Base	PCT	G	PO	A	E	DP
Camargo	1.000	10	5	28	0	2
Hechavarria	.714	8	2	8	4	0
Riley	.955	46	31	95	6	6
Sandoval	1.000	1	0	3	0	0

Shortstop	PCT	G	PO	A	E	DP
Hechavarria	1.000	4	1	3	0	0
Swanson	.991	60	74	152	2	39

Outfield	PCT	G	PO	A	E	DP
Acuna Jr.	1.000	46	102	0	0	0
Duvall	.976	56	79	1	2	0
Inciarte	.986	46	70	1	1	0
Markakis	1.000	34	54	0	0	0
Ozuna	.955	21	42	0	2	0
Pache	1.000	2	3	0	0	0
Riley	1.000	4	4	0	0	0
Schebler	--	1	0	0	0	0

ATLANTA BRAVES

Baltimore Orioles

SEASON IN A SENTENCE: The Orioles remained remarkably competitive through the first two-thirds of the shortened season and finished in fourth place in the American League East, the first time they avoided last place since 2016, giving fans reason to think brighter days are around the corner.

HIGH POINT: The Orioles won three straight games against the Yankees from Sept. 4-6—outscoring them 17-5 in the process—and followed with an 11-2 pounding of the Mets on Sept. 8. The stretch moved the O's just a half-game back of a playoff spot with less than three weeks remaining in the season.

LOW POINT: The Orioles trailed the Yankees by just 1.5 games in the standings entering a four-game series on Sept. 11, but were summarily swept to put a dent in their playoff hopes. The series was the start of a 5-13 tailspin to end the season.

NOTABLE ROOKIES: Outfielder Ryan Mountcastle made his debut on Aug. 21 and immediately asserted himself as one of the top rookies in the American League. The 23-year-old hit .333/.386/.492 with five home runs and 23 RBIs in 35 games and was batting third in the Orioles' lineup by the end of the season. Righthander Dean Kremer (1-1, 4.82) and lefthander Keegan Akin (1-2, 4.56) each made their major league debuts and held their own in the starting rotation. Righthander Cole Sulser, 30, led all rookies with five saves.

KEY TRANSACTIONS: The Orioles traded righthander Dylan Bundy and infielder Jonathan Villar before the season as they continued their ongoing rebuild. Even as they contended for a wild card spot, they traded lefthanded starter Tommy Milone to the Braves, longtime reliever Mychal Givens to the Rockies and fellow reliever Miguel Castro to the Mets at the Aug. 31 trade deadline for prospects. In Milone's case, they turned a minor league free agent into a useful trade chip. Shortstop Jose Iglesias, their most significant free

agent signing during the offseason, played only 39 games due to the pandemic and injuries to his wrist and quadriceps, but hit .373/.400/.556 when he was healthy. Most significantly, outfielder Trey Mancini was diagnosed with colon cancer in March and spent the year on the 60-day injured list as he underwent surgery and treatment. He completed his final chemotherapy treatment in September and is expected to be back for the 2021 season.

OPENING DAY PAYROLL: $23,918,577 (30th)

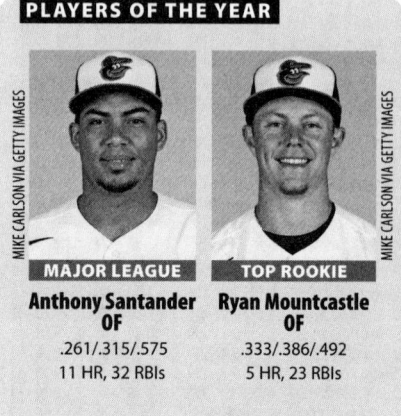

PLAYERS OF THE YEAR

MIKE CARLSON VIA GETTY IMAGES

MAJOR LEAGUE	TOP ROOKIE
Anthony Santander OF	**Ryan Mountcastle** OF
.261/.315/.575	.333/.386/.492
11 HR, 32 RBIs	5 HR, 23 RBIs

ORGANIZATION LEADERS

Batting		*Minimum 100 AB
MAJORS		
* AVG	Jose Iglesias	.373
* OPS	Jose Iglesias	.956
HR	Renato Nunez	12
RBI	Rio Ruiz	32

PITCHING		#Minimum 30 IP
MAJORS		
W	Thomas Eshelman	3
W	Travis Lakins	3
# ERA	Alex Cobb	4.30
SO	John Means	42
SV	Cole Sulser	5

ORGANIZATION STATISTICS

BALTIMORE ORIOLES
AMERICAN LEAGUE

Batting	B-T	HT	WT	DOB	AVG	vLH	vRH	G	AB	R	H	2B	3B	HR	RBI	BB	HBP	SH	SF	SO	SB	CS	SLG	OBP
Alberto, Hanser	R-R	5-11	215	10-17-92	.283	.375	.257	54	219	35	62	15	0	3	22	5	3	2	2	30	3	0	.393	.306
Davis, Chris	L-R	6-3	245	3-17-86	.115	.000	.128	16	52	3	6	3	0	0	1	3	0	0	0	17	0	0	.173	.164
Hays, Austin	R-R	6-0	205	7-5-95	.279	.250	.287	33	122	20	34	2	0	4	9	8	2	0	2	25	2	3	.393	.328
Herrera, Dilson	R-R	5-10	210	3-3-94	.000	.000	.000	3	5	0	0	0	0	0	0	0	1	0	0	4	0	0	.000	.167

Batting

Batting	B-T	HT	WT	DOB	AVG	vLH	vRH	G	AB	R	H	2B	3B	HR	RBI	BB	HBP	SH	SF	SO	SB	CS	SLG	OBP
Holaday, Bryan	R-R	6-0	215	11-19-87	.161	.083	.211	20	31	5	5	1	0	0	4	2	0	0	0	9	0	0	.194	.212
Iglesias, Jose	R-R	5-11	195	1-5-90	.373	.375	.373	39	142	16	53	17	0	3	24	3	4	0	1	17	0	0	.556	.400
Mountcastle, Ryan	R-R	6-3	210	2-18-97	.333	.267	.354	35	126	12	42	5	0	5	23	11	1	0	2	30	0	1	.492	.386
Mullins, Cedric	B-L	5-8	175	10-1-94	.271	.171	.305	48	140	16	38	4	3	3	12	8	1	4	0	37	7	2	.407	.315
Nunez, Renato	R-R	6-1	220	4-4-94	.256	.220	.266	52	195	29	50	10	0	12	31	17	3	0	1	64	0	0	.492	.324
Ruiz, Rio	L-R	6-1	215	5-22-94	.222	.289	.204	54	185	25	41	11	0	9	32	17	0	1	1	46	1	2	.427	.286
Santander, Anthony	B-R	6-2	225	10-19-94	.261	.167	.285	37	153	24	40	13	1	11	32	10	2	0	0	25	0	1	.575	.315
Severino, Pedro	R-R	6-1	220	7-20-93	.250	.162	.276	48	160	17	40	5	1	5	21	16	1	1	0	40	1	0	.388	.322
Sisco, Chance	L-R	6-2	195	2-24-95	.214	.167	.221	36	98	11	21	4	0	4	10	17	6	0	0	41	0	0	.378	.364
Smith, Dwight	L-R	6-0	210	10-26-92	.222	.250	.218	21	63	9	14	3	0	2	6	7	1	0	1	19	1	0	.365	.306
Stewart, DJ	L-R	6-0	230	11-30-93	.193	.125	.208	31	88	13	17	2	0	7	15	20	2	2	0	38	0	0	.455	.355
Urias, Ramon	R-R	5-11	180	6-3-94	.360	.429	.333	10	25	3	9	2	0	1	3	2	0	0	0	6	0	0	.560	.407
Valaika, Pat	R-R	5-11	210	9-9-92	.277	.279	.276	52	141	24	39	4	0	8	16	8	0	1	0	34	0	2	.475	.315
Velazquez, Andrew	B-R	5-9	170	7-14-94	.159	.250	.116	40	63	11	10	1	1	0	3	10	0	4	0	23	4	2	.206	.274
Williams, Mason	L-R	6-1	195	8-21-91	.111	1.000	.059	10	18	0	2	0	1	0	0	0	0	0	0	9	0	1	.222	.111

Pitching

Pitching	B-T	HT	WT	DOB	W	L	ERA	G	GS	CG	SV	IP	H	R	ER	HR	BB	SO	AVG	vLH	vRH	K/9	BB/9
Akin, Keegan	L-L	6-0	225	4-1-95	1	2	4.56	8	6	0	0	26	27	17	13	3	10	35	.262	.240	.269	12.27	3.51
Armstrong, Shawn	R-R	6-2	225	9-11-90	2	0	1.80	14	0	0	0	15	9	6	3	1	3	14	.170	.176	.167	8.40	1.80
Bleier, Richard	L-L	6-3	215	4-16-87	0	0	0.00	2	0	0	0	3	1	0	0	0	0	4	.100	.143	.000	12.00	0.00
Carroll, Cody	R-R	6-5	215	10-15-92	0	0	54.00	3	0	0	0	2	9	12	12	0	5	3	.643	.667	.625	13.50	22.50
Castro, Miguel	R-R	6-7	205	12-24-94	1	0	4.02	16	0	0	1	16	17	7	7	3	5	24	.266	.389	.217	13.79	2.87
Cobb, Alex	R-R	6-3	205	10-7-87	2	5	4.30	10	10	0	0	52	52	27	25	8	18	38	.252	.271	.236	6.54	3.10
Eshelman, Thomas	R-R	6-3	210	6-20-94	3	1	3.89	12	4	0	0	35	34	17	15	7	9	16	.260	.321	.218	4.15	2.34
Fry, Paul	L-L	6-0	205	7-26-92	1	0	2.45	22	0	0	0	22	22	7	6	3	9	29	.250	.273	.227	11.86	3.68
Fulmer, Carson	R-R	6-0	215	12-13-93	0	0	0.00	3	0	0	0	4	0	0	0	0	2	4	.000	.000	.000	9.82	4.91
2-team total (7 Detroit Tigers)					0	0	4.35	10	0	0	0	10	8	5	5	1	5	11	.205	.158	.250	9.58	4.35
Givens, Mychal	R-R	6-0	230	5-13-90	0	1	1.38	12	0	0	0	13	7	2	2	1	6	19	.159	.250	.125	13.15	4.15
Harvey, Hunter	R-R	6-3	210	12-9-94	0	2	4.15	10	0	0	0	9	8	6	4	2	2	6	.242	.182	.273	6.23	2.08
Hess, David	R-R	6-1	215	7-10-93	0	0	6.43	3	0	0	0	7	10	5	5	1	2	1	.333	.308	.353	1.29	2.57
Holaday, Bryan	R-R	6-0	215	11-19-87	0	0	0.00	1	0	0	0	2	0	0	0	0	0	0	.667	1.000	.500	0.00	0.00
Kline, Branden	R-R	6-3	210	9-29-91	0	0	1.80	3	0	0	0	5	2	1	1	0	3	7	.118	.200	.083	12.60	5.40
Kremer, Dean	R-R	6-3	185	1-7-96	1	1	4.82	4	4	0	0	19	15	10	10	0	12	22	.214	.152	.270	10.61	5.79
Lakins, Travis	R-R	6-1	215	6-29-94	3	2	2.81	22	0	0	1	26	25	11	8	2	13	25	.250	.133	.300	8.77	4.56
LeBlanc, Wade	L-L	6-3	215	8-7-84	1	1	8.06	6	6	0	0	22	27	20	20	6	8	13	.293	.188	.316	5.24	3.22
Lopez, Jorge	R-R	6-2	205	2-10-93	2	2	6.34	9	6	0	0	38	43	30	27	7	12	28	.287	.260	.312	6.57	2.82
2-team total (1 Kansas City Royals)					2	2	6.69	10	6	0	0	39	46	32	29	7	12	28	.297	.286	.308	6.46	2.77
Means, John	L-L	6-3	230	4-24-93	2	4	4.53	10	10	0	0	44	36	22	22	12	7	42	.220	.244	.210	8.66	1.44
Milone, Tommy	L-L	6-0	215	2-16-87	1	4	3.99	6	6	0	0	29	33	18	13	5	4	31	.273	.194	.300	9.51	1.23
Phillips, Evan	R-R	6-2	215	9-11-94	1	1	5.02	14	0	0	0	14	14	8	8	1	10	20	.250	.158	.297	12.56	6.28
Scott, Tanner	R-L	6-2	220	7-22-94	0	0	1.31	25	0	0	1	21	12	5	3	1	10	23	.164	.154	.176	10.02	4.35
Sulser, Cole	R-R	6-1	190	3-12-90	1	5	5.56	19	0	0	5	23	17	18	14	2	17	19	.210	.143	.282	7.54	6.75
Tate, Dillon	R-R	6-2	195	5-1-94	1	1	3.24	12	0	0	0	17	9	7	6	1	5	14	.164	.294	.105	7.56	2.70
Valdez, Cesar	R-R	6-2	200	3-17-85	1	1	1.26	9	0	0	3	14	7	3	2	0	3	12	.143	.190	.107	7.53	1.88
Wojciechowski, Asher	R-R	6-4	235	12-21-88	1	3	6.81	10	7	0	0	37	45	29	28	11	15	31	.308	.293	.324	7.54	3.65
Zimmermann, Bruce	L-L	6-2	215	2-9-95	0	0	7.71	2	1	0	0	7	6	6	6	2	2	7	.222	.250	.211	9.00	2.57

Fielding

Catcher	PCT	G	PO	A	E	DP	PB
Holaday	1.000	10	51	2	0	0	0
Severino	.986	35	272	11	4	1	5
Sisco	.989	26	172	6	2	0	0

First Base	PCT	G	PO	A	E	DP
Davis	.974	15	105	7	3	8
Herrera	1.000	2	11	1	0	0
Holaday	1.000	6	11	3	0	2
Mountcastle	.982	10	48	6	1	6
Nunez	.995	28	193	9	1	18
Valaika	1.000	13	63	1	0	6

Second Base	PCT	G	PO	A	E	DP
Alberto	.990	52	84	107	2	24
Ruiz	1.000	1	0	1	0	0
Urias	.900	4	5	4	1	2
Valaika	1.000	13	14	26	0	5
Velazquez	1.000	2	4	5	0	2

Third Base	PCT	G	PO	A	E	DP
Alberto	1.000	4	1	11	0	2
Nunez	.750	4	0	6	2	0
Ruiz	.958	53	37	100	6	13
Valaika	1.000	4	2	6	0	0

Shortstop	PCT	G	PO	A	E	DP
Iglesias	.986	24	24	44	1	6
Urias	.850	5	6	11	3	6
Valaika	.911	24	13	38	5	8
Velazquez	1.000	30	25	54	0	8

Outfield	PCT	G	PO	A	E	DP
Hays	1.000	33	67	3	0	0
Herrera	--	1	0	0	0	0
Mountcastle	1.000	25	33	0	0	0
Mullins	1.000	47	103	1	0	1
Ruiz	--	1	0	0	0	0
Santander	.963	36	75	4	3	0
Smith	.963	16	26	0	1	0
Stewart	.956	30	64	1	3	0
Valaika	1.000	4	8	0	0	0
Velazquez	1.000	9	5	0	0	0
Williams	1.000	9	6	0	0	0

BALTIMORE ORIOLES

Boston Red Sox

SEASON IN A SENTENCE: After trading Mookie Betts and David Price and losing Chris Sale and Eduardo Rodriguez for health reasons, the outlook was not bright and the Red Sox lived up to those expectations as they plummeted to their lowest winning percentage since 1965 and finished in last place in the American League East.

HIGH POINT: The Red Sox won five of their final seven games to avoid the ignominy of gaining the first overall draft pick for the first time in franchise history. Young righthanders Tanner Houck and Nick Pivetta delivered solid starts the final two days, giving the franchise some semblance of hope on the mound after posting a 5.58 ERA as a team during the season.

LOW POINT: The Red Sox officially announced on Feb. 9 they had traded Betts, a franchise icon in the prime of his career, to the Dodgers along with Price. Betts quickly signed a contract extension with the Dodgers and led them to the World Series, cementing the trade as a low point in Red Sox franchise history.

NOTABLE ROOKIES: First baseman Bobby Dalbec made his major league debut on Aug. 30 and hit eight home runs in 23 games to provide a late-season spark. He homered in his major league debut and added a string of five consecutive games with a home run the following week. Righthander Tanner Houck went 3-0, 0.53 in three starts after a late callup and finished with a 10-strikeout performance against the Braves in his final outing. Infielder Jonathan Arauz, a Rule 5 draft selection, stuck on the roster and hit a respectable .250 while seeing time at second base, third base and shortstop. Righthander Phillips Valdez emerged as one of the team's most reliable relievers with a 3.26 ERA in 24 appearances.

KEY TRANSACTIONS: The Red Sox set the course for their season when they traded Betts, Price and cash to the Dodgers for outfielder Alex Verdugo and prospects Jeter Downs and Connor Wong in February. Sale went on the 60-day injured list after having Tommy John surgery in March and Rodriguez missed the season after he became ill with the coronavirus and developed myocarditis, a heart condition linked to COVID-19. With the season spiraling, the Red Sox traded relievers Brandon Workman and Heath Hembree to the Phillies, first baseman Mitch Moreland to the Padres and outfielder Kevin Pillar to the Rockies at the Aug. 31 trade deadline, primarily for prospects.

OPENING DAY PAYROLL: $84,478,422 (3rd)

PLAYERS OF THE YEAR

MAJOR LEAGUE
Xander Bogaerts
SS
.300/.364/.502
11 HR, 28 RBIs, 8 SB

TOP ROOKIE
Bobby Dalbec
1B/3B
.263/.359/.600
8 HR, 16 RBIs in 23 games

ORGANIZATION LEADERS

Batting		*Minimum 100 AB
MAJORS		
* AVG	Alex Verdugo	.308
* OPS	Xander Bogaerts	.867
HR	Rafael Devers	11
HR	Xander Bogaerts	11
RBI	Rafael Devers	43

Pitching		#Minimum 30 IP
MAJORS		
W	Nathan Eovaldi	4
# ERA	Nathan Eovaldi	3.72
SO	Nathan Eovaldi	52
SV	Matt Barnes	9

ORGANIZATION STATISTICS

BOSTON RED SOX
AMERICAN LEAGUE

Batting	B-T	HT	WT	DOB	AVG	vLH	vRH	G	AB	R	H	2B	3B	HR	RBI	BB	HBP	SH	SF	SO	SB	CS	SLG	OBP
Arauz, Jonathan	B-R	6-0	195	8-3-98	.250	.290	.220	25	72	8	18	2	0	1	9	8	0	0	0	21	0	0	.319	.325
Arroyo, Christian	R-R	6-1	210	5-30-95	.240	.158	.290	14	50	7	12	1	0	3	8	4	0	0	0	11	0	0	.440	.296
2-team total (1 Cleveland Indians)					.240	.158	.290	15	50	7	12	1	0	3	8	4	0	0	0	11	0	0	.440	.296
Benintendi, Andrew	L-L	5-9	180	7-6-94	.103	.000	.125	14	39	4	4	1	0	0	1	11	1	1	0	17	1	2	.128	.314

Batting

Batting	B-T	HT	WT	DOB	AVG	vLH	vRH	G	AB	R	H	2B	3B	HR	RBI	BB	HBP	SH	SF	SO	SB	CS	SLG	OBP
Bogaerts, Xander	R-R	6-2	218	10-1-92	.300	.375	.266	56	203	36	61	8	0	11	28	21	0	0	1	41	8	0	.502	.364
Bradley Jr., Jackie	L-R	5-10	196	4-19-90	.283	.288	.280	55	191	32	54	11	0	7	22	23	2	0	1	48	5	2	.450	.364
Chavis, Michael	R-R	5-10	210	8-11-95	.212	.212	.213	42	146	16	31	5	2	5	19	8	2	0	2	50	3	0	.377	.259
Dalbec, Bobby	R-R	6-4	227	6-29-95	.263	.296	.245	23	80	13	21	3	0	8	16	10	2	0	0	39	0	0	.600	.359
Devers, Rafael	L-R	6-0	240	10-24-96	.263	.222	.285	57	232	32	61	16	1	11	43	13	3	0	0	67	0	0	.483	.310
Grullon, Deivy	R-R	5-11	240	2-17-96	.333	--	.333	1	3	0	1	0	0	0	1	0	0	0	0	1	0	0	.333	.500
Lin, Tzu-Wei	L-R	5-9	180	2-15-94	.154	.000	.174	26	52	2	8	1	0	0	3	1	2	0	2	17	0	0	.173	.182
Lucroy, Jonathan	R-R	6-0	200	6-13-86	--	--	--	1	0	0	0	0	0	0	0	0	0	0	0	0	0	0	--	--
Martinez, J.D.	R-R	6-3	230	8-21-87	.213	.214	.213	54	211	22	45	16	0	7	27	22	2	0	2	59	1	0	.389	.291
Moreland, Mitch	L-L	6-3	245	9-6-85	.328	.375	.322	22	67	14	22	4	0	8	21	11	1	0	0	18	0	0	.746	.430
Munoz, Yairo	R-R	5-11	200	1-23-95	.333	.375	.324	12	45	6	15	5	0	1	4	0	0	0	0	11	2	0	.511	.333
Peraza, Jose	R-R	6-0	210	4-30-94	.225	.196	.246	34	111	13	25	8	1	1	8	5	3	0	1	18	1	1	.342	.275
Pillar, Kevin	R-R	6-0	200	1-4-89	.274	.286	.265	30	117	20	32	7	2	4	13	8	1	0	0	23	1	1	.470	.325
Plawecki, Kevin	R-R	6-2	208	2-26-91	.341	.367	.327	24	82	8	28	5	1	1	17	5	2	0	0	14	1	0	.463	.393
Puello, Cesar	R-R	6-2	220	4-1-91	.375	.000	.600	5	8	1	3	0	0	0	0	2	0	1	0	2	0	0	.375	.500
Vazquez, Christian	R-R	5-9	205	8-21-90	.283	.236	.305	47	173	22	49	9	0	7	23	16	0	0	3	43	4	3	.457	.344
Verdugo, Alex	L-L	6-0	192	5-15-96	.308	.320	.302	53	201	36	62	16	0	6	15	17	2	0	1	45	4	0	.478	.367

Pitching

Pitching	B-T	HT	WT	DOB	W	L	ERA	G	GS	CG	SV	IP	H	R	ER	HR	BB	SO	AVG	vLH	vRH	K/9	BB/9
Barnes, Matt	R-R	6-4	208	6-17-90	1	3	4.30	24	0	0	0	23	18	13	11	4	14	31	.214	.167	.250	12.13	5.48
Brasier, Ryan	R-R	6-0	227	8-26-87	1	0	3.96	25	1	0	0	25	24	12	11	2	11	30	.245	.270	.230	10.80	3.96
Brewer, Colten	R-R	6-4	222	10-29-92	0	3	5.61	11	4	0	0	26	31	17	16	6	14	25	.290	.234	.333	8.77	4.91
Brice, Austin	R-R	6-4	238	6-19-92	1	0	5.95	21	1	0	0	17	13	13	13	3	13	25	.236	.308	.196	11.44	5.95
Covey, Dylan	R-R	6-1	215	8-14-91	0	0	7.07	8	0	0	0	14	18	11	11	2	2	11	.310	.300	.316	7.07	1.29
Eovaldi, Nathan	R-R	6-2	217	2-13-90	4	2	3.72	9	9	0	0	48	51	20	20	8	7	52	.273	.191	.355	9.68	1.30
Godley, Zack	R-R	6-3	250	4-21-90	0	4	8.16	8	7	0	0	29	42	26	26	9	14	28	.336	.295	.375	8.79	4.40
Hall, Matt	L-L	6-0	200	7-23-93	0	3	18.69	4	1	0	0	9	17	18	18	2	10	9	.395	.476	.318	9.35	10.38
Hart, Kyle	L-L	6-5	200	11-23-92	0	1	15.55	4	3	0	0	11	24	21	19	4	10	13	.429	.429	.429	10.64	8.18
Hembree, Heath	R-R	6-4	220	1-13-89	2	0	5.59	11	0	0	0	10	9	6	6	2	3	10	.243	.364	.192	9.31	2.79
Hernandez, Darwinzon	L-L	6-2	255	12-17-96	1	0	2.16	7	0	0	0	8	5	2	2	0	8	13	.161	.143	.167	14.04	8.64
Houck, Tanner	R-R	6-5	230	6-29-96	3	0	0.53	3	3	0	0	17	6	2	1	1	9	21	.113	.111	.114	11.12	4.76
Kickham, Mike	L-L	6-4	220	12-12-88	1	1	7.71	6	2	0	0	14	21	12	12	6	5	17	.333	.235	.370	10.93	3.21
Leyer, Robinson	R-R	6-2	185	3-13-93	0	0	21.21	6	1	0	0	5	12	11	11	3	8	9	.462	.643	.250	17.36	15.43
Lin, Tzu-Wei	L-R	5-9	180	2-15-94	0	0	27.00	1	0	0	0	1	4	3	3	1	0	0	.571	.000	.800	0.00	0.00
Mazza, Chris	R-R	6-4	190	10-17-89	1	2	4.80	9	6	0	0	30	34	18	16	3	15	29	.288	.294	.284	8.70	4.50
Osich, Josh	L-L	6-2	235	9-3-88	1	1	5.74	13	1	0	0	16	16	10	10	6	5	20	.250	.231	.263	11.49	2.87
Peraza, Jose	R-R	6-0	210	4-30-94	0	0	27.00	1	0	0	0	2	1	0	0	0	1	0	.667	.000	1.000	0.00	0.00
Perez, Martin	L-L	6-0	200	4-4-91	3	5	4.50	12	12	0	0	62	55	33	31	8	28	46	.240	.231	.242	6.68	4.06
Pivetta, Nick	R-R	6-5	214	2-14-93	2	0	1.80	2	2	0	0	10	8	2	2	1	5	13	.216	.250	.190	11.70	4.50
Plawecki, Kevin	R-R	6-2	208	2-26-91	0	0	0.00	1	0	0	0	1	0	0	0	0	1	0	.000	.000	.000	0.00	13.50
Springs, Jeffrey	L-L	6-3	218	9-20-92	0	2	7.08	16	0	0	0	20	30	18	16	5	7	28	.333	.316	.346	12.39	3.10
Stock, Robert	L-R	6-1	214	11-21-89	0	1	4.73	10	0	0	0	13	16	9	7	0	10	14	.320	.217	.407	9.45	6.75
Tapia, Domingo	R-R	6-3	263	8-4-91	0	0	2.08	5	0	0	0	4	4	1	1	1	2	4	.235	.286	.200	8.31	4.15
Taylor, Josh	L-L	6-5	245	3-2-93	1	1	9.82	8	0	0	0	7	7	8	8	2	5	7	.233	.182	.263	8.59	6.14
Triggs, Andrew	R-R	6-4	233	3-16-89	0	1	4.50	4	2	0	0	8	8	4	4	3	3	7	.250	.105	.462	7.88	3.38
Valdez, Phillips	R-R	6-2	160	11-16-91	1	1	3.26	24	0	0	0	30	33	16	11	3	16	30	.282	.175	.338	8.90	4.75
Walden, Marcus	R-R	5-10	198	9-13-88	0	2	9.45	15	0	0	1	13	18	14	14	5	9	10	.371	.393	.353	6.75	6.08
Weber, Ryan	R-R	6-1	175	8-12-90	1	3	4.40	17	5	0	0	43	44	23	21	8	14	27	.265	.227	.297	5.65	2.93
Workman, Brandon	R-R	6-5	235	8-13-88	0	0	4.05	7	0	0	4	7	8	3	3	0	4	8	.296	.308	.286	10.80	5.40

Fielding

Catcher	PCT	G	PO	A	E	DP	PB
Grullon	1.000	1	4	1	0	0	0
Lin	.000	1	0	0	0	0	0
Lucroy	1.000	1	2	0	0	0	0
Plawecki	.994	20	168	7	1	0	1
Vazquez	.997	42	370	19	1	3	4

First Base	PCT	G	PO	A	E	DP
Chavis	1.000	24	161	7	0	20
Dalbec	.981	21	143	10	3	16
Moreland	.993	22	137	9	1	17
Plawecki	1.000	2	2	1	0	0

Second Base	PCT	G	PO	A	E	DP
Arauz	.965	16	27	28	2	9
Arroyo	1.000	13	19	39	0	10
Chavis	.931	8	10	17	2	6
Lin	1.000	6	5	8	0	3
Peraza	.972	27	43	61	3	17
Vazquez	.000	1	0	0	0	0

Third Base	PCT	G	PO	A	E	DP
Arauz	1.000	6	4	5	0	1
Dalbec	1.000	2	1	1	0	0
Devers	.891	57	30	84	14	12
Peraza	.333	1	1	0	2	0

Shortstop	PCT	G	PO	A	E	DP
Arauz	1.000	4	2	10	0	4
Arroyo	1.000	2	2	1	0	0
Bogaerts	.974	53	59	130	5	26
Lin	.929	12	12	14	2	8
Peraza	1.000	3	1	3	0	1

Outfield	PCT	G	PO	A	E	DP
Benintendi	1.000	13	20	0	0	0
Bradley Jr.	1.000	55	120	3	0	0
Chavis	.895	12	16	1	2	1
Lin	1.000	9	16	0	0	0
Martinez	1.000	6	9	0	0	0
Munoz	1.000	11	18	2	0	0
Peraza	1.000	5	5	0	0	0
Pillar	1.000	29	56	3	0	0
Puello	1.000	5	8	2	0	2
Verdugo	.959	50	86	7	4	1

Chicago Cubs

SEASON IN A SENTENCE: The Cubs showed new life and energy under first-year manager David Ross and cruised to the National League Central division title, but an early playoff exit against the Marlins ended the season on a sour note and raised questions over whether the end is near for the core group of Cubs that led the team to the 2016 World Series win.

HIGH POINT: Righthander Alec Mills pitched a no-hitter against the Brewers on Sept. 13, becoming just the third Cubs pitcher to throw a no-hitter since 1972 (Jake Arrieta and Carlos Zambrano are the others). The unheralded 28-year-old, who spent the previous two years bouncing back and forth between Triple-A and the majors, walked three, struck out five and allowed only one batter to reach base after the fourth inning as the Cubs rolled to a 12-0 win.

LOW POINT: The Cubs managed only one run in two games as they were swept at home by the Marlins in the Wild Card Series. They had more strikeouts (16) than hits (nine) and walks (five) combined in the series, the final chapter in a year of poor performances by the offense.

NOTABLE ROOKIES: Infielder Nico Hoerner split time with Jason Kipnis at second base but never got going offensively, batting .222 with zero home runs in 48 games. Righthander Adbert Alzolay went up and down between Chicago and the alternate training site but made major strides by the end of the season and finished with a 2.95 ERA in six appearances (four starts). Righthander Duane Underwood Jr. made 17 relief appearances and posted a 5.66 ERA, while righthanders James Norwood (three appearances) and Tyson Miller (two) and lefthanders Matt Dermody and Brailyn Marquez (one each) appeared for the Cubs as well.

KEY TRANSACTIONS: The Cubs remained relatively quiet in the offseason, signing reliever Jeremy Jeffress to a one-year deal and bringing in Kipnis on a minor league deal. They sought to beef up their bullpen during the season by signing former closers Cody Allen, A.J. Ramos and Kelvin Herrera, but all were released before they could pitch in a single game for the Cubs. The Cubs remained similarly low-key at the trade deadline, acquiring veteran outfielders Jose Martinez from the Rays and Cameron Maybin from the Tigers in minor trades and acquiring lefthanded relievers Andrew Chafin from the D-backs and Josh Osich from the Red Sox for players to be named later. The trades didn't cost much, but they didn't bring in much either.

OPENING DAY PAYROLL: $76,166,963 (6th)

PLAYERS OF THE YEAR

ADAM GLANZMAN VIA GETTY IMAGES

MAJOR LEAGUE
Yu Darvish
RHP
8-3, 2.01
93 SO, 14 BB in 76 IP

TOP ROOKIE
Adbert Alzolay
RHP
1-1, 2.95
29 SO in 21.1 IP

ORGANIZATION LEADERS

Batting		*Minimum 100 AB
MAJORS		
* AVG	Jason Heyward	.265
* OPS	Ian Happ	.866
HR	Ian Happ	12
RBI	David Bote	29

Pitching		#Minimum 30 IP
MAJORS		
W	Yu Darvish	8
# ERA	Yu Darvish	2.01
SO	Yu Darvish	93
SV	Jeremy Jeffress	8

ORGANIZATION STATISTICS

CHICAGO CUBS
NATIONAL LEAGUE

Batting	B-T	HT	WT	DOB	AVG	vLH	vRH	G	AB	R	H	2B	3B	HR	RBI	BB	HBP	SH	SF	SO	SB	CS	SLG	OBP
Almora Jr., Albert	R-R	6-2	190	4-16-94	.167	.200	.150	28	30	4	5	1	0	0	1	3	1	0	0	9	0	0	.200	.265
Baez, Javier	R-R	6-0	190	12-1-92	.203	.218	.198	59	222	27	45	9	1	8	24	7	4	0	2	75	3	0	.360	.238
Bote, David	R-R	6-1	205	4-7-93	.200	.122	.238	45	125	15	25	3	1	7	29	17	2	0	1	40	2	0	.408	.303
Bryant, Kris	R-R	6-5	230	1-4-92	.206	.286	.184	34	131	20	27	5	1	4	11	12	4	0	0	40	0	0	.351	.293

Batting	B-T	HT	WT	DOB	AVG	vLH	vRH	G	AB	R	H	2B	3B	HR	RBI	BB	HBP	SH	SF	SO	SB	CS	SLG	OBP
Caratini, Victor	B-R	6-1	215	8-17-93	.241	.292	.228	44	116	10	28	7	0	1	16	12	4	0	0	31	0	1	.328	.333
Contreras, Willson	R-R	6-1	225	5-13-92	.243	.186	.260	57	189	37	46	10	0	7	26	20	14	0	2	57	1	2	.407	.356
Hamilton, Billy	B-R	6-0	155	9-9-90	.300	.333	.286	14	10	6	3	0	0	1	1	0	0	0	4	3	1	.600	.364	
2-team total (17 New York Mets)					.125	.091	.143	31	32	10	4	0	0	1	2	2	0	1	1	7	6	2	.219	.171
Happ, Ian	B-R	6-0	205	8-12-94	.258	.250	.260	57	198	27	51	11	1	12	28	30	2	1	0	63	1	3	.505	.361
Heyward, Jason	L-L	6-5	240	8-9-89	.265	.167	.297	50	147	20	39	6	2	6	22	30	2	0	2	37	2	0	.456	.392
Hoerner, Nico	R-R	6-1	200	5-13-97	.222	.257	.205	48	108	19	24	4	0	0	13	12	3	0	2	24	3	2	.259	.312
Kipnis, Jason	L-R	5-11	200	4-3-87	.237	.091	.272	44	114	13	27	8	1	3	16	18	1	0	2	41	1	0	.404	.341
Martinez, Jose	R-R	6-6	215	7-25-88	.000	.000	.000	10	21	0	0	0	0	0	0	1	0	0	0	7	0	0	.000	.045
Maybin, Cameron	R-R	6-3	215	4-4-87	.250	.100	.286	18	52	3	13	4	1	0	5	3	1	0	0	12	3	0	.365	.304
Miller, Ian	L-R	6-0	170	2-21-92	--	--	--	1	0	0	0	0	0	0	0	0	0	0	0	0	0	0	--	--
Perez, Hernan	R-R	6-1	213	3-26-91	.167	.200	.000	3	6	0	1	0	0	0	0	0	0	0	0	2	0	0	.167	.167
Phegley, Josh	R-R	5-10	225	2-12-88	.063	.083	.000	11	16	4	1	0	0	1	2	1	1	0	0	3	0	0	.250	.167
Rizzo, Anthony	L-L	6-3	240	8-8-89	.222	.204	.227	58	203	26	45	6	0	11	24	28	10	0	2	38	3	1	.414	.342
Schwarber, Kyle	L-R	6-0	225	3-5-93	.188	.189	.188	59	191	30	36	6	0	11	24	30	3	0	0	66	1	0	.393	.308
Souza, Steven	R-R	6-4	225	4-24-89	.148	.200	.118	11	27	3	4	2	0	1	5	4	0	0	0	15	1	0	.333	.258
Vargas, Ildemaro	B-R	6-0	180	7-16-91	.222	.250	.200	6	9	1	2	0	0	1	1	0	0	0	0	3	0	0	.556	.222
2-team total (8 Arizona Diamondbacks)					.172	.133	.214	14	29	3	5	0	0	1	1	1	0	0	0	8	0	0	.276	.200
Wisdom, Patrick	R-R	6-2	220	8-27-91	.000	.000	--	2	2	0	0	0	0	0	0	0	0	0	0	0	0	0	.000	.000

Pitching	B-T	HT	WT	DOB	W	L	ERA	G	GS	CG	SV	IP	H	R	ER	HR	BB	SO	AVG	vLH	vRH	K/9	BB/9
Adam, Jason	R-R	6-3	229	8-4-91	2	1	3.29	13	0	0	0	14	9	7	5	2	8	21	.180	.172	.190	13.83	5.27
Alzolay, Adbert	R-R	6-1	208	3-1-95	1	1	2.95	6	4	0	0	21	12	8	7	1	13	29	.169	.219	.128	12.23	5.48
Brothers, Rex	L-L	6-0	205	12-18-87	0	0	8.10	3	0	0	0	3	2	3	3	2	3	8	.167	.000	.333	21.60	8.10
Chafin, Andrew	R-L	6-2	235	6-17-90	0	1	3.00	4	0	0	1	3	2	1	1	1	1	3	.182	.200	.167	9.00	3.00
2-team total (11 Arizona Diamondbacks)					1	2	6.52	15	0	0	1	10	11	7	7	2	5	13	.275	.273	.278	12.10	4.66
Chatwood, Tyler	R-R	5-11	200	12-16-89	2	2	5.30	5	5	0	0	19	22	11	11	2	9	25	.289	.265	.333	12.05	4.34
Darvish, Yu	R-R	6-5	220	8-16-86	8	3	2.01	12	12	0	0	76	59	18	17	5	14	93	.211	.211	.211	11.01	1.66
Dermody, Matt	R-L	6-5	190	7-4-90	0	0	0.00	1	0	0	0	1	0	0	0	0	0	1	.000	--	.000	9.00	0.00
Hendricks, Kyle	R-R	6-3	190	12-7-89	6	5	2.88	12	12	1	0	81	73	26	26	10	8	64	.240	.209	.274	7.08	0.89
Jeffress, Jeremy	R-R	6-0	205	9-21-87	4	1	1.54	22	0	0	8	23	10	5	4	1	12	17	.137	.136	.138	6.56	4.63
Kimbrel, Craig	R-R	6-0	215	5-28-88	0	1	5.28	18	0	0	2	15	10	9	9	2	12	28	.182	.207	.154	16.43	7.04
Lester, Jon	L-L	6-4	240	1-7-84	3	3	5.16	12	12	0	0	61	64	35	35	11	17	42	.262	.233	.266	6.20	2.51
Maples, Dillon	R-R	6-2	230	5-9-92	0	0	18.00	2	0	0	0	1	3	2	2	0	4	1	.200	.000	.500	9.00	36.00
Marquez, Brailyn	L-L	6-4	185	1-30-99	0	0	67.50	1	0	0	0	1	2	5	5	0	3	1	.500	1.000	.333	13.50	40.50
Miller, Tyson	R-R	6-4	225	7-29-95	0	0	5.40	2	1	0	0	5	2	3	3	1	3	0	.125	.111	.143	0.00	5.40
Mills, Alec	R-R	6-4	205	11-30-91	5	5	4.48	11	11	1	0	62	53	31	31	13	19	46	.230	.275	.163	6.64	2.74
Norwood, James	R-R	6-2	215	12-24-93	0	0	16.20	3	0	0	0	2	4	5	4	1	3	0	.500	.500	.500	0.00	5.40
Osich, Josh	L-L	6-2	235	9-3-88	0	0	10.13	4	0	0	0	3	5	6	3	0	0	4	.333	.143	.500	13.50	0.00
Quintana, Jose	R-L	6-1	220	1-24-89	0	0	4.50	4	1	0	0	10	5	5	5	1	3	12	.263	.364	.222	10.80	2.70
Rea, Colin	R-R	6-5	235	7-1-90	1	1	5.79	9	2	0	0	14	15	9	9	3	2	10	.254	.172	.333	6.43	1.29
Ryan, Kyle	L-L	6-5	215	9-25-91	1	0	5.17	18	0	0	1	16	16	9	9	5	6	11	.267	.240	.286	6.32	3.45
Sadler, Casey	R-R	6-3	205	7-13-90	0	0	5.79	10	0	0	0	9	8	6	6	2	8	9	.229	.067	.350	8.68	7.71
Tepera, Ryan	R-R	6-1	195	11-3-87	0	1	3.92	21	0	0	0	21	17	9	9	2	12	31	.227	.188	.256	13.50	5.23
Underwood Jr., Duane	R-R	6-2	210	7-20-94	1	0	5.66	17	0	0	0	21	25	13	13	5	6	27	.313	.289	.333	11.76	2.61
Wick, Rowan	L-R	6-3	234	11-9-92	0	1	3.12	19	0	0	4	17	18	6	6	1	6	20	.265	.290	.243	10.38	3.12
Wieck, Brad	L-L	6-8	257	10-14-91	0	0	18.00	1	0	0	0	1	1	2	2	1	1	2	.250	.500	.000	18.00	9.00
Winkler, Dan	R-R	6-3	205	2-2-90	0	0	2.95	18	0	0	0	18	11	7	6	3	11	18	.175	.100	.209	8.84	5.40

Fielding

Catcher	PCT	G	PO	A	E	DP	PB
Caratini	.995	22	198	5	1	1	0
Contreras	.994	41	311	13	2	0	0
Phegley	1.000	4	21	0	0	0	1

First Base	PCT	G	PO	A	E	DP
Bote	1.000	1	8	1	0	1
Bryant	1.000	1	10	0	0	1
Caratini	1.000	3	6	1	0	1
Happ	1.000	2	5	0	0	0
Kipnis	1.000	1	6	0	0	1
Perez	1.000	2	1	0	0	0
Rizzo	.998	57	418	44	1	39
Wisdom	1.000	2	3	0	0	0

Second Base	PCT	G	PO	A	E	DP
Bote	.950	7	9	10	1	5
Hoerner	.977	37	27	58	2	6
Kipnis	.972	36	29	75	3	12
Perez	1.000	1	0	1	0	0
Vargas	1.000	5	4	8	0	1

Third Base	PCT	G	PO	A	E	DP
Bote	.941	33	21	43	4	6
Bryant	.937	27	15	44	4	4
Hoerner	1.000	6	1	7	0	0
Vargas	1.000	1	2	0	0	0

Shortstop	PCT	G	PO	A	E	DP
Baez	.968	56	86	159	8	34
Hoerner	1.000	10	4	15	0	3

Outfield	PCT	G	PO	A	E	DP
Almora Jr.	1.000	28	30	0	0	0
Baez	--	1	0	0	0	0
Bryant	1.000	4	5	1	0	0
Hamilton	1.000	12	6	0	0	0
Happ	.989	56	87	3	1	1
Heyward	1.000	50	98	2	0	1
Hoerner	1.000	2	2	0	0	0
Maybin	1.000	14	24	2	0	0
Perez	1.000	1	1	0	0	0
Schwarber	1.000	48	70	3	0	0
Souza	1.000	9	12	0	0	0

Chicago White Sox

SEASON IN A SENTENCE: After getting to the playoffs for the first time since 2008, the White Sox saw their season crumble in the Wild Card Series against the Athletics while a pair of their brightest young players succumbed to injuries.

HIGH POINT: On Aug. 25, 26-year-old ace Lucas Giolito threw his first career no-hitter. He bedeviled the Pirates for 101 pitches, including 13 strikeouts, to record the first of two no-nos in the pandemic-shortened season.

LOW POINT: The final game of the season, against the Athletics, could not have gone much worse. Lefty Garrett Crochet got hurt and lasted just 0.2 innings after relieving Dane Dunning. From there, Codi Heuer and Carlos Rodon combined to allow four runs in the fourth inning, and Evan Marshall gave up two more in the fifth, giving Oakland all the cushion it needed to advance to the next round. Slugging outfielder Eloy Jimenez also left the game after reaggravating an injury to his right foot.

NOTABLE ROOKIES: The White Sox were chock-full of potentially impactful rookies, led by Cuban sensation Luis Robert, who finished among the AL's three finalists for the Rookie of the Year award. Robert, who inked an eight-figure deal before the season, started the season strong but took a swan dive late as the league adjusted to him. Second baseman Nick Madrigal performed to his scouting report in his debut season, which was sandwiched around a shoulder injury that required offseason surgery. The White Sox also got a burst of energy from lefty Garrett Crochet, whom the team took with the 11th overall pick. Crochet finished the year with eight strikeouts in six relief innings thanks to a fastball that averaged 100 mph and a filthy slider. Righthander Dane Dunning, recovered from Tommy John surgery, made his debut on Aug. 19 and went 2-0, 3.97 in seven starts. Less-heralded rookies like Matt Foster and Codi Heuer each provided key innings out of the bullpen during the season. Utilityman Danny Mendick was solid all season, as well.

KEY TRANSACTIONS: The White Sox made a host of additions before the season, including the signings of catcher Yasmani Grandal and lefty Dallas Keuchel, which provided jolts of veteran production to a lineup built around a strong core of young players. Grandal hit .230/.351/.422 with eight homers while Keuchel went 6-2, 1.99 in 11 starts. Robert's extension also solidified his role as one of their cornerstone players.

OPENING DAY PAYROLL: $51,404,630 (18th)

PLAYERS OF THE YEAR

DAVE DUROCHIK VIA GETTY IMAGES

DAVE DUROCHIK VIA GETTY IMAGES

MAJOR LEAGUE	TOP ROOKIE
Jose Abreu	**Luis Robert**
1B	**OF**
.317/.370/.617	.233/.302/.436
Led AL in hits (76), RBIs (60), SLG	11 HR, 31 RBIs, 9 SB

ORGANIZATION LEADERS

Batting		*Minimum 100 AB
MAJORS		
* AVG	Nick Madrigal	.340
* OPS	Jose Abreu	.987
HR	Jose Abreu	19
RBI	Jose Abreu	60
Pitching		**#Minimum 30 IP**
MAJORS		
W	Matt Foster	6
W	Dallas Keuchel	6
# ERA	Dallas Keuchel	1.99
SO	Lucas Giolito	97
SV	Alex Colome	12

ORGANIZATION STATISTICS

CHICAGO WHITE SOX
AMERICAN LEAGUE

Batting	B-T	HT	WT	DOB	AVG	vLH	vRH	G	AB	R	H	2B	3B	HR	RBI	BB	HBP	SH	SF	SO	SB	CS	SLG	OBP
Abreu, Jose	R-R	6-3	250	1-29-87	.317	.250	.335	60	240	43	76	15	0	19	60	18	3	0	1	59	0	0	.617	.370
Anderson, Tim	R-R	6-1	185	6-23-93	.322	.449	.283	49	208	45	67	11	1	10	21	10	2	0	1	50	5	2	.529	.357
Collins, Zack	L-R	6-3	230	2-6-95	.063	.000	.067	9	16	1	1	1	0	0	0	2	0	0	0	5	0	0	.125	.167
Cuthbert, Cheslor	R-R	6-1	205	11-16-92	.000	.000	--	1	1	0	0	0	0	0	0	0	0	0	0	0	0	0	.000	.000

Batting

Batting	B-T	HT	WT	DOB	AVG	vLH	vRH	G	AB	R	H	2B	3B	HR	RBI	BB	HBP	SH	SF	SO	SB	CS	SLG	OBP
Delmonico, Nicky	L-R	6-3	230	7-12-92	.150	--	.150	6	20	0	3	0	0	0	3	2	0	0	0	2	0	0	.150	.227
Dyson, Jarrod	L-R	5-9	165	8-15-84	.300	.500	.250	11	10	3	3	0	0	0	0	0	0	1	0	1	2	0	.300	.300
Encarnacion, Edwin	R-R	6-1	230	1-7-83	.157	.121	.167	44	159	19	25	5	0	10	19	16	4	0	1	54	0	0	.377	.250
Engel, Adam	R-R	6-2	220	12-9-91	.295	.303	.291	36	88	11	26	5	1	3	12	3	2	0	0	19	1	0	.477	.333
Garcia, Leury	B-R	5-8	185	3-18-91	.271	.500	.235	16	59	6	16	1	0	3	8	4	0	0	0	9	0	0	.441	.317
Goins, Ryan	L-R	5-10	180	2-13-88	.000	.000	.000	14	9	4	0	0	0	0	0	1	0	0	0	1	0	0	.000	.100
Gonzalez, Luis	L-L	6-1	180	9-10-95	.000	--	.000	3	1	1	0	0	0	0	0	0	1	0	0	1	0	0	.000	.500
Grandal, Yasmani	B-R	6-2	230	11-8-88	.230	.286	.218	46	161	27	37	7	0	8	27	30	1	0	2	58	0	0	.422	.351
Jimenez, Eloy	R-R	6-4	235	11-27-96	.296	.289	.298	55	213	26	63	14	0	14	41	12	0	0	1	56	0	0	.559	.332
Madrigal, Nick	R-R	5-8	175	3-5-97	.340	.227	.370	29	103	8	35	3	0	0	11	4	2	0	0	7	2	1	.369	.376
Mazara, Nomar	L-L	6-4	215	4-26-95	.228	.333	.205	42	136	13	31	6	0	1	15	10	3	0	0	44	0	1	.294	.295
McCann, James	R-R	6-3	220	6-13-90	.289	.429	.232	31	97	20	28	3	0	7	15	8	4	0	2	30	1	1	.536	.360
Mendick, Danny	R-R	5-10	195	9-28-93	.243	.194	.263	33	107	11	26	4	1	3	6	6	0	0	1	25	0	1	.383	.281
Mercedes, Yermin	R-R	5-11	235	2-14-93	.000	--	.000	1	1	0	0	0	0	0	0	0	0	0	0	0	0	0	.000	.000
Moncada, Yoan	B-R	6-2	225	5-27-95	.225	.222	.226	52	200	28	45	8	3	6	24	28	1	0	2	72	0	0	.385	.320
Robert, Luis	R-R	6-2	210	8-3-97	.233	.273	.222	56	202	33	47	8	0	11	31	20	1	0	2	73	9	2	.436	.302
Sanchez, Yolmer	B-R	5-8	205	6-29-92	.313	.000	.333	11	16	7	5	3	0	1	1	5	0	0	0	5	0	0	.688	.476

Pitching

Pitching	B-T	HT	WT	DOB	W	L	ERA	G	GS	CG	SV	IP	H	R	ER	HR	BB	SO	AVG	vLH	vRH	K/9	BB/9
Anderson, Drew	R-R	6-3	205	3-22-94	0	1	40.50	1	0	0	0	1	4	6	6	2	2	2	.500	.333	.600	13.50	13.50
Bummer, Aaron	L-L	6-3	215	9-21-93	1	0	0.96	9	0	0	0	9	5	1	1	0	5	14	.152	.231	.100	13.50	4.82
Burdi, Zack	R-R	6-3	210	3-9-95	0	1	11.05	8	0	0	0	7	11	11	9	4	3	11	.324	.188	.444	13.50	3.68
Cease, Dylan	R-R	6-2	200	12-28-95	5	4	4.01	12	12	0	0	58	50	30	26	12	34	44	.234	.256	.202	6.79	5.25
Cishek, Steve	R-R	6-6	215	6-18-86	0	0	5.40	22	0	0	0	20	21	12	12	4	9	21	.269	.194	.319	9.45	4.05
Colome, Alex	R-R	6-1	225	12-31-88	2	0	0.81	21	0	0	12	22	13	3	2	0	8	16	.163	.098	.231	6.45	3.22
Cordero, Jimmy	R-R	6-4	235	10-19-91	1	2	6.08	30	0	0	0	27	33	21	18	2	9	22	.300	.426	.179	7.43	3.04
Crochet, Garrett	L-L	6-6	218	6-21-99	0	0	0.00	5	0	0	0	6	3	0	0	0	0	8	.143	.143	.143	12.00	0.00
Detwiler, Ross	R-L	6-5	210	3-6-86	1	1	3.20	16	0	0	0	20	19	8	7	2	5	15	.253	.194	.295	6.86	2.29
Dunning, Dane	R-R	6-4	225	12-20-94	2	0	3.97	7	7	0	0	34	25	17	15	4	13	35	.197	.246	.152	9.26	3.44
Flores Jr., Bernardo	L-L	6-4	190	8-23-95	0	0	9.00	2	0	0	0	2	4	2	2	0	0	2	.400	.000	.500	9.00	0.00
Foster, Matt	R-R	6-0	210	1-27-95	6	1	2.20	23	2	0	0	29	16	8	7	2	9	31	.162	.188	.137	9.73	2.83
Fry, Jace	L-L	6-1	220	7-9-93	0	1	3.66	18	0	0	0	20	16	9	8	3	12	24	.225	.231	.222	10.98	5.49
Giolito, Lucas	R-R	6-6	245	7-14-94	4	3	3.48	12	12	1	0	72	47	31	28	8	28	97	.184	.180	.190	12.07	3.48
Gonzalez, Gio	R-L	6-0	205	9-19-85	1	2	4.83	12	4	0	0	32	40	19	17	6	19	34	.305	.278	.316	9.66	5.40
Hamilton, Ian	R-R	6-1	200	6-16-95	0	0	4.50	4	0	0	0	4	4	2	2	0	5	4	.267	.222	.333	9.00	11.25
Herrera, Kelvin	R-R	5-10	220	12-31-89	0	0	15.43	2	0	0	0	2	3	4	4	2	1	3	.300	.250	.500	11.57	3.86
Heuer, Codi	R-R	6-5	190	7-3-96	3	0	1.52	21	0	0	1	24	12	4	4	1	9	25	.145	.130	.162	9.51	3.42
Keuchel, Dallas	L-L	6-2	205	1-1-88	6	2	1.99	11	11	0	0	63	52	15	14	2	17	42	.218	.171	.228	5.97	2.42
Lail, Brady	R-R	6-2	200	8-9-93	0	0	0.00	1	0	0	0	1	2	0	0	0	1	.333	.250	.500	6.75	0.00
2-team total (7 Seattle Mariners)					0	0	4.41	8	0	0	0	16	14	8	8	5	7	12	.226	.200	.250	6.61	3.86
Lambert, Jimmy	R-R	6-2	190	11-18-94	0	0	0.00	2	0	0	0	2	2	0	0	0	2	.250	.333	.000	9.00	0.00
Lopez, Reynaldo	R-R	6-1	220	1-4-94	1	3	6.49	8	8	0	0	26	28	21	19	9	15	24	.269	.208	.333	8.20	5.13
Marshall, Evan	R-R	6-2	235	4-18-90	2	1	2.38	23	0	0	0	23	17	6	6	1	7	30	.198	.119	.273	11.91	2.78
McRae, Alex	R-R	6-2	220	4-6-93	0	0	0.00	2	0	0	0	3	1	0	0	0	2	.000	.000	.167	6.00	0.00
Rodon, Carlos	L-L	6-3	250	12-10-92	0	2	8.22	4	2	0	0	8	9	7	7	1	3	6	.290	.333	.286	7.04	3.52
Ruiz, Jose	R-R	6-1	250	10-21-94	0	0	2.25	5	0	0	0	4	2	1	1	0	5	.143	.143	.143	11.25	0.00
Sanchez, Yolmer	B-R	5-8	205	6-29-92	0	0	9.00	1	0	0	0	1	2	1	1	0	0	.500	.333	1.000	0.00	0.00
Stiever, Jonathan	R-R	6-2	215	5-12-97	0	1	9.95	2	2	0	0	6	7	7	7	4	4	3	.280	.286	.273	4.26	5.68

Fielding

Catcher	PCT	G	PO	A	E	DP	PB
Collins	1.000	2	11	0	0	0	0
Grandal	.993	32	271	13	2	2	4
McCann	.985	30	250	7	4	0	2

First Base	PCT	G	PO	A	E	DP
Abreu	.989	54	430	27	5	39
Collins	1.000	1	1	0	0	0
Grandal	.983	6	56	2	1	6

Second Base	PCT	G	PO	A	E	DP
Garcia	1.000	5	7	14	0	2
Goins	1.000	1	0	1	0	0
Madrigal	.964	29	32	74	4	12
Mendick	.991	28	39	66	1	15
Sanchez	1.000	1	2	3	0	0

Third Base	PCT	G	PO	A	E	DP
Cuthbert	1.000	1	1	0	0	0
Goins	1.000	2	0	5	0	0
Mendick	1.000	3	3	5	0	1
Moncada	.957	52	33	101	6	17
Sanchez	.889	5	1	7	1	0

Shortstop	PCT	G	PO	A	E	DP
Anderson	.967	49	65	109	6	23
Garcia	1.000	10	11	27	0	6
Goins	1.000	2	0	1	0	0
Mendick	1.000	4	2	4	0	2
Sanchez	1.000	3	2	2	0	0

Outfield	PCT	G	PO	A	E	DP
Delmonico	1.000	6	9	0	0	0
Dyson	1.000	8	5	0	0	0
Engel	.974	35	35	2	1	0
Garcia	1.000	3	2	0	0	0
Gonzalez	.500	2	0	1	1	0
Jimenez	.986	54	68	0	1	0
Mazara	1.000	42	72	1	0	0
Robert	.994	56	151	2	1	0

Cincinnati Reds

SEASON IN A SENTENCE: A slow start almost torpedoed the Reds' playoff chances, but a furious 11-3 finish to the season helped Cincinnati slide into the playoffs for the first time since 2013.

HIGH POINT: Righthander Trevor Bauer became the first pitcher in Reds history to win the Cy Young Award, capping off a season that saw him lead the National League in ERA (1.73) and WHIP (0.795). Bauer (5-4, 1.73) was just one key part of an excellent rotation that also included Luis Castillo (4-6, 3.12), Sonny Gray (5-3, 3.70) and Tyler Mahle (2-2, 3.59). Bauer, Castillo and Gray all initially came to the Reds in trades. The excellent pitching allowed Cincinnati to survive despite a surprisingly ineffective lineup. The Reds hit .212/.312/.403 as a team and finished 13th in the National League in runs scored.

LOW POINT: A 16-2 loss to the Cardinals on Sept. 1 dropped the Reds to 6.5 games back in the National League Central. At that point, the team's postseason chances seemed incredibly bleak. Even with the expanded playoff format, Cincinnati had to leapfrog four teams to get into the postseason, which it did by winning 16 of its last 24 games.

NOTABLE ROOKIES: Outfielder Shogo Akiyama showed he was capable of getting on base, but didn't show an ability to put any fear into pitchers. Akiyama had seven extra-base hits in 183 plate appearances. The 32-year-old was a Gold Glove finalist in left field in his first year in the U.S. Righthander Tejay Antone made the team as an extra reliever, but quickly showed himself capable of handling a long-relief and spot starter role. Catcher Tyler Stephenson was largely limited to a DH role, hitting two home runs in just eight games. Shortstop Jose Garcia jumped from Class A in 2019 to the majors in 2020. His glove at shortstop was excellent, but his approach at the plate offered reminders that he needs more seasoning in the minors.

KEY TRANSACTIONS: Free agent signee outfielder Nick Castellanos provided power in his

Reds debut. His 14 home runs were second most on the team, although his .225/.298/.486 stat line was in line with many of his new teammates. The Reds signed second baseman Mike Moustakas as a free agent and saw him hit .230/.331/.468 with eight home runs. Akiyama provided excellent outfield defense after signing with the Reds in January. The Reds acquired righthander Archie Bradley and outfielder Brian Goodwin at the August trade deadline.

OPENING DAY PAYROLL: $53,315,987 (17th)

PLAYERS OF THE YEAR

MAJOR LEAGUE
Trevor Bauer
RHP
5-4, 1.73 in 11 GS
LED NL in ERA+ (276)

TOP ROOKIE
Tejay Antone
RHP
0-3, 2.80, 13 G
45 SO in 35.1 IP

ORGANIZATION LEADERS

Batting		*Minimum 100 AB
MAJORS		
* AVG	Jesse Winker	.255
* OPS	Jesse Winker	.932
HR	Eugenio Suarez	15
RBI	Eugenio Suarez	38

Pitching		#Minimum 30 IP
MAJORS		
W	Trevor Bauer	5
W	Sonny Gray	5
# ERA	Trevor Bauer	1.73
SO	Trevor Bauer	100
SV	Raisel Iglesias	8

ORGANIZATION STATISTICS

CINCINNATI REDS
NATIONAL LEAGUE

Batting	B-T	HT	WT	DOB	AVG	vLH	vRH	G	AB	R	H	2B	3B	HR	RBI	BB	HBP	SH	SF	SO	SB	CS	SLG	OBP
Akiyama, Shogo	L-R	6-0	190	4-16-88	.245	.190	.254	54	155	16	38	6	1	0	9	25	2	0	0	34	7	3	.297	.357
Aquino, Aristides	R-R	6-4	220	4-22-94	.170	.190	.154	23	47	7	8	1	0	2	8	6	3	0	0	18	1	0	.319	.304
Barnhart, Tucker	L-R	5-11	192	1-7-91	.204	.053	.241	38	98	10	20	3	0	5	13	12	0	0	0	28	0	0	.388	.291
Casali, Curt	R-R	6-2	220	11-9-88	.224	.290	.178	31	76	10	17	3	0	6	8	14	3	0	0	29	2	0	.500	.366

Batting	B-T	HT	WT	DOB	AVG	vLH	vRH	G	AB	R	H	2B	3B	HR	RBI	BB	HBP	SH	SF	SO	SB	CS	SLG	OBP
Castellanos, Nick	R-R	6-4	203	3-4-92	.225	.235	.222	60	218	37	49	11	2	14	34	19	4	0	1	69	0	2	.486	.298
Colon, Christian	R-R	5-10	215	5-14-89	.130	.200	.077	11	23	3	3	1	0	0	2	1	0	0	0	3	1	0	.174	.167
Davidson, Matt	R-R	6-3	230	3-26-91	.163	.214	.067	20	43	3	7	1	0	3	11	4	0	0	0	13	0	0	.395	.234
Ervin, Phillip	R-R	5-10	207	7-15-92	.086	.095	.071	19	35	5	3	0	0	0	0	6	1	0	0	8	1	0	.086	.238
Farmer, Kyle	R-R	6-0	205	8-17-90	.266	.400	.179	32	64	4	17	3	0	0	4	5	1	0	0	13	1	0	.313	.329
Galvis, Freddy	B-R	5-10	195	11-14-89	.220	.229	.217	47	141	18	31	5	0	7	16	13	5	0	0	30	1	1	.404	.308
Garcia, Jose	R-R	6-2	175	4-5-98	.194	.300	.149	24	67	4	13	0	0	0	2	1	0	0	0	26	1	1	.194	.206
Goodwin, Brian	L-R	6-0	200	11-2-90	.163	.000	.222	20	49	5	8	2	0	2	5	5	0	0	1	19	4	0	.327	.236
Jankowski, Travis	L-R	6-2	190	6-15-91	.067	.000	.083	16	15	3	1	0	0	0	0	2	0	0	0	7	2	1	.067	.176
Moustakas, Mike	L-R	6-0	225	9-11-88	.230	.214	.237	44	139	13	32	9	0	8	27	18	4	0	2	36	1	0	.468	.331
Payton, Mark	L-L	5-8	180	12-7-91	.167	.000	.176	8	18	0	3	1	0	0	2	0	0	0	5	1	0	.222	.250
Senzel, Nick	R-R	6-1	205	6-29-95	.186	.074	.256	23	70	8	13	6	0	2	8	6	0	0	1	15	2	1	.357	.247
Stephenson, Tyler	R-R	6-4	225	8-16-96	.294	.111	.500	8	17	4	5	0	0	2	6	2	1	0	0	9	0	0	.647	.400
Suarez, Eugenio	R-R	5-11	213	7-18-91	.202	.176	.211	57	198	29	40	8	0	15	38	30	2	0	1	67	2	0	.470	.312
VanMeter, Josh	L-R	5-11	190	3-10-95	.059	.000	.065	14	34	3	2	1	0	1	1	3	1	0	0	16	1	0	.176	.158
2-team total (12 Arizona Diamondbacks)					.129	.182	.119	26	70	9	9	3	0	2	6	7	2	0	0	24	1	0	.257	.228
Votto, Joey	L-R	6-2	220	9-10-83	.226	.178	.241	54	186	32	42	8	0	11	22	37	0	0	0	43	0	0	.446	.354
Winker, Jesse	L-L	6-3	215	8-17-93	.255	.265	.252	54	149	27	38	7	0	12	23	28	5	0	1	46	1	0	.544	.388

Pitching	B-T	HT	WT	DOB	W	L	ERA	G	GS	CG	SV	IP	H	R	ER	HR	BB	SO	AVG	vLH	vRH	K/9	BB/9
Antone, Tejay	R-R	6-4	230	12-5-93	0	3	2.80	13	4	0	0	35	20	11	11	4	16	45	.165	.210	.119	11.46	4.08
Bauer, Trevor	R-R	6-1	205	1-17-91	5	4	1.73	11	11	2	0	73	41	17	14	9	17	100	.159	.170	.146	12.33	2.10
Biddle, Jesse	L-L	6-5	220	10-22-91	0	0	0.00	1	0	0	0	1	1	0	0	0	1	1	.333	.000	.500	13.50	13.50
Bradley, Archie	R-R	6-4	215	8-10-92	1	0	1.17	6	0	0	0	8	4	1	1	1	0	6	.143	.000	.267	7.04	0.00
2-team total (10 Arizona Diamondbacks)					2	0	2.95	16	0	0	6	18	17	6	6	1	3	18	.246	.176	.314	8.84	1.47
Castillo, Luis	R-R	6-2	200	12-12-92	4	6	3.21	12	12	1	0	70	62	31	25	5	24	89	.233	.244	.221	11.44	3.09
Davidson, Matt	R-R	6-3	230	3-26-91	0	0	5.40	3	0	0	0	3	4	2	2	1	2	1	.308	.167	.429	2.70	5.40
De Leon, Jose	R-R	6-2	215	8-7-92	0	0	18.00	5	0	0	0	6	6	12	12	1	11	10	.250	.250	.250	15.00	16.50
DeSclafani, Anthony	R-R	6-1	200	4-18-90	1	2	7.22	9	7	0	0	34	41	27	27	7	16	25	.301	.333	.255	6.68	4.28
Garrett, Amir	R-L	6-5	239	5-3-92	1	0	2.45	21	0	0	1	18	10	5	5	4	7	26	.161	.043	.231	12.76	3.44
Gray, Sonny	R-R	5-10	195	11-7-89	5	3	3.70	11	11	0	0	56	42	26	23	4	26	72	.203	.202	.205	11.57	4.18
Iglesias, Raisel	R-R	6-2	190	1-4-90	4	3	2.74	22	0	0	8	23	16	11	7	1	5	31	.193	.237	.156	12.13	1.96
Jones, Nate	R-R	6-5	230	1-28-86	0	1	6.27	21	0	0	0	19	25	13	13	5	6	23	.325	.273	.364	11.09	2.89
Kuhnel, Joel	R-R	6-4	280	2-19-95	1	0	6.00	3	0	0	0	3	4	2	2	2	0	3	.308	.250	.400	9.00	0.00
Lorenzen, Michael	R-R	6-3	220	1-4-92	3	1	4.28	18	2	0	0	34	30	17	16	3	17	35	.236	.250	.220	9.36	4.54
Mahle, Tyler	R-R	6-3	210	9-29-94	2	2	3.59	10	9	0	0	48	34	21	19	6	21	60	.198	.176	.218	11.33	3.97
Miley, Wade	L-L	6-2	220	11-13-86	0	3	5.65	6	4	0	0	14	15	10	9	1	9	12	.268	.067	.341	7.53	5.65
Raley, Brooks	L-L	6-3	200	6-29-88	0	0	9.00	4	0	0	0	4	5	4	4	0	2	6	.294	.000	.333	13.50	4.50
Reed, Cody	L-L	6-5	230	4-15-93	0	1	5.79	9	0	0	0	9	10	6	6	2	8	10	.270	.333	.250	9.64	7.71
Romano, Sal	R-R	6-5	255	10-12-93	1	0	0.00	2	0	0	0	1	0	0	0	0	0	0	.000	.000	.000	0.00	0.00
Sims, Lucas	R-R	6-2	225	5-10-94	3	0	2.45	20	0	0	0	26	13	10	7	3	11	34	.146	.106	.190	11.92	3.86
Stephenson, Robert	R-R	6-3	205	2-24-93	0	0	9.90	10	0	0	0	10	11	11	11	8	3	13	.282	.263	.300	11.70	2.70
Strop, Pedro	R-R	6-1	220	6-13-85	0	0	3.86	4	0	0	0	2	1	3	1	0	6	3	.125	.333	.000	11.57	23.14
Thornburg, Tyler	R-R	5-11	190	9-29-88	0	0	3.86	7	0	0	0	7	6	3	3	0	5	10	.222	.235	.200	12.86	6.43

Fielding

Catcher	PCT	G	PO	A	E	DP	PB
Barnhart	1.000	36	341	15	0	0	2
Casali	.996	29	258	9	1	1	3
Stephenson	1.000	4	23	1	0	0	0

First Base	PCT	G	PO	A	E	DP
Barnhart	1.000	2	5	0	0	2
Colon	.000	1	0	0	0	0
Davidson	1.000	2	10	1	0	2
Farmer	.000	1	0	0	0	0
Moustakas	.980	10	48	1	1	5
VanMeter	1.000	3	7	1	0	0
Votto	.985	50	299	40	5	25

Second Base	PCT	G	PO	A	E	DP
Colon	1.000	7	6	10	0	3
Farmer	.935	13	8	21	2	6
Galvis	1.000	16	11	28	0	4
Moustakas	1.000	32	38	43	0	7
VanMeter	.958	7	10	13	1	3

Third Base	PCT	G	PO	A	E	DP
Farmer	1.000	2	1	2	0	1
Moustakas	1.000	2	0	4	0	1
Suarez	.961	57	47	75	5	10

Shortstop	PCT	G	PO	A	E	DP
Farmer	1.000	15	11	21	0	7
Galvis	.967	33	29	60	3	9
Garcia	.969	21	17	46	2	10

Outfield	PCT	G	PO	A	E	DP
Akiyama	1.000	52	87	2	0	0
Aquino	1.000	18	22	0	0	0
Castellanos	.963	57	78	1	3	0
Ervin	1.000	16	11	0	0	0
Farmer	--	2	0	0	0	0
Goodwin	.957	18	21	1	1	0
Jankowski	1.000	13	11	0	0	0
Lorenzen	1.000	3	1	0	0	0
Payton	1.000	6	6	0	0	0
Senzel	.976	23	39	2	1	1
Winker	1.000	16	20	0	0	0

Cleveland Indians

SEASON IN A SENTENCE: On the field, the Indians followed a familiar script in 2020: their strong pitching and defense led them to the playoffs, but they fell short on the big stage of October and were swept in the best-of-three Wild Card Series by the Yankees, who scored 22 runs in those two games.

HIGH POINT: Shane Bieber continued to establish himself as one of the best pitchers in the game and was unanimously voted the AL Cy Young Award winner. He won the pitching triple crown, leading the major leagues in wins (eight), ERA (1.63) and strikeouts (122). After producing just one winner in the Cy Young Award's first 40 years, an Indians' pitcher has now won it five times since 2007. As a staff the Indians led the American League in ERA (3.29), strikeouts (621) and hits allowed (440). Additionally, the Indians won seven out of their final eight games in the regular season, including four straight against the White Sox, to take second place in the AL Central and the No. 4 seed in the playoffs.

LOW POINT: As good as Indians' pitchers were on the field in 2020, they didn't escape controversy off it. Mike Clevinger and Zach Plesac were both found to have broken MLB protocols while on the road in Chicago in August and the duo was briefly exiled to the alternate team site as a result. Clevinger was eventually traded to the Padres in a deal at the Aug. 31 trade deadline.

NOTABLE ROOKIES: Righthander Triston McKenzie, the team's No. 1 prospect in 2019, was excellent in his major league debut, going 2-1, 3.24 with 42 strikeouts in 33.1 innings and helping fill the rotation void created when Clevinger and Plesac were demoted. Righthander James Karinchak quickly became one of the team's most trusted relievers, appearing in a team-high 27 games and striking out 53 batters in 27 innings. Lefthander Logan Allen made a trio of multi-inning relief appearances, allowing four runs in 10.2 innings while striking out seven and walking seven.

KEY TRANSACTIONS: Before the season the Indians traded one-time ace Corey Kluber to the Rangers for righthander Emmanuel Clase and outfielder Delino DeShields Jr. For the third straight year, the Indians made a major in-season deal with the Padres. This year, they sent Clevinger and center fielder Greg Allen to San Diego in exchange for catcher Austin Hedges, outfielder Josh Naylor and righthander Cal Quantrill, as well as prospects Gabriel Arias, Joey Cantillo and Owen Miller.

OPENING DAY PAYROLL: $37,642,966 (24th)

PLAYERS OF THE YEAR

Photo credit: JASON HANNA VIA GETTY IMAGES

MAJOR LEAGUE
Shane Bieber
RHP
8-1, 1.63, 122 SO
Triple Crown Winner

TOP ROOKIE
James Karinchak
RHP
1-2, 2.67, 27 G
17.7 SO/9

ORGANIZATION LEADERS

Batting		*Minimum 100 AB
MAJORS		
* AVG	Jose Ramirez	.292
* OPS	Jose Ramirez	.993
HR	Jose Ramirez	17
RBI	Jose Ramirez	46
Pitching		#Minimum 30 IP
MAJORS		
W	Shane Bieber	8
# ERA	Shane Bieber	1.63
SO	Shane Bieber	122
SV	Brad Hand	16

ORGANIZATION STATISTICS

CLEVELAND INDIANS
AMERICAN LEAGUE

Batting	B-T	HT	WT	DOB	AVG	vLH	vRH	G	AB	R	H	2B	3B	HR	RBI	BB	HBP	SH	SF	SO	SB	CS	SLG	OBP
Allen, Greg	B-R	6-0	185	3-15-93	.160	.000	.222	15	25	3	4	1	0	1	4	1	1	0	1	9	1	0	.320	.214
Arroyo, Christian	R-R	6-1	210	5-30-95	--	--	--	1	0	0	0	0	0	0	0	0	0	0	0	0	0	0	--	--
2-team total (14 Boston Red Sox)					.240	.158	.290	15	50	7	12	1	0	3	8	4	0	0	0	11	0	0	.440	.296
Chang, Yu	R-R	6-1	180	8-18-95	.182	.286	.000	10	11	1	2	0	0	0	1	2	0	0	0	4	0	0	.182	.308

CLEVELAND INDIANS

Batting	B-T	HT	WT	DOB	AVG	vLH	vRH	G	AB	R	H	2B	3B	HR	RBI	BB	HBP	SH	SF	SO	SB	CS	SLG	OBP
DeShields, Delino	R-R	5-9	190	8-16-92	.252	.222	.263	37	107	10	27	3	2	0	7	9	0	4	0	29	3	2	.318	.310
Freeman, Mike	L-R	6-0	195	8-4-87	.237	.500	.222	24	38	5	9	3	0	0	3	3	1	0	1	11	0	0	.316	.302
Hedges, Austin	R-R	6-1	223	8-18-92	.083	.000	.125	6	12	0	1	0	0	0	0	0	0	0	0	5	0	0	.083	.083
Hernandez, Cesar	B-R	5-10	195	5-23-90	.283	.246	.297	58	233	35	66	20	0	3	20	24	2	1	0	57	0	0	.408	.355
Johnson, Daniel	L-L	5-10	200	7-11-95	.083	--	.083	5	12	0	1	0	0	0	0	1	0	0	0	5	0	0	.083	.154
Leon, Sandy	B-R	5-10	235	3-13-89	.136	.143	.135	25	66	4	9	1	0	2	4	14	1	0	0	21	0	0	.242	.296
Lindor, Francisco	B-R	5-11	190	11-14-93	.258	.293	.247	60	236	30	61	13	0	8	27	24	4	0	2	41	6	2	.415	.335
Luplow, Jordan	R-R	6-1	195	9-26-93	.192	.270	.122	29	78	8	15	5	1	2	8	12	1	0	1	19	0	1	.359	.304
Mercado, Oscar	R-R	6-2	197	12-16-94	.128	.107	.138	36	86	6	11	1	0	1	6	5	0	1	1	27	3	0	.174	.174
Naquin, Tyler	L-R	6-2	195	4-24-91	.218	.000	.257	40	133	15	29	8	1	4	20	5	1	0	2	40	0	1	.383	.248
Naylor, Josh	L-L	5-11	250	6-22-97	.230	.200	.232	22	61	9	14	3	0	2	14	6	0	0	0	8	0	0	.279	.277
Perez, Roberto	R-R	5-11	220	12-23-88	.165	.154	.169	32	97	6	16	2	0	1	5	11	2	0	0	38	0	0	.216	.264
Ramirez, Jose	B-R	5-9	190	9-17-92	.292	.386	.259	58	219	45	64	16	1	17	46	31	3	0	1	43	10	3	.607	.386
Reyes, Franmil	R-R	6-5	265	7-7-95	.275	.261	.279	59	211	27	58	10	0	9	34	24	1	0	5	69	0	0	.450	.344
Santana, Carlos	B-R	5-11	210	4-8-86	.199	.246	.179	60	206	34	41	7	0	8	30	47	1	0	1	43	0	0	.350	.349
Santana, Domingo	R-R	6-5	232	8-5-92	.157	.056	.192	24	70	6	11	3	0	2	12	13	1	0	0	25	0	0	.286	.298
Taylor, Beau	L-R	5-11	205	2-13-90	.048	.000	.063	7	21	1	1	0	0	0	2	2	0	1	0	9	0	0	.048	.130
Zimmer, Bradley	L-R	6-5	220	11-27-92	.162	.167	.161	20	37	3	6	0	0	1	3	7	5	0	1	14	2	1	.243	.360

Pitching	B-T	HT	WT	DOB	W	L	ERA	G	GS	CG	SV	IP	H	R	ER	HR	BB	SO	AVG	vLH	vRH	K/9	BB/9
Allen, Logan	R-L	6-3	220	5-23-97	0	0	3.38	3	0	0	0	11	12	4	4	1	7	7	.293	.111	.344	5.91	5.91
Bieber, Shane	R-R	6-3	200	5-31-95	8	1	1.63	12	12	0	0	77	46	15	14	7	21	122	.167	.153	.181	14.20	2.44
Carrasco, Carlos	R-R	6-4	224	3-21-87	3	4	2.91	12	12	0	0	68	55	22	22	8	27	82	.221	.224	.218	10.85	3.57
Cimber, Adam	R-R	6-3	195	8-15-90	0	1	3.97	14	0	0	0	11	13	5	5	1	2	5	.289	.143	.355	3.97	1.59
Civale, Aaron	R-R	6-2	215	6-12-95	4	6	4.74	12	12	1	0	74	82	39	39	11	16	69	.282	.231	.333	8.39	1.95
Clevinger, Mike	R-R	6-4	215	12-21-90	1	1	3.18	4	4	0	0	23	20	8	8	5	11	21	.247	.269	.207	8.34	4.37
Hand, Brad	L-L	6-3	215	3-20-90	2	1	2.05	23	0	0	16	22	13	8	5	0	4	29	.169	.125	.174	11.86	1.64
Hill, Cam	R-R	6-1	200	5-24-94	2	0	4.91	18	0	0	1	18	11	11	10	4	5	16	.175	.176	.172	7.85	2.45
Karinchak, James	R-R	6-3	215	9-22-95	1	2	2.67	27	0	0	1	27	14	9	8	1	16	53	.159	.179	.143	17.67	5.33
Leone, Dominic	R-R	5-10	215	10-26-91	0	0	8.38	12	0	0	0	10	14	9	9	3	5	16	.333	.389	.292	14.90	4.66
Maton, Phil	R-R	6-2	206	3-25-93	3	3	4.57	23	0	0	0	22	23	14	11	1	6	32	.267	.267	.268	13.29	2.49
McKenzie, Triston	R-R	6-5	165	8-2-97	2	1	3.24	8	6	0	0	33	21	12	12	6	9	42	.179	.222	.143	11.34	2.43
Nelson, Kyle	L-L	6-1	175	7-8-96	0	0	54.00	1	0	0	0	1	3	4	4	1	1	0	.600	1.000	.500	0.00	13.50
Perez, Oliver	L-L	6-3	225	8-15-81	1	1	2.00	21	0	0	1	18	13	5	4	0	6	14	.210	.185	.229	7.00	3.00
Plesac, Zach	R-R	6-3	220	1-21-95	4	2	2.28	8	8	0	0	55	38	14	14	8	6	57	.191	.205	.180	9.27	0.98
Plutko, Adam	R-R	6-3	215	10-3-91	2	2	4.88	10	4	0	1	28	30	15	15	5	7	15	.280	.239	.311	4.88	2.28
Quantrill, Cal	L-R	6-3	195	2-10-95	0	0	1.84	8	2	0	0	15	14	6	3	2	2	13	.246	.148	.333	7.98	1.23
Wittgren, Nick	R-R	6-2	216	5-29-91	2	0	3.42	25	0	0	0	24	18	9	9	4	6	28	.209	.178	.244	10.65	2.28

Fielding

Catcher	PCT	G	PO	A	E	DP	PB
Hedges	1.000	6	37	0	0	0	0
Leon	.978	24	213	14	5	0	0
Perez	1.000	32	291	21	0	2	0
Taylor	.988	7	73	6	1	0	0

First Base	PCT	G	PO	A	E	DP
Freeman	1.000	1	1	0	0	1
Naylor	1.000	2	1	0	0	0
Santana	.991	60	413	36	4	44

Second Base	PCT	G	PO	A	E	DP
Chang	.917	2	4	7	1	1
Freeman	1.000	4	4	4	0	1
Hernandez	.981	58	67	139	4	33

Third Base	PCT	G	PO	A	E	DP
Arroyo	.000	1	0	0	0	0
Chang	1.000	3	0	1	0	0
Freeman	.900	6	3	6	1	0
Ramirez	.945	57	39	65	6	13

Shortstop	PCT	G	PO	A	E	DP
Chang	1.000	4	1	4	0	1
Freeman	1.000	3	0	2	0	0
Lindor	.995	58	79	128	1	30

Outfield	PCT	G	PO	A	E	DP
Allen	1.000	14	18	0	0	0
DeShields	1.000	35	86	2	0	0
Freeman	.875	4	7	0	1	0
Johnson	1.000	5	2	0	0	0
Luplow	1.000	29	35	2	0	0
Mercado	1.000	32	65	0	0	0
Naquin	1.000	39	66	5	0	0
Naylor	1.000	19	23	0	0	0
Reyes	--	1	0	0	0	0
Santana	1.000	23	35	1	0	0
Zimmer	.917	20	22	0	2	0

Colorado Rockies

SEASON IN A SENTENCE: The Rockies were one of the hottest teams in baseball out of the gate, but they ran out of gas quickly, won just two series after early August and finished the season out of the postseason.

HIGH POINT: On Aug. 8, the Rockies one-hit the Mariners in a 5-0 win, pushing the team's record to a high-water mark of 11-3 as they led the NL West by 1.5 games. Rookie righthander Ryan Castellani started and threw four no-hit innings that day in his major league debut.

LOW POINT: Anything after Aug. 31, which is the date on which the Rockies were still holding on to the second wild card. A 23-5 loss to Seattle on Sept. 1 was a harbinger of a bad month to come. The Rockies were eliminated from playoff contention on Sept. 25 as they lost both ends of a doubleheader to the last-place Diamondbacks by a combined score of 15-5.

NOTABLE ROOKIES: It wasn't a standout year for Rockies rookies, but 27-year-old infielder Josh Fuentes took advantage of his opportunities and hit .306 in 30 games after hitting just .218 in 24 games in his debut in 2019. The debut of top prospect Brendan Rodgers as a full-time player was delayed again by a shoulder injury that limited him to seven games. Castellani faded right along with the team down the stretch, but he was outstanding in his first two outings of the season, which should give him and the club confidence that he can parlay that into more success moving forward. After showing well in a small sample in 2019, outfielder Sam Hilliard struggled in 2020, hitting .210 with 42 strikeouts in 114 plate appearances.

KEY TRANSACTIONS: In an effort to push for the postseason, the Rockies made a deadline deal to acquire righthanded reliever Mychal Givens from the Orioles in exchange for two prospects, first baseman Tyler Nevin and shortstop Terrin Vavra. Nevin was ranked 13th in the Rockies' midseason prospects update prior to the trade, while Vavra was the team's 17th-ranked prospect.

PLAYERS OF THE YEAR

ROBERT BINDER VIA GETTY IMAGES

ROBERT BINDER VIA GETTY IMAGES

MAJOR LEAGUE	TOP ROOKIE
Trevor Story	**Josh Fuentes**
SS	1B/3B
.289/.355/.519	.306/.320/.439
11 HR, Led NL in SB	9 XBH, 17 RBIs
(15), 3B (4)	

ORGANIZATION LEADERS

Batting		*Minimum 100 AB
MAJORS		
* AVG	Raimel Tapia	.321
* OPS	Trevor Story	.874
HR	Trevor Story	11
RBI	Charlie Blackmon	42

Pitching		#Minimum 30 IP
MAJORS		
W	Antonio Senzatela	5
# ERA	Antonio Senzatela	3.44
SO	German Marquez	73
SV	Daniel Bard	6

After putting up a 1.38 ERA in 12 games for the Orioles, Givens had a 6.75 ERA for the Rockies in 10 appearances after the trade. Prior to the season, the Rockies signed righthander Daniel Bard, who ended up as one of the feelgood stories of the season. After a long battle with the yips and an early retirement, Bard returned to the big leagues in 2020 to serve as the Rockies' primary closer. In January, the team signed shortstop Trevor Story to a two-year extension, which bought out his remaining arbitration years.

OPENING DAY PAYROLL: $60,330,370 (16th)

ORGANIZATION STATISTICS

COLORADO ROCKIES
NATIONAL LEAGUE

Batting	B-T	HT	WT	DOB	AVG	vLH	vRH	G	AB	R	H	2B	3B	HR	RBI	BB	HBP	SH	SF	SO	SB	CS	SLG	OBP
Arenado, Nolan	R-R	6-2	215	4-16-91	.253	.264	.248	48	182	23	46	9	0	8	26	15	0	0	4	20	0	0	.434	.303
Blackmon, Charlie	L-L	6-3	221	7-1-86	.303	.375	.262	59	221	31	67	12	1	6	42	19	2	0	5	44	2	1	.448	.356
Butera, Drew	R-R	6-1	212	8-9-83	.154	.143	.167	28	39	4	6	2	0	0	4	2	0	1	1	11	0	0	.205	.190
Dahl, David	L-R	6-2	197	4-1-94	.183	.156	.197	24	93	9	17	2	2	0	9	4	1	0	1	28	1	0	.247	.222

Batting

Batting	B-T	HT	WT	DOB	AVG	vLH	vRH	G	AB	R	H	2B	3B	HR	RBI	BB	HBP	SH	SF	SO	SB	CS	SLG	OBP
Diaz, Elias	R-R	6-1	223	11-17-90	.235	.231	.238	26	68	4	16	2	0	2	9	5	0	0	0	15	0	0	.353	.288
Fuentes, Josh	R-R	6-2	209	2-19-93	.306	.258	.328	30	98	14	30	7	0	2	17	2	1	0	2	29	1	0	.439	.320
Hampson, Garrett	R-R	5-11	196	10-10-94	.234	.212	.248	53	167	25	39	4	3	5	11	13	0	3	1	60	6	1	.383	.287
Hilliard, Sam	L-L	6-5	236	2-21-94	.210	.194	.216	36	105	13	22	2	2	6	10	9	0	0	0	42	3	0	.438	.272
Kemp, Matt	R-R	6-4	225	9-23-84	.239	.300	.194	43	117	18	28	3	0	6	21	15	0	0	0	41	1	0	.419	.326
McMahon, Ryan	L-R	6-2	219	12-14-94	.215	.192	.225	52	172	23	37	6	1	9	26	18	2	0	1	66	0	1	.419	.295
Murphy, Daniel	L-R	6-1	223	4-1-85	.236	.200	.250	40	123	10	29	3	0	3	16	7	0	0	1	21	0	0	.333	.275
Owings, Chris	R-R	5-10	185	8-12-91	.268	.250	.286	17	41	9	11	1	0	2	5	3	0	0	0	11	1	0	.439	.318
Pillar, Kevin	R-R	6-0	200	1-4-89	.308	.444	.250	24	91	14	28	5	1	2	13	5	1	0	0	18	4	1	.451	.351
Rodgers, Brendan	R-R	6-0	204	8-9-96	.095	.111	.083	7	21	1	2	1	0	0	2	0	0	0	0	6	0	0	.143	.095
Story, Trevor	R-R	6-2	213	11-15-92	.289	.328	.275	59	235	41	68	13	4	11	28	24	0	0	0	63	15	3	.519	.355
Tapia, Raimel	L-L	6-3	175	2-4-94	.321	.364	.302	51	184	26	59	8	2	1	17	14	2	1	3	38	8	2	.402	.369
Wolters, Tony	L-R	5-10	207	6-9-92	.230	.158	.247	42	100	10	23	4	0	0	8	6	1	2	0	30	0	0	.270	.280

Pitching

Pitching	B-T	HT	WT	DOB	W	L	ERA	G	GS	CG	SV	IP	H	R	ER	HR	BB	SO	AVG	vLH	vRH	K/9	BB/9
Almonte, Yency	B-R	6-5	223	6-4-94	3	0	2.93	24	0	0	1	28	25	13	9	2	6	23	.243	.264	.220	7.48	1.95
Bard, Daniel	R-R	6-4	197	6-25-85	4	2	3.65	23	0	0	6	25	22	10	10	2	10	27	.237	.265	.205	9.85	3.65
Butera, Drew	R-R	6-1	212	8-9-83	0	0	5.40	1	0	0	0	2	3	1	1	0	0	1	.375	.500	.250	5.40	0.00
Castellani, Ryan	R-R	6-4	218	4-1-96	1	4	5.82	10	9	0	0	43	37	30	28	12	26	25	.236	.229	.241	5.19	5.40
Davis, Wade	R-R	6-5	225	9-7-85	0	1	20.77	5	0	0	2	4	9	10	10	3	3	3	.409	.286	.625	6.23	6.23
Diaz, Jairo	R-R	6-0	254	5-27-91	1	2	7.65	24	0	0	4	20	31	21	17	4	14	17	.365	.317	.409	7.65	6.30
Diehl, Phillip	L-L	6-2	169	7-16-94	0	0	10.50	6	0	0	0	6	7	7	7	2	1	4	.292	.250	.333	6.00	1.50
Doyle, Tommy	R-R	6-6	244	5-1-96	0	0	23.14	3	0	0	0	2	6	6	6	0	4	2	.462	.429	.500	7.71	15.43
Estevez, Carlos	R-R	6-6	277	12-28-92	1	3	7.50	26	0	0	1	24	33	21	20	6	9	27	.317	.313	.321	10.13	3.38
Freeland, Kyle	L-L	6-4	204	5-14-93	2	3	4.33	13	13	0	0	71	77	34	34	9	23	46	.278	.279	.278	5.86	2.93
Givens, Mychal	R-R	6-0	230	5-13-90	1	0	6.75	10	0	0	1	9	9	8	7	4	4	6	.250	.118	.368	5.79	3.86
Gonzalez, Chi Chi	R-R	6-3	210	1-15-92	0	2	6.86	6	4	0	0	20	22	16	15	3	10	16	.289	.333	.256	7.32	4.58
Goudeau, Ashton	R-R	6-6	210	7-23-92	0	0	7.56	4	0	0	0	8	15	7	7	3	2	2	.441	.308	.524	2.16	2.16
Gray, Jon	R-R	6-4	225	11-5-91	2	4	6.69	8	8	0	0	39	45	31	29	6	11	22	.281	.265	.306	5.08	2.54
Harvey, Joe	R-R	6-2	236	1-9-92	0	0	0.00	4	0	0	0	3	3	0	0	0	2	2	.231	.286	.167	5.40	0.00
Hoffman, Jeff	R-R	6-5	215	1-8-93	2	1	9.28	16	0	0	1	21	32	23	22	3	9	20	.352	.378	.326	8.44	3.80
Kinley, Tyler	R-R	6-4	220	1-31-91	0	2	5.32	24	0	0	0	24	13	15	14	2	12	26	.167	.111	.242	9.89	4.56
Marquez, German	R-R	6-1	230	2-22-95	4	6	3.75	13	13	0	0	82	78	41	34	6	25	73	.247	.253	.239	8.04	2.76
Mujica, Jose	R-R	6-2	249	6-29-96	0	0	12.46	2	0	0	0	4	10	7	6	2	2	1	.476	.500	.444	2.08	4.15
Pazos, James	R-L	6-2	252	5-5-91	0	0	16.88	6	0	0	0	5	10	10	10	3	5	1	.435	.333	.500	1.69	8.44
Ramos, AJ	R-R	5-10	200	9-20-86	0	0	3.38	3	0	0	0	3	4	1	1	1	3	1	.333	.667	.000	3.38	10.13
Santos, Antonio	R-R	6-3	223	10-6-96	0	1	16.50	3	1	0	0	6	14	11	11	1	4	4	.483	.462	.500	6.00	6.00
Senzatela, Antonio	R-R	6-1	236	1-21-95	5	3	3.44	12	12	1	0	73	71	29	28	9	18	41	.254	.247	.264	5.03	2.21
Tinoco, Jesus	R-R	6-4	258	4-30-95	0	0	2.45	3	0	0	0	4	3	1	1	0	4	3	.231	.250	.200	7.36	9.82
2-team total (3 Miami Marlins)					0	0	1.04	6	0	0	0	9	3	1	1	0	7	6	.120	.133	.100	6.23	7.27

Fielding

Catcher	PCT	G	PO	A	E	DP	PB
Butera	1.000	25	91	3	0	1	1
Diaz	1.000	24	79	9	0	1	0
Wolters	.996	39	230	13	1	2	4

First Base	PCT	G	PO	A	E	DP
Butera	1.000	5	3	0	0	1
Fuentes	.996	26	200	22	1	27
McMahon	.989	12	84	8	1	15
Murphy	.985	29	228	27	4	29

Second Base	PCT	G	PO	A	E	DP
Hampson	.981	26	39	65	2	22
McMahon	.947	33	43	83	7	21
Owings	1.000	8	10	17	0	5
Rodgers	1.000	5	8	5	0	2
Wolters	1.000	4	2	2	0	0

Third Base	PCT	G	PO	A	E	DP
Arenado	.982	48	43	117	3	19
Fuentes	1.000	6	4	1	0	0
McMahon	.946	14	3	32	2	2
Owings	.500	2	1	1	2	1

Shortstop	PCT	G	PO	A	E	DP
Hampson	1.000	6	4	8	0	1
McMahon	.000	2	0	0	0	0
Owings	1.000	1	0	5	0	2
Rodgers	1.000	1	1	0	0	0
Story	.961	57	88	161	10	49

Outfield	PCT	G	PO	A	E	DP
Blackmon	1.000	50	101	4	0	2
Dahl	.980	22	50	0	1	0
Fuentes	--	2	0	0	0	0
Hampson	1.000	26	38	1	0	0
Hilliard	1.000	34	73	1	0	1
Kemp	1.000	1	2	0	0	0
Owings	1.000	6	7	0	0	0
Pillar	.978	21	42	2	1	0
Tapia	.971	38	65	3	2	0

Detroit Tigers

SEASON IN A SENTENCE: The Tigers remained impressively competitive for just over half of the abbreviated season, but a 6-19 finish dropped them into last place in the American League Central for the second straight year and the fourth time in the last six seasons.

HIGH POINT: The Tigers won six straight games from Aug. 25-Sept. 1, including a sweep of the first-place Twins, to pull within a half-game of a playoff spot with less than a month remaining in the season. The Tigers outscored their opponents 41-14 during the stretch, their longest win streak in four years.

LOW POINT: The Tigers awoke the morning of Sept. 9 just one game out of a wild card spot, but the Brewers embarrassed the Tigers 19-0 that afternoon—the largest shutout loss in franchise history. The Tigers never recovered, losing their next game 12-2 and suffering losses of 14-0 and 10-3 within the next eight days as their season quickly spiraled our of their control.

NOTABLE ROOKIES: Shortstop Willi Castro made his debut on Aug. 12 and hit .349/.381/.550 in 36 games, leading all rookies with at least 100 at-bats in all three slash-line categories. Top pitching prospects Casey Mize and Tarik Skubal made their long-awaited major league debuts but struggled in their first stints in the Tigers rotation. Mize went 0-3, 6.99 in seven starts and Skubal went 1-4, 5.63 in eight appearances (seven starts). There was more rookie success in the bullpen, where lefthander Gregory Soto and righthander Bryan Garcia successfully assumed high-leverage roles in the late innings. Rule 5 draft pick Rony Garcia and former top draft selections Kyle Funkouser and Beau Burrows also made their debuts in relief, but struggled. Third baseman Isaac Paredes and right fielder Daz Cameron debuted and took over as starters by the end of the season, though both made little impact. Infielder Sergio Alcantara, outfielder Derek Hill and catcher Eric Haase appeared in limited reserve roles.

PLAYERS OF THE YEAR

MAJOR LEAGUE
Jeimer Candelario
1B
.297/.369/.503
7 HR, 29 RBIs

TOP ROOKIE
Willi Castro
SS/3B
.349/.381/.550
6 HR, 24 RBIs

ORGANIZATION LEADERS

Batting		*Minimum 100 AB
MAJORS		
* AVG	Willi Castro	.349
* OPS	Willi Castro	.932
HR	Miguel Cabrera	10
RBI	Miguel Cabrera	35

Pitching		#Minimum 30 IP
MAJORS		
W	Spencer Turnbull	4
# ERA	Tyler Alexander	3.96
SO	Matthew Boyd	60
SV	Joe Jimenez	5

KEY TRANSACTIONS: The Tigers signed first baseman C.J. Cron, second baseman Jonathan Schoop and righthander Ivan Nova in the off-season to provide some veteran anchors for their rebuild. Cron and Nova both got hurt early, but Schoop performed well as their everyday second baseman. The Tigers made just one minor move at the trade deadline, dealing veteran outfielder Cameron Maybin—another offseason signee— to the Cubs in exchange for minor league shortstop Zack Short.

OPENING DAY PAYROLL: $43,069,928 (22nd)

ORGANIZATION STATISTICS

DETROIT TIGERS
AMERICAN LEAGUE

Batting	B-T	HT	WT	DOB	AVG	vLH	vRH	G	AB	R	H	2B	3B	HR	RBI	BB	HBP	SH	SF	SO	SB	CS	SLG	OBP
Alcantara, Sergio	B-R	5-9	151	7-10-96	.143	.333	.111	10	21	2	3	0	1	1	1	2	0	0	0	4	0	0	.381	.217
Bonifacio, Jorge	R-R	6-1	220	6-4-93	.221	.316	.194	30	86	8	19	3	0	2	17	5	2	0	1	26	0	0	.326	.277
Cabrera, Miguel	R-R	6-4	249	4-18-83	.250	.400	.219	57	204	28	51	4	0	10	35	24	1	0	2	51	1	0	.417	.329
Cameron, Daz	R-R	6-2	185	1-15-97	.193	.143	.200	17	57	4	11	2	1	0	3	2	0	0	0	19	1	0	.263	.220

Batting

Batting	B-T	HT	WT	DOB	AVG	vLH	vRH	G	AB	R	H	2B	3B	HR	RBI	BB	HBP	SH	SF	SO	SB	CS	SLG	OBP
Candelario, Jeimer	B-R	6-1	221	11-24-93	.297	.400	.269	52	185	30	55	11	3	7	29	20	1	0	0	49	1	1	.503	.369
Castro, Harold	L-R	5-10	151	11-30-93	.347	.333	.348	22	49	6	17	4	0	0	3	5	0	0	0	11	0	0	.429	.407
Castro, Willi	B-R	6-1	170	4-24-97	.349	.391	.340	36	129	21	45	4	2	6	24	7	1	1	2	38	0	1	.550	.381
Cron, C.J.	R-R	6-4	235	1-5-90	.190	.154	.207	13	42	9	8	3	0	4	8	9	1	0	0	16	0	0	.548	.346
Demeritte, Travis	R-R	6-0	180	9-30-94	.172	.231	.125	18	29	5	5	1	0	0	4	3	1	0	0	14	0	0	.207	.273
Dixon, Brandon	R-R	6-2	215	1-29-92	.077	.000	.111	5	13	0	1	0	0	0	2	1	0	0	0	4	0	0	.154	.143
Goodrum, Niko	B-R	6-3	198	2-28-92	.184	.333	.144	43	158	15	29	7	1	5	20	18	0	0	3	69	7	1	.335	.263
Greiner, Grayson	R-R	6-6	239	10-11-92	.118	.100	.122	18	51	8	6	2	0	3	8	3	1	0	0	20	0	0	.333	.182
Haase, Eric	R-R	5-10	210	12-18-92	.176	--	.176	7	17	1	3	0	0	0	2	1	0	0	1	6	0	0	.176	.211
Hill, Derek	R-R	6-2	190	12-30-95	.091	.000	.111	15	11	3	1	0	0	0	0	1	0	0	0	6	0	0	.091	.167
Jones, JaCoby	R-R	6-2	201	5-10-92	.268	.286	.263	30	97	19	26	9	0	5	14	7	3	0	1	34	1	1	.515	.333
Lugo, Dawel	R-R	6-0	190	12-31-94	.200	.400	.000	9	10	3	2	0	0	0	1	1	0	0	0	1	0	0	.200	.273
Maybin, Cameron	R-R	6-3	215	4-4-87	.244	.444	.188	14	41	5	10	4	0	1	2	4	0	0	0	13	0	0	.415	.311
Mercer, Jordy	R-R	6-3	210	8-27-86	.222	.250	.200	3	9	1	2	0	0	0	0	0	0	0	0	1	0	0	.222	.222
2-team total (6 New York Yankees)					.200	.333	.143	9	20	2	4	0	0	0	2	0	0	0	0	2	0	0	.200	.273
Paredes, Isaac	R-R	5-11	213	2-18-99	.220	.438	.179	34	100	7	22	4	0	1	6	8	0	0	0	24	0	0	.290	.278
Reyes, Victor	B-R	6-5	194	10-5-94	.277	.342	.262	57	202	30	56	7	2	4	14	9	2	0	0	45	8	2	.391	.315
Romine, Austin	R-R	6-1	216	11-22-88	.238	.318	.222	37	130	12	31	5	0	2	17	4	0	0	1	47	0	0	.323	.259
Schoop, Jonathan	R-R	6-1	225	10-16-91	.278	.281	.277	44	162	26	45	4	2	8	23	8	4	0	2	39	0	0	.475	.324
Stewart, Christin	L-R	6-0	220	12-10-93	.167	.222	.160	36	90	6	15	3	0	3	9	5	2	0	1	30	0	0	.300	.224

Pitching

Pitching	B-T	HT	WT	DOB	W	L	ERA	G	GS	CG	SV	IP	H	R	ER	HR	BB	SO	AVG	vLH	vRH	K/9	BB/9
Alexander, Tyler	R-L	6-2	200	7-14-94	2	3	3.96	14	2	0	0	36	39	16	16	8	9	34	.283	.225	.306	8.42	2.23
Boyd, Matthew	L-L	6-3	234	2-2-91	3	7	6.71	12	12	1	0	60	67	46	45	15	22	60	.278	.135	.304	8.95	3.28
Burrows, Beau	R-R	6-2	210	9-18-96	0	0	5.40	5	0	0	0	7	8	4	4	3	1	3	.286	.154	.400	4.05	1.35
Castro, Anthony	R-R	6-2	182	4-13-95	0	0	18.00	1	0	0	0	1	1	2	2	1	1	1	.250	.500	.000	9.00	9.00
Cisnero, Jose	R-R	6-3	245	4-11-89	3	3	3.03	29	0	0	0	30	23	10	10	1	10	34	.209	.184	.222	10.31	3.03
Demeritte, Travis	R-R	6-0	180	9-30-94	0	0	36.00	1	0	0	0	1	4	4	4	2	0	0	.571	.000	.667	0.00	0.00
Farmer, Buck	L-R	6-4	232	2-20-91	1	0	3.80	23	0	0	0	21	20	9	9	3	5	14	.244	.289	.189	5.91	2.11
Fulmer, Carson	R-R	6-0	215	12-13-93	0	0	6.75	7	0	0	0	7	8	5	5	1	3	7	.286	.188	.417	9.45	4.05
2-team total (3 Baltimore Orioles)					0	0	4.35	10	0	0	0	10	8	5	5	1	5	11	.205	.158	.250	9.58	4.35
Fulmer, Michael	R-R	6-3	246	3-15-93	0	2	8.78	10	10	0	0	28	45	27	27	8	12	20	.375	.258	.519	6.51	3.90
Funkhouser, Kyle	R-R	6-2	225	3-16-94	1	1	7.27	13	0	0	0	17	22	14	14	3	11	12	.319	.300	.333	6.23	5.71
Garcia, Bryan	R-R	6-1	215	4-19-95	2	1	1.66	26	0	0	4	22	18	6	4	0	10	12	.222	.225	.220	4.98	4.15
Garcia, Rony	R-R	6-3	200	12-19-97	1	0	8.14	15	2	0	0	21	25	20	19	7	9	14	.287	.154	.396	6.00	3.86
Jimenez, Joe	R-R	6-3	272	1-17-95	1	3	7.15	25	0	0	5	23	25	19	18	7	6	22	.284	.324	.255	8.74	2.38
McKay, David	R-R	6-3	205	3-31-95	0	0	54.00	1	0	0	0	1	2	2	2	1	0	0	.500	1.000	.000	0.00	27.00
Mize, Casey	R-R	6-3	220	5-1-97	3	6	6.99	7	7	0	0	28	29	25	22	7	13	26	.252	.300	.200	8.26	4.13
Norris, Daniel	L-L	6-2	185	4-25-93	3	1	3.25	14	1	0	0	28	25	10	10	2	7	28	.231	.154	.256	9.11	2.28
Nova, Ivan	R-R	6-5	250	1-12-87	1	1	8.53	4	4	0	0	19	22	18	18	4	9	9	.278	.267	.294	4.26	4.26
Ramirez, Nick	L-L	6-4	232	8-1-89	0	0	5.91	5	0	0	0	11	8	7	7	3	4	11	.200	.167	.206	9.28	3.38
Schreiber, John	R-R	6-2	210	3-5-94	0	1	6.32	15	0	0	0	16	19	11	11	2	4	14	.297	.360	.256	8.04	2.30
Skubal, Tarik	L-L	6-3	215	11-20-96	1	4	5.63	8	7	0	0	32	28	21	20	9	11	37	.235	.136	.258	10.41	3.09
Soto, Gregory	L-L	6-1	236	2-11-95	0	1	4.30	27	0	0	2	23	16	11	11	2	13	29	.193	.095	.226	11.35	5.09
Turnbull, Spencer	R-R	6-3	211	9-18-92	4	4	3.97	11	11	0	0	57	47	25	25	2	29	51	.226	.218	.236	8.10	4.61
Zimmermann, Jordan	R-R	6-2	225	5-23-86	0	0	7.94	3	2	0	0	6	11	6	5	0	2	6	.423	.563	.200	9.53	3.18

Fielding

Catcher	PCT	G	PO	A	E	DP	PB
Greiner	1.000	18	134	4	0	0	2
Haase	.982	7	52	2	1	0	0
Romine	1.000	37	269	7	0	1	2

First Base	PCT	G	PO	A	E	DP
Candelario	.988	43	297	19	4	35
Castro	1.000	2	5	1	0	0
Cron	.984	13	113	12	2	9
Dixon	1.000	4	16	2	0	1
Mercer	1.000	2	6	0	0	0
Romine	1.000	1	5	1	0	0

Second Base	PCT	G	PO	A	E	DP
Alcantara	1.000	6	5	3	0	2
Castro	1.000	2	1	0	0	0
Castro	1.000	1	1	1	0	0
Dixon	1.000	1	1	0	0	0
Goodrum	.976	11	18	23	1	2
Lugo	.000	1	0	0	0	0
Schoop	.994	44	60	113	1	25

Third Base	PCT	G	PO	A	E	DP
Alcantara	.818	6	2	7	2	1
Candelario	1.000	10	4	25	0	3
Castro	1.000	4	2	3	0	0
Castro	.938	8	3	12	1	0
Lugo	1.000	5	0	9	0	0
Mercer	1.000	2	0	1	0	0
Paredes	.975	33	22	56	2	8

Shortstop	PCT	G	PO	A	E	DP
Castro	1.000	2	0	7	0	0
Castro	.941	27	24	56	5	10
Goodrum	.991	31	29	87	1	17

Outfield	PCT	G	PO	A	E	DP
Bonifacio	.981	29	49	2	1	0
Cameron	.972	16	35	0	1	0
Castro	1.000	12	17	0	0	0
Demeritte	.960	14	24	0	1	0
Dixon	1.000	2	1	0	0	0
Hill	.900	10	9	0	1	0
Jones	1.000	28	61	0	0	0
Maybin	.957	12	22	0	1	0
Reyes	.992	56	117	0	1	0
Stewart	1.000	32	40	3	0	0

Houston Astros

SEASON IN A SENTENCE: A cheating scandal shook up the organization and led to the departures of general manager Jeff Luhnow and manager A.J. Hinch, but despite a 29-31 finish, the Astros sneaked into the expanded playoffs and were one win away from the World Series, falling to the Rays in seven games in the American League Championship Series.

HIGH POINT: The Astros went on an eight-game winning streak starting Aug. 12 that jumped their record to 15-10. But in an otherwise sluggish regular season, the Astros played their best baseball in the playoffs. They swept the Twins 2-0 in the Wild Card Series, made quick work of the A's (3-1) in the Division Series and pushed the Rays to seven games in the ALCS. George Springer, Michael Brantley and Kyle Tucker carried the offense, while homegrown pitchers Framber Valdez, Cristian Javier and Lance McCullers played key roles in a starting rotation that lost Gerrit Cole to free agency and Justin Verlander to Tommy John surgery.

LOW POINT: The true low point for the Astros came before the season in January, when the commissioner's office penalized the organization for its sign-stealing violations, costing them their first- and second-round picks in the 2020 and 2021 drafts and leading to the dismissal of their GM and manager that same day. On the field, the Astros lost eight of nine games in an early September stretch against the Angels and A's to drop them 6.5 games back in the AL West, then limped into the playoffs by losing five of seven games to the Angels and Rangers to finish the season.

NOTABLE ROOKIES: Houston's pitching pipeline from Latin America came through in 2020, led by righthander Cristian Javier. Javier posted a 3.48 ERA and struck out nearly a batter per inning in a strong rookie campaign. Two more righthanders the Astros signed in 2015—Enoli Paredes from the Dominican Republic and Jose Urquidy from Mexico—were productive as well.

KEY TRANSACTIONS: The major moves for the Astros involved bringing in new leadership, with James Click taking over as GM and Dusty Baker as manager. Otherwise the moves were relatively minor. They signed catcher Martin Maldonado as a free agent before the season and traded outfielder Jake Marisnick to the Mets for lefthander Blake Taylor and infielder Kenedy Corona. The Astros added to their bullpen in August when they acquired lefthander Brooks Raley from the Reds for a player to be named later.

OPENING DAY PAYROLL: $81,848,621 (4th)

PLAYERS OF THE YEAR

MAJOR LEAGUE
George Springer
OF
.265/.359/.540
14 HR, 32 RBIs

TOP ROOKIE
Cristian Javier
RHP
5-2, 3.48 in 12 G
54 SO in 54.1 IP

MARY DECICCO VIA GETTY IMAGES

ORGANIZATION LEADERS

Batting		*Minimum 100 AB
MAJORS		
* AVG	Michael Brantley	.300
* OPS	George Springer	.899
HR	George Springer	14
RBI	Kyle Tucker	42

Pitching		#Minimum 30 IP
MAJORS		
W	Cristian Javier	5
W	Framber Valdez	5
# ERA	Cristian Javier	3.48
SO	Framber Valdez	76
SV	Ryan Pressly	12

ORGANIZATION STATISTICS

HOUSTON ASTROS
AMERICAN LEAGUE

Batting	B-T	HT	WT	DOB	AVG	vLH	vRH	G	AB	R	H	2B	3B	HR	RBI	BB	HBP	SH	SF	SO	SB	CS	SLG	OBP
Altuve, Jose	R-R	5-6	166	5-6-90	.219	.167	.236	48	192	32	42	9	0	5	18	17	1	0	0	39	2	3	.344	.286
Alvarez, Yordan	L-R	6-5	225	6-27-97	.250	.400	.000	2	8	2	2	0	0	1	4	0	1	0	0	1	0	0	.625	.333
Brantley, Michael	L-L	6-2	209	5-15-87	.300	.231	.331	46	170	24	51	15	0	5	22	17	0	0	0	28	2	0	.476	.364
Bregman, Alex	R-R	6-0	192	3-30-94	.242	.319	.208	42	153	19	37	12	1	6	22	24	2	0	1	26	0	0	.451	.350

Batting

Batting	B-T	HT	WT	DOB	AVG	vLH	vRH	G	AB	R	H	2B	3B	HR	RBI	BB	HBP	SH	SF	SO	SB	CS	SLG	OBP
Correa, Carlos	R-R	6-4	220	9-22-94	.264	.279	.257	58	201	22	53	9	0	5	25	16	3	0	1	49	0	0	.383	.326
Diaz, Aledmys	R-R	6-1	195	8-1-90	.241	.200	.263	17	58	8	14	5	0	3	6	1	0	0	0	12	0	0	.483	.254
Garneau, Dustin	R-R	6-2	205	8-13-87	.158	.111	.172	17	38	4	6	0	1	1	4	6	0	2	0	15	0	0	.289	.273
Gurriel, Yuli	R-R	6-0	215	6-9-84	.232	.290	.208	57	211	27	49	12	1	6	22	12	2	0	5	27	0	1	.384	.274
Jones, Taylor	R-R	6-7	230	12-6-93	.190	.000	.235	7	21	3	4	1	0	1	3	1	0	0	0	7	0	0	.381	.227
Maldonado, Martin	R-R	6-0	230	8-16-86	.215	.279	.185	47	135	19	29	4	0	6	24	27	1	2	0	51	1	0	.378	.350
Mayfield, Jack	R-R	5-11	190	9-30-90	.190	.111	.212	21	42	5	8	1	0	0	3	2	1	1	1	14	0	0	.214	.239
Reddick, Josh	L-R	6-2	197	2-19-87	.245	.262	.236	56	188	22	46	11	1	4	23	20	0	0	1	42	1	0	.378	.316
Springer, George	R-R	6-3	221	9-19-89	.265	.229	.277	51	189	37	50	6	2	14	32	24	5	0	2	38	1	2	.540	.359
Straw, Myles	R-R	5-10	178	10-17-94	.207	.033	.308	33	82	8	17	4	0	0	8	4	0	0	0	22	6	2	.256	.244
Stubbs, Garrett	L-R	5-10	170	5-26-93	.125	.000	.143	14	8	1	1	0	0	0	1	0	0	1	0	1	0	0	.125	.111
Toro, Abraham	B-R	6-0	206	12-20-96	.149	.174	.141	33	87	13	13	2	0	3	9	3	7	0	0	23	1	1	.276	.237
Tucker, Kyle	L-R	6-4	199	1-17-97	.268	.217	.293	58	209	33	56	12	6	9	42	18	0	0	1	46	8	1	.512	.325

Pitching

Pitching	B-T	HT	WT	DOB	W	L	ERA	G	GS	CG	SV	IP	H	R	ER	HR	BB	SO	AVG	vLH	vRH	K/9	BB/9
Abreu, Bryan	R-R	6-1	225	4-22-97	0	0	2.70	4	0	0	0	3	1	2	1	0	7	3	.091	.000	.250	8.10	18.90
Bailey, Brandon	R-R	5-10	195	10-19-94	0	0	2.45	5	0	0	0	7	6	2	2	1	3	4	.231	.200	.273	4.91	3.68
Biagini, Joe	R-R	6-5	235	5-29-90	0	0	20.77	4	0	0	0	4	10	10	10	1	4	4	.435	.462	.400	8.31	8.31
Bielak, Brandon	L-R	6-2	208	4-2-96	3	3	6.75	12	6	0	0	32	39	26	24	9	17	26	.305	.229	.397	7.31	4.78
Castellanos, Humberto	R-R	5-11	218	4-3-98	0	1	6.75	8	0	0	0	11	12	8	8	2	5	12	.273	.200	.310	10.13	4.22
De Jong, Chase	L-R	6-4	230	12-29-93	0	1	14.73	3	2	0	0	7	12	12	12	2	4	9	.375	.400	.333	11.05	4.91
Devenski, Chris	R-R	6-3	219	11-13-90	0	1	14.73	4	0	0	0	4	7	6	6	1	3	5	.389	.125	.600	12.27	7.36
Garcia, Luis	R-R	6-1	244	12-13-96	0	1	2.92	5	1	0	0	12	7	4	4	1	5	9	.167	.286	.048	6.57	3.65
2-team total (11 Texas Rangers)					0	3	4.79	16	3	0	0	21	17	13	11	2	14	20	.218	.333	.103	8.71	6.10
Greinke, Zack	R-R	6-2	200	10-21-83	3	3	4.03	12	12	0	0	67	67	30	30	6	9	67	.256	.206	.305	9.00	1.21
James, Josh	R-R	6-3	234	3-8-93	1	0	7.27	13	2	0	0	15	14	14	14	4	17	21	.234	.286	.194	10.90	8.83
Javier, Cristian	R-R	6-1	213	3-26-97	5	2	3.48	12	10	0	0	54	36	21	21	11	18	54	.188	.248	.101	8.94	2.98
McCullers Jr., Lance	L-R	6-1	202	10-2-93	3	3	3.93	11	11	0	0	55	44	29	24	5	20	56	.220	.190	.253	9.16	3.27
Osuna, Roberto	R-R	6-2	217	2-7-95	0	0	2.08	4	0	0	1	4	3	1	1	0	0	3	.188	.333	.000	6.23	0.00
Paredes, Enoli	R-R	5-11	171	9-28-95	3	3	3.05	22	0	0	0	23	18	9	7	1	11	20	.237	.143	.353	8.71	4.79
Peacock, Brad	R-R	6-1	207	2-2-88	0	0	7.71	3	0	0	0	2	3	2	2	0	1	3	.300	.667	.143	11.57	3.86
Perez, Cionel	L-L	5-11	162	4-21-96	0	0	2.84	7	0	0	0	6	7	2	2	0	6	8	.269	.000	.412	11.37	8.53
Pressly, Ryan	R-R	6-2	206	12-15-88	1	3	3.43	23	0	0	12	21	21	10	8	2	7	29	.253	.227	.282	12.43	3.00
Raley, Brooks	L-L	6-3	200	6-29-88	0	1	3.94	17	0	0	1	16	8	7	7	3	4	21	.143	.129	.160	11.81	2.25
Rodriguez, Nivaldo	R-R	6-1	214	4-16-97	0	1	6.23	5	0	0	0	9	15	7	6	3	6	8	.385	.318	.471	8.31	6.23
Sanabria, Carlos	R-R	6-3	165	1-24-97	0	0	9.00	2	0	0	0	2	3	2	2	1	3	2	.333	.400	.250	9.00	13.50
Scrubb, Andre	R-R	6-4	270	1-13-95	1	0	1.90	20	0	0	1	24	15	5	5	1	20	24	.190	.211	.171	9.13	7.61
Sneed, Cy	R-R	6-4	213	10-1-92	0	3	5.71	18	0	0	0	17	22	15	11	3	10	21	.310	.357	.279	10.90	5.19
Taylor, Blake	L-L	6-3	220	8-17-95	2	1	2.18	22	0	0	1	21	13	7	5	2	12	17	.173	.171	.175	7.40	5.23
Urquidy, Jose	R-R	6-0	217	5-1-95	1	1	2.73	5	0	0	0	30	22	9	9	4	8	17	.206	.136	.292	5.16	2.43
Valdez, Framber	L-L	5-11	239	11-19-93	5	3	3.57	11	10	0	0	71	63	32	28	5	16	76	.240	.243	.238	9.68	2.04
Verlander, Justin	R-R	6-5	235	2-20-83	1	0	3.00	1	1	0	0	6	3	2	2	2	1	7	.150	.154	.143	10.50	1.50

Fielding

Catcher	PCT	G	PO	A	E	DP	PB
Garneau	.969	17	120	6	4	1	1
Maldonado	.995	47	375	22	2	0	3
Stubbs	1.000	8	24	0	0	0	0

First Base	PCT	G	PO	A	E	DP
Diaz	1.000	2	10	1	0	0
Gurriel	.998	55	412	50	1	40
Jones	1.000	3	16	0	0	3
Toro	1.000	4	18	3	0	2

Second Base	PCT	G	PO	A	E	DP
Altuve	.979	48	64	126	4	36
Diaz	1.000	10	14	19	0	3
Mayfield	1.000	5	3	6	0	1
Toro	1.000	1	1	1	0	0

Third Base	PCT	G	PO	A	E	DP
Bregman	.979	42	23	72	2	2
Diaz	1.000	3	3	1	0	1
Mayfield	1.000	8	4	15	0	0
Toro	1.000	14	9	22	0	3

Shortstop	PCT	G	PO	A	E	DP
Correa	.995	57	69	142	1	35
Mayfield	1.000	8	3	7	0	0
Straw	.000	1	0	0	0	0

Outfield	PCT	G	PO	A	E	DP
Brantley	1.000	19	39	2	0	1
Diaz	1.000	1	1	0	0	0
Reddick	.978	50	89	1	2	0
Springer	1.000	47	86	0	0	0
Straw	1.000	27	44	0	0	0
Stubbs	1.000	3	2	0	0	0
Tucker	.989	47	89	2	1	1

Kansas City Royals

SEASON IN A SENTENCE: The Royals slogged their way to fourth place in their first year under manager Mike Matheny, but the emergence of some promising young pitchers provided hope for the future.

HIGH POINT: As teams throughout MLB began implementing pay cuts, furloughing employees and releasing minor leaguers en masse in response to the coronavirus pandemic, the Royals announced they would not lay off or furlough any employees and or release any of their minor leaguers. More significant than anything on the field, the decisions elevated the Royals' status to a model organization that takes care of its people and has the right priorities in place.

LOW POINT: The Royals suffered three walkoff losses in a span of four games at the end of August. They blew a 5-2 lead in the ninth inning against the Cardinals on Aug. 26, surrendered a walkoff home run in the bottom of the ninth to Yasmani Grandal against the White Sox on Aug. 28 and allowed another walkoff homer to Chicago's Luis Robert in the bottom of the 10th on Aug. 30.

NOTABLE ROOKIES: Righthander Brady Singer made the Opening Day roster and went 4-5, 4.06 in 12 starts while leading all rookies with 61 strikeouts. Singer's brightest moment occurred Sept. 10 when he came within four outs of a no-hitter against the Indians. Lefthander Kris Bubic joined the rotation despite never pitching above high Class A and posted a 4.32 ERA in 10 starts with 49 strikeouts in 50 innings. Righthander Josh Staumont posted a 2.45 ERA in 26 relief appearances while firing 100-plus mph fastballs and more strikes than expected. Former first-round pick Kyle Zimmer posted a 1.57 ERA in 16 relief appearances. First baseman Ryan McBroom hit six home runs in 36 games to headline the Royals rookie position players.

KEY TRANSACTIONS: The Royals signed third baseman Maikel Franco and reliever Trevor Rosenthal in the offseason and also brought former closer Greg Holland back to the organization on a one-year deal. The Royals hooked up with the Padres twice on trades during the year, sending lefthanded reliever Tim Hill to San Diego in July for outfielder Franchy Cordero and pitching prospect Ronald Bolaños and trading Rosenthal to the Padres in August for outfielder Edward Olivares. They also acquired shortstop prospect Lucius Fox from the Rays for outfielder Brett Phillips, who became Tampa Bay's unlikely Game 4 World Series hero.

OPENING DAY PAYROLL: $35,631,531 (25th)

PLAYERS OF THE YEAR

MAJOR LEAGUE
Salvador Perez
C
.333/.353/.633
11 HR, 32 RBIs

TOP ROOKIE
Brady Singer
RHP
4-5, 4.06 in 12 GS
61 SO in 64.1 IP

Photos: JENNIFER STEWART VIA GETTY IMAGES

ORGANIZATION LEADERS

Batting		*Minimum 100 AB
MAJORS		
* AVG	Salvador Perez	.333
* OPS	Salvador Perez	.986
HR	Salvador Perez	11
RBI	Maikel Franco	38
Pitching		#Minimum 30 IP
MAJORS		
W	Brad Keller	5
# ERA	Brad Keller	2.47
SO	Brady Singer	61
SV	Trevor Rosenthal	7

ORGANIZATION STATISTICS

KANSAS CITY ROYALS
AMERICAN LEAGUE

Batting	B-T	HT	WT	DOB	AVG	vLH	vRH	G	AB	R	H	2B	3B	HR	RBI	BB	HBP	SH	SF	SO	SB	CS	SLG	OBP
Cordero, Franchy	L-R	6-3	226	9-2-94	.211	.000	.250	16	38	7	8	3	0	2	7	4	0	0	0	4	1	0	.447	.286
Dozier, Hunter	R-R	6-4	220	8-22-91	.228	.250	.224	44	158	29	36	4	2	6	12	27	1	0	0	48	4	0	.392	.344
Franco, Maikel	R-R	6-1	225	8-26-92	.278	.318	.268	60	223	23	62	16	0	8	38	16	0	0	4	38	1	0	.457	.321
Gallagher, Cam	R-R	6-3	230	12-6-92	.283	.200	.292	25	53	10	15	5	0	1	3	6	0	1	0	11	0	0	.434	.356

Batting	B-T	HT	WT	DOB	AVG	vLH	vRH	G	AB	R	H	2B	3B	HR	RBI	BB	HBP	SH	SF	SO	SB	CS	SLG	OBP
Gordon, Alex	L-R	6-1	220	2-10-84	.209	.214	.207	50	163	15	34	4	0	4	11	18	3	0	0	37	0	0	.307	.299
Gutierrez, Kelvin	R-R	6-2	220	8-28-94	.111	.000	.143	4	9	0	1	0	0	0	0	3	0	0	0	6	0	0	.111	.333
Heath, Nick	L-L	6-1	190	11-27-93	.154	1.000	.083	15	13	2	2	1	0	0	3	2	1	1	0	6	2	2	.231	.313
Hernandez, Oscar	R-R	6-1	230	7-9-93	.500	.000	.667	4	4	1	2	0	0	0	0	0	0	0	0	1	0	0	.500	.500
Lopez, Nicky	L-R	5-11	175	3-13-95	.201	.136	.224	56	169	15	34	8	0	1	13	18	2	3	0	41	0	5	.266	.286
McBroom, Ryan	R-L	6-3	225	4-9-92	.247	.267	.235	36	81	8	20	3	0	6	10	4	0	0	0	30	0	0	.506	.282
Mejia, Erick	B-R	5-11	155	11-9-94	.071	.000	.143	8	14	1	1	1	0	0	0	0	0	1	0	7	1	0	.143	.071
Merrifield, Whit	R-R	6-1	195	1-24-89	.282	.296	.278	60	248	38	70	12	0	9	30	12	4	0	1	33	12	3	.440	.325
Mondesi, Adalberto	B-R	6-1	200	7-27-95	.256	.321	.235	59	219	33	56	11	3	6	22	11	1	2	0	70	24	8	.416	.294
O'Hearn, Ryan	L-L	6-3	220	7-26-93	.195	.333	.178	42	113	7	22	6	0	2	18	18	0	0	1	37	0	0	.301	.303
Olivares, Edward	R-R	6-2	188	3-6-96	.274	.136	.350	18	62	5	17	1	1	2	7	2	0	0	1	11	0	1	.419	.292
Perez, Salvador	R-R	6-3	250	5-10-90	.333	.257	.357	37	150	22	50	12	0	11	32	3	2	0	1	36	1	0	.633	.353
Phillips, Brett	L-R	6-0	195	5-30-94	.226	.750	.148	18	31	8	7	0	1	1	2	3	0	0	0	8	3	1	.387	.294
2-team total (17 Tampa Bay Rays)					.196	.429	.159	35	51	10	10	0	2	2	5	8	0	0	0	15	6	1	.392	.305
Reynolds, Matt	R-R	6-1	200	12-3-90	.000	.000	.000	3	11	1	0	0	0	0	0	0	0	0	0	7	0	0	.000	.000
Soler, Jorge	R-R	6-4	235	2-25-92	.228	.263	.223	43	149	17	34	8	0	8	24	19	3	0	1	60	0	0	.443	.326
Starling, Bubba	R-R	6-4	215	8-3-92	.169	.083	.229	35	59	5	10	1	0	1	5	4	0	0	1	27	0	0	.237	.219
Viloria, Meibrys	L-R	5-11	225	2-15-97	.190	.500	.118	15	21	1	4	1	0	0	2	1	0	0	0	9	0	0	.238	.292

Pitching	B-T	HT	WT	DOB	W	L	ERA	G	GS	CG	SV	IP	H	R	ER	HR	BB	SO	AVG	vLH	vRH	K/9	BB/9
Adams, Chance	R-R	6-1	215	8-10-94	0	0	9.35	6	0	0	0	9	15	9	9	1	0	6	.375	.350	.400	6.23	0.00
Barlow, Scott	R-R	6-3	215	12-18-92	2	1	4.20	32	0	0	2	30	27	14	14	4	9	39	.239	.228	.250	11.70	2.70
Blewett, Scott	R-R	6-6	245	4-10-96	0	0	6.00	2	0	0	0	3	6	2	2	0	1	4	.400	.500	.364	12.00	3.00
Bolanos, Ronald	R-R	6-2	230	8-23-96	0	2	12.27	2	2	0	0	4	8	7	5	2	3	2	.471	.571	.400	4.91	7.36
Bubic, Kris	L-L	6-3	220	8-19-97	1	6	4.32	10	10	0	0	50	52	29	24	8	22	49	.263	.320	.254	8.82	3.96
Duffy, Danny	L-L	6-3	185	12-21-88	4	4	4.95	12	11	0	0	56	53	33	31	10	22	57	.249	.219	.254	9.11	3.51
Griffin, Foster	R-L	6-3	225	7-27-95	1	0	0.00	1	0	0	0	2	0	0	0	0	1	0	.000	--	.000	5.40	0.00
Hahn, Jesse	R-R	6-5	210	7-30-89	1	0	0.52	18	0	0	3	17	4	1	1	0	8	19	.071	.000	.143	9.87	4.15
Harvey, Matt	R-R	6-4	220	3-27-89	0	3	11.57	7	4	0	0	12	27	15	15	6	5	10	.450	.471	.423	7.71	3.86
Hernandez, Carlos	R-R	6-4	250	3-11-97	0	1	4.91	5	3	0	0	15	19	9	8	4	6	13	.317	.313	.321	7.98	3.68
Holland, Greg	R-R	5-10	205	11-20-85	3	0	1.91	28	0	0	6	28	20	8	6	1	7	31	.200	.179	.227	9.85	2.22
Junis, Jakob	R-R	6-3	220	9-16-92	0	2	6.39	8	6	0	0	25	35	18	18	7	6	19	.333	.354	.300	6.75	2.13
Keller, Brad	R-R	6-5	250	7-27-95	5	3	2.47	9	9	1	0	55	39	16	15	2	17	35	.202	.214	.184	5.76	2.80
Kennedy, Ian	R-R	6-0	210	12-19-84	0	2	9.00	15	1	0	0	14	20	17	14	7	5	15	.323	.259	.371	9.64	3.21
Lopez, Jorge	R-R	6-2	205	2-10-93	0	0	27.00	1	0	0	0	1	3	2	2	0	0	0	.600	.750	.000	0.00	0.00
2-team total (9 Baltimore Orioles)					2	2	6.69	10	6	0	0	39	46	32	29	7	12	28	.297	.286	.308	6.46	2.77
Lovelady, Richard	L-L	6-0	185	7-7-95	0	0	9.00	1	0	0	0	1	1	1	1	1	0	2	.333	--	.333	9.00	9.00
McCarthy, Kevin	R-R	6-3	210	2-22-92	0	0	4.50	5	0	0	0	6	10	3	3	1	2	2	.385	.333	.429	3.00	3.00
Montgomery, Mike	L-L	6-5	220	7-1-89	0	0	5.06	3	1	0	0	5	6	5	3	1	1	4	.286	.000	.333	6.75	1.69
Newberry, Jake	R-R	6-2	205	11-20-94	1	0	4.09	20	0	0	1	22	20	12	10	3	12	24	.256	.267	.250	9.82	4.91
Rosario, Randy	L-L	6-1	210	5-18-94	0	1	8.10	4	0	0	0	3	7	3	3	1	3	4	.438	.400	.455	10.80	8.10
Rosenthal, Trevor	R-R	6-2	230	5-29-90	0	0	3.29	14	0	0	7	14	9	5	5	2	7	21	.188	.111	.286	13.83	4.61
Singer, Brady	R-R	6-5	210	8-4-96	4	5	4.06	12	12	0	0	64	52	29	29	8	23	61	.220	.217	.224	8.53	3.22
Sparkman, Glenn	R-R	6-2	215	5-11-92	0	0	5.40	4	0	0	0	5	9	6	3	0	1	2	.360	.571	.278	3.60	1.80
Speier, Gabe	L-L	5-11	175	4-12-95	0	1	7.94	8	0	0	0	6	9	5	5	1	4	6	.346	.000	.529	9.53	6.35
Staumont, Josh	R-R	6-3	205	12-21-93	2	1	2.45	26	0	0	0	26	20	8	7	2	16	37	.215	.268	.173	12.97	5.61
Zimmer, Kyle	R-R	6-3	225	9-13-91	1	0	1.57	16	1	0	0	23	14	4	4	0	10	26	.175	.150	.200	10.17	3.91
Zuber, Tyler	R-R	5-11	175	6-16-95	1	2	4.09	23	0	0	0	22	15	11	10	4	20	30	.197	.270	.128	12.27	8.18

Fielding

Catcher	PCT	G	PO	A	E	DP	PB
Gallagher	.994	25	156	4	1	0	1
Hernandez	1.000	3	7	2	0	0	0
Perez	1.000	34	295	6	0	1	0
Viloria	.985	15	62	3	1	0	1

First Base	PCT	G	PO	A	E	DP
Dozier	1.000	28	182	9	0	24
Franco	1.000	2	8	0	0	2
McBroom	.985	10	62	2	1	7
Merrifield	1.000	1	3	0	0	1
O'Hearn	.990	27	192	8	2	22
Perez	1.000	3	15	0	0	4

Second Base	PCT	G	PO	A	E	DP
Lopez	.991	53	74	135	2	34
Mejia	.000	1	0	0	0	0
Merrifield	.966	15	20	36	2	11

Third Base	PCT	G	PO	A	E	DP
Dozier	.000	1	0	0	0	0
Franco	.952	51	29	89	6	17
Gutierrez	1.000	3	2	5	0	2
Lopez	.000	2	0	0	0	0
Mejia	.875	4	2	5	1	1
Reynolds	1.000	3	3	2	0	0

Shortstop	PCT	G	PO	A	E	DP
Lopez	1.000	4	2	8	0	1
Mondesi	.983	59	85	144	4	37

Outfield	PCT	G	PO	A	E	DP
Cordero	.882	12	15	0	2	0
Dozier	1.000	20	33	0	0	0
Gordon	1.000	49	81	4	0	1
Heath	1.000	7	7	0	0	0
McBroom	1.000	4	2	0	0	0
Mejia	1.000	2	1	0	0	0
Merrifield	.990	51	95	1	1	0
Olivares	.973	18	36	0	1	0
Phillips	1.000	16	22	1	0	0
Soler	1.000	8	12	0	0	0
Starling	1.000	31	32	0	0	0

Los Angeles Angels

SEASON IN A SENTENCE: A season that started with promise ended short of the postseason for the sixth consecutive year as the pitching staff struggled to a 5.09 ERA, Albert Pujols and Justin Upton continued to struggle and the Angels turned sellers at the trade deadline.

HIGH POINT: On July 25, optimism was still in the air as the Angels cruised past the Athletics, 4-1, thanks to a sterling start from Dylan Bundy and key contributions from David Fletcher, Justin Upton and Andrelton Simmons. The win moved the Angels to 1-1, marking the only time all season they had a .500 record.

LOW POINT: After beating the A's in two consecutive games to move to 7-11 on Aug. 11, the Angels dropped 11 of their next 13 games to fall 11.5 games back in the division with 29 games left in the season, all but ensuring they would be sellers at the trade deadline.

KEY ROOKIES: Jared Walsh excelled in his second big league stint, taking over first base duties for good at the end of August and hitting .293/.324/.646 with nine home runs and 26 RBIs in just 99 at-bats. Jo Adell, one of the game's top prospects, arrived in the big leagues in early August and struggled to the tune of a .161/.212/.266 slash line with three home runs and seven RBIs in 38 games. Lefthander Patrick Sandoval started the season with back-to-back promising starts before allowing 14 earned runs in 12.2 innings over his next three starts, resulting in a demotion to the alternate site in late August. He was better in his return in mid-September, including striking out 12 in 7.1 innings over a two-game span.

KEY TRANSACTIONS: The Angels signed star third baseman Anthony Rendon to a seven-year, $245 million deal in the offseason and he looked well worth the money, posting a .915 OPS and a 151 OPS+ in 52 games. In desperate need of starting pitchers, the Angels dealt for righthander Dylan Bundy from the Orioles for four pitching prospects in December. Bundy turned out to be one of the bright spots for the Angels, posting career highs in multiple categories. The Angels also acquired righthanders Julio Teheran and Matt Andriese, but both struggled to varying degrees. Before the trade deadline, the Angels made a trio of trades, dealing outfielder Brian Goodwin to the Reds for pitching prospects Packy Naughton and Jose Salvador, sending catcher Jason Castro to the Padres for righthander Gerardo Reyes and trading utilityman Tommy La Stella to the A's for middle infielder Franklin Barreto.

OPENING DAY SALARY: $69,282,429 (11th)

PLAYERS OF THE YEAR

MAJOR LEAGUE
Mike Trout
OF
.281/.390/.603
17 HR, 46 RBIs,
168 OPS+

TOP ROOKIE
Jared Walsh
1B
.293/.324/.646
9 HR, 26 RBIs in 32 G

ORGANIZATION LEADERS

Batting		*Minimum 100 AB
MAJORS		
* AVG	David Fletcher	.319
* OPS	Mike Trout	.993
HR	Mike Trout	17
RBI	Mike Trout	46

Pitching		#Minimum 30 IP
MAJORS		
W	Dylan Bundy	6
# ERA	Dylan Bundy	3.29
SO	Dylan Bundy	72
SV	Ty Buttrey	5

ORGANIZATION STATISTICS

LOS ANGELES ANGELS
AMERICAN LEAGUE

Batting	B-T	HT	WT	DOB	AVG	vLH	vRH	G	AB	R	H	2B	3B	HR	RBI	BB	HBP	SH	SF	SO	SB	CS	SLG	OBP
Adell, Jo	R-R	6-3	215	4-8-99	.161	.171	.157	38	124	9	20	4	0	3	7	7	1	0	0	55	0	1	.266	.212
Barreto, Franklin	R-R	5-10	208	2-27-96	.118	.250	.077	6	17	0	2	0	0	0	2	0	1	0	0	8	1	0	.118	.167
2-team total (15 Oakland Athletics)					.074	.083	.067	21	27	5	2	0	0	0	2	0	1	0	0	15	1	0	.074	.107
Bemboom, Anthony	L-R	6-2	200	1-18-90	.208	.111	.267	21	48	9	10	1	0	3	5	7	2	2	1	13	0	1	.417	.328

Batting

Batting	B-T	HT	WT	DOB	AVG	vLH	vRH	G	AB	R	H	2B	3B	HR	RBI	BB	HBP	SH	SF	SO	SB	CS	SLG	OBP
Briceno, Jose	R-R	6-1	225	9-19-92	.200	.000	.250	2	5	0	1	0	0	0	0	1	0	0	0	1	0	0	.200	.333
Castro, Jason	L-R	6-3	215	6-18-87	.192	.167	.200	18	52	5	10	4	0	2	6	10	0	0	0	23	0	0	.385	.323
Fletcher, David	R-R	5-9	185	5-31-94	.319	.348	.304	49	207	31	66	13	0	3	18	20	0	1	2	25	2	1	.425	.376
Goodwin, Brian	L-R	6-0	200	11-2-90	.242	.240	.243	30	95	12	23	7	1	4	17	12	1	0	1	35	1	0	.463	.330
Hermosillo, Michael	R-R	6-0	205	1-17-95	.250	.400	.000	7	8	0	2	0	0	0	2	1	0	0	1	1	1	0	.250	.300
Jones, Jahmai	R-R	6-0	204	8-4-97	.429	.000	.500	3	7	2	3	0	0	0	1	0	0	0	0	2	0	0	.429	.429
La Stella, Tommy	L-R	5-11	180	1-31-89	.273	.185	.306	28	99	15	27	8	0	4	14	15	1	1	1	7	1	0	.475	.371
2-team total (27 Oakland Athletics)					.281	.216	.303	55	196	31	55	14	2	5	25	27	2	1	2	12	1	0	.449	.370
Pujols, Albert	R-R	6-3	235	1-16-80	.224	.231	.218	39	152	15	34	8	0	6	25	9	1	0	1	25	0	0	.395	.270
Rendon, Anthony	R-R	6-1	200	6-6-90	.286	.288	.285	52	189	29	54	11	1	9	31	38	5	0	0	31	0	0	.497	.418
Rengifo, Luis	B-R	5-10	195	2-26-97	.156	.111	.185	33	90	12	14	1	0	1	3	14	0	2	0	26	3	1	.200	.269
Simmons, Andrelton	R-R	6-2	195	9-4-89	.297	.270	.309	30	118	19	35	7	0	0	10	8	1	0	0	16	2	0	.356	.346
Soto, Elliot	R-R	5-9	160	8-21-89	.333	1.000	.200	3	6	2	2	1	0	0	1	0	0	0	0	1	0	0	.500	.429
Stassi, Max	R-R	5-10	200	3-15-91	.278	.295	.261	31	90	12	25	2	0	7	20	11	1	0	3	21	0	0	.533	.352
Thaiss, Matt	L-R	6-0	215	5-6-95	.143	.400	.063	8	21	3	3	0	0	1	1	4	0	0	0	8	0	0	.286	.280
Trout, Mike	R-R	6-2	235	8-7-91	.281	.245	.295	53	199	41	56	9	2	17	46	35	3	0	4	56	1	1	.603	.390
Upton, Justin	R-R	6-1	215	8-25-87	.204	.219	.193	42	147	20	30	5	0	9	22	11	7	0	1	43	0	2	.422	.289
Walsh, Jared	L-L	6-0	210	7-30-93	.293	.324	.277	32	99	19	29	4	2	9	26	5	1	0	3	15	0	0	.646	.324
Ward, Taylor	R-R	6-1	200	12-14-93	.277	.256	.291	34	94	16	26	6	2	0	5	8	0	0	0	28	2	0	.383	.333

Pitching

Pitching	B-T	HT	WT	DOB	W	L	ERA	G	GS	CG	SV	IP	H	R	ER	HR	BB	SO	AVG	vLH	vRH	K/9	BB/9
Andriese, Matt	R-R	6-2	215	8-28-89	2	4	4.50	16	1	0	2	32	21	17	16	5	11	33	.184	.204	.169	9.28	3.09
Bard, Luke	R-R	6-3	200	11-13-90	0	0	6.75	6	0	0	0	5	7	4	4	2	0	7	.304	.250	.333	11.81	0.00
Barnes, Jacob	R-R	6-2	231	4-14-90	0	2	5.50	18	0	0	0	18	19	13	11	1	4	24	.257	.167	.333	12.00	2.00
Barria, Jaime	R-R	6-1	210	7-18-96	1	0	3.62	7	5	0	0	32	27	13	13	3	9	27	.223	.273	.164	7.52	2.51
Bedrosian, Cam	R-R	6-1	225	10-2-91	0	0	2.45	11	0	0	0	15	10	4	4	0	6	11	.196	.192	.200	6.75	3.68
Bemboom, Anthony	L-R	6-2	200	1-18-90	0	0	0.00	1	0	0	0	1	0	0	0	0	1	0	.000	.000	.000	0.00	9.00
Buchter, Ryan	L-L	6-4	232	2-13-87	2	0	4.50	10	0	0	0	6	5	4	3	2	6	8	.217	.273	.167	12.00	9.00
Bundy, Dylan	B-R	6-1	225	11-15-92	6	3	3.29	11	11	1	0	66	51	27	24	5	17	72	.208	.217	.196	9.87	2.33
Buttrey, Ty	L-R	6-6	240	3-31-93	2	3	5.81	27	0	0	5	26	28	18	17	4	9	18	.283	.273	.291	6.15	3.08
Canning, Griffin	R-R	6-2	180	5-11-96	2	3	3.99	11	11	0	0	56	54	29	25	8	23	56	.257	.232	.278	8.95	3.67
Heaney, Andrew	L-L	6-2	200	6-5-91	4	3	4.46	12	12	0	0	67	63	35	33	9	19	70	.246	.268	.236	9.45	2.57
Keller, Kyle	R-R	6-4	205	4-28-93	0	0	7.71	2	0	0	0	2	3	2	2	0	2	1	.273	.000	.375	3.86	7.71
Mayers, Mike	R-R	6-2	220	12-6-91	2	0	2.10	29	0	0	2	30	18	10	7	2	9	43	.162	.100	.235	12.90	2.70
Middleton, Keynan	R-R	6-3	215	9-12-93	0	1	5.25	13	0	0	0	12	12	8	7	2	6	11	.273	.235	.296	8.25	4.50
Milner, Hoby	L-L	6-3	175	1-13-91	0	0	8.10	19	0	0	0	13	13	12	12	5	6	13	.250	.256	.231	8.78	4.05
Ohtani, Shohei	L-R	6-4	210	7-5-94	0	1	37.80	2	2	0	0	2	3	7	7	0	8	3	.375	.500	.333	16.20	43.20
Pena, Felix	R-R	6-2	220	2-25-90	3	0	4.05	25	0	0	2	27	27	12	12	2	8	29	.255	.225	.273	9.79	2.70
Peters, Dillon	L-L	5-11	190	8-31-92	0	0	16.20	1	1	0	0	2	3	4	3	2	0	2	.333	.250	.400	10.80	0.00
Quijada, Jose	L-L	5-11	215	11-9-95	0	1	7.36	6	0	0	0	4	4	3	1	2	6	.375	.200	.667	14.73	4.91
Ramirez, Noe	R-R	6-3	205	12-22-89	1	0	3.00	21	0	0	0	21	15	7	7	2	9	14	.203	.273	.173	6.00	3.86
Robles, Hansel	R-R	6-0	220	8-13-90	0	2	10.26	18	0	0	1	17	19	20	19	4	10	20	.284	.360	.238	10.80	5.40
Rodriguez, Jose	R-R	6-2	175	8-29-95	0	0	0.00	1	0	0	0	2	2	0	0	0	1	0	.286	.500	.200	0.00	5.40
Sandoval, Patrick	L-L	6-3	190	10-18-96	1	5	5.65	9	6	0	0	37	37	26	23	10	12	33	.252	.233	.264	8.10	2.95
Suarez, Jose	L-L	5-10	225	1-3-98	0	2	38.57	2	2	0	0	2	10	10	10	1	5	2	.588	.750	.538	7.71	19.29
Teheran, Julio	R-R	6-2	205	1-27-91	0	4	10.05	10	9	0	0	31	39	35	35	12	16	20	.305	.284	.328	5.74	4.60

Fielding

Catcher	PCT	G	PO	A	E	DP	PB
Bemboom	1.000	20	143	8	0	2	0
Briceno	.941	2	16	0	1	0	1
Castro	1.000	17	131	7	0	0	1
Stassi	.996	31	242	14	1	1	1

First Base	PCT	G	PO	A	E	DP
La Stella	1.000	10	64	10	0	4
Pujols	.989	26	164	20	2	16
Thaiss	1.000	2	14	1	0	2
Walsh	.994	29	157	11	1	10
Ward	1.000	2	2	0	0	0

Second Base	PCT	G	PO	A	E	DP
Barreto	1.000	2	3	4	0	1
Fletcher	.983	15	22	35	1	3
Jones	1.000	2	1	3	0	1
La Stella	.944	15	29	22	3	10
Rengifo	.981	32	40	62	2	11
Soto	1.000	1	1	1	0	0
Thaiss	.750	1	0	3	1	0

Third Base	PCT	G	PO	A	E	DP
Barreto	1.000	2	2	3	0	0
Fletcher	.944	8	6	11	1	2
Rendon	.976	52	48	73	3	7
Rengifo	1.000	1	2	1	0	1
Thaiss	.000	1	0	0	0	0

Shortstop	PCT	G	PO	A	E	DP
Barreto	.667	1	1	1	1	0
Fletcher	.972	27	38	65	3	10
Rengifo	.500	1	0	1	1	0
Simmons	.960	30	25	71	4	10
Soto	1.000	2	2	5	0	2

Outfield	PCT	G	PO	A	E	DP
Adell	.961	38	72	2	3	0
Barreto	1.000	1	3	0	0	0
Fletcher	.500	1	1	0	1	0
Goodwin	1.000	28	57	0	0	0
Hermosillo	1.000	6	13	0	0	0
Thaiss	1.000	1	1	0	0	0
Trout	1.000	52	120	0	0	0
Upton	.970	39	65	0	2	0
Walsh	1.000	2	3	0	0	0
Ward	1.000	32	49	0	0	0

Los Angeles Dodgers

SEASON IN A SENTENCE: Bolstered by the off-season acquisition of Mookie Betts, the Dodgers posted the majors' best record and ended their postseason misery by besting the Rays in the World Series for their first championship since 1988.

HIGH POINT: The Dodgers entered Game 6 of the World Series one win from a title and didn't let the opportunity pass them by. After being stymied by Rays starter Blake Snell for 5.1 innings, they jumped when Rays manager Kevin Cash pulled Snell and quickly turned a 1-0 deficit into a 2-1 lead. Betts added a solo home run in the eighth and, when Julio Urias struck out Willy Adames looking at a fastball to end the ninth, the Dodgers had their first World Series title in 32 years.

LOW POINT: Third baseman Justin Turner was removed in the eighth inning of Game 6 of the World Series after MLB learned he tested positive for COVID-19. Turner initially isolated in the clubhouse, but went back on the field to celebrate after the final out. Turner interacted with teammates and took off his mask during team pictures despite the positive test, an incident that resulted in a stern rebuke from Major League Baseball and led to a league investigation.

NOTABLE ROOKIES: Righthanders Tony Gonsolin (2-2, 2.31) and Dustin May (3-1, 2.57) became full-fledged members of the Dodgers rotation and finished third and fourth among rookies in ERA, respectively. Lefthander Victor Gonzalez logged a 1.33 ERA in 15 relief appearances and was the winning pitcher in the clinching game of the World Series. Third baseman Edwin Rios hit eight home runs in only 32 games and added two more home runs in the playoffs. He was the player that replaced Turner at third base in Game 6.

KEY TRANSACTIONS: The Dodgers made the offseason's biggest splash by acquiring Betts and lefthander David Price from the Red Sox on Feb. 9 in exchange for outfielder Alex Verdugo and prospects Jeter Downs and Connor Wong. The Dodgers signed Betts to a 12-year, $365 mil-lion extension in July. They also acquired hard-throwing righthander Brusdar Graterol from the Twins for righthander Kenta Maeda, a move that bolstered their bullpen in conjunction with signing righthander Blake Treinen to a one-year deal and claiming lefthander Jake McGee off waivers. With May and Gonsolin emerging in the rotation, the Dodgers traded Ross Stripling to the Blue Jays for pitching prospect Kendall Williams at the trade deadline.

OPENING DAY PAYROLL: $105,747,176 (2nd)

PLAYERS OF THE YEAR

MAJOR LEAGUE
Mookie Betts
OF
.292/.366/.592
16 HR, 39 RBIs
47 R, 10 SB

TOP ROOKIE
Tony Gonsolin
RHP
2-2, 2.31 in 9 G
46 SO in 46.2 IP

ORGANIZATION LEADERS

Batting		*Minimum 100 AB
MAJORS		
* AVG	Justin Turner	.307
* OPS	Will Smith	.980
HR	Mookie Betts	16
HR	AJ Pollock	16
RBI	Corey Seager	41

Pitching		#Minimum 30 IP
MAJORS		
W	Clayton Kershaw	6
# ERA	Clayton Kershaw	2.16
SO	Clayton Kershaw	62
SV	Kenley Jansen	11

ORGANIZATION STATISTICS

LOS ANGELES DODGERS
NATIONAL LEAGUE

Batting	B-T	HT	WT	DOB	AVG	vLH	vRH	G	AB	R	H	2B	3B	HR	RBI	BB	HBP	SH	SF	SO	SB	CS	SLG	OBP
Barnes, Austin	R-R	5-10	187	12-28-89	.244	.316	.224	29	86	14	21	3	0	1	9	13	2	2	1	24	3	0	.314	.353
Beaty, Matt	L-R	6-0	215	4-28-93	.220	.333	.205	21	50	8	11	1	0	2	5	2	2	0	0	14	0	0	.360	.278
Bellinger, Cody	L-L	6-4	203	7-13-95	.239	.216	.252	56	213	33	51	10	0	12	30	30	0	0	0	42	6	1	.455	.333
Betts, Mookie	R-R	5-9	180	10-7-92	.292	.200	.323	55	219	47	64	9	1	16	39	24	2	0	1	38	10	2	.562	.366

Batting

Batting	B-T	HT	WT	DOB	AVG	vLH	vRH	G	AB	R	H	2B	3B	HR	RBI	BB	HBP	SH	SF	SO	SB	CS	SLG	OBP
Gore, Terrance	R-R	5-7	160	6-8-91	--	--	--	2	0	0	0	0	0	0	0	0	0	0	0	0	0	0	--	--
Hernandez, Enrique	R-R	5-11	190	8-24-91	.230	.217	.237	48	139	20	32	8	1	5	20	6	2	0	1	31	0	1	.410	.270
Lux, Gavin	L-R	6-2	190	11-23-97	.175	.100	.189	19	63	8	11	2	0	3	8	6	0	0	0	19	1	0	.349	.246
McKinstry, Zach	L-R	6-0	180	4-29-95	.286	--	.286	4	7	1	2	1	0	0	0	0	0	0	0	3	0	0	.429	.286
Muncy, Max	L-R	6-0	215	8-25-90	.192	.239	.169	58	203	36	39	4	0	12	27	39	4	0	2	60	1	0	.389	.331
Pederson, Joc	L-L	6-1	220	4-21-92	.190	.333	.179	43	121	21	23	4	0	7	16	11	5	0	0	34	1	0	.397	.285
Pollock, AJ	R-R	6-1	210	12-5-87	.276	.345	.248	55	196	30	54	9	0	16	34	12	0	0	2	45	2	2	.566	.314
Rios, Edwin	L-R	6-3	220	4-21-94	.250	.313	.233	32	76	13	19	6	0	8	17	4	2	0	1	18	0	0	.645	.301
Ruiz, Keibert	B-R	6-0	225	7-20-98	.250	--	.250	2	8	1	2	0	0	1	1	0	0	0	0	3	0	0	.625	.250
Seager, Corey	L-R	6-4	215	4-27-94	.307	.275	.322	52	212	38	65	12	1	15	41	17	1	0	2	37	1	0	.585	.358
Smith, Will	R-R	5-10	195	3-28-95	.289	.294	.288	37	114	23	33	9	0	8	25	20	2	0	1	22	0	0	.579	.401
Taylor, Chris	R-R	6-1	196	8-29-90	.270	.200	.296	56	185	30	50	10	2	8	32	26	2	1	0	55	3	2	.476	.366
Turner, Justin	R-R	5-11	202	11-23-84	.307	.234	.340	42	150	26	46	9	1	4	23	18	6	0	1	26	1	0	.460	.400

Pitching

Pitching	B-T	HT	WT	DOB	W	L	ERA	G	GS	CG	SV	IP	H	R	ER	HR	BB	SO	AVG	vLH	vRH	K/9	BB/9
Alexander, Scott	L-L	6-2	195	7-10-89	2	0	2.92	13	0	0	0	12	9	6	4	2	9	9	.214	.056	.333	6.57	6.57
Baez, Pedro	R-R	6-0	232	3-11-88	0	0	3.18	18	0	0	2	17	10	8	6	2	7	13	.159	.097	.219	6.88	3.71
Buehler, Walker	R-R	6-2	185	7-28-94	1	0	3.44	8	8	0	0	37	24	18	14	7	11	42	.178	.176	.180	10.31	2.70
Ferguson, Caleb	R-L	6-3	226	7-2-96	2	1	2.89	21	1	0	0	19	16	7	6	4	3	27	.222	.280	.191	13.02	1.45
Floro, Dylan	L-R	6-2	203	12-27-90	3	0	2.59	25	0	0	0	24	23	7	7	1	4	19	.250	.188	.283	7.03	1.48
Gonsolin, Tony	R-R	6-3	205	5-14-94	2	2	2.31	9	8	0	0	47	32	13	12	2	7	46	.193	.179	.207	8.87	1.35
Gonzalez, Victor	L-L	6-0	180	11-16-95	3	0	1.33	15	1	0	0	20	13	3	3	0	2	23	.176	.143	.205	10.18	0.89
Graterol, Brusdar	R-R	6-1	265	8-26-98	1	2	3.09	23	2	0	0	23	18	9	8	1	3	13	.225	.360	.164	5.01	1.16
Jansen, Kenley	B-R	6-5	265	9-30-87	3	1	3.33	27	0	0	11	24	19	11	9	2	9	33	.211	.159	.261	12.21	3.33
Kelly, Joe	R-R	6-1	174	6-9-88	0	0	1.80	12	1	0	0	10	8	3	2	0	7	9	.235	.235	.235	8.10	6.30
Kershaw, Clayton	L-L	6-4	225	3-19-88	6	2	2.16	10	10	0	0	58	41	18	14	8	8	62	.194	.180	.199	9.57	1.23
Kolarek, Adam	L-L	6-3	215	1-14-89	3	0	0.95	20	0	0	1	19	11	2	2	1	4	13	.164	.077	.286	6.16	1.89
May, Dustin	R-R	6-6	180	9-6-97	3	1	2.57	12	10	0	0	56	45	18	16	9	16	44	.220	.242	.198	7.07	2.57
McGee, Jake	L-L	6-4	229	8-6-86	3	1	2.66	24	0	0	0	20	14	6	6	2	3	33	.187	.304	.135	14.61	1.33
Santana, Dennis	R-R	6-2	190	4-12-96	1	2	5.29	12	0	0	0	17	15	11	10	4	7	18	.234	.143	.279	9.53	3.71
Sborz, Josh	R-R	6-3	215	12-17-93	0	0	2.08	4	0	0	0	4	2	1	1	1	1	2	.133	.167	.111	4.15	2.08
Stripling, Ross	R-R	6-3	220	11-23-89	3	1	5.61	7	7	0	0	34	38	26	21	11	12	27	.279	.225	.338	7.22	2.94
Treinen, Blake	R-R	6-5	225	6-30-88	3	3	3.86	27	0	0	1	26	23	15	11	1	8	22	.240	.233	.242	7.71	2.81
Urias, Julio	L-L	6-0	225	8-12-96	3	0	3.27	11	10	0	0	55	45	20	20	5	18	45	.220	.137	.247	7.36	2.95
White, Mitch	R-R	6-3	210	12-28-94	1	0	0.00	2	0	0	0	3	1	0	0	0	1	2	.100	.000	.200	6.00	3.00
Wood, Alex	R-L	6-4	215	1-12-91	0	1	6.39	9	2	0	0	13	17	11	9	2	6	15	.304	.300	.306	10.66	4.26

Fielding

Catcher	PCT	G	PO	A	E	DP	PB
Barnes	.992	28	245	6	2	0	0
Ruiz	1.000	2	12	1	0	0	0
Smith	1.000	34	270	10	0	3	1

First Base	PCT	G	PO	A	E	DP
Beaty	1.000	13	68	3	0	8
Bellinger	1.000	19	143	7	0	11
Hernandez	1.000	2	9	1	0	0
Muncy	.988	35	232	14	3	18
Rios	1.000	6	41	1	0	4

Second Base	PCT	G	PO	A	E	DP
Betts	1.000	1	0	2	0	0
Hernandez	.960	30	44	75	5	19
Lux	.958	18	22	46	3	11
McKinstry	.000	1	0	0	0	0
Muncy	1.000	12	10	19	0	5
Taylor	.973	13	12	24	1	3

Third Base	PCT	G	PO	A	E	DP
Muncy	.975	16	6	33	1	5
Rios	.939	21	9	22	2	2
Turner	.952	32	17	63	4	7

Shortstop	PCT	G	PO	A	E	DP
Hernandez	1.000	2	3	3	0	1
Seager	.952	43	46	113	8	16
Taylor	1.000	20	12	40	0	4

Outfield	PCT	G	PO	A	E	DP
Beaty	1.000	2	3	0	0	0
Bellinger	.990	39	103	1	1	0
Betts	.966	52	113	1	4	0
Gore	--	1	0	0	0	0
Hernandez	1.000	17	21	0	0	0
Kolarek	--	1	0	0	0	0
McKinstry	1.000	1	3	0	0	0
Pederson	1.000	29	46	2	0	1
Pollock	.984	42	60	0	1	0
Taylor	.978	24	43	2	1	1

Miami Marlins

SEASON IN A SENTENCE: The Marlins suffered a widespread COVID-19 outbreak just four days into the season, but patched together a makeshift roster and managed to reach the playoffs for the first time since 2003.

HIGH POINT: On the verge of a postseason berth, the Marlins overcame a blown three-run lead and beat the Yankees 4-3 in 10 innings on Sept. 25 to clinch their first playoff appearance in 17 years. Jesus Aguilar lifted the tiebreaking sacrifice fly in the top of the 10th inning and Brandon Kintzler got DJ LeMaheiu to ground into a game-ending double play with the bases loaded in the bottom of the inning to end it.

LOW POINT: The Marlins played July 26 against the Phillies knowing four of their players had tested positive for COVID-19. Within days, the outbreak grew to affect 18 Marlins players and a visiting clubhouse attendant in Philadelphia. The Marlins' next eight games were postponed and the entire MLB schedule was reshuffled as a result of the outbreak.

NOTABLE ROOKIES: Eighteen different players made their major league debut for the Marlins with the team in desperate need of healthy players following their coronavirus outbreak. Righthander Sixto Sanchez went 3-2, 3.46 in the regular season and started and won the clinching game of the Wild Card Series against the Cubs. Lefthanders Daniel Castano (1-2, 3.03), Trevor Rogers (1-2, 6.11) and Braxton Garrett (1-1, 5.87) all took turns in the rotation, as did righthander Humberto Mejia despite having never pitched above high Class A. Infielder Jazz Chisholm, first baseman Lewin Diaz and outfielders Monte Harrison and Jesus Sanchez were among the top position player prospects who debuted. Second baseman Eddy Alvarez, a former Olympic speed skater, made his debut at age 30 and played in 12 games.

KEY TRANSACTIONS: The Marlins bulked up their roster by trading for Jonathan Villar, claim-ing Jesus Aguilar off waivers and signing Corey Dickerson and Francisco Cervelli in the offseason. They signed, claimed or traded for 12 players in 19 days following their outbreak. With the team contending at the trade deadline, they acquired outfielder Starling Marte from the D-backs in exchange for lefthander Caleb Smith, pitching prospect Julio Frias and Mejia, but also traded Villar to the Blue Jays for outfield prospect Griffin Conine, the son of Marlins legend Jeff Conine.

OPENING DAY PAYROLL: $28,560,819 (28th)

PLAYERS OF THE YEAR

MAJOR LEAGUE

Jesus Aguilar
1B
.277/.352/.457
8 HR, 34 RBIs

TOP ROOKIE

Sixto Sanchez
RHP
3-2, 3.46 in 7 GS
33 SO in 39 IP

ORGANIZATION LEADERS

Batting		*Minimum 100 AB
MAJORS		
* AVG	Miguel Rojas	.304
* OPS	Miguel Rojas	.888
HR	Brian Anderson	11
RBI	Brian Anderson	38

Pitching		#Minimum 30 IP
MAJORS		
W	Pablo Lopez	6
# ERA	Sandy Alcantara	3.00
SO	Pablo Lopez	59
SV	Brandon Kintzler	12

ORGANIZATION STATISTICS

MIAMI MARLINS
NATIONAL LEAGUE

Batting	B-T	HT	WT	DOB	AVG	vLH	vRH	G	AB	R	H	2B	3B	HR	RBI	BB	HBP	SH	SF	SO	SB	CS	SLG	OBP
Aguilar, Jesus	R-R	6-3	277	6-30-90	.277	.321	.259	51	188	31	52	10	0	8	34	23	1	0	4	40	0	1	.457	.352
Alfaro, Jorge	R-R	6-3	230	6-11-93	.226	.258	.210	31	93	12	21	2	0	3	16	4	3	0	0	36	2	0	.344	.280
Alvarez, Eddy	B-R	5-9	185	1-30-90	.189	.000	.226	12	37	6	7	1	0	0	2	3	1	0	0	16	2	0	.216	.268
Anderson, Brian	R-R	6-3	208	5-19-93	.255	.286	.243	59	200	27	51	7	1	11	38	22	6	0	1	66	0	0	.465	.345
Berti, Jon	R-R	5-10	190	1-22-90	.258	.220	.278	39	120	21	31	5	0	2	14	23	3	2	1	37	9	2	.350	.388

Batting

Batting	B-T	HT	WT	DOB	AVG	vLH	vRH	G	AB	R	H	2B	3B	HR	RBI	BB	HBP	SH	SF	SO	SB	CS	SLG	OBP
Brinson, Lewis	R-R	6-5	212	5-8-94	.226	.260	.196	47	106	14	24	6	0	3	12	6	0	0	0	30	4	0	.368	.268
Cervelli, Francisco	R-R	6-0	220	3-6-86	.245	.211	.265	16	53	10	13	2	0	3	7	8	1	0	0	14	1	0	.453	.355
Chisholm, Jazz	L-R	5-11	184	2-1-98	.161	.286	.119	21	56	8	9	1	1	2	6	5	1	0	0	19	2	2	.321	.242
Cooper, Garrett	R-R	6-5	235	12-25-90	.283	.350	.250	34	120	20	34	8	0	6	20	11	2	0	0	31	0	0	.500	.353
Diaz, Isan	L-R	5-11	201	5-27-96	.182	.667	.105	7	22	3	4	0	0	0	1	0	0	0	0	7	0	0	.182	.182
Diaz, Lewin	L-L	6-4	217	11-19-96	.154	.000	.222	14	39	2	6	2	0	0	3	2	0	0	0	12	0	0	.205	.195
Dickerson, Corey	L-R	6-1	200	5-22-89	.258	.212	.275	52	194	25	50	5	1	7	17	15	0	0	0	35	1	1	.402	.311
Forsythe, Logan	R-R	6-1	205	1-14-87	.118	.214	.050	12	34	2	4	1	0	1	2	4	0	0	0	12	0	0	.235	.211
Harrison, Monte	R-R	6-3	225	8-10-95	.170	.111	.207	32	47	8	8	1	0	1	3	4	0	0	0	26	6	0	.255	.235
Joyce, Matt	L-R	6-2	194	8-3-84	.252	.154	.263	46	127	16	32	4	0	2	14	20	0	0	1	41	1	0	.331	.351
Lavarnway, Ryan	R-R	6-3	239	8-7-87	.364	.000	.444	5	11	0	4	0	0	0	0	0	0	0	0	2	0	0	.364	.364
Marte, Starling	R-R	6-1	195	10-9-88	.245	.212	.260	28	106	13	26	6	0	4	13	2	4	0	0	22	5	0	.415	.286
2-team total (33 Arizona Diamondbacks)					.281	.290	.277	64	228	36	64	14	1	6	27	12	9	0	1	41	10	2	.430	.340
Navarreto, Brian	R-R	6-0	237	12-29-94	.400	.000	.500	2	5	0	2	0	0	0	2	0	0	0	0	1	0	0	.400	.400
Ramirez, Harold	R-R	5-10	232	9-6-94	.200	.250	.167	3	10	2	2	0	0	0	1	1	0	0	0	2	0	1	.200	.273
Rodriguez, Sean	R-R	6-0	199	4-26-85	.154	.250	.111	4	13	0	2	0	0	0	0	0	0	0	0	6	0	0	.154	.154
Rojas, Miguel	R-R	6-0	188	2-24-89	.304	.500	.225	40	125	20	38	10	1	4	20	16	2	0	0	18	5	1	.496	.392
Sanchez, Jesus	L-R	6-3	222	10-7-97	.040	.000	.056	10	25	1	1	1	0	0	2	4	0	0	0	11	0	0	.080	.172
Sierra, Magneuris	L-L	5-11	178	4-7-96	.250	.250	.250	19	44	8	11	3	1	0	7	5	1	2	1	9	4	1	.364	.333
Villar, Jonathan	B-R	6-0	233	5-2-91	.259	.279	.247	30	116	10	30	4	0	2	9	10	0	1	1	32	9	5	.345	.315
Wallach, Chad	R-R	6-2	246	11-4-91	.227	.500	.147	15	44	4	10	3	0	0	3	2	1	0	0	12	0	0	.364	.277

Pitching

Pitching	B-T	HT	WT	DOB	W	L	ERA	G	GS	CG	SV	IP	H	R	ER	HR	BB	SO	AVG	vLH	vRH	K/9	BB/9
Alcantara, Sandy	R-R	6-5	200	9-7-95	3	2	3.00	7	7	0	0	42	35	22	14	4	15	39	.226	.268	.190	8.36	3.21
Bleier, Richard	L-L	6-3	215	4-16-87	1	1	2.63	19	0	0	0	14	13	6	4	0	4	7	.250	.161	.381	4.61	2.63
Boxberger, Brad	R-R	5-10	211	5-27-88	1	0	3.00	23	0	0	0	18	17	7	6	3	8	18	.246	.192	.279	9.00	4.00
Brigham, Jeff	R-R	6-0	195	2-16-92	0	0	9.00	1	0	0	0	1	2	1	1	0	0	0	.400	.500	.333	0.00	0.00
Castano, Daniel	L-L	6-3	231	9-17-94	1	2	3.03	7	6	0	0	30	30	12	10	3	11	12	.263	.313	.244	3.64	3.34
Dugger, Robert	R-R	6-0	198	7-3-95	0	0	12.66	4	1	0	0	11	21	16	15	5	3	4	.396	.522	.300	3.38	2.53
Eibner, Brett	R-R	6-4	215	12-2-88	0	0	13.50	3	0	0	0	3	7	7	5	2	4	4	.412	.500	.333	10.80	10.80
Forsythe, Logan	R-R	6-1	205	1-14-87	0	0	9.00	1	0	0	0	1	2	1	1	0	1	0	.500	.333	1.000	0.00	9.00
Garcia, Yimi	R-R	6-2	228	8-18-90	3	0	0.60	14	0	0	1	15	9	1	1	0	5	19	.164	.217	.125	11.40	3.00
Garrett, Braxton	L-L	6-2	202	8-5-97	1	1	5.87	2	2	0	0	8	8	6	5	3	5	8	.276	.400	.250	9.39	5.87
Guzman, Jorge	R-R	6-1	246	1-28-96	0	0	18.00	1	0	0	0	1	2	2	2	1	0	0	.400	.500	.333	0.00	9.00
Hernandez, Eliezer	R-R	6-0	214	5-3-95	1	0	3.16	6	6	0	0	26	21	10	9	5	5	34	.212	.240	.184	11.92	1.75
Holloway, Jordan	R-R	6-6	230	6-13-96	0	0	0.00	1	0	0	0	2	0	0	0	1	0	.667	.500	1.000	0.00	27.00
Hoyt, James	R-R	6-6	230	9-30-86	2	0	1.23	24	0	0	0	15	9	2	2	1	8	20	.173	.267	.135	12.27	4.91
Kintzler, Brandon	R-R	5-10	200	8-1-84	2	3	2.22	24	0	0	12	24	21	7	6	3	11	14	.236	.300	.184	5.18	4.07
Leibrandt, Brandon	L-L	6-4	190	12-13-92	0	0	2.00	5	0	0	0	9	3	2	2	0	7	3	.103	.118	.083	3.00	7.00
Lopez, Pablo	L-R	6-4	225	3-7-96	6	4	3.61	11	11	0	0	57	50	27	23	4	18	59	.230	.269	.184	9.26	2.83
Mejia, Humberto	R-R	6-4	235	3-3-97	0	2	5.40	3	3	0	0	10	13	8	6	3	6	11	.310	.304	.316	9.90	5.40
Moran, Brian	L-L	6-4	225	9-30-88	1	0	12.27	5	0	0	0	4	5	5	5	1	6	3	.313	.333	.300	14.73	14.73
Morin, Mike	R-R	6-4	220	5-3-91	1	0	0.00	3	0	0	0	4	1	0	0	0	1	2	.091	.250	.000	4.50	2.25
Neidert, Nick	R-R	6-1	202	11-10-96	0	0	5.40	4	0	0	0	8	10	5	5	1	2	4	.313	.400	.273	4.32	2.16
Quezada, Johan	R-R	6-9	255	8-25-94	0	0	9.00	3	0	0	0	3	4	3	3	1	1	2	.400	.400	.333	6.00	3.00
Rogers, Trevor	L-L	6-5	217	11-13-97	1	2	6.11	7	7	0	0	28	32	20	19	5	13	39	.283	.265	.291	12.54	4.18
Sanchez, Sixto	R-R	6-0	234	7-29-98	3	2	3.46	7	7	1	0	39	36	15	15	3	11	33	.250	.232	.267	7.62	2.54
Shafer, Justin	R-R	6-2	205	9-18-92	0	0	12.71	5	0	0	0	6	8	8	8	2	6	3	.333	.600	.143	7.94	6.35
Sharp, Sterling	R-R	6-3	182	5-30-95	0	0	10.13	4	0	0	0	5	7	6	6	1	5	3	.304	.222	.357	5.06	8.44
Smith, Caleb	R-L	6-2	206	7-31-91	1	1	3.00	1	1	0	0	3	1	1	1	1	6	2	.111	.333	.000	9.00	18.00
2-team total (4 Arizona Diamondbacks)					0	0	2.57	5	4	0	0	14	6	4	4	3	12	15	.125	.143	.118	9.64	7.71
Smith, Josh A.	R-R	6-2	210	8-7-87	1	1	6.84	16	1	0	1	26	33	21	20	3	11	18	.314	.293	.328	6.15	3.76
Smith, Josh D.	L-L	6-2	200	10-11-89	0	0	10.80	2	0	0	0	2	2	2	2	1	1	4	.286	.250	.333	21.60	5.40
Stanek, Ryne	R-R	6-4	226	7-26-91	0	0	7.20	9	0	0	0	10	11	8	8	3	8	11	.275	.556	.194	9.90	7.20
Tarpley, Stephen	R-L	6-0	202	2-17-93	2	2	9.00	12	0	0	1	11	11	12	11	2	8	11	.282	.316	.250	9.00	6.55
Tinoco, Jesus	R-R	6-4	258	4-30-95	0	0	0.00	3	0	0	0	5	0	0	0	3	3	.000	.000	.000	5.40	5.40
2-team total (3 Colorado Rockies)					0	0	1.04	6	0	0	0	9	3	1	1	0	7	6	.120	.133	.100	6.23	7.27
Urena, Jose	R-R	6-2	208	9-12-91	0	3	5.40	5	5	0	0	23	22	15	14	4	13	15	.247	.406	.158	5.79	5.01
Venditte, Pat	L-B	6-0	186	6-30-85	0	0	0.00	3	0	0	0	4	1	0	0	0	0	5	.077	.125	.000	10.38	0.00
Vesia, Alex	L-L	6-1	209	4-11-96	0	1	18.69	4	0	0	0	4	7	10	9	3	7	5	.350	.400	.300	10.38	14.54
Vincent, Nick	R-R	5-10	185	7-12-86	1	2	4.43	21	0	0	3	22	23	11	11	5	6	17	.271	.219	.302	6.85	2.42
Yamamoto, Jordan	R-R	6-0	185	5-11-96	0	1	18.26	4	3	0	0	11	27	24	23	8	7	13	.458	.500	.432	10.32	5.56

Fielding

Catcher	PCT	G	PO	A	E	DP	PB
Alfaro	.990	29	182	9	2	0	4
Cervelli	.992	16	124	3	1	0	2
Lavarnway	1.000	5	35	1	0	0	0
Navarreto	1.000	2	13	1	0	0	0
Wallach	1.000	15	110	4	0	1	0

First Base	PCT	G	PO	A	E	DP
Aguilar	.989	31	243	20	3	36
Anderson	1.000	1	6	0	0	1
Cooper	1.000	15	108	11	0	10
Diaz	1.000	11	88	6	0	10
Forsythe	1.000	4	23	1	0	1
Rojas	.000	1	0	0	0	0

Second Base	PCT	G	PO	A	E	DP
Alvarez	1.000	9	10	13	0	5
Anderson	.000	1	0	0	0	0
Berti	.988	21	33	46	1	15
Chisholm	1.000	13	18	25	0	10
Diaz	1.000	7	11	18	0	6
Forsythe	1.000	6	6	13	0	4
Rodriguez	1.000	3	3	4	0	1
Villar	.941	12	20	28	3	7

Third Base	PCT	G	PO	A	E	DP
Aguilar	.000	1	0	0	0	0
Alvarez	1.000	3	0	6	0	0
Anderson	.944	56	32	119	9	11
Berti	1.000	5	3	5	0	0
Rojas	1.000	1	0	1	0	0

Shortstop	PCT	G	PO	A	E	DP
Alvarez	1.000	1	2	5	0	1
Berti	1.000	2	1	7	0	1
Chisholm	.962	9	7	18	1	3

Outfield	PCT	G	PO	A	E	DP
Alfaro	.000	1	0	0	1	0
Berti	1.000	16	20	1	0	1
Brinson	.984	46	63	0	1	0
Dickerson	.970	46	62	3	2	0
Harrison	1.000	28	42	0	0	0
Joyce	.952	36	40	0	2	0
Marte	.981	28	52	1	1	0
Ramirez	1.000	3	4	0	0	0
Rodriguez	--	1	0	0	0	0
Sanchez	.944	10	17	0	1	0
Sierra	1.000	17	41	1	0	1
Villar	.500	2	1	0	1	0

MIAMI MARLINS

Milwaukee Brewers

SEASON IN A SENTENCE: The expanded play-offs allowed the Brewers to finish 29-31, never spend a day above .500 and still make the playoffs, but it was a swift exit in a 2-0 sweep against the Dodgers in the Wild Card Series.

HIGH POINT: After sinking to 21-25 on Sept. 15, the Brewers bludgeoned the Cardinals with an 18-3 victory the next day, then won five of their next eight games to get back to .500 at 27-27 with six games left in the season. Righthanders Brandon Woodruff and Corbin Burnes anchored the starting rotation, with Woodruff ranking ninth in the National League in ERA (3.05) and seventh in strikeouts (91) over 73.2 innings. Burnes was one of the best pitchers in the NL and posted a 2.11 ERA but didn't qualify for the league leaders. A strained left oblique he suffered at the end of September kept him out of the postseason.

LOW POINT: The Pirates were the worst team in baseball, but after the Brewers lost two of three games to the Twins, they went on to lose three straight in Pittsburgh, dropping them to 11-15 on Aug. 23. Throughout the season, the Brewers' offense struggled, ranking 26th in the majors in runs scored. Steep declines in production from Christian Yelich, Ryan Braun and Keston Hiura hurt Milwaukee's offense, as did the departures of Yasmani Grandal, Eric Thames and Mike Moustakas.

NOTABLE ROOKIES: It's difficult for relievers to accumulate enough innings to put themselves in the Rookie of the Year picture, but in a 60-game season, Devin Williams' performance was so spectacular that he forced his way into that discussion as one of the game's elite bullpen arms and ended up winning NL Rookie of the Year. Williams averaged a remarkable 17.7 K/9, with a 53-9 K-BB mark in 22 innings and an ERA of 0.33 on the strength of a devastating changeup.

KEY TRANSACTIONS: One of Milwaukee's first big moves after the 2019 season was trading outfielder Trent Grisham and righthander Zach Davies to the Padres for second baseman Luis Urias and lefthander Eric Lauer. While Urias and Lauer struggled, Grisham was one of the top outfielders in the NL in his age-23 season. With the Brewers struggling to score runs, his bat would have been a useful boost. Davies was also missed, as he went 7-4, 2.73 with the Padres. At the Aug. 31 trade deadline, the Brewers sent reliever David Phelps to the Phillies for righthanders Brandon Ramey, Israel Puello and Juan Geraldo.

OPENING DAY PAYROLL: $39,405,276 (23rd)

PLAYERS OF THE YEAR

MAJOR LEAGUE
Corbin Burnes
RHP
4-1, 2.11, 12 G
88 SO in 59.2 IP

TOP ROOKIE
Devin Williams
RHP
4-1, 0.33, 22 G
17.7 K/9, 2.7 H/9

ORGANIZATION LEADERS

Batting		*Minimum 100 AB
MAJORS		
* AVG	Orlando Arcia	.260
* OPS	Jedd Gyorko	.838
HR	Keston Hiura	13
RBI	Keston Hiura	32
Pitching		#Minimum 30 IP
MAJORS		
W	Brett Anderson	4
W	Corbin Burnes	4
W	Devin Williams	4
# ERA	Corbin Burnes	2.11
SO	Brandon Woodruff	91
SV	Josh Hader	13

ORGANIZATION STATISTICS

MILWAUKEE BREWERS
NATIONAL LEAGUE

Batting	B-T	HT	WT	DOB	AVG	vLH	vRH	G	AB	R	H	2B	3B	HR	RBI	BB	HBP	SH	SF	SO	SB	CS	SLG	OBP
Arcia, Orlando	R-R	6-0	187	8-4-94	.260	.191	.286	59	173	22	45	10	1	5	20	14	1	0	1	32	2	0	.416	.317
Braun, Ryan	R-R	6-2	205	11-17-83	.233	.233	.233	39	129	14	30	7	1	8	26	7	2	0	1	27	1	0	.488	.281
Cain, Lorenzo	R-R	6-2	214	4-13-86	.333	.500	.286	5	18	4	6	1	0	0	2	3	0	0	0	2	0	0	.389	.429
Gamel, Ben	L-L	5-11	177	5-17-92	.237	.238	.237	40	114	13	27	8	1	3	10	13	0	0	0	39	0	2	.404	.315

Batting	B-T	HT	WT	DOB	AVG	vLH	vRH	G	AB	R	H	2B	3B	HR	RBI	BB	HBP	SH	SF	SO	SB	CS	SLG	OBP
Garcia, Avisail	R-R	6-4	250	6-12-91	.238	.291	.214	53	181	20	43	10	0	2	15	20	6	0	0	49	1	3	.326	.333
Gyorko, Jedd	R-R	5-10	205	9-23-88	.248	.267	.236	42	117	19	29	3	0	9	17	15	1	0	2	38	0	0	.504	.333
Healy, Ryon	R-R	6-4	230	1-10-92	.143	.000	.500	4	7	0	1	0	0	0	0	0	0	0	0	2	0	0	.143	.143
Hiura, Keston	R-R	6-0	202	8-2-96	.212	.241	.202	59	217	30	46	4	0	13	32	16	11	0	2	85	3	2	.410	.297
Holt, Brock	L-R	5-10	180	6-11-88	.100	.000	.103	16	30	1	3	0	0	0	1	4	1	0	1	9	0	0	.100	.222
2-team total (20 Washington Nationals)					.211	.357	.185	36	95	12	20	6	0	0	5	9	1	0	1	24	1	0	.274	.283
Mathias, Mark	R-R	6-0	200	8-2-94	.278	.238	.333	16	36	2	10	3	0	0	4	0	0	0	0	7	1	0	.361	.278
Morrison, Logan	L-L	6-3	245	8-25-87	.120	.000	.136	9	25	3	3	1	0	1	2	3	0	0	0	8	0	0	.280	.214
Narvaez, Omar	L-R	5-11	220	2-10-92	.176	.211	.169	40	108	8	19	4	0	2	10	16	2	0	0	39	0	0	.269	.294
Nottingham, Jacob	R-R	6-2	220	4-3-95	.188	.286	.147	20	48	8	9	1	0	4	13	5	1	0	0	20	0	0	.458	.278
Peterson, Jace	L-R	6-0	215	5-9-90	.200	.000	.209	26	45	6	9	1	0	2	5	15	0	0	1	20	1	0	.356	.393
Pina, Manny	R-R	6-0	222	6-5-87	.231	.211	.250	15	39	4	9	1	0	2	5	3	3	0	0	11	0	0	.410	.333
Smoak, Justin	B-L	6-4	220	12-5-86	.186	.167	.191	33	113	14	21	7	0	5	15	10	2	0	1	40	0	0	.381	.262
2-team total (3 San Francisco Giants)					.176	.167	.179	36	119	14	21	7	0	5	16	10	2	0	1	42	0	0	.361	.250
Sogard, Eric	L-R	5-10	180	5-22-86	.209	.182	.212	43	115	10	24	5	0	1	10	11	1	0	1	20	0	0	.278	.281
Taylor, Tyrone	R-R	6-0	194	1-22-94	.237	.250	.227	22	38	6	9	4	0	2	6	2	1	0	0	8	0	0	.500	.293
Urias, Luis	R-R	5-9	186	6-3-97	.239	.265	.227	41	109	11	26	4	1	0	11	10	1	0	0	32	2	2	.294	.308
Vogelbach, Daniel	L-R	6-0	270	12-17-92	.328	.167	.346	19	58	13	19	2	0	4	12	8	1	0	0	18	0	0	.569	.418
Yelich, Christian	L-R	6-3	195	12-5-91	.205	.293	.169	58	200	39	41	7	1	12	22	46	1	0	0	76	4	2	.430	.356

Pitching	B-T	HT	WT	DOB	W	L	ERA	G	GS	CG	SV	IP	H	R	ER	HR	BB	SO	AVG	vLH	vRH	K/9	BB/9
Anderson, Brett	L-L	6-4	230	2-1-88	4	4	4.21	10	10	0	0	47	50	24	22	6	10	32	.270	.257	.273	6.13	1.91
Arcia, Orlando	R-R	6-0	187	8-4-94	0	0	18.00	2	0	0	0	2	4	4	4	1	1	0	.444	.333	.667	0.00	4.50
Bickford, Phil	R-R	6-4	200	7-10-95	0	0	36.00	1	0	0	0	1	4	4	4	0	0	2	.571	.500	.667	18.00	0.00
Black, Ray	R-R	6-3	230	6-26-90	0	0	3.00	3	0	0	0	3	2	1	1	0	3	3	.182	.250	.143	9.00	9.00
Burnes, Corbin	R-R	6-3	225	10-22-94	4	1	2.11	12	9	0	0	60	37	15	14	2	24	88	.174	.200	.140	13.27	3.62
Claudio, Alex	L-L	6-3	188	1-31-92	0	0	4.26	20	0	0	1	19	18	10	9	2	6	15	.243	.212	.268	7.11	2.84
Feyereisen, J.P.	R-R	6-2	215	2-7-93	0	0	5.79	6	0	0	0	9	4	6	6	3	5	7	.138	.167	.091	6.75	4.82
Grimm, Justin	R-R	6-3	210	8-16-88	0	0	17.36	4	0	0	0	5	9	9	9	4	4	6	.391	.556	.286	11.57	7.71
Gyorko, Jedd	R-R	5-10	205	9-23-88	0	0	0.00	1	0	0	0	1	1	0	0	0	0	0	.250	.000	.000	0.00	0.00
Hader, Josh	L-L	6-3	180	4-7-94	1	2	3.79	21	0	0	13	19	8	8	8	3	10	31	.123	.154	.115	14.68	4.74
Houser, Adrian	R-R	6-3	222	2-2-93	1	6	5.30	12	11	0	0	56	63	41	33	8	21	44	.285	.336	.219	7.07	3.38
Knebel, Corey	R-R	6-3	224	11-26-91	0	0	6.08	15	0	0	0	13	15	9	9	4	8	15	.278	.290	.261	10.13	5.40
Lauer, Eric	R-L	6-3	228	6-3-95	0	2	13.09	4	2	0	0	11	17	16	16	2	9	12	.347	.333	.351	9.82	7.36
Lindblom, Josh	R-R	6-4	240	6-15-87	2	4	5.16	12	10	0	0	45	42	26	26	6	16	52	.244	.284	.195	10.32	3.18
Peralta, Freddy	R-R	5-11	199	6-4-96	3	1	3.99	15	1	0	0	29	22	14	13	2	12	47	.204	.186	.224	14.42	3.68
Perdomo, Angel	L-L	6-8	265	5-7-94	0	0	20.25	3	0	0	0	3	3	7	6	0	7	5	.273	.250	.286	16.88	23.63
Phelps, David	R-R	6-2	198	10-9-86	2	3	2.77	12	0	0	0	13	7	5	4	2	2	20	.156	.133	.200	13.85	1.38
2-team total (10 Philadelphia Phillies)					2	4	6.53	22	0	0	0	21	19	16	15	7	5	31	.241	.190	.297	13.50	2.18
Rasmussen, Drew	R-R	6-1	211	7-27-95	1	0	5.87	12	0	0	0	15	17	10	10	3	9	21	.274	.375	.167	12.33	5.28
Suter, Brent	L-L	6-4	213	8-29-89	2	0	3.13	16	4	0	0	32	30	13	11	4	5	38	.244	.250	.241	10.80	1.42
Topa, Justin	R-R	6-4	200	3-7-91	0	1	2.35	6	0	0	0	8	7	3	2	1	0	12	.233	.273	.211	14.09	0.00
Wahl, Bobby	R-R	6-3	216	3-21-92	0	1	11.57	3	0	0	0	2	4	3	3	2	0	1	.400	.600	.200	3.86	0.00
Williams, Devin	R-R	6-2	200	9-21-94	4	1	0.33	22	0	0	0	27	8	4	1	1	9	53	.090	.075	.111	17.67	3.00
Woodruff, Brandon	L-R	6-4	243	2-10-93	3	5	3.05	13	13	1	0	74	55	26	25	9	18	91	.204	.194	.220	11.12	2.20
Yardley, Eric	R-R	6-0	170	8-18-90	2	0	1.54	24	0	0	0	23	19	6	4	2	10	19	.224	.243	.208	7.33	3.86

Fielding

Catcher	PCT	G	PO	A	E	DP	PB
Narvaez	.991	39	333	9	3	1	0
Nottingham	.989	19	178	7	2	0	2
Pina	1.000	13	117	7	0	2	0

First Base	PCT	G	PO	A	E	DP
Braun	.000	1	0	0	0	0
Gyorko	.994	30	163	10	1	9
Healy	1.000	2	12	0	0	3
Mathias	1.000	1	2	1	0	1
Morrison	1.000	2	14	0	0	1
Peterson	1.000	4	13	0	0	1
Smoak	.986	31	208	11	3	26
Vogelbach	1.000	2	15	2	0	1

Second Base	PCT	G	PO	A	E	DP
Hiura	.961	49	66	83	6	15
Mathias	.000	1	0	0	0	0
Peterson	.833	3	2	3	1	1
Sogard	1.000	9	7	10	0	6
Urias	.980	10	19	30	1	7

Third Base	PCT	G	PO	A	E	DP
Gyorko	1.000	11	2	15	0	2
Holt	1.000	13	4	11	0	1
Peterson	.818	4	2	7	2	0
Sogard	.962	30	23	52	3	9
Urias	.981	30	15	38	1	2

Shortstop	PCT	G	PO	A	E	DP
Arcia	.983	57	58	120	3	26
Sogard	.941	7	7	9	1	2
Urias	.929	8	3	10	1	0

Outfield	PCT	G	PO	A	E	DP
Arcia	--	1	0	0	0	0
Braun	.963	20	26	0	1	0
Cain	1.000	5	11	0	0	0
Gamel	1.000	37	50	1	0	0
Garcia	1.000	49	67	2	0	1
Holt	1.000	4	7	1	0	0
Mathias	1.000	11	17	0	0	0
Peterson	1.000	17	16	0	0	0
Sogard	--	2	0	0	0	0
Taylor	1.000	20	15	0	0	0
Yelich	1.000	51	60	1	0	0

Minnesota Twins

SEASON IN A SENTENCE: The Twins won the American League Central for the second straight year thanks to a run differential (+54) that was third-best in the AL, but continued to shrink in the postseason with a 2-0 Wild Card Series loss to the Astros.

HIGH POINT: Minnesota extended its winning streak to six games—its largest of the season—after taking three of four against the Indians and then winning the first three games of a four-game series against the Pirates in early August. The Twins were one of just two teams (along with the Cubs) with 10 wins by Aug. 5 and their success came despite a slow start for third baseman Josh Donaldson.

LOW POINT: The Twins continue to haunt their fans in the postseason and extended their North American pro sports record of consecutive postseason losses to 18. Despite earning a wild card matchup against the sub-.500 Astros, the Twins dropped the first two games of the series and scored just one run in each game. The Mariners are the only MLB team to not win a postseason game since the Twins' most recent postseason victory, which came against the Yankees on Oct. 5, 2004.

NOTABLE ROOKIES: Minnesota's 2018 second-round pick Ryan Jeffers continues to look excellent. He is the first player drafted in the second round that year to make the majors and hit close to 20% better than league average while playing 26 games and starting both playoff games. Righthander Randy Dobnak started 10 games and posted a 4.05 ERA, despite one of the lowest strikeout rates among starting pitchers. Righthanders Cody Stashak and Jorge Alcala were both effective relievers. Outfielder Brent Rooker hit well (.316/.381/.579), but his brief callup was cut short when he was hit by a pitch which fractured his forearm.

KEY TRANSACTIONS: The biggest transaction for the Twins this season was signing Donaldson to a four-year, $92 million contract and while he did manage a 131 OPS+ when on the field, inju-

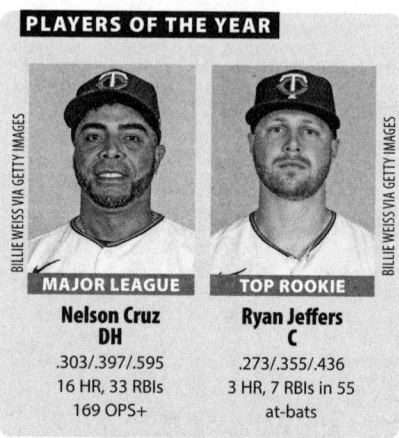

PLAYERS OF THE YEAR

MAJOR LEAGUE
Nelson Cruz
DH
.303/.397/.595
16 HR, 33 RBIs
169 OPS+

TOP ROOKIE
Ryan Jeffers
C
.273/.355/.436
3 HR, 7 RBIs in 55
at-bats

ORGANIZATION LEADERS

Batting		*Minimum 100 AB
MAJORS		
* AVG	Luis Arraez	.321
* OPS	Nelson Cruz	.992
HR	Nelson Cruz	16
RBI	Eddie Rosario	42

Pitching		#Minimum 30 IP
MAJORS		
W	Randy Dobnak	6
W	Kenta Maeda	6
# ERA	Kenta Maeda	2.70
SO	Kenta Maeda	80
SV	Taylor Rogers	9

ries limited him to just 28 games. Minnesota re-signed righthander Michael Pineda to a two-year, $20 million deal and he was the team's third-best pitcher per fWAR (1.1) despite throwing just 26.2 innings. Perhaps an under-the-radar choice for best transaction is the Oct. 29 waiver claim of Matt Wisler from the Mariners. Wisler had arguably his best pro season as a reliever and spot-starter, posting a 1.07 ERA thanks to the highest slider rate of his career.

OPENING DAY PAYROLL: $48,747,770 (20th)

ORGANIZATION STATISTICS

MINNESOTA TWINS
AMERICAN LEAGUE

Batting	B-T	HT	WT	DOB	AVG	vLH	vRH	G	AB	R	H	2B	3B	HR	RBI	BB	HBP	SH	SF	SO	SB	CS	SLG	OBP
Adrianza, Ehire	B-R	6-1	195	8-21-89	.191	.162	.212	44	89	10	17	7	0	0	3	11	1	0	0	23	1	0	.270	.287
Arraez, Luis	L-R	5-10	175	4-9-97	.321	.231	.349	32	112	16	36	9	0	0	13	8	0	0	1	11	0	0	.402	.364
Astudillo, Willians	R-R	5-9	225	10-14-91	.250	.000	.267	8	16	4	4	1	0	1	3	0	0	0	0	2	0	0	.500	.250
Avila, Alex	L-R	5-11	210	1-29-87	.184	.250	.162	23	49	6	9	2	0	1	2	11	2	0	0	22	0	0	.286	.355

Batting

Batting	B-T	HT	WT	DOB	AVG	vLH	vRH	G	AB	R	H	2B	3B	HR	RBI	BB	HBP	SH	SF	SO	SB	CS	SLG	OBP
Blankenhorn, Travis	L-R	6-2	235	8-3-96	.333	--	.333	1	3	0	1	1	0	0	0	0	1	0	0	0	0	0	.667	.500
Buxton, Byron	R-R	6-2	190	12-18-93	.254	.250	.255	39	130	19	33	3	0	13	27	2	1	0	2	36	2	1	.577	.267
Cave, Jake	L-L	6-0	200	12-4-92	.221	.188	.235	42	113	17	25	3	2	4	15	5	5	0	0	44	0	2	.389	.285
Cruz, Nelson	R-R	6-2	230	7-1-80	.303	.465	.254	53	185	33	56	6	0	16	33	25	4	0	0	58	0	0	.595	.397
Donaldson, Josh	R-R	6-1	210	12-8-85	.222	.067	.258	28	81	14	18	2	0	6	11	18	2	0	1	24	0	0	.469	.373
Garver, Mitch	R-R	6-1	220	1-15-91	.167	.304	.102	23	72	8	12	1	0	2	5	7	1	0	1	37	0	0	.264	.247
Gonzalez, Marwin	B-R	6-1	205	3-14-89	.211	.217	.209	53	175	15	37	4	0	5	22	17	3	0	4	41	0	0	.320	.286
Jeffers, Ryan	R-R	6-4	235	6-3-97	.273	.300	.257	26	55	5	15	0	0	3	7	5	2	0	0	19	0	0	.436	.355
Kepler, Max	L-L	6-4	225	2-10-93	.228	.128	.266	48	171	27	39	9	0	9	23	22	2	0	1	36	3	0	.439	.321
Polanco, Jorge	B-R	5-11	208	7-5-93	.258	.345	.227	55	209	22	54	8	0	4	19	13	1	2	1	35	4	2	.354	.304
Rooker, Brent	R-R	6-3	225	11-1-94	.316	.333	.308	7	19	4	6	2	0	1	5	0	2	0	0	5	0	0	.579	.381
Rosario, Eddie	L-R	6-1	180	9-28-91	.257	.236	.265	57	210	31	54	7	0	13	42	19	0	0	2	34	3	1	.476	.316
Sano, Miguel	R-R	6-4	272	5-11-93	.204	.159	.218	53	186	31	38	12	0	13	25	18	1	0	0	90	0	0	.478	.278
Vargas, Ildemaro	B-R	6-0	180	7-16-91	.227	.077	.444	10	22	3	5	1	1	0	2	1	0	0	1	2	0	0	.364	.250
Wade Jr., LaMonte	L-L	6-1	205	1-1-94	.231	.000	.257	16	39	3	9	3	0	0	1	4	1	0	0	9	1	1	.308	.318
Whitefield, Aaron	R-R	6-4	210	9-2-96	.000	--	.000	3	1	1	0	0	0	0	0	0	0	0	0	1	0	0	.000	.000

Pitching

Pitching	B-T	HT	WT	DOB	W	L	ERA	G	GS	CG	SV	IP	H	R	ER	HR	BB	SO	AVG	vLH	vRH	K/9	BB/9
Adrianza, Ehire	B-R	6-1	195	8-21-89	0	0	9.00	1	0	0	0	1	1	1	1	1	0	0	.250	.000	.333	0.00	0.00
Alcala, Jorge	R-R	6-3	205	7-28-95	2	1	2.63	16	0	0	0	24	21	8	7	3	8	27	.244	.364	.170	10.13	3.00
Bailey, Homer	R-R	6-4	223	5-3-86	1	0	3.38	2	2	0	0	8	6	3	3	1	3	7	.207	.308	.125	7.88	3.38
Berrios, Jose	R-R	6-0	205	5-27-94	5	4	4.00	12	12	0	0	63	57	28	28	8	26	68	.238	.180	.287	9.71	3.71
Clippard, Tyler	R-R	6-3	200	2-14-85	2	1	2.77	26	2	0	0	26	19	9	8	2	4	26	.202	.213	.191	9.00	1.38
Colina, Edwar	R-R	5-11	240	5-3-97	0	0	81.00	1	0	0	0	0	4	3	3	1	2	0	.800	1.000	.500	0.00	54.00
Coulombe, Danny	L-L	5-10	190	10-26-89	0	0	0.00	2	0	0	0	3	2	0	0	0	3	3	.200	.333	.143	10.13	10.13
Dobnak, Randy	R-R	6-1	230	1-17-95	6	4	4.05	10	10	0	0	47	50	21	21	3	13	27	.278	.296	.263	5.21	2.51
Duffey, Tyler	R-R	6-3	220	12-27-90	1	1	1.88	22	0	0	0	24	13	6	5	2	6	31	.153	.171	.136	11.63	2.25
Gearrin, Cory	R-R	6-1	205	4-14-86	0	0	0.00	1	0	0	0	2	0	0	0	0	2	1	.000	.000	.000	4.50	9.00
Hill, Rich	L-L	6-5	221	3-11-80	2	2	3.03	8	8	0	0	39	28	13	13	3	17	31	.204	.176	.208	7.22	3.96
Littell, Zack	R-R	6-4	220	10-5-95	0	0	9.95	6	0	0	0	6	12	7	7	5	3	3	.444	.273	.563	4.26	4.26
Maeda, Kenta	R-R	6-1	185	4-11-88	6	1	2.70	11	11	0	0	67	40	20	20	9	10	80	.168	.182	.149	10.80	1.35
May, Trevor	R-R	6-5	240	9-23-89	1	0	3.86	24	0	0	2	23	20	11	10	5	7	38	.227	.200	.256	14.66	2.70
Odorizzi, Jake	R-R	6-2	190	3-27-90	0	1	6.59	4	4	0	0	14	16	10	10	5	3	12	.291	.190	.353	7.90	1.98
Pineda, Michael	R-R	6-7	280	1-18-89	2	0	3.38	5	5	0	0	27	25	10	10	0	7	25	.248	.308	.184	8.44	2.36
Poppen, Sean	R-R	6-3	205	3-15-94	0	0	4.70	6	0	0	0	8	9	4	4	0	4	10	.290	.235	.357	11.74	4.70
Rogers, Taylor	L-L	6-3	190	12-17-90	2	4	4.05	21	0	0	9	20	26	14	9	2	4	24	.302	.250	.311	10.80	1.80
Romo, Sergio	R-R	5-11	185	3-4-83	1	2	4.05	24	0	0	5	20	16	9	9	3	7	23	.211	.219	.205	10.35	3.15
Smeltzer, Devin	R-L	6-3	195	9-7-95	2	0	6.75	7	1	0	0	16	19	12	12	2	5	15	.292	.385	.269	8.44	2.81
Stashak, Cody	R-R	6-2	180	6-4-94	1	0	3.00	11	0	0	0	15	11	5	5	2	3	17	.204	.154	.250	10.20	1.80
Thielbar, Caleb	R-L	6-0	205	1-31-87	2	1	2.25	17	0	0	0	20	14	6	5	0	9	22	.192	.136	.216	9.90	4.05
Thorpe, Lewis	R-L	6-1	218	11-23-95	0	1	6.06	7	1	0	0	16	24	12	11	4	10	10	.358	.444	.345	5.51	5.51
Wisler, Matt	R-R	6-3	215	9-12-92	0	1	1.07	18	4	0	1	25	15	3	3	2	14	35	.165	.121	.190	12.43	4.97

Fielding

Catcher	PCT	G	PO	A	E	DP	PB
Astudillo	1.000	6	40	1	0	0	2
Avila	.981	22	153	6	3	1	1
Garver	1.000	22	173	11	0	2	3
Jeffers	1.000	25	183	4	0	1	1

First Base	PCT	G	PO	A	E	DP
Garver	1.000	1	2	0	0	0
Gonzalez	1.000	14	59	2	0	5
Sano	.989	52	355	13	4	30
Wade Jr.	1.000	4	19	0	0	0

Second Base	PCT	G	PO	A	E	DP
Adrianza	1.000	5	7	5	0	2
Arraez	.992	31	50	68	1	16
Blankenhorn	1.000	1	1	1	0	1
Gonzalez	.984	21	24	36	1	5
Vargas	.970	8	14	18	1	8

Third Base	PCT	G	PO	A	E	DP
Adrianza	.978	23	14	30	1	3
Donaldson	1.000	26	17	37	0	4
Gonzalez	1.000	23	14	31	0	2
Vargas	1.000	1	0	1	0	0

Shortstop	PCT	G	PO	A	E	DP
Adrianza	1.000	9	8	16	0	4
Polanco	.988	53	49	117	2	17

Outfield	PCT	G	PO	A	E	DP
Buxton	1.000	39	104	1	0	0
Cave	1.000	38	57	1	0	0
Gonzalez	.900	8	9	0	1	0
Kepler	.987	46	74	2	1	0
Rooker	1.000	5	4	0	0	0
Rosario	.978	51	84	5	2	1
Wade Jr.	.917	8	10	1	1	0
Whitefield	1.000	2	3	0	0	0

New York Mets

SEASON IN A SENTENCE: The Mets' offense led the major leagues with a 122 park-adjusted OPS+, but the club's 86 ERA+ was fourth worst in baseball, resulting in a 26-34 record and a fourth straight October-free season in Queens.

HIGH POINT: The Mets stood at 3-2 after five games, lost the next day and never again nosed above .500. Aside from righthander Jacob deGrom's Cy Young-worthy season and big steps forward from first baseman Dominic Smith (169 OPS+), right fielder Michael Conforto (156) and center fielder Brandon Nimmo (146), the Mets' high point occurred off the field. On Nov. 6, the franchise's $2.475 billion sale to hedge fund manager Steve Cohen was approved by owners.

LOW POINT: Injuries exposed the lack of depth in the Mets' rotation behind ace deGrom. Righthander Noah Syndergaard missed the season after having Tommy John surgery in late March, while righthander Marcus Stroman tore a calf muscle just prior to Opening Day and later opted out of the season, citing Covid-19 concerns. Lefthander Steven Matz ran up a 9.68 ERA and was moved to the bullpen.

NOTABLE ROOKIES: Two bright spots in a lost season were rookies Andres Gimenez and David Peterson, who both finished 2019 in Double-A but proved more big league ready than expected. Gimenez, a natural shortstop, wrested playing time from Amed Rosario in September and hit .263/.333/.398 with three home runs and eight stolen bases in nine tries. The 22-year-old Venezuelan filled in admirably at second base and third base, too, ranking 10th among all infielders with five outs above average, according to MLB Statcast. Peterson, the Mets' first-round pick out of Oregon in 2017, became the club's de facto No. 2 starter by going 6-2, 3.44 in 10 games (nine starts) and striking out 40 in 49.2 innings. The 25-year-old lefthander throws a nasty slider, the 18th most valuable slider by Statcast run value, but needs to improve his control—particularly

throwing strike one—after walking 4.3 per nine innings as a rookie.

KEY TRANSACTIONS: Mathematically alive for one of eight National League postseason berths, the Mets made three minor moves at the 2020 trade deadline. They acquired catcher Robinson Chirinos and third baseman Todd Frazier from the Rangers in separate deals and righthanded reliever Miguel Castro from the Orioles for 23-year-old lefthander Kevin Smith, who had been the organization's minor league pitcher of the year in 2019.

OPENING DAY PAYROLL: $80,296,949 (5th)

PLAYERS OF THE YEAR

MAJOR LEAGUE

Jacob deGrom
RHP
4-2, 2.38 in 12 starts,
NL-leading 104 SO
finalist for Cy Young

TOP ROOKIE

Andres Gimenez
SS/2B
.263/.333/.398
3 HR, 8-for-9 SB
plus glove at SS/2B/3B

ORGANIZATION LEADERS

Batting		*Minimum 100 AB
MAJORS		
* AVG	Michael Conforto	.322
* OPS	Dominic Smith	.993
HR	Pete Alonso	16
RBI	Dominic Smith	42

Pitching		#Minimum 30 IP
MAJORS		
W	David Peterson	6
# ERA	Jacob deGrom	2.38
SO	Jacob deGrom	104
SV	Edwin Diaz	6

ORGANIZATION STATISTICS

NEW YORK METS
NATIONAL LEAGUE

Batting	B-T	HT	WT	DOB	AVG	vLH	vRH	G	AB	R	H	2B	3B	HR	RBI	BB	HBP	SH	SF	SO	SB	CS	SLG	OBP
Alonso, Pete	R-R	6-3	245	12-7-94	.231	.194	.248	57	208	31	48	6	0	16	35	24	6	0	1	61	1	0	.490	.326
Cano, Robinson	L-R	6-0	212	10-22-82	.316	.264	.339	49	171	23	54	9	0	10	30	9	1	0	1	24	0	0	.544	.352
Cespedes, Yoenis	R-R	5-11	225	10-18-85	.161	.000	.238	8	31	3	5	1	0	2	4	2	1	0	0	15	0	0	.387	.235
Chirinos, Robinson	R-R	6-1	220	6-5-84	.219	.500	.091	12	32	1	7	2	0	1	5	1	0	0	0	9	0	0	.375	.242

Batting

Batting	B-T	HT	WT	DOB	AVG	vLH	vRH	G	AB	R	H	2B	3B	HR	RBI	BB	HBP	SH	SF	SO	SB	CS	SLG	OBP
Conforto, Michael	L-R	6-1	215	3-1-93	.322	.284	.344	54	202	40	65	12	0	9	31	24	7	0	0	57	3	3	.515	.412
Cordell, Ryan	R-R	6-4	200	3-31-92	.125	.250	.000	5	8	0	1	0	0	0	0	0	0	0	0	3	1	0	.125	.125
Davis, J.D.	R-R	6-3	218	4-27-93	.247	.235	.254	56	190	26	47	9	0	6	19	31	7	0	1	56	0	0	.389	.371
Dozier, Brian	R-R	5-11	200	5-15-87	.133	.077	.500	7	15	1	2	0	0	0	1	0	0	0	0	5	0	0	.133	.188
Frazier, Todd	R-R	6-3	220	2-12-86	.224	.217	.231	14	49	5	11	2	0	2	5	1	1	0	0	16	0	0	.388	.255
Gimenez, Andres	L-R	5-11	161	9-4-98	.263	.261	.263	49	118	22	31	3	2	3	12	7	6	0	1	28	8	1	.398	.333
Guillorme, Luis	L-R	5-10	190	9-27-94	.333	.125	.367	29	57	6	19	6	0	0	9	10	0	0	1	17	2	0	.439	.426
Hamilton, Billy	B-R	6-0	155	9-9-90	.045	.000	.071	17	22	4	1	0	0	0	1	0	1	1	1	3	3	1	.045	.083
2-team total (14 Chicago Cubs)					.125	.091	.143	31	32	10	4	0	0	1	2	2	0	1	1	7	6	2	.219	.171
Heredia, Guillermo	R-L	5-10	195	1-31-91	.235	.167	.273	7	17	4	4	0	0	2	3	1	0	0	0	5	0	0	.588	.278
2-team total (8 Pittsburgh Pirates)					.212	.250	.190	15	33	6	7	0	0	2	5	3	0	0	0	9	1	0	.394	.278
Lagares, Juan	R-R	6-2	219	3-17-89	--	--	--	2	0	0	0	0	0	0	0	0	0	0	0	0	0	0	--	--
Marisnick, Jake	R-R	6-4	220	3-30-91	.333	.375	.294	16	33	4	11	3	0	2	5	1	0	0	0	10	0	0	.606	.353
McNeil, Jeff	L-R	6-1	195	4-8-92	.311	.303	.316	52	183	19	57	14	0	4	23	20	3	0	3	24	0	2	.454	.383
Nido, Tomas	R-R	6-0	211	4-12-94	.292	.500	.188	7	24	4	7	1	0	2	6	2	0	0	0	6	0	0	.583	.346
Nimmo, Brandon	L-R	6-3	206	3-27-93	.280	.196	.311	55	186	33	52	8	3	8	18	33	6	0	0	43	1	2	.484	.404
Nunez, Eduardo	R-R	6-0	195	6-15-87	.500	1.000	.000	2	2	0	1	0	0	0	0	0	0	0	0	0	1	0	.500	.500
Ramos, Wilson	R-R	6-1	245	8-10-87	.239	.275	.225	45	142	13	34	6	0	5	15	10	2	0	1	31	0	0	.387	.297
Rivera, Rene	R-R	5-10	215	7-31-83	.250	1.000	.000	2	4	0	1	0	0	0	0	0	0	0	0	3	0	0	.250	.250
Rosario, Amed	R-R	6-2	190	11-20-95	.252	.316	.209	46	143	20	36	3	1	4	15	4	0	0	0	34	0	1	.371	.272
Sanchez, Ali	R-R	6-1	200	1-20-97	.111	.000	.143	5	9	0	1	0	0	0	0	1	0	0	0	3	0	0	.111	.200
Smith, Dominic	L-L	6-0	239	6-15-95	.316	.283	.331	50	177	27	56	21	1	10	42	14	5	0	3	45	0	0	.616	.377

Pitching

Pitching	B-T	HT	WT	DOB	W	L	ERA	G	GS	CG	SV	IP	H	R	ER	HR	BB	SO	AVG	vLH	vRH	K/9	BB/9
Betances, Dellin	R-R	6-8	265	3-23-88	0	1	7.71	15	0	0	0	12	12	10	10	0	12	11	.267	.375	.207	8.49	9.26
Brach, Brad	R-R	6-6	215	4-12-86	1	0	5.84	14	0	0	0	12	8	8	8	2	14	14	.186	.250	.161	10.22	10.22
Castro, Miguel	R-R	6-7	205	12-24-94	1	2	4.00	10	0	0	0	9	11	5	4	1	8	14	.297	.200	.364	14.00	8.00
deGrom, Jacob	L-R	6-4	180	6-19-88	4	2	2.38	12	12	0	0	68	47	21	18	7	18	104	.190	.184	.195	13.76	2.38
Diaz, Edwin	R-R	6-3	165	3-22-94	2	1	1.75	26	0	0	6	26	18	6	5	2	14	50	.191	.178	.204	17.53	4.91
Familia, Jeurys	R-R	6-3	240	10-10-89	2	3	3.71	25	0	0	0	27	20	11	11	2	19	23	.204	.278	.161	7.76	6.41
Frazier, Todd	R-R	6-3	220	2-12-86	0	0	0.00	1	0	0	0	1	0	0	0	0	0	1	.000	--	.000	9.00	0.00
Gsellman, Robert	R-R	6-4	200	7-18-93	0	0	9.64	6	4	0	0	14	22	15	15	4	8	9	.361	.385	.343	5.79	5.14
Guillorme, Luis	L-R	5-10	190	9-27-94	0	0	0.00	1	0	0	0	1	0	0	0	0	0	0	.000	--	.000	0.00	0.00
Hughes, Jared	R-R	6-7	240	7-4-85	1	2	4.84	18	0	0	0	22	23	17	12	3	14	21	.256	.297	.226	8.46	5.64
Jurado, Ariel	R-R	6-2	240	1-30-96	0	0	11.25	1	1	0	0	4	9	5	5	1	0	2	.450	.455	.444	4.50	0.00
Kilome, Franklyn	R-R	6-6	175	6-25-95	0	1	11.12	4	0	0	1	11	14	14	14	5	9	13	.298	.286	.308	10.32	7.15
Lockett, Walker	R-R	6-5	225	5-3-94	1	0	5.63	2	1	0	0	8	9	5	5	1	3	8	.281	.286	.278	9.00	3.38
Lugo, Seth	R-R	6-4	225	11-17-89	3	4	5.15	16	7	0	3	37	40	22	21	8	10	47	.274	.275	.273	11.54	2.45
Matz, Steven	R-L	6-2	201	5-29-91	0	5	9.68	9	6	0	0	31	42	33	33	14	10	36	.323	.333	.320	10.57	2.93
Oswalt, Corey	R-R	6-5	250	9-3-93	0	0	4.85	4	1	0	0	13	14	7	7	3	2	11	.269	.250	.286	7.62	1.38
Peterson, David	L-L	6-6	240	9-3-95	6	2	3.44	10	9	0	0	50	36	20	19	5	24	40	.202	.161	.211	7.25	4.35
Porcello, Rick	R-R	6-5	205	12-27-88	1	7	5.64	12	12	0	0	59	74	41	37	5	15	54	.303	.278	.324	8.24	2.29
Ramirez, Erasmo	R-R	6-0	220	5-2-90	0	0	0.63	6	0	0	1	14	8	1	1	1	4	9	.163	.143	.179	5.65	2.51
Sewald, Paul	R-R	6-3	207	5-26-90	0	0	13.50	5	0	0	0	6	12	9	9	1	4	2	.414	.444	.400	3.00	6.00
Shreve, Chasen	L-L	6-4	195	7-12-90	1	0	3.96	17	0	0	0	25	17	12	11	4	12	34	.191	.063	.263	12.24	4.32
Smith, Drew	R-R	6-2	190	9-24-93	0	1	6.43	8	0	0	0	7	6	6	5	2	2	7	.222	.182	.250	9.00	2.57
Strickland, Hunter	R-R	6-3	225	9-24-88	0	1	8.10	4	0	0	0	3	5	4	3	0	1	4	.333	.143	.500	10.80	2.70
Wacha, Michael	R-R	6-6	215	7-1-91	1	4	6.62	8	7	0	0	34	46	26	25	9	7	37	.313	.275	.346	9.79	1.85
Wilson, Justin	L-L	6-2	205	8-18-87	2	1	3.66	23	0	0	0	20	18	10	8	1	9	23	.240	.115	.306	10.53	4.12

Fielding

Catcher	PCT	G	PO	A	E	DP	PB
Chirinos	1.000	12	93	2	0	0	0
Nido	.983	7	57	1	1	0	1
Ramos	.998	41	396	9	1	3	4
Rivera	1.000	1	7	1	0	0	0
Sanchez	1.000	5	29	0	0	0	1

First Base	PCT	G	PO	A	E	DP
Alonso	.982	39	264	14	5	21
Smith	.988	25	144	15	2	14

Second Base	PCT	G	PO	A	E	DP
Cano	.989	34	35	58	1	11
Dozier	.941	5	9	7	1	3
Gimenez	1.000	19	11	17	0	2
Guillorme	1.000	17	23	30	0	9
McNeil	1.000	12	13	20	0	5

Third Base	PCT	G	PO	A	E	DP
Davis	.958	34	11	57	3	5
Frazier	.974	14	9	29	1	3
Gimenez	.923	10	3	9	1	1
Guillorme	1.000	4	5	4	0	0
McNeil	.865	9	5	27	5	5

Shortstop	PCT	G	PO	A	E	DP
Gimenez	.987	23	33	43	1	9
Guillorme	1.000	3	2	4	0	1
Rosario	.981	44	33	72	2	11

Outfield	PCT	G	PO	A	E	DP
Conforto	1.000	52	92	6	0	1
Cordell	1.000	5	5	0	0	0
Davis	.900	8	8	1	1	0
Hamilton	1.000	13	13	2	0	0
Heredia	1.000	7	13	0	0	0
Lagares	1.000	2	3	0	0	0
Marisnick	.968	16	30	0	1	0
McNeil	1.000	30	46	1	0	1
Nimmo	.981	55	98	3	2	0
Nunez	1.000	1	2	0	0	0
Smith	1.000	23	16	1	0	0

NEW YORK METS

New York Yankees

SEASON IN A SENTENCE: The team endured injuries to key contributors—Luis Severino, Aaron Judge, Giancarlo Stanton, James Paxton—to make the playoffs, but fell to the Rays in the fifth game of the Division Series.

HIGH POINT: In the opening game of the playoffs, the Yankees tagged Cleveland ace Shane Bieber for seven earned runs over 4.2 innings, including home runs from Judge and Gleyber Torres, en route to a 12-3 win in an eventual two-game sweep of the Wild Card Series.

LOW POINT: Mike Brosseau's pinch-hit home run off of Aroldis Chapman in the final game of the Division Series sent the Yankees home. The moment was made even more poignant because of an incident between the teams earlier in the season when Chapman threw a fastball behind Brosseau and sparked a benches-clearing incident at Yankee Stadium.

NOTABLE ROOKIES: Righthander Deivi Garcia, one of the organization's top pitching prospects, made a handful of excellent starts in the season's final stretch and got the opening nod in a Division Series game against the Rays. In all, Garcia finished the year 3-2, 4.98 with 33 strikeouts in 34.1 innings. Righties Clarke Schmidt, Albert Abreu, Nick Nelson, Brooks Kriske and Miguel Yajuire were each up and down throughout the season. Schmidt, the organization's highest-rated pitcher entering the year, struck out seven and allowed five runs over 6.1 innings spread among one start and three relief appearances. Both Schmidt and Garcia should battle for rotation spots come 2021.

KEY TRANSACTIONS: In the offseason, the Yankees finally got their man. After drafting and being spurned by Gerrit Cole in the first round in 2008, then failing to acquire him via trade on multiple occasions, Cole inked with New York in December for nine years and $324 million. Cole went 7-3, 2.84 with 94 strikeouts in 73 innings in his first year with his new team. He was also a little bit homer-happy in 2020, allowing 1.7

per nine innings, a mark that stands as the worst of his career. Going forward, Cole will be tasked with leading a pitching staff in flux. Righthander Masahiro Tanaka and lefties James Paxton and J.A. Happ (the Yankees declined Happ's $17 million option) are free agents, leaving rehabbing righty Luis Severino, lefty Jordan Montgomery and possibly Garcia and Schmidt to battle for spots in the rotation behind Cole.

OPENING DAY PAYROLL: $110,852,878 (1st)

PLAYERS OF THE YEAR

MIKE CARLSON VIA GETTY IMAGES

MAJOR LEAGUE

DJ LeMahieu
2B/3B
.364/.421/.590
Led AL in AVG, OBP,
OPS+ (177)

TOP ROOKIE

Deivi Garcia
RHP
3-2, 4.98 in 6 GS
33 SO in 34.1 IP

ORGANIZATION LEADERS

Batting		*Minimum 100 AB
MAJORS		
* AVG	DJ LeMahieu	.364
* OPS	DJ LeMahieu	1.011
HR	Luke Voit	22
RBI	Luke Voit	52

Pitching		#Minimum 30 IP
MAJORS		
W	Gerrit Cole	7
# ERA	Gerrit Cole	2.84
SO	Gerrit Cole	94
SV	Zack Britton	8

ORGANIZATION STATISTICS

NEW YORK YANKEES
AMERICAN LEAGUE

Batting	B-T	HT	WT	DOB	AVG	vLH	vRH	G	AB	R	H	2B	3B	HR	RBI	BB	HBP	SH	SF	SO	SB	CS	SLG	OBP
Andujar, Miguel	R-R	6-0	211	3-2-95	.242	.308	.194	21	62	5	15	2	1	1	5	3	0	0	0	9	0	0	.355	.277
Estrada, Thairo	R-R	5-10	185	2-22-96	.167	.286	.074	26	48	8	8	0	0	1	3	1	3	0	0	19	1	0	.229	.231
Florial, Estevan	L-R	6-1	195	11-25-97	.333	--	.333	1	3	0	1	0	0	0	0	0	0	0	0	2	0	0	.333	.333
Ford, Mike	L-R	6-0	225	7-4-92	.135	.000	.152	29	74	5	10	4	0	2	11	7	2	0	1	16	0	0	.270	.226

Batting

Batting	B-T	HT	WT	DOB	AVG	vLH	vRH	G	AB	R	H	2B	3B	HR	RBI	BB	HBP	SH	SF	SO	SB	CS	SLG	OBP
Frazier, Clint	R-R	5-11	212	9-6-94	.267	.273	.265	39	131	24	35	6	1	8	26	25	3	0	1	44	3	0	.511	.394
Gardner, Brett	L-L	5-11	195	8-24-83	.223	.190	.229	49	130	20	29	5	1	5	15	26	1	0	1	35	3	3	.392	.354
Hicks, Aaron	B-R	6-1	205	10-2-89	.225	.244	.218	54	169	28	38	10	2	6	21	41	1	0	0	38	4	1	.414	.379
Higashioka, Kyle	R-R	6-1	202	4-20-90	.250	.125	.313	16	48	7	12	1	0	4	10	0	0	0	0	11	0	0	.521	.250
Judge, Aaron	R-R	6-7	282	4-26-92	.257	.240	.263	28	101	23	26	3	0	9	22	10	2	0	0	32	0	1	.554	.336
Kratz, Erik	R-R	6-4	250	6-15-80	.321	.364	.294	16	28	2	9	2	0	0	4	2	0	0	0	6	0	0	.393	.367
LeMahieu, DJ	R-R	6-4	220	7-13-88	.364	.400	.355	50	195	41	71	10	2	10	27	18	2	0	1	21	3	0	.590	.421
Mercer, Jordy	R-R	6-3	210	8-27-86	.182	.500	.111	6	11	1	2	0	0	0	0	2	0	0	0	1	0	0	.182	.308
2-team total (3 Detroit Tigers)					.200	.333	.143	9	20	2	4	0	0	0	2	0	0	0	0	2	0	0	.200	.273
Sanchez, Gary	R-R	6-2	230	12-2-92	.147	.094	.161	49	156	19	23	4	0	10	24	18	4	0	0	64	0	0	.365	.253
Stanton, Giancarlo	R-R	6-6	245	11-8-89	.250	.176	.271	23	76	12	19	7	0	4	11	15	2	0	0	27	1	1	.500	.387
Tauchman, Mike	L-L	6-2	220	12-3-90	.242	.100	.280	43	95	18	23	6	0	0	14	14	1	0	1	26	6	0	.305	.342
Torres, Gleyber	R-R	6-1	205	12-13-96	.243	.235	.245	42	136	17	33	8	0	3	16	22	2	0	0	28	1	0	.368	.356
Urshela, Gio	R-R	6-0	215	10-11-91	.298	.233	.314	43	151	24	45	11	0	6	30	18	1	0	4	25	1	0	.490	.368
Voit, Luke	R-R	6-3	255	2-13-91	.277	.229	.291	56	213	41	59	5	0	22	52	17	3	0	1	54	0	0	.610	.338
Wade, Tyler	L-R	6-1	188	11-23-94	.170	.043	.215	52	88	19	15	3	0	3	10	12	3	1	1	22	4	1	.307	.288

Pitching

Pitching	B-T	HT	WT	DOB	W	L	ERA	G	GS	CG	SV	IP	H	R	ER	HR	BB	SO	AVG	vLH	vRH	K/9	BB/9
Abreu, Albert	R-R	6-2	190	9-26-95	0	1	20.25	2	0	0	0	1	4	4	3	1	2	2	.500	.250	.750	13.50	13.50
Avilan, Luis	L-L	6-2	220	7-19-89	0	0	4.32	10	0	0	0	8	9	4	4	2	5	9	.265	.176	.353	9.72	5.40
Britton, Zack	L-L	6-1	200	12-22-87	1	2	1.89	20	0	0	8	19	12	6	4	0	7	16	.174	.077	.196	7.58	3.32
Cessa, Luis	R-R	6-0	208	4-25-92	0	0	3.32	16	0	0	1	22	20	10	8	2	7	17	.235	.234	.234	7.06	2.91
Chapman, Aroldis	L-L	6-4	218	2-28-88	1	1	3.09	13	0	0	3	12	6	4	4	2	4	22	.150	.077	.185	16.97	3.09
Cole, Gerrit	R-R	6-4	220	9-8-90	7	3	2.84	12	12	2	0	73	53	27	23	14	17	94	.197	.191	.201	11.59	2.10
Garcia, Deivi	R-R	5-9	163	5-19-99	3	2	4.98	6	6	0	0	34	35	20	19	6	6	33	.254	.226	.276	8.65	1.57
Green, Chad	L-R	6-3	215	5-24-91	3	3	3.51	22	0	0	1	26	13	13	10	5	8	32	.144	.075	.200	11.22	2.81
Hale, David	R-R	6-2	210	9-27-87	0	0	3.00	5	0	0	1	6	7	2	2	0	3	7	.304	.273	.333	10.50	4.50
Happ, J.A.	L-L	6-5	205	10-19-82	2	2	3.47	9	9	0	0	49	37	19	19	8	15	42	.208	.204	.209	7.66	2.74
Heller, Ben	R-R	6-3	210	8-5-91	0	0	3.00	6	0	0	0	6	5	2	2	2	6	7	.231	.200	.900	9.00	3.00
Holder, Jonathan	R-R	6-2	232	6-9-93	3	0	4.98	18	0	0	0	22	25	13	12	3	11	14	.281	.350	.224	5.82	4.57
Kahnle, Tommy	R-R	6-1	230	8-7-89	0	0	0.00	1	0	0	0	1	1	0	0	0	1	3	.200	.500	.000	27.00	9.00
King, Michael	R-R	6-3	210	5-25-95	1	2	7.76	9	4	0	0	27	30	23	23	5	11	26	.278	.255	.295	8.78	3.71
Kratz, Erik	R-R	6-4	250	6-15-80	0	0	9.00	2	0	0	0	2	2	2	2	0	0	0	.250	.000	.500	0.00	0.00
Kriske, Brooks	R-R	6-3	190	2-3-94	0	0	14.73	4	0	0	0	4	3	6	6	1	7	8	.200	.333	.000	19.64	17.18
Loaisiga, Jonathan	R-R	5-11	165	11-2-94	3	0	3.52	12	3	0	0	23	21	11	9	3	7	22	.241	.257	.231	8.61	2.74
Lyons, Tyler	L-L	6-2	210	2-21-88	0	0	21.60	1	0	0	0	2	3	4	4	0	1	0	.375	.667	.200	0.00	5.40
Montgomery, Jordan	L-L	6-6	228	12-27-92	2	3	5.11	10	10	0	0	44	48	27	25	7	9	47	.265	.229	.278	9.61	1.84
Nelson, Nick	R-R	6-1	205	12-5-95	1	0	4.79	11	0	0	0	21	20	13	11	4	11	18	.256	.270	.244	7.84	4.79
Ottavino, Adam	B-R	6-5	246	11-22-85	2	3	5.89	24	0	0	0	18	20	12	12	2	9	25	.270	.294	.263	12.27	4.42
Paxton, James	L-L	6-4	227	11-6-88	1	1	6.64	5	5	0	0	20	23	17	15	4	7	26	.284	.286	.283	11.51	3.10
Schmidt, Clarke	R-R	6-1	200	2-20-96	0	1	7.11	3	1	0	0	6	7	5	5	0	5	7	.269	.231	.308	9.95	7.11
Tanaka, Masahiro	R-R	6-3	218	11-1-88	3	3	3.56	10	10	0	0	48	48	25	19	9	8	44	.257	.188	.330	8.25	1.50
Yajure, Miguel	R-R	6-1	175	5-1-98	0	0	1.29	3	0	0	0	7	3	1	1	1	5	8	.130	.200	.077	10.29	6.43

Fielding

Catcher	PCT	G	PO	A	E	DP	PB
Higashioka	.983	14	108	7	2	1	1
Kratz	1.000	12	74	3	0	1	0
Sanchez	.984	41	347	14	6	2	5

First Base	PCT	G	PO	A	E	DP
Ford	.969	13	59	3	2	6
Kratz	1.000	4	6	1	0	1
LeMahieu	1.000	11	24	0	0	1
Voit	.991	48	308	20	3	23

Second Base	PCT	G	PO	A	E	DP
Estrada	1.000	20	20	28	0	6
LeMahieu	.971	37	51	82	4	19
Wade	.983	31	21	36	1	7

Third Base	PCT	G	PO	A	E	DP
Andujar	.750	6	4	5	3	2
Estrada	.800	6	1	3	1	1
LeMahieu	.929	11	10	16	2	2
Urshela	.992	43	34	86	1	10

Shortstop	PCT	G	PO	A	E	DP
Estrada	.000	3	0	0	0	0
Mercer	1.000	6	7	4	0	1
Torres	.933	40	40	86	9	13
Wade	1.000	22	23	24	0	3

Outfield	PCT	G	PO	A	E	DP
Andujar	.800	7	4	0	1	0
Florial	1.000	1	1	0	0	0
Frazier	.984	34	62	1	1	0
Gardner	.972	48	69	1	2	0
Hicks	.980	50	97	3	2	2
Judge	1.000	25	45	1	0	1
Tauchman	1.000	41	63	2	0	0

Oakland Athletics

SEASON IN A SENTENCE: The A's overtook the Astros in the AL West to win their first division title since 2013, but the Astros beat the A's in the Division Series in the club's latest in a long string of postseason disappointments.

HIGH POINT: The A's won their first playoff series in 14 years with a stirring win over the White Sox in Game 3 of the Wild Card Series. Trailing 3-0 early, the A's battled back and took the lead for good on Chad Pinder's tiebreaking two-run single in the fifth that sent them on their way to a 6-4 victory.

LOW POINT: A's owner John Fisher, with an estimated net worth of $2.1 billion, announced in May the team would not continue paying its minor leaguers $400 per week. His announcement came at a time that most other franchises had committed to paying their players. For a while the A's were the only team of the 30 MLB clubs that was opting to not pay its minor leaguers. After a torrent of public criticism, Fisher eventually reversed course, but the damage to the franchise's standing was done.

NOTABLE ROOKIES: Lefthander Jesus Luzardo took his place in the A's rotation and went 3-2, 4.12 with 59 strikeouts in 59 innings. He earned the start in the A's playoff opener. Catcher Sean Murphy finished second on the team with an .821 OPS and played standout defense to solidify his place as the franchise's long-term catcher. Rule 5 draft selection Vimael Machin stuck on the roster as a utility infielder and catchers Austin Allen and Jonah Heim each got their first significant major league time. Righthander Jordan Weems, a converted catcher-turned-pitcher, made the Opening Day roster and logged a 3.22 ERA in nine relief appearances.

KEY TRANSACTIONS: The A's swapped out second basemen in the offseason, trading Jurickson Profar to the Padres in exchange for prospects and acquiring Tony Kemp from the Cubs to replace him. They continued tweaking the posi-

tion throughout the year, trading Jorge Mateo to the Padres in July and acquiring Tommy La Stella from the Angels in exchange for Franklin Barreto at the Aug. 31 trade deadline. They also added lefthander Mike Minor in a trade with the Rangers for the stretch run. The A's made their most impactful addition when they signed Jake Lamb as a free agent in September after Matt Chapman suffered a season-ending injury. Lamb posted an .882 OPS with seven extra-base hits in 13 games after signing.

OPENING DAY PAYROLL: $35,520,598(26th)

PLAYERS OF THE YEAR

MAJOR LEAGUE
Liam Hendriks
RHP
3-1, 1.78, 14 SV
37 SO, 3 BB in 25.1 IP

TOP ROOKIE
Sean Murphy
C
.233/.364/.457
7 HR, 14 RBIs,
24 BB

ORGANIZATION LEADERS

Batting		*Minimum 100 AB
MAJORS		
* AVG	Tommy La Stella	.289
* OPS	Robbie Grossman	.826
HR	Matt Olson	14
RBI	Matt Olson	42
Pitching		#Minimum 30 IP
MAJORS		
W	Mike Fiers	6
# ERA	Chris Bassitt	2.29
SO	Frankie Montas	60
SV	Liam Hendriks	14

ORGANIZATION STATISTICS

OAKLAND ATHLETICS
AMERICAN LEAGUE

Batting	B-T	HT	WT	DOB	AVG	vLH	vRH	G	AB	R	H	2B	3B	HR	RBI	BB	HBP	SH	SF	SO	SB	CS	SLG	OBP
Allen, Austin	L-R	6-2	219	1-16-94	.194	--	.194	14	31	1	6	1	0	1	3	1	0	0	0	14	0	0	.323	.219
Barreto, Franklin	R-R	5-10	208	2-27-96	.000	.000	.000	15	10	5	0	0	0	0	0	0	0	0	0	7	0	0	.000	.000
2-team total (6 Los Angeles Angels)					.074	.083	.067	21	27	5	2	0	0	0	2	1	0	0	1	15	1	0	.074	.107
Brown, Seth	L-L	6-1	223	7-13-92	.000	--	.000	7	5	0	0	0	0	0	0	0	0	0	0	2	0	0	.000	.000

OAKLAND ATHLETICS

KELLY GAVIN VIA GETTY IMAGES

KELLY GAVIN VIA GETTY IMAGES

OAKLAND ATHLETICS

Batting	B-T	HT	WT	DOB	AVG	vLH	vRH	G	AB	R	H	2B	3B	HR	RBI	BB	HBP	SH	SF	SO	SB	CS	SLG	OBP
Canha, Mark	R-R	6-2	209	2-15-89	.246	.333	.221	59	191	32	47	12	2	5	33	37	10	0	5	54	4	0	.408	.387
Chapman, Matt	R-R	6-0	215	4-28-93	.232	.190	.240	37	142	22	33	9	2	10	25	8	1	0	1	54	0	0	.535	.276
Davis, Khris	R-R	5-11	205	12-21-87	.200	.303	.135	30	85	9	17	5	0	2	10	10	3	0	1	26	0	0	.329	.303
Grossman, Robbie	B-L	6-0	216	9-16-89	.241	.100	.260	51	166	23	40	12	2	8	23	21	5	0	0	38	8	1	.482	.344
Heim, Jonah	B-R	6-4	220	6-27-95	.211	.333	.172	13	38	5	8	0	0	0	3	0	0	0	0	3	0	0	.211	.268
Kemp, Tony	L-R	5-6	160	10-31-91	.247	.000	.267	49	93	15	23	5	0	0	4	15	3	1	2	14	3	1	.301	.363
La Stella, Tommy	L-R	5-11	180	1-31-89	.289	.250	.301	27	97	16	28	6	2	1	11	12	1	0	1	5	0	0	.423	.369
2-team total (28 Los Angeles Angels)					.281	.216	.303	55	196	31	55	14	2	5	25	27	2	1	2	12	1	0	.449	.370
Lamb, Jake	L-R	6-3	215	10-9-90	.267	.188	.310	13	45	5	12	4	0	3	9	2	0	0	0	8	0	0	.556	.327
Laureano, Ramon	R-R	5-11	203	7-15-94	.213	.205	.216	54	183	27	39	8	1	6	25	24	12	0	3	58	2	1	.366	.338
Machin, Vimael	L-R	5-11	185	9-25-93	.206	.143	.214	24	63	11	13	2	0	0	0	8	0	0	0	10	0	0	.238	.296
Murphy, Sean	R-R	6-3	228	10-4-94	.233	.235	.232	43	116	21	27	5	0	7	14	24	0	0	0	37	0	0	.457	.364
Olson, Matt	L-R	6-5	225	3-29-94	.195	.208	.191	60	210	28	41	4	1	14	42	34	1	0	0	77	1	0	.424	.310
Orf, Nate	R-R	5-8	181	2-1-90	.000	.000	.000	6	7	1	0	0	0	0	0	0	0	0	0	1	0	0	.000	.000
Pinder, Chad	R-R	6-2	210	3-29-92	.232	.160	.290	24	56	8	13	3	0	2	8	5	0	0	0	13	0	0	.393	.295
Piscotty, Stephen	R-R	6-4	211	1-14-91	.226	.229	.225	45	159	17	36	6	0	5	29	9	1	1	1	53	4	0	.358	.271
Semien, Marcus	R-R	6-0	195	9-17-90	.223	.224	.222	53	211	28	47	9	1	7	23	25	0	0	0	50	4	0	.374	.305

Pitching	B-T	HT	WT	DOB	W	L	ERA	G	GS	CG	SV	IP	H	R	ER	HR	BB	SO	AVG	vLH	vRH	K/9	BB/9
Bassitt, Chris	R-R	6-5	217	2-22-89	5	2	2.29	11	11	0	0	63	56	18	16	6	17	55	.233	.248	.223	7.86	2.43
Blackburn, Paul	R-R	6-1	196	12-4-93	0	1	27.00	1	1	0	0	2	5	7	7	0	2	2	.417	.400	.429	7.71	7.71
Diekman, Jake	L-L	6-4	195	1-21-87	2	0	0.42	21	0	0	0	21	8	2	1	1	12	31	.114	.185	.070	13.08	5.06
Fiers, Mike	R-R	6-2	211	6-15-85	6	3	4.58	11	11	0	0	59	65	31	30	9	16	37	.275	.244	.308	5.64	2.44
Hendriks, Liam	R-R	6-0	230	2-10-89	3	1	1.78	24	0	0	14	25	14	6	5	1	3	37	.161	.200	.135	13.14	1.07
Jefferies, Daulton	L-R	6-0	182	8-2-95	0	1	22.50	1	1	0	0	2	5	5	5	2	2	1	.455	.500	.429	4.50	9.00
Kaprielian, James	R-R	6-3	225	3-2-94	0	0	7.36	2	0	0	0	4	4	3	3	2	2	4	.267	.375	.143	9.82	4.91
Luzardo, Jesus	L-L	6-0	218	9-30-97	3	2	4.12	12	9	0	0	59	58	27	27	9	17	59	.257	.260	.256	9.00	2.59
Manaea, Sean	R-L	6-5	245	2-1-92	4	3	4.50	11	11	0	0	54	57	32	27	7	8	45	.270	.250	.277	7.50	1.33
McFarland, T.J.	L-L	6-3	200	6-8-89	2	0	4.35	23	0	0	0	21	26	10	10	5	5	9	.302	.289	.313	3.92	2.18
Mengden, Daniel	R-R	6-1	215	2-19-93	0	1	3.65	4	1	0	0	12	14	5	5	2	7	10	.286	.250	.333	7.30	5.11
Minor, Mike	R-L	6-4	210	12-26-87	1	1	5.48	5	4	1	0	21	15	13	13	4	7	27	.197	.250	.179	11.39	2.95
2-team total (7 Texas Rangers)					1	6	5.56	12	11	1	0	57	50	36	35	11	20	62	.230	.231		9.85	3.18
Montas, Frankie	R-R	6-2	255	3-21-93	3	5	5.60	11	11	0	0	53	57	35	33	10	23	60	.270	.350	.198	10.19	3.91
Petit, Yusmeiro	R-R	6-1	252	11-22-84	2	1	1.66	26	0	0	0	22	19	4	4	3	5	17	.232	.077	.304	7.06	2.08
Smith, Burch	R-R	6-4	225	4-12-90	2	0	2.25	6	0	0	1	12	7	3	3	1	1	13	.163	.231	.133	9.75	0.75
Soria, Joakim	R-R	6-3	208	5-18-84	2	2	2.82	22	0	0	2	22	18	8	7	1	10	24	.217	.130	.250	9.67	4.03
Trivino, Lou	R-R	6-5	235	10-1-91	0	0	3.86	20	0	0	0	23	16	10	10	3	10	26	.193	.235	.163	10.03	3.86
Weems, Jordan	L-R	6-3	175	11-7-92	0	0	3.21	9	0	0	0	14	10	5	5	1	7	18	.200	.273	.143	11.57	4.50
Wendelken, J.B.	R-R	6-1	242	3-24-93	1	1	1.80	21	0	0	0	25	17	8	5	2	11	31	.183	.194	.175	11.16	3.96

Fielding

Catcher	PCT	G	PO	A	E	DP	PB
Allen	1.000	14	76	1	0	0	0
Heim	1.000	12	105	6	0	0	0
Murphy	.994	43	334	14	2	1	4

First Base	PCT	G	PO	A	E	DP
Brown	1.000	3	3	0	0	0
Canha	1.000	3	5	0	0	0
Machin	1.000	2	2	0	0	1
Olson	.998	60	393	48	1	30

Second Base	PCT	G	PO	A	E	DP
Barreto	1.000	4	1	3	0	0
Kemp	.990	43	49	55	1	12
La Stella	.982	18	19	35	1	7
Machin	1.000	3	4	4	0	1
Orf	1.000	2	0	2	0	1
Pinder	.972	13	16	19	1	4

Third Base	PCT	G	PO	A	E	DP
Chapman	.944	36	28	57	5	9
La Stella	1.000	6	2	7	0	1
Lamb	.957	11	9	13	1	2
Machin	1.000	10	3	7	0	0
Pinder	1.000	7	2	9	0	0

Shortstop	PCT	G	PO	A	E	DP
Barreto	1.000	3	1	2	0	1
Chapman	1.000	1	1	2	0	0
Machin	.931	6	9	18	2	2
Orf	1.000	3	2	0	0	0
Semien	.967	53	59	147	7	17

Outfield	PCT	G	PO	A	E	DP
Canha	.988	37	84	1	1	0
Grossman	1.000	47	86	1	0	0
Kemp	1.000	3	2	0	0	0
Laureano	1.000	53	144	2	0	0
Pinder	1.000	3	1	0	0	0
Piscotty	1.000	44	73	2	0	0

Philadelphia Phillies

SEASON IN A SENTENCE: One of the most expensive teams in baseball looked on its way to a playoff bid with a 19-15 record through the first 34 games, but an abysmal bullpen proved too much for the team to overcome as it missed the postseason for the ninth straight year.

HIGH POINT: The Phillies stood at 19-15 after 34 games, overcoming a sluggish start to win 10 of 11 heading into a Sept. 5 contest against the Mets. Stars Bryce Harper, Rhys Hoskins, Didi Gregorius and J.T. Realmuto all had an OPS at .828 or higher and the team was getting contributions from top prospects Alec Bohm and Spencer Howard.

LOW POINT: Any time a Phillies reliever jogged into the game, Phillies fans had reasons to worry. Philadelphia's starting pitching was good enough to drive the team to the playoffs, but the pen never gave the Phillies a chance. Phillies relievers posted a 7.09 ERA and a 1.790 WHIP. Opponents hit .315/.391/.555 against the Phillies relievers.

NOTABLE ROOKIES: Third baseman Alec Bohm looked the part of an all-star hitter after making his big league debut in mid-August, hitting .338/.400/.481 with four home runs and 23 RBIs in 44 games. Bohm is a plus hitter with plus power, but questions remain regarding whether his glove will give him a chance to stick at third base long term. Righthander Spencer Howard, meanwhile, struggled at times, but still showed an impressive arsenal—a plus-plus fastball and three above-average secondary offerings. He finished the year with a 1-2, 5.92 mark in six starts and the Phillies are confident he will lead the rotation for years to come. Righthanders Connor Brogdon and Adonis Medina, catcher Rafael Marchan and outfielder Mickey Moniak were among those who also made their debuts.

KEY TRANSACTIONS: The Phillies traded No. 2 prospect Sixto Sanchez for J.T. Realmuto before the 2019 season for a playoff run. Instead, the team missed out on the postseason in consecutive years and Realmuto entered free agency after the

2020 season. Sanchez, meanwhile, is one of the top pitching prospects in baseball and looked the part of a top-end starter for the Marlins, posting a 3.46 ERA in seven starts. The Phillies made three trades during the season to beef up their bullpen, including acquiring righthanders Brandon Workman and Heath Hembree from the Red Sox for righthanders Nick Pivetta and Connor Seabold and trading righthander Addison Russ for righthander David Hale from the Yankees.

OPENING DAY PAYROLL: $74,604,761 (7th).

PLAYERS OF THE YEAR

MAJOR LEAGUE	TOP ROOKIE
Bryce Harper OF	**Alec Bohm** 3B
.268/.420/.542	.338/.400/.481
13 HR, 33 RBIs	4 HR, 23 RBIs,
MLB-best 49 walks	11 2B

ORGANIZATION LEADERS

Batting		*Minimum 100 AB
MAJORS		
* AVG	Alec Bohm	.338
* OPS	Bryce Harper	.962
HR	Bryce Harper	13
RBI	Didi Gregorius	40
Pitching		#Minimum 30 IP
MAJORS		
W	Aaron Nola	5
# ERA	Zack Wheeler	2.92
SO	Aaron Nola	96
SV	Hector Neris	5
SV	Brandon Workman	5

ORGANIZATION STATISTICS

PHILADELPHIA PHILLIES
NATIONAL LEAGUE

Batting	B-T	HT	WT	DOB	AVG	vLH	vRH	G	AB	R	H	2B	3B	HR	RBI	BB	HBP	SH	SF	SO	SB	CS	SLG	OBP
Bohm, Alec	R-R	6-5	218	8-3-96	.338	.270	.358	44	160	24	54	11	0	4	23	16	2	0	2	36	1	1	.481	.400
Bruce, Jay	L-L	6-3	230	4-3-87	.198	.111	.218	32	96	11	19	4	2	6	14	7	0	0	0	24	0	0	.469	.252
Garlick, Kyle	R-R	6-1	210	1-26-92	.136	.125	.143	12	22	0	3	1	0	0	3	0	1	0	0	7	0	0	.182	.174
Gosselin, Phil	R-R	6-1	188	10-3-88	.250	.278	.211	39	92	14	23	5	0	3	12	10	0	0	0	27	0	0	.402	.324

Batting

Batting	B-T	HT	WT	DOB	AVG	vLH	vRH	G	AB	R	H	2B	3B	HR	RBI	BB	HBP	SH	SF	SO	SB	CS	SLG	OBP
Gregorius, Didi	L-R	6-3	205	2-18-90	.284	.203	.318	60	215	34	61	10	2	10	40	15	4	1	2	28	3	2	.488	.339
Harper, Bryce	L-R	6-3	210	10-16-92	.268	.281	.263	58	190	41	51	9	2	13	33	49	2	1	2	43	8	2	.542	.420
Haseley, Adam	L-L	6-1	190	4-12-96	.278	.400	.261	40	79	7	22	5	0	0	13	7	2	3	1	17	0	0	.342	.348
Hoskins, Rhys	R-R	6-4	245	3-17-93	.245	.341	.209	41	151	35	37	9	0	10	26	29	5	0	0	43	1	0	.503	.384
Kingery, Scott	R-R	5-10	180	4-29-94	.159	.121	.175	36	113	12	18	5	0	3	6	9	1	1	0	35	0	0	.283	.228
Knapp, Andrew	B-R	6-1	189	11-9-91	.278	.313	.268	33	72	9	20	4	1	2	15	15	1	0	1	19	0	0	.444	.404
Marchan, Rafael	B-R	5-9	170	2-25-99	.500	--	.500	3	8	3	4	0	0	1	3	1	0	0	0	2	0	0	.875	.556
McCutchen, Andrew	R-R	5-11	195	10-10-86	.253	.283	.242	57	217	32	55	9	0	10	34	22	1	0	1	48	4	0	.433	.324
Moniak, Mickey	L-R	6-2	195	5-13-98	.214	.000	.273	8	14	3	3	0	0	0	4	0	0	0	0	6	0	0	.214	.389
Quinn, Roman	B-R	5-10	175	5-14-93	.213	.206	.216	41	108	14	23	3	1	2	7	5	2	1	0	39	12	0	.315	.261
Realmuto, J.T.	R-R	6-1	212	3-18-91	.266	.386	.225	47	173	33	46	6	0	11	32	16	6	0	0	48	4	1	.491	.349
Segura, Jean	R-R	5-10	220	3-17-90	.266	.273	.263	54	192	28	51	5	2	7	25	23	1	1	0	45	2	2	.422	.347
Torreyes, Ronald	R-R	5-8	155	9-2-92	.143	.000	.250	4	7	1	1	0	0	0	0	0	0	0	0	0	0	0	.286	.143
Walker, Neil	B-R	6-2	214	9-10-85	.231	.000	.290	18	39	5	9	3	0	0	3	1	0	0	1	13	0	0	.308	.244

Pitching

Pitching	B-T	HT	WT	DOB	W	L	ERA	G	GS	CG	SV	IP	H	R	ER	HR	BB	SO	AVG	vLH	vRH	K/9	BB/9
Alvarez, Jose	L-L	5-11	195	5-6-89	0	0	1.42	8	0	0	0	6	7	1	1	0	3	6	.292	.444	.200	8.53	4.26
Arrieta, Jake	R-R	6-4	230	3-6-86	4	4	5.08	9	9	0	0	44	51	25	25	6	16	32	.298	.304	.293	6.50	3.25
Brogdon, Connor	R-R	6-6	205	1-29-95	1	0	3.97	9	0	0	0	11	5	5	5	3	5	17	.128	.133	.125	13.50	3.97
Cleavinger, Garrett	R-L	6-1	220	4-23-94	0	0	13.50	1	0	0	0	1	2	1	1	1	0	1	.500	.667	.000	13.50	9.00
Davis, Austin	L-L	6-4	225	2-3-93	0	0	21.00	4	0	0	0	3	10	7	7	1	1	2	.526	.857	.333	6.00	3.00
2-team total (5 Pittsburgh Pirates)					0	0	10.80	9	0	0	0	7	11	8	8	1	2	5	.367	.636	.211	6.75	2.70
Eflin, Zach	R-R	6-6	220	4-8-94	4	2	3.97	11	10	1	0	59	60	28	26	8	15	70	.263	.279	.250	10.68	2.29
Guerra, Deolis	R-R	6-5	245	4-17-89	1	3	8.59	9	0	0	0	7	10	9	7	3	2	8	.313	.077	.474	9.82	2.45
Hale, David	R-R	6-2	210	9-27-87	0	0	4.09	6	2	0	0	11	16	5	5	2	1	7	.333	.211	.414	5.73	0.82
Hembree, Heath	R-R	6-4	220	1-13-89	1	0	12.54	11	0	0	0	9	17	13	13	7	5	10	.405	.231	.483	9.64	4.82
Howard, Spencer	R-R	6-3	210	7-28-96	1	2	5.92	6	6	0	0	24	30	17	16	6	10	23	.300	.333	.265	8.51	3.70
Hunter, Tommy	R-R	6-3	250	7-3-86	0	1	4.01	24	0	0	0	25	22	11	11	2	6	25	.239	.295	.188	9.12	2.19
Irvin, Cole	L-L	6-4	217	1-31-94	0	1	17.18	3	0	0	0	4	11	7	7	1	1	4	.524	.800	.438	9.82	2.45
Kelley, Trevor	R-R	6-2	210	10-20-93	0	0	10.80	4	0	0	0	3	8	4	4	2	1	5	.444	.250	.600	13.50	2.70
Llovera, Mauricio	R-R	5-11	224	4-17-96	0	0	36.00	1	0	0	0	1	5	4	4	0	1	1	.625	.667	.500	9.00	9.00
McClain, Reggie	R-R	6-2	180	11-16-92	0	0	5.06	5	0	0	0	5	9	6	3	1	3	4	.360	.375	.353	3.38	5.06
Medina, Adonis	R-R	6-1	187	12-18-96	0	1	4.50	1	1	0	0	4	3	2	2	0	3	4	.200	.154	.900	9.00	6.75
Morgan, Adam	L-L	6-1	200	2-27-90	1	0	5.54	17	0	0	0	13	14	8	8	3	6	16	.269	.200	.364	11.08	4.15
Neris, Hector	R-R	6-2	227	6-14-89	2	2	4.57	24	0	0	5	22	24	15	11	0	13	27	.267	.275	.260	11.22	5.40
Nola, Aaron	R-R	6-2	200	6-4-93	5	5	3.28	12	12	2	0	71	54	31	26	9	23	96	.205	.210	.201	12.11	2.90
Parker, Blake	R-R	6-3	225	6-19-85	3	0	2.81	14	1	0	0	16	12	7	5	2	9	25	.203	.258	.143	14.06	5.06
Phelps, David	R-R	6-2	198	10-9-86	0	1	12.91	10	0	0	0	8	12	11	11	5	3	11	.353	.333	.364	12.91	3.52
2-team total (12 Milwaukee Brewers)					2	4	6.53	22	0	0	0	21	19	16	15	7	5	31	.241	.190	.297	13.50	2.18
Pivetta, Nick	R-R	6-5	214	2-14-93	0	0	15.88	3	0	0	0	6	10	10	10	3	1	4	.385	.455	.333	6.35	1.59
Romero, JoJo	L-L	5-11	200	9-9-96	0	0	7.59	12	0	0	0	11	13	10	9	1	2	10	.310	.227	.400	8.44	1.69
Rosso, Ramon	R-R	6-4	240	6-9-96	0	1	6.52	7	1	0	0	10	9	7	7	1	8	11	.243	.389	.105	10.24	7.45
Suarez, Ranger	L-L	6-1	217	8-26-95	0	1	20.25	3	0	0	0	4	10	9	9	1	4	1	.476	.500	.462	2.25	9.00
Velasquez, Vince	R-R	6-3	212	6-7-92	1	1	5.56	9	7	0	0	34	36	21	21	5	17	46	.269	.315	.238	12.18	4.50
Walker, Neil	B-R	6-2	214	9-10-85	0	0	0.00	1	0	0	0	1	0	0	0	0	1	0	.000	--	.000	0.00	13.50
Wheeler, Zack	L-R	6-4	195	5-30-90	4	2	2.92	11	11	0	0	71	67	26	23	3	16	53	.254	.250	.258	6.72	2.03
Workman, Brandon	R-R	6-5	235	8-13-88	1	4	6.92	14	0	0	5	13	23	11	10	4	9	15	.377	.323	.433	10.38	6.23

Fielding

Catcher	PCT	G	PO	A	E	DP	PB
Knapp	.991	29	218	13	2	1	4
Marchan	.963	3	25	1	1	0	0
Realmuto	.993	36	296	8	2	3	1

First Base	PCT	G	PO	A	E	DP
Bohm	1.000	7	55	4	0	6
Bruce	1.000	2	13	1	0	0
Gosselin	1.000	8	39	2	0	5
Hoskins	.988	40	315	21	4	34
Knapp	1.000	1	6	0	0	2
Realmuto	1.000	6	16	0	0	0
Walker	1.000	3	19	1	0	3

Second Base	PCT	G	PO	A	E	DP
Gosselin	1.000	4	1	7	0	2
Kingery	.952	29	40	59	5	23
Segura	1.000	32	27	85	0	20
Torreyes	1.000	1	1	2	0	1
Walker	1.000	9	5	8	0	1

Third Base	PCT	G	PO	A	E	DP
Bohm	.957	38	26	64	4	6
Gosselin	1.000	2	1	1	0	0
Segura	.964	24	13	40	2	4
Walker	1.000	2	1	4	0	0

Shortstop	PCT	G	PO	A	E	DP
Gregorius	.968	59	79	132	7	34
Kingery	.000	1	0	0	0	0
Segura	.909	4	2	8	1	2
Torreyes	1.000	2	0	3	0	0

Outfield	PCT	G	PO	A	E	DP
Bruce	1.000	17	26	2	0	1
Garlick	1.000	10	2	0	0	0
Gosselin	.875	14	7	0	1	0
Harper	.986	48	67	2	1	0
Haseley	1.000	39	37	0	0	0
Kingery	1.000	9	8	0	0	0
McCutchen	1.000	39	47	0	0	0
Moniak	.857	6	12	0	2	0
Quinn	.984	39	60	3	1	1
Torreyes	1.000	1	1	0	0	0
Walker	--	1	0	0	0	0

Pittsburgh Pirates

SEASON IN A SENTENCE: The Pirates traded Starling Marte before the season to signal the start of their rebuild and plummeted even further than expected, losing 17 of their first 21 games and finishing with MLB's worst record at 19-41.

HIGH POINT: The debut of third baseman Ke'Bryan Hayes on Sept. 1 at least gave the Pirates a sense of hope for the future. Hayes hit a double and a home run and scored three times against the Cubs in his major league debut. It was the start of a sensational month in which Hayes hit .376 with seven doubles, two triples and five home runs in only 24 games.

LOW POINT: The Pirates nadir came on Aug. 25 when they were no-hit by White Sox righthander Lucas Giolito. It wasn't just that Giolito threw a no-hitter, but how feebly the Pirates went down against him. Giolito struck out 13 batters, allowed only one baserunner and needed just 101 pitches to complete the feat.

NOTABLE ROOKIES: Hayes starred at the plate and in the field after his callup to establish himself as the Pirates' third baseman of the future. His defensive excellence was expected, but his power at the plate was a nice surprise. Righthander Mitch Keller bounced back from a rough debut in 2019 to post a 2.91 ERA in five starts wrapped around an oblique injury. Righthander JT Brubaker took over a rotation spot and went 1-3, 4.94 in 11 appearances (nine starts). Another righthander, Cody Ponce, moved into the starting rotation and went 1-1, 3.18 in five appearances (three starts). Relievers Geoff Hartlieb, Nik Turley and Sam Howard all got their first extended major league action and pitched well out of the bullpen. Outfielder Jared Oliva and first baseman Will Craig each made their major league debut.

KEY TRANSACTIONS: The Pirates traded Marte, their all-star and two-time Gold Glove-winning center fielder, to the D-backs in late January for pitching prospect Brennan Malone and shortstop prospect Liover Peguero. The Pirates then spent most of the season claiming players off waivers, including pitchers Nick Tropeano and Carson Fulmer and outfielders Anthony Alford and Guillermo Heredia. Despite their poor record, the Pirates avoided selling and made only two minor moves at the trade deadline. They acquired reliever Austin Davis from the Phillies for pitching prospect Joel Cesar and sent outfielder Jarrod Dyson to the White Sox for a player to be named later.

OPENING DAY PAYROLL: $24,770,928 (29th)

PLAYERS OF THE YEAR

MAJOR LEAGUE

Richard Rodriguez
RHP
3-2, 2.70, 4 SV
34 SO, 5 BB in 23.1 IP

TOP ROOKIE

Ke'Bryan Hayes
3B
.376/.442/.682
14 XBH, 11 RBIs in 24 G

ORGANIZATION LEADERS

Batting		*Minimum 100 AB
MAJORS		
* AVG	Jacob Stallings	.248
* OPS	Colin Moran	.797
HR	Colin Moran	10
RBI	Adam Frazier	23
RBI	Colin Moran	23
Pitching		**#Minimum 30 IP**
MAJORS		
W	Richard Rodriguez	3
# ERA	Steven Brault	3.38
SO	Joe Musgrove	55
SV	Richard Rodriguez	4

ORGANIZATION STATISTICS

PITTSBURGH PIRATES
NATIONAL LEAGUE

Batting	B-T	HT	WT	DOB	AVG	vLH	vRH	G	AB	R	H	2B	3B	HR	RBI	BB	HBP	SH	SF	SO	SB	CS	SLG	OBP
Alford, Anthony	R-R	6-1	210	7-20-94	.250	.000	.273	5	12	2	3	0	1	1	4	1	0	0	0	1	0	0	.667	.308
Bell, Josh	B-R	6-4	250	8-14-92	.226	.180	.241	57	195	22	44	3	0	8	22	22	2	0	4	59	0	0	.364	.305
Craig, Will	R-R	6-3	220	11-16-94	.000	.000	.000	2	4	0	0	0	0	0	0	0	0	0	0	1	0	0	.000	.000
Dyson, Jarrod	L-R	5-9	165	8-15-84	.157	.200	.152	21	51	6	8	0	0	0	5	4	0	0	0	10	4	0	.157	.218

Batting	B-T	HT	WT	DOB	AVG	vLH	vRH	G	AB	R	H	2B	3B	HR	RBI	BB	HBP	SH	SF	SO	SB	CS	SLG	OBP
Evans, Phillip	R-R	5-10	210	9-10-92	.359	.429	.320	11	39	6	14	2	0	1	9	5	1	0	0	7	0	1	.487	.444
Frazier, Adam	L-R	5-10	185	12-14-91	.230	.200	.238	58	209	22	48	7	0	7	23	17	3	1	0	35	1	3	.364	.297
Gonzalez, Erik	R-R	6-3	210	8-31-91	.227	.304	.200	50	181	14	41	13	1	3	20	8	0	1	3	51	2	3	.359	.255
Hayes, Ke'Bryan	R-R	5-10	205	1-28-97	.376	.500	.333	24	85	17	32	7	2	5	11	9	1	0	0	20	1	0	.682	.442
Heredia, Guillermo	R-L	5-10	195	1-31-91	.188	.333	.100	8	16	2	3	0	0	0	2	2	0	0	0	4	1	0	.188	.278
2-team total (7 New York Mets)					.212	.250	.190	15	33	6	7	0	0	2	5	3	0	0	0	9	1	0	.394	.278
Martin, Jason	L-R	5-9	185	9-5-95	.000	.000	.000	7	9	2	0	0	0	0	0	2	0	0	0	4	0	0	.000	.182
Moran, Colin	L-R	6-4	200	10-1-92	.247	.231	.254	52	178	28	44	10	0	10	23	19	2	0	1	52	0	0	.472	.325
Murphy, John Ryan	R-R	5-11	200	5-13-91	.172	.429	.137	25	58	6	10	2	0	0	2	4	0	1	0	28	0	0	.207	.226
Newman, Kevin	R-R	6-0	200	8-4-93	.224	.276	.213	44	156	12	35	5	0	1	10	12	1	1	2	21	0	1	.276	.281
Oliva, Jared	R-R	6-2	195	11-27-95	.188	.000	.200	6	16	0	3	0	0	0	0	0	0	0	0	6	1	0	.188	.188
Osuna, Jose	R-R	6-2	235	12-12-92	.205	.292	.167	26	78	6	16	3	0	4	11	4	0	0	0	16	1	0	.397	.244
Polanco, Gregory	L-L	6-5	235	9-14-91	.153	.139	.157	50	157	12	24	6	0	7	22	13	0	0	3	65	3	1	.325	.214
Reynolds, Bryan	B-R	6-3	205	1-27-95	.189	.195	.188	55	185	24	35	6	2	7	19	21	1	0	0	57	1	1	.357	.275
Riddle, JT	L-R	6-1	190	10-12-91	.149	.222	.138	23	67	8	10	2	0	1	1	2	0	0	0	13	1	0	.224	.174
Stallings, Jacob	R-R	6-5	220	12-22-89	.248	.324	.220	42	125	13	31	7	0	3	18	15	0	2	1	40	0	0	.376	.326
Susac, Andrew	R-R	6-1	220	3-22-90	.000	--	.000	1	2	0	0	0	0	0	0	2	0	0	0	0	0	0	.000	.500
Tucker, Cole	B-R	6-3	205	7-3-96	.220	.258	.205	37	109	17	24	3	0	1	8	5	0	1	1	31	1	0	.275	.252

Pitching	B-T	HT	WT	DOB	W	L	ERA	G	GS	CG	SV	IP	H	R	ER	HR	BB	SO	AVG	vLH	vRH	K/9	BB/9
Bashlor, Tyler	R-R	6-0	195	4-16-93	0	0	8.64	8	0	0	0	8	9	8	8	2	4	6	.281	.294	.267	6.48	4.32
Brault, Steven	L-L	6-0	195	4-29-92	1	3	3.38	11	10	1	0	43	29	17	16	2	22	38	.195	.217	.190	8.02	4.64
Brubaker, JT	R-R	6-3	185	11-17-93	1	3	4.94	11	9	0	0	47	48	27	26	6	17	48	.262	.287	.232	9.13	3.23
Burdi, Nick	R-R	6-3	225	1-19-93	0	1	3.86	3	0	0	1	2	2	1	1	0	2	4	.250	.250	.250	15.43	7.71
Cederlind, Blake	R-R	6-4	215	1-4-96	0	0	4.50	5	0	0	0	4	3	2	2	0	1	4	.200	.222	.167	9.00	2.25
Crick, Kyle	R-R	6-4	225	11-30-92	0	1	1.59	7	0	0	0	6	6	1	1	0	4	7	.280	.375	.235	11.12	6.35
Davis, Austin	L-L	6-4	225	2-3-93	0	0	2.45	5	0	0	0	4	1	1	1	0	1	3	.091	.250	.000	7.36	2.45
2-team total (4 Philadelphia Phillies)					0	0	10.80	9	0	0	0	7	11	8	8	1	2	5	.367	.636	.211	6.75	2.70
Del Pozo, Miguel	L-L	6-1	205	10-14-92	0	0	17.18	9	0	0	0	4	7	7	7	0	8	2	.412	.333	.429	4.91	19.64
Erlin, Robbie	R-L	5-11	200	10-8-90	0	0	5.40	2	0	0	0	3	5	2	2	0	1	4	.333	.333	.333	10.80	2.70
2-team total (7 Atlanta Braves)					0	0	8.10	9	5	0	0	27	33	24	24	8	7	25	.295	.424	.241	8.44	2.36
Feliz, Michael	R-R	6-4	240	6-28-93	0	0	32.40	3	0	0	0	2	4	6	6	1	2	2	.444	.333	.667	10.80	10.80
Hartlieb, Geoff	R-R	6-5	235	12-9-93	0	0	3.63	21	0	0	0	22	16	11	9	1	19	19	.205	.182	.222	7.66	7.66
Holland, Derek	B-L	6-2	213	10-9-86	1	3	6.86	12	5	0	0	41	42	33	31	12	15	45	.261	.161	.285	9.96	3.32
Holmes, Clay	R-R	6-5	230	3-27-93	0	0	0.00	1	0	0	0	1	2	0	0	0	0	1	.333	.333	.333	6.75	0.00
Howard, Sam	R-L	6-4	200	3-5-93	2	3	3.86	22	0	0	0	21	17	10	9	4	9	27	.221	.259	.200	11.57	3.86
Kela, Keone	R-R	6-1	220	4-16-93	0	0	4.50	3	0	0	0	2	3	1	1	1	1	3	.333	.333	.333	13.50	4.50
Keller, Mitch	R-R	6-2	205	4-4-96	1	1	2.91	5	5	0	0	22	9	7	7	4	18	16	.132	.179	.069	6.65	7.48
Kuhl, Chad	R-R	6-3	215	9-10-92	2	3	4.27	11	9	0	0	46	35	26	22	8	28	44	.212	.196	.233	8.55	5.44
Mears, Nick	R-R	6-2	215	10-7-96	0	0	5.40	4	0	0	0	5	4	3	3	1	7	7	.222	.143	.273	12.60	12.60
Murphy, John Ryan	R-R	5-11	200	5-13-91	0	0	0.00	1	0	0	0	1	0	0	0	0	0	0	.000	.000	.000	0.00	0.00
Musgrove, Joe	R-R	6-5	235	12-4-92	1	5	3.86	8	8	0	0	40	33	17	17	5	16	55	.226	.183	.281	12.48	3.63
Neverauskas, Dovydas	R-R	6-3	225	1-14-93	0	3	7.11	17	0	0	0	19	24	17	15	5	10	23	.304	.382	.244	10.89	4.74
Ponce, Cody	R-R	6-5	255	4-25-94	1	1	3.18	5	3	0	0	17	12	7	6	5	6	12	.200	.212	.185	6.35	3.18
Rios, Yacksel	R-R	6-3	215	6-27-93	0	0	9.00	3	0	0	0	4	3	4	4	0	2	3	.214	.125	.333	6.75	4.50
Rodriguez, Richard	R-R	6-4	218	3-4-90	3	2	2.70	24	0	0	4	23	15	8	7	5	5	34	.179	.140	.220	13.11	1.93
Stratton, Chris	R-R	6-2	210	8-22-90	2	1	3.90	27	0	0	0	30	26	19	13	3	13	39	.224	.204	.242	11.70	3.90
Tropeano, Nick	R-R	6-4	205	8-27-90	1	0	1.15	7	0	0	0	16	14	2	2	1	4	19	.233	.067	.289	10.91	2.30
Turley, Nik	L-L	6-4	235	9-11-89	0	3	4.98	25	0	0	1	22	13	13	12	1	11	20	.173	.227	.151	8.31	4.57
Waddell, Brandon	L-L	6-3	180	6-3-94	0	0	2.70	2	0	0	0	3	2	1	1	0	2	2	.167	.200	.143	5.40	5.40
Williams, Trevor	R-R	6-3	235	4-25-92	2	8	6.18	11	11	0	0	55	66	42	38	15	21	49	.296	.260	.344	7.97	3.42

Fielding

Catcher	PCT	G	PO	A	E	DP	PB
Murphy	.988	23	159	11	2	3	0
Stallings	.990	42	379	22	4	2	3
Susac	1.000	1	5	0	0	0	0

First Base	PCT	G	PO	A	E	DP
Bell	.984	35	215	26	4	24
Craig	1.000	2	9	0	0	1
Evans	.750	1	3	0	1	0
Moran	.988	22	152	15	2	16
Osuna	1.000	9	47	1	0	3
Riddle	1.000	1	2	0	0	0

Second Base	PCT	G	PO	A	E	DP
Frazier	.994	41	63	90	1	24
Newman	.960	20	33	39	3	8
Riddle	1.000	1	0	2	0	0
Tucker	.000	1	0	0	0	0

Third Base	PCT	G	PO	A	E	DP
Evans	.882	8	6	9	2	1
Gonzalez	.967	13	5	24	1	1
Hayes	.985	24	17	50	1	3
Moran	.923	4	5	7	1	1
Osuna	1.000	5	1	7	0	2
Riddle	.885	11	7	16	3	2

Shortstop	PCT	G	PO	A	E	DP
Gonzalez	.957	38	32	79	5	22
Newman	.930	23	20	46	5	10
Riddle	.917	3	6	5	1	2

Outfield	PCT	G	PO	A	E	DP
Alford	1.000	5	2	0	0	0
Dyson	.974	21	37	1	1	0
Evans	1.000	2	3	0	0	0
Frazier	1.000	14	26	2	0	0
Heredia	1.000	7	14	1	0	1
Martin	1.000	5	6	0	0	0
Oliva	1.000	5	4	0	0	0
Osuna	1.000	11	18	2	0	0
Polanco	.971	39	67	1	2	1
Reynolds	.980	53	95	5	2	1
Riddle	1.000	6	9	0	0	0
Tucker	1.000	30	54	0	0	0

St. Louis Cardinals

SEASON IN A SENTENCE: The Cardinals suffered a COVID-19 outbreak that decimated their roster and led to 17 straight games being postponed, but they recovered to finish strong and made the playoffs as a wild card.

HIGH POINT: Needing a win on the season's final day to clinch a playoff berth, Paul Goldschmidt went 3-for-4, Harrison Bader homered and four pitchers combined for 10 strikeouts to lead the Cardinals to a 5-2 win over the Brewers to punch their ticket to the postseason.

LOW POINT: A COVID-19 outbreak began amongst the team on July 30 and eventually spread to 18 members of the organization, including players, coaches and staff members. The team was shut down from playing for more than two weeks and five consecutive series had to be postponed, forcing the team to endure a long run of makeup games.

NOTABLE ROOKIES: Largely because the COVID-19 outbreak hollowed out the roster, the Cardinals used 21 different rookies in 2020, including 14 on their pitching staff. Outfielder Dylan Carlson had a rocky first stint in the majors but excelled after returning in September and batted cleanup during the Cardinals' Wild Card Series against the Padres. He joined Stan Musial and Albert Pujols as the only players in franchise history to bat cleanup at age 21 or younger in a playoff game. Lefthander Kwang Hyun Kim went 3-0, 1.62 in eight appearances (seven starts) and had the lowest ERA of any qualified rookie. Lefthander Genesis Cabrera went 4-1, 2.42 in 19 appearances and emerged as one of the Cardinals' top setup men. Righthander Johan Oviedo joined the rotation in August and made five starts, while righthanders Jake Woodford and Seth Elledge each made 12 appearances, most among Cardinals pitchers who debuted in 2020.

KEY TRANSACTIONS: The Cardinals signed Kim to a two-year, $8 million deal in December 2019 after a decorated career in South Korea. The 31-year-old was a star pitcher in the Korea Baseball

PLAYERS OF THE YEAR

MAJOR LEAGUE

Paul Goldschmidt
1B
.304/.417/.466
37 BB, 43 K

TOP ROOKIE

Johan Oviedo
RHP
0-3, 5.47 in 5 GS
16 SO in 24.2 IP

MARY DECICCO VIA GETTY IMAGES

ORGANIZATION LEADERS

Batting		*Minimum 100 AB
MAJORS		
* AVG	Paul Goldschmidt	.304
* OPS	Paul Goldschmidt	.883
HR	Tyler O'Neill	7
HR	Brad Miller	7
RBI	Tommy Edman	26
Pitching		#Minimum 30 IP
MAJORS		
W	Adam Wainwright	5
# ERA	Kwang Hyun Kim	1.62
SO	Adam Wainwright	54
SV	Giovanny Gallegos	4
SV	Andrew Miller	4

Organization and in international competition for his home country, including in the Olympics and World Baseball Classic. In January, the Cardinals traded outfielders Jose Martinez and Randy Arozarena to the Rays for a package headlined by top pitching prospect Matthew Liberatore. Arozarena went on to set the record for most hits and home runs in a single postseason while leading Tampa Bay to the World Series.

OPENING DAY PAYROLL: $70,452,778 (9th)

ORGANIZATION STATISTICS

ST. LOUIS CARDINALS
NATIONAL LEAGUE

Batting	B-T	HT	WT	DOB	AVG	vLH	vRH	G	AB	R	H	2B	3B	HR	RBI	BB	HBP	SH	SF	SO	SB	CS	SLG	OBP
Bader, Harrison	R-R	6-0	210	6-3-94	.226	.360	.185	50	106	21	24	7	2	4	11	13	5	0	1	40	3	1	.443	.336
Carlson, Dylan	B-L	6-2	205	10-23-98	.200	.182	.202	35	110	11	22	7	1	3	16	8	0	0	1	35	1	1	.364	.252
Carpenter, Matt	L-R	6-4	210	11-26-85	.186	.190	.185	50	140	22	26	6	0	4	24	23	6	0	0	48	0	0	.314	.325
Dean, Austin	R-R	6-0	215	10-14-93	.250	0	.333	3	4	1	1	1	0	0	0	3	0	0	0	2	0	0	.500	.571

Batting

Batting	B-T	HT	WT	DOB	AVG	vLH	vRH	G	AB	R	H	2B	3B	HR	RBI	BB	HBP	SH	SF	SO	SB	CS	SLG	OBP
DeJong, Paul	R-R	6-0	205	8-2-93	.250	.125	.273	45	152	17	38	6	0	3	25	17	1	0	4	50	1	0	.349	.322
Edman, Tommy	B-R	5-10	180	5-9-95	.250	.317	.233	55	204	29	51	7	1	5	26	16	5	0	2	48	2	4	.368	.317
Fowler, Dexter	B-R	6-5	205	3-22-86	.233	.118	.260	31	90	14	21	2	0	4	15	10	1	0	0	28	1	1	.389	.317
Goldschmidt, Paul	R-R	6-3	220	9-10-87	.304	.286	.307	58	191	31	58	13	0	6	21	37	1	0	1	43	1	0	.466	.417
Knizner, Andrew	R-R	6-1	225	2-3-95	.250	.200	.273	8	16	1	4	1	0	0	4	0	0	0	1	5	0	0	.313	.235
Miller, Brad	L-R	6-2	195	10-18-89	.232	.176	.240	48	142	21	33	8	1	7	25	25	3	0	1	46	1	0	.451	.357
Molina, Yadier	R-R	5-11	225	7-13-82	.262	.192	.277	42	145	12	38	2	0	4	16	6	3	1	1	21	0	0	.359	.303
Nogowski, John	R-L	6-0	245	1-5-93	.250	.333	0	1	4	0	1	0	0	0	0	0	0	0	0	1	0	0	.250	.250
O'Neill, Tyler	R-R	5-11	200	6-22-95	.173	.154	.177	50	139	20	24	5	0	7	19	15	2	0	1	43	3	1	.360	.261
Ravelo, Rangel	R-R	6-1	235	4-24-92	.171	.188	.158	13	35	5	6	1	0	1	6	4	0	0	2	6	0	0	.286	.244
Schrock, Max	L-R	5-9	185	10-12-94	.176	1.000	.067	11	17	1	3	0	0	1	1	0	0	0	0	6	0	0	.353	.176
Thomas, Lane	R-R	6-0	185	8-23-95	.111	.125	.107	18	36	5	4	2	0	1	2	4	0	0	0	13	0	0	.250	.200
Wieters, Matt	B-R	6-5	235	5-21-86	.200	.143	.214	19	35	3	7	1	0	0	4	3	2	1	0	10	0	0	.229	.300
Williams, Justin	L-R	6-1	235	8-20-95	.200	--	.200	3	5	0	1	0	0	0	0	1	0	0	0	2	0	0	.200	.333
Wong, Kolten	L-R	5-7	185	10-10-90	.265	.294	.259	53	181	26	48	4	2	1	16	20	4	2	1	30	5	2	.326	.350

Pitching

Pitching	B-T	HT	WT	DOB	W	L	ERA	G	GS	CG	SV	IP	H	R	ER	HR	BB	SO	AVG	vLH	vRH	K/9	BB/9
Cabrera, Genesis	L-L	6-2	180	10-10-96	4	1	2.42	19	0	0	1	22	10	9	6	3	16	32	.132	.069	.170	12.90	6.45
Crismatt, Nabil	R-R	6-1	220	12-25-94	0	0	3.24	6	0	0	0	8	6	3	3	2	1	8	.200	.286	.125	8.64	1.08
Cruz, Jesus	R-R	6-1	230	4-1-95	0	0	18.00	1	0	0	0	1	3	2	2	0	1	2	.600	.667	.500	18.00	9.00
Elledge, Seth	R-R	6-3	240	5-20-96	1	0	4.63	12	0	0	0	12	11	6	6	2	8	14	.262	.316	.217	10.8	6.17
Fernandez, Junior	R-R	6-3	215	3-2-97	0	0	18.00	3	0	0	0	3	6	6	6	1	2	2	.429	.333	.500	6.00	6.00
Flaherty, Jack	R-R	6-4	225	10-15-95	4	3	4.91	9	9	0	0	40	33	22	22	6	16	49	.221	.232	.209	10.93	3.57
Gallegos, Giovanny	R-R	6-2	215	8-14-91	2	2	3.60	16	0	0	4	15	9	6	6	1	4	21	.170	.158	.176	12.60	2.40
Gant, John	R-R	6-4	200	8-6-92	0	3	2.40	17	0	0	0	15	9	6	4	0	7	18	.167	.176	.162	10.80	4.20
Gomber, Austin	L-L	6-5	220	11-23-93	1	1	1.86	14	4	0	0	29	19	6	6	1	15	27	.190	.192	.189	8.38	4.66
Helsley, Ryan	R-R	6-2	230	7-18-94	1	1	5.25	12	0	0	1	12	8	8	7	3	8	10	.186	.222	.160	7.50	6.00
Hudson, Dakota	R-R	6-5	215	9-15-94	3	2	2.77	8	8	0	0	39	24	13	12	5	15	31	.178	.130	.241	7.15	3.46
Kaminsky, Rob	R-L	6-0	195	9-2-94	0	0	1.93	5	0	0	0	5	3	3	1	0	2	3	.188	.250	.167	5.79	3.86
Kim, Kwang Hyun	L-L	6-2	195	7-22-88	3	0	1.62	8	7	0	1	39	28	9	7	3	12	24	.197	.192	.198	5.54	2.77
Martinez, Carlos	R-R	6-0	200	9-21-91	0	3	9.90	5	5	0	0	20	32	26	22	6	10	17	.352	.310	.388	7.65	4.50
Meisinger, Ryan	R-R	6-4	235	5-4-94	0	0	0.00	2	0	0	0	3	1	0	0	0	4	3	.125	.333	.000	10.13	13.50
Miller, Andrew	L-L	6-7	200	5-21-85	1	1	2.77	16	0	0	4	13	9	4	4	0	5	16	.191	.158	.214	11.08	3.46
Oviedo, Johan	R-R	6-5	245	3-2-98	0	3	5.47	5	5	0	0	25	24	18	15	3	10	16	.253	.200	.311	5.84	3.65
Ponce de Leon, Daniel	R-R	6-3	200	1-16-92	1	3	4.96	9	8	0	0	33	23	18	18	8	20	45	.190	.175	.207	12.40	5.51
Ramirez, Roel	R-R	6-0	235	5-26-95	0	0	81.00	1	0	0	0	1	6	6	6	4	1	1	.857	1.000	.750	13.50	13.50
Reyes, Alex	R-R	6-4	220	8-29-94	2	1	3.20	15	1	0	1	20	14	10	7	1	14	27	.197	.172	.214	12.36	6.41
Sanchez, Ricardo	L-L	5-10	220	4-11-97	0	0	6.75	3	0	0	0	5	5	4	4	1	5	4	.250	.000	.333	6.75	8.44
Schrock, Max	L-R	5-9	185	10-12-94	0	0	0.00	1	0	0	0	1	0	0	0	0	0	0	.000	.000	.000	0	0
Wainwright, Adam	R-R	6-7	230	8-30-81	5	3	3.15	10	10	2	0	66	54	25	23	9	15	54	.221	0.217	.226	7.40	2.06
Webb, Tyler	L-L	6-5	240	7-20-90	1	1	2.08	21	0	0	1	22	17	5	5	2	7	19	.218	.100	.292	7.89	2.91
Whitley, Kodi	R-R	6-3	220	2-21-95	0	0	1.93	4	0	0	0	5	2	1	1	1	1	5	.125	.250	.000	9.64	1.93
Woodford, Jake	R-R	6-4	215	10-28-96	1	0	5.57	12	1	0	0	21	20	13	13	7	5	16	.253	.194	.302	6.86	2.14

Fielding

Catcher	PCT	G	PO	A	E	DP	PB
Knizner	.979	7	40	6	1	0	1
Molina	.985	42	307	16	5	1	3
Wieters	1.000	18	119	2	0	0	2

First Base	PCT	G	PO	A	E	DP
Carpenter	1.000	6	21	1	0	1
Dean	1.000	1	2	0	0	0
Goldschmidt	.998	52	383	27	1	41
Molina	1.000	2	3	0	0	0
Nogowski	1.000	1	6	1	0	0
Ravelo	1.000	3	16	1	0	2

Second Base	PCT	G	PO	A	E	DP
Edman	.964	8	9	18	1	2
Miller	1.000	1	0	2	0	0
Schrock	1.000	5	3	5	0	0
Wong	.989	53	59	129	2	29

Third Base	PCT	G	PO	A	E	DP
Carpenter	.960	30	16	56	3	6
Edman	.946	31	18	35	3	4
Miller	.783	15	2	16	5	2
Schrock	1.000	2	1	2	0	0

Shortstop	PCT	G	PO	A	E	DP
DeJong	.974	45	52	100	4	24
Edman	.946	13	14	21	2	4
Miller	1.000	2	1	2	0	1

Outfield	PCT	G	PO	A	E	DP
Bader	.975	49	75	2	2	0
Carlson	1.000	34	64	4	0	2
Dean	1.000	2	2	0	0	0
Edman	.960	21	24	0	1	0
Fowler	1.000	27	38	0	0	0
O'Neill	1.000	48	89	0	0	0
Ravelo	1.000	5	5	1	0	0
Thomas	.957	18	21	1	1	1
Williams	1.000	2	1	0	0	0

San Diego Padres

SEASON IN A SENTENCE: The Padres rebuild finally came to fruition with their first playoff berth since 2006, highlighted by their emergence as "Slam Diego" and arguably baseball's most exciting team.

HIGH POINT: The Padres hit a grand slam in four consecutive games from Aug. 17-20, setting a new major league record and earning them the "Slam Diego" moniker.

LOW POINT: The Padres lost their top two starting pitchers to injury within a week of the playoffs in late September. Mike Clevinger left his Sept. 23 start with an elbow injury and Dinelson Lamet exited his Sept. 26 start with biceps tightness. Clevinger briefly returned in the National League Division Series, but the injuries effectively ended any hope of an extended playoff run.

NOTABLE ROOKIES: Infielder Jake Cronenworth emerged as one of baseball's top rookies after coming over in an offseason trade with Tampa Bay. He hit .285/.354/.477, led all rookies with 22 extra-base hits and played standout defense at both first and second base. Catcher Luis Campusano made his debut and homered in his first major league game, but a wrist sprain sidelined him for the rest of the regular season. Righthander Javy Guerra (14 appearances) and lefthander Adrian Morejon (nine) took on larger roles on the pitching staff after debuting in 2019, while righthander Luis Patiño made 11 appearances in his first major league action.

KEY TRANSACTIONS: The Padres were baseball's busiest team from the end of the 2019 season through the 2020 trade deadline. In the offseason, they acquired Cronenworth and outfielder Tommy Pham in a trade with the Rays, center fielder Trent Grisham and righthander Zach Davies from the Brewers and utilityman Jurickson Profar from the Athletics. They also signed relievers Drew Pomeranz and Pierce Johnson and acquired fellow reliever Emilio Pagan in a separate trade with the Rays. All would emerge as key contributors in the Padres' turnaround. With the team in the thick of contention at the August trade deadline, general manager A.J. Preller went on another spree, making six trades involving 26 players. Clevinger, closer Trevor Rosenthal, catchers Austin Nola and Jason Castro and designated hitter Mitch Moreland headlined the players acquired. Righthander Cal Quantrill, outfielder Josh Naylor, catcher Austin Hedges, infielder Ty France and 10 prospects were among those sent away in exchange.

OPENING DAY PAYROLL: $69,465,574 (10th)

PLAYER OF THE YEAR

MAJOR LEAGUE
Fernando Tatis Jr.
SS
.277/.366/.571
11 HR, 45 RBIs
11 SB

TOP ROOKIE
Jake Cronenworth
2B/SS
.285/.354/.477
26 R, 20 RBIs,
22 XBH

ORGANIZATION LEADERS

Batting		*Minimum 100 AB
MAJORS		
* AVG	Manny Machado	.304
* OPS	Wil Myers	.959
HR	Fernando Tatis Jr.	17
RBI	Manny Machado	47

Pitching		#Minimum 30 IP
MAJORS		
W	Zach Davies	7
# ERA	Dinelson Lamet	2.09
SO	Dinelson Lamet	93
SV	Drew Pomeranz	4
SV	Trevor Rosenthal	4

ORGANIZATION STATISTICS

SAN DIEGO PADRES
NATIONAL LEAGUE

Batting	B-T	HT	WT	DOB	AVG	vLH	vRH	G	AB	R	H	2B	3B	HR	RBI	BB	HBP	SH	SF	SO	SB	CS	SLG	OBP
Allen, Greg	B-R	6-0	185	3-15-93	.000	--	.000	1	1	1	0	0	0	0	0	2	1	0	0	1	1	0	.000	.750
Almonte, Abraham	B-R	5-10	223	6-27-89	.091	.500	.000	7	11	0	1	0	0	0	0	2	0	0	0	4	1	1	.091	.231
Campusano, Luis	R-R	5-11	232	9-29-98	.333	.500	.000	1	3	2	1	0	0	1	1	0	1	0	0	2	0	0	1.333	.500
Castro, Jason	L-R	6-3	215	6-18-87	.179	.167	.182	9	28	3	5	5	0	0	3	2	0	0	0	10	0	0	.357	.233

Batting	B-T	HT	WT	DOB	AVG	vLH	vRH	G	AB	R	H	2B	3B	HR	RBI	BB	HBP	SH	SF	SO	SB	CS	SLG	OBP
Cronenworth, Jake	L-R	6-0	187	1-21-94	.285	.218	.316	54	172	26	49	15	3	4	20	18	1	0	1	30	3	1	.477	.354
France, Ty	R-R	5-11	217	7-13-94	.309	.259	.357	20	55	9	17	4	0	2	10	5	1	0	0	15	0	0	.491	.377
Garcia, Greg	L-R	6-0	200	8-8-89	.200	.000	.222	35	60	6	12	3	0	0	11	7	0	3	1	18	1	0	.250	.279
Grisham, Trent	L-L	5-11	224	11-1-96	.251	.267	.245	59	215	42	54	8	3	10	26	31	3	1	1	64	10	1	.456	.352
Hedges, Austin	R-R	6-1	223	8-18-92	.158	.158	.158	29	57	7	9	1	0	3	6	6	2	5	1	18	1	1	.333	.258
Hosmer, Eric	L-L	6-4	226	10-24-89	.287	.204	.330	38	143	23	41	6	0	9	36	9	2	0	2	28	4	0	.517	.333
Machado, Manny	R-R	6-3	218	7-6-92	.304	.313	.300	60	224	44	68	12	1	16	47	26	0	0	4	37	6	3	.580	.370
Mateo, Jorge	R-R	6-0	182	6-23-95	.154	.176	.111	22	26	4	4	3	0	0	2	1	0	1	0	11	1	0	.269	.185
Mejia, Francisco	B-R	5-8	188	10-27-95	.077	.083	.074	17	39	5	3	1	0	1	2	2	0	0	0	9	0	0	.179	.143
Moreland, Mitch	L-L	6-3	245	9-6-85	.203	.176	.212	20	69	8	14	5	0	2	8	4	0	0	0	14	0	0	.362	.247
Myers, Wil	R-R	6-3	207	12-10-90	.288	.328	.269	55	198	34	57	14	2	15	40	18	2	0	0	56	2	1	.606	.353
Naylor, Josh	L-L	5-11	250	6-22-97	.278	.667	.242	18	36	4	10	0	1	1	4	1	1	0	0	4	1	0	.417	.316
Nola, Austin	R-R	6-0	197	12-28-89	.222	.120	.289	19	63	9	14	4	0	2	9	9	1	0	1	17	0	0	.381	.324
Olivares, Edward	R-R	6-2	188	3-6-96	.176	.231	.143	13	34	4	6	1	0	1	3	2	0	0	0	14	0	1	.294	.222
Ona, Jorge	R-R	6-0	235	12-31-96	.250	.400	.143	5	12	3	3	1	0	1	2	2	1	0	0	7	0	0	.583	.400
Pham, Tommy	R-R	6-1	223	3-8-88	.211	.300	.177	31	109	13	23	2	0	3	12	15	1	0	0	27	6	0	.312	.312
Profar, Jurickson	B-R	6-0	184	2-20-93	.278	.294	.268	56	180	28	50	6	0	7	25	15	4	1	2	28	7	1	.428	.343
Tatis Jr., Fernando	R-R	6-3	217	1-2-99	.277	.242	.290	59	224	50	62	11	2	17	45	27	5	0	1	61	11	3	.571	.366
Torrens, Luis	R-R	6-0	208	5-2-96	.273	.000	.375	7	11	0	3	1	0	0	1	0	1	0	0	2	0	0	.364	.333

Pitching	B-T	HT	WT	DOB	W	L	ERA	G	GS	CG	SV	IP	H	R	ER	HR	BB	SO	AVG	vLH	vRH	K/9	BB/9
Adams, Austin	R-R	6-3	220	5-5-91	0	0	4.50	3	0	0	0	4	3	2	2	1	2	7	.200	.500	.091	15.75	4.50
Altavilla, Dan	R-R	5-11	226	9-8-92	1	1	3.12	9	0	0	0	9	6	3	3	0	5	10	.200	.000	.250	10.38	5.19
Baez, Michel	R-R	6-8	220	1-21-96	0	0	7.71	3	1	0	0	5	7	4	4	0	2	1	.333	.300	.364	13.50	3.86
Bednar, David	L-R	6-1	249	10-10-94	0	0	7.11	4	0	0	0	6	11	6	5	1	2	5	.367	.313	.429	7.11	2.84
Clevinger, Mike	R-R	6-4	215	12-21-90	2	1	2.84	4	4	1	0	19	14	6	6	1	3	19	.212	.214	.211	9.00	1.42
Davies, Zach	R-R	6-0	180	2-7-93	7	4	2.73	12	12	0	0	69	55	26	21	9	19	63	.216	.171	.254	8.18	2.47
Guerra, Javy	L-R	6-0	185	9-25-95	1	0	10.13	14	0	0	0	13	25	16	15	1	5	12	.417	.520	.343	8.10	3.38
2-team total (14 Washington Nationals)					1	0	6.83	28	0	0	0	29	44	23	22	3	12	25	.358	.377	.343	7.76	3.72
Hill, Tim	R-L	6-4	200	2-10-90	3	0	4.50	23	0	0	0	18	17	9	9	3	6	20	.239	.225	.258	10.00	3.00
Johnson, Pierce	R-R	6-2	202	5-10-91	3	1	2.70	24	0	0	0	20	15	7	6	2	9	27	.214	.087	.277	12.15	4.05
Lamet, Dinelson	R-R	6-3	228	7-18-92	3	1	2.09	12	12	0	0	69	39	18	16	5	20	93	.163	.196	.127	12.13	2.61
Lucchesi, Joey	L-L	6-5	225	6-6-93	0	1	7.94	3	2	0	0	6	13	5	5	0	2	5	.464	.400	.500	7.94	3.18
Morejon, Adrian	L-L	5-11	224	2-27-99	2	2	4.66	9	4	0	0	19	20	11	10	7	4	25	.267	.294	.244	11.64	1.86
Paddack, Chris	R-R	6-5	217	1-8-96	4	5	4.73	12	12	0	0	59	60	33	31	14	12	58	.262	.270	.252	8.85	1.83
Pagan, Emilio	R-R	6-2	208	5-7-91	0	1	4.50	22	0	0	2	22	14	11	11	4	9	23	.182	.205	.158	9.41	3.68
Patino, Luis	R-R	6-1	192	10-26-99	1	0	5.19	11	1	0	0	17	18	10	10	3	14	21	.257	.188	.316	10.90	7.27
Perdomo, Luis	R-R	6-2	201	5-9-93	0	0	5.71	10	1	0	0	17	13	12	11	3	10	16	.203	.100	.294	8.31	5.19
Pomeranz, Drew	R-L	6-5	246	11-22-88	1	0	1.45	20	0	0	4	19	9	3	3	1	10	29	.145	.143	.146	13.98	4.82
Quantrill, Cal	L-R	6-3	195	2-10-95	2	0	2.60	10	1	0	1	17	17	6	5	2	6	18	.262	.259	.263	9.35	3.12
Richards, Garrett	R-R	6-2	210	5-27-88	2	2	4.03	14	10	0	0	51	47	23	23	7	17	46	.244	.296	.189	8.06	2.98
Rosenthal, Trevor	R-R	6-2	230	5-29-90	1	0	0.00	9	0	0	4	10	3	1	0	0	1	17	.091	.133	.000	15.30	0.90
Stammen, Craig	R-R	6-2	228	3-9-84	4	2	5.63	24	0	0	0	24	27	16	15	2	4	20	.278	.262	.291	7.50	1.50
Strahm, Matt	R-L	6-2	190	11-12-91	0	1	2.61	19	0	0	0	21	14	6	6	3	4	15	.189	.116	.290	6.53	1.74
Williams, Taylor	B-R	5-11	185	7-21-91	0	0	9.00	1	0	0	0	1	2	1	1	0	1	1	.400	.000	.500	9.00	0.00
Yates, Kirby	L-R	5-10	205	3-25-87	0	1	12.46	6	0	0	2	4	7	6	6	1	4	8	.350	.417	.250	16.62	8.31

Fielding

Catcher	PCT	G	PO	A	E	DP	PB
Castro	.989	9	85	7	1	0	0
Hedges	.990	28	183	15	2	0	4
Mejia	.990	16	93	7	1	0	1
Nola	1.000	17	157	9	0	2	1
Torrens	1.000	7	38	3	0	0	3

First Base	PCT	G	PO	A	E	DP
Cronenworth	1.000	10	63	5	0	4
France	1.000	5	30	3	0	2
Hosmer	.992	32	215	19	2	24
Moreland	.991	16	108	4	1	13
Myers	1.000	2	9	1	0	1
Naylor	1.000	3	7	2	0	0
Profar	1.000	1	1	0	0	0

Second Base	PCT	G	PO	A	E	DP
Cronenworth	.984	38	47	76	2	19
Garcia	.963	11	10	16	1	2
Mateo	1.000	5	5	9	0	1
Profar	.979	17	18	29	1	7

Third Base	PCT	G	PO	A	E	DP
Cronenworth	1.000	1	0	1	0	0
France	1.000	2	0	6	0	0
Garcia	1.000	10	0	10	0	1
Machado	.987	56	44	105	2	10

Shortstop	PCT	G	PO	A	E	DP
Cronenworth	.917	11	6	5	1	0
Tatis Jr.	.984	57	72	116	3	32

Outfield	PCT	G	PO	A	E	DP
Allen	1.000	1	2	0	0	0
Almonte	1.000	3	6	0	0	0
Grisham	.986	59	134	3	2	1
Mateo	1.000	7	8	0	0	0
Myers	.968	52	89	2	3	0
Naylor	1.000	7	5	0	0	0
Olivares	.947	12	18	0	1	0
Ona	--	0	0	0	0	0
Pham	.967	18	28	1	1	0
Profar	1.000	39	52	3	0	0

San Francisco Giants

SEASON IN A SENTENCE: Led by second-year sensation Mike Yastrzemski, the Giants put together a surprisingly potent offense fueled by upstarts like Alex Dickerson, Donovan Solano and Wilmer Flores and finished just shy of a playoff berth, providing encouragement for what's yet to come.

HIGH POINT: On Sept. 1, the Giants put on their hitting shoes and took full advantage of the thin air at Coors Field. They rapped out 27 hits to rout the Rockies 23-5. The outburst included a three-home run game from Alex Dickerson as part of a five-hit day for the 30-year-old outfielder.

LOW POINT: The Giants needed one win in their final three games to secure a spot in the playoffs, which had been expanded to 16 teams because of the bizarre nature of the 2020 season. Instead, they were swept by the Padres and fell to 29-31, which tied them with the Brewers, who had the tiebreaker and earned the right to play the eventual World Series-champion Dodgers in the first round.

NOTABLE ROOKIES: Catcher Joey Bart, the game's second-best backstop prospect, was called up on Aug. 20 and went through highs and lows during his first taste of the big leagues. Bart, the No. 2 overall pick in the 2018 draft out of Georgia Tech, doubled in each of his first three games before going 1-for-20 to close the month of August. Bart rebounded in September and started the month 8-for-19. He finished .233/.288/.320 with 41 strikeouts against just three walks. Mauricio Dubon, a trade piece acquired from the Brewers, showed the versatility to play center field and both middle-infield positions and provided a light blend of speed and occasional pop. Lefty Logan Webb exhausted his rookie credentials during the season while going 3-4, 5.47 and Caleb Baragar picked up five wins while mostly working in relief.

KEY TRANSACTIONS: The Giants made several small transactions which turned out to be quite impactful. Darin Ruf, a former Phillies farmhand who had been playing overseas, signed a minor league deal in January and hit for an .887 OPS and five home runs. Lefty Trevor Cahill also got a minor league deal, then provided 25 solid innings. The Giants also made a pair of small deals during the season, netting them a pair of mid-range prospects in outfielder Luis Alexander Basabe (White Sox) and righthander Jordan Humphreys (Mets). Humphreys was acquired in exchange for speedy outfielder Billy Hamilton, while Basabe was a cash deal after he was designated for assignment in Chicago.

OPENING DAY PAYROLL: $71,170,857 (8th)

PLAYERS OF THE YEAR

MAJOR LEAGUE
Mike Yastrzemski
OF
.297/.400/.568
10 HR, 35 RBIs
Led NL in 3B (4)

TOP ROOKIE
Mauricio Dubon
CF/2B/SS
.274/.337/.389
9 XBH, 19 RBIs

ORGANIZATION LEADERS

Batting		*Minimum 100 AB
MAJORS		
* AVG	Donovan Solano	.326
* OPS	Brandon Belt	1.015
HR	Wilmer Flores	12
RBI	Mike Yastrzemski	35
Pitching		#Minimum 30 IP
MAJORS		
W	Caleb Baragar	5
# ERA	Kevin Gausman	3.62
SO	Kevin Gausman	79
SV	Trevor Gott	4

ORGANIZATION STATISTICS

SAN FRANCISCO GIANTS
NATIONAL LEAGUE

Batting	B-T	HT	WT	DOB	AVG	vLH	vRH	G	AB	R	H	2B	3B	HR	RBI	BB	HBP	SH	SF	SO	SB	CS	SLG	OBP
Alexander Basabe, Luis	B-R	6-0	180	8-26-96	.143	.286	.000	9	14	5	2	0	0	0	1	4	0	0	0	5	2	0	.143	.333
Bart, Joey	R-R	6-2	238	12-15-96	.233	.185	.250	33	103	15	24	5	2	0	7	3	5	0	0	41	0	0	.320	.288
Belt, Brandon	L-L	6-3	231	4-20-88	.309	.115	.350	51	149	25	46	13	1	9	30	30	0	0	0	36	0	0	.591	.425
Brantly, Rob	L-R	6-0	191	7-14-89	.000	.000	.000	1	3	0	0	0	0	0	0	0	0	0	0	0	0	0	.000	.000

Batting	B-T	HT	WT	DOB	AVG	vLH	vRH	G	AB	R	H	2B	3B	HR	RBI	BB	HBP	SH	SF	SO	SB	CS	SLG	OBP
Crawford, Brandon	L-R	6-1	223	1-21-87	.256	.226	.262	54	172	26	44	12	0	8	28	15	4	0	2	47	1	2	.465	.326
Davis, Jaylin	R-R	5-11	205	7-1-94	.167	.000	.286	4	12	2	2	0	0	1	1	0	0	0	0	6	0	0	.417	.167
Dickerson, Alex	L-L	6-2	226	5-26-90	.298	.273	.300	52	151	28	45	10	1	10	27	16	2	0	1	30	0	0	.576	.371
Dubon, Mauricio	R-R	6-0	173	7-19-94	.274	.341	.248	54	157	21	43	4	1	4	19	15	1	1	2	36	2	3	.389	.337
Duggar, Steven	L-R	6-1	187	11-4-93	.176	.000	.188	21	34	3	6	2	0	0	3	1	1	0	0	11	1	0	.235	.222
Flores, Wilmer	R-R	6-2	213	8-6-91	.268	.274	.265	55	198	30	53	11	1	12	32	13	1	0	1	36	1	0	.515	.315
Heineman, Tyler	B-R	5-10	199	6-19-91	.190	.286	.171	15	42	3	8	1	0	0	1	4	2	2	0	6	1	0	.214	.292
Longoria, Evan	R-R	6-1	213	10-7-85	.254	.308	.234	53	193	26	49	10	1	7	28	11	2	0	3	39	0	1	.425	.297
McCarthy, Joe	L-L	6-3	220	2-23-94	.000	--	.000	4	10	0	0	0	0	0	0	0	0	0	0	5	0	0	.000	.000
Pence, Hunter	R-R	6-4	216	4-13-83	.096	.107	.083	17	52	4	5	0	1	2	6	3	1	0	0	15	0	0	.250	.161
Rickard, Joey	R-L	6-0	192	5-21-91	.000	.000	.000	4	5	1	0	0	0	0	1	0	0	0	0	1	0	0	.000	.167
Robertson, Daniel	R-R	5-11	210	3-22-94	.333	.364	.300	13	21	4	7	0	0	0	2	3	0	0	0	6	0	0	.333	.417
Ruf, Darin	R-R	6-2	232	7-28-86	.276	.259	.310	40	87	11	24	6	0	5	18	13	0	0	0	23	1	0	.517	.370
Sandoval, Pablo	B-R	5-10	268	8-11-86	.220	.300	.208	33	82	5	18	1	0	1	6	6	1	0	1	18	0	0	.268	.278
2-team total (1 Atlanta Braves)					.214	.300	.203	34	84	5	18	1	0	1	6	6	8	1	0	1	19	0	0	.262	.287
Slater, Austin	R-R	6-1	204	12-13-92	.282	.316	.255	31	85	18	24	2	1	5	7	16	2	1	0	22	8	1	.506	.408
Smoak, Justin	B-L	6-4	220	12-5-86	.000	--	.000	3	6	0	0	0	0	0	0	0	0	0	0	2	0	0	.000	.000
2-team total (33 Milwaukee Brewers)					.176	.167	.179	36	119	14	21	7	0	5	15	10	2	0	1	42	0	0	.361	.250
Solano, Donovan	R-R	5-8	210	12-17-87	.326	.350	.315	54	190	22	62	15	1	3	29	10	2	0	1	39	0	0	.463	.365
Tromp, Chadwick	R-R	5-8	221	3-21-95	.213	.321	.121	24	61	11	13	1	0	4	10	1	0	0	2	20	0	0	.426	.219
Yastrzemski, Mike	L-L	5-10	178	8-23-90	.297	.284	.304	54	192	39	57	14	4	10	35	30	3	0	0	55	2	1	.568	.400

Pitching	B-T	HT	WT	DOB	W	L	ERA	G	GS	CG	SV	IP	H	R	ER	HR	BB	SO	AVG	vLH	vRH	K/9	BB/9
Anderson, Shaun	R-R	6-4	228	10-29-94	0	0	3.52	18	0	0	0	15	10	6	6	3	12	18	.182	.143	.206	10.57	7.04
Anderson, Tyler	L-L	6-2	213	12-30-89	4	3	4.37	13	11	1	0	60	58	32	29	5	25	41	.256	.309	.233	6.18	3.77
Baragar, Caleb	R-L	6-3	215	4-9-94	5	1	4.03	24	1	0	0	22	17	10	10	3	5	19	.210	.161	.240	7.66	2.01
Cahill, Trevor	R-R	6-4	223	3-1-88	1	2	3.24	11	6	0	0	25	16	10	9	3	14	31	.184	.111	.262	11.16	5.04
Coonrod, Sam	R-R	6-1	229	9-22-92	0	2	9.82	18	0	0	3	15	17	16	16	2	7	15	.283	.304	.270	9.20	4.30
Cueto, Johnny	R-R	5-11	229	2-15-86	2	3	5.40	12	12	0	0	63	61	41	38	9	26	56	.248	.265	.233	7.96	3.69
Garcia, Jarlin	L-L	6-3	215	1-18-93	2	1	0.49	19	0	0	0	18	11	6	1	0	7	14	.180	.172	.188	6.87	3.44
Garcia, Rico	R-R	5-9	201	1-10-94	1	1	5.40	12	0	0	0	10	13	6	6	1	4	7	.333	.200	.379	6.30	3.60
Gausman, Kevin	L-R	6-2	190	1-6-91	3	3	3.62	12	10	0	0	60	50	26	24	8	16	79	.221	.217	.225	11.92	2.41
Gott, Trevor	R-R	5-10	182	8-26-92	1	2	10.03	15	0	0	4	12	13	13	13	7	8	8	.271	.350	.214	6.17	6.17
Heineman, Tyler	B-R	5-10	199	6-19-91	0	0	0.00	1	0	0	0	1	1	0	0	0	1	0	.333	.000	.500	0.00	9.00
Jimenez, Dany	R-R	6-1	182	12-23-93	0	0	6.75	2	0	0	0	1	1	1	1	0	3	1	.200	.000	.250	6.75	20.25
Menez, Conner	L-L	6-2	206	5-29-95	1	0	2.38	7	0	0	0	11	6	4	3	2	5	8	.158	.188	.136	6.35	3.97
Peralta, Wandy	L-L	6-0	217	7-27-91	1	1	3.29	25	0	0	0	27	22	13	10	3	11	25	.220	.171	.254	8.23	3.62
Rodriguez, Dereck	R-R	6-0	208	6-5-92	0	0	13.50	2	0	0	0	4	6	6	6	2	3	2	.476	.400	.500	4.50	6.75
Rogers, Tyler	R-R	6-3	181	12-17-90	3	3	4.50	29	0	0	3	28	31	16	14	2	6	27	.277	.250	.292	8.68	1.93
Samardzija, Jeff	R-R	6-4	233	1-23-85	0	2	9.72	4	4	0	0	17	21	19	18	7	4	6	.296	.226	.350	3.24	2.16
Selman, Sam	R-L	6-2	198	11-14-90	1	1	3.72	24	0	0	1	19	13	8	8	2	9	23	.186	.100	.250	10.71	4.19
Smyly, Drew	L-L	6-2	188	6-13-89	0	1	3.42	7	5	0	0	26	20	11	10	6	9	42	.198	.083	.262	14.35	3.08
Suarez, Andrew	L-L	6-0	202	9-11-92	0	0	3.72	6	0	0	0	10	9	4	4	1	6	5	.250	.214	.273	4.66	5.59
Triggs, Andrew	R-R	6-4	233	3-16-89	0	1	81.00	1	0	0	0	0	0	3	3	0	3	0	.000	--	.000	0.00	81.00
Watson, Tony	L-L	6-3	224	5-30-85	1	0	2.50	21	0	0	2	18	13	8	5	3	3	15	.191	.174	.200	7.50	1.50
Webb, Logan	R-R	6-1	220	11-18-96	3	4	5.47	13	11	0	0	54	61	38	33	4	24	46	.288	.291	.284	7.62	3.98

Fielding

Catcher	PCT	G	PO	A	E	DP	PB
Bart	.992	32	234	12	2	0	2
Brantly	1.000	1	4	1	0	0	0
Heineman	.975	15	110	9	3	0	0
Tromp	.993	23	144	3	1	1	3

First Base	PCT	G	PO	A	E	DP
Belt	.994	47	278	28	2	2
Flores	.989	14	86	6	1	7
Ruf	1.000	4	11	1	0	2
Sandoval	1.000	8	44	6	0	4

Second Base	PCT	G	PO	A	E	DP
Dubon	.963	8	10	16	1	2
Flores	1.000	14	19	35	0	9
Robertson	.000	3	0	0	0	0
Solano	.951	45	56	79	7	19

Third Base	PCT	G	PO	A	E	DP
Flores	.778	3	2	5	2	0
Longoria	.984	52	41	84	2	9
Robertson	1.000	2	0	1	0	0
Sandoval	1.000	4	1	1	0	0
Solano	.692	5	3	6	4	0

Shortstop	PCT	G	PO	A	E	DP
Crawford	.960	53	69	124	8	24
Dubon	.947	8	7	11	1	3
Robertson	1.000	5	6	8	0	3
Solano	1.000	2	4	3	0	1

Outfield	PCT	G	PO	A	E	DP
Alexander Basabe	1.000	8	12	0	0	0
Davis	.900	4	8	1	1	0
Dickerson	.985	46	63	1	1	0
Dubon	.989	44	87	1	1	1
Duggar	1.000	20	22	0	0	0
McCarthy	1.000	4	3	0	0	0
Pence	1.000	10	17	0	0	0
Rickard	1.000	3	4	0	0	0
Robertson	1.000	3	0	1	0	0
Ruf	.962	24	25	0	1	0
Slater	1.000	12	28	1	0	0
Yastrzemski	1.000	53	120	2	0	1

Seattle Mariners

SEASON IN A SENTENCE: The Mariners rebuild took a step forward with the emergence of several young contributors, who helped the club remain in playoff contention through the final week of the abbreviated season.

HIGH POINT: With the Mariners hanging on to their playoff hopes, standout rookie Kyle Lewis delivered a go-ahead, two-run home run in the bottom of the sixth inning against the A's on Sept. 14 to complete a five-run, comeback victory in the first game of a doubleheader. The win pulled the Mariners within one game of the Astros for second place in the AL West and the final American League playoff spot.

LOW POINT: The Mariners bullpen was a problem all season and had its worst moment Aug. 27 against the Padres. Leading 7-3 with two outs and no one on base in the final inning, the Mariners allowed seven consecutive runs with two outs, including a walkoff three-run home run by Wil Myers, for a stunning 10-7 loss.

NOTABLE ROOKIES: Lewis emerged as arguably baseball's top rookie in 2020, finishing either first or second among all rookies in runs, hits, home runs, RBIs and walks and playing highlight-reel defense in center field. Lefthanded pitcher Justus Sheffield (4-3, 3.58) and righthander Justin Dunn (4-1, 4.34) settled nicely into the starting rotation. First baseman Evan White was named a finalist for a Gold Glove award, although he hit just .176/.252/.376. Rule 5 draft selection Yohan Ramirez logged a 2.61 ERA in 16 appearances, the lowest ERA of any Mariners reliever.

KEY TRANSACTIONS: The Mariners continued their rebuild by trading veterans for prospects or young major leaguers at every turn. They began the offseason by trading catcher Omar Narvaez to the Brewers for prospect Adam Hill and a draft pick. They brought righthander Taijuan Walker back to Seattle on a one-year deal in the offseason and, as soon as he pitched well, traded him to the Blue Jays near the deadline for minor league outfielder Alberto Rodriguez. Their biggest moves came on deadline day, Aug. 31, when they traded catcher Austin Nola and relievers Austin Adams, Dan Altavilla and Taylor Williams to the Padres in two separate deals and received infielder Ty France, catcher Luis Torrens and prospects Taylor Trammell, Andres Muñoz and Matt Brash in return. Seattle landed significant talent in return for Nola, who had signed with the team as an under-the-radar free agent acqusition in November 2018.

OPENING DAY PAYROLL: $48,421,623 (21st)

PLAYERS OF THE YEAR

MAJOR LEAGUE

Marco Gonzales
LHP

7-2, 3.10 in 11 GS
Led team in W, ERA,
IP (69.2), SO (64)

TOP ROOKIE

Kyle Lewis
OF

.262/.364/.437
11 HR, 28 RBIs, 34 BB
AL Rookie of the Year

ORGANIZATION LEADERS

Batting		*Minimum 100 AB
MAJORS		
* AVG	Austin Nola	.306
* OPS	Austin Nola	.903
HR	Kyle Lewis	11
RBI	Kyle Seager	40

Pitching		#Minimum 30 IP
MAJORS		
W	Marco Gonzales	7
# ERA	Marco Gonzales	3.10
SO	Marco Gonzales	64
SV	Taylor Williams	6

ORGANIZATION STATISTICS

SEATTLE MARINERS
AMERICAN LEAGUE

Batting	B-T	HT	WT	DOB	AVG	vLH	vRH	G	AB	R	H	2B	3B	HR	RBI	BB	HBP	SH	SF	SO	SB	CS	SLG	OBP
Bishop, Braden	R-R	6-1	178	8-22-93	.167	.235	.077	12	30	2	5	2	0	0	4	2	1	1	0	10	1	0	.233	.242
Crawford, J.P.	L-R	6-2	199	1-11-95	.255	.242	.261	53	204	33	52	7	2	2	24	23	3	0	2	39	6	3	.338	.336
Ervin, Phillip	R-R	5-10	207	7-15-92	.205	.150	.263	18	39	5	8	3	0	0	4	8	0	0	0	14	0	0	.282	.340
Fraley, Jake	L-L	6-0	195	5-25-95	.154	.000	.200	7	26	3	4	1	1	0	0	2	1	0	0	11	2	1	.269	.241

SEATTLE MARINERS

Batting	B-T	HT	WT	DOB	AVG	vLH	vRH	G	AB	R	H	2B	3B	HR	RBI	BB	HBP	SH	SF	SO	SB	CS	SLG	OBP
France, Ty	R-R	5-11	217	7-13-94	.302	.167	.375	23	86	10	26	5	1	2	13	6	2	0	0	22	0	0	.453	.362
Haggerty, Sam	B-R	5-11	175	5-26-94	.260	.333	.219	13	50	7	13	4	0	1	6	4	0	1	0	16	4	0	.400	.315
Hudson, Joe	R-R	6-0	210	5-21-91	.176	--	.176	9	17	0	3	0	0	0	2	0	1	0	5	0	0	.176	.263
Lewis, Kyle	R-R	6-4	205	7-13-95	.262	.224	.277	58	206	37	54	3	0	11	28	34	0	0	2	71	5	1	.437	.364
Long, Shed	L-R	5-8	184	8-22-95	.171	.063	.212	34	117	10	20	5	0	3	9	11	0	0	0	37	4	0	.291	.242
Lopes, Tim	R-R	5-11	180	6-24-94	.238	.218	.250	46	143	16	34	12	0	2	15	6	2	0	0	34	5	0	.364	.278
Marmolejos, Jose	L-L	6-2	239	1-2-93	.206	.167	.217	35	107	12	22	4	0	6	18	7	1	0	0	32	0	1	.411	.261
Moore, Dylan	R-R	6-0	185	8-2-92	.255	.234	.267	38	137	26	35	9	0	8	17	14	8	0	0	43	12	5	.496	.358
Nola, Austin	R-R	6-0	197	12-28-89	.306	.259	.324	29	98	15	30	5	1	5	19	9	2	0	1	17	0	0	.531	.373
Odom, Joseph	R-R	6-2	215	1-9-92	.128	.000	.167	18	39	2	5	0	0	2	5	4	0	1	0	20	0	0	.128	.209
Seager, Kyle	L-R	6-0	216	11-3-87	.241	.185	.268	60	203	35	49	12	0	9	40	32	7	0	6	33	5	0	.433	.355
Smith, Mallex	L-R	5-10	180	5-6-93	.133	.000	.146	14	45	2	6	2	0	0	3	2	0	0	0	13	2	0	.178	.170
Strange-Gordon, Dee	L-R	5-11	166	4-22-88	.200	.077	.265	33	75	12	15	1	0	0	3	5	2	0	0	13	3	2	.213	.268
Torrens, Luis	R-R	6-0	208	5-2-96	.254	.231	.273	18	59	5	15	4	0	1	6	6	0	0	0	13	0	0	.373	.323
Vogelbach, Daniel	L-R	6-0	270	12-17-92	.094	.000	.102	18	53	3	5	1	0	2	4	11	0	0	0	13	0	0	.226	.250
2-team total (2 Toronto Blue Jays)					.088	.000	.098	20	57	3	5	1	0	2	4	12	0	0	0	15	0	0	.211	.246
Walton, Donovan	L-R	5-10	175	5-25-94	.154	.667	.000	5	13	0	2	1	0	0	3	1	0	0	0	5	0	1	.231	.214
White, Evan	R-L	6-3	220	4-26-96	.176	.140	.192	54	182	19	32	7	0	8	26	18	1	0	1	84	1	2	.346	.252

Pitching	B-T	HT	WT	DOB	W	L	ERA	G	GS	CG	SV	IP	H	R	ER	HR	BB	SO	AVG	vLH	vRH	K/9	BB/9
Altavilla, Dan	R-R	5-11	226	9-8-92	1	2	7.71	13	0	0	1	12	12	11	10	3	7	14	.255	.357	.212	10.80	5.40
Brennan, Brandon	R-R	6-4	207	7-26-91	0	0	3.68	5	0	0	0	7	3	3	2		5	7	.250	.222	.263	8.59	6.14
Cortes, Nestor	R-L	5-11	210	12-10-94	0	1	15.26	5	1	0	0	8	12	14	13	6	6	8	.343	.444	.308	9.39	7.04
Dunn, Justin	R-R	6-2	185	9-22-95	4	1	4.34	10	10	0	0	46	31	23	22	10	31	38	.189	.193	.185	7.49	6.11
Edwards Jr., Carl	R-R	6-3	170	9-3-91	0	0	1.93	5	0	0	1	5	2	1	1	0	1	6	.125	.333	.077	11.57	1.93
Fletcher, Aaron	L-L	6-0	220	2-25-96	0	0	12.46	6	0	0	0	4	7	6	6	1	7	7	.350	.000	.500	14.54	14.54
Frankoff, Seth	R-R	6-5	215	8-27-88	0	0	16.88	2	0	0	0	3	6	5	5	0	2	0	.429	.625	.167	0.00	6.75
Gerber, Joey	R-R	6-4	215	5-3-97	1	1	4.02	17	0	0	0	16	13	8	7	1	5	6	.241	.278	.222	3.45	2.87
Gonzales, Marco	L-L	6-1	197	2-16-92	7	2	3.10	11	11	1	0	70	59	27	24	8	7	64	.222	.274	.202	8.27	0.90
Graveman, Kendall	R-R	6-2	200	12-21-90	1	3	5.79	11	2	0	0	19	15	13	12	2	8	15	.221	.115	.286	7.23	3.86
Grotz, Zac	R-R	6-2	195	2-17-93	0	0	14.73	5	0	0	0	7	11	12	12	4	11	4	.367	.429	.348	4.91	13.50
Guilbeau, Taylor	L-L	6-4	190	5-12-93	0	0	1.17	8	0	0	0	8	8	1	1	0	6	3	.267	.385	.176	3.52	7.04
Hirano, Yoshihisa	R-R	6-1	185	3-8-84	0	1	5.84	13	0	0	4	12	18	9	8	2	8	11	.340	.300	.391	8.03	5.84
Kikuchi, Yusei	L-L	6-0	200	6-17-91	2	4	5.17	9	9	0	0	47	41	27	27	3	20	47	.238	.265	.228	9.00	3.83
Lail, Brady	R-R	6-2	200	8-9-93	0	0	4.80	7	0	0	0	15	12	8	8	5	7	11	.214	.192	.233	6.60	4.20
2-team total (1 Chicago White Sox)					0	0	4.41	8	0	0	0	16	14	8	8	5	7	12	.226	.200	.250	6.61	3.86
Lockett, Walker	R-R	6-5	225	5-3-94	0	0	4.32	5	0	0	0	8	12	4	4	1	1	3	.343	.294	.389	3.24	1.08
Lopes, Tim	R-R	5-11	180	6-24-94	0	0	18.00	1	0	0	0	1	2	2	2	0	1	0	.500	.333	1.000	0.00	9.00
Magill, Matt	R-R	6-3	210	11-10-89	0	1	6.10	11	0	0	0	10	9	7	7	3	6	11	.231	.167	.259	9.58	5.23
Margevicius, Nick	L-L	6-5	220	6-18-96	2	3	4.57	10	7	0	0	41	38	21	21	6	14	36	.244	.205	.259	7.84	3.05
Misiewicz, Anthony	R-L	6-1	200	11-1-94	0	2	4.05	21	0	0	0	20	20	9	9	2	6	25	.263	.216	.308	11.25	2.70
Newsome, Ljay	R-R	5-11	210	11-8-96	0	1	5.17	5	4	0	0	16	20	9	9	4	1	9	.303	.379	.243	5.17	0.57
Ramirez, Yohan	R-R	6-4	190	5-6-95	0	0	2.61	16	0	0	3	21	9	6	6	3	20	26	.130	.222	.071	11.32	8.71
Sadler, Casey	R-R	6-3	205	7-13-90	1	2	4.50	7	0	0	0	10	7	7	5	1	4	12	.184	.261	.067	10.80	3.60
Shaw, Bryan	B-R	6-1	226	11-8-87	1	0	18.00	6	0	0	0	6	13	12	12	1	6	4	.433	.273	.526	6.00	9.00
Sheffield, Justus	L-L	5-10	195	5-13-96	4	3	3.58	10	10	0	0	55	52	23	22	2	20	48	.251	.154	.284	7.81	3.25
Swanson, Erik	R-R	6-3	220	9-4-93	0	2	12.91	9	0	0	0	8	11	12	11	3	2	9	.344	.353	.333	10.57	2.35
Walker, Taijuan	R-R	6-4	235	8-13-92	2	2	4.00	5	5	0	0	27	21	13	12	5	8	25	.210	.289	.145	8.33	2.67
2-team total (6 Toronto Blue Jays)					4	3	2.70	11	11	0	0	53	43	23	16	8	19	50	.214	.265	.178	8.44	3.21
Williams, Taylor	B-R	5-11	185	7-21-91	1	1	5.93	14	0	0	6	14	12	9	9	1	7	19	.231	.222	.240	12.51	4.61
Yacabonis, Jimmy	R-R	6-3	225	3-21-92	0	1	3.86	2	1	0	0	2	2	1	1	0	3	1	.222	.167	.333	3.86	11.57

Fielding

Catcher	PCT	G	PO	A	E	DP	PB
Hudson	1.000	9	57	3	0	0	1
Nola	.990	27	195	4	2	1	3
Odom	1.000	18	110	3	0	0	2
Torrens	1.000	17	118	3	0	1	3

First Base	PCT	G	PO	A	E	DP
Marmolejos	1.000	5	28	2	0	5
Moore	1.000	3	20	0	0	3
Nola	1.000	2	17	1	0	0
White	.998	54	370	32	1	36

Second Base	PCT	G	PO	A	E	DP
France	.971	10	13	21	1	6
Long	.991	32	50	55	1	17
Moore	.957	10	20	25	2	4
Strange-Gordon	.923	13	10	14	2	2
Walton	1.000	1	2	1	0	1

Third Base	PCT	G	PO	A	E	DP
France	.950	4	11	8	1	2
Haggerty	1.000	1	2	3	0	0
Lopes	.833	1	3	2	1	0
Moore	1.000	2	2	1	0	0
Nola	1.000	1	0	1	0	0
Seager	.975	53	39	115	4	11

Shortstop	PCT	G	PO	A	E	DP
Crawford	.986	53	73	145	3	31
Moore	.800	3	1	3	1	0
Strange-Gordon	1.000	3	2	4	0	0
Walton	1.000	3	4	6	0	2

Outfield	PCT	G	PO	A	E	DP
Bishop	1.000	12	19	0	0	0
Ervin	1.000	18	32	1	0	0
Fraley	1.000	7	19	1	0	0
Haggerty	1.000	11	25	0	0	0
Lewis	.985	57	133	1	2	0
Long	1.000	1	3	0	0	0
Lopes	1.000	28	36	4	0	1
Marmolejos	.966	19	28	0	1	0
Moore	1.000	24	42	2	0	1
Smith	.958	14	23	0	1	0
Strange-Gordon	1.000	13	20	1	0	0

Tampa Bay Rays

SEASON IN A SENTENCE: It was a magical year for the Rays as they posted the best record in the American League (40-20), rolled through the Blue Jays, Yankees and Astros to earn their second World Series appearance, then pushed the Dodgers to six games before falling short.

HIGH POINT: There have been few World Series games more thrilling than the Rays' 8-7 win in Game 4. The Dodgers jumped out to an early lead, but the Rays rallied back to take the lead on a three-run homer by Brandon Lowe in the sixth inning. The teams handed the lead back and forth three more times before Brett Phillips came to the plate with two out in the ninth trailing by one. Phillips' unlikely bloop single scored two thanks to a Dodgers' error, giving Tampa Bay an unlikely win and a moment to remember for years to come.

LOW POINT: In a must-win Game 6 of the World Series, Rays manager Kevin Cash decided to pull a dominant Blake Snell midway through the sixth after he gave up his second hit of the game. Less than 10 pitches later reliever Nick Anderson had given back the Rays' tenuous one-run lead thanks to a Mookie Betts' double, a wild pitch and a Corey Seager fielder's choice. Cash's decision will long be debated, but a later Mookie Betts home run and Julio Urias' dominant relief outing meant the Rays may have been knocked out that night whether Snell was pulled or not.

NOTABLE ROOKIES: Outfielder Randy Arozarena was excellent in September and even better in the postseason. Lefthander Josh Fleming (5-0, 2.78) stepped in and filled a void in the starting rotation created by lefthander Brendan McKay's shoulder injury. Outfielder Yoshi Tsutsugo hit eight home runs but struggled with consistency in his U.S. debut.

KEY TRANSACTIONS: When the Rays acquired Arozarena in a deal that sent highly-regarded pitching prospect Matthew Liberatore to the Cardinals, it was seen as a high price to pay for an outfielder who seemed ticketed for a fourth-outfield role in

St. Louis. No one is questioning the price tag any more. Arozarena was one of the Rays best players during spring training in March. He tested positive for coronavirus when the Rays returned to action in July, but once he was called up, he proved to be their best power hitter. His 10 home runs in the postseason set an MLB record. Outfielder Manuel Margot, acquired for RHP Emilio Pagan in February, had a rather unimpressive regular season, but his five postseason home runs helped push the Rays to the World Series.

OPENING DAY PAYROLL: $28,735,222 (27th)

PLAYERS OF THE YEAR

MAJOR LEAGUE
Nick Anderson
RHP
2-1, 0.55 in 19 G
26 SO in 16.1 IP

TOP ROOKIE
Randy Arozarena
OF
.281/.382/.641
7 HR, 11 RBIs in 23 G
ALCS MVP

ORGANIZATION LEADERS

Batting		*Minimum 100 AB
MAJORS		
* AVG	Yandy Diaz	.307
* OPS	Brandon Lowe	.916
HR	Brandon Lowe	14
RBI	Brandon Lowe	37
Pitching		**#Minimum 30 IP**
MAJORS		
W	Pete Fairbanks	6
# ERA	Blake Snell	3.24
SO	Tyler Glasnow	91
SV	Nick Anderson	6

ORGANIZATION STATISTICS

TAMPA BAY RAYS
AMERICAN LEAGUE

Batting	B-T	HT	WT	DOB	AVG	vLH	vRH	G	AB	R	H	2B	3B	HR	RBI	BB	HBP	SH	SF	SO	SB	CS	SLG	OBP
Adames, Willy	R-R	6-0	210	9-2-95	.259	.319	.239	54	185	29	48	15	1	8	23	20	0	0	0	74	2	1	.481	.332
Arozarena, Randy	R-R	5-11	185	2-28-95	.281	.400	.227	23	64	15	18	2	0	7	11	6	5	0	1	22	4	0	.641	.382
Brosseau, Mike	R-R	5-10	205	3-15-94	.302	.333	.273	36	86	12	26	5	1	5	12	8	3	0	1	31	2	0	.558	.378
Choi, Ji-Man	L-R	6-1	260	5-19-91	.230	.118	.248	42	122	16	28	13	0	3	16	20	0	0	3	36	0	0	.410	.331

Batting	B-T	HT	WT	DOB	AVG	vLH	vRH	G	AB	R	H	2B	3B	HR	RBI	BB	HBP	SH	SF	SO	SB	CS	SLG	OBP
Diaz, Yandy	R-R	6-2	215	8-8-91	.307	.265	.325	34	114	16	35	3	0	2	11	23	1	0	0	17	0	0	.386	.428
Kiermaier, Kevin	L-R	6-1	210	4-22-90	.217	.158	.227	49	138	16	30	5	3	3	22	20	1	0	0	42	8	1	.362	.321
Lowe, Brandon	L-R	5-10	185	7-6-94	.269	.300	.259	56	193	36	52	9	2	14	37	25	4	0	2	58	3	0	.554	.362
Lowe, Nate	L-R	6-4	220	7-7-95	.224	.133	.250	21	67	10	15	2	0	4	11	9	0	0	0	28	1	0	.433	.316
Margot, Manuel	R-R	5-11	180	9-28-94	.269	.222	.284	47	145	19	39	9	0	1	16	13	0	0	1	25	12	4	.352	.327
Martinez, Jose	R-R	6-6	215	7-25-88	.239	.229	.250	24	67	10	16	4	0	2	10	9	0	0	0	20	0	0	.388	.329
Meadows, Austin	L-L	6-3	225	5-3-95	.205	.143	.227	36	132	19	27	8	1	4	13	17	1	0	2	50	2	1	.371	.296
O'Grady, Brian	L-R	6-2	215	5-17-92	.400	.000	.500	2	5	2	2	1	0	0	0	0	0	0	0	1	1	0	.600	.400
Perez, Michael	L-R	5-10	195	8-7-92	.167	.500	.132	38	84	7	14	3	0	1	13	7	1	0	1	27	0	0	.238	.237
Phillips, Brett	L-R	6-0	195	5-30-94	.150	.000	.176	17	20	2	3	0	1	1	3	5	0	0	0	7	3	0	.400	.320
2-team total (18 Kansas City Royals)					.196	.429	.159	35	51	10	10	0	2	2	5	8	0	0	0	15	6	1	.392	.305
Renfroe, Hunter	R-R	6-1	230	1-28-92	.156	.146	.160	42	122	18	19	5	0	8	22	14	2	0	1	37	2	0	.393	.252
Smith, Kevan	R-R	6-4	230	6-28-88	.258	.100	.333	17	31	3	8	3	0	1	8	5	1	0	0	11	0	0	.452	.378
Tsutsugo, Yoshi	L-R	6-1	225	11-26-91	.197	.243	.183	51	157	27	31	5	1	8	24	26	1	0	1	50	0	0	.395	.314
Wendle, Joey	L-R	6-1	195	4-26-90	.286	.294	.284	50	168	24	48	9	2	4	17	10	5	0	1	35	8	2	.435	.342
Zunino, Mike	R-R	6-2	235	3-25-91	.147	.045	.189	28	75	8	11	4	0	4	10	6	3	0	0	37	0	0	.360	.238

Pitching	B-T	HT	WT	DOB	W	L	ERA	G	GS	CG	SV	IP	H	R	ER	HR	BB	SO	AVG	vLH	vRH	K/9	BB/9
Alvarado, Jose	L-L	6-2	245	5-21-95	0	0	6.00	9	0	0	0	9	9	7	6	2	6	13	.250	.000	.333	13.00	6.00
Anderson, Nick	R-R	6-4	205	7-5-90	2	1	0.55	19	0	0	6	16	5	2	1	1	3	26	.091	.154	.034	14.33	1.65
Banda, Anthony	L-L	6-2	230	8-10-93	1	0	10.29	4	0	0	1	7	10	9	8	1	5	4	.345	.222	.400	5.14	6.43
Beeks, Jalen	L-L	5-11	215	7-10-93	1	1	3.26	12	0	0	1	19	21	9	7	1	4	26	.276	.240	.294	12.10	1.86
Brosseau, Mike	R-R	5-10	205	3-15-94	0	0	0.00	1	0	0	0	0	0	0	0	0	0	1	.000	--	.000	27.00	0.00
Castillo, Diego	R-R	6-3	250	1-18-94	3	0	1.66	22	0	0	4	22	12	4	4	3	11	23	.156	.136	.164	9.55	4.57
Chirinos, Yonny	R-R	6-2	225	12-26-93	0	0	2.38	3	3	0	0	11	14	4	3	2	4	10	.304	.250	.364	7.94	3.18
Curtiss, John	R-R	6-5	220	4-5-93	3	0	1.80	17	3	0	2	25	21	7	5	3	3	25	.223	.184	.250	9.00	1.08
Drake, Oliver	R-R	6-4	220	1-13-87	0	2	5.73	11	0	0	2	11	7	8	7	2	6	7	.189	.200	.176	5.73	4.91
Fairbanks, Pete	R-R	6-6	225	12-16-93	6	3	2.70	27	2	0	0	27	23	9	8	2	14	39	.228	.191	.259	13.16	4.73
Fleming, Josh	R-L	6-2	220	5-18-96	5	0	2.78	7	5	0	0	32	28	10	10	5	7	25	.230	.270	.212	6.96	1.95
Garcia, Edgar	R-R	6-1	205	10-4-96	0	0	10.80	4	0	0	1	3	3	4	4	2	4	1	.250	.000	.375	2.70	10.80
Gilmartin, Sean	L-L	6-2	205	5-8-90	0	0	8.31	2	0	0	0	4	7	4	4	2	4	5	.350	.222	.455	10.38	8.31
Glasnow, Tyler	L-R	6-8	225	8-23-93	5	1	4.08	11	11	0	0	57	43	26	26	11	22	91	.200	.200	.200	14.38	3.45
Kittredge, Andrew	R-R	6-1	230	3-17-90	0	0	2.25	8	1	0	1	8	8	2	2	0	2	3	.276	.250	.286	3.38	2.25
Loup, Aaron	L-L	5-11	210	12-19-87	3	2	2.52	24	0	0	0	25	17	9	7	3	4	22	.200	.212	.192	7.92	1.44
Morton, Charlie	R-R	6-5	215	11-12-83	2	2	4.74	9	9	0	0	38	43	21	20	4	10	42	.279	.242	.304	9.95	2.37
Reed, Cody	L-L	6-5	230	4-15-93	0	0	0.00	2	0	0	0	3	1	0	0	0	2	1	.100	.125	.000	6.75	0.00
Richards, Trevor	R-R	6-2	195	5-15-93	0	0	5.91	9	4	0	0	32	44	24	21	6	11	27	.321	.259	.361	7.59	3.09
Roe, Chaz	R-R	6-5	190	10-9-86	2	0	2.89	10	0	0	1	9	10	4	3	0	3	9	.294	.143	.333	8.68	2.89
Sherriff, Ryan	L-L	6-1	190	5-25-90	1	0	0.00	10	0	0	1	6	6	0	0	2	2	6	.188	.154	.211	1.86	1.86
Slegers, Aaron	R-R	6-10	260	9-4-92	0	0	3.46	11	1	0	2	26	18	10	10	1	5	19	.194	.222	.175	6.58	1.73
Snell, Blake	L-L	6-4	225	12-4-92	4	2	3.24	11	11	0	0	50	42	19	18	10	18	63	.228	.217	.232	11.34	3.24
Thompson, Ryan	R-R	6-5	210	6-26-92	1	2	4.44	25	1	0	1	26	29	15	13	4	8	23	.274	.250	.284	7.86	2.73
Yarbrough, Ryan	R-L	6-5	205	12-31-91	1	4	3.56	11	9	0	0	56	54	22	22	5	12	44	.256	.259	.255	7.11	1.94

Fielding

Catcher	PCT	G	PO	A	E	DP	PB
Perez	.996	38	222	25	1	2	1
Smith	1.000	16	73	3	0	0	1
Zunino	.996	28	244	15	1	2	5

First Base	PCT	G	PO	A	E	DP
Brosseau	1.000	12	51	8	0	9
Choi	.989	38	255	11	3	25
Diaz	1.000	2	9	0	0	0
Lowe	.000	1	0	0	0	0
Lowe	1.000	15	110	6	0	8
Martinez	1.000	6	31	2	0	2
O'Grady	1.000	1	1	0	0	0
Perez	1.000	1	10	2	0	2
Renfroe	1.000	2	5	2	0	0

Second Base	PCT	G	PO	A	E	DP
Brosseau	1.000	9	15	17	0	8
Lowe	.984	44	54	68	2	21
Wendle	1.000	20	26	36	0	7

Third Base	PCT	G	PO	A	E	DP
Brosseau	.935	11	6	23	2	1
Diaz	.981	25	12	41	1	4
Lowe	1.000	2	0	4	0	1
Tsutsugo	.846	14	6	16	4	3
Wendle	.934	28	17	40	4	5

Shortstop	PCT	G	PO	A	E	DP
Adames	.953	53	53	131	9	27
Wendle	.974	10	7	30	1	5

Outfield	PCT	G	PO	A	E	DP
Arozarena	1.000	17	17	1	0	1
Brosseau	1.000	3	5	0	0	0
Kiermaier	1.000	46	86	6	0	0
Lowe	1.000	12	21	0	0	0
Margot	.979	46	92	0	2	0
Meadows	1.000	26	38	0	0	0
O'Grady	--	1	0	0	0	0
Phillips	1.000	15	15	0	0	0
Renfroe	.953	39	60	1	3	0
Tsutsugo	1.000	16	15	0	0	0

Texas Rangers

SEASON IN A SENTENCE: The Rangers opened brand new Globe Life Field anticipating they would contend and welcome plenty of fans in the first year of the new stadium, but those hopes were quickly dashed as they skidded to the American League's worst record and fans were kept out of ballparks because of the novel coronavirus pandemic.

HIGH POINT: After losing eight of 11 games to open the season, the Rangers pushed their record back over .500 with a 7-1 stretch from Aug. 7-15. Kyle Gibson capped it off with a quality start in a 6-4 win over the Rockies that put the Rangers record at 10-9.

LOW POINT: After a 14-4 loss to the Padres on Aug. 17, manager Chris Woodward and Rangers players criticized Padres shortstop Fernando Tatis Jr. for swinging on a 3-0 pitch and hitting a grand slam with the Padres holding a seven-run lead. Their complaints energized the Padres, who went on to hit a grand slam in a major league-record four straight games—all against the Rangers.

NOTABLE ROOKIES: Utilityman Nick Solak bounced between left field, second base and center field and hit wherever he played. He led all rookies with 56 hits and batted .268/.326/.344 overall. Outfielder Leody Taveras made the Opening Day roster and took over as the Rangers everyday center fielder. He hit .227 with four home runs but played standout defense. Shortstop Anderson Tejeda made his debut and homered in his first career game on Aug. 6. Catcher Sam Huff, who had never played above high Class A, debuted in September and hit three doubles and three home runs in 10 games. Righthander Kyle Cody (1-1, 1.59) buttressed the starting rotation and righthander Jonathan Hernandez went 5-1, 2.90 in a team-high 27 relief appearances.

KEY TRANSACTIONS: The Rangers bulked up their starting rotation before the season by acquiring Corey Kluber from the Indians in exchange for Delino DeShields and Emmanuel Clase and

signing Gibson and Jordan Lyles as free agents. Kluber made it through only one inning in his first start before suffering a season-ending shoulder injury, while Gibson (5.35 ERA) and Lyles (7.02) disappointed. The Rangers also traded outfielder Nomar Mazara to the White Sox for outfielder Steele Walker. At the trade deadline, they traded catcher Robinson Chirinos and infielder Todd Frazier to the Mets and lefthander Mike Minor to the A's, all for prospects.

OPENING DAY PAYROLL: $63,687,408 (15th)

PLAYERS OF THE YEAR

MAJOR LEAGUE
Lance Lynn
RHP
6-3, 3.32
89 SO, 25 BB in 84 IP

TOP ROOKIE
Leody Taveras
OF
.227/.308/.395
4 HR, 6 RBIs, 8-8 SB in 33 games

ORGANIZATION LEADERS

Batting		*Minimum 100 AB
MAJORS		
* AVG	Isiah Kiner-Falefa	.280
* OPS	Shin-Soo Choo	.723
HR	Rougned Odor	10
HR	Joey Gallo	10
RBI	Rougned Odor	30

Pitching		#Minimum 30 IP
MAJORS		
W	Lance Lynn	6
# ERA	Lance Lynn	3.32
SO	Lance Lynn	89
SV	Rafael Montero	8

ORGANIZATION STATISTICS

TEXAS RANGERS
AMERICAN LEAGUE

Batting	B-T	HT	WT	DOB	AVG	vLH	vRH	G	AB	R	H	2B	3B	HR	RBI	BB	HBP	SH	SF	SO	SB	CS	SLG	OBP
Andrus, Elvis	R-R	6-0	210	8-26-88	.194	.206	.188	29	103	11	20	5	0	3	7	8	0	0	0	15	3	1	.330	.252
Apostel, Sherten	R-R	6-4	235	3-11-99	.100	.091	.111	7	20	1	2	1	0	0	0	1	0	0	0	9	0	0	.150	.143
Calhoun, Willie	L-R	5-8	200	11-4-94	.190	.368	.148	29	100	3	19	2	1	1	13	5	1	0	2	17	0	0	.260	.231
Chirinos, Robinson	R-R	6-1	220	6-5-84	.119	.118	.120	14	42	3	5	1	0	0	2	5	1	0	1	12	0	0	.143	.224

Batting	B-T	HT	WT	DOB	AVG	vLH	vRH	G	AB	R	H	2B	3B	HR	RBI	BB	HBP	SH	SF	SO	SB	CS	SLG	OBP
Choo, Shin-Soo	L-L	5-11	205	7-13-82	.236	.222	.243	33	110	13	26	3	0	5	15	13	2	0	2	33	6	2	.400	.323
Dietrich, Derek	L-R	6-2	205	7-18-89	.197	.286	.185	25	61	9	12	1	0	5	8	9	5	0	0	21	1	1	.459	.347
Frazier, Todd	R-R	6-3	220	2-12-86	.241	.343	.192	31	108	11	26	7	1	2	10	3	0	0	26	1	1	.380	.322
Gallo, Joey	L-R	6-5	250	11-19-93	.181	.143	.203	57	193	23	35	8	0	10	26	29	4	0	0	79	2	0	.378	.301
Garcia, Adolis	R-R	6-1	205	3-2-93	.000	.000	.000	3	6	0	0	0	0	0	0	1	0	0	0	4	0	0	.000	.143
Guzman, Ronald	L-L	6-5	235	10-20-94	.244	.167	.267	26	78	10	19	1	1	4	9	7	1	0	0	24	1	0	.436	.314
Heineman, Scott	R-R	6-1	205	12-4-92	.154	.154	.154	24	52	6	8	3	0	1	7	2	0	0	0	11	3	0	.269	.185
Huff, Sam	R-R	6-5	240	1-14-98	.355	.286	.375	10	31	5	11	3	0	3	4	2	0	0	0	11	0	0	.742	.394
Kiner-Falefa, Isiah	R-R	5-11	190	3-23-95	.280	.373	.243	58	211	28	59	4	3	3	10	14	2	0	1	32	8	5	.370	.329
Mathis, Jeff	R-R	6-0	205	3-31-83	.161	.067	.191	24	62	6	10	1	1	3	9	5	0	0	1	24	1	0	.355	.221
Odor, Rougned	L-R	5-11	200	2-3-94	.167	.104	.200	38	138	15	23	4	0	10	30	7	1	0	2	47	0	1	.413	.209
Refsnyder, Rob	R-R	6-0	205	3-26-91	.200	.235	.154	15	30	4	6	1	0	0	1	2	1	0	1	11	0	0	.233	.265
Rivera, Yadiel	R-R	6-3	190	5-2-92	.000	.000	.000	4	5	0	0	0	0	0	0	0	0	0	0	1	1	0	.000	.000
Romine, Andrew	B-R	6-1	190	12-24-85	.250	--	.250	2	4	1	1	1	0	0	0	0	0	0	0	1	0	0	.500	.250
Santana, Danny	B-R	5-11	195	11-7-90	.145	.105	.167	15	55	6	8	4	0	1	7	7	0	0	1	24	2	0	.273	.238
Solak, Nick	R-R	5-11	185	1-11-95	.268	.313	.246	58	209	27	56	10	0	2	23	18	2	0	4	42	7	1	.344	.326
Taveras, Leody	B-R	6-2	195	9-8-98	.227	.282	.200	33	119	20	27	6	1	4	14	14	0	1	0	43	8	0	.395	.308
Tejeda, Anderson	B-R	6-0	200	5-1-98	.253	.190	.278	23	75	7	19	4	1	3	8	2	0	0	0	30	4	1	.453	.273
Trevino, Jose	R-R	5-11	210	11-28-92	.250	.273	.233	24	76	10	19	8	0	2	9	3	1	1	2	15	0	0	.434	.280
White, Eli	R-R	6-3	195	6-26-94	.188	.048	.296	19	48	5	9	2	0	3	3	0	0	1	1	16	1	1	.229	.231

Pitching	B-T	HT	WT	DOB	W	L	ERA	G	GS	CG	SV	IP	H	R	ER	HR	BB	SO	AVG	vLH	vRH	K/9	BB/9
Allard, Kolby	L-L	6-1	195	8-13-97	0	6	7.75	11	8	0	0	34	31	29	29	4	20	32	.238	.263	.228	8.55	5.35
Benjamin, Wes	R-L	6-2	210	7-26-93	2	1	4.84	8	1	0	0	22	24	12	12	4	7	21	.264	.200	.288	8.46	2.82
Chavez, Jesse	R-R	6-1	175	8-21-83	0	0	6.88	18	0	0	0	17	20	13	13	6	7	13	.303	.222	.359	6.88	3.71
Cody, Kyle	R-R	6-7	225	8-9-94	1	1	1.59	8	5	0	0	23	15	5	4	1	13	18	.190	.133	.224	7.15	5.16
Evans, Demarcus	R-R	6-5	265	10-22-96	0	0	2.25	4	0	0	0	4	3	1	1	1	0	4	.231	.000	.300	9.00	0.00
Farrell, Luke	L-R	6-6	200	6-7-91	0	0	8.44	4	0	0	0	5	5	5	5	1	5	8	.250	.222	.273	13.50	8.44
Garcia, Luis	R-R	6-2	240	1-30-87	0	2	7.56	11	2	0	0	8	10	9	7	1	9	11	.278	.389	.167	11.88	9.72
2-team total (5 Houston Astros)					0	3	4.79	16	3	0	0	21	17	13	11	2	14	20	.218	.333	.103	8.71	6.10
Gibaut, Ian	R-R	6-3	250	11-19-93	0	1	6.57	14	0	0	0	12	11	10	9	2	9	14	.229	.192	.273	10.22	6.57
Gibson, Kyle	R-R	6-6	215	10-23-87	2	6	5.35	12	12	1	0	67	73	44	40	12	30	58	.275	.265	.283	7.75	4.01
Goody, Nick	R-R	5-11	200	7-6-91	0	2	9.00	17	1	0	1	14	14	12	11	3	8	13	.304	.357	.281	10.64	6.55
Hearn, Taylor	L-L	6-6	230	8-30-94	0	0	3.63	14	0	0	0	17	13	8	7	2	11	23	.206	.261	.175	11.94	5.71
Herget, Jimmy	R-R	6-3	170	9-9-93	1	0	3.20	20	1	0	0	20	13	7	7	2	14	17	.188	.087	.239	7.78	6.41
Hernandez, Jonathan	R-R	6-3	190	7-6-96	5	1	2.90	27	0	0	0	31	24	10	10	2	8	31	.218	.244	.200	9.00	2.32
King, John	L-L	6-2	215	9-14-94	1	0	6.10	6	0	0	0	10	13	8	7	2	4	9	.289	.333	.267	7.84	3.48
Kluber, Corey	R-R	6-4	215	4-10-86	0	0	0.00	1	1	0	0	1	0	0	0	0	1	1	.000	.000	--	9.00	9.00
Leclerc, Jose	R-R	6-0	195	12-19-93	0	0	4.50	2	0	0	1	2	1	1	1	0	2	3	.250	.286	.000	13.50	9.00
Lyles, Jordan	R-R	6-5	230	10-19-90	1	6	7.02	12	9	0	0	58	67	49	45	12	23	36	.285	.292	.279	5.62	3.59
Lynn, Lance	B-R	6-5	250	5-12-87	6	3	3.32	13	13	1	0	84	64	34	31	13	25	89	.206	.182	.229	9.54	2.68
Martin, Brett	L-L	6-4	200	4-28-95	1	1	1.84	15	0	0	0	15	8	5	3	2	9	8	.157	.176	.147	4.91	5.52
Minor, Mike	L-R	6-4	210	12-26-87	0	5	5.60	7	7	0	0	35	35	23	22	7	13	35	.248	.220	.260	8.92	3.31
2-team total (5 Oakland Athletics)					1	6	5.56	12	11	0	0	57	50	36	35	11	20	62	.230	.230	.231	9.85	3.18
Montero, Rafael	R-R	6-0	190	10-17-90	0	1	4.08	17	0	0	8	18	12	11	8	2	6	19	.190	.188	.194	9.68	3.06
Nicasio, Juan	R-R	6-4	255	8-31-86	0	0	40.50	2	0	0	0	1	5	6	6	1	2	1	.556	.667	.500	6.75	13.50
Palumbo, Joe	L-L	6-0	195	10-26-94	0	1	11.57	2	0	0	0	3	3	3	3	1	3	5	.273	.143	.500	19.29	11.57
Rodriguez, Joely	L-L	6-1	200	11-14-91	0	0	2.13	12	0	0	0	13	8	3	3	0	5	17	.174	.188	.167	12.08	3.55
Volquez, Edinson	R-R	6-0	220	7-3-83	2	1	6.35	7	0	0	0	6	6	4	4	0	2	3	.261	.273	.250	4.76	3.18

Fielding

Catcher	PCT	G	PO	A	E	DP	PB
Chirinos	1.000	13	117	4	0	0	2
Huff	.970	10	62	2	2	1	2
Mathis	.989	24	169	15	2	1	2
Trevino	.994	21	153	3	1	0	0

First Base	PCT	G	PO	A	E	DP
Apostel	.973	5	32	4	1	4
Dietrich	.977	6	40	2	1	5
Frazier	1.000	16	106	5	0	9
Guzman	.995	24	169	14	1	14
Heineman	1.000	1	7	1	0	0
Refsnyder	1.000	4	17	0	0	2
Rivera	1.000	1	4	0	0	1
Santana	1.000	9	58	2	0	3
Solak	.000	1	0	0	0	0
Trevino	1.000	1	1	0	0	0

Second Base	PCT	G	PO	A	E	DP
Dietrich	1.000	3	2	2	0	0
Odor	.972	37	54	86	4	18
Rivera	1.000	1	3	3	0	2
Solak	.981	17	21	30	1	5
Tejeda	1.000	4	7	6	0	1

Third Base	PCT	G	PO	A	E	DP
Apostel	.500	2	1	0	1	0
Dietrich	1.000	3	0	4	0	0
Frazier	.935	15	6	23	2	2
Kiner-Falefa	.957	46	32	79	5	4

Shortstop	PCT	G	PO	A	E	DP
Andrus	.969	29	33	61	3	10
Kiner-Falefa	1.000	15	12	31	0	6
Rivera	1.000	2	0	2	0	0
Romine	1.000	1	0	3	0	1
Tejeda	.944	18	12	39	3	8

Outfield	PCT	G	PO	A	E	DP
Calhoun	1.000	8	11	0	0	0
Choo	.976	19	41	0	1	0
Gallo	1.000	53	120	3	0	1
Garcia	1.000	3	8	0	0	0
Heineman	.974	21	38	0	1	0
Refsnyder	1.000	3	6	1	0	1
Santana	1.000	4	14	0	0	0
Solak	.986	36	69	1	1	0
Taveras	.976	33	81	1	2	1
White	1.000	17	22	0	0	0

Toronto Blue Jays

SEASON IN A SENTENCE: A talented young lineup and an expanded playoff system helped the Blue Jays reach their first postseason since 2016—with all their "home" games played in Buffalo—though it was a quick 2-0 exit against the Rays in the Wild Card Series.

HIGH POINT: After starting the season a sluggish 7-11, the Blue Jays ripped off a six-game winning streak against the Orioles, Phillies and Rays, bringing them to 13-11. They never sank below .500 the rest of the season, climbing to 24-18 on Sept. 8 after back-to-back wins against the Yankees. A lineup built around young players in their 20s such as Bo Bichette, Teoscar Hernandez, Lourdes Gurriel, Cavan Biggio, Rowdy Tellez and Vladimir Guerrero Jr. helped the Blue Jays rank seventh in the majors in runs scored.

LOW POINT: The Blue Jays were 26-20 and 3.5 games back in the AL East before they lost three straight to the Yankees followed by three more consecutive losses to the Phillies, dropping them back to 26-26 and 8.5 games back in the division. While Hyun-Jin Ryu was one of the best pitchers in baseball, the Blue Jays largely struggled to prevent runs when he wasn't on the mound, finishing 25th in MLB in runs allowed.

NOTABLE ROOKIES: The Blue Jays were counting on Nate Pearson to play a pivotal role in their starting rotation in 2020. A flexor strain in his right elbow limited him to just 18 innings. Catcher Alejandro Kirk made the jump from high Class A in 2019 to the big leagues in September 2020, showing exceptional bat control and plate discipline to become a regular in the Blue Jays lineup down the stretch. While older for a rookie at 27, righthander Jordan Romano proved an effective reliever, posting a 21-5 strikeout-to-walk mark in 14.2 innings with a 1.23 ERA.

KEY TRANSACTIONS: The biggest move for the Blue Jays was the offseason signing of Ryu, who was one of the most effective starters in the majors with a 2.69 ERA that ranked fourth in the AL. He

posted a stellar 72-17 K-BB mark in 67 innings, tied for ninth in the AL in strikeouts. The Blue Jays added one of their most effective starters down the stretch when they traded 20-year-old outfield prospect Alberto Rodriguez to the Mariners for righthander Taijuan Walker, who in six starts for the Blue Jays had a 2-1 record and a 1.37 ERA. Toronto also traded for lefthander Robbie Ray at the Aug. 31 deadline, sending lefthander Travis Bergen to the D-backs as the return. Ray provided some useful innings as a starter.

OPENING DAY PAYROLL: $50,989,164 (19th)

PLAYERS OF THE YEAR

MAJOR LEAGUE	ROOKIE
Hyun Jin Ryu LHP	**Thomas Hatch** RHP
5-2, 2.69, 12 GS 72 SO in 67 IP	3-1, 2.73, 17 G 23 SO in 26.1 IP

ORGANIZATION LEADERS

Batting		*Minimum 100 AB
MAJORS		
* AVG	Lourdes Gurriel Jr.	.308
* OPS	Teoscar Hernandez	.919
HR	Teoscar Hernandez	16
RBI	Randal Grichuk	35
Pitching		#Minimum 30 IP
MAJORS		
W	Hyun Jin Ryu	5
# ERA	Hyun Jin Ryu	2.69
SO	Hyun Jin Ryu	72
SV	Anthony Bass	7

ORGANIZATION STATISTICS

TORONTO BLUE JAYS
AMERICAN LEAGUE

Batting	B-T	HT	WT	DOB	AVG	vLH	vRH	G	AB	R	H	2B	3B	HR	RBI	BB	HBP	SH	SF	SO	SB	CS	SLG	OBP
Alford, Anthony	R-R	6-1	210	7-20-94	.188	.222	.143	13	16	3	3	0	0	1	3	0	0	0	0	7	3	0	.375	.188
Bichette, Bo	R-R	6-0	185	3-5-98	.301	.333	.290	29	123	18	37	9	1	5	23	5	0	0	0	27	4	1	.512	.328
Biggio, Cavan	L-R	6-2	200	4-11-95	.250	.299	.229	59	220	41	55	16	0	8	28	41	3	0	0	61	6	0	.432	.375
Davis, Jonathan	R-R	5-8	190	5-12-92	.259	.125	.316	13	27	4	7	2	0	1	6	3	2	0	1	11	1	0	.444	.364

Batting

Batting	B-T	HT	WT	DOB	AVG	vLH	vRH	G	AB	R	H	2B	3B	HR	RBI	BB	HBP	SH	SF	SO	SB	CS	SLG	OBP
Drury, Brandon	R-R	6-2	230	8-21-92	.152	.261	.043	21	46	3	7	1	0	0	1	2	0	0	1	9	0	0	.174	.184
Espinal, Santiago	R-R	5-10	181	11-13-94	.267	.324	.192	26	60	10	16	4	0	0	6	4	0	1	1	16	1	0	.333	.308
Fisher, Derek	L-R	6-3	215	8-21-93	.226	.400	.192	16	31	5	7	2	1	1	7	7	0	0	1	11	0	1	.452	.359
Grichuk, Randal	R-R	6-2	216	8-13-91	.273	.328	.252	55	216	38	59	9	0	12	35	13	0	0	2	49	1	1	.481	.312
Guerrero Jr., Vladimir	R-R	6-2	250	3-16-99	.262	.224	.276	60	221	34	58	13	2	9	33	20	2	0	0	38	1	0	.462	.329
Gurriel Jr., Lourdes	R-R	6-4	215	10-10-93	.308	.286	.317	57	208	28	64	14	0	11	33	14	0	0	2	48	3	1	.534	.348
Hernandez, Teoscar	R-R	6-2	205	10-15-92	.289	.275	.295	50	190	33	55	7	0	16	34	14	1	0	1	63	6	1	.579	.340
Jansen, Danny	R-R	6-2	225	4-15-95	.183	.103	.222	43	120	18	22	3	0	6	20	21	2	3	1	31	0	0	.358	.313
Joseph, Caleb	R-R	6-3	205	6-18-86	.125	.000	.200	3	8	2	1	0	0	1	2	1	0	0	0	1	0	0	.500	.222
Kirk, Alejandro	R-R	5-8	265	11-6-98	.375	.143	.471	9	24	4	9	2	0	1	3	1	0	0	0	4	0	0	.583	.400
McGuire, Reese	L-R	6-0	215	3-2-95	.073	.000	.125	19	41	2	3	0	0	1	1	0	0	4	0	11	0	0	.146	.073
McKinney, Billy	L-L	6-1	205	8-23-94	.667	--	.667	2	3	1	2	0	0	0	0	0	0	0	0	0	0	0	.667	.667
Panik, Joe	L-R	6-1	205	10-30-90	.225	.303	.195	41	120	18	27	6	0	1	7	20	1	0	0	27	0	0	.300	.340
Shaw, Travis	L-R	6-4	230	4-16-90	.239	.295	.218	50	163	17	39	10	0	6	17	16	0	0	1	50	0	0	.411	.306
Tellez, Rowdy	L-L	6-4	255	3-16-95	.283	.333	.267	35	113	20	32	5	0	8	23	11	1	0	2	20	0	1	.540	.346
Villar, Jonathan	B-R	6-0	233	5-2-91	.188	.158	.200	22	69	3	13	1	0	0	6	9	0	0	1	22	7	0	.203	.278
Vogelbach, Daniel	L-R	6-0	270	12-17-92	.000	.000	.000	2	4	0	0	0	0	0	1	0	0	0	2	0	0	0	.000	.200
2-team total (18 Seattle Mariners)					.088	.000	.098	20	57	3	5	1	0	2	4	12	0	0	0	15	0	0	.211	.246

Pitching

Pitching	B-T	HT	WT	DOB	W	L	ERA	G	GS	CG	SV	IP	H	R	ER	HR	BB	SO	AVG	vLH	vRH	K/9	BB/9
Anderson, Chase	R-R	6-1	210	11-30-87	1	2	7.22	10	7	0	0	34	45	29	27	11	10	38	.315	.328	.305	10.16	2.67
Bass, Anthony	R-R	6-2	200	11-1-87	2	3	3.51	26	0	0	7	26	17	13	10	2	9	21	.189	.161	.203	7.36	3.16
Bergen, Travis	L-L	6-1	215	10-8-93	0	0	0.00	1	0	0	0	2	1	0	0	0	1	3	.200	.000	.333	16.20	5.40
Borucki, Ryan	L-L	6-4	215	3-31-94	1	1	2.70	21	0	0	0	17	12	5	5	1	12	21	.200	.125	.286	11.34	6.48
Cole, A.J.	R-R	6-5	240	1-5-92	3	0	3.09	24	0	0	1	23	19	9	8	3	9	20	.226	.139	.292	7.71	3.47
Dolis, Rafael	R-R	6-4	235	1-10-88	2	2	1.50	24	0	0	5	24	16	9	4	1	14	31	.193	.162	.217	11.63	5.25
Espinal, Santiago	R-R	5-10	181	11-13-94	0	0	9.00	2	0	0	0	2	3	2	2	1	1	0	.333	.400	.250	0.00	4.50
Font, Wilmer	R-R	6-4	255	5-24-90	1	3	9.92	21	0	0	0	16	28	19	18	2	9	15	.378	.400	.367	8.27	4.96
Gaviglio, Sam	R-R	6-1	215	5-22-90	0	1	9.00	4	0	0	0	3	3	3	3	0	5	1	.273	.333	.250	3.00	15.00
Giles, Ken	R-R	6-3	210	9-20-90	0	0	9.82	4	0	0	1	4	4	4	4	2	4	6	.267	.143	.375	14.73	9.82
Hatch, Thomas	R-R	6-1	205	9-29-94	3	1	2.73	17	1	0	0	26	18	11	8	2	13	23	.191	.200	.185	7.86	4.44
Kay, Anthony	L-L	6-0	225	3-21-95	2	0	5.14	13	0	0	0	21	22	13	12	3	14	22	.268	.350	.190	9.43	6.00
Merryweather, Julian	R-R	6-4	215	10-14-91	0	0	4.15	8	3	0	0	13	11	6	6	0	6	15	.224	.111	.290	10.38	4.15
Moran, Brian	L-L	6-4	225	9-30-88	0	0	0.00	2	0	0	0	1	1	0	0	0	1	1	.250	.333	.000	9.00	9.00
Murphy, Patrick	R-R	6-5	235	6-10-95	0	0	1.50	4	0	0	0	6	6	1	1	0	2	5	.261	.375	.200	7.50	3.00
Pearson, Nate	R-R	6-6	250	8-20-96	1	0	6.00	5	4	0	0	18	14	15	12	5	13	16	.209	.313	.114	8.00	6.50
Perez, Hector	R-R	6-3	223	6-6-96	0	0	10.80	1	0	0	0	2	3	2	2	1	3	1	.429	.000	.600	5.40	16.20
Ray, Robbie	L-L	6-2	215	10-1-91	1	1	4.79	5	4	0	0	21	22	13	11	4	14	25	.265	.174	.300	10.89	6.10
Reid-Foley, Sean	R-R	6-3	230	8-30-95	1	0	1.35	5	0	0	0	7	3	3	1	0	6	6	.125	.000	.176	8.10	8.10
Roark, Tanner	R-R	6-2	238	10-5-86	2	3	6.80	11	11	0	0	48	60	39	36	14	23	41	.309	.218	.383	7.74	4.34
Romano, Jordan	R-R	6-5	225	4-21-93	2	1	1.23	15	0	0	2	15	8	3	2	2	5	21	.154	.083	.214	12.89	3.07
Ryu, Hyun Jin	R-L	6-3	255	3-25-87	5	2	2.69	12	12	0	0	67	60	22	20	6	17	72	.234	.220	.238	9.67	2.28
Shoemaker, Matt	R-R	6-2	225	9-27-86	0	1	4.71	6	6	0	0	29	22	16	15	8	9	26	.210	.194	.233	8.16	2.83
Stripling, Ross	R-R	6-3	220	11-23-89	0	2	6.32	5	2	0	0	16	18	11	11	1	3	13	.286	.207	.353	7.47	4.02
Thornton, Trent	R-R	6-0	195	9-30-93	0	0	11.12	3	3	0	0	6	15	7	7	0	3	6	.517	.385	.625	9.53	4.76
Waguespack, Jacob	R-R	6-6	235	11-5-93	0	0	8.15	11	0	0	0	18	27	20	16	2	9	16	.346	.282	.410	8.15	4.58
Walker, Taijuan	R-R	6-4	235	8-13-92	2	1	1.37	6	6	0	0	26	22	10	4	3	11	25	.218	.237	.206	8.54	3.76
2-team total (5 Seattle Mariners)					4	3	2.70	11	11	0	0	53	43	23	16	8	19	50	.214	.265	.178	8.44	3.21
Yamaguchi, Shun	R-R	6-2	225	7-11-87	2	4	8.06	17	0	0	0	26	28	25	23	6	17	26	.283	.238	.316	9.12	5.96
Zeuch, T.J.	R-R	6-7	245	8-1-95	1	0	1.59	3	1	0	0	11	9	2	2	1	4	3	.209	.400	.152	2.38	3.18

Fielding

Catcher	PCT	G	PO	A	E	DP	PB
Jansen	.994	43	332	20	2	2	3
Joseph	.900	3	18	0	2	0	1
Kirk	1.000	7	48	1	0	0	
McGuire	.978	18	131	5	3	1	2

First Base	PCT	G	PO	A	E	DP
Guerrero Jr.	.990	34	265	22	3	25
Gurriel Jr.	1.000	1	3	0	0	0
Shaw	.986	14	67	6	1	5
Tellez	1.000	19	132	4	0	15

Second Base	PCT	G	PO	A	E	DP
Biggio	.977	37	54	74	3	22
Drury	1.000	4	4	5	0	0
Panik	.980	18	28	20	1	6
Villar	.959	13	13	34	2	7

Third Base	PCT	G	PO	A	E	DP
Biggio	.964	10	5	22	1	1
Drury	1.000	16	5	17	0	3
Espinal	1.000	2	1	1	0	0
Panik	1.000	12	4	9	0	0
Shaw	.977	37	20	64	2	7

Shortstop	PCT	G	PO	A	E	DP
Bichette	.971	26	34	66	3	11
Drury	1.000	2	1	2	0	1
Espinal	.975	21	22	57	2	12
Panik	1.000	14	13	29	0	5
Villar	.917	7	7	15	2	2

Outfield	PCT	G	PO	A	E	DP
Alford	1.000	8	6	0	0	0
Biggio	.968	18	30	0	1	0
Davis	1.000	13	20	0	0	0
Fisher	.929	15	13	0	1	0
Grichuk	.990	48	96	2	1	0
Gurriel Jr.	.990	53	100	3	1	0
Hernandez	.965	46	76	7	3	2
McKinney	1.000	1	1	0	0	0

Washington Nationals

SEASON IN A SENTENCE: With Juan Soto testing positive for COVID-19 on Opening Day, Stephen Strasburg suffering an injury in his second start and Ryan Zimmerman opting out of the season, the defending World Series champions stumbled out of the gate and never recovered as they finished tied for last place in the National League East.

HIGH POINT: Soto returned from his positive test and summarily laid waste to opposing pitchers. On the final day of the season, the 21-year-old went 1-for-1 with a single and walk to raise his batting average to .351 and become the youngest player to ever win an MLB batting title.

LOW POINT: The Nationals sat just three games out of second place—and the resulting automatic playoff spot—in the NL East a month into the season, but they lost seven straight games from Aug. 29-Sept. 4 to all but end their playoff hopes. It was the franchise's longest losing streak in four years.

NOTABLE ROOKIES: With Anthony Rendon departing in free agency, the Nationals installed Carter Kieboom as their everyday third baseman but didn't get nearly the production they had hoped for. Kieboom hit just .202 with zero home runs and was demoted to the alternate training site for a chunk of the season. Second baseman Luis Garcia's first season in D.C. was much more promising. The 20-year-old jumped straight from Double-A and hit .276 over 40 games to cement his place as the Nationals' everyday second baseman moving forward. Outfielder Yadiel Hernandez, a 32-year-old signed out of Cuba in 2016, received his first callup and hit a walkoff two-run home run to beat the Phillies on Sept. 22 for his first career home run. Starting pitcher Wil Crowe and relievers Dakota Bacus and Seth Romero made their debuts to limited success. Lefthanded reliever Ben Braymer was the best of the Nationals rookie pitchers with one run allowed in 7.1 innings.

KEY TRANSACTIONS: The Nationals lost Rendon to the Angels in free agency, but they did as much as they could to keep the core of the 2019 World Series winners together. They re-signed Strasburg, infielders Howie Kendrick, Ryan Zimmerman and Asdrubal Cabrera and catcher Yan Gomes from their World Series team and also added infielder Starlin Castro and reliever Will Harris in the offseason. Zimmerman eventually opted out of the season and Strasburg developed season-ending carpal tunnel neuritis in his right hand.

OPENING DAY PAYROLL: $66,525,837 (12th)

PLAYERS OF THE YEAR

MARY DECICCO VIA GETTY IMAGES

MAJOR LEAGUE
Trea Turner
SS
.335/.394/.588
12 HR, 41 RBIs, 12 SB
MLB-best 78 hits

TOP ROOKIE
Luis Garcia
2B/SS
.276/.302/.366
6 2B, 16 RBIs
in 40 G

ORGANIZATION LEADERS

Batting		*Minimum 100 AB
MAJORS		
* AVG	Juan Soto	.351
* OPS	Juan Soto	1.185
HR	Juan Soto	13
RBI	Trea Turner	41
Pitching		**#Minimum 30 IP**
MAJORS		
W	Max Scherzer	5
# ERA	Max Scherzer	3.74
SO	Max Scherzer	92
SV	Daniel Hudson	10

ORGANIZATION STATISTICS

WASHINGTON NATIONALS
NATIONAL LEAGUE

Batting	B-T	HT	WT	DOB	AVG	vLH	vRH	G	AB	R	H	2B	3B	HR	RBI	BB	HBP	SH	SF	SO	SB	CS	SLG	OBP
Bonifacio, Emilio	B-R	5-10	200	4-23-85	.000	--	.000	3	3	1	0	0	0	0	0	0	0	0	0	2	0	1	.000	.000
Cabrera, Asdrubal	B-R	6-0	205	11-13-85	.242	.314	.216	52	190	23	46	9	3	8	31	19	0	0	4	40	0	0	.447	.305
Castro, Starlin	R-R	6-2	220	3-24-90	.267	.500	.182	16	60	9	16	3	1	2	4	3	0	0	0	13	0	0	.450	.302
Difo, Wilmer	B-R	5-11	200	4-2-92	.071	.000	.111	12	14	1	1	0	0	0	1	3	0	0	1	4	0	0	.071	.222

Batting

Batting	B-T	HT	WT	DOB	AVG	vLH	vRH	G	AB	R	H	2B	3B	HR	RBI	BB	HBP	SH	SF	SO	SB	CS	SLG	OBP
Eaton, Adam	L-L	5-9	176	12-6-88	.226	.103	.267	41	159	22	36	11	1	4	17	12	1	4	0	32	3	0	.384	.285
Garcia, Luis	L-R	6-2	211	5-16-00	.276	.143	.323	40	134	18	37	6	0	2	16	5	0	0	0	29	1	1	.366	.302
Gomes, Yan	R-R	6-2	215	7-19-87	.284	.308	.277	30	109	14	31	6	1	4	13	6	1	0	3	22	1	0	.468	.319
Harrison, Josh	R-R	5-8	190	7-8-87	.278	.278	.279	33	79	11	22	2	0	3	14	4	4	0	2	12	1	2	.418	.352
Hernandez, Yadiel	L-R	5-9	185	10-9-87	.192	.167	.200	12	26	3	5	3	0	1	6	1	0	0	1	12	0	0	.423	.214
Holt, Brock	L-R	5-10	180	6-11-88	.262	.385	.231	20	65	11	17	6	0	0	4	5	0	0	0	15	1	0	.354	.314
2-team total (16 Milwaukee Brewers)					.211	.357	.185	36	95	12	20	6	0	0	5	9	1	0	1	24	1	0	.274	.283
Kendrick, Howie	R-R	5-11	225	7-12-83	.275	.200	.303	25	91	11	25	4	0	2	14	7	0	0	2	17	0	0	.385	.320
Kieboom, Carter	R-R	6-2	210	9-3-97	.202	.343	.125	33	99	15	20	1	0	0	9	17	5	0	1	33	0	1	.212	.344
Noll, Jake	R-R	6-2	215	3-8-94	.353	.364	.333	7	17	2	6	1	0	0	0	0	0	0	0	4	0	0	.412	.353
Robles, Victor	R-R	6-0	205	5-19-97	.220	.326	.180	52	168	20	37	5	1	3	15	9	9	1	2	53	4	1	.315	.293
Soto, Juan	L-L	6-1	220	10-25-98	.351	.360	.346	47	154	39	54	14	0	13	37	41	1	0	0	28	6	2	.695	.490
Stevenson, Andrew	L-L	6-0	192	6-1-94	.366	.000	.375	15	41	11	15	7	1	2	12	5	1	0	0	11	2	0	.732	.447
Suzuki, Kurt	R-R	5-11	210	10-4-83	.270	.345	.244	33	111	15	30	8	0	2	17	11	4	0	3	19	1	0	.396	.349
Taylor, Michael A.	R-R	6-4	215	3-26-91	.196	.172	.206	38	92	11	18	6	0	5	16	6	1	0	0	27	0	0	.424	.253
Thames, Eric	L-R	5-11	235	11-10-86	.203	.182	.208	41	123	10	25	5	0	3	14	3	0	0	2	42	1	0	.317	.300
Turner, Trea	R-R	6-2	185	6-30-93	.335	.375	.322	59	233	46	78	15	4	12	41	22	2	0	2	36	12	4	.588	.394

Pitching

Pitching	B-T	HT	WT	DOB	W	L	ERA	G	GS	CG	SV	IP	H	R	ER	HR	BB	SO	AVG	vLH	vRH	K/9	BB/9
Bacus, Dakota	R-R	6-2	220	4-2-91	0	0	7.94	11	0	0	0	11	14	10	10	1	9	7	.298	.250	.314	5.56	7.15
Barrett, Aaron	R-R	6-3	230	1-2-88	0	0	10.80	2	0	0	0	2	2	2	2	0	2	1	.333	.000	.500	5.40	10.80
Bourque, James	R-R	6-4	215	7-9-93	1	0	6.75	6	0	0	0	4	3	3	3	1	5	1	.214	.000	.300	2.25	11.25
Braymer, Ben	L-L	6-2	220	4-28-94	1	0	1.23	3	1	0	0	7	7	1	1	0	5	8	.241	.300	.211	9.82	6.14
Corbin, Patrick	L-L	6-3	210	7-19-89	2	7	4.66	11	11	0	0	66	85	35	34	10	18	60	.308	.262	.321	8.22	2.47
Crowe, Wil	R-R	6-2	228	9-9-94	0	2	11.88	3	3	0	0	8	14	13	11	5	8	8	.378	.538	.292	8.64	8.64
Doolittle, Sean	L-L	6-2	204	9-26-86	0	2	5.87	11	0	0	0	8	9	6	5	3	4	6	.300	.214	.375	7.04	4.70
Espino, Paolo	R-R	5-10	215	1-10-87	0	0	4.50	2	1	0	0	6	8	3	3	1	2	7	.320	.333	.313	10.50	3.00
Fedde, Erick	R-R	6-4	200	2-25-93	2	4	4.29	11	8	0	0	50	47	25	24	10	22	28	.241	.188	.278	5.01	3.93
Finnegan, Kyle	R-R	6-2	200	9-4-91	1	0	2.92	25	0	0	0	25	21	10	8	2	13	27	.226	.179	.259	9.85	4.74
Freeman, Sam	R-L	5-11	180	6-24-87	0	0	1.80	7	0	0	0	5	2	1	1	0	7	6	.111	.091	.143	10.80	12.60
Guerra, Javy	R-R	6-1	216	10-31-85	0	0	4.02	14	0	0	0	16	19	7	7	2	7	13	.302	.250	.343	7.47	4.02
2-team total (14 San Diego Padres)					1	0	6.83	28	0	0	0	29	44	23	22	3	12	25	.358	.377	.343	7.76	3.72
Harper, Ryne	R-R	6-3	215	3-27-89	1	0	7.61	23	0	0	0	24	29	21	20	5	9	25	.290	.361	.250	9.51	3.42
Harris, Will	R-R	6-4	240	8-28-84	0	1	3.06	20	0	0	1	18	21	9	6	3	9	21	.280	.343	.225	10.70	4.58
Holt, Brock	L-R	5-10	180	6-11-88	0	0	13.50	2	0	0	0	1	5	2	2	1	0	0	.500	1.000	.444	0.00	0.00
Hudson, Daniel	R-R	6-3	215	3-9-87	3	2	6.10	21	0	0	10	21	15	15	14	6	11	28	.195	.139	.244	12.19	4.79
McGowin, Kyle	R-R	6-3	195	11-27-91	1	0	4.91	9	0	0	1	11	9	6	6	2	5	16	.214	.100	.250	13.09	4.09
Rainey, Tanner	R-R	6-2	235	12-25-92	1	1	2.66	20	0	0	0	20	8	6	6	4	7	32	.119	.107	.128	14.16	3.10
Romero, Seth	L-L	6-3	240	4-19-96	0	0	13.50	3	0	0	0	3	5	4	4	1	3	5	.333	.250	.429	16.88	10.13
Sanchez, Anibal	R-R	6-0	205	2-27-84	4	5	6.62	11	11	0	0	53	70	40	39	11	18	43	.313	.300	.327	7.30	3.06
Scherzer, Max	R-R	6-3	215	7-27-84	5	4	3.74	12	12	1	0	67	70	30	28	10	23	92	.260	.312	.206	12.30	3.07
Strasburg, Stephen	R-R	6-5	235	7-20-88	0	1	10.80	2	2	0	0	5	8	6	6	1	1	2	.364	.400	.333	3.60	1.80
Suero, Wander	R-R	6-4	211	9-15-91	2	0	3.80	22	0	0	0	24	20	10	10	1	10	28	.227	.163	.289	10.65	3.80
Voth, Austin	R-R	6-2	210	6-26-92	2	5	6.34	11	11	1	0	50	57	36	35	14	18	44	.281	.295	.269	7.97	3.26

Fielding

Catcher	PCT	G	PO	A	E	DP	PB
Gomes	.992	30	229	15	2	0	2
Suzuki	1.000	30	271	10	0	2	1

First Base	PCT	G	PO	A	E	DP
Cabrera	.995	25	171	10	1	19
Harrison	1.000	1	1	0	0	0
Holt	.950	4	13	6	1	2
Kendrick	.970	6	28	4	1	3
Noll	1.000	4	26	2	0	2
Thames	.989	27	163	9	2	20

Second Base	PCT	G	PO	A	E	DP
Castro	.955	16	26	37	3	9
Difo	1.000	4	1	1	0	0
Garcia	.954	37	54	49	5	15
Harrison	1.000	12	10	18	0	4

Third Base	PCT	G	PO	A	E	DP
Cabrera	1.000	17	4	27	0	2
Difo	1.000	2	0	2	0	0
Harrison	.944	10	7	10	1	3
Holt	.900	5	1	8	1	0
Kieboom	.966	31	16	69	3	4
Noll	1.000	1	0	1	0	0

Shortstop	PCT	G	PO	A	E	DP
Difo	1.000	4	3	3	0	1
Garcia	.889	3	3	5	1	0
Turner	.956	59	77	120	9	33

Outfield	PCT	G	PO	A	E	DP
Bonifacio	1.000	1	4	0	0	0
Eaton	.988	41	81	0	1	0
Harrison	1.000	6	12	0	0	0
Hernandez	1.000	1	2	0	0	0
Holt	1.000	8	10	0	0	0
Robles	1.000	52	121	1	0	1
Soto	1.000	42	64	1	0	0
Stevenson	1.000	14	24	0	0	0
Taylor	.984	35	63	0	1	0

MINOR
LEAGUES

The Minor League Baseball season was canceled due to the coronavirus pandemic, leaving stadiums empty across the country.

Ahead Of Big Changes, Pandemic Guts Season

BY JOSH NORRIS AND J.J. COOPER

For Minor League Baseball, there had never been a year like 2020. For the sake of baseball, one hopes it will never be repeated.

Even under normal circumstances, 2020 was expected to be a testy season in the minor leagues. The Professional Baseball Agreement was up at the end of the year, and Major League Baseball was attempting to install a plan that would reduce the minors by 40 teams.

Those negotiations had been brewing for years, and a list of the initial group of teams to be cut was leaked in November 2019. The list set off panic around the municipalities that could wind up losing their clubs. That alone would have been enough to place a shroud over the season.

Then came the coronavirus pandemic.

The sports world came to a halt on March 12, when Major League Baseball shut down its spring training and sent most everybody home. Minor league spring training, which takes place on back fields away from the stadiums in the Grapefruit and Cactus leagues, had only just begun, so prospects who weren't invited to big league camp were just beginning their seasons when they had to turn around and enter what would become a prolonged state of limbo.

Minor leaguers only get paid in-season, so an extended absence without games meant there were questions about how teams would handle compensation. To begin, MLB announced on March 31 that its clubs would pay their minor

COURTESY OF PENSACOLA BLUE WAHOOS

The Pensacola Blue Wahoos' decision to set up an Airbnb at their stadium was a huge success.

leaguers a stipend of $400 a week. Because there was no certainty about how long the season would be paused, the plan was only in place until the end of May.

Afterward, teams had to choose whether they'd be willing to extend the payments another 30 days. Some did so readily. Others dragged their feet. At one point, the A's announced they'd be halting payments to their minor leaguers. A few days later, after the franchise and owner John Fisher were thoroughly reamed in the media, the team reversed course and reinstalled the payments.

While the players waited to see whether the payments would be extended, a bigger question loomed: Could the virus be controlled enough to allow the minor league season to begin? The issue affected a lot more than simply whether players would get a chance to develop in 2020. Jobs for minor league staff, both full-time and part-time, hung in the balance.

If there was no season, and thus nearly no revenue flowing to 160 teams across the country, then teams were going to have to make even deeper cuts and enact even more layoffs and furloughs than were already in place.

For nearly three months, teams did what they could to tread water. They sold food via stadium drive-ups, turned their Jumbotrons into movie theaters and held farmers markets on their outfield grass. Two teams—the Pensacola Blue Wahoos and the Salem-Keizer Volcanoes—spruced up their clubhouses and put their entire stadiums up for rent on Airbnb.

Though the speed and variety of the promotions was a perfect display of the creativity and dexterity for which the minor leagues are famous, the revenue produced did little to salve the wounds caused by a lack of games.

All the while, executives grew impatient at the lack of a final decision—or at least a formalizing of the obvious—from Minor League Baseball. Then, on June 30, the worst fear to which everybody had already become resigned was made official.

Because MLB had informed MiLB teams it would not be providing players in 2020, MiLB had no choice but to cancel the season.

The announcement, made via video conference call, showed MiLB president Pat O'Conner sounding a dire tone about the present and future of the sport.

"It's extremely difficult for us to project, because there is no end in sight in the immediate future," O'Conner said, referring to MiLB's future given the uncertain timeline of the pandemic. "Our clubs are committed. They are capitalized as best can be expected. We are in dire straits, and I still have grave concerns. What happens every day doesn't alleviate any of my concerns."

The cancellation of the entire season meant that there was no minor league baseball for the first time since professional baseball began to emerge in the mid-1870s. The National Association bound the most successful minor leagues together in 1901, and there had been minor league baseball every year since.

In 1918, during World War I and a global flu pandemic, all but one of the 10 operating minor leagues suspended operations in June or July, but the International League managed to play a full season. Until 2020, that was the sparsest season in minor league history, but in 1918 hundreds of minor league games were played. In 2020, there were none.

Early in the pandemic, many teams applied for and received payroll protection loans as part of the government's response to the shutdown. Those loans allowed teams to keep many of their staff members employed, but it wasn't a permanent solution. Once the loans ran out, those same workers were imperiled once more.

During the same call that announced the season's cancellation, O'Conner expressed hope for a second lifeline from Congress, via H.R. Bill 7023, which would provide support for sports facilities, museums and theaters. The legislation, which was introduced by Lori Trahan (D-Ill.) on May 27, stalled and no additional legislative support for MiLB teams passed before the 2020 election.

In the meantime, with the finality of the season's cancellation, teams were free to unleash their creativity without the chance of the season suddenly restarting and their plans needing to quickly shift.

Dozens of teams returned to what they did best—baseball. Makeshift college and high school tournaments and leagues popped up around the country, including the wacky Lemonade League in Lansing, Mich., and the Texas Collegiate League in ballparks scattered throughout the footprints of the Texas and Pacific Coast Leagues.

The lack of a minor league season also meant that some MLB prospects played in the newly formed leagues. Blue Jays righthander Adam Kloffenstein and Tigers 2020 third-rounder Trei Cruz each participated in the TCL, while former top White Sox pick Jake Burger spent time in

MiLB President Pat O'Conner stepped down in September after a 13-year run.

BRIAN WESTERHOLT

the Carshield Collegiate League in the Midwest. Others played in independent leagues, which MLB teams were allowed to give their players permission to play in if the players requested the opportunity.

Though the competition varied, the leagues gave players valuable at-bats to at least kick off some of the rust that accumulated while everybody was on lockdown.

For other minor leaguers, including members of the 40-man roster and other invitees, reps came at each big league club's alternate training site (ATS). The ATS concept was established by MLB especially for a stunted season that everybody knew would feature plenty of roster shakeup because of COVID-19 protocols and other injuries.

While the 40-man MLB roster rules remained, teams were allowed to have a total of 60 players between the MLB roster and the ATS. Teams used the ATS camps—held mostly at MiLB parks—to keep a series of reserves ready and on-call. The composition of the ATS rosters were dependent on the outlook for each big league team.

A team without much hope of making even a playoff expanded to 16 teams, for example, might choose to use many of their available spots for the highest-priority prospects. A team with eyes toward October, however, might fill its ATS with upper-level players who could more capably fill a big league spot when needed.

There were notable exceptions, of course. The Giants brought top prospect Marco Luciano, the Mariners included high-upside shortstop Noelvi Marte and the Yankees included reliever Alexander Vizcaino. Neither Luciano nor Marte had ever played a game in full-season ball, while Vizcaino had only a cameo at high Class A.

None of the trio was on his team's 40-man roster, yet their parent clubs saw fit to make sure they got a chance to develop while most other players were stuck at home.

For everyone not at the ATS or in a makeshift league, the summer was a wash for their development. Many prospects simply did not get on the field in any meaningful way. Many did keep in touch with their MLB clubs and continued to work out, but a bullpen session is not the same as getting into a game and competing.

For a number of those players, a small glimpse of opportunity did arise when MLB approved teams to run instructional leagues. The instructional league was especially significant in 2020 because, unlike previous years, teams were required to pay the players they invited. The compensation was determined by the level where a player would have been assigned if everything had proceeded as normal. The league also somewhat made up for the void created by the cancellation of the Arizona Fall League.

Given how certain teams had consistently been reluctant to extend the $400 per week payments to their minor leaguers during the summer, it wouldn't have been particularly surprising to see those same teams opt not to participate in the instructional league. In the end, just two teams declined to hold camps: The Yankees and the Cardinals.

Everyone else participated, and some teams went above and beyond. The Royals held a pair of camps—one in their big league park in Kansas City and another at their spring training home in Surprise, Ariz.

MLB also gave the OK for teams to hold instructional leagues at their complexes in the Dominican Republic, where players had been mostly stagnant for the spring and summer; teams were allowed to house their players at the complex but were not permitted to hold any formal baseball activity.

Behind the scenes, MLB and MiLB were jostling over the future of the minors once the COVID era had passed. The negotiations behind the scenes were both contentious and public, but the pandemic sapped MiLB of enough revenue that it allowed MLB to more or less put it over a barrel.

In the middle of all that, O'Conner announced his retirement after 13 years as the league's president. In any environment, that news would have been significant. In the context of the PBA negotiations, it was a watershed moment.

In the weeks prior, O'Conner had made multiple changes to MiLB's negotiating committee before the PBA expired, but that was only staving off the inevitable: Not only was MLB going to get its way in terms of contraction, it was also going to take over the day-to-day operations of the minor leagues as part of its "One Baseball" plan, under which MLB would gain greater influence over baseball and softball in the high school, college, affiliated and independent ranks.

Eventually, MiLB capitulated and signaled its willingness to go forth with the plan that would reduce the league to 120 full-season teams. Along with the culling of the clubs—including the short-season and Rookie-level classifications outside of a Gulf Coast or Arizona League club for each big league team—the leagues themselves were going to be restructured and reorganized.

There were plenty of rumors about how things would look when the dust settled, though none was entirely confirmed by the time the Almanac went to press.

Among the proposed changes were the flipping of Class A levels (the Florida State, Carolina and California leagues becoming low Class A while the Midwest, South Atlantic, Northwest and perhaps a new "Mid-Atlantic" league becoming high Class A), the shortening of seasons at some of the lower levels (independent of any havoc COVID played on the 2021 season) and the removal of midseason all-star games.

While plenty of rumors had flown around about who was going to be affiliated with whom in the new-look minor leagues, only the Yankees and Mets had anything officially settled at press time.

A day after Baseball America reported it would happen, the Yankees announced on Nov. 7 that their four affiliates would play at Scranton/Wilkes-Barre (Triple-A), Somerset (Double-A), Hudson Valley (high Class A) and Tampa (low Class A).

During new owner Steve Cohen's introductory press conference, he revealed that the Mets would place their affiliates at Syracuse (Triple-A), Binghamton (Double-A), Brooklyn (high Class A) and St. Lucie (low Class A).

Those two announcements seemed to signal that, yes, the FSL would flip its classification from high Class A to low Class A, and that teams would be more than willing to look beyond the stalwarts when finding their affiliates.

No matter how the final 120 teams shook out, 40-plus teams were going to lose their affiliations. Throughout the negotiations, MLB had been firm that although teams weren't going to be a part of the affiliated minor leagues, they would not go without baseball.

The Appalachian League, for example, agreed to become a summer college wood-bat league for rising sophomores akin to the Cape Cod League. The New York-Penn League, which was also eliminated (though some of its teams survived), was given the same opportunity, as were former full-season teams which were cut from affiliated baseball under the plan.

Beyond settling on the final 120 teams, MLB also proposed a laundry list of new standards for upgraded facilities. The requested changes included things like expanded clubhouses, separated areas for food preparation and dining, mandatory weight rooms, brighter lights, all-weather hitting and pitching tunnels equipped with power and WiFi and a separate locker room area for female staff members.

If accepted, all of those changes would be extraordinarily expensive for minor league teams, especially considering the severe lack of revenue they've seen since September 2019.

Once the details for the new-look minor leagues are hammered out, attention will turn to 2021 and what the season might look like if the coronavirus still lingers. There is already speculation of a staggered spring training and a late start to the season, perhaps in the middle of May, dependent on the development and distribution of any combination of a vaccine, advanced rapid testing or therapeutic treatments.

In the absence of a return to semi-normalcy, teams will have to begin to consult with local officials about how many fans can be let into games—teams in some summer leagues welcomed fans—safely dependent on how the area is doing with regard to the virus.

Whenever the games do return, it will mark the beginning of a new era.

In 1901, minor league teams banded together to form the National Association because they were unhappy with how National League and American League clubs were raiding their teams for players. The National Association (later rebranded to become Minor League Baseball) provided the protection and stability that the minor leagues wanted, as the NL and AL agreed in 1903 to respect minor league teams' contracts and set up an organized manner for players to move up through the minors to the major

Alan Trammell spent his summer at the Tigers alternate site in Toledo.

MARK CUNNINGHAM/MLB PHOTOS VIA GETTY IMAGES

leagues.

That system remained in place with many modifications for decades. But the symbiotic relationship between independent minor league operators and MLB clubs slowly shifted to a much more dependent relationship.

When the National Association was formed, every MiLB club was fully independent from the major leagues. At the time, minor league teams scouted, signed and paid their own players. By the 1962 reorganization of the minors, baseball had shifted to the "farm system" approach. MiLB teams were independent when it came to the business side of their operations, but were fully dependent on MLB teams paying player salaries.

Now, MLB's decisions have created an entirely new system. After the Professional Baseball Agreement between MLB and MiLB expired on Oct. 1, 2020, MLB made clear it had no intention of continuing to negotiate with MiLB's corporate offices. Any agreement would be made with MiLB owners, but the many responsibilities that had been retained by MiLB and MiLB league presidents (scheduling, umpire assignments, intra-league disputes, etc.) would now be the responsibility of MLB.

So 2020 will be forever remembered in the minors as the year without any games. But it will also forever be the year that MLB fully consolidated its power over the minor leagues.

Here is where every MLB team held its 2020 alternate training site camp

After the Minor League Baseball season was canceled due to the coronavirus pandemic, all 30 teams had to decide what to do with their top prospects and other minor league players in their system.

As directed by MLB, each organization established an alternate site location, with the requirement that the location must be within 100 miles of its home ballpark, to send players who otherwise would spend the summer working out at home.

The alternate sites provided an additional place for players to prepare during spring training 2.0 and later were used for non-major leaguers on the 60-man roster to train and play as a substitute for the MiLB season. Some of the alternate sites were comprised of players who could be needed at the big league level, while others were stuffed with the organization's top prospects.

Below is a list of the alternate site locations for all 30 MLB teams.

Lefthander Shane McClanahan spent time at the Rays alternate site.

CLIFF WELCH/ICON SPORTSWIRE VIA GETTY IMAGES

TEAM	LOCATION
Angels	Long Beach State University
Astros	University of Houston (first weeks); Whataburger Field, Corpus Christi, Texas Athletics Excite Ballpark, San Jose, Calif.
Athletics	Excite Ballpark, San Jose, Calif.
Braves	Coolray Field, Gwinnett, Ga.
Brewers	Fox Cities Stadium, Appleton, Wisc.
Blue Jays	Frontier Field, Rochester, N.Y.
Cardinals	Hammons Field, Springfield, Mo.
Cubs	Four Winds Field, South Bend, Ind.
Diamondbacks	Salt River Fields, Scottsdale, Ariz.
Dodgers	University of Southern California, Los Angeles; LoanMart Field, Rancho Cucamonga, Calif.
Giants	Sutter Health Park, West Sacramento, Calif.
Indians	Classic Park, Eastlake, Ohio
Mariners	Cheney Stadium, Tacoma, Wash.
Marlins	Roger Dean Stadium, Jupiter, Fla.
Mets	MCU Park, Brooklyn, N.Y.
Nationals	New Fredericksburg Ballpark, Fredericksburg, Va.
Orioles	Prince George's Stadium, Bowie, Md.
Padres	University of San Diego
Phillies	Coca-Cola Park, Allentown, Pa.
Pirates	People's Natural Gas Field, Altoona, Pa.
Rangers	Globe Life Park, Arlington, Texas
Rays	Charlotte Sports Park, Port Charlotte, Fla.
Reds	Prasco Park and Legacy Field, Mason, Ohio
Red Sox	Boston College; McCoy Stadium, Pawtucket, R.I.
Rockies	Metro State University, Denver; Isotopes Park, Albuquerque, N.M.
Royals	T-Bones Stadium, Kansas City, Kan.
Tigers	Fifth Third Field, Toledo, Ohio
Twins	CHS Field, St. Paul, Minn.
White Sox	Boomers Stadium, Schaumburg, Ill.
Yankees	PNC Field, Moosic, Pa.

INDEPENDENT
LEAGUES

Independent Leagues Came Full Circle in 2020

BY J.J. COOPER

A form of baseball created in the aftermath of a bitter negotiation between Major League Baseball and Minor League Baseball, the independent leagues were known most for their independence. It was in their name. They were the rebels who operated outside of the structure of what was at the time called "organized" baseball.

But in 2020, as Minor League Baseball and Major League Baseball conducted yet another contentious negotiation, independent baseball dropped its independence. Even before the final structure of Major League Baseball's restructuring of Minor League Baseball had been completed, MLB and the independent Atlantic, American Association and Frontier Leagues announced that they had come to an agreement by which the previously independent leagues were now partner leagues of MLB.

The partnership ensures that the leagues will have significantly closer ties to MLB with new-found business and baseball relationships. These leagues' stats will be gathered and distributed by MLB. They will share analytical data with MLB (and MLB teams) and their transactions will be more closely connected with MLB.

The final details will need to be worked out, but it means that while these leagues will not be part of affiliated baseball (with players provided by MLB), they also will not be as independent as they were in the past.

This is a reversal of how independent league baseball was birthed. MLB and MiLB had faced off and stared into a seemingly unthinkable abyss in 1990. The two sides had failed to come to an agreement on a new Professional Baseball Agreement. During the worst moments of the negotiations, the two sides began to make plans to operate in 1991 independently. MLB looked at operating at college stadiums or spring training complexes to fill out schedules for its minor leaguers.

At the same time, MiLB teams started to look at the possibility of fielding teams of players picked by, and paid for by, the MiLB clubs.

In the end, the two sides patched up their differences and came to a resolution. But the idea of teams forging their own paths stuck with a

Fernando Rodney pitched in the Constellation League in 2020.

few MiLB owners. There had been independent teams operating within the structure of Minor League Baseball in the past, and the idea of forming a new league fully independent from MLB and MiLB took hold. The increased facility standards of the new PBA as well as expansive MiLB territorial rules prevented many cities from having the option of getting into affiliated baseball and created a list of available stadiums/markets.

The Northern League and Frontier League kicked off the idea in 1993 and it soon spread elsewhere.

There will still be baseball outside of the structure of affiliated baseball, but beginning in 2021, it will no longer be exactly what it was before. A new era is upon what was independent baseball.

The final year of the era of independent baseball ended in an unconventional manner as many leagues had to cancel their seasons because of the novel coronavirus pandemic. But several leagues adapted and managed to field seasons of some sort. Fans were strictly limited and travel was also reduced, but there were leagues that played while most of the rest of baseball below the MLB level did not.

AMERICAN ASSOCIATION

The American Association and the United Shores Professional Baseball League were the only two independent leagues that were able to operate as their normal entities in 2020. The American Association had six teams that were capable of playing, although a few of them had to play entirely on the road until they were cleared to play home games. Attendance was strictly limited throughout the season, but the league managed to successfully complete a season.

And with no affiliated minor league teams playing, some MLB teams gave approval for their prospects to play in an independent league, creating a unique crossover.

In just its second year in the league, Milwaukee finished the regular season with the league's best record and rolled to a dominating win over Sioux Falls in the playoffs.

After the season the Grand Prairie Airhogs announced that they would not return to the league in 2021.

Team	W	L	PCT	GB
Milwaukee Milkmen	34	26	.567	—
Sioux Falls Canaries	31	27	.534	2
St. Paul Saints	30	30	.500	4
Winnipeg Goldeyes	29	31	.483	5
Fargo-Moorhead RedHawks	28	32	.467	6
Chicago Dogs	26	32	.448	7

PLAYOFFS: Milwaukee defeated Sioux Falls 3-1 in best-of-five series.

All-Star Team: C: Chris Chinea, St. Paul. **1B:** Kyle Martin, Winnipeg. **2B:** Edwin Arroyo, Chicago. **3B:** Damek Tomscha, Sioux Falls. **SS:** Andrew Ely, Sioux Falls. **OF:** Adam Brett Walker II, Milwaukee; Logan Landon, Sioux Falls; Mikey Reynolds, St. Paul. **DH:** Drew Ward, Fargo-Moorhead.
SP: Mike Devine, St. Paul. **RP:** Peyton Gray, Milwaukee.

Player of the Year: Adam Brett Walker, Milwaukee. **Rookie of the Year:** Peyton Gray, Milwaukee. **Manager of the Year:** Rick Forney, Winnipeg.

BATTING LEADERS

Player, Team	Team	AVG	AB	R	H	HR	RBI
Corelle Prime	FM	.335	248	37	83	4	31
Drew Ward	FM	.335	218	42	73	17	45
Logan Landon	SF	.333	228	37	76	10	43
Mikey Reynolds	STP	.332	238	36	79	7	28
Roy Morales	SF	.331	154	19	51	2	22
Alay Lago	SF	.321	246	41	79	4	35
Damek Tomscha	SF	.320	231	36	74	10	49
Josh Allen	STP	.304	158	36	48	6	24
Kyle Martin	WPG	.301	226	40	68	16	51
Edwin Arroyo	CHI	.300	220	34	66	4	23

PITCHING LEADERS

Player, Team	Team	W	L	ERA	IP	H	BB	SO
David Holmberg	MKE	6	1	2.34	73	60	31	76
Mike Devine	STP	4	3	2.58	80	70	13	89
Matt Tomshaw	FM	5	3	2.69	80	69	15	62
John Anderson	FM	2	2	2.87	53	53	14	49
Jake Zokan	SF	4	2	3	51	49	19	41
Luke Westphal	CHI	3	2	3.42	53	39	24	75
Bradin Hagens	FM	4	3	3.43	60	48	22	64
Thomas Dorminy	CHI	7	1	3.63	62	61	16	62
Tyler Pike	FM	4	5	3.88	70	76	31	87
Matt Solter	STP	4	4	3.89	81	84	23	77

CHICAGO DOGS

Name	AVG	AB	R	H	HR	RBI	BB	SO	SB
Brett Milazzo	.310	29	3	9	0	1	4	11	0
Edwin Arroyo	.300	220	34	66	4	23	24	40	6
Logan Moore	.299	67	10	20	4	9	11	19	0
Joey Terdoslavich	.296	213	38	63	15	46	44	29	0
Blake Allemand	.263	209	32	55	6	30	28	35	6
Mike Crouse	.262	221	42	58	10	30	41	78	20
K.C. Hobson	.226	212	32	48	8	43	27	37	2
Tyler Ladendorf	.223	206	33	46	13	38	21	51	6

Harrison Smith	.223	103	18	23	6	16	8	36	3
Victor Roache	.221	226	36	50	16	34	15	88	2
Ryan Lidge	.217	23	1	5	1	2	2	5	0
Ryan Haug	.209	43	9	9	0	4	9	8	0
Tony Rosselli	.204	49	4	10	1	4	9	20	0
Kelly Dugan	.192	26	3	5	2	3	3	6	0
Garrett Hope	.155	71	9	11	2	5	6	31	0

Name	W	L	ERA	G	SV	IP	H	BB	SO
Jake Cousins	1	1	3.38	15	3	16	10	5	25
Luke Westphal	3	2	3.42	10	0	52.2	39	24	75
Thomas Dorminy	7	1	3.63	11	0	62	61	16	62
Harrison Smith	0	0	3.86	8	0	7	3	4	4
Jalen Miller	4	3	3.89	29	0	37	27	16	52
Adam Choplick	1	2	4.26	20	5	19	21	4	31
Wes Helsabeck	0	3	4.31	17	1	31.1	25	15	34
Justin Goossen-Brown	0	1	5.14	8	1	14	13	6	9
Jake Dahlberg	4	4	5.52	13	0	58.2	85	16	45
Eddie Butler	0	7	5.65	12	0	65.1	87	24	40
Paul Schwendel	0	1	5.81	23	1	26.1	32	10	33
Garrett Granitz	1	0	6.43	8	0	7	16	0	3
J.D. Busfield	4	3	6.66	12	0	48.2	45	15	37
Jamie Callahan	0	1	8.10	4	1	3.1	3	4	2
Scott Shuman	0	1	8.10	9	0	10	13	4	16
Casey Crosby	0	0	8.37	24	0	23.2	29	31	32
Eric Stout	1	1	9.45	3	0	13.1	16	5	8
K.C. Hobson	0	0	12.00	3	0	3	3	5	2
Jeff Thompson	0	0	20.25	1	0	1.1	2	2	2

FARGO-MOORHEAD REDHAWKS

Name	AVG	AB	R	H	HR	RBI	BB	SO	SB
Bret Helton	1.000	1	1	1	0	0	0	0	0
Dylan Kelly	.336	140	15	47	5	21	5	18	1
Correlle Prime	.335	248	37	83	4	31	12	42	7
Drew Ward	.335	218	42	73	17	45	23	63	1
Forrestt Allday	.310	126	27	39	8	19	12	20	0
Sam Dexter	.309	81	11	25	2	13	4	13	0
Dario Pizzano	.286	112	15	32	1	15	15	15	0
Leobaldo Pina	.275	236	23	65	6	32	13	46	3
Christian Ibarra	.268	194	22	52	3	25	28	39	2
Cito Culver	.258	31	3	8	0	5	4	11	0
Trey Hair	.254	138	16	35	2	16	9	28	4
Brennan Metzger	.252	226	43	57	5	19	44	59	3
Alex Boxwell	.246	118	17	29	4	10	4		3
Blake Grant-Parks	.244	41	2	10	2	6	4	6	0
Nick Kahle	.232	56	6	13	1	2	4	16	0
Alex Crosby	.185	27	3	5	0	1	2	4	0
Jordan Patterson	.122	41	2	5	0	0	0	11	0
Brent Jones	.000	1	1	0	0	0	0	1	0

Name	W	L	ERA	G	SV	IP	H	BB	SO
Christian Ibarra	0	0	0.00	1	0	0.2	1	2	1
Brent Jones	1	1	2.66	16	0	23.2	27	14	21
Matt Tomshaw	5	3	2.69	12	0	80.1	69	15	62
John Anderson	2	2	2.87	10	0	53.1	53	14	49
Bradin Hagens	4	3	3.43	12	0	60.1	48	22	64
Bret Helton	4	3	3.46	17	1	39	33	19	32
Tyler Pike	4	5	3.88	12	0	69.2	76	31	87
Ryan Williams	4	3	3.92	12	1	64.1	58	12	35
Ryan Flores	0	2	4.50	16	0	26	19	21	34
Tyler Wilson	1	2	4.61	15	2	13.2	8	9	16
Jake Cosart	0	0	5.63	8	0	8	12	7	10
Ryan Thurston	1	2	5.68	16	0	19	25	8	29
Kevin McGovern	1	1	6.00	4	0	15	14	6	15
Mitchell Osnowitz	1	2	8.64	17	9	16.2	19	8	20
Dustin Beggs	0	2	9.28	2	0	10.2	16	7	5
Cale Coshow	0	1	11.25	5	0	4	6	2	2
Tanner Kiest	0	0	20.77	5	0	4.1	9	9	4
Ben Strahm	0	0	21.60	1	0	1.2	2	3	1
Jackson Sigman	0	0	22.50	1	0	2	6	1	4

MILWAUKEE MILKMEN

Name	AVG	AB	R	H	HR	RBI	BB	SO	SB
Christ Conley	.333	36	4	12	0	3	3	10	0
Chase Simpson	.313	16	1	5	0	0	1	1	0
Brett Vertigan	.293	229	31	67	1	16	33	39	10
Adam Walker	.268	220	42	59	22	50	16	75	3
Dylan Tice	.248	222	29	55	4	24	22	48	9
David Washington	.245	237	32	58	8	34	19	89	3
Logan Trowbridge	.231	199	20	46	3	21	22	52	9
Mason Davis	.224	210	31	47	5	29	9	46	15
Christian Correa	.211	161	14	34	4	20	11	33	0
Aaron Hill	.198	96	18	19	3	11	24	42	8
Jose Sermo	.197	142	17	28	5	13	16	55	0
Zach Nehrir	.196	209	23	41	3	19	15	65	8

Name	W	L	ERA	G	SV	IP	H	BB	SO
Jack Alkire	0	0	0.00	2	0	2	2	2	2
Peyton Gray	3	0	0.00	30	14	32	10	14	56
Jack Maynard	0	0	0.00	2	0	3	1	0	4
A.J. Schugel	0	0	1.03	28	1	26.1	10	9	23
Myles Smith	2	1	1.88	23	1	24	12	13	36
David Holmberg	6	1	2.34	12	0	73	60	31	76
Henderson Alvarez III	2	1	2.90	5	0	31	21	3	22
Tim Dillard	2	1	3.12	5	0	26	26	5	19
Zach Hartman	1	1	3.89	18	0	34.2	43	13	25
Taylor Ahearn	1	5	4.06	13	0	51	50	16	46
Drew Hutchison	2	2	4.09	6	0	22	17	13	33
Karch Kowalczyk	2	4	4.10	26	2	26.1	27	15	23
Ryan Kussmaul	5	2	4.83	13	0	63.1	61	23	75
Dylan Baker	0	1	4.95	8	0	20	24	5	19
Hayden Carter	0	0	5.40	1	0	3.1	3	1	2
Angel Ventura	2	3	5.45	7	0	33	39	7	24
Anthony Bender	2	1	5.48	22	0	21.1	24	11	25
Jake Matthys	4	2	6.81	15	0	35.2	43	12	24
Christian Correa	0	1	27.00	1	0	0.1	2	0	0

ST. PAUL SAINTS

Name	AVG	AB	R	H	HR	RBI	BB	SO	SB
Sebastian Zawada	.438	16	5	7	1	3	3	4	0
Mikey Reynolds	.332	238	36	79	7	28	21	42	8
Justin Byrd	.311	61	11	19	1	8	8	11	6
Josh Allen	.304	158	36	48	6	24	20	26	1
Chris Chinea	.293	239	31	70	4	37	11	38	0
Chesny Young	.286	206	25	59	1	20	29	32	0
J.C. Millan	.280	50	3	14	1	6	3	13	0
Drew Stankiewicz	.271	70	10	19	1	5	9	7	0
Mitch Ghelfi	.263	95	10	25	3	20	7	32	1
Troy Alexander	.260	96	14	25	6	17	3	36	0
Nate Samson	.257	191	16	49	1	22	12	15	7
Max Murphy	.256	223	38	57	5	27	21	65	4
Alonzo Harris	.246	179	29	44	7	18	20	26	8
Chuck Taylor	.233	43	5	10	2	6	4	18	0
John Silviano	.231	225	40	52	14	40	21	70	1
Cody Young	.167	6	0	1	0	0	0	4	0
Connor Justus	.161	31	1	5	0	2	3	9	1

Name	W	L	ERA	G	SV	IP	H	BB	SO
Tanner Kiest	0	0	0.00	3	0	3	1	1	2
Aaron Brown	1	0	1.84	11	0	14.2	10	5	17
Jameson McGrane	1	1	2.33	26	16	27	14	19	41
Mike Devine	4	3	2.58	12	0	80.1	70	13	89
Brian Glowicki	3	0	2.78	25	1	32.1	22	7	36
Matt Pobereyko	1	0	3.00	13	0	21	18	8	22
Jose Velez	2	0	3.63	23	0	22.1	21	7	35
Matt Solter	4	4	3.89	13	0	81	84	23	77
Nick Belzer	4	3	4.21	13	0	36.1	36	22	31
Paul Voelker	3	2	4.46	24	1	36.1	39	8	44
Ryan Zimmerman	4	4	5.64	12	0	67	57	37	58
Spencer Jones	1	0	6.95	10	0	22	29	8	19
Matt Quintana	1	3	7.14	8	0	29	41	6	36
Eddie Medina	1	7	7.46	9	0	50.2	62	17	38
Drew Stankiewicz	0	0	9.00	2	0	2	5	1	1
Pete Tago	0	1	11.05	2	0	7.1	11	7	7
Chris Nunn	0	2	14.21	3	0	6.1	10	7	7

SIOUX FALLS CANARIES

Name	AVG	AB	R	H	HR	RBI	BB	SO	SB
Madison Younginer	.375	8	2	3	0	1	0	2	0
Logan Landon	.333	228	37	76	10	43	20	46	3
Roy Morales	.330	97	11	32	2	12	9	8	2
Alay Lago	.321	246	41	79	4	35	11	36	5
Damek Tomscha	.320	231	36	74	10	49	12	55	1
Andrew Ely	.295	244	55	72	9	30	26	54	1
Matt Morales	.286	7	1	2	0	0	0	2	0
Clint Coulter	.264	220	32	58	11	41	10	67	0
Grant Kay	.262	141	20	37	3	18	17	43	4
Jabari Henry	.260	177	34	46	9	31	21	61	0
Ryan Brett	.243	140	24	34	1	14	6	37	3
Mike Hart	.243	177	33	43	7	26	17	60	4
KC Huth	.211	76	6	16	2	13	3	10	4
Ryan Long	.198	86	10	17	2	8	5	26	0
Sebastian Zawada	.167	6	0	1	0	0	0	2	0

Name	W	L	ERA	G	SV	IP	H	BB	SO
Ryan Long	0	0	0.00	3	0	4	1	1	0
Tyler Danish	4	0	2.13	7	0	38	36	12	26
Nicco Blank	1	1	2.66	19	0	20.1	13	16	24
Jake Zokan	4	2	3.00	9	0	51	49	19	41
Ryan Fritze	2	1	3.14	28	2	28.2	21	16	32
Michael Gunn	0	0	4.50	4	0	4	3	4	3
Keaton Steele	0	1	4.55	30	16	29.2	34	10	16
Tyler Herron	7	1	4.60	12	0	76.1	95	21	55
Madison Younginer	0	0	4.70	13	0	15.1	14	16	18
D.J. Sharabi	1	4	4.80	28	0	30	33	20	32
Grady Wood	2	1	5.45	10	0	33	38	11	27
Eddie Medina	0	2	6.00	2	0	9	15	4	8
Ty Culbreth	3	2	6.32	7	0	37	49	11	27
Kevin Folman	3	1	6.53	21	0	40	48	20	37
Dakota Freese	0	0	6.75	3	0	5.1	6	6	8
Casey Delgado	0	2	6.92	4	0	13	16	4	10
Kurt Heyer	2	4	7.58	11	0	29.2	44	19	11
Sam Bragg	1	2	7.65	8	0	20	38	9	12
Tanner Anderson	1	2	10.64	4	0	11	22	5	6
Alex Boshers	0	1	11.15	4	0	15.1	35	9	14
Will Solomon	0	0	13.50	5	0	5.1	9	8	5

WINNIPEG GOLDEYES

Name	AVG	AB	R	H	HR	RBI	BB	SO	SB
Roy Morales	.333	57	8	19	0	10	10	9	3
Kyle Martin	.301	226	40	68	16	51	23	46	8
Dario Pizzano	.297	64	11	19	0	1	13	10	0
Darnell Sweeney	.277	238	40	66	14	38	26	75	14
Jonathan Moroney	.272	191	27	52	3	17	9	58	4
Logan Hill	.270	204	32	55	6	22	18	68	3
Wes Darvill	.268	209	32	56	5	31	16	60	13
Kevin Lachance	.262	172	35	45	5	16	21	42	8
John Nester	.259	189	20	49	6	31	16	43	0
Nick Oddo	.250	24	2	6	0	0	1	9	0
Jordan George	.223	184	21	41	7	31	32	39	3
Eric Wood	.216	176	21	38	2	21	25	57	3
Breland Almadova	.152	33	5	5	0	1	3	16	2
Ryan Lidge	.000	4	0	0	0	0	0	0	0

Name	W	L	ERA	G	SV	IP	H	BB	SO
Josh Lucas	0	0	1.20	3	0	15	12	2	18
Victor Capellan	1	1	1.69	27	12	26.2	26	6	26
Kent Hasler	3	2	1.84	22	0	29.1	13	8	41
Jose Jose	1	0	2.08	22	0	21.2	12	1	25
Ryan Thurston	0	0	2.25	3	0	4	4	6	2
Nate Antone	1	0	3.55	22	0	25.1	17	11	29
John Gorman	2	2	4.05	12	0	26.2	26	11	33
Dylan Rheault	0	1	4.20	12	1	15	21	8	9
Brandon Cumpton	2	3	4.53	9	0	43.2	49	15	34
Kevin McGovern	1	1	4.78	7	0	26.1	33	8	22
Mitchell Lambson	4	4	4.82	12	0	74.2	91	14	65
Frank Duncan	5	7	4.85	13	0	78	98	21	55
Evan Grills	3	2	4.89	11	0	38.2	36	9	44
Kevin Hilton	5	4	5.20	11	0	55.1	73	12	27
Ryan Flores	0	0	8.44	3	0	5.1	9	2	4

Justin Kamplain	1	1	10.00	8	0	9	12	6	12
John Nester	0	0	11.25	4	0	4	9	0	3
McKenzie Mills	0	2	17.18	3	0	7.1	16	5	6
Garrett Harris	0	1	27.00	2	0	1	8	0	1

CONSTELLATION LEAGUE

When it became clear that the Atlantic League as a whole would not be able to operate in 2020, the Sugar Land Skeeters decided to create a league of their own. The Constellation League ended up landing a significant amount of talent.

Freedom Division	W	L	PCT	GB
Eastern Reyes del Tigre	14	9	.589	—
Sugar Land Skeeters	14	11	.554	1
Sugar Land Lightning Sloths	11	13	.466	3.5
Team Texas	9	15	.397	5.5

All-Star Team: C: Jake Romanski, Skeeters. **1B:** Casey Gillaspie, Tigre. **2B:** Dustin Peterson, Skeeters. **SS:** Ford Proctor, Tigre. **3B:** Ryder Jones, Skeeters. **OF:** Courtney Hawkins, Skeeters; Evan Marzilli, Tigre; Jamie Westbrook, Sloths. **DH:** Jared Walker, Tigre. **UTL:** Kody Clemens, Texas. **UTL:** David Hamilton, Texas. **SP:** Matt Dermody, Skeeters; Anthony Vasquez, Tigre; Joe Wieland, Sloths. **RP:** Alejandro Mateo, Texas; Zac Rosscup, Sloths; Robby Scott, Skeeters.

BATTING LEADERS

Player	Team	AVG	AB	R	H	HR	RBI
Ford Proctor	EAS	.346	81	18	28	4	21
Breland Almadova	LIG, EAS	.317	180	45	57	0	12
Josh Altmann	LIG	.314	70	10	22	3	10
Dustin Peterson	SLS	.309	94	15	29	3	11
David Hamilton	TEX	.296	81	14	24	0	10
Jamie Westbrook	LIG	.294	85	8	25	5	18
Jake Romanski	SLS, EAS	.288	240	42	69	6	36
Dondrei Hubbard	LI	.276	29	2	8	0	2
Ryder Jones	SLS	.276	76	11	21	3	17
Dakota Phillips	LIG	.276	29	7	8	2	3

PITCHING LEADERS

Player	Team	W	L	ERA	IP	H	BB	SO
Matt Dermody	SLS	3	0	0.52	17	13	6	23
Zac Rosscup	LIG	2	0	0.71	13	7	9	21
Beau Ridgeway	TEX	1	0	0.82	11	7	3	10
Akeem Bostick	SLS	1	0	0.90	10	7	5	11
Robby Scott	SLS	0	0	1.80	15	13	5	21
Chris Dula	EAS	0	0	1.86	10	4	10	9
Turner Larkins	TEX	4	0	2.16	17	17	1	17
Jeff Johnson	SLS	0	0	2.40	15	9	11	19

EASTERN REYES DEL TIGRE

Name	AVG	AB	R	H	HR	RBI	BB	SO	SB
Romanski, Jake	.357	14	3	5	0	6	6	5	0
Proctor, Ford	.346	81	18	28	4	21	24	16	7
Taylor, Chuck	.333	3	0	1	0	1	0	1	0
Kemmer, Jon	.255	47	6	12	0	5	6	16	1
Breaux, Josh	.250	16	2	4	1	5	2	8	0
Almadova, Breland	.250	4	1	1	0	0	0	1	1
Gillaspie, Casey	.218	78	15	17	5	18	13	27	2
Marzilli, Evan	.209	91	17	19	2	11	18	35	6
Walker, Jared	.203	79	11	16	3	10	6	34	2
Mitchell, Jared	.171	35	4	6	0	1	6	18	9
Weisz, Keaton	.170	47	4	8	0	2	3	22	1
Eibner, Brett	.167	6	3	1	0	0	3	0	0
Lancaster, Seth	.160	50	7	8	1	6	10	20	5
Cruz, Trei	.155	71	6	11	1	5	15	21	7
Mcelroy, CJ	.115	52	7	6	0	5	5	21	9
Jenista, Greyson	.106	47	5	5	1	5	5	25	1
Groshans, Jaxx	.091	11	1	1	0	0	3	3	0
Almond, Zach	.088	34	3	3	0	1	5	12	1

Name	W	L	ERA	G	SV	IP	H	BB	SO
Eibner, Brett	0	0	0.00	5	0	5.1	0	1	8
Gillies, Darin	0	0	1.17	7	1	7.2	4	4	11
Dula, Chris	0	0	1.86	11	0	9.2	4	10	9
Self, Derek	0	0	2.63	12	6	13.2	11	3	8
Taylor, Cory	3	0	2.74	10	0	23	16	4	34

SUGAR LAND LIGHTNING SLOTHS

Name	AVG	AB	R	H	HR	RBI	BB	SO	SB
Borenstein, Zach	.353	17	3	6	0	2	6	8	0
Almadova, Breland	.321	56	14	18	0	4	12	15	12
Altmann, Josh	.314	70	10	22	3	10	9	15	6
Westbrook, Jamie	.294	85	8	25	5	18	6	19	0
Phillips, Dakota	.276	29	7	8	2	3	8	14	2
Aviles, Luis	.267	30	4	8	0	4	6	10	4
Palmeiro, Preston	.261	46	7	12	1	3	5	13	2
Dugan, Kelly	.231	52	10	12	4	9	7	12	0
Hinojosa, CJ	.222	63	6	14	1	5	8	13	1
Barnes, Barrett	.218	55	9	12	2	4	10	13	2
Cordero, Albert	.211	19	3	4	0	0	2	5	0
Bell, Brantley	.197	71	11	14	2	9	7	12	5
Erceg, Lucas	.180	89	8	16	0	7	8	24	4
Sullivan, Brett	.154	13	1	2	0	3	5	4	0
Maxwell, Carson	.136	44	5	6	2	8	4	17	2
Pabst, Arden	.125	16	1	2	0	1	1	4	0
Pompey, Dalton	.071	14	0	1	0	2	1	4	0

Name	W	L	ERA	G	SV	IP	H	BB	SO
Altmann, Josh	0	0	0.00	1	0	1	2	1	0
Ross, Robbie	1	0	0.00	5	0	5	0	0	7
Barbato, Johnny	0	0	0.00	5	1	7	2	1	9
Rosscup, Zac	2	0	0.71	11	0	12.2	7	9	21
Newell, Ryan	1	0	1.29	8	1	7	3	4	8
Mccanna, Kevin	1	1	2.40	14	3	15	8	2	16
Weiland, Joe	2	1	2.41	9	0	37.1	27	13	56
Ball, Matt	0	1	2.70	5	0	10	7	6	14
Huff, David	0	0	3.14	14	1	14.1	12	2	22
Ledet, Pat	1	2	4.70	7	0	23	19	9	21
Mckinley, Jayson	0	1	5.14	11	0	14	14	14	18
Mcgowen, Kevin	0	1	5.79	7	0	9.1	8	9	8
Kelly, Parker	0	2	7.20	9	0	10	12	8	7
Smith, Patrick	2	1	8.53	9	0	12.2	15	7	18
Gambrell, Grant	0	0	9.00	1	0	1	2	5	1
Rodriguez, Orlando	1	3	10.38	11	0	21.2	17	25	19
Mahle, Greg	0	0	15.43	2	0	2.1	5	1	2
Owens, Henry	0	0	22.09	3	0	3.2	7	9	6
Koch, Brandon	0	0	99.00	1	0	0	0	0	0

SUGAR LAND SKEETERS

Name	AVG	AB	R	H	HR	RBI	BB	SO	SB
Peterson, Dustin	.309	94	15	29	3	11	15	21	3
Jones, Ryder	.276	76	11	21	3	17	10	26	1
Peterson, DJ	.275	91	11	25	4	14	6	20	0
Romanski, Jake	.273	66	11	18	2	6	8	10	0
Bernard, Wynton	.270	74	11	20	2	9	6	20	6
Sturgeon, Cole	.257	70	9	18	0	5	7	15	6
Hawkins, Courtney	.247	73	15	18	6	18	16	31	1
Giansanti, Anthony	.217	46	6	10	1	4	7	11	2
Cordero, Albert	.214	42	7	9	2	8	6	6	1
Cecchini, Gavin	.213	75	10	16	1	10	8	23	0
Borenstein, Zach	.200	35	4	7	1	4	8	15	2
Romano, Ramsey	.133	30	4	4	0	0	2	11	0
Gray, Tristan	.111	27	4	3	2	7	6	10	1
Palmeiro, Preston	.071	14	1	1	0	0	1	7	0

Name									
Gage, Matt	0	0	3.07	11	0	14.2	14	7	16
Rhoades, Jeremy	3	0	3.24	9	0	8.1	7	7	10
House, TJ	1	2	3.38	7	0	29.1	21	15	29
Vasquez, Anthony	2	1	3.65	7	0	24.2	26	3	17
Machado, Andres	0	0	4.15	7	0	8.2	6	3	9
Kazmir, Scott	2	1	4.20	4	0	15	16	4	10
Kipper, Jordan	2	2	4.20	12	0	15	18	5	9
Gorst, Matthew	1	0	4.35	10	0	10.1	9	2	9
Marsh, Alec	0	1	4.50	3	0	4	2	5	6
Blair, Aaron	0	1	6.75	4	0	8	5	11	9
Mcgowan, Kevin	0	0	9.00	2	0	3	4	2	3
Dowdy, Kyle	0	1	10.13	2	0	5.1	7	4	5
Dirks, Caleb	0	0	10.29	7	0	7	10	4	7
Boyles, Ty	0	0	27.00	2	0	1.1	1	8	4

INDEPENDENT LEAGUES

Name	W	L	ERA	G	SV	IP	H	BB	SO
Rodney, Fernando	0	0	0.00	1	0	1	0	1	1
Norris, Bud	0	0	0.00	2	0	2	0	1	2
Dermody, Matt	3	0	0.52	5	0	17.1	13	6	23
Bostick, Akeem	1	0	0.90	8	0	10	7	5	11
Scott, Robby	0	0	1.80	13	0	15	13	5	21
Johnson, Jeff	0	0	2.40	15	3	15	9	11	19
De jong, Chase	1	2	3.18	6	0	17	10	6	27
Jungmann, Taylor	1	0	3.38	8	0	26.2	19	15	30
Cervenka, Hunter	4	1	3.97	9	0	11.1	10	7	16
Nix, Michael	0	1	4.01	8	0	24.2	27	13	24
Stapler, Cole	1	1	4.15	5	0	13	16	5	14
Gibson, Daniel	0	1	4.20	14	1	15	13	12	21
Latz, Jake	2	1	4.35	6	0	10.1	4	10	15
Kloffenstein, Adam	0	0	4.91	2	0	3.2	6	4	2
Weiss, Zack	1	0	5.40	5	0	6.2	9	2	7
Muller, Chris	0	0	5.63	7	2	8	5	4	9
Paulino, Felipe	0	1	12.00	4	0	3	1	5	2
West, Matt	0	1	12.00	6	0	6	12	2	6
Martin, Josh	0	1	13.50	2	0	2	3	2	2
Martin, Kyle	0	0	16.88	3	0	2.2	1	5	5
Beachy, Brandon	0	1	18.00	1	0	1	3	1	0
Gillaspie, Casey	0	0	99.00	1	0	0	0	0	0

TEAM TEXAS

Name	AVG	AB	R	H	HR	RBI	BB	SO	SB
Joseph, Tommy	.333	15	3	5	1	2	2	3	0
Hamilton, David	.296	81	14	24	0	10	19	16	20
Hubbard, Dondrei	.276	29	2	8	0	2	2	2	2
Reynolds, Ryan	.267	75	7	20	1	14	8	22	4
Martinson, Jason	.256	39	5	10	2	13	7	17	3
Clemens, Kacy	.236	72	11	17	1	13	10	24	0
Gurwitz, Zane	.233	60	10	14	1	7	7	24	1
Clemens, Kody	.233	90	14	21	4	12	9	20	2
Capel, Conner	.200	85	9	17	1	6	8	25	3
Lopez, BJ	.196	56	5	11	0	6	4	20	0
Davidson, Braxton	.196	51	12	10	2	7	18	27	0
Sherley, Luke	.150	40	6	6	0	1	4	7	4
Benson, Will	.143	56	11	8	2	4	13	27	5
Rupp, Cameron	.136	22	2	3	0	1	5	6	0
Cribbs, Galli	.105	19	2	2	0	1	1	7	1

Name	W	L	ERA	G	SV	IP	H	BB	SO
Ridgeway, Beau	1	0	0.82	8	0	11	7	3	10
Larkins, Turner	4	0	2.16	10	0	16.2	17	1	17
Mateo, Alejandro	0	0	2.45	12	1	11	11	4	18
Crockett, Kyle	0	2	3.14	14	3	14.1	11	4	22
Mcguire, Andy	1	0	3.21	10	0	14	16	1	7
Lakind, Jared	1	3	3.86	9	0	30.1	29	17	33
Lavendier, Winston	0	1	3.93	10	0	18.1	13	7	22
Shetter, Ryan	1	0	3.95	9	0	13.2	10	8	11
Clarkin, Ian	0	4	4.35	7	0	20.2	13	9	33
Clemens, Kacy	0	0	4.50	1	0	2	1	2	2
Kloffenstein, Adam	0	2	4.58	7	0	17.2	14	8	18
Young, Patrick	0	1	7.23	8	0	18.2	15	25	22
Brickhouse, Bryan	0	0	7.62	11	1	13	15	5	15
Crawford, Jonathan	1	2	14.73	7	0	7.1	8	15	9
Benson, Will	0	0	27.00	2	0	0.1	0	0	0

PECOS LEAGUE

Tucson was the dominant team in the Pecos League from day one until the end of the season, winning so many games that second-place Salina finished only one game above .500.

Team	W	L	PCT	GB
Tucson Saguaros	26	4	.866	—
Salina Stockade	16	15	.516	11
Roswell Invaders	10	19	.344	15
Houston Apollos	7	21	.250	17

Playoffs: Tucson defeated Salina 2-0 in a best-of-three series.

HOUSTON APOLLOS

Name	AVG	AB	R	H	HR	RBI	BB	SO	SB
Yale Hughes	.389	54	16	21	5	18	10	9	6
Jordan Gonzalez	.385	26	3	10	1	8	5	4	0
Aaron Stubblefield	.356	73	17	26	0	16	25	12	8
Ben Tingen	.323	31	6	10	0	4	3	6	5
Isaiah Garza	.321	28	5	9	0	3	3	9	0
Mark Traylor	.313	16	2	5	0	3	0	3	0
Mike Million	.298	57	8	17	4	15	6	5	0
Tevin Brown	.280	93	19	26	1	13	12	18	9
Kellen Hatheway	.276	29	5	8	0	3	6	8	3
Aaron Thor	.273	22	1	6	0	2	2	7	0
Jamal Washington	.250	28	5	7	0	3	3	5	3
Harrison Moore	.222	9	3	2	0	0	3	4	1
Trey Silmon	.216	37	7	8	1	8	6	12	1
Michael Flohr	.196	56	10	11	0	3	15	21	0
Rodney Goldsmith	.178	45	8	8	0	3	4	14	4
Jalin Lawson	.174	23	3	4	0	2	6	4	0
Daniel Arroyo	.167	12	1	2	0	1	1	2	0
Myles Waley	.105	19	3	2	0	2	8	9	0
Marcus Lopez	.100	10	2	1	0	0	0	5	1
Eric Olivo	.000	3	0	0	0	0	0	1	0
Julian Hunt	.000	3	0	0	1	0	2	0	0

Name	W	L	ERA	G	SV	IP	H	BB	SO
David Towler	1	1	0.81	5	0	24.1	26	17	19
Nick Coffman	1	1	5.31	8	0	26	23	18	16
Kyle Atkinson	1	3	5.87	6	0	22	14	31	18
Derrick Sylve	2	5	6.83	13	0	46	61	46	40
Mike Wilson	0	2	12.70	5	0	20.1	31	6	20
Yale Hughes	2	0	15.00	5	0	8	12	8	7
Marshall Mindieta	0	2	24.50	7	0	13.2	23	18	4

ROSWELL INVADERS

Name	AVG	AB	R	H	HR	RBI	BB	SO	SB
Ausar Rankin	.369	65	16	24	1	11	21	14	4
Coleton Horner	.340	103	29	35	4	28	24	16	1
Ian Yetsko	.320	97	26	31	7	34	17	24	6
Jacob Lentz	.316	38	7	12	0	4	2	9	0
Taichi Nakamura	.309	97	27	30	0	11	33	18	14
Rene Moreda	.260	50	10	13	1	6	6	11	1
Seth Strong	.255	51	15	13	4	17	11	13	0
Logan Rycraft	.233	86	7	20	0	7	13	11	6
Scott Martinez	.211	38	7	8	1	5	6	14	0
Collins Robinson	.179	39	6	7	0	4	7	15	1
Anthony Todaro	.083	12	0	1	0	0	0	4	0
Marcus Hanson	.000	2	1	0	0	0	1	1	0
Daryl Donerson	.000	1	0	0	0	0	0	0	0

Name	W	L	ERA	G	SV	IP	H	BB	SO
Stephen Keller	0	1	0.00	6	1	17.2	4	3	19
Troy Whitty	0	1	0.00	6	0	9	9	4	9
Joshua Welcher	0	1	0.00	3	0	12	9	8	8
Jonathan Fleckenstein	2	0	3.00	7	0	20	23	12	18
Tyler Schmidt	1	1	3.26	14	1	42.1	36	26	46
Joe Slocum	1	1	3.50	3	0	18	24	6	9
Matt Cronin	3	3	4.05	10	0	28	33	14	30
Zachary Love	0	0	5.40	6	0	7	10	3	1
Elvin Jorge	1	3	5.92	5	0	13.2	19	20	18
Max Maarleveld	1	2	6.42	7	0	7	10	4	6
Alexander Merithew	1	2	9.52	11	0	32	51	16	41

SALINA STOCKADE

Name	AVG	AB	R	H	HR	RBI	BB	SO	SB
Aaron Takacs	.386	83	29	32	3	20	22	17	11
Lance Myers	.383	47	18	18	1	14	23	5	6
Ernie Geraci	.370	46	16	17	0	16	14	8	3
Hudson Bilodeau	.357	112	29	40	3	25	19	6	4
Drew Schutt	.348	69	21	24	1	19	13	14	5
Alex Nielson	.340	103	25	35	0	19	13	8	0
Eddie Grimaldo	.326	89	16	29	1	28	17	10	6
Brian Dansereau	.318	44	12	14	1	7	5	7	8
Jared Gay	.316	79	18	25	3	20	16	29	4
Khalyd Cox	.283	60	14	17	2	11	6	21	8

Butch Hobson and the Chicago Dogs managed to successfully play a 60-game schedule in front of socially distanced fans.

Jose Tejeda	.273	44	8	12	0	4	10	17	1
Keaven Diaz	.269	26	6	7	0	8	9	7	0
Jordan Dicks	.269	104	29	28	1	21	27	27	12
Kyree Tekra	.000	2	0	0	0	0	0	0	0

Name	W	L	ERA	G	SV	IP	H	BB	SO
Mark Simon	2	0	0.00	4	0	12.2	4	8	19
Reid Frase	1	1	0.00	5	0	22.1	26	21	8
Matthew Fountain	2	3	0.79	15	0	16	22	13	11
Kenneth Pierson	1	0	2.59	6	0	17.1	18	6	15
Blake Garrett	1	0	2.61	9	1	10.2	8	11	16
Ben Butler	1	2	3.64	9	0	15.1	3	21	20
Tommy Giunta	1	4	6.06	10	1	35.2	40	24	21
Joey Deperno	0	1	6.75	9	0	17	17	23	19
Ryan Osborne	0	1	7.71	3	1	4.2	12	4	2
Alex Clayton	1	1	8.16	6	0	14.1	16	4	10
Jesus Grimaldo	0	0	9.00	4	0	6.1	9	8	3
Eddie Grimaldo	0	0	9.00	4	0	6.1	9	8	3
Jacob Williams	3	2	9.00	11	0	28.1	30	33	23
Trevor Wick	0	0	11.70	12	1	19.1	35	20	17
Nicholas Ray	1	0	13.50	13	0	19.2	36	10	15

TUCSON SAGUAROS

Name	AVG	AB	R	H	HR	RBI	BB	SO	SB
Thomas DeBonville	.455	110	38	50	2	32	21	17	9
Nathan Etheridge	.438	130	39	57	5	59	17	10	1
Noah Mahoney	.429	21	3	9	2	11	7	4	0
Erwin Real	.397	68	18	27	2	24	10	8	0
Chris Caffery	.378	90	32	34	5	39	28	7	1
Danny Kerr	.352	91	24	32	4	24	24	9	2
Cody Earl	.345	58	19	20	1	12	17	7	0
Blaze Speas	.304	23	7	7	0	6	6	5	0

Christopher Eusay	.297	91	43	27	3	14	28	22	7
Gary Mason Jr.	.292	48	17	14	3	11	3	5	3
Caleb Pyscher	.286	7	3	2	0	1	3	1	0
James Prockish	.286	112	30	32	0	22	27	11	2
Marcus Catalano	.274	62	12	17	1	14	16	16	0
Blake Berry	.259	54	19	14	2	19	19	15	0
Carlo Francisco	.200	10	3	2	1	1	1	1	0
Edison Cabrera	.000	4	0	0	0	0	0	0	0

Name	W	L	ERA	G	SV	IP	H	BB	SO
Ryan Porras	0	0	0.67	9	0	21.1	15	22	25
Martin Alcoverde	3	0	2.25	13	4	14.1	8	10	18
Erwin Real	3	0	2.81	3	0	16	19	9	19
Cody Earl	5	0	3.49	12	1	55.2	54	27	37
Darian Fleming	3	0	4.23	3	0	17	26	11	7
Aleq McMullin	1	0	4.76	2	0	6.2	10	8	8
Jake Lialios	3	0	5.92	11	0	29.1	22	16	37
Jim Kennedy	0	0	8.10	3	0	6.2	15	3	8
Jay Causey	2	0	9.00	10	0	13.1	4	8	24
Sati Santa Cruz	0	1	10.90	7	0	23.1	32	31	18
Eli Straw	4	2	11.50	16	0	29	30	19	23

U.S. PRO BASEBALL LEAGUE

Team	W	L	PCT	GB
Unicorns	22	13	.629	—
Diamond Hoppers	21	14	.597	1
Beavers	15	21	.419	7.5
Woolly Mammoths	10	20	.333	9.5

Playoffs—First round: Beavers defeated Mammoths. **Second round:** Beavers defeated Hoppers. **Finals:** Unicorns defeated Beavers.

INDEPENDENT LEAGUES

Pandemic Forces Halt Of International Events

Hyun Jin Ryu and South Korea remain the defending Olympic champions, at least until 2021.

BY J.J. COOPER

When baseball was dropped from the Olympics schedule in 2005, it was a significant blow to the growth of the sport internationally.

For all the success of the World Baseball Classic, which lands a much larger swath of the best players from around the world, it is the Olympics that provides the impetus to grow the game worldwide. Being an Olympic sport means that countries fund sports development at a higher level than happens for non-Olympic sports.

So after baseball was dropped from the Olympics, the sport's international community made many efforts to get the sport back on the docket. The International Baseball Federation (IBAF) and the International Softball Federation merged and became the World Baseball Softball Confederation, which helped provide a unified effort to get baseball and softball back into the Olympics.

It worked. Baseball and softball were supposed to have their triumphant return to the Olympics in 2020 in Tokyo, one of baseball's biggest hotbeds.

Instead, this was the first year without a sig-nificant sanctioned international baseball event since the IBAF was founded in 1938. The Olympics and every other WBSC-scheduled international tournament had to be delayed to 2021 because of the worldwide novel coronavirus pandemic. That meant that the only international competition of the year was the Caribbean Series, which wrapped up before the coronavirus pandemic had widely spread to Central America.

In addition to the postponement of the Olympics, the Women's World Cup, U-15 Baseball World Cup and U-23 Baseball World Cup all had to be moved to 2021. The Americas qualifier and the Baseball final qualifier also were delayed into 2021. The U.S. does not currently have a spot in the Olympics field. It will play Puerto Rico, Cuba, Canada, the Dominican Republic, Nicaragua, Colombia and Venezuela for the Americas Qualifier. The winner will advance to the Olympics.

The second- and third-place finishers in that tournament will be invited to participate in the Final Qualifier against Australia, Taiwan, China and the Netherlands, with the winner of that tournament earning the last Olympics bid.

INTERNATIONAL

Hawks Win Fourth Straight Title

BY J.J. COOPER

Once again, the Fukuoka SoftBank Hawks were the class of Japanese baseball. The Hawks wrapped up their fourth straight Japan Series title and their seventh since 2011 with a relatively easy four-games-to-one win over Yomiuri.

Even as stars like Yu Darvish and Shohei Ohtani have left for Major League Baseball, the Hawks continue to be the class of the league year after year. Ryoya Kurihara was the playoff MVP for Fukuoka. Yuki Yanigita was the regular-season star for the Hawks. He hit .342 with 29 home runs.

Because of the novel coronavirus pandemic, the season got off to a late start. The regular season was cut to 120 games (reduced from the normal 143 games) and the Central League decided to eliminate its playoffs, deeming the champion of the regular season as its representative for the Japan Series.

But for all the upheaval, there was some familiarity to how the season finished. The Yomiuri Giants won their 38th league crown, easily trouncing Hanshin and Chunichi for the Central League's top spot.

Tomoyuki Sugano (14-2, 1.97) was Yomiuri's ace. Sugano won his first 13 decisions before finally picking up his first loss. Import Rubby de la Rosa, the former Red Sox pitcher, picked up 17 saves for the Giants in 32 appearances.

The Hawks ran away with the Pacific League crown and rolled to an easy sweep in their Climax Series matchup against Lotte. This was SoftBank's eighth consecutive playoff appearance.

Yuki Yanagita led SoftBank at the plate with a .342-29-86 season. Koudai Senga, (11-6, 2.16) was the team's ace and led the PL in ERA.

There were some notable retirements in 2020. Righthander Kyuji Fujikawa, a former Rangers and Cubs reliever, announced that at age 40 it was time to step away from the mound. His 243 NPB saves are fourth most all-time.

Giants pitcher Hisashi Iwakuma also announced that his career was coming to an end. Iwakuma did not appear in a game for Yomiuri in 2020, but technically he was still active.

Iwakuma was once one of the best pitchers in Japan before coming to the U.S. to pitch for the Mariners after 11 excellent years in the NPB.

Former Orioles mainstay Adam Jones began his career in the Central League, with the Orix Buffaloes. Jones finished the year by hitting .258 with 12 home runs and 43 RBIs over the course of 302 at-bats with his new club.

CENTRAL LEAGUE

Team	W	L	T	PCT	GB
Yomiuri Giants	67	45	8	.598	—
Hanshin Tigers	60	53	7	.531	7.5
Chunichi Dragons	60	55	5	.522	8.5
DeNA BayStars	56	58	6	.491	12
Hiroshima Carp	52	56	12	.481	13
Yakult Swallows	41	69	10	.373	25

Playoffs: Canceled due to COVID-19. Yomiuri advanced directly to Japan series. **Japan Series:** Fukuoka defeated Yomiuri 4-1 in best-of-seven series.

CENTRAL LEAGUE BATTING LEADERS

Player, Team	AVG	AB	R	H	HR	RBI	SB
Keita Sano, BS	.328	402	48	132	20	69	0
Takayuki Kajitani, BS	.323	433	88	140	19	53	14
Norichika Aoki, Swall.	.317	357	64	113	18	51	2
Yohei Ohshima, Drag.	.316	462	58	146	1	30	16
Munetaka Murakami, Swall.	.307	424	70	130	28	86	11
Shuhei Takahashi, Drag.	.305	394	46	120	7	46	1
Toshiro Miyazaki, BS	.301	429	47	129	14	53	0
Seiya Suzuki, Carp	.300	430	85	129	25	75	6
Koji Chikamoto, Tigers	.293	474	81	139	9	45	31
Hayato Sakamoto, Giants	.289	412	64	119	19	65	4
Yusuke Ohyama, Tigers	.288	423	66	122	28	85	1
Yoshihiro Maru, Giants	.284	423	63	120	27	77	8
Shota Dohbayashi, Carp	.279	401	55	112	14	58	17
Ryuhei Matsuyama, Carp	.277	404	38	112	9	67	0
Kazuma Okamoto, Giants	.275	440	79	121	31	97	2
Naoki Yoshikawa, Giants	.274	354	47	97	8	32	11
Alcides Escobar, Swall.	.273	377	27	103	1	30	6
Ryosuke Kikuchi, Carp	.271	376	43	102	10	41	3
Dayan Viciedo, Drag.	.267	409	48	109	17	82	3
Toshiki Abe, Drag.	.257	421	44	108	13	61	2
Jerry Sands, Tigers	.257	377	47	97	19	64	2
Tetsuto Yamada, Swall.	.254	334	52	85	12	52	8
Neftali Soto, BS	.252	428	59	108	25	78	0
Kosuke Tanaka, Carp	.251	378	51	95	8	39	8
Yota Kyoda, Drag.	.247	442	43	109	5	29	8
Tomotaka Sakaguchi, Swall	.246	398	55	98	9	36	4
Justin Bour, Tigers	.243	329	27	80	17	45	1

OTHER NOTABLE HITTERS

Player, Team	AVG	AB	R	H	HR	RBI	SB
Adam Jones, Buff.	.258	302	29	78	12	43	1
Jose Pirela, Carp	.266	316	47	84	11	34	2
Jose Lopez, BS	.246	293	26	72	12	42	0
Zelous Wheeler, Giants	.247	263	26	65	12	36	3
Tyler Austin, BS	.286	238	36	68	20	56	0
Zoilo Almonte, Dragons	.294	214	32	63	9	29	1
Aderlin Rodriguez, Buff.	.218	193	11	42	6	25	1
Steven Moya, Buff.	.274	164	20	45	12	38	0
Gerardo Parra, Giants	.267	146	14	39	4	13	0

CENTRAL LEAGUE PITCHING LEADERS

Pitcher, Team	W	L	ERA	IP	H	HR	BB	SO
Yudai Ohno, Drag.	11	6	1.82	149	106	13	23	148
Masato Morishita, Carp	10	3	1.91	123	102	6	32	124
Tomoyuki Sugano, Giants	14	2	1.97	137	97	8	25	131
Yuki Nishi, Tigers	11	5	2.26	148	116	15	28	115
Aren Kuri, Carp	8	6	2.96	131	116	11	44	106
Koyo Aoyagi, Tigers	7	9	3.36	121	111	4	44	88

OTHER NORTH AMERICAN PITCHERS

Pitcher, Team	W	L	ERA	IP	H	HR	BB	SO
Rubby De La Rosa, Giants	2	0	2.56	32	23	3	16	28
Nattino Diplan, Giants	0	0	19.29	2	7	3	2	2
Jon Edwards, Tigers	0	1	2.38	23	17	2	3	17
Edwin Escobar, BS	1	4	2.33	54	39	3	17	58
Jose Flores, Giants	2	2	7.66	22	27	3	16	25
Onelki Garcia, Tigers	2	6	4.42	75	71	9	35	51
Luis Gonzalez, Dragons	0	0	4.78	26	34	3	9	27
Joe Gunkel, Tigers	2	4	3.18	58	54	6	13	39
Frank Herrmann, Giants	3	2	2.15	38	28	2	12	37
DJ Johnson, Carp	0	0	4.61	14	19	0	8	13
Kris Johnson, Carp	0	7	6.10	52	60	3	25	35
Matt Koch, Swall.	0	3	7.88	16	29	2	3	6
Raidel Martinez, Dragons	2	0	1.13	40	24	2	12	49
Scott McGough, Swall.	4	1	3.91	46	42	4	15	52
Spencer Patton, BS	3	2	4.92	53	52	6	27	65
Michael Peoples, BS	2	2	4.97	38	40	6	13	29
Yariel Rodriguez, Dragons	3	4	4.12	59	50	4	21	67
Tayler Scott, Carp	0	3	15.75	8	17	1	8	7
Robert Suarez, Tigers	3	1	2.24	52	36	2	19	50
Albert Suarez, Swall.	4	4	2.67	67	56	4	27	52
Thyago Vieira, Giants	0	1	3.28	25	27	3	17	29
Gabriel Ynoa, Swall.	0	3	10.13	24	45	8	10	15

PACIFIC LEAGUE

Team	W	L	T	PCT	GB
Fukuoka SoftBank Hawks	73	42	5	.635	—
Chiba Lotte Marines	60	57	3	.513	14
Seibu Lions	58	58	4	.500	15.5
Rakuten Golden Eagles	55	57	8	.491	16.5
Nippon-Ham Fighters	53	62	5	.461	20
ORIX Buffaloes	45	68	7	.398	27

Playoffs: Fukuoka defeated Lotte 3-0 in best-of-five series. **Japan Series:** Fukuoka defeated Yomiuri 4-1 in best-of-seven series.

PACIFIC LEAGUE BATTING LEADERS

Player, Team	AVG	AB	R	H	HR	RBI	SB
Masataka Yoshida, Buff.	.350	408	55	143	14	64	8
Yuki Yanagita, Hawks	.342	427	90	146	29	86	7
Kensuke Kondoh, Fight.	.340	371	56	126	5	60	4
Haruki Nishikawa, Fight.	.306	422	82	129	5	39	42
Daichi Suzuki, Eagles	.295	478	71	141	4	55	1
Hiroto Kobukata, Eagles	.288	378	61	109	3	31	17
Ryo Watanabe, Fight.	.283	414	49	117	6	39	4
Hiroaki Shimauchi, Eagles	.281	406	50	114	8	53	9
Hideto Asamura, Eagles	.280	432	72	121	32	104	1
Taishi Ohta, Fight.	.275	455	57	125	14	68	3
Stefen Romero, Eagles	.272	356	46	97	24	63	0
Takumi Kuriyama, Lions	.272	372	37	101	12	67	0
Akira Nakamura, Hawks	.271	362	43	98	6	50	0
Sosuke Genda, Lions	.270	455	67	123	1	21	18
Cory Spangenberg, Lions	.268	407	51	109	15	57	12
Takahiro Okada, Buff.	.256	328	36	84	16	55	5
Tomoya Mori, Lions	.251	358	46	90	9	38	4
Shogo Nakamura, Marines	.249	422	57	105	8	49	6
Shuta Tonosaki, Lions	.247	433	62	107	8	43	21
Seiya Inoue, Marines	.245	376	44	92	15	67	0
Ryoya Kurihara, Hawks	.243	440	52	107	17	73	5
Sho Nakata, Fight.	.239	440	52	105	31	108	1
Leonys Martin, Marines	.234	359	72	84	25	65	7
Nobuhiro Matsuda, Hawks	.228	395	36	90	13	46	1
Hisanori Yasuda, Marines	.221	393	32	87	6	54	2
Hotaka Yamakawa, Lions	.205	322	47	66	24	73	0

OTHER NORTH AMERICAN HITTERS

Player, Team	AVG	AB	R	H	HR	RBI	SB
Yurisbel Gracial, Hawks	.277	256	30	71	10	35	2
Stefen Romero, Eagles	.272	356	46	97	24	63	0
Cory Spangenberg, Lions	.268	407	51	109	15	57	12
Jabari Blash, Eagles	.235	119	25	28	2	18	1

The NPB completed a successful but shortened 120-game season.

CARL COURT/GETTY IMAGES

Brandon Laird, Marines	.233	133	15	31	6	15	0	
Alfredo Despaigne, Hawks	.224	85	9	19	6	12	0	
Christian Villanueva, Fight.	.220	168	11	37	4	19	1	
Ernesto Mejia, Lions	.207	237	20	49	11	33	0	

PACIFIC LEAGUE PITCHING LEADERS

Pitcher, Team	W	L	ERA	IP	H	HR	BB	SO
Koudai Senga, Hawks	11	6	2.16	121	90	4	57	149
Yoshinobu Yamamoto, Buff.	8	4	2.20	127	82	6	37	149
Kohei Arihara, Fight.	8	9	3.46	133	125	11	30	106
Hideaki Wakui, Eagles	11	4	3.60	130	110	17	38	110
Kona Takahashi, Lions	8	8	3.74	120	100	9	44	100
Manabu Mima, Marines	10	4	3.95	123	130	9	25	88
Daiki Tajima, Buff.	4	6	4.05	122	102	14	42	89
Ayumu Ishikawa, Marines	7	6	4.25	133	138	19	26	77

OTHER NORTH AMERICAN PITCHERS

Pitcher, Team	W	L	ERA	IP	H	HR	BB	SO
Andrew Albers, Buff.	4	8	3.94	89	93	12	22	66
Alan Busenitz, Eagles	1	4	2.86	44	46	2	18	32
J.T. Chargois, Eagles	0	3	5.81	26	23	2	14	19
Brandon Dickson, Buff.	0	4	3.28	36	34	2	16	32
Jose Flores, Marines	2	2	7.66	22	27	3	16	25
Reed Garrett, Lions	3	2	3.10	49	52	2	20	45
Frank Herrmann, Marines	3	2	2.15	38	28	2	12	37
Tyler Higgins, Buff.	3	3	2.40	41	37	2	20	45
Jay Jackson, Marines	0	0	3.86	7	4	1	3	12
DJ Johnson, Eagles	1	0	3.07	15	13	2	6	16
Livan Moinelo, Hawks	2	3	1.69	48	26	1	25	77
Matt Moore, Hawks	6	3	2.65	78	64	7	22	89
Zach Neal, Lions	6	8	5.22	112	125	13	35	66
Sean Nolin, Lions	1	2	6.75	21	22	3	10	21
Bryan Rodriguez, Fight	0	0	2.25	8	7	0	3	9
Rick van den Hurk, Hawks	2	2	6.92	26	28	6	10	20

Aaron Altherr hit 31 home runs.

CHUNG SUNG-JUN/GETTY IMAGES

KBO Fills The Void In The U.S.

The Korean Baseball Organization went about as mainstream in the U.S. as possible in 2020.

With U.S. baseball (and all other sports) shut down, the KBO managed to land a distribution deal on ESPN when its season began in May.

For a while, until the Japanese leagues and eventually Major League Baseball returned, it was the most prominent baseball league in the world that was playing games.

That may not have turned into massive TV ratings in the U.S. (the time difference meant most of the games were aired live in the overnight hours in the U.S., although some were then rebroadcast at more TV-friendly times), but it did provide the highest profile the league has ever received in the States.

U.S. fans saw is what fans in Korea have long known—KBO provides an entertaining, hitter-heavy brand of baseball.

KT Wiz outfielder Mel Rojas Jr.'s fourth season in Korea proved to be his best. He led the league with 47 home runs. He has averaged 33 home runs a season since coming to Korea.

While Rojas was the league's big bat, it was the NC Dinos who were the class of the league. After eight seasons in the league, the Dinos won their first KBO title. The Dinos also had the league's best record. Dinos ace Drew Rucinski was on the mound for the title-clinching Game 6 win. The Dinos shut out Doosan in Games 4 and 5 of the series and won Game 6, 4-2.

STANDINGS & LEADERS

Team	W	L	T	PCT	GB
NC Dinos	83	55	6	.601	—
KT Wiz	81	62	1	.566	4.5
Doosan Bears	79	61	4	.564	5
LG Twins	79	61	4	.564	5
Kiwoom Heroes	80	63	1	.559	5.5
Kia Tigers	73	71	0	.507	13
Lotte Giants	71	72	1	.497	14.5
Samsung Lions	64	75	5	.460	19.5
SK Wyverns	51	92	1	.357	34.5
Hanwha Eagles	46	95	3	.326	38.5

Playoffs—First Round: Doosan defeated LG 2-0 in best-of-three series. **Semifinals**: Doosan defeated KT 3-1 in best-of-five series. **Finals:** NC Dinos defeated Doosan 4-2 in best-of-seven series.

BATTING LEADERS

Player, Team	AVG	AB	R	H	HR	RBI	SB
Choi Hyoung Woo, Kia	.354	522	93	185	28	115	0
Son Ah Seop, Lotte	.352	540	98	190	11	85	5
Mel Rojas Jr., KT	.349	550	116	192	47	135	0
Park Min Woo, NC	.345	467	82	161	8	63	13
Jose Fernandez, Doosan	.340	586	104	199	21	105	0
Lee Jung Hoo, Kiwoom	.333	544	85	181	15	101	12
Heo Kyoung Min, Doosan	.332	437	70	145	7	58	14
Kim Hyun Soo, LG	.331	547	98	181	22	119	14
Kang Baek Ho, KT	.330	500	95	165	23	89	7
Yang Eui Ji, NC	.328	461	86	151	33	124	5
Na Sung Bum, NC	.324	525	115	170	34	112	3
Hwang Jae Gyun, KT	.312	541	108	169	21	97	11
Kim Dong Yub, Samsung	.312	413	60	129	20	74	4
Oh Jae Il, Doosan	.312	471	62	147	16	89	2
Koo Ja Wook, Samsung	.307	446	70	137	15	78	19
Choi Joo Hwan, Doosan	.306	509	63	156	16	88	2
Preston Tucker, Kia	.306	542	100	166	32	113	0
Park Sok Min, NC	.306	356	58	109	14	63	0
Lee Myung Ki, NC	.306	477	82	146	2	45	12
Kim Ha Seong, Kiwoom	.306	533	111	163	30	109	23

PITCHING LEADERS

Player, Team	W	L	ERA	G	IP	H	BB	SO
Eric Jokisch, Kiwoom	12	7	2.14	27	160	144	25	115
Dan Straily, Lotte	15	4	2.50	31	195	148	51	205
Aaron Brooks, Kia	11	4	2.50	23	151	131	24	130
Raul Alcantara, Doosan	20	2	2.54	31	199	174	30	182
Drew Rucinski, NC	19	5	3.05	30	183	173	57	167
Casey Kelly, LG	15	7	3.32	28	173	160	40	134
David Buchanan, Samsung	15	7	3.45	27	175	172	50	121
Choi Chae Heung, Samsung	11	8	3.58	26	146	131	51	123
Moon Seung Won, SK	6	8	3.65	25	146	136	45	117
Im Chan Kyu, LG	10	9	4.08	27	148	143	65	138
William Cuevas, KT	10	8	4.10	27	158	152	46	110
Odrisamer Despaigne, KT	15	8	4.33	35	208	233	68	152
Andrew Gagnon, Kia	11	8	4.34	28	160	162	64	141
Tyler Wilson, LG	10	8	4.42	25	145	161	39	109
Dennis Wright , NC	11	9	4.68	29	158	164	63	125
Yang Hyeon Jong, Kia	11	10	4.70	31	172	180	64	149
Park Se Woong, Lotte	8	10	4.70	28	147	177	47	108
Park Jong Hun, SK	13	11	4.81	29	157	146	78	134
Warwick Saupold, Hanwha	10	13	4.91	28	165	203	42	97
Ricardo Pinto, Sk	6	15	6.17	30	162	198	90	112

INTERNATIONAL

Uni-President celebrated winning the CPBL for the first time in seven years.

CPBL Lands Added Attention

Normally, the Chinese Professional Baseball League, Taiwan's four-team professional league, operates in the shadow of both the Nippon Professional Baseball League and the Korean Baseball Organization.

But thanks to the global coronavirus pandemic, for a while in 2020, the CPBL was the only professional baseball being played anywhere. The start of the season was delayed a few weeks, but on April 11, the CPBL opened up in fanless stadiums.

The league drew attention from baseball-starved fans in the U.S., as games were streamed on Twitter and other services with English-language broadcasters. By May 6, teams were allowed to have up to 1,000 fans in the stands. Those capacity limits were largely removed by June.

The Uni-President 7-Eleven Lions won their first CPBL title in seven years by coming back from a 3-1 deficit against CTBC Brothers in the best-of-seven Taiwan Series. The Lions won three straight must-win games, including a come-from-behind 7-4 win in Game 7.

Teddy Stankiewicz gave up all four of CTBC's runs in 6.2 innings. Relievers Huang Chun-Yen and Brock Dykxhoorn held CTBC scoreless for the final 2.1 innings to finish off the deciding game.

The Uni-Lions were led all season by the best outfield in the CPBL. Chen Chieh-Hsien, Uni-Lions; Su Chih-Chieh were two of the best position players in the league, but the surprising star was rookie Lin An-Ko. Lin led the league with 32 home runs while hitting .310/.390/.590. Lin was the overwhelming and easy choice as the league's rookie of the year.

Jose De Paula was named the league MVP. The CTBC ace led the league in wins (16), ERA (3.20) and strikeouts (192).

STANDINGS & LEADERS

Team	W	L	T	PCT	GB
*CTBC Brothers	67	51	2	.568	—
Rakuten Monkeys	59	61	0	.492	9
& Uni President 7-Eleven Lions	58	61	1	.487	9.5
Fubon Guardians	54	65	1	.454	13

* First half champion &Second half champion
Finals: Uni-Lions defeated CTBC 4-3 in best-of-seven series.

All-Star Team C: Liao Chien-Fu, Rakuten. **1B:** Hsu Chi-Hong, CTBC. **2B:** Wu Tung-Jung, CTBC. **3B:** Wang Wei-Chen, CTBC. **SS:** Lee Tsung-Hsien, Fubon. **OF:** Lin An-Ko; Uni-Lions; Chen Chieh-Hsien, Uni-Lions; Su Chih-Chieh, Uni-Lions. **DH:** Chou Szu-Chi, CTBC. **SP:** Jose De Paula, CTBC.

BATTING LEADERS

Player, Team	AVG	OBP	SLG	AB	R	H	HR	RBI	SB
Chen Chieh-Hsien, Uni-Lions	.360	.419	.461	484	99	174	3	67	21
Lin Li, Rakuten	358	.414	.613	416	92	149	25	86	22
Chu Yu-Hsien, Rakuten	.353	.405	.641	357	62	126	27	70	0
Wang Wei-Chen, CTBC	.339	.386	.433	501	90	170	4	47	17
Chan Tzu-Hsien, CTBC	.333	.403	.529	420	74	140	20	80	4
Chou Szu-Chi, CTBC	.324	.386	.589	355	75	115	22	81	6
Hsu Chih-Hong, CTBC	.322	.389	.556	351	64	113	19	65	1
Su Chih-Chieh, Uni-Lions	.313	.394	.594	438	104	137	28	98	13
Lin Hung-Yu, Rakuten	.312	.344	.466	397	57	124	13	70	1
Lin Yi-Chuan, Fubon	.312	.361	.527	391	52	122	22	78	1
Chen Chun-Hsiu, Rakuten	.311	.381	.469	341	58	106	12	54	3
Lin An-Ko, Uni-Lions	.310	.395	.590	432	90	134	32	99	10
Lee Tsung-Hsien, Fubon	.309	.351	.408	488	78	151	5	46	26
Chiang Kun-Yu, CTBC	.309	.356	.410	395	61	122	4	44	7
Kao Kuo-Hui, Fubon	.303	.358	.598	343	59	104	25	70	3
Chang Chih-hao, CTBC	.298	.373	.564	369	66	110	27	88	4
Chen Chen-Wei, Rakuten	.284	.331	.394	472	89	134	4	52	42
Kuo Yen-Wen, Rakuten	.268	.320	.407	351	52	94	10	54	2

PITCHING LEADERS

Player, Team	W	L	ERA	G	IP	H	BB	SO
Jose De Paula, CTBC	16	9	3.20	27	174	154	48	192
Henry Sosa, Fubon	15	5	3.38	29	194	230	37	172
Ariel Miranda, CTBC	10	8	3.80	25	156	149	60	170
Ryan Carpenter, Rakuten	10	7	4.00	26	157	181	33	150
Mike Loree, Fubon	6	11	5.00	23	137	172	28	126
Lisalverto Bonilla, Rakuten	10	9	5.24	28	173	198	63	139

OTHER NORTH AMERICAN PITCHERS

Player, Team	W	L	ERA	G	IP	H	BB	SO
Esmil Rogers, CTBC	6	4	3.47	17	109	111	28	113
Josh Roenicke, Uni-Lions	5	4	4.94	14	75	98	13	50
Elih Villanueva, Rakuten	1	7	7.13	12	71	95	28	45
Brock Dykxhoorn, Uni-Lions	5	3	5.68	13	70	69	28	48
Tim Melville, Uni-Lions	4	3	2.93	10	61	49	32	46
Teddy Stankiewicz, Uni-Lions	6	0	3.81	10	54	62	13	47
Manny Bañuelos, Fubon	6	3	2.60	10	52	39	26	62
Mitch Lively, CTBC	6	1	3.94	9	48	56	7	36
Justin Nicolino, Rakuten	1	3	5.90	8	40	50	11	39
Logan Darnell, Uni-Lions	2	2	8.01	10	39	70	8	36
Brandon Mann, Rakuten	0	2	7.08	10	20	26	10	25
Arturo Reyes, CTBC	1	1	6.23	4	17	15	6	14
Yoanys Quiala, Fubon	0	1	2.76	3	16	13	11	13

INTERNATIONAL

GENE WANG/GETTY IMAGES

Bologna Wins Serie A1 Title

BY HARVEY SAHKER

Series A1 was smaller in 2020. The league included just six clubs, down one from last year and two from 2018. All games were also shortened to just seven innings.

But that didn't change the story at the top of the league. Bologna prevailed yet again, defeating San Marino, 4-3, in the best-of-seven Italy Series. It was Bologna's fifth national championship in the last seven years and its 14th overall.

Two pitchers shared a no-hitter in Game 6 of the series, a 6-1 San Marino victory. Former Tampa Bay and St. Louis farmhand Fernando Baez started on the mound and went five innings, striking out six and walking five. Baez was relieved by ex-Mercer and independent league hurler Dimitri Kourtis, who whiffed four Bologna batters and walked one.

San Marino outfielder Federico Celli, 25, won the Serie A1 triple crown after batting .473 with 10 home runs and 36 RBIs. A minor leaguer in the Dodgers system from 2014 to 2016, Celli also led the league in slugging, on-base percentage, runs, hits, doubles and total bases. His batting average was the highest in the league since Federico Bassi hit .474 for Modena in 1998. Aluminum bats were used in Serie A1 when Bassi reached his mark.

German Markus Solbach (3-0, 0.23) and Italian Alessandro Maestri (7-0, 0.82) anchored the San Marino pitching staff. Solbach, 29, was a farm hand for the Twins, Diamondbacks and Dodgers, and played in the Can-Am League. Maestri, 35, spent five years in the Cubs system, four years in Japan and has since played pro ball in South Korea, Mexico and Australia.

Solbach and Kourtis shared a no-hitter in a 1-0, eight-inning win over Collecchio in late July. Solbach started, went 3.2 innings, struck out 11 and walked one. Kourtis pitched the rest of the game, faced the minimum number of batters and struck out six. Celli singled in the only run of the game in the bottom of the eighth.

Its no-hit defeat against San Marino underscored Collechio's offensive woes. Joint basement dwellers in Serie A1, Collecchio sported a league worst .166 batting average with zero home runs and Collecchio pitching staff's 5.99 ERA was also last in the loop.

Alessandro Maestri was 7-0, 0.82 this season.

DOUG BENC/WBCI

Ray-Patrick Didder, a minor leaguer in the Atlanta system between 2013 and 2019, joined Bologna in 2020. The Aruba native finished second in the race for the Serie A1 batting crown and led the league with 15 stolen bases.

STANDINGS

Team	W	L	PCT	GB
San Marino	23	4	.852	—
Bologna	23	6	.793	1
Parma	16	11	.593	7
Macerata	6	17	.261	15
Godo	6	21	.222	17
Collecchio	6	21	.222	17

Italy Series: Bologna beat San Marino 4-3 in best-of-seven series.

INDVIDUAL BATTING LEADERS

Player, Team	AVG	AB	R	H	2B	3B	HR	RBI	SB
Celli, Federico, RSM	.473	93	38	44	11	1	10	36	2
Didder, Ray-Patrick, BOL	.413	75	28	31	6	1	2	18	15
Caseres, Maikel, RSM	.380	71	17	27	3	0	2	22	3
Morresi, Lorenzo, MAC	.373	67	7	25	2	1	0	10	0
Reginato, Mattia, RSM	.369	65	27	24	4	0	3	23	0
Desimoni, Stefano, PAR	.333	63	11	21	4	1	0	9	3
Garbella, Giovanni, RSM	.329	79	13	26	5	1	1	20	2
Paolini, Segundo, PAR	.325	83	17	27	5	0	1	10	5
Avagnina, Lorenzo, RSM	.325	77	17	25	5	0	1	10	0
Moredo, Eduardo, MAC	.314	70	19	22	1	0	0	7	9

INDIVIDUAL PITCHING LEADERS

Player	W	L	ERA	IP	H	R	ER	BB	SO
Solbach, Markus, RSM	3	0	0.23	30	15	2	1	8	53
Maestri, Alessandro, RSM	7	0	0.82	43	19	5	5	20	60
Brolo, Gouvea Murilo, BOL	5	0	1.12	31	19	5	5	6	46
Bassani, Alex, BOL	4	2	1.34	37	22	8	7	10	40
Lugo, Luis E., PAR	3	3	1.40	40	26	12	8	10	69
Kourtis, Dimitri, RSM	3	2	1.88	26	12	8	7	11	42
Pomponi, Michele, PAR	2	3	2.47	40	34	17	14	20	48
Bocchi, Matteo, BOL	7	1	2.58	43	39	20	16	12	44
Zotti, Matthias, BOL	4	0	2.68	31	32	19	12	19	29
Garbella, Nicola, RSM	4	1	2.71	31	23	13	12	13	25

Coronavirus Wrecks Season

BY HARVEY SAHKER

The coronavirus wreaked havoc on the Dutch Major League season. Because of the pandemic, the season started three months later than planned, which meant that the regular season was halved.

Neptunus and the Amsterdam Pirates finished atop the league's semifinal round to earn berths in the Holland Series. The Pirates won the first two games of the best-of-seven series, but the series was then shut down as part of the Dutch government's response to a surge in coronavirus cases. A few days later, the Royal Netherlands Baseball and Softball Association (KNBSB) ruled that no DML champion would be declared.

One of the few highlights of the season for the last-place Haag Storks was a triple play that they turned against Neptunus in late August. With runners on first and second via walks, Benjamin Dille hit a hard grounder to third baseman Jurian Hansen, who stepped on the bag and threw to Jason Netten at second. Netten then fired the ball to Joost van den Bergh at first to complete the triple killing. It was the first DML triple play since 2016, when HCAW turned one against Neptunus. It, too, was an around the horn, 5-4-3 triple play. Amazingly, the hitter in that triple play was also Dille.

Outfielder Roger Bernadina joined Amersfoort near the end of the regular season. A veteran of 548 major league games between 2008 and 2014, the 36-year-old Curacao native played seven games with Amersfoort and batted .286 with a home run.

Amersfoort outfielder Taylor Clemensia tied a DML record when he hit three homers in a road game against DSS. His second dinger came in the sixth inning, part of a 10-run rally that gave Amersfoort a 13-3 lead. Going into the bottom of the seventh, DSS was down by 10 runs. The league's mercy rule would be invoked if they failed to score, in which case Clemensia would not get a chance to tie the record. But the home team obliged Clemensia by scoring four times, thus prolonging the game. Clemensia hit his third homer in the top of the ninth.

In early September, Amsterdam righthand-er Rob Cordemans became the first DML pitcher to win 200 career regular-season games. Cordemans, 45, reached two other significant milestones in 2020. He became the first DML hurler to pitch 2,000 innings and he broke the league record for most games pitched (334).

Rob Cordemans

Cordemans and Amsterdam relievers Nick Veltkamp and Matz Schutte shared a no-hitter in the semifinals. It was the team's first no-hitter in the top flight. It was a 10-0 win over HCAW where the mercy rule was invoked after seven innings. Cordemans went five innings while Veltkamp and Schutte each pitched one inning.

DML batting crown-winner Victor Draijer of the Hoofddorp Pioniers became the first DML player to hit .500 since 1984.

STANDINGS

Team	W	L	T	GB
Neptunus	18	2	1	-
Amsterdam Pirates	16	5	0	2.5
Hoofddorp Pioniers	13	7	1	5
HCAW	12	8	1	6
Oosterhout Twins	8	13	0	10.5
Amersfoort	6	14	1	12
DSS	6	15	0	12.5
The Hague Storks	3	18	0	15.5

Holland Series: Canceled with Amsterdam leading Neptunus, 2-0.

INDIVIDUAL BATTING LEADERS

Player, Team	AVG	AB	R	H	2B	3B	HR	RBI	SB
Draijer, Victor, PIO	.500	84	19	42	14	1	1	24	2
Muller, Gregory, NEP	.417	36	20	15	5	1	1	13	3
Richardson, Denzel, AMS	.412	85	23	35	8	0	5	26	4
Kemp, Dwayne, NEP	.404	89	18	36	5	0	4	19	14
Polonius, John, NEP	.367	79	27	29	4	0	3	22	7
Berkenbosch, Kenny, AMS	.365	63	12	23	4	0	1	17	1
Sams, Kalian, AMS	.359	64	20	23	5	0	8	27	6
Collins, Darryl, NEP	.352	54	13	19	4	3	0	12	5
Schoop, Sharlon, AMS	.350	60	19	21	7	1	2	17	4
Silberie, Diamond, TWI	.347	49	9	17	2	0	2	10	1

INDIVIDUAL PITCHING LEADERS

Player, Team	W	L	ERA	IP	H	R	ER	BB	SO
Yntema, Orlando, NEP	6	1	0.86	42	22	4	4	15	41
Graauw, De Gio, HCAW	2	0	1.17	23	17	5	3	7	28
Huijer, Lars, PIO	2	0	1.50	24	14	5	4	10	31
Floranus, Wendell, QUI	0	2	1.52	24	16	13	4	13	39
Groot, De Aaron, NEP	3	1	1.93	23	13	7	5	9	26
Beek, Ter Luuk, HCAW	4	1	2.32	43	38	14	11	18	22
Burgersdijk, Dennis, HCAW	4	2	2.44	48	36	14	13	14	34
Markwell, Diegomar, NEP	3	0	3.00	33	33	12	11	17	12
Sakashita, Sora, TWI	3	2	3.10	41	39	19	14	18	26
Ploeger, Jim, AMS	2	2	3.33	27	29	10	10	8	25

INTERNATIONAL

Steady Matanzas Takes Title

Matanzas was consistent from start to finish, going 26-19 in both the first half and the second half of the 59th regular season en route to winning the Serie Nacional championship. After finishing with the best run differential in Serie Nacional during the regular season, Matanzas quickly bounced Las Tunas in four games in the semifinals before taking down the team with the best regular season record, Camaguey, in six games for the title.

Matanzas did it with a familiar name at shortstop—former Dodgers prospect Barbaro Erisbel Arruebarrena, who led the league with 19 home runs and a .634 slugging average. Arruebarrena had signed a five-year, $25 million contract with the Dodgers in 2014 and played briefly in Los Angeles that year, his only time in the big leagues before being released in 2018 and eventually returning to Cuba.

STANDINGS

Team	W	L	PCT	GB
Camaguey	53	37	.589	-
Matanzas	52	38	.578	1
Las Tunas	52	38	.578	1
Industriales	52	38	.578	1
Santiago de Cuba	47	43	.523	6
Cienfuegos	45	45	.500	8

ELIMINATED IN FIRST HALF

Team	W	L	PCT	GB
Granma	26	19	.578	3
Santi Spiritus	26	19	.578	3
Pinar del Rio	23	21	.523	5.5
Isla de la Juventud	21	23	.478	7.5
Ciego de Avila	19	26	.423	10
Holguin	19	26	.423	10
Villa Clara	17	27	.387	11.5
Mayabeque	16	29	.356	13
Artemisa	15	29	.341	13.5
Guantanamo	10	35	.223	19

Wild Card: Matanzas defeated Santi Spiritus 2-1 and Industriales defeated Granma 2-1 in best-of-three series ensuring the two teams advanced to the second phase of the season.

Playoffs: Semifinals: Camaguey defeated Industriales 3-0 and Matanzas defeated Las Tunas 3-0. Finals: Matanzas defeated Camaguey 4-2 in best-of-seven series.

BATTING LEADERS

Player, Team	AVG	AB	R	H	2B	3B	HR	RBI
Yordanis Alarcon, LTU	.378	341	48	129	18	0	15	83
Jefferson Delgado, MTZ	.360	327	59	118	13	2	9	61
Edilse Silva, SCU	.358	302	52	108	16	0	16	75
Pavel Quesada, CFG	.356	264	51	94	18	1	8	50
Yasiel Santoya, MTZ	.356	315	56	112	30	0	11	57
Alexander Ayala, CMG	.355	228	35	81	12	0	8	45
Cesar Prieto, MTZ	.352	273	50	96	13	5	4	42
Yosvanhi Penalver, IND	.350	323	65	113	14	0	7	42
Frederich Cepeda, IND	.349	232	55	81	8	0	18	59
Yasniel Gonzalez, LTU	.346	280	52	97	17	1	12	54
Raico Santos, SCU	.344	311	51	107	23	0	5	48
Dayan Garcia, IND	.342	321	45	110	22	0	4	50
Alberto Calderon, IND	.341	296	55	101	17	3	3	39
Yorbis Borroto, CMG	.336	220	44	74	13	1	2	29
Yoandry Urgelles, IND	.335	224	39	75	16	1	3	41
Rudens Sanhez, SCU	.328	287	37	94	20	0	12	59
Adriel Labrada, SCU	.322	267	41	86	15	1	8	37
Barbaro Arruebarrena, MTZ	.322	227	47	73	14	0	19	50
Juan Soriano, CFG	.319	320	52	102	18	0	6	65
Yosvani Alarcon, LTU	.317	227	43	70	16	1	6	43
Santiago Torres, CMG	.314	343	66	108	26	2	3	31
Javier Camero, MTZ	.313	290	38	91	18	1	9	50
Yusniel Ibanez, LTU	.311	347	62	108	23	2	15	78
Denis Pena, LTU	.311	238	38	74	15	0	7	37
Eduardo Blanco, MTZ	.305	333	61	102	12	5	7	50
Leonel Segura, CMG	.303	333	37	101	15	0	5	45
Luis Mateo, IND	.302	298	51	90	10	0	4	38
Yoelkis Guibert, CMG	.301	256	51	77	11	6	8	45
Danel Castro, LTU	.300	247	40	74	10	0	11	50
Yuniesky Larduert, LTU	.300	333	55	100	13	4	2	33
Ricardo Ramos, SCU	.297	269	46	80	20	5	6	45
Carlos Benitez, LTU	.295	227	30	67	12	0	4	43
Daniel Perez, CFG	.293	276	34	81	13	2	2	33
Humberto Bravo, CMG	.292	257	37	75	6	3	2	23
Loidel Chapelli, CMG	.288	205	37	59	12	2	0	32
Andres Quiala, LTU	.286	329	55	94	23	0	2	42
Dainier Galvez, MTZ	.282	227	40	64	7	0	7	38
Jorge Pena, CMG	.281	295	39	83	16	0	15	48
Richel Lopez, CFG	.271	277	64	75	13	1	7	48
Jorge Aloma, IND	.262	248	41	65	13	2	5	37

PITCHING LEADERS

Player, Team	W	L	ERA	G	IP	H	HR	BB	SO
Carlos Juan Viera, LTU	11	5	2.37	21	129	110	4	36	92
Frank Madan, CMG	8	2	2.65	22	92	82	6	19	55
Yamichel Perez, MTZ	13	3	2.74	21	121	118	8	29	73
Frank Medina, CMG	10	8	2.93	21	132	130	3	44	62
Vladimir Banos, IND	9	4	3.09	16	93	88	3	26	46
Bryan Chi, IND	7	5	3.27	20	110	101	5	55	82
Carlos Santiesteban, SCU	9	8	3.59	24	113	120	8	30	51
Yordi Rodriguez, CMG	7	6	3.61	18	100	91	3	54	93
Carlos Font, SCU	9	4	3.83	25	110	110	9	44	70
Lazaro Blanco, CMG	5	7	3.9	16	97	101	3	25	73
Yosimar Cousin, CMG	6	7	4.02	17	94	98	11	37	71
Alberto Bicet, SCU	8	5	4.04	27	111	147	8	36	42
Cesar Garcia, CFG	8	4	4.05	23	104	117	9	43	49
Yander Guevara, LTU	7	6	4.44	17	103	123	8	35	44
Misael Villa, IND	4	11	4.51	22	122	149	4	35	48
Yadian Martinez, CMG	5	8	4.53	25	115	143	8	54	71
Danny Betancourt, SCU	7	8	4.69	21	96	104	13	41	46
Wilson Paredes, LTU	5	6	4.72	27	109	116	13	55	56
Yoalkis Cruz, LTU	8	9	5.09	29	124	139	14	32	64
Carlos Ramirez, CFG	3	7	5.45	23	99	112	6	54	57

The Toros del Este won their first Caribbean Series title and delivered the 20th title for the Dominican Republic.

D.R. Adds Another Caribbean Series Championship

BY BEN BADLER

The Toros del Este of the Dominican Republic won their first Caribbean Series title, beating the Cardenales de Lara 9-3 in the final game. It was the 20th title for the Dominican Republic, the most championships for any country, and the first title for the Dominican Republic since 2012.

The Toros reached the championship after a narrow comeback victory over Puerto Rico in the semifinal game. With the Toros trailing Santurce 3-2 heading to the bottom of the eighth inning, Jordany Valdespin singled, then went to third on a Peter O'Brien double. Valdespin scored the tying run on a wild pitch, then O'Brien came home with the go-ahead run on an Abraham Almonte sacrifice fly, with the Toros holding on in the ninth for a 4-3 victory.

For the first time in history, Colombia participated in the Caribbean Series, replacing the Cuban team that could not travel to San Juan, Puerto Rico due to visa issues.

AUSTRALIAN BASEBALL LEAGUE

Southwest	W	L	PCT	GB
Adelaide Giants	24	12	.667	—
Melbourne Aces	23	17	.575	3
Perth Heat	23	17	.575	3
Geelong-Korea	11	29	.275	15

Northeast	W	L	PCT	GB
Auckland Tuatara	21	18	.538	—
Canberra Cavalry	17	17	.500	1.5
Brisbane Bandits	18	20	.474	2.5
Sydney Blue Sox	16	23	.410	5

Playoffs—Semifinals: Adelaide defeated Canberra 2-1 and Melbourne defeated Auckland 2-0 in best-of-three series. **Finals:** Melbourne defeated Adelaide 2-0 in a best-of-three series.

INDIVIDUAL BATTING LEADERS

Player, Team	AVG	AB	R	H	2B	3B	HR	RBI	BB	SO	SB
Colin Willis, MEL	.427	103	32	44	10	0	3	28	22	16	7
Yuma Mune, MEL	.387	93	19	36	3	1	3	12	8	8	6
Aaron Whitefield, ADE	.376	125	28	47	9	2	2	24	17	23	23
Zach Wilson, CAN	.368	136	25	50	11	0	7	26	9	18	0
Delmon Young, MEL	.345	148	28	51	8	0	13	42	10	29	0
Jared Walker, AUC	.344	122	31	42	11	0	8	33	20	25	9
D.J. Burt, MEL	.338	65	12	22	2	1	0	4	6	8	3
Robbie Glendinning, PER	.335	155	30	52	12	0	7	31	18	29	3
Chang-ki Hong, GEE	.333	123	29	41	11	0	3	21	27	38	0
Josh Morgan, AUC	.330	103	24	34	6	0	4	20	15	12	2

INDIVIDUAL PITCHING LEADERS

Player, Team	W	L	ERA	G	SV	IP	H	BB	SO	AVG
Jon Kennedy, MEL	1	1	0.35	17	1	26	20	11	18	.217
Kih-Yun Yang, GEE	1	0	0.86	15	1	21	19	5	18	.241
Frank Gailey, CAN	0	0	0.90	2	0	10	8	6	8	.211
Darin Downs, MEL	3	0	0.95	4	0	19	10	5	13	.159
Elliot Johnstone, AUC	4	1	1.09	12	1	25	14	10	28	.167
Ryan Chaffee, ADE	2	0	1.25	13	6	22	16	6	27	.198
Cody Mincey, MEL	0	0	1.29	6	4	7	4	1	7	.160
Daina Ono, ADE	1	1	1.42	9	3	13	10	8	19	.213

DOMINICAN LEAGUE

Team	W	L	PCT	GB
Toros del Este	34	16	.680	—
Tigres del Licey	27	23	.540	7
Aguilas Cibaenas	24	26	.480	10
Leones del Escogido	24	26	.480	10
Gigantes del Cibao	21	29	.420	13
Estrellas Orientales	20	30	.400	14

Playoffs—Round Robin: Toros del Este, Tigres del Licey, Aguilas Cibaenas and Leones del Escogido advance. **Finals:** Toros del Este defeated Tigres del Licey 5-3 in best-of-nine series.

INTERNATIONAL

INDIVIDUAL BATTING LEADERS

Player, Team	AVG	AB	R	H	2B	3B	HR	RBI	BB	SO	SB
Moises Sierra, GIG	.348	135	18	47	7	1	2	21	21	32	2
Jordany Valdespin, TOR	.340	144	22	49	6	0	5	22	20	18	5
John Nogowski, AGU	.316	114	13	36	6	0	4	22	17	12	1
Eric Filia, LIC	.301	156	24	47	6	0	1	9	23	16	1
Socrates Brito, LIC	.296	186	30	55	10	4	2	17	24	42	4
Richard Urena, GIG	.292	137	17	40	4	0	2	19	15	34	2
Dairon Blanco, TOR	.283	145	21	41	3	3	0	11	11	48	8
Edmundo Sosa, AGU	.274	175	27	48	7	0	3	14	7	41	3
Yamaico Navarro, TOR	.273	128	19	35	5	0	5	18	21	26	4
Erick Mejia, LIC	.273	132	23	36	5	0	1	5	20	22	8

INDIVIDUAL PITCHING LEADERS

Player, Team	W	L	ERA	G	SV	IP	H	BB	SO	AVG
Cesar Valdez, LIC	4	1	1.11	7	0	41	31	4	40	.204
Carlos Hernandez, TOR	6	1	1.94	9	0	46	39	11	18	.231
Jorge Martinez, TOR	4	2	1.96	10	0	46	46	3	32	.256
Esmil Rogers, LIC	3	2	2.34	11	0	50	38	13	42	.210
Raul Valdes, TOR	5	2	2.51	10	0	61	46	22	30	.210
Forrest Snow, EST	2	1	2.76	11	0	46	40	12	37	.238
David Kubiak, ESC	4	3	2.81	12	0	51	39	20	52	.207
Jose De Paula, LIC	3	3	3.26	11	0	50	53	12	38	.273

MEXICAN PACIFIC LEAGUE

Team	W	L	PCT	GB
Yaquis de Obregon	43	22	.662	—
Charros de Jalisco	38	26	.594	4.5
Naranjeros de Hermosillo	38	27	.585	5
Tomateros de Culiacan	36	29	.554	7
Aguilas de Mexicali	32	32	.500	10.5
Caneros de los Mochis	32	36	.471	12.5
Venados de Mazatlan	31	36	.463	13
Algodoneros de Guasave	26	38	.406	16.5
Mayos de Navojoa	25	40	.385	18
Sultanes de Monterrey	25	40	.385	18

Playoffs—Semifinals: Tomateros de Culiacan defeated Caneros de los Mochis 4-3 and Venados de Mazatlan defeated Yaquis de Obregon 4-3 in best-of-seven series. **Finals:** Tomateros de Culiacan defeated Venados de Mazatlan 4-3 in a best-of-seven series.

INDIVIDUAL BATTING LEADERS

Player, Team	AVG	AB	R	H	2B	3B	HR	RBI	BB	SO	SB
Francisco Peguero, HER	.352	216	27	76	15	2	6	44	9	43	0
Jasson Atondo, MAZ	.351	231	39	81	11	0	0	21	11	21	1
Jesus Valdez, OBR	.325	240	30	78	13	1	6	43	33	41	2
Victor Mendoza, OBR	.323	186	29	60	15	1	6	30	29	29	0
I. Rodriguez Salazar, MOC	.318	245	41	78	11	2	1	18	37	32	9
Ramon Urias, MOC	.318	173	31	55	7	0	10	34	34	35	5
Dariel Alvarez, JAL	.315	219	33	69	12	1	14	38	18	22	0
Manny Rodriguez, JAL	.313	256	41	80	9	0	13	52	22	37	2
Leandro Castro, MOC	.303	241	49	73	15	2	13	45	36	42	12
Alonzo Harris, JAL	.302	248	51	75	10	1	7	22	32	55	28

INDIVIDUAL PITCHING LEADERS

Player, Team	W	L	ERA	G	SV	IP	H	BB	SO	AVG
Javier Solano, MXC	3	5	2.23	16	2	77	76	15	51	.264
Yoanys Quiala, MOC	9	2	2.57	14	0	88	70	16	71	.215
Joe Van Meter, MXC	3	4	2.75	12	0	75	62	15	62	.224
Mitch Atkins, MTY	5	6	2.92	13	0	77	72	13	44	.249
Juan Pablo Oramas, MAZ	5	3	3.09	13	0	70	66	25	76	.245
Raul Carrillo, NAV	4	3	3.47	13	0	70	77	19	46	.282
Andre Rienzo, OBR	6	2	3.62	14	0	75	74	23	71	.261
Dustin Crenshaw, OBR	3	4	3.71	13	0	78	86	17	54	.285

PUERTO RICAN LEAGUE

Team	W	L	PCT	GB
Cangrejeros de Santurce	21	9	.700	—
Gigantes de Carolina	17	15	.531	5
Indios de Mayaguez	15	16	.484	6.5

Antenienses de Manati	13	18	.419	8.5
Criollos de Caguas	11	19	.367	10

Playoffs—Semifinals: Indios de Mayaguez defeated Gigantes de Carolina 4-2 in a best-of-seven series. **Finals:** Cangrejeros de Santurce defeated Indios de Mayaguez 4-1 in a best-of-seven series.

INDIVIDUAL BATTING LEADERS

Player, Team	AVG	AB	R	H	2B	3B	HR	RBI	BB	SO	SB
Vimael Machin, SAN	.333	96	9	32	7	3	0	10	5	16	0
Ivan De Jesus Jr., SAN	.329	85	13	28	7	2	1	17	22	8	0
Jose Sermo, MAN	.317	101	15	32	8	0	5	18	13	24	1
Henry Ramos, MAY	.314	121	28	38	9	1	3	16	19	13	4
Emmanuel Rivera, MAY	.309	123	14	38	3	2	3	14	6	16	2
Juan Centeno, MAN	.306	85	9	26	1	0	2	9	6	7	1
Kennys Vargas, MAY	.272	103	14	28	9	0	5	25	27	33	0
Mario Feliciano, MAN	.269	93	2	25	6	0	0	4	5	20	0
Anthony Garcia, CAR	.263	76	10	20	1	0	3	10	26	17	1
Chris Sharpe, MAN	.261	69	8	18	1	3	1	9	15	21	3

INDIVIDUAL PITCHING LEADERS

Player, Team	W	L	ERA	G	SV	IP	H	BB	SO	AVG
Hector Santiago, CAR	4	2	0.73	8	0	49	30	9	40	.176
Eric Stout, MAY	1	1	1.62	9	0	33	14	15	42	.128
Miguel A. Martinez, CAR	1	4	1.69	7	0	37	29	4	20	.218
Giovanni Soto, SAN	4	1	1.77	8	0	41	36	13	30	.243
Hosei Takata, MAY	1	2	2.00	8	0	36	25	16	20	.200
Yuri Furukawa, MAY	2	2	2.04	7	0	35	28	9	29	.217
Hector Hernandez, MAN	1	1	2.45	8	0	37	34	15	27	.245
Carlos Sierra, MAN	0	3	2.45	8	0	33	23	12	26	.200

VENEZUELAN LEAGUE

Team	W	L	PCT	GB
Tiburones de La Guaira	25	18	.581	—
Aguilas del Zulia	24	18	.571	0.5
Cardenales de Lara	24	18	.571	0.5
Caribes de Anzoategui	22	20	.524	2.5
Navegantes del Magallanes	21	21	.500	3.5
Leones del Caracas	21	22	.488	4
Tigres de Aragua	17	25	.405	7.5
Bravos de Margarita	15	27	.357	9.5

Playoffs—Semifinals: Cardenales de Lara defeated Aguilas de Zulia 4-1 and Caribes de Anzoategui defeated Tiburones de la Guaira 4-0 in best-of-seven series. **Finals:** Cardenales de Lara defeated Caribes de Anzoategui 4-3 in a best-of-seven series.

INDIVIDUAL BATTING LEADERS

Player, Team	AVG	AB	R	H	2B	3B	HR	RBI	BB	SO	SB
Jay Austin, ZUL	.392	102	19	40	4	3	1	8	9	11	9
Yosmany Guerra, ZUL	.388	139	26	54	6	2	0	31	30	11	0
Yojhan Quevedo, LAR	.372	129	12	48	5	0	0	22	3	18	0
Danry Vasquez, LAG	.368	136	27	50	5	1	5	24	15	9	7
Olmo Rosario, ZUL	.355	155	40	55	12	2	2	33	21	15	1
Cesar Valera, ORI	.351	148	34	52	6	3	2	22	13	20	3
Leonardo Reginatto, LAG	.338	157	25	53	13	2	1	22	16	24	5
Angel Reyes, ZUL	.333	126	27	42	11	2	3	28	12	31	3
Osman Marval, LAR	.329	140	22	46	9	3	2	31	16	23	0
Alberto Gonzalez, LAG	.327	159	26	52	9	1	0	23	17	8	2

INDIVIDUAL PITCHING LEADERS

Player, Team	W	L	ERA	G	SV	IP	H	BB	SO	AVG
Henry Centeno, LAR	4	0	1.34	9	0	47	37	20	30	.220
Angelo Palumbo, LAR	2	1	1.87	8	0	34	30	13	21	.240
Yohan Pino, MAG	5	0	2.11	11	0	55	42	8	40	.203
Guillermo Moscoso, LAG	2	1	2.13	8	0	38	34	10	28	.238
Raul Rivero, LAR	3	2	2.37	7	0	38	39	7	26	.271
Tiago Da Silva, ARA	4	1	2.55	16	4	35	32	5	20	.244
Francisley Bueno, ORI	4	1	2.70	8	0	37	31	6	21	.233
Nestor Molina, LAR	6	0	3.09	11	0	58	53	14	39	.234

COLLEGE

The cancellation of the College World Series left TD Ameritrade Park empty in June.

COVID Abruptly Halts Season, Cancels CWS

BY TEDDY CAHILL

On a surreal day in a surreal week in what turned into a surreal year, college baseball on March 12 saw its season come to a sudden, wrenching end. Amid the coronavirus outbreak, the NCAA cancelled all winter and spring championships, including the College World Series.

The decision to cancel the CWS was unprecedented. The NCAA delivered the news with a brief statement that afternoon.

"Today, NCAA President Mark Emmert and the Board of Governors canceled the Division I men's and women's 2020 basketball tournaments, as well as all remaining winter and spring NCAA championships. This decision is based on the evolving COVID-19 public health threat, our ability to ensure the events do not contribute to spread of the pandemic, and the impracticality of hosting such events at any time during this academic year given ongoing decisions by other entities."

The cancellation of the CWS came after a day of conferences announcing they had suspended the spring sports seasons. A few others, including the Big Ten, had already canceled their spring seasons before the NCAA announcement, following the Ivy League's decision on March 11 to do so.

COACHING CAROUSEL

School	In (Previous Job)	Out (Reason/New Job)
Alabama A&M	Elliot Jones (Grambling State assistant)	Manny Lora (fired)
Alabama-Birmingham	Perry Roth (interim, UAB assistant)	Brian Shoop (retired)
Bowling Green State	Kyle Hallock (Bowling Green State assistant)	Danny Schmitz (retired)
Charleston Southern	Marc MacMillian (Mississippi assistant)	Adam Ward (resigned)
Eastern Kentucky	Chris Prothro (South Alabama assistant)	Edwin Thompson (Georgetown head coach)
Georgetown	Edwin Thompson (Eastern Kentucky head coach)	Pete Wilk (resigned)
Holy Cross	Ed Kahovec (Holy Cross assistant)	Greg DiCenzo (Indians MiLB manager)
Lafayette	Tim Reilly (Lafayette assistant)	Joe Kinney (retired)
North Carolina	Scott Forbes (North Carolina assistant)	Mike Fox (retired)
Oakland	Jordon Banfield (Akron assistant)	Colin Kaline (resigned)
Pacific	Chris Rodriguez (Pacific assistant)	Ryan Garko (Angels coaching staff)
St. John's	Mike Hampton (St. John's assistant)	Ed Blankmeyer (Mets MiLB manager)
UC Riverside	Justin Johnson (interim, UCR assistant)	Troy Percival (resigned)

Because of the bureaucracy of college sports, the NCAA could only cancel its championships and not the regular season. As a result, some conferences briefly held out hope for their seasons to resume in a couple weeks, but that optimisim quickly withered within a few days and the sad reality of the season's end set in around the country.

The day's fast-moving news began around noon, as conference basketball tournaments were scheduled to tip off around the country. Those were cancelled en masse, hinting at what was to come. Soon after, spring sports were suspended by one conference after another.

At Louisiana State, which was scheduled to open SEC play at Mississippi, the news came an hour before the team was slated to leave. Players pulled their bags off the bus and went into a team meeting where they learned the news. Assistant coaches who were out recruiting were pulled off the road. And around baseball, everyone wondered what came next.

Like everything else with COVID-19, the situation in college sports escalated quickly throughout the week. At the start of the week, the NCAA was consulting with its panel of doctors about the outbreak but felt that it could go ahead with everything as scheduled. But that would rapidly change.

On March 10, universities began moving to online classes and extending spring breaks to prepare for the change. Central Connecticut State canceled its weekend series at Creighton because it would not be allowed to travel out of state. The talk soon turned to playing games with no fans in attendance.

By the following day, the concern was growing and playing in front of empty stadiums became the standard response around the country. The Ivy League took the additional step of cancelling its season.

That night, things rapidly changed again. The NBA had to postpone a game between the Utah Jazz and Oklahoma City Thunder when Rudy Gobert tested positive for COVID-19. The league soon after announced it would go on hiatus. Meanwhile, at the Big Ten men's basketball tournament in Indianapolis, Nebraska coach Fred Hoiberg visibly appeared to be sick during a game and was taken to the hospital at halftime. While he was later diagnosed with influenza A, it was a scary scene that played out live on television.

With the NBA shut down, it seemed inevitable that colleges would follow. That came to pass March 12, with conference after conference announcing suspensions. The Big Ten, Metro Atlantic Athletic Conference and Patriot League joined the Ivy League in cancelling the entire season.

The announcements left many unanswered questions that would be grappled with in ensuing weeks. How the cancelation would affect players' eligibility and baseball's roster construction rules were at the front of many minds around the country. What would become of the draft, of recruiting classes, of everything that the baseball season involves became an open question, albeit one that took on a secondary concern amid the immediate health concerns facing so many.

One thing was clear, however. The season was over and the Road to Omaha was closed for 2020.

NCAA Grants Eligibility Relief

The NCAA's Division I Council on March 30 approved a proposal to give eligibility relief to all spring sports athletes, effectively granting athletes an extra year of college eligibility to account for the cancellation of the 2020 season due to the pandemic.

With the vote, Division I joined all other collegiate sports governing bodies in granting extra eligibility due to the loss of the 2020 season. Division II, Division III, NAIA and the National Junior College Athletics Association previously ruled in favor of eligibility relief.

For players who already had eligibility remaining after the 2020 season, their aid will be required to remain at the same level. For 2020 seniors, the NCAA will leave it up to individual schools on a case-by-case basis to determine how much aid to offer athletes. They will be able to offer less aid than they offered a player in 2020 or match it, but not exceed it. That could mean that within one program that a player gets offered a spot back, but none of his scholarship money, while another player is brought back at 100 percent of what he received in 2020.

The Council also adjusted rules to ease baseball's restrictions of a maximum 35 players on the roster and a maximum of 27 players on scholarship. In effect, returning seniors will not count toward either cap.

The Council's decision affirmed the position of the Division I Council Coordination Committee. On March 13, the day after the NCAA cancelled the College World Series along with every other winter and spring championship, the coordination committee came out in support in principle of eligibility relief. A week later, it doubled down in a

statement. The Student-Athlete Advisory Council also came out publicly in favor of eligibility relief on the eve of the Council's vote, and SEC commissioner Greg Sankey publicly backed it as well.

The final decision lay with the Council, which is primarily composed of athletic directors, representing every conference. In an uncertain financial time, there was a lot of apprehension before the vote that they would not see it the same way.

USA Today estimated that granting seniors an extra year of eligibility would cost Power Five Conference schools anywhere from $500,000 to $900,000. Smaller schools might still incur costs of up to $400,000. Costs to grant every spring athlete an extra year of eligibility will rise even higher.

That's not insignificant money in the best of times financially and these are not the best financial times. The stock market's downturn hurt schools' endowments and boosters' ability to donate as much as they have in recent years. Another pinch on budgets came when the NCAA lowered its annual payout to schools from the $600 million it had budgeted to $225 million following the cancellation of its winter and spring championships. With

COLLEGE WORLD SERIES CHAMPIONS

Year	Champion	Coach	Record	Runner-Up	Most Outstanding Player
1948	Southern California	Sam Barry	40-12	Yale	None selected
1949	Texas*	Bibb Falk	23-7	Wake Forest	Charles Teague, 2B, Wake Forest
1950	Texas	Bibb Falk	27-6	Washington State	Ray VanCleef, OF, Rutgers
1951	Oklahoma*	Jack Baer	19-9	Tennessee	Sid Hatfield, 1B/P, Tennessee
1952	Holy Cross	Jack Barry	21-3	Missouri	Jim O'Neill, P, Holy Cross
1953	Michigan	Ray Fisher	21-9	Texas	J.L. Smith, P, Texas
1954	Missouri	Hi Simmons	22-4	Rollins	Tom Yewcic, C, Michigan State
1955	Wake Forest	Taylor Sanford	29-7	Western Michigan	Tom Borland, P, Oklahoma State
1956	Minnesota	Dick Siebert	33-9	Arizona	Jerry Thomas, P, Minnesota
1957	California*	George Wolfman	35-10	Penn State	Cal Emery, 1B/P, Penn State
1958	Southern California	Rod Dedeaux	35-7	Missouri	Bill Thom, P, Southern California
1959	Oklahoma State	Toby Greene	27-5	Arizona	Jim Dobson, 3B, Oklahoma State
1960	Minnesota	Dick Siebert	34-7	Southern California	John Erickson, 2B, Minnesota
1961	Southern California*	Rod Dedeaux	43-9	Oklahoma State	Littleton Fowler, P, Oklahoma State
1962	Michigan	Don Lund	31-13	Santa Clara	Bob Garibaldi, P, Santa Clara
1963	Southern California	Rod Dedeaux	37-16	Arizona	Bud Hollowell, C, Southern California
1964	Minnesota	Dick Siebert	31-12	Missouri	Joe Ferris, P, Maine
1965	Arizona State	Bobby Winkles	54-8	Ohio State	Sal Bando, 3B, Arizona State
1966	Ohio State	Marty Karow	27-6	Oklahoma State	Steve Arlin, P, Ohio State
1967	Arizona State	Bobby Winkles	53-12	Houston	Ron Davini, C, Arizona State
1968	Southern California*	Rod Dedeaux	45-14	Southern Illinois	Bill Seinsoth, 1B, Southern California
1969	Arizona State	Bobby Winkles	56-11	Tulsa	John Dolinsek, OF, Arizona State
1970	Southern California	Rod Dedeaux	51-13	Florida State	Gene Ammann, P, Florida State
1971	Southern California	Rod Dedeaux	53-13	Southern Illinois	Jerry Tabb, 1B, Tulsa
1972	Southern California	Rod Dedeaux	50-13	Arizona State	Russ McQueen, P, Southern California
1973	Southern California*	Rod Dedeaux	51-11	Arizona State	Dave Winfield, OF/P, Minnesota
1974	Southern California	Rod Dedeaux	50-20	Miami	George Milke, P, Southern California
1975	Texas	Cliff Gustafson	56-6	South Carolina	Mickey Reichenbach, 1B, Texas
1976	Arizona	Jerry Kindall	56-17	Eastern Michigan	Steve Powers, DH/P, Arizona
1977	Arizona State	Jim Brock	57-12	South Carolina	Bob Horner, 3B, Arizona State
1978	Southern California*	Rod Dedeaux	54-9	Arizona State	Rod Boxberger, P, Southern California
1979	Cal State Fullerton	Augie Garrido	60-14	Arkansas	Tony Hudson, P, Cal State Fullerton
1980	Arizona	Jerry Kindall	45-21	Hawaii	Terry Francona, OF, Arizona
1981	Arizona State	Jim Brock	55-13	Oklahoma State	Stan Holmes, OF, Arizona State
1982	Miami	Ron Fraser	57-18	Wichita State	Dan Smith, P, Miami
1983	Texas	Cliff Gustafson	66-14	Alabama	Calvin Schiraldi, P, Texas

the pandemic continuing into the fall, schools also lost revenue due to reduced seating capacity at fall and winter sports events.

In the end, however, the Council found a way to satisfy both the financial crunch athletic departments will be operating under in the immediate future and still provide student-athletes with a do-over for a lost 2020 season. Athletes, after all, due to an unprecedented action had seen their season canceled less than a third of the way into the schedule. In baseball, if a player had gone down with a season-ending injury on March 12, the day the College World Series was canceled, he would have been eligible for a medical redshirt. So, in any other year, a player who had his season end at the same time would have gotten an extra year of eligibility.

Around the country, conferences and athletic departments had to determine their path forward under the NCAA's new guidelines. Coaches and players alike had some difficult decisions to make.

Even without the draft's complications, this year's seniors were already facing a difficult decision. Many already made plans for graduate school or lined up a job for after graduation. They had to decide whether playing another season of college baseball—and the additional cost that inherently comes with that in a partial scholarship sport—is worth it.

Because of those decisions, many seniors did not return for another season. But between the returning seniors and the shortened draft, which led to both fewer high school seniors and college juniors being selected, college baseball still faces a roster crunch. The restrictions on the maximum number of players on a roster were relaxed, enabling teams to bring in larger rosters than normal.

The difference between schools' ability to bring seniors back for an extra year also led to a robust transfer market over the summer, especially for players who had already graduated and therefore automatically are granted immediate eligibility after transferring.

While the changes left some players scrambling and will affect college baseball for years to come as teams slowly work back to their normal roster constructions, they also represented a clear victory for spring athletes and could produce a college baseball season for the ages in 2021.

Year	Champion	Coach	Record	Runner-Up	MOST OUTSTANDING PLAYER
1984	Cal State Fullerton	Augie Garrido	66-20	Texas	John Fishel, OF, Cal State Fullerton
1985	Miami*	Ron Fraser	64-16	Texas	Greg Ellena, DH, Miami
1986	Arizona	Jerry Kindall	49-19	Florida State	Mike Senne, OF, Arizona
1987	Stanford	Mark Marquess	53-17	Oklahoma State	Paul Carey, OF, Stanford
1988	Stanford	Mark Marquess	46-23	Arizona State	Lee Plemel, P, Stanford
1989	Wichita State	Gene Stephenson	68-16	Texas	Greg Brummett, P, Wichita State
1990	Georgia	Steve Webber	52-19	Oklahoma State	Mike Rebhan, P, Georgia
1991	Louisiana State*	Skip Bertman	55-18	Wichita State	Gary Hymel, C, Louisiana State
1992	Pepperdine*	Andy Lopez	48-11	Cal State Fullerton	Phil Nevin, 3B, Cal State Fullerton
1993	Louisiana State	Skip Bertman	53-17	Wichita State	Todd Walker, 2B, Louisiana State
1994	Oklahoma*	Larry Cochell	50-17	Georgia Tech	Chip Glass, OF, Oklahoma
1995	Cal State Fullerton*	Augie Garrido	57-9	Southern California	Mark Kotsay, OF/P, Cal State Fullerton
1996	Louisiana State*	Skip Bertman	52-15	Miami	Pat Burrell, 3B, Miami
1997	Louisiana State*	Skip Bertman	57-13	Alabama	Brandon Larson, SS, Louisiana State
1998	Southern California	Mike Gillespie	49-17	Arizona State	Wes Rachels, 2B, Southern California
1999	Miami*	Jim Morris	50-13	Florida State	Marshall McDougall, 2B, Florida State
2000	Louisiana State*	Skip Bertman	52-17	Stanford	Trey Hodges, P, Louisiana State
2001	Miami*	Jim Morris	53-12	Stanford	Charlton Jimerson, OF, Miami
2002	Texas*	Augie Garrido	57-15	South Carolina	Huston Street, P, Texas
2003	Rice	Wayne Graham	58-12	Stanford	John Hudgins, P, Stanford
2004	Cal State Fullerton	George Horton	47-22	Texas	Jason Windsor, P, Cal State Fullerton
2005	Texas*	Augie Garrido	56-16	Florida	David Maroul, 3B, Texas
2006	Oregon State	Pat Casey	50-16	North Carolina	Jonah Nickerson, P, Oregon State
2007	Oregon State*	Pat Casey	49-18	North Carolina	Jorge Reyes, P, Oregon State
2008	Fresno State	Mike Batesole	47-31	Georgia	Tommy Mendonca, 3B, Fresno State
2009	Louisiana State	Paul Mainieri	56-17	Texas	Jared Mitchell, OF, Louisiana State
2010	South Carolina	Ray Tanner	54-16	UCLA	Jackie Bradley Jr., OF, South Carolina
2011	South Carolina*	Ray Tanner	55-14	Florida	Scott Wingo, 2B, South Carolina
2012	Arizona*	Andy Lopez	48-17	South Carolina	Robert Refsnyder, OF, Arizona
2013	UCLA*	John Savage	49-17	Mississippi State	Adam Plutko, P, UCLA
2014	Vanderbilt	Tim Corbin	51-21	Virginia	Dansby Swanson, 2B, Vanderbilt
2015	Virginia	Brian O'Connor	44-24	Vanderbilt	Josh Sborz, P, Virginia
2016	Coastal Carolina	Gary Gilmore	55-18	Arizona	Andrew Beckwith, P, Coastal Carolina
2017	Florida	Kevin O'Sullivan	52-19	Louisiana State	Alex Faedo, P, Florida
2018	Oregon State	Pat Casey	55-12-1	Arkansas	Adley Rutschman, C, Oregon State
2019	Vanderbilt	Tim Corbin	59-12	Michigan	Kumar Rocker, RHP, Vanderbilt

Four Schools Eliminate Baseball Programs

The financial crunch that followed in the wake of the pandemic led four colleges to eliminate their baseball programs. Boise State, Chicago State and Furman were all immediately cut over the summer, while La Salle announced in September that the 2021 season would be the last for its baseball program.

In addition, Bowling Green State cut its program before reversing course two weeks later after an alumni group raised enough money to save the team. UC Riverside, meanwhile, was seriously mulling eliminating its entire athletic department due to its poor finances.

While other sports—swimming and tennis especially—were hit harder over the summer by cuts, losing four programs made for an especially difficult offseason for baseball.

In the case of Chicago State and La Salle, economics were a factor, but in both cases the athletic departments were also making a move to be more competitive as a whole. At Chicago State, baseball was replaced by men's soccer, which the university says will help cut costs and be a better fit. At La Salle, baseball was one of seven sports the university eliminated. It is cutting back from an atheltic department that sponsors 25 sports to 18, the average number for a Division I school.

Boise State was the most shocking of the cuts. The decision came three years after the school moved to restart its long-dormant baseball program and less than five months after the Broncos made their official return to the diamond.

In 2017, Boise State announced it would restart its baseball program, which had been eliminated in 1980. It cut wrestling at the same time, partially to free up some budget space and in part because the Mountain West Conference sponsors baseball but not wrestling.

The Broncos seemed determined to make the venture a success and hired Gary Van Tol, who spent his whole career playing and coaching in the Northwest, as their head coach. They found quick success, winning three series this spring and were 9-5 when the season was halted.

Furman was historically the most successful of the programs cut. The Paladins produced nine big leaguers, won the Southern Conference regular-season title four times and advanced to the NCAA Tournament five times, most recently in 2005.

BGSU had the strangest offseason of any program in the nation. It was the first program to be shuttered (May 15), when athletic director Bob Moosbrugger, who played baseball at the school and serves on the

RPI RANKINGS

The Ratings Percentage Index is an important tool used by the NCAA in selecting at-large teams for the 64-team Division I tournament. These were the top 100 finishers for 2020. A team's rank in the final Baseball America Top 25 is indicated in parentheses.

Rank School	Record	Rank School	Record
1. UCLA (4)	13-2	51. Col. of Charleston	12-2
2. Florida (1)	16-1	52. Oregon St.	5-9
3. Alabama	16-1	53. Utah	6-7
4. Mississippi (8)	16-1	54. Northwestern St.	12-4
5. East Carolina (24)	13-4	55. Georgia Tech	11-5
6. Oklahoma (9)	14-4	56. East Tennessee St.	12-3
7. Miami (5)	12-4	57. Virginia Tech	11-5
8. Clemson (22)	14-3	58. Vanderbilt (11)	13-5
9. Oklahoma St.	13-5	59. Pennsylvania	3-5
10. Cal St. Northridge	10-5	60. Eastern Illinois	8-6
11. Northeastern	10-5	61. Virginia (17)	14-4
12. N.C. St. (18)	14-3	62. Appalachian St.	10-6
13. Texas A&M	15-3	63. Western Michigan	9-6
14. Texas-Arlington	12-4	64. Michigan (25)	8-7
15. Texas Christian	11-4	65. New Mexico	14-4
16. Wichita St.	13-2	66. Illinois	8-5
17. Wright St.	6-9	67. Louisiana Tech	11-6
18. Florida St. (19)	12-5	68. North Carolina	12-7
19. West Virginia	11-5	69. Louisiana-Monroe	12-5
20. UC Santa Barbara	13-2	70. Northwestern	6-7
21. Georgia (3)	14-4	71. Rhode Island	8-5
22. Central Florida (15)	15-3	72. UNC Greensboro	12-4
23. Xavier	5-10	73. Connecticut	8-5
24. San Diego	12-4	74. UNC Wilmington	11-5
25. Illinois State	7-9	75. Long Beach St. (12)	10-5
26. Dallas Baptist (21)	12-4	76. Abilene Christian	7-8
27. Tulane	15-2	77. New Mexico St.	12-4
28. Kent State	7-7	78. Duke (10)	12-4
29. Georgia Southern	11-5	79. Maryland	10-5
30. Florida Atlantic	10-6	80. New Orleans	10-6
31. Notre Dame	11-2	81. Belmont	14-3
32. Pepperdine (16)	12-3	82. Hawaii	9-6
33. Coastal Carolina	11-5	83. Lipscomb	11-5
34. Texas	14-3	84. Brigham Young	7-9
35. Louisville (6)	13-4	85. UC Riverside	9-7
36. Southern Miss.	12-4	86. Incarnate Word	9-7
37. Louisiana St. (20)	12-5	87. Missouri	11-5
38. Iowa	9-5	88. Kentucky	11-6
39. Indiana	9-6	89. Villanova	9-5
40. Mercer	13-3	90. Liberty	10-7
41. Santa Clara	12-5	91. Grand Canyon	9-9
42. Arizona St. (7)	13-4	92. Youngstown St.	7-7
43. San Diego St.	10-6	93. Tennessee (23)	15-2
44. Texas Tech (2)	16-3	94. Central Michigan	11-6
45. Arizona	10-5	95. UC Irvine	8-7
46. Southern California	10-5	96. Western Kentucky	10-6
47. Arkansas (14)	11-5	97. Hartford	6-6
48. Middle Tennessee St.	7-10	98. Samford	13-2
49. Southern Illinois	12-6	99. Wofford	14-3
50. Mississippi St. (13)	12-4	100. Indiana St.	8-6

NCAA's Division I Baseball Committee, made the difficult decision. Players began to plan to move and some went through the transfer process.

But, on June 2, after a fundraising campaign by the program's alumni, BGSU announced it was reinstating baseball. Donors committed $1.5 million over the next three years and the university committed to working with the group to find a long-term funding solution.

COLLEGE ALL-AMERICA TEAM

FIRST TEAM

Pos. Name	Year	AVG	OBP	SLG	AB	HR	RBI
C Patrick Bailey, North Carolina State	Jr.	.288	.390	.513	236	10	46
1B Spencer Torkelson, Arizona State	Jr.	.351	.446	.707	242	23	66
2B Nick Gonzales, New Mexico State	Jr.	.432	.532	.773	220	16	80
3B Austin Martin, Vanderbilt	Jr.	.392	.486	.604	268	10	46
SS Casey Martin, Arkansas	Jr.	.286	.364	.548	283	15	57
OF Daniel Cabrera, Louisiana State	Jr.	.284	.359	.516	225	12	50
OF Heston Kjerstad, Arkansas	Jr.	.327	.400	.575	266	17	51
OF Garrett Mitchell, UCLA	Jr.	.349	.418	.566	258	6	41
UTL Max Meyer, Minnesota	Jr.	.256	.323	.314	121	1	12

	Year	W	L	ERA	IP	SO	SV
SP Garrett Crochet, Tennessee	Jr.	5	3	4.02	65	81	3
SP JT Ginn, Mississippi State	Jr.	8	4	3.13	86	105	0
SP Emerson Hancock, Georgia	Jr.	8	3	1.99	90	97	0
SP Asa Lacy, Texas A&M	Jr.	8	4	2.13	89	130	0
RP Burl Carraway, Dallas Baptist	Jr.	4	2	2.81	42	72	6
UTL Max Meyer, Minnesota	Jr.	5	3	2.11	77	87	2

SECOND TEAM

Pos. Name	Year	AVG	OBP	SLG	AB	HR	RBI
C Austin Wells, Arizona	So.	.353	.462	.552	221	5	60
1B Aaron Sabato, North Carolina	So.	.343	.453	.696	230	18	63
2B Justin Foscue, Mississippi State	Jr.	.331	.395	.564	275	14	60
3B Gage Workman, Arizona State	Jr.	.330	.413	.528	218	8	42
SS Alika Williams, Arizona State	Jr.	.333	.429	.474	213	4	53
OF Parker Chavers, Coastal Carolina	Jr.	.316	.435	.612	209	15	54
OF Jesse Franklin, Michigan	Jr.	.262	.388	.477	260	13	55
OF Alerick Soularie, Tennessee	Jr.	.357	.466	.602	196	11	46
UTL Logan Allen, Florida International	Jr.	.276	.321	.434	76	3	5

	Year	W	L	ERA	IP	SO	SV
SP Reid Detmers, Louisville	Jr.	13	4	2.78	113	167	0
SP Carmen Mlodzinski, South Carolina	R-So.	0	0	5.91	11	11	0
SP Kumar Rocker, Vanderbilt	So.	12	5	3.25	100	114	0
SP C.J. Van Eyk, Florida State	Jr.	10	4	3.81	99	129	0
RP Tyler Brown, Vanderbilt	Jr.	3	1	2.19	49	65	17
UTL Logan Allen, Florida International	Jr.	4	6	3.11	84	120	0

THIRD TEAM

Pos. Name	Year	AVG	OBP	SLG	AB	HR	RBI
C Casey Opitz, Arkansas	Jr.	.243	.379	.311	177	3	33
1B Alex Toral, Miami	Jr.	.293	.400	.656	215	24	67
2B Noah Campbell, South Carolina	Jr.	.239	.324	.378	188	6	19
3B Niko Kavadas, Notre Dame	Jr.	.274	.390	.517	201	12	43
SS Nick Loftin, Baylor	Jr.	.323	.380	.502	235	6	41
OF Colton Cowser, Sam Houston State	So.	.361	.450	.602	216	7	54
OF Zach DeLoach, Texas A&M	Jr.	.200	.318	.294	160	3	16
OF Joey Wiemer, Cincinnati	Jr.	.263	.360	.408	240	6	28
UTL Casey Schmitt, San Diego State	Jr.	.315	.415	.450	200	5	36

	Year	W	L	ERA	IP	SO	SV
SP Tanner Burns, Auburn	Jr.	4	4	2.82	80	101	0
SP Cade Cavalli, Oklahoma	Jr.	5	3	3.28	60	59	0
SP Slade Cecconi, Miami	Jr.	5	4	4.16	80	89	0
SP Cole Wilcox, Georgia	So.	3	2	4.07	60	64	0
RP Joe Boyle, Notre Dame	Jr.	3	3	5.96	26	39	2
UTL Casey Schmitt, San Diego State	Jr.	3	3	3.77	43	44	8

Stats from the 2019 season.

A 'New Model'?

A group of prominent coaches, led by Michigan's Erik Bakich, developed a detailed proposal to alter college baseball's calendar in an effort to make the sport more financially stable. At the crux of the plan is a proposal to push the season back about a month, moving Opening Day from mid-February to the third weekend of March and the start of the NCAA Tournament to the end of June.

Similar plans to push the season back have been made over the years. This proposal is different, however, both in its scope—it makes a case from a financial, academic and student-welfare standpoint —and in its support. Whereas previous proposals

OWEN MAIN/COURTESY OF MICHIGAN

Michigan first baseman Matt Schmidt homered on Opening Day against Vanderbilt.

were typically led by one coach or one conference, the latest proposal quickly captured broad-reaching support, involving many of the game's most prominent coaches from across the country.

The proposal is in part a reaction to the financial crisis in college sports that has followed the coronavirus pandemic. With all but about half a dozen baseball programs losing money, the coaches are concerned about the future of the sport and are looking for ways to bring it more stability and turn it into a revenue producer.

"The Covid-19 pandemic and resultant economic turmoil has created a financial crisis for higher education," the proposal states. "The landscape of college athletics has changed. Implementing modernized business models has never been more important than today.

"In order for college baseball to survive, grow and thrive in uncertain times, we must make these necessary adjustments."

Those adjustments are, 1) pushing the season back four weeks, 2) expanded preseason, 3) shortened fall ball, 4) moving fall scrimmages to the preseason. Opening Day in March? Selection Monday in late June? The College World Series in July? They would all be the new reality under this proposal.

A later start date to the season has long been debated in college baseball. Proponents note that while baseball is technically a spring sport, the cur-rent mid-February Opening Day (this year's was Feb. 14) occurs during the thick of winter. This reality forces many teams to play on the road for the first several weeks of the season, piling up travel costs and missed class time, while they wait for better weather at their home ballparks.

Even for schools that can play at home early in the season, the weather is still not optimal for fans who want to watch a three-hour baseball game outdoors. Programs tend to schedule more day games early in the season, even on Friday series openers, which hurts attendance, which means they aren't maximizing their revenue potential.

According to the coaches' proposal, a Big Ten or "competitive northern team" spent an average of $233,728 over the last five years on travel in the first four weeks of the season. In that same time period, the last four weeks of the regular season, when teams are in conference play and playing a more regional schedule, travel costs were an average of $88,864.

Meanwhile, schools in better weather in the south and west typically saw their attendance increase in April and May vs. February and March. The comparison isn't perfect, as fans may simply be more interested in conference games than in less competitive nonconference series. But college baseball attendance figures are almost always taken off of "paid attendance," which isn't a true reflection of how many fans are actually in the stands, and, anecdotally, attendance can tick up in the second half of the season.

For every school, a February start date also places the first-half of the season in a crowded sports calendar. College basketball is reaching its fever pitch by mid-February and, as it stands, the start of conference play in baseball, which should be a big event, overlaps with conference basketball tournaments and the start of the NCAA Tournament. The result is college baseball gets lost in the shuffle, even on conference TV networks and social media channels.

Pushing the season back isn't without complications, however. The season already lasts well past the end of the spring semester (at schools on semester schedules) and keeping players on campus while school is out of session is a significant expense. This plan would keep players on campus four extra weeks. Northern schools would also get more home games in this arrangement, which also adds expenses like umpires and game-day staff to their budgets.

The draft must also be accounted for in any proposal looking at pushing the season back. But with MLB having pushed back its draft into mid-July in accordance with its plan to scale back the minor leagues, that becomes much less of a problem for college baseball.

The proposal has some significant academic merits—less travel time means more time players are in class. Reduced fall ball would give players more time to focus on their studies and an extended preseason would lighten the load at the start of the spring semester.

Michigan righthander Isaiah Paige supports the academic benefits.

"This proposal grants the opportunity for collegiate baseball programs to reach new heights on the field and allows the athletes to maximize all the resources of their university off the field," he said.

But pushing the season back a month also reduces academic opportunities for players who are mostly on partial scholarships. Already, players on teams that advance to the NCAA Tournament cannot start an internship until June, about a month after their classmates who aren't playing baseball. While every Division I player may harbor ambitions to play professional baseball, the reality is most will not and are pursuing other professions, which may require work in the summer.

What will happen to summer leagues is also a question that is always raised during any debate about pushing the season back. Many leagues were set to this season begin their season in the last week of May, though Opening Day in the Cape Cod League, the premier summer league, wasn't until June 13. Summer leagues that could push their start

Oklahoma righthander Dane Acker.

BRIAN WESTERHOLT

date back to the end of June would have as many players as usual to choose. But the reality is that a player on a team that regularly made the NCAA Tournament may never play in a summer league.

As the coaches lay out in the proposal, that may simply be a necessary tradeoff to maximize college baseball's potential.

"The Covid-19 pandemic and changing landscape of college athletics has created the need for the game of college baseball to self-audit and make adjustments," it states. "Almost all schools operate at a significant financial net loss because we start our season in February. The attendance data and inflated travel budgets prove that. College baseball is also losing valuable developmental time during one of the peak weather months for our sport.

"Our student-athletes should be developing on our campuses in June, especially with the amount of resources many institutions have invested into our programs. Our fans should be watching our student-athletes in our stadiums, and those revenue dollars should go to our athletic departments.

"We need to do what is best for the long-term health and growth of college baseball."

That argument is what the new model comes down to. There are still many details to be hammered out and the coaches will have to get their athletic directors on board with the idea to get it passed through the NCAA legislative process.

What's clear is that this proposal has momentum where others have floundered and that its supporters are determined to see it advance.

HITTING (MINIMUM 25 AT-BATS)

BATTING AVERAGE

Rk.	Player, School	AVG	OBP	SLG	G	AB	2B	3B	HR	RBI	BB	SO	SB
1.	Brendyn Stillman, St. Bonaventure	.519	.594	1.259	7	27	2	0	6	13	5	4	0
2.	Brooks Carlson, Samford	.500	.644	.760	15	50	4	0	3	19	20	4	0
3.	Jake Holcroft, Portland	.484	.522	.758	15	62	7	2	2	11	5	7	4
4.	Juan Teixeira, Florida International	.482	.508	.643	15	56	3	0	2	14	3	3	5
5.	Eduardo Malinowski, Pennsylvania	.471	.526	.735	8	34	1	1	2	10	3	8	0
6.	Bailey Peterson, Michigan State	.464	.537	.571	14	56	4	1	0	15	10	6	8
7.	Zack Raabe, Minnesota	.463	.526	.612	17	67	7	0	1	10	7	7	0
8.	Daniel Harris, Eastern Kentucky	.460	.541	.680	14	50	3	1	2	16	6	6	5
9.	Peter Matt, Pennsylvania	.457	.525	.543	8	35	3	0	0	9	4	7	4
10.	Brandt Belk, Missouri	.457	.544	.652	13	46	3	0	2	9	9	13	4
11.	Jason Coules, Fordham	.453	.492	.660	16	53	5	0	2	18	6	4	6
12.	Jackson Coutts, Rhode Island	.451	.525	.824	13	51	7	0	4	12	8	7	2
13.	A.J. Lewis, Eastern Kentucky	.451	.541	.843	13	51	7	2	3	21	9	11	3
14.	Michael Guldberg, Georgia Tech	.450	.521	.533	16	60	5	0	0	9	5	3	3
15.	Jacob Young, Florida	.450	.514	.517	17	60	4	0	0	9	7	9	6
16.	Cody Morissette, Boston College	.448	.522	.655	15	58	6	0	2	11	9	6	3
17.	Nick Gonzales, New Mexico State	.448	.610	1.155	16	58	3	1	12	36	21	10	4
18.	Heston Kjerstad, Arkansas	.448	.513	.791	16	67	5	0	6	20	7	9	1
19.	Vinnie Martin, Mass.-Lowell	.447	.581	.660	14	47	4	0	2	7	14	7	2
20.	Nick Shumski, Merrimack	.443	.469	.508	15	61	4	0	0	12	3	10	3
21.	Kyler McMahan, Oregon State	.439	.492	.544	14	57	6	0	0	4	5	17	3
22.	Brian Cordell, Maryland-Eastern Shore	.438	.578	.604	15	48	2	0	2	9	15	7	2
23.	Anthony Warneke, Long Island	.438	.491	.542	12	48	3	1	0	3	4	3	9
24.	Kyle Manzardo, Washington State	.435	.500	.694	16	62	7	0	3	14	6	12	0
25.	Jaylyn Williams, Jackson State	.434	.508	.528	15	53	5	0	0	13	8	8	4
26.	Maxwell Costes, Maryland	.432	.620	.750	15	44	2	0	4	15	16	7	3
27.	Braden Zarbnisky, West Virginia	.431	.486	.538	16	65	3	2	0	9	7	9	13
28.	Will Knight, Virginia Military	.431	.484	.586	15	58	7	1	0	6	5	7	1
29.	Nick Hassan, Kennesaw State	.431	.463	.549	15	51	4	1	0	10	3	4	2
30.	Spencer Myers, Notre Dame	.431	.492	.466	12	58	2	0	0	8	7	5	15
31.	Colby Higgerson, Radford	.431	.513	.492	17	65	2	1	0	15	9	11	4
32.	Carson Taylor, Virginia Tech	.431	.541	.690	16	58	7	1	2	20	12	5	2
33.	Tyler Gentry, Alabama	.429	.554	.750	17	56	6	0	4	21	10	10	2
34.	Noah Levin, George Washington	.429	.522	.500	16	56	4	0	0	13	10	7	0
35.	Bryson Bloomer, Murray State	.429	.468	.554	16	56	4	0	1	10	4	4	1
36.	Equon Smith, Jackson State	.429	.500	.595	14	42	0	2	1	9	5	6	8
37.	Kenyon Yovan, Oregon	.429	.566	.714	15	56	2	1	4	9	15	9	0
38.	Jake Evans, Binghamton	.429	.451	.449	12	49	1	0	0	5	2	3	0
39.	John Rhodes, Kentucky	.426	.485	.672	17	61	10	1	1	19	2	5	1
40.	Branden Comia, Illinois	.426	.526	.702	13	47	3	2	2	10	6	12	1
41.	Chandler Dillard, Jackson State	.426	.486	.541	16	61	1	3	0	7	7	10	11
42.	Scott Dubrule, Jacksonville	.426	.500	.544	18	68	5	0	1	6	10	5	3
43.	Pres Cavenaugh, UNC Greensboro	.425	.479	.525	15	40	2	1	0	7	6	3	6
44.	Jack Cunningham, Boston College	.424	.478	.576	15	59	3	0	2	13	6	12	2
45.	Grant Richardson, Indiana	.424	.453	.797	14	59	3	2	5	17	4	16	1
46.	Parker Bates, Louisiana Tech	.422	.531	.891	17	64	4	1	8	28	11	9	2
47.	Zach DeLoach, Texas A&M	.421	.547	.789	18	57	3	0	6	17	14	3	6
48.	Bryce Kelley, Michigan State	.421	.492	.439	14	57	1	0	0	4	7	6	8
49.	Aaron Zavala, Oregon	.418	.493	.491	15	55	1	0	1	22	8	3	2
50.	Kale Emshoff, Arkansas-Little Rock	.417	.527	.800	17	60	2	0	7	12	14	11	0
51.	Kyle Landers, New Mexico	.417	.532	.567	17	60	6	0	1	18	14	5	5
52.	Jordan Cozart, Murray State	.417	.486	.750	16	60	5	0	5	19	9	8	0
53.	Spencer Gedestad, UC Davis	.417	.463	.517	15	60	6	0	0	8	6	21	2
54.	Jimmy Glowenke, Dallas Baptist	.415	.458	.509	13	53	2	0	1	7	5	5	1
55.	Jake Dickerson, McNeese State	.415	.487	.662	17	65	4	0	4	18	9	12	3
56.	Joe Suozzi, Boston College	.414	.471	.638	15	58	4	3	1	16	8	16	4
57.	Jason Hinchman, Tennessee Tech	.414	.485	.793	15	58	4	0	6	13	7	15	3
58.	Ben Anderson, Georgia	.414	.544	.552	18	58	6	1	0	13	15	11	5
59.	Justin Dirden, Southeast Missouri State	.414	.471	.900	17	70	3	2	9	26	8	11	9
60.	Aharon Modlin, Pepperdine	.413	.472	.571	15	63	5	1	1	11	8	11	3
61.	Kyler Fedko, Connecticut	.412	.434	.627	13	51	3	1	2	12	2	4	0
62.	Matt Scheffler, Auburn	.412	.516	.549	16	51	4	0	1	14	8	4	1
63.	Rankin Woley, Auburn	.412	.487	.618	18	68	8	0	2	22	8	14	0
64.	Ian Walters, Southern Illinois	.411	.516	.562	18	73	6	1	1	14	13	14	9
65.	Levi Usher, Louisville	.411	.484	.571	16	56	3	0	2	10	7	14	11
66.	Austin Gauthier, Hofstra	.411	.515	.714	14	56	6	1	3	11	11	17	2

Rank	Player, Team	AVG	OBP	SLG									
67.	Max Hewitt, Oklahoma State	.410	.479	.525	18	61	5	1	0	10	7	5	0
68.	Ben Wanger, Southern California	.410	.500	.564	13	39	4	1	0	8	7	10	1
69.	Drew Frederic, Troy	.409	.500	.545	17	66	4	1	1	13	11	16	11
70.	Angel Zarate, North Carolina	.408	.477	.493	19	71	4	1	0	18	11	4	5
71.	Alex Baratta, Binghamton	.408	.492	.510	12	49	5	0	0	11	7	7	2
72.	Chris Newell, Virginia	.407	.545	.729	18	59	5	1	4	20	13	21	8
73.	Kole Kaler, Hawaii	.407	.486	.661	17	59	9	3	0	17	10	13	4
74.	Anthony Donofrio, Hofstra	.407	.508	.519	14	54	4	1	0	15	10	8	5
75.	Elian Merejo, Georgia State	.407	.527	.763	16	59	6	0	5	13	15	14	5
76.	Steele Netterville, Louisiana Tech	.407	.500	.797	16	59	5	0	6	22	7	13	1
77.	Tyler Wilber, Southeast Missouri State	.406	.494	.696	17	69	9	1	3	12	11	8	3
78.	Jared McKenzie, Baylor	.406	.453	.449	16	69	3	0	0	5	5	7	4
79.	Ryan Humeniuk, Louisiana-Monroe	.406	.481	.594	17	69	2	1	3	14	9	14	4
80.	Dominic Pilolli, Charlotte	.403	.481	.567	17	67	3	1	2	14	9	10	2
81.	Tyler Keenan, Mississippi	.403	.488	.791	17	67	5	0	7	33	9	14	1
82.	Connor Norby, East Carolina	.403	.439	.500	17	62	1	1	1	10	4	10	6
83.	Charles Middleton, Pacific	.403	.494	.657	17	67	5	0	4	20	12	9	1
84.	Connor Kokx, Long Beach State	.400	.491	.511	15	45	5	0	0	5	1	6	3
85.	Kyler Castillo, New Mexico	.400	.465	.480	18	75	6	0	0	12	8	7	9
86.	Darryn Davis, Toledo	.400	.532	.550	16	60	4	1	1	17	13	6	1
87.	Denzel Clarke, Cal State Northridge	.400	.529	.775	15	40	4	1	3	9	5	15	5
88.	Andrew Keck, Southeast Missouri State	.400	.463	.500	17	70	4	0	1	19	8	12	7
89.	Andrew Beesley, Louisiana-Monroe	.400	.565	.600	14	45	4	1	1	15	13	5	5
90.	Izaya Fullard, Iowa	.400	.449	.583	15	60	3	1	2	21	5	7	2
91.	Gavin Homer, Penn State	.400	.500	.689	14	45	6	2	1	17	8	9	8
92.	Johnny Piacentino, Penn State	.400	.511	.686	13	35	4	0	2	11	10	4	4
93.	Reese Alexiades, Pepperdine	.397	.458	.571	15	63	6	1	1	15	8	15	2
94.	Matt McLain, UCLA	.397	.422	.621	13	58	4	0	3	19	4	13	1
95.	Tucker Bradley, Georgia	.397	.513	.703	18	63	3	0	6	23	13	4	8
96.	Connor Emmet, Central Arkansas	.397	.449	.571	16	63	6	1	1	7	6	9	1
97.	Jack Rogers, Sam Houston State	.396	.450	.698	14	53	7	3	1	14	6	16	4
98.	Gio Diaz, Saint Mary's	.396	.442	.417	13	48	1	0	0	2	4	2	3
99.	William Sullivan, Troy	.396	.468	.547	15	53	6	1	0	12	6	13	0
100.	Matt Arceo, Towson	.395	.490	.442	12	43	2	0	0	7	6	9	2

ON-BASE PERCENTAGE

Rank	Player, Pos., Team	OBP
1.	Brooks Carlson, INF, Samford	.644
2.	Maxwell Costes, OF, Maryland	.620
3.	Nick Gonzales, SS, New Mexico St.	.610
4.	Spencer Torkelson, 1B, Arizona St.	.598
5.	Brendyn Stillman, OF, St. Bonaventure	.594
6.	Vinnie Martin, OF, Mass.-Lowell	.581
7.	Jake Dukart, INF, Oregon St.	.580
8.	Brian Cordell, OF, Md.-Eastern Shore	.578
9.	Anthony Servideo, SS, Mississippi	.575
10.	Vinny Zavolta, OF, Utah	.571

SLUGGING PERCENTAGE

Rank	Player, Pos., Team	SLG
1.	Brendyn Stillman, OF, St. Bonaventure	1.259
2.	Nick Gonzales, SS, New Mexico St.	1.155
3.	Tyler Kelder, INF, St. Bonaventure	1.097
4.	Justin Dirden, OF, Southeast Mo. St.	.900
5.	Parker Bates, OF, Louisiana Tech	.891
6.	Dan Bolt, OF, Bradley	.881
7.	A.J. Lewis, C, Eastern Kentucky	.843
8.	Roderick Coffee, OF, Texas Southern	.830
9.	Jackson Coutts, UTL, Rhode Island	.824
10.	Zach Presno, C, Fresno St.	.804

RUNS BATTED IN

Rank	Player, Pos., Team	RBI
1.	Nick Gonzales, SS, New Mexico St.	36
2.	Tyler Keenan, 3B, Mississippi	33
3.	Hunter Goodman, C, Memphis	31
4.	Parker Bates, OF, Louisiana Tech	28
4.	Elijah Cabell, OF, Florida St.	28
6.	Nate Rombach, C, Texas Tech	27
7.	Justin Dirden, OF, Southeast Mo. St.	26
8.	Cal Conley, SS, Texas Tech	24
8.	Luis DeLeon, INF, N.C. Central	24
8.	Oscar Ponce, UTL, Texas Southern	24

HOME RUNS

Rank	Player, Pos., Team	HR
1.	Nick Gonzales, SS, New Mexico St.	12
2.	Justin Dirden, OF, Southeast Mo. St.	9
3.	Brock Anderson, OF, Murray St.	8
3.	Parker Bates, OF, Louisiana Tech	8
3.	Wes Clarke, C, South Carolina	8
3.	Hunter Goodman, C, Memphis	8
3.	Zach Presno, C, Fresno St.	8
8.	10 players tied	7

DOUBLES

Rank	Player, Pos., Team	2B
1.	Zach Britton, OF, Louisville	11
2.	Cole Blatchford, INF, Air Force	10
2.	Brian Klein, 2B, Texas Tech	10
2.	John Rhodes, OF, Kentucky	10
2.	Jack Wilson, INF, Western Kentucky	10
6.	Nine players tied	9

TRIPLES

Rank	Player, Pos., Team	3B
1.	Peter Brookshaw, INF, N. Dakota St.	4
1.	Max Cotier, INF, Virginia	4
1.	Ashton Easley, OF, Air Force	4
1.	Ty Johnson, OF, Tulane	4
1.	Garrett Kocis, 1B, Wichita State	4
1.	Brandon Raquet, OF, William & Mary	4
1.	Tanner Treadaway, INF, Oklahoma St.	4
1.	Caeden Trenkle, OF, Oklahoma St.	4
1.	Jabronski Williams, OF, Alabama St.	4
10.	29 players tied	3

STOLEN BASES

Rank	Player, Pos., Team	SB
1.	Spencer Myers, INF, Notre Dame	15
2.	Gephry Pena, OF, Central Florida	13
2.	Tyler Villaroman, OF, San Francisco	13
2.	Braden Zabrinsky, UTL, West Virginia	13
5.	Brett Auerbach, UTL, Alabama	12
5.	Zack Budzik, INF, UNC Greensboro	12
5.	Ashton Easley, OF, Air Force	12
5.	Jake Lyle, INF, East Tennessee St.	12
5.	Dylan Neuse, OF, Texas Tech	12
10.	Five players tied	11

RUNS

Rank	Player, Pos., Team	R
1.	Nick Gonzales, SS, New Mexico St.	28
2.	Tyler Wilber, INF, Southeast Mo. St.	26
3.	Zach DeLoach, OF, Texas A&M	25
4.	Ben Anderson, OF, Georgia	24
4.	Zack Gelof, OF, Virginia	24
4.	Julian Rip, OF, South Carolina-Upstate	24
4.	Anthony Servideo, SS, Mississippi	24
4.	Spencer Torkelson, 1B, Arizona St.	24
9.	Peyton Chatagnier, 2B, Mississippi	23
9.	Jackson Swiney, OF, Western Kentucky	23

HITS

Rank	Player, Pos., Team	H
1.	Zack Raabe, SS, Minnesota	31
2.	Kyler Castillo, INF, New Mexico	30
2.	Jake Holcroft, OF, Portland	30
2.	Heston Kjerstad, OF, Arkansas	30
2.	Ian Walters, INF, Southern Illinois	30
6.	Ryan Bliss, SS, Auburn	29
6.	Juan Colato, UTL, Grand Canyon	29
6.	Justin Dirden, OF, Southeast Mo. St.	29
6.	Scott Dubrule, INF, Jacksonville	29
6.	Danny Wright, OF, Southeast Mo. St.	29
6.	Angel Zarate, OF, North Carolina	29

TOTAL BASES

Rank	Player, Pos., Team	TB
1.	Nick Gonzales, SS, New Mexico St.	67
2.	Justin Dirden, OF, Southeast Mo. St.	63
3.	Parker Bates, OF, Louisiana Tech	57
4.	Tyler Keenan, 3B, Mississippi	53
4.	Heston Kjerstad, OF, Arkansas	53
6.	Hunter Goodman, C, Memphis	52
7.	Tanner Treadaway, INF, Oklahoma	51
8.	Juan Colato, UTL, Grand Canyon	49
9.	Kale Emshoff, C, Arkansas-Little Rock	49
9.	Tyler Wilber, INF, Southeast Mo. St.	49

WALKS

Rank	Player, Pos., Team	BB
1.	Spencer Torkelson, 1B, Arizona St.	31
2.	Anthony Servideo, SS, Mississippi	24
3.	Aaron Sabato, 1B, North Carolina	22
4.	Nick Gonzales, SS, New Mexico St.	21
4.	Matthew Guidry, INF, Southern Miss.	21
6.	Brooks Carlson, INF, Samford	20
6.	Trevor Hauver, OF, Arizona St.	20
8.	Sky Duff, INF, Pittsburgh	19
8.	Kaden Polcovich, UTL, Oklahoma St.	19
10.	Six players tied	18

TOUGHEST TO STRIKE OUT

Rank	Player, Pos., Team	AB/SO
1.	Jim Weglarz, 2B, Delaware St.	53.0
2.	Trevor Austin, INF, Mercer	44.0
3.	Alsander Womack, INF, Norfolk St.	33.5
4.	Jake MacKenzie, INF, Fordham	29.5
5.	Matthew Williams, 1B, St. Bonaventure	29.0
6.	Austin Martin, OF, Vanderbilt	26.5
7.	Owen Wosleger, OF, Mount St. Mary's	26.0
8.	Ari Sechopoulos, INF, Charleston	25.0
9.	Gio Diaz, INF, Saint Mary's	24.0
10.	Francisco Urbaez, INF, Fla. Atlantic	21.7

HIT BY PITCH

Rank	Player, Pos., Team	HBP
1.	Elijah Cabell, OF, Florida St.	15
2.	Waldy Arias, INF, Campbell	12
2.	George Callil, SS, South Carolina	12
2.	Conrado Diaz, C, UTRGV	12
5.	Tucker Flint, OF, Maryland	11
5.	Bennett Hostetler, INF, N. Dakota St.	11
5.	Garrett Matheny, OF, Radford	11
5.	Immanuel Wilder, OF, W. Carolina	11
9.	Maxwell Costes, OF, Maryland	9
9.	Cam Locklear, SS, Liberty	9
9.	Fox Semones, UTL, James Madison	9

SACRIFICE BUNTS

Rank	Player, Pos., Team	SAC
1.	Pat O'Neill, INF, Villanova	6
1.	Kamron Willman, INF, Kansas St.	6
3.	Matt Bottcher, INF, Illinois-Chicago	5
3.	Jack Capobianco, INF, Belmont	5
3.	Blake Colvin, OF, Air Force	5
3.	Collier Cranford, INF, Louisiana St.	5
3.	Kyle Dockus, INF, Mercer	5
3.	Dallas Duarte, C, Hawaii	5
3.	Dakota Julylia, INF, Jacksonville	5
3.	Kyle Lovelace, C, Houston	5
3.	Andrew Meggs, INF, Creighton	5
3.	Cole Roberts, INF, Loyola Marymount	5
3.	Caeden Trenkle, OF, Oklahoma State	5

SACRIFICE FLYS

Rank	Player, Pos., Team	SF
1.	Alvin Melendez, UTL, Fordham	6
2.	Peter Brookshaw, INF, N. Dakota St.	5
2.	Sonny DiChiara, 1B, Samford	5
2.	Danny Oriente, OF, Louisville	5
2.	Donta Williams, OF, Arizona	5
2.	Zach Zubia, 1B, Texas	5
7.	12 players tied	4

PITCHING (MINIMUM 5 INNINGS PITCHED)

Rk.	Pitcher, Team	W	L	ERA	G	GS	SV	IP	H	R	ER	BB	SO
1.	Mac McCarty, Alabama-Birmingham	0	0	0.00	10	0	5	16	3	0	0	2	16
2.	Pete Hansen, Texas	2	0	0.00	6	1	1	17	9	1	0	2	18
3.	Logan Hofmann, Northwestern State	4	0	0.00	4	4	0	28	14	3	0	5	38
4.	Christian Scafidi, Pennsylvania	2	0	0.00	2	2	0	15	9	2	0	5	13
5.	Joshua Loeschorn, Long Island	2	0	0.00	3	3	0	15	9	2	0	6	14
6.	Haylen Green, Texas Christian	1	0	0.00	8	0	1	18	7	0	0	5	19
7.	Wyatt Divis, Texas-Arlington	1	0	0.00	4	0	2	16	7	0	0	7	15
8.	Connor Prielipp, Alabama	3	0	0.00	4	4	0	21	5	0	0	6	35
9.	Braden Olthoff, Tulane	4	0	0.32	4	4	0	28	12	4	1	3	47
10.	Jordan Wicks, Kansas State	3	0	0.35	4	4	0	26	13	1	1	4	26
11.	Trevor McMurray, Murray State	3	0	0.35	4	4	0	26	15	1	1	8	23
12.	Zach Torra, UC Santa Barbara	3	0	0.36	4	4	0	25	11	1	1	9	39
13.	Nick Krauth, Connecticut	4	0	0.37	4	4	0	25	14	4	1	9	24
14.	Levi Thomas, Troy	2	1	0.39	4	4	0	23	9	1	1	6	42
15.	Cooper Stinson, Duke	3	0	0.42	4	4	0	22	16	1	1	4	24
16.	Chris Farrell, William & Mary	2	0	0.42	4	4	0	21	14	1	1	16	19
17.	Brandon Fox, Central Connecticut State	1	2	0.43	3	3	0	21	16	6	1	2	14
18.	Mason Hickman, Vanderbilt	2	0	0.48	3	3	0	19	8	2	1	3	26
19.	Alec Huertas, Long Island	1	1	0.50	3	3	0	18	14	6	1	6	13
20.	Alex Williams, Stanford	2	1	0.51	3	3	0	18	11	5	1	4	18
21.	Tyler Owens, Georgia Southern	2	0	0.51	5	3	0	18	9	2	1	3	15
22.	Antonio Velez, Florida State	1	0	0.52	6	1	0	17	7	1	1	3	21
23.	Mike Entzona, Florida Atlantic	3	0	0.55	10	0	0	16	10	2	1	5	27
24.	Christian Peters, Portland	3	1	0.63	4	4	0	29	19	3	2	3	35
25.	Bryce Jarvis, Duke	3	1	0.67	4	4	0	27	11	3	2	2	40
26.	David Moffat, Texas-Arlington	1	0	0.67	4	4	0	27	13	3	2	4	16
27.	Justin Showalter, James Madison	4	0	0.68	5	4	0	27	13	4	2	4	21
28.	Brian Van Belle, Miami	2	0	0.68	4	4	0	26	16	3	2	4	38
29.	Jackson Kelley, Mercer	3	0	0.70	4	4	0	26	22	5	2	2	20
30.	Boyd Vander Kooi, Arizona State	2	1	0.70	5	2	0	26	19	5	2	2	20
31.	Austin Temple, Jacksonville	2	1	0.71	4	4	0	25	14	2	2	10	29
32.	Jaret Bennett, Charleston Southern	2	0	0.71	4	4	0	25	14	5	2	10	24
33.	Jordan Patty, Central Michigan	3	0	0.72	4	4	0	25	12	3	2	13	17
34.	Asa Lacy, Texas A&M	3	0	0.75	4	4	0	24	9	2	2	8	46
35.	Sam Weatherly, Clemson	2	0	0.79	4	4	0	23	7	4	2	14	43
36.	Stevie Emanuels, Washington	3	1	0.79	4	4	0	23	17	6	2	9	38
37.	John Natoli, Cornell	1	0	0.82	3	3	0	11	10	1	1	3	13
38.	Christian Chamberlain, Oregon State	2	1	0.82	4	4	0	22	6	4	2	11	34
39.	Carter Rustad, San Diego	4	0	0.84	4	4	0	22	5	2	2	8	24
40.	Brett Walker, Oregon	3	0	0.84	5	3	0	22	13	2	2	1	10
41.	Mike Doherty, Northwestern	1	0	0.86	4	4	0	21	17	2	2	5	20
42.	Christian MacLeod, Mississippi State	4	0	0.86	4	4	0	21	9	2	2	6	35
43.	Nick Rogers, Bethune-Cookman	0	2	0.87	4	4	0	21	11	4	2	15	16

44. Nicholas Dombkowski, Hartford	3	0	0.90	3	3	0	20	7	2	2	4	20
45. Gabe Levy, Davidson	3	1	0.91	4	4	0	30	19	7	3	10	28
46. Jaylyn Whitehead, Central Florida	1	1	0.95	6	3	1	19	8	2	2	5	18
47. Michael McGreevy, UC Santa Barbara	2	0	0.99	4	4	0	27	19	4	3	7	26
48. Cooper Chandler, Pepperdine	3	0	1.00	3	3	0	18	14	4	2	5	20
49. Cameron Reeves, The Citadel	4	0	1.04	4	4	0	26	18	6	3	5	32
50. Jake Kates, Western Kentucky	2	0	1.04	6	0	1	17	10	4	2	6	29
51. Austin Koehn, UNC Greensboro	1	0	1.04	4	2	0	17	15	3	2	4	19
52. Alec Mendez, Bethune-Cookman	2	0	1.04	4	4	0	26	18	3	3	4	22
53. Charlie Connolly, Navy	1	0	1.04	4	4	0	26	20	3	3	3	32
54. Mason Erla, Michigan State	2	0	1.04	4	4	0	26	20	4	3	6	42
55. Chris McMahon, Miami	3	0	1.05	4	4	0	26	19	3	3	5	38
56. Zach Pettway, UCLA	3	0	1.05	4	4	0	26	13	4	3	1	29
57. Jackson Wolf, West Virginia	3	1	1.05	4	4	0	26	14	4	3	5	27
58. Corley Woods, Jacksonville State	1	2	1.06	7	0	1	17	13	3	2	3	10
59. Jesse Schmit, Utah Valley	2	0	1.08	4	4	0	25	13	3	3	7	27
60. Landon Knack, East Tennessee State	4	0	1.08	4	4	0	25	12	3	3	1	51
61. Brandon Young, Louisiana-Lafayette	3	0	1.10	4	3	0	25	13	6	3	9	37
62. Luke Dawson, Holy Cross	1	1	1.11	4	4	0	24	25	8	3	8	20
63. Matt Gilbertson, Pittsburgh	2	1	1.13	4	4	0	24	26	9	3	6	20
64. Caleb Bolden, Arkansas	1	0	1.13	4	2	0	16	14	2	2	3	15
65. John Beller, Southern California	3	0	1.13	4	2	1	24	10	4	3	6	25
66. Hunter Swift, Oral Roberts	2	0	1.13	3	2	0	16	10	4	2	3	18
67. Parker Brahms, Sacramento State	2	1	1.14	4	4	0	24	18	4	3	0	32
68. Justin Armbruester, New Mexico	1	0	1.14	4	4	0	24	14	5	3	3	24
69. Lance Lusk, Sam Houston State	2	0	1.15	6	0	1	16	16	2	2	3	17
70. Gunnar Hoglund, Mississippi	3	0	1.16	4	4	0	23	18	5	3	4	37
71. Will Saxton, Florida International	1	1	1.17	4	0	0	15	14	10	2	8	13
72. Mason Studstill, Florida Gulf Coast	3	0	1.17	4	4	0	23	11	4	3	10	35
73. Jonah Jenkins, Dartmouth	0	1	1.17	2	1	0	8	4	1	1	4	3
74. Samuel Strickland, Stanford	3	0	1.17	4	4	0	23	20	4	3	1	30
75. Trevor Holloway, Central Florida	3	1	1.19	4	4	0	23	12	3	3	6	37
76. Isaac Esqueda, Southern California	0	1	1.20	3	2	0	15	14	3	2	6	13
77. Justin Sorokowski, Virginia Commonwealth	0	1	1.23	6	6	0	22	18	7	3	4	15
78. Adam Seminaris, Long Beach State	1	0	1.23	4	3	0	22	9	3	3	3	36
79. Dominic Robinson, Sam Houston State	1	1	1.23	4	3	0	22	12	4	3	5	30
80. Reid Detmers, Louisville	3	0	1.23	4	4	0	22	16	3	3	6	48
81. Trey Shaffer, Southeastern Louisiana	3	1	1.23	4	4	0	22	8	3	3	12	32
82. Walker Powell, Southern Mississippi	3	0	1.24	4	4	0	29	22	6	4	2	22
83. Jesse Bergin, UCLA	4	0	1.27	4	4	0	21	13	3	3	7	27
84. Matt Mikulski, Fordham	2	1	1.29	4	4	0	21	19	10	3	9	18
85. Nick Swiney, North Carolina State	4	0	1.29	4	4	0	28	13	4	4	6	42
86. Gavin Stone, Central Arkansas	3	1	1.30	4	4	0	28	15	5	4	6	31
87. Trent Palmer, Jacksonville	2	1	1.30	4	4	0	28	12	4	4	5	41
88. CJ Van Eyk, Florida State	1	1	1.31	4	4	0	21	11	4	3	12	25
89. Carter Robinson, Louisiana-Lafayette	2	1	1.31	4	4	0	21	15	4	3	6	15
90. Ty Weber, Illinois	2	0	1.31	4	4	0	21	17	6	3	2	15
91. Kenny Serwa, Southern Illinois-Edwardsville	4	0	1.33	4	4	0	27	20	5	4	4	42
92. Caswell Smith, College of Charleston	3	0	1.35	4	4	0	20	14	5	3	8	20
93. Tim Williamson, Harvard	1	0	1.35	2	0	0	7	6	2	1	5	4
94. Griff McGarry, Virginia	3	0	1.35	4	4	0	20	5	3	3	19	31
95. Hunter Dobbins, Texas Tech	2	0	1.35	6	3	0	20	17	3	3	5	25
96. Cole Kirschsieper, Illinois	3	0	1.35	4	2	0	20	18	3	3	5	12
97. Kevin Davis, South Carolina-Upstate	1	0	1.35	7	0	3	20	10	6	3	5	28
98. Luke Jannetta, Tulane	3	0	1.37	7	2	1	20	12	3	3	1	16
99. Justin Murray, Dartmouth	1	1	1.39	2	2	0	13	8	4	2	2	8
100. Hunter Barco, Florida	2	0	1.40	5	4	0	19	11	3	3	6	26

WINS

Rank Pitcher, Team	W
1. Kyle Brennan, Belmont	5
2. 22 players tied	4

SAVES

Rank Pitcher, Team	SV
1. Garrett Acton, Illinois	6
1. Luke Boyd, Baylor	6
1. Michael Kirian, Louisville	6
1. Jeffrey Hakanson, Central Florida	6
1. Tyler Guilfoil, Lipscomb	6
1. Casey Schmitt, San Diego State	6
1. Conner Williams, Central Arkansas	6
8. Nine players tied	5

STRIKEOUTS

Rank Pitcher, Team	SO
1. Landon Knack, East Tennessee State	51
2. Reid Detmers, Louisville	48
3. Aaron Bailey, Mississippi Valley State	47
3. Braden Olthoff, Tulane	47
5. Asa Lacy, Texas A&M	46
5. Max Meyer, Minnesota	46
7. Ryan Cusick, Wake Forest	43
7. Jared Shuster, Wake Forest	43
7. Sam Weatherly, Clemson	43
10. Mason Erla, Michigan State	42
10. Seth Lonsway, Ohio State	42
10. Kenny Serwa, SIU-Edwardsville	42
10. Nick Swiney, North Carolina State	42
10. Levi Thomas, Troy	42

STRIKEOUTS PER NINE

Rank Pitcher, Team	SO/9
1. Seth Lonsway, Ohio State	21.00
2. Reid Detmers, Louisville	19.64
3. Landon Knack, East Tennessee St.	18.36
4. Ian Seymour, Virginia Tech	17.70
5. Carson Ragsdale, South Florida	17.53
6. Ryan Cusick, Wake Forest	17.33
7. Asa Lacy, Texas A&M	17.25
8. Sam Weatherly, Clemson	17.07
9. Levi Thomas, Troy	16.43
10. Will Dion, McNeese State	16.11

FEWEST HITS PER NINE

Rank Pitcher, Team	H/9
1. Mac McCarty, Ala.-Birmingham	1.69
2. Carter Rustad, San Diego	2.11
3. Connor Prielipp, Alabama	2.14
4. Griff McGarry, Virginia	2.25
5. Christian Chamberlain, Oregon St.	2.45
6. Tommy Vail, Notre Dame	2.60

7. Sam Weatherly, Clemson	2.78
8. Tristan Weaver, Indiana State	2.96
9. Brannon Jordan, South Carolina	3.00
10. Nicholas Dombkowski, Hartford	3.15

FEWEST WALKS PER NINE

Rank Pitcher, Team	BB/9
1. Parker Brahms, Sacramento State	0.00
1. Nathan Skinner, Dartmouth	0.00

3. Pierson Ohl, Grand Canyon	0.32
4. Nick Durgin, Stetson	0.33
5. Carlos Lomeli, Saint Mary's	0.34
6. Zach Pettway, UCLA	0.35
6. Scott Randall, Sacramento State	0.35
8. Landon Knack, East Tennessee St.	0.36
9. Samuel Strickland, Samford	0.39
10. Brett Walker, Oregon	0.42

TEAM LEADERS

SCORING

Rank Team	G	R	R/G
1. Tennessee	17	180	10.6
2. New Mexico State	16	153	9.6
3. Mississippi	17	161	9.5
4. Texas Tech	19	177	9.3
5. Louisiana-Monroe	17	155	9.1
6. Texas A&M	18	164	9.1
7. Virginia	18	162	9.0
8. North Carolina State	17	153	9.0
9. Notre Dame	13	116	8.9
10. Auburn	18	158	8.8
11. Alabama	17	148	8.7
12. Western Michigan	15	129	8.6
13. Louisville	17	146	8.6
14. Coastal Carolina	16	135	8.4
15. Eastern Kentucky	14	118	8.4
16. Murray State	17	143	8.4
17. Rhode Island	13	106	8.2
18. Old Dominion	16	129	8.1
19. Louisiana Tech	17	137	8.1
20. Florida State	17	135	7.9
20. Kentucky	17	135	7.9
22. Wofford	17	134	7.9
22. McNeese State	17	134	7.9
24. Samford	15	118	7.9
25. East Tennessee State	15	117	7.8
26. Tulane	17	132	7.8
27. Oklahoma State	18	137	7.6
28. Southeast Missouri State	17	129	7.6
29. South Carolina-Upstate	18	136	7.6
30. Arizona	15	113	7.5
31. Cincinnati	15	113	7.5
32. UCLA	15	112	7.5
33. Pepperdine	15	112	7.5
34. Maryland	15	111	7.4
35. Arkansas	16	118	7.4
36. Troy	17	125	7.4
37. Boston College	15	110	7.3
38. Pittsburgh	16	117	7.3
39. New Mexico	18	131	7.3
40. Western Kentucky	16	116	7.3
41. Arizona State	17	123	7.2
42. Florida	17	123	7.2
43. Boise State	14	101	7.2
44. North Carolina	19	137	7.2
45. Iowa	15	108	7.2
46. Hofstra	14	100	7.1
47. Texas Christian	15	107	7.1
48. Georgia	18	128	7.1
49. Bradley	10	71	7.1
50. Florida International	15	106	7.1

BATTING AVERAGE

Rank Team	AVG
1. Auburn	.330
2. North Carolina State	.323
3. Louisville	.323
4. Jackson State	.321
5. Tennessee	.320
6. New Mexico State	.320
7. Texas Tech	.319
8. East Carolina	.317
9. Wofford	.316
10. Boston College	.316

HOME RUNS

Rank Team	HR
1. Mississippi	37
2. Tennessee	31
3. North Carolina State	28
4. Louisiana Tech	26
5. Wake Forest	24
5. Murray State	24
7. Texas Tech	23
7. Fresno State	23
7. Portland	23
10. Virginia	22
10. Alabama	22
10. Kentucky	22

DOUBLES

Rank Team	2B
1. Louisville	54
1. Texas Tech	54
3. Auburn	51
4. Pittsburgh	46
4. Troy	46
6. North Carolina State	43
6. Tennessee	43
8. Air Force	42
8. Tulane	42
10. New Mexico	41
10. Oklahoma	41
10. Western Kentucky	41

TRIPLES

Rank Team	3B
1. William & Mary	12
1. Tulane	12
3. Miami (Ohio)	11
4. Nevada-Las Vegas	10
4. New Mexico State	10
4. Oklahoma State	10
4. Virginia	10
8. Alabama State	9
8. East Tennessee State	9
8. South Carolina-Upstate	9
8. Southeast Missouri State	9
8. The Citadel	9
8. Wichita State	9

SLUGGING PERCENTAGE

Rank Team	SLG
1. North Carolina State	.557
2. Tennessee	.556
3. Mississippi	.549
4. Texas Tech	.527
5. East Tennessee State	.524
6. Virginia	.514
7. Murray State	.513
8. New Mexico State	.511
9. Louisville	.508
10. Louisiana Tech	.508

STOLEN BASES

Rank Team	SB
1. Wofford	47
2. Air Force	46
3. Fordham	45
4. Southern Illinois	44
5. Jackson State	42
6. North Carolina State	41
7. Charleston Southern	40
8. Bryant	39
8. West Virginia	39
10. Five teams teid	36

WALKS

Rank Team	BB
1. Texas Tech	128
2. Tennessee	124
3. Florida State	116
4. Alabama State	105
4. Louisian-Monroe	105
4. New Mexico State	105
7. Alabama	104
7. Mississippi	104
9. William & Mary	100
10. North Carolina	99

PITCHING

EARNED RUN AVERAGE

Rank Team	ERA
1. Vanderbilt	1.84
2. UC Santa Barbara	1.84
3. UCLA	1.88
4. Tennessee	2.00
5. Northwestern State	2.05
6. Kansas State	2.07
7. College of Charleston	2.13
8. Penn State	2.16
9. Central Florida	2.17
10. Georgia Southern	2.17
11. Alabama	2.24
12. Long Beach State	2.38
13. Louisiana State	2.38
14. Duke	2.39
15. Texas Christian	2.40
16. Florida	2.41
17. Southern California	2.42
18. Texas-Arlington	2.42
19. West Virginia	2.43
20. Florida State	2.50
21. Georgia	2.52
22. Washington	2.54
23. Bethune-Cookman	2.56
24. Sacramento State	2.58
25. Texas	2.59
26. Clemson	2.60
27. Portland	2.62
28. Stetson	2.67
29. Mercer	2.69
30. Davidson	2.71
31. Villanova	2.78
32. Winthrop	2.79
33. Miami	2.80
34. Auburn	2.81
34. South Carolina	2.81
36. Texas State	2.85
37. Oklahoma	2.85
38. Mississippi State	2.85
39. Wichita State	2.91
40. Pepperdine	2.91
41. Mississippi	2.92
42. New Orleans	2.93
43. Texas A&M	2.94
44. Memphis	3.02
45. Sam Houston State	3.02
46. Louisiana Tech	3.03
47. Liberty	3.04
48. Virginia Tech	3.05
49. Tulane	3.06
50. Saint Mary's	3.06

STRIKEOUTS PER NINE

Rank Team	SO/9
1. Ohio State	12.7
2. Texas A&M	12.5
3. Oklahoma	12.4
4. Vanderbilt	12.1
5. Florida State	12.1
6. Southern Illinois-Edwardsville	12.1
7. Louisville	12.0
8. Miami	12.0
9. Virginia Tech	11.9
10. Texas Tech	11.8

FEWEST WALKS PER NINE

Rank Team	BB/9
1. Sacramento State	1.32
2. Cal State Fullerton	1.95
3. Tennessee	2.06
4. Stetson	2.09
5. Central Arkansas	2.35
6. Long Beach State	2.38
7. Saint Mary's	2.49
8. Monmouth	2.56
9. Oklahoma	2.68
10. East Tennessee State	2.69

FIELDING

FIELDING PERCENTAGE

Rank Team	PCT
1. East Carolina	.990
2. Nebraska-Omaha	.990
3. Navy	.989
4. Duke	.988
5. Georgia Southern	.988
6. Lamar	.986
7. Oklahoma	.986
8. UC Santa Barbara	.985
9. Alabama	.985
10. Florida	.984
11. Auburn	.983
12. South Alabama	.983
13. Texas Christian	.983
14. Florida Atlantic	.983
15. Southern Illinois	.982
16. Nevada	.982
17. Appalachian State	.981
18. Tennessee	.981
19. San Diego	.981
20. Western Kentucky	.981
21. Evansville	.980
22. New Mexico State	.980
23. Hawaii	.980
24. Incarnate Word	.980
25. Iowa	.980
26. Portland	.980
27. Kansas State	.980
28. Oklahoma State	.980
29. Nebraska	.980
30. West Virginia	.979
31. Louisiana State	.979
32. South Florida	.979
33. San Francisco	.979
34. Indiana State	.979
35. North Carolina A&T	.978
36. Monmouth	.978
37. Pepperdine	.978
38. Yale	.978
39. Washington	.978
40. Saint Mary's	.978
41. Sacramento State	.978
42. Missouri State	.977
43. Texas State	.977
44. South Dakota State	.977
45. Campbell	.977
46. Virginia Commonwealth	.977
47. George Washington	.977
48. Sacred Heart	.977
49. Texas-Arlington	.977
50. Texas Tech	.977

DOUBLE PLAYS

Rank Team	DP
1. Bethune-Cookman	24
2. Coastal Carolina	22
2. North Carolina State	22
4. Austin Peay State	20
4. Jacksonville State	20
6. Belmont	19
6. Chicago State	19
6. Texas-Arlington	19
9. Seven teams tied	18

1. FLORIDA

Coach: Kevin O'Sullivan. **Record:** 16-1

Player, Pos., Year	AVG	OBP	SLG	AB	R	2B	3B	HR	RBI	SB
Acton, Cory, INF, So.	.192	.364	.269	52	7	1	0	1	4	4
Armstrong, Kris, INF, So.	.250	.368	.438	32	5	1	1	1	6	0
Blasucci, Nick, INF, R-Sr.	.333	.333	.500	6	2	1	0	0	1	0
Butler, Jordan, 1B, Jr.	.333	.370	.571	42	6	4	0	2	12	1
Calilao, Kendrick, UT, So.	.262	.319	.357	42	9	1	0	1	10	1
Edge, Brock, OF, Jr.	.333	.429	.333	6	0	0	0	0	1	1
Fabian, Jud, OF, So.	.294	.407	.603	68	19	6	0	5	13	2
Greenfield, Cal, C, Jr.	.233	.333	.400	30	9	2	0	1	7	0
Hickey, Nathan, UT, Fr.	.311	.439	.622	45	12	2	0	4	7	1
Langworthy, Austin, OF, Sr.	.246	.316	.348	69	11	4	0	1	8	4
McMullen, Kirby, INF, Jr.	.278	.458	.407	54	14	4	0	1	10	1
Nunez, Isaac, INF, Fr.	.167	.167	.167	6	0	0	0	0	1	0
Rivera, Josh, INF, Fr.	.298	.385	.439	57	12	2	0	2	9	1
Smith, Brady, UT, Jr.	.167	.235	.367	30	5	0	0	2	7	2
Specht, Ben, UT, Jr.	1.000	1.000	1.000	1	0	0	0	0	1	0
Young, Jacob, OF, So.	.450	.514	.517	60	12	4	0	0	9	6

Pitcher, Year	W	L	ERA	G	GS	SV	IP	H	BB	SO
Alintoff, Justin, Jr.	0	0	3.72	5	0	0	9.2	9	2	13
Barco, Hunter, Fr.	2	0	1.40	5	4	0	19.1	11	6	26
Butler, Jordan, Jr.	0	0	6.23	3	2	0	4.1	10	1	4
Cabarcas, Ryan, Fr.	0	0	1.29	7	0	1	7	4	2	10
Ficarrotta, Nick, Fr.	1	0	2.70	2	0	0	3.1	1	0	1
Leftwich, Jack, Jr.	2	0	4.15	4	4	0	21.2	16	8	23
Luethje, David, So.	2	0	5.19	6	0	0	8.2	6	4	9
Mace, Tommy, Jr.	3	0	1.67	4	4	0	27	21	5	26
Mink, Hunter, Fr.	0	0		1	0	0	1	1	0	1
Nesbitt, Tyler, Fr.	1	0	0.00	5	1	0	11.2	7	3	17
Pogue, Nick, So.	1	1	5.23	7	2	1	10.1	15	3	17
Scott, Christian, So.	2	0	1.20	7	0	0	15	11	6	16

	W	L	ERA	G	GS	SV	IP	H	BB	SO
Specht, Ben, So.	2	0	0.75	9	0	3	12	6	4	16
Sproat, Brandon, Fr.	0	0	1.50	4	0	0	6	2	3	8

2. TEXAS TECH

Coach: Tim Tadlock. **Record:** 16-3

Player, Pos., Year	AVG	OBP	SLG	AB	R	2B	3B	HR	RBI	SB
Baker, Dru, UT, So.	.266	.392	.469	64	13	3	2	2	8	3
Carter, Dillon, OF, Fr.	.280	.448	.380	50	12	3	1	0	4	7
Conley, Cal, INF, R-Fr.	.371	.444	.643	70	15	8	1	3	24	5
Cushing, Jared, INF, Fr.	.250	.400	.250	4	1	0	0	0	0	0
Fulford, Braxton, C, Jr.	.227	.379	.273	44	6	2	0	0	11	0
Jung, Jace, INF, Fr.	.264	.438	.604	53	16	4	1	4	23	1
Kelly, Parker, INF, Jr.	.429	.455	.619	21	8	1	0	1	3	0
Klein, Brian, INF, Sr.	.391	.494	.580	69	20	10	0	1	13	0
Marusak, Max, OF, Jr.	.286	.318	.286	21	3	0	0	0	6	3
Masters, Cody, OF, Jr.	.194	.316	.548	31	13	2	0	3	11	1
Neuse, Dylan, UT, Jr.	.355	.438	.487	76	22	5	1	1	12	12
O'Tremba, Tanner, OF, So.	.313	.333	.625	16	5	3	1	0	2	1
Rombach, Nate, UT, Fr.	.308	.440	.677	65	20	4	1	6	27	0
Rumfield, T.J., INF, R-Fr.	.417	.481	.542	24	6	3	0	0	3	0
Stilwell, Cole, UT, So.	.345	.500	.564	55	15	6	0	2	18	0
Willis, Bo, C, Fr.	.250	.400	.250	4	2	0	0	0	0	0
Wilson, Kurt, OF, Jr.	1.000	1.000	1.000	1	0	0	0	0	1	0

Pitcher, Year	W	L	ERA	G	GS	SV	IP	H	BB	SO
Barrera, Jon, Fr.	0	0	13.50	2	0	0	2	3	5	3
Becker, Austin, So.	1	0	6.08	5	4	0	13.1	9	14	11
Beeter, Clayton, R-So.	2	1	2.14	4	4	0	21	13	4	33
Bonnin, Bryce, Jr.	2	0	7.36	4	4	0	14.2	19	6	27
Brustoski, Jakob, Jr.	1	1	1.80	7	0	0	10	5	4	13
Dallas, Micah, So.	1	0	0.57	5	0	3	15.2	7	1	23
Devine, Andrew, Fr.	1	0	1.23	6	0	1	7.1	4	2	10
Dobbins, Hunter, Fr.	2	0	1.35	6	3	0	20	17	5	25
Hamilton, Tyler, Fr.	0	0	18.00	1	0	0	1	4	0	1
Hendrix, Brandon, Fr.	0	0	6.00	5	0	0	6	7	1	5
McMillon, John, Sr.	1	0	3.86	7	0	0	9.1	9	8	20
Montgomery, Mason, So.	3	1	3.00	4	4	0	18	12	7	20
Queen, Connor, Sr.	0	0	1.50	3	0	0	6	5	1	1
Ramsey, Riley, Jr.	0	0	0.00	2	0	0	1.1	1	0	2
Riechmann, Eli, Jr.	0	0	3.00	5	0	0	6	6	1	6
Sublette, Ryan, Jr.	2	0	3.86	6	0	0	9.1	7	5	15
Wilson, Kurt, Jr.	0	0	4.50	5	0	0	8	6	4	7

3. GEORGIA

Coach: Scott Stricklin. **Record:** 14-4

Player, Pos., Year	AVG	OBP	SLG	AB	R	2B	3B	HR	RBI	SB
Anderson, Ben, OF, R-So.	.414	.544	.552	58	24	6	1	0	13	5
Blaylock, Garrett, INF, Jr.	.180	.261	.426	61	8	3	0	4	8	0
Bradley, Tucker, OF, R-Jr.	.397	.513	.730	63	17	3	0	6	23	8
Floyd, Buddy, INF, Fr.	.207	.395	.207	29	5	0	0	0	3	1
Fowler, Kaden, UT, R-Fr.	.333	.600	.778	9	4	1	0	1	2	0
Jernigan, Randon, OF, So.	.273	.467	.273	11	2	0	0	0	2	0
King, Riley, UT, R-Jr.	.203	.306	.203	59	8	0	0	0	11	2
Ledford, Kale, C, Jr.	.143	.333	.143	7	2	0	0	0	0	0
Marshall, Shane, C, So.	.179	.361	.214	28	7	1	0	0	3	0
Meadows, Mason, C, R-Jr.	.150	.292	.150	20	2	0	0	0	3	0
Rogers, Chaney, UT, Jr.	.297	.395	.351	37	5	2	0	0	2	0
Shepherd, Cam, SS, Sr.	.268	.372	.493	71	18	4	0	4	21	7
Sullivan, Patrick, 1B, R-Sr.	.298	.385	.351	57	6	3	0	0	8	0
Tate, Cole, INF, Jr.	.339	.350	.536	56	11	5	0	2	14	1
Tate, Connor, INF, R-So.	.243	.396	.351	37	9	1	0	1	5	2

Pitcher, Year	W	L	ERA	G	GS	SV	IP	H	BB	SO
Bradley, Tucker, R-Jr.	0	0	0.00	3	0	1	4.1	2	1	6
Brown, Garrett, R-Fr.	1	2	4.96	4	4	0	16.1	16	4	13
Cannon, Jonathan, Fr.	3	0	0.00	5	0	0	11.1	4	2	12
Childers, Will, Fr.	1	0	0.79	5	1	0	11.1	8	6	13
Glover, Justin, Sr.	1	0	2.70	5	0	0	10	6	5	8
Gowen, Jack, So.	0	0	3.18	4	0	0	5.2	2	5	10
Hancock, Emerson, Jr.	2	0	3.75	4	4	0	24	22	3	34
Moody, Logan, R-Sr.	1	0	0.00	3	1	0	8	3	4	7
Pasqua, Darryn, R-So.	0	1	7.71	4	0	0	4.2	9	2	3
Polk, Michael, Fr.	0	0	0.00	5	0	0	5	1	3	7
Smith, Brandon, Fr.	0	0	13.50	3	0	0	2	3	2	1
Smith, C.J., Jr.	0	1	3.32	4	4	0	19	12	10	20
Tatum, Cain, Fr.	0	0	2.08	5	0	0	4.1	4	1	5
Webb, Ryan, Jr.	2	0	1.20	5	0	1	15	13	5	26
Wilcox, Cole, So.	3	0	1.57	4	4	0	23	18	2	32

4. UCLA

Coach: John Savage. **Record:** 13-2

Player, Pos., Year	AVG	OBP	SLG	AB	R	2B	3B	HR	RBI	SB
Cardenas, Noah, C, So.	.237	.367	.289	38	6	2	0	0	10	0
Caulfield, Pat, OF, Jr.	.302	.362	.442	43	8	3	0	1	9	1
Cuellar, Kyle, OF, Sr.	.341	.451	.537	41	8	2	0	2	9	0
Curialle, Michael, INF, Fr.	.325	.357	.525	40	9	2	0	2	9	2
Hahn, Josh, OF, Fr.	.176	.300	.176	17	1	0	0	0	0	1
McInerny, Will, C, Sr.	.348	.360	.348	23	4	0	0	0	5	0
McLain, Matt, INF, So.	.397	.422	.621	58	15	4	0	3	19	1
Mitchell, Garrett, OF, Jr.	.355	.425	.484	62	18	6	1	0	9	5
Moberg, Jake, INF, So.	.265	.391	.265	49	10	0	0	0	6	1
Perez, Mikey, INF, So.	.333	.476	.455	33	15	4	0	0	6	1
Perry, Darius, C, Fr.	.000	.000	.000	4	0	0	0	0	0	0
Prendiz, Jordan, OF, R-Jr.	.071	.263	.071	14	3	0	0	0	1	0
Schwartz, J.T., INF, R-Fr.	.328	.380	.391	64	11	4	0	0	8	2
Silva, Jarron, OF, R-Jr.	.276	.382	.379	29	4	0	0	1	8	2
Teijeiro, R.J., INF, Jr.	.250	.250	.250	4	0	0	0	0	1	0

Pitcher, Year	W	L	ERA	G	GS	SV	IP	H	BB	SO
Bergin, Jesse, So.	4	0	1.27	4	4	0	21.1	13	7	27
Chaidez, Adrian, Jr.	1	1	8.10	4	0	0	3.1	2	3	7
Colwell, Daniel, So.	0	0	10.80	4	0	0	1.2	4	1	2
Filby, Jack, So.	0	0	0.00	3	0	0	2.1	0	2	2
Harrison, Charles, Fr.	0	0	0.00	3	0	0	1.2	0	1	0
Karros, Jared, Fr.	2	0	3.86	4	3	0	14	9	2	16
Mora, Kyle, Sr.	0	0	0.96	11	0	9	9.1	7	3	15
Mullen, Sean, So.	0	0	0.93	7	0	0	9.2	5	6	10
Nastrini, Nick, So.	2	1	4.60	4	0	0	15.2	12	10	19
Pettway, Zach, Jr.	3	0	1.05	4	4	0	25.2	13	1	29
Powell, Holden, Jr.	0	0	0.00	8	0	3	9.1	3	2	20
Rubi, Felix, Sr.	0	0	0.00	5	0	0	5	4	0	5
Saum, Jake, Fr.	0	0	3.00	4	0	0	3	1	3	2
Townsend, Michael, Jr.	1	0	0.00	11	0	0	12	1	2	12

5. MIAMI

Coach: Gino DiMare. **Record:** 12-4

Player, Pos., Year	AVG	OBP	SLG	AB	R	2B	3B	HR	RBI	SB
Carmona, Yordani, UT, Fr.	.000	.000	.000	1	0	0	0	0	0	0
Crosbie, Chad, OF, Sr.	.167	.375	.333	6	1	1	0	0	0	0
Del Castillo, Adrian, C, So.	.358	.478	.547	53	13	2	1	2	15	1
Gates, J.P., UT, So.	.184	.244	.263	38	4	0	0	1	2	0
Gil, Raymond, INF, Jr.	.179	.300	.375	56	9	2	0	3	11	0
Jenkins, Tony, OF, Jr.	.300	.417	.380	50	11	1	0	1	5	3
Lala, Jordan, OF, So.	.232	.419	.286	56	12	3	0	0	6	4
Lauck, Josh, INF, Jr.	.500	.833	.500	2	0	0	0	0	3	0
Moore, Chet, OF, So.	.167	.286	.167	6	1	0	0	0	0	0
Paige, Tyler, INF, Jr.	.107	.194	.107	28	1	0	0	0	2	0
Pollak, Austin, INF, Jr.	.000	.000	.000	3	0	0	0	0	0	0
Quinones, Isaac, C, Jr.	.231	.333	.231	13	1	0	0	0	0	0
Rivera, Gabe, OF, Jr.	.317	.404	.415	41	6	1	0	1	5	2
Thomas, Jared, UT, Fr.	.188	.278	.313	32	7	1	0	1	3	1
Toral, Alex, 1B, Jr.	.296	.435	.593	54	13	1	0	5	16	0
Tuero, Luis, INF, R-Fr.	.323	.364	.355	31	6	1	0	0	8	0
Valdez, Mykanthony, UT, Fr.	.200	.200	.200	5	1	0	0	0	0	0
Vilar, Anthony, INF, So.	.297	.361	.469	64	12	5	2	0	15	3

Pitcher, Year	W	L	ERA	G	GS	SV	IP	H	BB	SO
Bodanza, Spencer, Jr.	0	0	3.60	5	0	0	5	2	4	7
Carmona, Yordani, Fr.	0	0	9.00	2	0	0	2	4	1	1
Cecconi, Slade, Jr.	2	1	3.80	4	4	0	21.1	15	7	30
Federman, Daniel, Jr.	0	1	2.08	7	0	3	8.2	7	2	11
Garland, Jake, Fr.	1	0	1.93	6	0	0	9.1	7	5	12
Gates, J.P., So.	1	0	0.82	9	0	0	11	2	1	13
Keysor, Tyler, Sr.	0	0	5.87	8	0	0	7.2	8	3	9
Maury, Jr., Albert, R-Jr.	0	0	7.36	5	0	0	3.2	9	1	3
McFarlane, Alex, Fr.	2	2	5.25	6	4	0	12	13	9	14
McMahon, Chris, Jr.	3	0	1.05	4	4	0	25.2	19	5	38
Munroe, Alex, Fr.	0	0	5.40	5	0	0	3.1	4	1	5
Palmquist, Carson, Fr.	1	0	2.31	8	0	0	11.2	6	5	15
Ruiz, Alex, R-So.	0	0	81.00	2	0	0	0.1	1	1	1
Van Belle, Brian, R-Sr.	2	0	0.68	4	4	0	26.1	16	4	38

6. LOUISVILLE

Coach: Dan McDonnell. **Record:** 13-4

Player, Pos., Year	AVG	OBP	SLG	AB	R	2B	3B	HR	RBI	SB
Benefield, Andrew, INF, So.	.286	.303	.393	28	3	3	0	0	6	1

Player, Pos., Year	AVG	OBP	SLG	AB	R	2B	3B	HR	RBI	SB
Bianco, Ben, UT, Jr.	.268	.388	.585	41	8	4	0	3	14	1
Binelas, Alex, INF, So.	.143	.143	.143	7	0	0	0	0	1	0
Borden II, Tim, INF, So.	.444	.516	.630	27	9	2	0	1	9	0
Britton, Zach, UT, Jr.	.322	.446	.542	59	14	11	1	0	12	1
Brown, Luke, OF, Jr.	.328	.384	.403	67	19	5	0	0	6	11
Davis, Henry, C, So.	.372	.481	.698	43	11	5	0	3	13	1
Dunn, Lucas, UT, Jr.	.273	.385	.455	11	3	0	1	0	4	0
Lavey, Justin, INF, Jr.	.316	.364	.526	57	11	7	1	1	17	4
Leonard, Trey, OF, Jr.	.250	.462	.250	8	6	0	0	0	1	0
Masterman, Cameron, UT, Jr.	.333	.400	.667	18	3	3	0	1	3	0
Metzinger, Ben, C, So.	.349	.417	.512	43	12	1	0	2	8	1
Oriente, Danny, OF, So.	.268	.378	.357	56	11	2	0	1	16	0
Poland, Jared, INF, So.	.281	.361	.500	32	7	4	0	1	7	2
Rushing, Dalton, UT, Fr.	.308	.419	.577	26	7	4	0	1	6	0
Seng, Chris, OF, So.	.167	.167	.167	6	5	0	0	0	0	3
Usher, Levi, OF, So.	.411	.484	.571	56	17	3	0	2	10	11

Pitcher, Year	W	L	ERA	G	GS	SV	IP	H	BB	SO
Albanese, Glenn, Jr.	0	0	2.08	5	0	0	8.2	5	5	18
Benefield, Andrew, So.	0	0	81.00	1	0	0	0.1	3	0	0
Detmers, Reid, Jr.	3	0	1.23	4	4	0	22	16	6	48
Elliott, Adam, Sr.	1	0	0.87	7	0	0	10.1	6	3	14
Hawks, Ryan, Fr.	0	0	5.40	5	0	0	5	0	4	4
Kirian, Michael, Jr.	0	0	0.00	6	0	6	6.1	2	1	11
Kuehner, Tate, Fr.	2	1	4.09	6	2	0	11	9	5	13
Lohman, Carter, So.	0	0	6.75	3	0	0	2.2	3	2	4
Miller, Bobby, Jr.	2	0	2.31	4	4	0	23.1	15	9	34
Poland, Jared, So.	0	1	12.71	5	0	0	5.2	11	3	7
Prosecky, Michael, Fr.	1	1	4.50	5	3	0	18	16	7	17
Smith, Luke, Sr.	3	0	3.42	4	4	0	23.2	21	4	18
Tulio, Kellan, Fr.	0	0	6.75	4	0	0	2.2	4	2	2
Webster, Evan, Fr.	1	1	1.04	5	0	0	8.2	5	5	9
Wright, Kerry, So.	0	0	0.00	3	0	0	2	1	2	2

7. ARIZONA STATE

Coach: Tracy Smith. **Record:** 13-4

Player, Pos., Year	AVG	OBP	SLG	AB	R	2B	3B	HR	RBI	SB
Baez, Nathan, INF, Fr.	.239	.321	.413	46	9	2	0	2	7	0
Cheema, Nick, C, Sr.	.255	.350	.275	51	9	1	0	0	2	0
Denson, Myles, OF, So.	.083	.154	.083	12	0	0	0	0	1	0
Ferri, Sam, C, Sr.	.400	.364	.400	10	0	0	0	0	2	0
Garcia, Dusty, OF, So.	.231	.412	.269	26	7	1	0	0	5	3
Hauver, Trevor, OF, Jr.	.339	.494	.695	59	18	6	0	5	20	0
Helmin, Alex, OF, Fr.	.333	.333	.333	3	0	0	0	0	2	0
Jump, Hunter, OF, Jr.	.317	.386	.524	63	10	7	0	2	15	0
Kalmer, Brian, INF, Fr.	.200	.467	.300	10	2	1	0	0	4	0
Marshall, Danny, UT, Fr.	.000	.143	.000	6	1	0	0	0	0	0
McLain, Sean, OF, Fr.	.000	.000	.000	0	1	0	0	0	0	0
Nager, Seth, OF, Fr.	.182	.308	.182	11	5	0	0	0	1	0
Swift, Drew, INF, Jr.	.365	.403	.460	63	10	3	0	1	16	1
Tolman, Erik, UT, So.	.071	.176	.071	14	0	0	0	0	1	0
Torkelson, Spencer, 1B, Jr.	.340	.598	.780	50	24	4	0	6	11	2
Wallerstedt, Nick, UT, Fr.	.000	.000	.000	1	1	0	0	0	0	0
Williams, Alika, SS, Jr.	.250	.359	.344	64	14	1	1	1	8	1
Workman, Gage, INF, Jr.	.250	.316	.471	68	12	4	1	3	14	3

Pitcher, Year	W	L	ERA	G	GS	SV	IP	H	BB	SO
Barnett, Bryce, Fr.	1	1	5.40	8	0	0	8.1	8	5	17
Benson, Cooper, Fr.	1	1	3.60	4	4	0	20	21	8	25
Bodlovich, Christian, Fr.	1	0	5.40	6	0	0	5	5	1	7
Burzell, Blake, So.	0	0	18.00	1	0	0	1	3	0	0
Corrigan, Brady, Jr.	0	0	54.00	1	0	0	0.1	2	1	1
Dabovich, R.J., Jr.	0	0	0.77	9	0	4	11.2	3	9	17
Dennie, Cam, Jr.	2	0	3.18	8	0	0	11.1	9	2	12
Fall, Justin, Jr.	1	0	5.68	4	4	0	19	16	13	17
La Flam, Luke, So.	0	0	0.00	1	0	0	0.2	0	2	0
Levine, Will, So.	1	0	5.40	3	0	0	3.1	3	3	1
Osman, Graham, Fr.	1	0	22.50	6	0	0	2	6	2	3
Thornton, Tyler, So.	2	0	3.38	4	4	0	24	20	7	25
Tolman, Erik, So.	1	1	2.50	4	3	0	18	9	12	30
Tomczak, Seth, Fr.	0	0	2.45	4	0	0	3.2	3	0	3
Vander Kooi, Boyd, Jr.	2	1	0.70	5	2	0	25.2	19	2	20

8. MISSISSIPPI

Coach: Mike Bianco. **Record:** 12-4

Player, Pos., Year	AVG	OBP	SLG	AB	R	2B	3B	HR	RBI	SB
Baker, Cael, UT, Jr.	.220	.349	.520	50	8	3	0	4	15	0
Bench, Justin, UT, So.	.295	.458	.386	44	13	1	0	1	11	3
Chatagnier, Peyton, UT, Fr.	.311	.449	.574	61	23	4	0	4	13	3
Dunhurst, Hayden, C, Fr.	.269	.355	.577	52	16	1	0	5	15	1
Ealy, Jerrion, OF, Fr.	.182	.321	.273	22	7	2	0	0	3	5
Elko, Tim, UT, Jr.	.354	.373	.667	48	12	4	1	3	15	3
Graham, Kevin, UT, So.	.237	.326	.579	38	11	4	0	3	9	1
Keenan, Tyler, INF, Jr.	.403	.488	.791	67	18	5	0	7	33	1
LaFleur, Trey, UT, Fr.	.000	.273	.000	8	2	0	0	0	1	0
Leatherwood, Hayden, OF, Jr.	.361	.477	.639	36	12	1	0	3	11	0
Loposer, Knox, C, So.	.154	.267	.615	13	3	0	0	2	5	0
Plumlee, John Rhys, OF, Fr.	.063	.111	.063	16	4	0	0	0	1	1
Sammons, Cade, OF, Fr.	.120	.241	.120	25	5	0	0	0	2	1
Servideo, Anthony, INF, Jr.	.390	.575	.695	59	24	3	0	5	17	9
Van Cleve, Ben, INF, Jr.	.385	.529	.500	26	3	3	0	0	1	0

Pitcher, Year	W	L	ERA	G	GS	SV	IP	H	BB	SO
Baker, Cole, Jr.	0	0	0.00	4	0	0	4.1	1	1	2
Broadway, Taylor, Sr.	2	0	0.56	7	0	0	16	16	3	18
Burton, Wes, Fr.	1	0	1.42	4	1	0	6.1	3	5	7
Cioffi, Max, Jr.	0	0	0.00	6	0	1	8	3	0	12
Diamond, Derek, Fr.	2	0	3.48	4	4	0	20.2	18	4	15
Forsyth, Braden, So.	1	0	1.23	6	0	5	7.1	5	4	9
Gilbert, Benji, Fr.	0	0	9.45	4	1	0	6.2	12	1	8
Hoglund, Gunnar, So.	3	0	1.16	4	4	0	23.1	18	4	37
Holston, Greer, Sr.	0	0	20.25	5	1	0	4	11	8	5
Kimbrell, Jackson, Fr.	2	0	2.45	5	2	0	11	11	3	9
McDaniel, Drew, Fr.	0	0	9.00	3	0	0	3	3	3	2
Miller, Austin, Sr.	2	0	2.08	7	0	0	13	7	5	19
Murrell, Mitch, Fr.	0	0	0.00	1	0	0	1	1	0	1
Nikhazy, Doug, So.	3	1	2.35	4	4	0	23	9	9	31
Savell, Logan, R-Fr.	0	0	10.80	5	0	0	3.1	5	1	4

9. OKLAHOMA

Coach: Skip Johnson. **Record:** 14-4

Player, Pos., Year	AVG	OBP	SLG	AB	R	2B	3B	HR	RBI	SB
Beichler, Connor, UT, Fr.	.364	.563	.455	11	4	1	0	0	3	4
Bohrofen, Braxton, INF, R-Fr.	.000	.667	.000	1	1	0	0	0	0	0
Bologna, Vincenzo, OF, Jr.	.182	.250	.273	11	1	1	0	0	0	0
Brown, Trent, INF, R-So.	.294	.350	.765	17	3	2	0	2	6	2
Godman, Jaret, INF, So.	1.000	1.000	1.000	2	0	0	0	0	0	0
Graham, Peyton, INF, Fr.	.358	.457	.612	67	19	8	0	3	10	8
Hardman, Tyler, INF, Jr.	.270	.333	.459	74	12	5	0	3	12	2
Harlan, Brady, OF, So.	.243	.417	.324	37	6	3	0	0	2	3
Kohler, Logan, INF, Fr.	.174	.200	.174	23	0	0	0	0	2	1
LaValley, Carter, INF, Fr.	.500	.667	.750	4	2	1	0	0	0	0
Lindsly, Brady, C, Sr.	.271	.358	.492	59	10	2	1	3	13	2
McKenna, Conor, INF, So.	.196	.260	.261	46	8	3	0	0	5	1
Mitchell, Justin, C, Jr.	.310	.392	.548	42	6	4	0	2	8	2
Muniz, Diego, UT, So.	.207	.314	.345	29	5	1	0	0	2	0
Pettis, Kendall, OF, Fr.	.276	.364	.448	29	4	0	1	1	4	1
Quick, Luke, OF, Jr.	.000	.000	.000	1	0	0	0	0	0	0
Tredaway, Tanner, UT, Jr.	.378	.392	.689	74	16	6	4	3	14	5
Vujovich, Jordan, OF, R-Jr.	.167	.278	.333	30	7	1	2	0	3	0
Zaragoza, Brandon, SS, Sr.	.250	.313	.304	56	9	3	0	0	9	1

Pitcher, Year	W	L	ERA	G	GS	SV	IP	H	BB	SO
Abram, Ben, So.	1	0	0.90	4	1	0	10	8	3	13
Acker, Dane, Jr.	1	1	3.51	4	4	0	25.2	15	5	28
Bennett, Jake, Fr.	3	0	0.75	3	3	0	12	6	3	19
Brooks, Aaron, Jr.	1	1	0.00	5	0	0	5	2	0	8
Carter, Carson, R-Jr.	0	0	5.79	5	0	0	4.2	6	3	9
Cavalli, Cade, Jr.	1	2	4.18	4	4	0	23.2	25	5	37
Demco, Brad, Sr.	0	0	3.00	5	0	0	3	2	3	4
Godman, Jaret, So.	0	0	5.00	7	0	1	9	11	2	9
Matthews, Zack, Jr.	1	0	4.50	4	0	0	6	6	3	7
Olds, Wyatt, So.	4	0	1.89	5	2	0	19	14	8	29
Prater, Levi, Jr.	1	0	3.42	4	4	0	23.2	20	10	33
Ruebeck, Christian, Fr.	0	0	5.40	4	0	0	3.1	3	1	6
Ruffcorn, Jason, Sr.	1	0	0.00	7	0	5	8	3	1	12
Smith, Ledgend, Jr.	0	0	0.00	6	0	0	6	2	0	4
Webb, Braxton, Sr.	0	0	4.50	3	0	0	2	2	1	4

10. DUKE

Coach: Chris Pollard. **Record:** 12-4

Player, Pos., Year	AVG	OBP	SLG	AB	R	2B	3B	HR	RBI	SB
Cheek, Chase, OF, Sr.	.250	.328	.333	60	10	2	0	1	5	2
Crabtree, Chris, INF, Jr.	.207	.368	.345	29	4	2	1	0	2	1
Dutra, Chris, C, Sr.	.375	.444	.500	8	1	1	0	0	2	0
Fuller, Britt, INF, Fr.	.333	.400	.333	3	0	0	0	0	1	0

Player	AVG	OBP	SLG	AB	R	2B	3B	HR	RBI	SB
Hoyle, Wil, INF, R-So.	.265	.324	.500	34	6	1	2	1	4	1
Knight, Chad, C, Fr.	.241	.241	.414	29	4	0	1	1	3	0
Loperfido, Joey, OF, Jr.	.264	.418	.358	53	12	1	2	0	6	5
Lux, Damon, OF, So.	.000	.000	.000	5	0	0	0	0	0	0
Maxwell, Rudy, C, So.	.195	.327	.293	41	6	2	1	0	7	1
Mervis, Matt, UT, Sr.	.304	.458	.589	56	9	5	1	3	15	1
Murray, Ethan, INF, So.	.222	.377	.352	54	11	4	0	1	6	2
Nichols, Erikson, INF, So.	.224	.274	.259	58	5	2	0	0	4	0
Norris, Grant, INF, Fr.	.111	.346	.111	18	3	0	0	0	2	0
Rothenberg, Michael, C, Jr.	.349	.551	.605	43	13	5	0	2	17	1
Schreck, R.J., OF, So.	.100	.308	.100	10	1	0	0	0	0	0
Topolski, Jake, INF, R-Fr.	.000	.000	.000	3	2	0	0	0	1	0

Pitcher, Year	W	L	ERA	G	GS	SV	IP	H	BB	SO
Beasley, Aaron, So.	0	1	10.80	4	0	0	5	8	1	6
Carey, Jack, So.	1	1	4.26	5	3	0	19	22	7	22
Chillari, Bill, Sr.	3	0	0.82	4	4	0	11	7	3	7
Dockman, Matt, Jr.	0	0	3.00	8	0	0	9	12	6	10
Girard, Thomas, Jr.	1	1	3.46	9	0	4	13	4	1	23
Herrick, Eli, Sr.	0	0	0.93	8	0	0	9.2	7	6	15
Jarvis, Bryce, Jr.	3	1	0.67	4	4	0	27	11	2	40
Johnson, Marcus, Fr.	0	0	3.86	3	0	0	2.1	3	1	4
Loper, Jimmy, R-Fr.	1	0	2.16	8	0	0	8.1	3	3	11
McCarthy, Oliver, R-Fr.	0	0	0.00	1	0	0	1	0	0	2
Mervis, Matt, Sr.	0	0	0.00	2	0	0	2	1	1	2
Nifong, Josh, Jr.	0	0	4.76	5	0	0	11.1	10	5	14
Salley, Kyle, So.	0	0	0.00	3	0	0	2.1	0	1	3
Stinson, Cooper, So.	3	0	0.42	4	4	0	21.2	16	4	24
Williams, Henry, Fr.	0	0	13.50	1	1	0	0.2	0	3	0

11. VANDERBILT
Coach: Tim Corbin. Record: 13-5

Player, Pos., Year	AVG	OBP	SLG	AB	R	2B	3B	HR	RBI	SB
Davis, Cooper, OF, Jr.	.348	.416	.435	69	14	2	2	0	5	5
Duff, Will, UT, Fr.	.267	.333	.333	15	2	1	0	0	3	1
Duvall, Ty, C, Sr.	.288	.415	.308	52	9	1	0	0	10	0
Hayes, Sterling, INF, So.	.000	.000	.000	1	0	0	0	0	0	0
Hogan, Matt, OF, So.	.000	.000	.000	2	0	0	0	0	0	0
Jones, Spencer, UT, Fr.	.206	.333	.324	34	8	4	0	0	3	2
Keegan, Dominic, UT, So.	.242	.324	.303	33	3	2	0	0	4	0
Kolwyck, Tate, OF, So.	.174	.296	.391	23	2	2	0	1	4	0
LaNeve, Troy, OF, Fr.	.000	.000	.000	1	0	0	0	0	0	0
Malloy, Justyn-Henry, UT, So.	.167	.487	.208	24	6	1	0	0	2	1
Martin, Austin, UT, Jr.	.377	.507	.660	53	15	6	0	3	11	3
McKenzie, T.J., UT, Fr.	.000	.500	.000	1	1	0	0	0	0	0
Noland, Parker, INF, Fr.	.259	.324	.310	58	8	3	0	0	11	2
Ray, Harrison, INF, Sr.	.242	.347	.355	62	9	4	0	1	13	9
Rodriguez, C.J., C, Fr.	.289	.370	.356	45	5	3	0	0	8	0
Thomas, Isaiah, OF, So.	.258	.313	.532	62	12	5	0	4	13	3
Young, Carter, INF, Fr.	.328	.373	.377	61	10	3	0	0	12	1

Pithcer, Year	W	L	ERA	G	GS	SV	IP	H	BB	SO
Brown, Tyler, Jr.	1	2	2.53	7	0	1	10.2	12	4	14
Doolin, Michael, Fr.	1	0	0.87	5	0	1	10.1	6	4	18
Eder, Jake, Jr.	1	1	3.60	4	4	0	20	20	9	27
Hickman, Mason, Jr.	2	0	0.48	3	3	0	18.2	8	3	26
Hliboki, Sam, Fr.	0	0	0.00	5	0	2	15.2	2	2	16
Kaiser, Erik, Jr.	1	0	0.00	4	0	0	5	2	2	10
Leiter, Jack, Fr.	2	0	1.72	4	3	0	15.2	5	8	22
Maldonado, Nick, Fr.	0	0	2.70	4	0	0	6.2	7	1	6
McElvain, Chris, Fr.	0	0	4.82	6	0	0	9.1	8	4	7
Murphy, Luke, R-Fr.	0	0	13.50	4	0	0	2	2	9	4
Rocker, Kumar, So.	2	1	1.80	3	3	0	15	6	8	28
Schultz, Thomas, Fr.	0	1	0.66	4	1	1	13.2	9	3	17
Smith, Ethan, So.	3	0	1.42	5	4	0	20	20	9	27

12. LONG BEACH STATE
Coach: Eric Valenzuela. Record: 10-5

Player, Pos., Year	AVG	OBP	SLG	AB	R	2B	3B	HR	RBI	SB
Carlino, Victor, INF, Sr.	.000	.083	.000	11	1	0	0	0	0	0
Carlson, Tanner, INF, So.	.250	.273	.250	20	5	0	0	0	1	0
DeSa, Riki, UT, Sr.	.235	.500	.471	17	5	1	0	1	7	0
Estrada, Calvin, OF, R-Sr.	.290	.362	.387	62	10	6	0	0	7	2
Greely, Thomas, C, Jr.	.333	.423	.333	21	4	0	0	0	2	1
Harrison, Devereaux, OF, Fr.	.000	.000	.000	1	0	0	0	0	0	0
Hogan, Kaden, INF, So.	.000	.000	.000	5	1	0	0	0	0	0
Hughey, Jacob, UT, R-Sr.	.116	.224	.116	43	4	0	0	0	4	0
Jones, Leonard, UT, R-So.	.327	.377	.509	55	7	2	1	2	9	2

Player	AVG	OBP	SLG	AB	R	2B	3B	HR	RBI	SB
Joy, Cole, UT, R-Sr.	.207	.303	.241	29	1	1	0	0	3	0
Kokx, Connor, OF, R-Fr.	.400	.491	.511	45	7	5	0	0	5	3
Lopez, Jesse, OF, Jr.	.000	.000	.000	3	2	0	0	0	0	1
Loust, Charlie, C, R-Fr.	.000	.167	.000	5	0	0	0	0	0	0
Luttrell, Chase, UT, So.	.370	.400	.444	27	3	2	0	0	4	1
Malm, Aidan, OF, Sr.	.306	.500	.389	36	3	1	1	0	8	3
Pimentel, Alex, OF, Fr.	.263	.333	.316	19	7	1	0	0	2	0
Porter, Tyler, INF, So.	.171	.275	.200	35	2	1	0	0	2	1
Rivera, Santino, INF, Jr.	.182	.265	.205	44	4	1	0	0	3	0
Rosales, Javier, OF, Jr.	.000	.000	.000	2	0	0	0	0	1	0
Rozell, Brennan, INF, So.	.100	.091	.100	10	0	0	0	0	1	0

Pitcher, Year	W	L	ERA	G	GS	SV	IP	H	BB	SO
Carlos, Jonathan, So.	0	1	7.71	5	1	0	9.1	14	2	6
Clough, Ethan, So.	0	1	4.15	3	0	0	4.1	4	0	3
Fields, Matt, R-Jr.	1	0	1.50	5	0	1	6	1	1	8
Gums, Tyler, Sr.	2	0	0.77	5	1	1	11.2	7	2	13
Harrison, Devereaux, Fr.	0	1	1.32	7	0	0	13.2	8	6	18
Lavallee, Jonathan, Jr.	1	0	3.27	5	1	0	11	11	3	7
Ramirez, Luis, Fr.	2	0	2.73	4	4	0	26.1	23	8	27
Riley, Connor, R-Jr.	0	0	0.00	1	0	0	1	0	0	1
Rons, Jake, Fr.	0	1	2.16	4	0	0	8.1	8	6	5
Ruiz, Alfredo, So.	3	1	1.80	4	4	0	25	15	5	24
Seminaris, Adam, Jr.	1	0	1.23	4	3	0	22	9	3	36
Taylor, Troy, Fr.	0	0	6.75	1	0	0	1.1	1	1	1

13. MISSISSIPPI STATE
Coach: Chris Lemonis. Record: 12-4

Player, Pos., Year	AVG	OBP	SLG	AB	R	2B	3B	HR	RBI	SB
Allen, Tanner, OF, Jr.	.240	.387	.400	25	6	2	1	0	5	0
Brock, Bryce, OF, So.	.000	.000	.000	3	0	0	0	0	1	0
Cumbest, Brad, OF, So.	.130	.167	.304	23	2	1	0	1	1	0
Foscue, Justin, INF, Jr.	.321	.464	.509	53	10	4	0	2	16	1
French, Hunter, OF, Fr.	.000	.000	.000	2	0	0	0	0	0	0
Hancock, Luke, C, So.	.231	.310	.308	26	0	2	0	0	3	0
Hatcher, Josh, UT, Jr.	.311	.338	.508	61	10	4	1	2	9	2
James, Kamren, INF, Fr.	.308	.339	.423	52	3	3	0	1	12	1
Jordan, Landon, INF, So.	.182	.341	.182	33	4	0	0	0	0	0
Jordan, Rowdey, OF, Jr.	.308	.395	.338	65	17	2	0	0	6	3
Land, Mason, INF, Fr.	.250	.400	.250	4	2	0	0	0	0	0
Leggett, Tanner, INF, Jr.	.118	.250	.118	17	3	0	0	0	0	0
McGowan, Drew, OF, Fr.	.100	.100	.100	10	0	0	0	0	1	0
Pimentel, Brandon, UT, So.	.184	.286	.265	49	5	1	0	1	8	2
Tanner, Logan, C, Fr.	.268	.388	.439	41	6	1	0	2	5	0
Westburg, Jordan, INF, Jr.	.317	.432	.517	60	17	4	0	2	16	1

Pitcher, Year	W	L	ERA	G	GS	SV	IP	H	BB	SO
Bednar, Will, Fr.	0	0	1.76	4	1	1	15.1	9	6	23
Cerantola, Eric, So.	1	1	3.18	4	4	0	17	17	11	22
Dunlavey, David, Sr.	2	1	1.69	5	0	0	10.2	8	8	11
Forrester, Jaxen, Jr.	0	0	2.57	7	0	0	7	5	3	9
Ginn, J.T., So.	0	0	6.00	1	1	0	3	3	2	4
Harding, Houston, Jr.	1	0	2.79	2	2	0	9.2	6	3	11
Hunt, K.C., Fr.	0	0	16.20	1	1	0	1.2	2	1	1
Koestler, Carlisle, Sr.	0	1	4.42	5	3	0	18.1	18	5	13
MacLeod, Christian, R-Fr.	4	0	0.86	4	4	0	21	9	6	25
Patrick, Chase, Jr.	2	0	4.50	4	0	0	6	4	3	7
Price, Spencer, Sr.	0	0	0.00	8	0	2	7.1	1	1	10
Self, Riley, Sr.	1	0	1.17	7	0	0	7.2	3	1	7
Shemper, Jared, Jr.	0	1	8.31	5	0	1	4.1	6	3	4
Sims, Landon, Fr.	1	0	3.46	5	0	0	13	5	7	23

14. ARKANSAS
Coach: Dave Van Horn. Record: 11-5

Player, Pos., Year	AVG	OBP	SLG	AB	R	2B	3B	HR	RBI	SB
Austin, Cole, INF, R-Sr.	.191	.269	.298	47	8	2	0	1	5	0
Franklin, Christian, OF, So.	.381	.467	.619	63	21	4	1	3	11	3
Goodheart, Matt, UT, Jr.	.302	.400	.492	63	14	3	0	3	18	1
Gregory, Zack, INF, R-Fr.	.136	.310	.136	22	1	0	0	0	2	1
Kjerstad, Heston, OF, Jr.	.448	.513	.791	67	19	5	0	6	20	1
Martin, Casey, SS, Jr.	.271	.386	.458	59	7	5	0	2	10	6
Matthews, Bryce, OF, Fr.	.250	.400	.500	4	1	1	0	0	0	0
Moore, Robert, INF, Fr.	.317	.403	.444	63	10	2	0	2	17	3
Nesbit, Jacob, INF, R-So.	.259	.348	.397	58	8	5	0	1	9	0
Opitz, Casey, C, Jr.	.302	.361	.509	53	10	6	1	1	11	0
Tamez, Dominic, UT, Fr.	.400	.455	.400	10	3	0	0	0	0	0
Tollett, Cason, UT, Fr.	.000	.000	.000	1	0	0	0	0	0	0
Washington, Jr., Curtis, UT, So.	.200	.500	.800	5	2	0	0	1	2	0

	AVG	OBP	SLG	AB	R	2B	3B	HR	RBI	SB
Webb, Braydon, UT, R-Jr.	.340	.452	.400	50	14	0	0	1	6	2

Pitcher, Year	W	L	ERA	G	GS	SV	IP	H	BB	SO
Adamiak, Mark, Fr.	0	0	16.20	2	0	0	1.2	4	0	2
Adams, Blake, Fr.	0	0	9.95	4	2	0	6.1	10	5	6
Bolden, Caleb, R-So.	1	0	1.12	4	2	0	16	14	3	15
Burton, Jacob, So.	0	0	4.15	5	0	0	4.1	1	7	6
Denton, Marshall, R-Jr.	1	0	1.50	6	0	0	6	7	2	6
Kopps, Kevin, R-Jr.	0	1	8.18	7	1	0	11	18	4	9
McEntire, Will, Fr.	1	0	1.12	2	1	0	8	7	0	7
Monke, Caden, So.	1	1	2.53	6	0	1	10.2	4	3	13
Morris, Zack, Fr.	1	0	3.18	5	0	0	5.2	4	1	1
Noland, Connor, So.	2	0	2.00	3	3	0	18	13	4	19
Pallette, Peyton, Fr.	0	0	1.59	4	0	1	5.2	5	3	3
Ramage, Kole, Jr.	1	1	4.40	5	3	0	14.1	17	5	14
Taylor, Evan, So.	0	0	9.00	2	0	0	2	1	2	3
Trest, Elijah, So.	0	0	1.93	7	0	0	9.1	7	3	10
Vermillion, Zebulon, Jr.	1	0	0.00	5	0	1	7.1	4	0	12
Wicklander, Patrick, So.	2	2	6.32	4	4	0	15.2	13	9	17

15. CENTRAL FLORIDA
Coach: Greg Lovelady. Record: 15-3

Player, Pos. Year	AVG	OBP	SLG	AB	R	2B	3B	HR	RBI	SB
Allen, Connor, INF, R-So.	.263	.364	.368	19	3	0	1	0	5	2
Archer, Matt, INF, Fr.	.291	.328	.364	55	10	1	0	1	10	2
Brait, Andrew, INF, Fr.	.226	.368	.226	31	5	0	0	0	3	2
Crouch, Josh, C, Jr.	.200	.256	.257	35	6	2	0	0	5	0
Josten, Tom, INF, So.	.196	.366	.429	56	13	4	0	3	10	0
McCabe, Ben, C, So.	.304	.385	.500	46	8	3	0	2	6	1
Orlando, Noah, INF, Jr.	.241	.353	.276	29	5	1	0	0	2	6
Pena, Gephry, OF, So.	.314	.415	.429	70	17	3	1	1	9	13
Rathbone, Jordan, UT, R-Sr.	.313	.382	.507	67	14	4	0	3	17	0
Romano, Nick, 1B, Jr.	.315	.373	.389	54	5	4	0	0	9	0
Ruiz, Pablo, UT, Fr.	.275	.302	.490	51	9	2	0	3	7	2
Rushing, Ben, UT, R-Fr.	.400	.400	1.400	5	1	0	1	1	4	0
Taylor, Trent, UT, Jr.	.000	.000	.000	3	4	0	0	0	1	2
Wingo, Dalton, OF, Jr.	.303	.338	.434	76	13	4	0	2	7	1

Pitcher, Year	W	L	ERA	G	GS	SV	IP	H	BB	SO
Gordon, Colton, R-So.	2	0	2.35	4	4	0	23	18	5	24
Gottilla, Nick, Fr.	0	0	0.00	6	0	0	6.1	0	4	8
Hakanson, Jeffrey, Jr.	0	0	0.00	7	0	6	8.1	1	1	20
Holloway, Trevor, R-Jr.	3	1	1.19	4	4	0	22.2	12	6	37
Hunsicker, Zack, So.	0	0	2.25	5	1	0	8	8	6	8
Lepkoske, Nolan, R-Fr.	0	0	0.00	1	0	0	0.1	0	1	0
Litchfield, David, R-Jr.	2	0	0.73	6	0	0	12.1	10	3	9
Luensmann, Chad, R-Sr.	0	0	22.50	2	0	0	2	5	1	2
McKay, Billy, R-Jr.	0	1	3.12	8	0	0	8.2	3	6	8
Patteson, Hunter, Fr.	1	0	4.91	4	2	0	14.2	13	8	12
Saltonstall, Ryan, R-Jr.	0	0	0.00	6	0	0	4.1	4	3	6
Sheridan, Joe, R-Jr.	2	0	3.32	4	4	0	19	16	10	18
Sinclair, Jack, Jr.	4	0	1.35	8	0	0	13.1	8	6	20
Whitehead Jaylyn, R-Sr.	1	1	0.95	6	3	1	19	8	5	18

16. PEPPERDINE
Coach: Rick Hirtensteiner. Record: 12-3

Player, Pos., Year	AVG	OBP	SLG	AB	R	2B	3B	HR	RBI	SB
Alexiades, Reese, OF, R-Jr.	.397	.458	.571	63	11	6	1	1	15	2
Caparis, Joe, C, Sr.	.164	.270	.218	55	4	0	0	1	7	0
Cook, Billy, OF, So.	.344	.452	.672	64	19	4	2	4	14	5
Johnson, Ryan, INF, Fr.	.286	.375	.429	56	16	3	1	1	12	6
Landis, Quintt, C, Fr.	.194	.324	.194	31	5	0	0	0	3	0
LeBioda, David, 1B, Fr.	.217	.280	.217	23	4	0	0	0	1	0
Lopez, Jesus, INF, Fr.	.000	.000	.000	10	0	0	0	0	0	0
Lutes, Justin, INF, Sr.	.328	.438	.655	58	16	3	2	4	21	0
Malinchak, Mike, OF, Jr.	.395	.458	.512	43	6	2	0	1	9	2
Modlin, Aharon, INF, Jr.	.413	.472	.571	63	17	5	1	1	11	3
Schoen, Grant, OF, Fr.	.000	.235	.000	13	1	0	0	0	1	1
Winaker, Michael, INF, So.	.000	.000	.000	1	0	0	0	0	0	0
Young, Wyatt, INF, So.	.299	.373	.299	67	13	0	0	0	4	0

Pitcher, Year	W	L	ERA	G	GS	SV	IP	H	BB	SO
Baird, Jack, So.	0	0	0.00	4	0	0	3	1	1	3
Castillo, Josiah, Fr.	0	0	0.00	3	0	0	5.1	2	5	3
Chandler, Cooper, R-So.	3	0	1.00	3	3	0	18	14	5	20
Chester, Jack, Fr.	1	0	4.15	3	0	0	4.1	4	3	2
Diamond, Nathan, Fr.	0	0	5.14	5	1	0	7	7	7	7
Franklin, Trevor, R-Jr.	0	1	1.64	5	0	0	11	9	3	5

	W	L	ERA	G	GS	SV	IP	H	BB	SO
Groen, Gunnar, R-So.	2	1	2.57	5	3	1	21	14	6	13
Jensen, Wil, R-So.	3	0	2.19	4	4	0	24.2	18	6	26
Kniskern, Trevor, So.	2	1	5.40	4	4	0	18.1	16	7	21
Mahony, Michael, R-Sr.	0	0	0.00	3	0	0	2	1	2	3
Morrow, Dane, Jr.	0	0	6.17	6	0	1	11.2	17	3	14
Murrah, Tyler, So.	0	0	0.00	1	0	0	1	0	0	0
Telfer, Shane, Fr.	1	0	3.12	6	0	1	8.2	11	7	7

17. VIRGINIA
Coach: Brian O'Connor. Record: 14-4

Player, Pos., Year	AVG	OBP	SLG	AB	R	2B	3B	HR	RBI	SB
Ballestero, Tate, UT, Fr.	.083	.214	.250	12	2	0	1	0	2	0
Cotier, Max, INF, Fr.	.338	.410	.527	74	21	3	4	1	15	3
Gelof, Zack, INF, So.	.349	.469	.746	63	24	6	2	5	18	4
Hamrock, Drew, UT, So.	.263	.483	.368	19	8	2	0	0	5	0
Hlinka, Christian, OF, Jr.	.320	.370	.880	25	7	0	1	4	9	0
Jenkins, Walker, INF, Jr.	.091	.167	.091	11	1	0	0	0	0	0
Kent, Nic, INF, So.	.328	.451	.433	67	17	4	0	1	7	6
Lebreux, Marc, OF, Jr.	.303	.425	.379	66	18	5	0	0	14	4
Michaels, Logan, C, Sr.	.316	.403	.474	57	17	6	0	1	16	2
Newell, Chris, OF, Fr.	.407	.545	.729	59	21	5	1	4	20	8
Ortiz, Devin, INF, Jr.	.255	.403	.418	55	11	3	0	2	14	3
Rivoli, Brendan, C, So.	.320	.390	.420	50	6	3	1	0	11	2
Sullivan, Jimmy, OF, So.	.233	.281	.633	30	7	0	0	4	7	2
Tappen, Alex, INF, Jr.	.235	.263	.294	17	2	1	0	0	1	0

Pitcher, Year	W	L	ERA	G	GS	SV	IP	H	BB	SO
Abbott, Andrew, Jr.	3	0	1.35	9	0	0	13.1	9	8	28
Baldino, Jacob, Fr.	0	0	18.00	4	0	0	4	6	3	5
Bales, Blake, Jr.	2	0	2.08	6	0	0	8.2	8	3	9
Harrington, Chesdin, Sr.	0	2	12.15	3	2	0	6.2	17	3	8
Hodorovich, Jake, Fr.	0	0	6.75	4	1	0	4	5	0	3
Hoopes, Jayson, Fr.	0	0	10.80	2	0	0	1.2	2	0	1
Kosanovich, Paul, So.	0	0	2.16	5	0	0	8.1	5	4	8
McGarry, Griff, Jr.	3	0	1.35	4	4	0	20	5	19	31
Messinger, Zach, So.	0	0	3.29	7	2	0	13.2	22	3	22
Neeck, Brandon, Fr.	0	0	4.50	3	0	0	2	2	4	4
Price, Billy, So.	0	0	0.00	2	0	0	3	1	1	2
Sanchez, Cristian, So.	0	0	18.00	2	0	0	2	2	2	1
Savino, Nate, Fr.	1	0	3.38	4	3	0	10.2	8	5	10
Schoch, Stephen, Sr.	1	1	1.62	11	0	5	16.2	10	5	24
Sperling, Evan, Sr.	0	0	6.00	4	0	0	3	3	3	3
Vasil, Mike, So.	2	0	2.45	4	4	0	22	21	10	23
Whitten, Kyle, Jr.	0	1	2.61	7	0	0	10.1	10	5	9
Wyatt, Matt, Fr.,	1	0	3.60	6	2	0	12	7	7	8

18. NORTH CAROLINA STATE
Coach: Elliott Avent. Record: 14-3

Player, Pos., Year	AVG	OBP	SLG	AB	R	2B	3B	HR	RBI	SB
Bailey, Patrick, C, Jr.	.296	.466	.685	54	20	3	0	6	20	1
Brown, Devonte, UT, Jr.	.338	.429	.692	65	19	6	1	5	19	4
Butler, Jonny, OF, Jr.	.290	.384	.468	62	7	4	2	1	14	9
Chlup, Marek, OF, So.	.500	.667	.750	4	2	1	0	0	0	0
Debo, Brad, C, Sr.	.263	.300	.316	19	3	1	0	0	0	0
Giles, DeAngelo, INF, Fr.	.500	.500	.500	2	0	0	0	0	1	0
Highfill, Sam, INF, Fr.	.200	.200	.200	5	0	0	0	1	0	
Jarrett, J.T. , INF, Jr.	.333	.388	.600	45	11	6	0	2	15	1
McArthur, Lawson, OF, Sr.	.200	.286	.240	25	5	1	0	0	3	1
McDonough, Tyler, UT, So.	.354	.457	.554	65	17	4	0	3	16	7
Mensik, Vojtech, INF, So.	.265	.359	.500	34	11	2	0	2	9	2
Murr, Austin, UT, Jr.	.306	.470	.629	62	21	7	2	3	14	5
Neese, C.J., INF, Fr.	.333	.333	.333	3	0	0	0	0	1	0
Soles, Noah, OF, Fr.	.600	.625	.733	15	5	2	0	0	5	1
Tatum, Terrell, OF, Jr.	.292	.500	.375	24	8	0	1	0	1	7
Torres, Jose, SS, Jr.	.333	.369	.533	60	11	3	0	3	13	2
Tresh, Luca, UT, Jr.	.405	.444	.690	42	11	3	0	3	9	1
Vazquez, David, INF, Jr.	.167	.375	.167	6	1	0	0	0	2	0
Willadsen, Matt, INF, Fr.	.500	.667	.500	2	1	0	0	0	1	0

Pitcher, Year	W	L	ERA	G	GS	SV	IP	H	BB	SO
Bender, Logan, R-Jr.	0	0	8.31	6	0	0	4.1	6	6	5
Feeney, Dalton, R-Jr.	2	0	2.35	5	0	0	7.2	8	2	3
Harrison, David, Jr.	2	1	2.75	5	3	0	19.2	15	4	23
Highfill, Sam, Fr.	3	1	3.21	6	0	0	14	18	2	15
Johnston, Reid, Jr.	0	1	5.68	4	3	0	12.2	11	4	17
Justice, Evan, Fr.	0	0	4.66	7	0	0	9.2	7	5	9
Klyman, Kent, Sr.	0	0	1.42	5	0	2	6.1	5	1	5
Nelson, Baker, So.	0	0	1.93	7	0	1	9.1	5	1	7

	W	L	ERA	G	GS	SV	IP	H	BB	SO
Pace, Austin, Fr.	1	0	1.23	3	2	0	7.1	4	0	9
Silver, Canaan, Jr.	0	0	5.40	7	0	0	8.1	9	6	6
Swiney, Nick, Jr.	4	0	1.29	4	4	0	28	13	6	42
Tillery, Andrew, So.	0	0	11.57	3	0	0	2.1	3	1	3
Villaman, Chris, Fr.	1	0	3.86	5	3	0	11.2	8	4	14
Willadsen, Matt, Fr.	1	0	10.57	6	2	0	7.2	9	3	7

	W	L	ERA	G	GS	SV	IP	H	BB	SO
Marceaux, Landon, So.	2	0	2.70	4	4	0	23.1	19	7	22
Storz, Nick, So.	0	0	1.04	6	0	0	8.2	5	3	9
Vietmeier, Trent, Jr.	1	0	3.38	4	0	0	5.1	5	2	3
Walker, Eric, Jr.	0	1	3.18	5	1	0	5.2	3	4	4

19. FLORIDA STATE

Coach: Mike Martin Jr. **Record:** 12-5

Player, Pos., Year	AVG	OBP	SLG	AB	R	2B	3B	HR	RBI	SB
Albert, Reese, OF, Jr.	.242	.407	.516	62	16	5	0	4	13	1
Baldor, Nico, UT, Sr.	.125	.222	.250	8	2	1	0	0	0	0
Brewer, Tyrell, UT, Fr.	.182	.471	.273	11	6	1	0	0	3	2
Cabell, Elijah, OF, So.	.263	.488	.649	57	18	1	0	7	28	3
De Sedas, Nander, INF, So.	.150	.307	.150	60	9	0	0	0	7	2
Greene, Jackson, INF, Jr.	.190	.373	.224	58	11	2	0	0	10	2
Kirkland, Doug, C, Fr.	.333	.333	.500	6	1	1	0	0	1	0
Lacey, Logan, UT, Jr.	.379	.438	.621	29	6	4	0	1	1	3
Martin, Robby, OF, So.	.324	.439	.412	68	10	4	1	0	14	1
Martin, Tyler, INF, Fr.	.310	.481	.431	58	17	5	1	0	13	1
Nelson, Matheu, C, So.	.250	.410	.383	60	16	5	0	1	14	2
Perry, Isaiah, OF, Jr.	.250	.20	.250	4	2	0	0	0	0	0
Simmons, Dylan, 1B, Fr.	.378	.489	.486	37	4	4	0	0	7	1
Smith, Carter, UT, So.	.233	.346	.349	43	11	2	0	1	9	0
Swanson, Cooper, INF, Jr.	.211	.423	.421	19	6	1	0	1	2	1

Pitcher, Year	W	L	ERA	G	GS	SV	IP	H	BB	SO
Ahearn, Tyler, Jr.	1	0	1.93	6	0	1	9.1	8	4	14
Anderson, Jack, So.	2	0	0.79	4	1	0	11.1	6	3	11
Drohan, Shane, Jr.	0	1	4.08	4	4	0	17.2	15	11	27
Grady, Conor, Jr.	2	0	3.00	4	4	0	15	10	8	15
Haney, Chase, R-Sr.	3	0	1.29	12	0	0	14	6	2	20
Hare, Davis, Jr.	1	1	4.66	7	0	0	9.2	8	4	15
Hubbart, Bryce, Fr.	0	1	6.48	7	3	0	8.1	8	8	13
Kirkland, Doug, Fr.	0	0	4.50	5	0	0	2	3	0	1
Kwiatkowski, Clayton, Sr.	0	0	2.45	7	0	0	7.1	8	3	11
Messick, Parker, Fr.	1	1	0.77	6	0	1	11.2	9	2	19
Scolaro, Jonah, Jr.	0	0	4.50	8	0	0	6	3	6	11
Simmons, Dylan, Fr.	0	0	10.12	3	0	0	2.2	4	2	2
Van Eyk, C.J., Jr.	1	1	1.31	4	4	0	20.2	11	12	25
Velez, Antonio, So.	1	0	0.52	6	1	0	17.1	7	3	21
Walker, Brandon, Fr.	0	0	0.00	2	0	0	2	2	0	3

20. LOUISIANA STATE

Coach: Paul Mainieri. **Record:** 12-5

Player, Pos., Year	AVG	OBP	SLG	AB	R	2B	3B	HR	RBI	SB
Arnold, Zach, INF, Fr.	.000	.000	.000	2	0	0	0	0	0	0
Beloso, Cade, 1B, So.	.313	.353	.453	64	6	4	1	1	12	0
Bianco, Drew, UT, Jr.	.074	.286	.111	27	9	1	0	0	2	2
Cabrera, Daniel, OF, Jr.	.345	.466	.500	58	14	3	0	2	12	6
Cranford, Collier, INF, Fr.	.286	.394	.357	28	5	2	0	0	6	0
DiGiacomo, Giovanni, OF, So.	.351	.429	.459	37	9	2	1	0	4	5
Doughty, Braden, UT, Fr.	.000	.000	.000	2	0	0	0	0	0	0
Doughty, Cade, INF, Fr.	.278	.365	.407	54	7	1	0	2	12	4
Dugas, Gavin, UT, Jr.	.286	.412	.460	28	6	0	0	3	5	0
Garza, Saul, C, Jr.	.229	.321	.479	48	9	1	1	3	12	0
Hampton, Jr., Maurice, OF, Jr.	.231	.310	.269	26	5	1	0	0	3	2
Hughes, Hal, INF, Jr.	.154	.200	.154	13	1	0	0	0	3	0
Mathis, Zack, INF, Jr.	.262	.368	.361	61	10	1	1	1	9	1
Milazzo, Alex, C, Fr.	.186	.340	.279	43	9	1	0	1	6	3
Sanford, Mitchell, OF, Fr.	.250	.400	.250	12	5	0	0	0	2	1
Toups, Wes, OF, Fr.	.222	.462	.444	9	1	2	0	0	0	0
Travinski, Hayden, C, Fr.	.059	.059	.235	17	1	0	0	1	1	0
Willis, C.J., UT, So.	.000	.200	.000	4	0	0	0	0	0	0

Pitcher, Year	W	L	ERA	G	GS	SV	IP	H	BB	SO
Beck, Matthew, Sr.	1	0	0.00	7	0	0	12	5	7	11
Costello, Chase, So.	0	0	7.71	3	0	0	2.1	5	1	1
Fontenot, Devin, Jr.	1	0	0.90	7	0	4	10	5	4	17
George, Aaron, Sr.	0	0	5.14	7	0	0	7	5	3	11
Gunter, Rye, So.	0	0	11.57	2	0	0	2.1	1	4	2
Hasty, Jacob, Fr.	0	0	0.00	7	0	0	4.2	1	7	4
Henry, Cole, So.	2	1	1.89	4	4	0	19	15	6	23
Hill, Jaden, So.	0	0	0.00	4	0	2	11.2	1	5	17
Hilliard, Ma'Khail, Jr.	0	0	0.00	1	0	0	1	0	1	1
Kaminer, Brandon, Jr.	3	1	2.84	7	4	0	12.2	12	5	12
Labas, A.J., So.	1	2	3.55	4	4	0	25.1	16	3	20
Lagarrigue, Michael, So.	0	0	0.00	1	0	0	0	1	1	0

21. DALLAS BAPTIST

Coach: Dan Heefner. **Record:** 12-4

Player, Pos., Year	AVG	OBP	SLG	AB	R	2B	3B	HR	RBI	SB
Bell, Austin, OF, R-Sr.	.241	.370	.362	58	16	1	0	2	10	2
Boulware, Christian, C, Sr.	.219	.308	.313	32	5	0	0	1	6	1
Burgarello, Nico, INF, Jr.	.056	.227	.056	18	1	0	0	0	0	1
David, Jeffrey, UT, Fr.	.351	.367	.526	57	10	4	0	2	15	2
Ebrecht, Hayden, UT, R-Fr.	.286	.394	.429	28	5	2	1	0	2	1
Freeman, Chandler, INF, Fr.	.167	.167	.167	6	0	0	0	0	0	0
Gaither, Ray, UT, R-Jr.	.250	.400	.250	4	0	0	0	0	0	0
Glenn, Jackson, INF, Sr.	.233	.370	.367	60	9	2	0	2	9	0
Glowenke, Jimmy, INF, Jr.	.415	.458	.509	53	7	2	0	1	7	1
Grady, Jace, OF, Fr.	.184	.295	.237	38	5	2	0	0	0	0
Hatton, Trevor, UT, R-Fr.	.000	.000	.000	1	0	0	0	0	1	0
Jones, Blayne, INF, Jr.	.286	.357	.619	63	14	4	1	5	16	1
McConnell, Ben, OF, Sr.	.100	.100	.100	10	0	0	0	0	0	4
Pruitt, Dan, UT, Jr.	.163	.294	.372	43	7	0	0	3	6	0
Russell, Zane, INF, Fr.	.000	.167	.000	5	0	0	0	0	0	0
Sosa, Andres, INF, Jr.	.286	.450	.500	14	5	0	0	1	5	0
Wrobleski, Ryan, C, R-Fr.	.271	.327	.563	48	8	5	0	3	9	0

Pitcher, Year	W	L	ERA	G	GS	SV	IP	H	BB	SO
Arnold, Chandler, So.	1	1	4.82	4	4	0	18.2	24	8	19
Baker, Alec, R-Fr.	0	0	0.00	1	0	0	0.1	1	1	0
Carraway, Burl, Jr.	2	0	0.96	8	0	5	9.1	5	6	17
Carver, Ross, Jr.	1	0	2.35	8	0	0	7.2	4	6	8
Gaither, Ray, R-Jr.	0	1	3.98	4	0	0	20.1	17	9	26
Hamel, Dominic, Jr.	2	0	4.58	4	4	0	19.2	13	7	27
Heaton, Zach, R-So.	1	2	7.50	4	4	0	12	14	5	12
Hines, MacGregor, R-Sr.	0	0	12.00	2	0	0	3	4	1	4
Kechely, Kragen, Sr.	3	0	1.42	9	0	0	12.2	8	4	15
Mullins, T.J., Jr.	0	0	37.80	4	0	0	1.2	8	6	2
Reeves, Cole, So.	0	0	0.00	5	0	1	6.2	3	2	7
Rich, Kyle, R-Fr.	1	0	2.57	3	0	0	7	5	1	6
Russell, Zane, Jr.	0	0	0.00	2	0	0	1.1	1	0	0
Sagedahl, Chas, Jr.	0	0	4.76	3	0	0	5.2	5	4	4
Sherlin, Peyton, Jr.	1	0	1.74	10	0	0	10.1	8	4	11
Trahan, Luke, So.	0	0	3.18	5	0	0	5.2	5	5	4

22. CLEMSON

Coach: Monte Lee. **Record:** 14-3

PLAYER, POS., YEAR	AVG	OBP	SLG	AB	R	2B	3B	HR	RBI	SB
Brewer, Dylan, UT, Fr.	.245	.413	.408	49	11	5	0	1	6	3
Cooper, Matt, UT, Jr.	.250	.429	.250	4	1	0	0	0	1	1
Donathan, Drew, C, R-So.	.000	.000	.000	2	0	0	0	0	0	0
Fairey, Chad, UT, So.	.233	.351	.367	30	4	1	0	1	3	0
Gallo, Pierce, INF, Fr.	.077	.200	.077	13	3	0	0	0	0	1
Hackenberg, Adam, C, So.	.295	.353	.344	61	3	3	0	0	15	1
Hall, Sam, UT, Jr.	.139	.244	.278	36	7	0	1	1	2	2
Hawkins, Bryar, INF, So.	.286	.309	.408	49	7	1	1	1	9	1
Henderson, Elijah, UT, R-So.	.323	.456	.435	62	10	7	0	0	12	3
Majkowski, Bo, OF, Jr.	.152	.222	.182	33	3	1	0	0	1	2
Meredith, Kier, OF, Jr.	.364	.455	.455	66	9	3	0	1	5	3
Parker, James, INF, So.	.294	.315	.392	51	10	2	0	1	7	3
Reid, Regan, UT, Fr.	1.000	1.000	1.000	1	0	0	0	0	0	0
Sharpe, Davis, UT, So.	.311	.436	.622	45	6	2	0	4	10	1
Starbuck, Mac, INF, R-Fr.	.154	.290	.231	26	5	2	0	0	0	2
Teodosio, Bryce, OF, Jr.	.167	.348	.222	18	2	1	0	0	1	3

Pitcher, Year	W	L	ERA	G	GS	SV	IP	H	BB	SO
Ammons, Ryan, Fr.	0	0	0.00	1	0	0	0.1	0	0	0
Anglin, Mack, Fr.	0	1	11.57	4	3	0	7	12	11	11
Askew, Keyshawn, So.	0	0	3.55	5	1	0	12.2	12	11	12
Clark, Mat, R-Jr.	2	0	3.00	4	0	0	12	11	3	14
Clayton, Nick, Fr.	1	0	0.00	6	0	1	8.2	4	4	8
Estridge, Evan, R-Jr.	0	0	4.91	2	0	0	3.2	3	3	1
Gilbert, Geoffrey, Fr.	1	0	0.71	8	0	0	12.2	7	7	14
Hoffmann, Nick, Fr.	2	1	1.64	7	0	0	11	10	0	11
Jones, Holt, So.	0	0	0.00	3	0	0	1.1	0	3	2
Labriola, Paul, Fr.	0	0	81.00	1	0	0	0.1	2	1	0
Lindley, Jackson, So.	1	0	1.17	3	1	0	7.2	7	0	6
O'Rear, Connor, R-So.	0	0	0.00	1	0	0	0	2	2	0
Raffield, Carter, R-Fr.	1	0	1.17	4	0	0	7.2	7	3	7

Pitcher	W	L	ERA	G	GS	SV	IP	H	BB	SO
Reed, Sheldon, R-Sr.	0	0	13.50	2	0	0	0.2	0	2	2
Sharpe, Davis, So.	1	1	3.93	4	4	0	18.1	20	4	20
Spiers, Carson, Sr.	3	0	0.00	9	0	4	15.1	5	3	17
Strider, Spencer, R-So.	0	0	4.50	4	4	0	12	13	3	19
Weatherly, Sam, Jr.	2	0	0.79	4	4	0	22.2	7	14	43

23. TENNESSEE

Coach: Tony Vitello. **Record:** 15-2

Player, Pos., Year	AVG	OBP	SLG	AB	R	2B	3B	HR	RBI	SB
Anderson, Ethan, OF, Fr.	.000	.333	.000	2	1	0	0	0	0	0
Beck, Jordan, OF, Fr.	.275	.396	.475	40	10	5	0	1	9	0
Daniels, Zach, OF, Jr.	.357	.478	.750	56	20	8	1	4	18	3
Derkay, Pete, UT, Sr.	.542	.633	.750	24	7	2	0	1	11	0
Ferguson, Max, INF, So.	.333	.462	.524	42	12	2	0	2	6	9
Gilbert, Drew, OF, Fr.	.350	.490	.500	40	15	3	0	1	8	2
Gray, Landon, C, Jr.	.318	.483	.636	22	10	1	0	2	8	0
Knight, Austin, INF, So.	.190	.292	.476	21	6	0	0	2	6	1
Lipcius, Luc, 1B, R-Jr.	.326	.525	.674	43	13	7	1	2	15	3
Lipscomb, Trey, INF, So.	.269	.400	.385	26	8	0	0	1	9	2
Pavolony, Connor, C, So.	.342	.395	.737	38	9	3	0	4	12	0
Rucker, Jake, INF, So.	.339	.425	.581	62	15	4	1	3	13	2
Russell, Evan, OF, Jr.	.271	.393	.458	48	14	3	0	2	12	3
Scott, Christian, OF, So.	.286	.313	.286	14	5	0	0	0	3	1
Soularie, Alerick, OF, Jr.	.267	.392	.533	60	16	1	0	5	17	2
Spence, Liam, INF, Jr.	.346	.462	.462	52	13	3	0	1	12	2
Turino, Matt, OF, Jr.	.308	.471	.385	13	6	1	0	0	1	0

Pitcher, Year	W	L	ERA	G	GS	SV	IP	H	BB	SO
Anderson, Ethan, Fr.	0	0	3.00	2	0	0	3	3	0	4
Connell, Kirby, Fr.	0	0	6.35	4	0	0	5.2	5	1	7
Crochet, Garrett, Jr.	0	0	0.00	1	1	0	3.1	2	0	6
Dallas, Chad, So.	3	0	2.53	4	4	0	21.1	19	6	21
Davidson, Kody, Jr.	0	0	0.00	6	0	0	5.1	3	0	8
Delashmit, Christian, Fr.	3	0	0.77	5	1	0	11.2	10	2	16
Gilbert, Drew, Fr.	1	0	5.63	4	0	0	8	9	2	9
Hunley, Sean, Jr.	0	0	0.54	6	1	3	16.2	8	2	14
Leath, Jackson, Jr.	4	0	1.45	5	2	0	18.2	11	5	29
Mabrey, Will, Fr.	0	0	2.25	5	0	0	4	2	1	3
McLaughlin, Mark, Fr.	1	0	1.80	5	1	0	10	5	1	12
Pleasants, Elijah, So.	1	0	1.42	7	2	0	12.2	13	5	9
Sewell, Camden, So.	0	0	3.00	1	1	0	3	1	1	5
Wallace, Chase, Fr.	1	1	3.50	4	4	0	18	13	7	18
Walsh, Redmond, R-Jr.	1	1	0.00	6	0	2	11.2	5	2	10

24. EAST CAROLINA

Coach: Cliff Godwin. **Record:** 13-4

Player, Pos., Year	AVG	OBP	SLG	AB	R	2B	3B	HR	RBI	SB
Agnos, Zach, INF, Fr.	.246	.333	.277	65	7	2	0	0	9	1
Barber, Nick, INF, Sr.	.235	.381	.353	17	5	2	0	0	3	1
Bridges, Matt, UT, R-Sr.	.000	.000	.000	1	0	0	0	0	0	0
Brooks, Skylar, INF, Jr.	.455	.667	.636	11	3	2	0	0	0	0
Burleson, Alec, 1B, Jr.	.375	.440	.547	64	17	2	0	3	12	2
Caddell, Seth, C, Jr.	.305	.344	.475	59	12	5	1	1	10	1
Francisco, Thomas, INF, So.	.423	.515	.538	26	5	0	0	1	7	0
Giles, Ryder, INF, So.	.239	.294	.283	46	6	2	0	0	10	0
Hoover, Lane, OF, So.	.353	.380	.456	68	15	2	1	1	12	6
James, Matt, C, Jr.	.250	.250	.500	12	1	0	0	1	2	0
Jayne, Christian, OF, So.	.233	.361	.233	30	10	0	0	0	4	5
Losito, Trevor, OF, Jr.	.125	.125	.250	8	2	1	0	0	1	0
Makarewicz, Alec, UT, Fr.	.250	.250	.375	4	1	0	0	0	1	0
Mayhue, C.J., UT, Fr.	.000	.000	.000	1	0	0	0	0	0	0
Newton, Ben, C, Jr.	.263	.500	.316	19	4	1	0	0	6	0
Norby, Connor, INF, So.	.403	.439	.500	62	14	1	1	1	10	6
Smallwood, Christian, OF, R-Jr.	.333	.474	.333	15	2	0	0	0	1	1
Whisenhunt, Carson, UT, Fr.	.000	.222	.000	7	0	0	0	0	0	0
Worrell, Bryson, OF, Jr.	.373	.465	.729	59	13	6	0	5	14	2

Pitcher, Year	W	L	ERA	G	GS	SV	IP	H	BB	SO
Agnos, Zach, Fr.	0	0	0.00	2	0	0	1.2	0	4	1
Boyle, Parker, Jr.	0	0	8.10	5	0	0	3.1	5	1	5
Bridges, Matt, R-Sr.	0	0	2.70	7	0	2	10	7	4	11
Brooks, Skylar, Fr.	0	0	0.00	3	0	0	1.0	0	1	3
Burleson, Alec, Jr.	2	1	4.24	4	4	0	23.1	24	4	22
Colmore, Cam, R-Sr.	1	0	0.00	6	0	1	12.1	4	3	10
Giles, Ryder, So.	0	1	10.38	4	0	2	4.1	6	1	7
Gill, Elijah, Jr.	0	1	10.13	4	2	0	5.1	9	1	8
Kimmel, Trystan, Jr.	0	0	4.00	8	3	0	9	8	8	7
Kuchmaner, Jake, Jr.	4	0	0.60	4	4	0	15	12	5	13
Lawson, Dylan, Fr.	0	0	0.00	1	0	0	1	0	0	1
Logusch, Nick, Jr.	0	0	4.50	5	0	0	4	2	1	7
Mayhue, C.J., Jr.	1	0	0.56	8	0	0	16	12	6	19
Nabholz, Nate, Fr.	0	0	6.75	3	0	0	2.2	6	1	2
Odum, Evan, R-Jr.	0	0	36.00	2	0	0	1	4	0	0
Saylor, Garrett, So.	3	0	0.82	7	0	0	11	5	6	18
Smith, Tyler, Sr.	2	1	1.96	4	4	0	18.1	9	10	19
Spivey, Carter, So.	0	0	7.36	5	0	0	3.2	6	1	4
Whisenhunt, Carson, Fr.	0	0	99.00	1	0	0	0	1	1	1
Williams, Gavin, Jr.	0	0	0.00	2	0	0	3	2	2	5
Wilson, A.J., Fr.	0	0	0.00	2	0	0	1.2	1	0	3
Wilson, Bradley, Fr.	0	0	0.00	3	0	0	4	5	0	5

25. MICHIGAN

Coach: Erik Bakich. **Record:** 8-7

Player, Pos., Year	AVG	OBP	SLG	AB	R	2B	3B	HR	RBI	SB
Bertram, Riley, INF, So.	.208	.290	.283	53	10	4	0	0	10	3
Blomgren, Jack, SS, So.	.286	.444	.393	56	11	3	0	1	6	6
Bullock, Christan, OF, Sr.	.111	.273	.111	9	0	0	0	0	0	1
Burton, Ted, INF, Fr.	.222	.275	.333	36	1	1	0	1	8	1
Clementi, Dominic, OF, Sr.	.225	.340	.300	40	4	3	0	0	7	1
Donovan, Joe, C, Jr.	.196	.318	.304	56	12	3	0	1	4	2
Elliott, Clark, UT, Fr.	.245	.369	.340	53	8	1	2	0	7	4
Flores, Tito, INF, Fr.	1.000	1.000	1.000	2	0	0	0	0	0	0
Hart, Cam, INF, So.	.217	.308	.217	23	1	0	0	0	1	0
Nwogu, Jordan, OF, Jr.	.353	.389	.456	68	11	1	0	2	4	3
Obertop, Jimmy, UT, Fr.	.265	.375	.353	34	3	3	0	0	2	0
Pollack, Logan, INF, Jr.	.000	.200	.000	4	0	0	0	0	0	0
Rogers, Jordon, C, R-Fr.	.500	.500	.500	2	0	0	0	0	0	1
Salter, Harrison, C, R-Jr.	.000	.000	.000	1	0	0	0	0	0	0
Schmidt, Matt, INF, R-Sr.	.212	.333	.364	33	4	2	0	1	4	0
Van Remort, Jack, INF, So.	.000	.000	.000	1	0	0	0	0	0	0
Velazquez, Joey, OF, Fr.	.364	.364	.455	11	2	1	0	0	1	0
Zimmerman, Danny, INF, R-So.	.212	.409	.364	33	5	2	0	1	5	0

Pitcher, Year	W	L	ERA	G	GS	SV	IP	H	BB	SO
Beers, Blake, Jr.	2	2	3.13	4	4	0	23	15	5	21
Carattini, Keaton, So.	0	0	7.71	2	0	0	2.1	2	2	5
Cleveland, Walker, So.	1	0	2.08	2	1	0	4.1	6	1	1
Criswell, Jeff, Jr.	0	1	4.50	4	4	0	24	18	9	26
Denner, Jacob, Fr.	0	0	3.75	5	0	1	12	12	3	7
Dragani, Ben, R-So.	0	0	27.00	1	0	0	0.1	0	2	1
Hajjar, Steve, R-Fr.	3	0	2.70	4	4	0	20	18	11	24
Keizer, Ben, R-Sr.	1	1	4.35	8	0	1	10.1	9	7	13
Pace, Joe, R-Sr.	0	0	3.86	5	0	0	4.2	6	5	4
Paige, Isaiah, R-So.	0	1	5.25	6	1	1	12	10	5	11
Smith, Angelo, Jr.	0	1	11.12	3	0	0	5.2	10	3	3
Weston, Cameron, Fr.	1	0	0.90	7	1	2	10	9	3	5
White, Jack, So.	0	1	5.79	3	0	1	4.2	6	3	1

CONFERENCE STANDINGS & LEADERS

AMERICA EAST CONFERENCE

	Conference		Overall	
	W	L	W	L
Albany	0	0	7	5
Hartford	0	0	6	6
Binghamton	0	0	5	7
Stony Brook	0	0	6	9
Massachusetts-Lowell	0	0	4	11
Maryland-Baltimore County	0	0	3	10
Maine	0	0	1	12

INDIVIDUAL BATTING LEADERS
(Minimum 40 at-bats)

	AVG	OBP	SLG	AB	2B	3B	HR	RBI	SB
Alex Baratta, Binghamton	.455	.528	.568	44	5	0	0	11	2
Jake Evans, Binghamton	.419	.444	.442	43	1	0	0	4	0
Tyler Coppo, Hartford	.370	.380	.587	46	4	0	2	10	0
Evan Giordano, Stony Brook	.368	.429	.561	57	5	0	2	3	4
Shane Marshall, Binghamton	.347	.400	.469	35	4	1	0	8	5
Gerry Siracusa, Mass.-Lowell	.341	.400	.415	41	1	1	0	5	5
Justin Drpich, Binghamton	.327	.365	.429	49	5	0	0	6	0
Alex Thul, Albany	.325	.426	.350	40	1	0	0	9	0
Dolan Ocasal, Albany	.317	.451	.341	41	1	0	0	4	3
Chris Hamilton, Stony Brook	.298	.394	.404	57	3	0	1	4	1

INDIVIDUAL PITCHING LEADERS
(Minimum 15 innings pitched)

	W	L	ERA	G	SV	IP	H	BB	SO
Nicholas Dombkowski, Hartford	3	0	0.90	3	0	20	7	4	20
Sam Turcotte, Stony Brook	0	2	3.32	4	0	21.2	18	10	21
Matt Draper, Mass.-Lowell	0	0	4.11	5	0	15.1	16	6	14
Reid Celata, UMBC	0	2	4.11	3	0	15.1	19	4	10
Cregg Scherrer, Albany	2	1	4.30	4	0	23	19	9	15
Thomas Babalis, Binghamton	2	1	4.64	4	0	21.1	18	8	21
Jared Milch, Stony Brook	1	2	4.91	4	0	22	25	5	19
Anthony Germinerio, Albany	0	2	5.40	4	0	15	17	9	7
Joe Nestel, UMBC	1	1	5.51	3	0	16.1	15	10	16
Nicholas Sinacola, Maine	0	4	5.57	4	0	21	21	13	23

AMERICAN ATHLETIC CONFERENCE

	Conference		Overall	
	W	L	W	L
Tulane	0	0	15	2
Wichita State	0	0	13	2
Central Florida	0	0	15	3
East Carolina	0	0	13	4
Connecticut	0	0	8	5
Memphis	0	0	10	7
Cincinnati	0	0	7	8
Houston	0	0	6	9
South Florida	0	0	6	11

INDIVIDUAL BATTING LEADERS
(Minimum 40 at-bats)

	AVG	OBP	SLG	AB	2B	3B	HR	RBI	SB
Kyler Fedko, Connecticut	.412	.434	.627	51	3	1	2	12	0
Connor Norby, East Carolina	.403	.439	.500	62	1	1	1	10	6
Alec Burleson, East Carolina	.375	.440	.547	64	2	0	3	12	2
Grant Mathews, Tulane	.373	.423	.612	67	4	0	4	22	0
Bryson Worrell, East Carolina	.373	.465	.729	59	6	0	5	14	2
Jeremy Johnson, Cincinnati	.370	.453	.696	46	6	3	1	13	2
Ben Brooks, Memphis	.368	.457	.603	68	5	1	3	18	1
Reggie Crawford, Connecticut	.365	.414	.558	52	7	0	1	16	1
Ty Johnson, Tulane	.362	.492	.681	47	4	4	1	6	4
Trevor Minder, Tulane	.359	.455	.609	64	5	1	3	14	3
Hunter Goodman, Memphis	.357	.416	.743	70	3	0	8	31	2

COURTESY OF VIRGINIA

Third baseman Zack Gelof helped Virginia take a step forward in 2020.

	AVG	OBP	SLG	AB	2B	3B	HR	RBI	SB
Couper Cornblum, Wichita State	.354	.492	.625	48	4	3	1	12	7
Lane Hoover, East Carolina	.353	.380	.456	68	2	1	1	12	6
Chris Winkel, Connecticut	.348	.404	.457	46	3	1	0	5	5
Hudson Haskin, Tulane	.333	.452	.500	66	6	1	1	14	1

INDIVIDUAL PITCHING LEADERS
(Minimum 15 innings pitched)

	W	L	ERA	G	SV	IP	H	BB	SO
Braden Olthoff, Tulane	4	0	0.32	4	0	28	12	3	47
Nick Krauth, Connecticut	4	0	0.36	4	0	24.2	14	9	24
C.J. Mayhue, East Carolina	1	0	0.56	8	0	16	12	6	19
Jake Kuchmaner, East Carolina	4	0	0.60	4	0	15	12	5	13
Jaylyn Whitehead, Central Florida	1	1	0.95	6	1	19	8	5	18
Trevor Holloway, Central Florida	3	1	1.19	4	0	22.2	12	6	37
Luke Jannetta, Tulane	3	0	1.37	7	1	19.2	12	1	16
Danny Denz, Memphis	2	0	1.50	4	0	18	7	9	26
Evan Shawver, Cincinnati	2	0	1.59	4	0	22.2	10	9	35
Clay Aguilar, Houston	2	0	1.59	4	0	22.2	27	9	17

ATLANTIC COAST CONFERENCE

	Conference		Overall	
Atlantic Division	W	L	W	L
Notre Dame	3	0	11	2
Clemson	3	0	14	3
Louisville	2	1	13	4
North Carolina State	1	2	14	3
Florida State	1	2	12	5
Wake Forest	1	2	10	8
Boston College	0	3	6	9

	Conference		Overall	
Coastal Division	W	L	W	L
Miami	3	0	12	4
Virginia	2	1	14	4
Duke	2	1	12	4
Georgia Tech	2	1	11	5
Virginia Tech	1	2	11	5
North Carolina	0	3	12	7
Pittsburgh	0	3	10	6

INDIVIDUAL BATTING LEADERS
(Minimum 40 at-bats)

	AVG	OBP	SLG	AB	2B	3B	HR	RBI	SB
Michael Guldberg, Georgia Tech	.450	.521	.533	60	5	0	0	9	3
Cody Morissette, Boston College	.448	.522	.655	58	6	0	2	11	3
Levi Usher, Louisville	.434	.500	.604	53	3	0	2	10	7
Carson Taylor, Virginia Tech	.431	.541	.690	58	7	1	2	20	2
Spencer Myers, Notre Dame	.431	.492	.466	58	2	0	0	8	15
Jack Cunningham, Boston College	.424	.478	.576	59	3	0	2	13	2
Joe Suozzi, Boston College	.414	.471	.638	58	4	3	1	16	4
Chris Newell, Virginia	.407	.545	.729	59	5	1	4	20	8
Angel Zarate, North Carolina	.395	.462	.474	76	4	1	0	18	5
William Simoneit, Wake Forest	.377	.462	.642	53	5	0	3	12	0
Kyle Hess, Pittsburgh	.373	.425	.627	67	9	1	2	20	1
Henry Davis, Louisville	.372	.481	.698	43	5	0	3	13	1
Gavin Cross, Virginia Tech	.369	.408	.385	65	1	0	0	8	7
Kier Meredith, Clemson	.364	.455	.455	66	3	0	1	5	3
Adrian Del Castillo, Miami	.358	.478	.547	53	2	1	2	15	1

INDIVIDUAL PITCHING LEADERS
(Minimum 15 innings pitched)

	W	L	ERA	G	SV	IP	H	BB	SO
Cooper Stinson, Duke	3	0	0.42	4	0	21.2	16	4	24
Antonio Velez, Florida State	1	0	0.52	6	0	17.1	7	3	21
Bryce Jarvis, Duke	3	1	0.67	4	0	27	11	2	40
Brian Van Belle, Miami	2	0	0.68	4	0	26.1	16	4	38
Sam Weatherly, Clemson	2	0	0.79	4	0	22.2	7	14	43
Chris McMahon, Miami	3	0	1.05	4	0	25.2	19	5	38
Matt Gilbertson, Pittsburgh	2	1	1.12	4	0	24	26	6	20
Reid Detmers, Louisville	3	0	1.23	4	0	22	16	6	48
Nick Swiney, North Carolina State	4	0	1.29	4	0	28	13	6	42
C.J. Van Eyk, Florida State	1	1	1.31	4	0	20.2	11	12	25

ATLANTIC SUN CONFERENCE

	Conference		Overall	
	W	L	W	L
Stetson	0	0	11	4
Lipscomb	0	0	11	5
Liberty	0	0	10	7
Florida Gulf Coast	0	0	9	7
Kennesaw State	0	0	10	8
Jacksonville	0	0	9	9
New Jersey Institute of Technology	0	0	6	10
North Florida	0	0	4	12
North Alabama	0	0	3	13

INDIVIDUAL BATTING LEADERS
(Minimum 40 at-bats)

	AVG	OBP	SLG	AB	2B	3B	HR	RBI	SB
Nick Hassan, Kennesaw State	.440	.472	.560	50	4	1	0	10	2
Scott Dubrule, Jacksonville	.426	.500	.544	68	5	0	1	6	3
Brandon Hylton, Stetson	.357	.451	.476	42	5	0	0	8	2
Haddon Adams, Lipscomb	.328	.416	.547	64	3	1	3	13	9
Alex Carballo, Kennesaw State	.323	.468	.597	62	5	0	4	21	1
Brian Ellis, FGCU	.321	.493	.429	56	4	1	0	5	7
Kyle Machado, FGCU	.320	.400	.460	50	4	0	1	5	0
Garrett Hodges, Kennesaw State	.319	.380	.458	72	4	0	2	11	1
David Marcano, NJIT	.317	.450	.444	63	6	1	0	8	6
Ben Highfill, Liberty	.317	.405	.600	60	6	1	3	12	0

INDIVIDUAL PITCHING LEADERS
(Minimum 15 innings pitched)

	W	L	ERA	G	SV	IP	H	BB	SO
Austin Temple, Jacksonville	2	1	0.71	4	0	25.1	14	10	29
Mason Studstill, FGCU	3	0	1.17	4	0	23	11	10	35
Trent Palmer, Jacksonville	2	1	1.30	4	0	27.2	12	5	41
Joe Adamez III, Liberty	1	1	1.59	4	0	22.2	24	4	21
Nick Durgin, Stetson	2	0	1.63	4	0	27.2	19	1	27
Robbie Peto, Stetson	3	0	1.78	4	0	25.1	15	13	41
Max Habegger, Lipscomb	2	0	1.80	4	0	20	12	11	19
Noah Skirrow, Liberty	1	1	1.96	4	0	23	14	13	20
Mason Hand, Liberty	3	1	2.18	5	0	20.2	17	9	15
Hunter McGarry, FGCU	3	1	2.53	9	3	2.1	21	4	16

COLLEGE

ATLANTIC 10 CONFERENCE

	Conference		Overall	
	W	L	W	L
St. Bonaventure	0	0	5	1
Davidson	0	0	13	3
Fordham	0	0	10	6
Saint Louis	0	0	10	6
Rhode Island	0	0	8	5
Virginia Commonwealth	0	0	9	8
George Washington	0	0	8	8
Dayton	0	0	6	8
La Salle	0	0	5	9
Saint Joseph's	0	0	5	10
Richmond	0	0	5	12
Massachusetts	0	0	1	8
George Mason	0	0	1	14

INDIVIDUAL BATTING LEADERS
(Minimum 40 at-bats)

	AVG	OBP	SLG	AB	2B	3B	HR	RBI	SB
Kyle Fitzgerald, Saint Louis	.477	.500	.750	44	3	0	3	11	0
Jason Coules, Fordham	.453	.492	.660	53	5	0	2	18	6
Jackson Coutts, Rhode Island	.451	.525	.824	51	7	0	4	12	2
Noah Levin, GW	.429	.522	.500	56	4	0	0	13	0
Alden Mathes, Richmond	.395	.469	.535	43	1	1	1	4	0
Steven Carpenter, VCU	.393	.500	.554	56	3	0	2	16	2
Alvin Melendez, Fordham	.392	.393	.549	51	6	1	0	15	6
Tyler Kelder, St. Bonaventure	.387	.4061	.097	31	1	0	7	13	0
Austin White, Rhode Island	.378	.549	.541	37	4	1	0	10	3
Anthony Videtto, Massachusetts	.375	.417	.656	32	4	1	1	6	0

INDIVIDUAL PITCHING LEADERS
(Minimum 15 innings pitched)

	W	L	ERA	G	SV	IP	H	BB	SO
Gabe Levy, Davidson	3	1	0.91	4	0	29.2	19	10	28
Justin Sorokowski, VCU	0	1	1.23	6	0	22	18	4	15
Matt Mikulski, Fordham	2	1	1.29	4	0	21	19	9	18
John Stankiewicz, Fordham	2	1	1.71	4	0	21	15	6	21
Harrison Cohen, GW	2	1	2.10	4	0	25.2	27	3	24
Jaret Edwards, GW	1	0	2.20	6	1	16.1	17	5	14
Michael Dailey, VCU	0	0	2.28	6	0	23.2	17	6	21
Jordan DiValerio, Saint Joseph's	3	1	2.38	4	0	22.2	16	5	33
Trevor Harris, Saint Louis	3	0	2.57	5	0	21	18	6	21
Justin Solt, George Washington	0	2	2.77	4	0	26	29	7	15

BIG EAST CONFERENCE

	Conference		Overall	
	W	L	W	L
Villanova	0	0	9	5
Butler	0	0	8	6
Seton Hall	0	0	6	8
St. John's	0	0	5	8
Creighton	0	0	5	10
Xavier	0	0	5	10
Georgetown	0	0	4	13

INDIVIDUAL BATTING LEADERS
(Minimum 40 at-bats)

	AVG	OBP	SLG	AB	2B	3B	HR	RBI	SB
Casey Dana, Seton Hall	.367	.458	.531	49	2	0	2	16	2
A.J. Lotsis, Georgetown	.343	.436	.537	67	1	0	4	13	1
David Vilches, Creighton	.333	.481	.595	42	3	1	2	8	0
Lucas Latrenta, Villanova	.333	.429	.595	42	0	1	3	10	0
Jake Lazzaro, St. John's	.327	.421	.408	49	4	0	0	3	3
Ryan Mantle, Creighton	.318	.429	.500	44	2	0	2	9	0
Connor Hood, Seton Hall	.305	.317	.356	59	3	0	0	10	0
Ty Shedler-McAvoy, Seton Hall	.304	.400	.375	56	0	2	0	3	7
Chris Rotondo, Villanova	.298	.485	.447	47	3	2	0	7	2
Dylan McNary, Villanova	.295	.407	.477	44	2	0	2	9	4
Justin Folz, St. John's	.294	.383	.471	51	1	1	2	12	0
Nick Ortega, Butler	.283	.469	.435	46	4	0	1	11	0
Pat O'Neill, Villanova	.280	.383	.340	50	3	0	0	6	0
John Simourian, Georgetown	.280	.327	.300	50	1	0	0	6	0
Brody McGrath, Butler	.280	.345	.300	50	1	0	0	7	1

INDIVIDUAL PITCHING LEADERS
(Minimum 15 innings pitched)

	W	L	ERA	G	SV	IP	H	BB	SO
Gordon Graceffo, Villanova	4	0	1.42	4	0	25.1	21	7	12
Jack Weeks, Georgetown	1	0	1.73	5	0	26	19	8	19
Dylan Tebrake, Creighton	3	2	2.05	5	0	26.1	18	5	24
Brandon Siegenthaler, Villanova	1	1	2.25	4	0	16	14	5	8
Noah Thompson, Seton Hall	0	2	2.29	4	0	19.2	19	6	12
Nick Zwack, Xavier	2	2	2.31	4	0	23.1	10	9	28
John Sakowski, Creighton	1	1	2.35	6	2	15.1	13	4	10
Connor Schultz, Butler	2	1	3.04	4	0	23.2	25	7	26
Jimmy Kingsbury, Villanova	2	1	3.08	4	0	26.1	21	8	20
Ryan McLinskey, Seton Hall	2	0	3.38	4	0	21.1	17	6	22

BIG SOUTH CONFERENCE

	Conference		Overall	
	W	L	W	L
Winthrop	0	0	11	4
USC Upstate	0	0	13	5
Radford	0	0	9	8
Gardner-Webb	0	0	8	8
Campbell	0	0	7	9
High Point	0	0	7	9
Charleston Southern	0	0	7	12
UNC Asheville	0	0	5	11
Longwood	0	0	4	13
Presbyterian	0	0	2	14

INDIVIDUAL BATTING LEADERS
(Minimum 40 at-bats)

	AVG	OBP	SLG	AB	2B	3B	HR	RBI	SB
Colby Higgerson, Radford	.431	.513	.492	65	2	1	0	15	4
J.D. Mundy, Radford	.385	.468	.662	65	6	0	4	19	1
Scout McFalls, Winthrop	.375	.478	.518	56	6	1	0	7	6
Julian Rip, USC Upstate	.368	.493	.561	57	4	2	1	11	7
Cullan Wadsworth, Longwood	.366	.447	.659	41	3	3	1	9	2
Andrew Jenner, Winthrop	.362	.431	.362	58	0	0	0	10	1
Dillon Morton, Winthrop	.362	.436	.511	47	4	0	1	7	0
Travis Holt, High Point	.348	.405	.409	66	4	0	0	9	1
Greg Gasparro, UNC Asheville	.344	.425	.557	61	4	0	3	16	5
Sam Zayicek, High Point	.344	.420	.508	61	4	0	2	12	1

INDIVIDUAL PITCHING LEADERS
(Minimum 15 innings pitched)

	W	L	ERA	G	SV	IP	H	BB	SO
Jaret Bennett, Charl. Southern	2	0	0.71	4	0	25.1	14	10	24
Kevin Davis, USC Upstate	1	0	1.35	7	3	20	10	5	28
Jordan Marks, USC Upstate	3	1	1.75	4	0	25.2	24	3	28
Blake Brown, UNC Asheville	1	1	1.89	4	0	19	9	18	26
Tyler Jones, Winthrop	0	0	2.25	4	1	16	12	9	18
Ryan Bywaters, Radford	0	0	2.29	5	0	19.2	15	9	17
Ryan Douglas, UNC Asheville	1	2	2.74	4	0	23	20	9	17
Thad Harris, Winthrop	1	1	2.95	3	0	18.1	13	5	15
Cam Cowan, Campbell	2	2	3.00	4	0	24	16	4	36
Kyle Schmitt, USC Upstate	2	0	3.00	5	0	18	16	6	14

BIG 12 CONFERENCE

	Conference		Overall	
	W	L	W	L
Texas Tech	0	0	16	3
Texas	0	0	14	3
Oklahoma	0	0	14	4
Texas Christian	0	0	11	4
Oklahoma State	0	0	13	5
West Virginia	0	0	11	5
Baylor	0	0	10	6
Kansas State	0	0	10	7
Kansas	0	0	7	10

INDIVIDUAL BATTING LEADERS
(Minimum 40 at-bats)

	AVG	OBP	SLG	AB	2B	3B	HR	RBI	SB
Braden Zarbnisky, West Virginia	.431	.486	.538	65	3	2	0	9	13
Max Hewitt, Oklahoma State	.410	.479	.525	61	5	1	0	10	0
Jared McKenzie, Baylor	.406	.453	.449	69	3	0	0	5	4
Brian Klein, Texas Tech	.391	.494	.580	69	10	0	1	13	0
Tanner Tredaway, Oklahoma	.378	.392	.689	74	6	4	3	14	5
Austin Todd, Texas	.375	.430	.500	72	4	1	1	15	2
Gray Rodgers, Texas Christian	.373	.464	.559	59	5	0	2	11	1
Daniel Carinci, Kansas State	.373	.409	.492	59	7	0	0	4	0
Cal Conley, Texas Tech	.371	.444	.643	70	8	1	3	24	5
Matt McCormick, West Virginia	.364	.470	.600	55	4	0	3	11	1
Peyton Graham, Oklahoma	.358	.457	.612	67	8	0	3	10	8
Dylan Neuse, Texas Tech	.355	.438	.487	76	5	1	1	12	12
Gene Wood, Texas Christian	.353	.514	.706	51	3	0	5	14	6
Kyle Nevin, Baylor	.350	.366	.450	40	0	2	0	3	1
Zach Kokoska, Kansas State	.349	.446	.540	63	5	2	1	9	5

INDIVIDUAL PITCHING LEADERS
(Minimum 15 innings pitched)

	W	L	ERA	G	SV	IP	H	BB	SO
Haylen Green, Texas Christian	1	0	0.00	8	1	17.2	7	5	19
Pete Hansen, Texas	2	0	0.00	6	1	17	9	2	18
Jordan Wicks, Kansas State	3	0	0.35	4	0	26	13	4	26
Micah Dallas, Texas Tech	1	0	0.57	5	3	15.2	7	1	23
Jackson Wolf, West Virginia	3	1	1.05	4	0	25.2	14	5	27
C.J. Varela, Oklahoma State	3	0	1.17	5	0	15.1	8	5	15
Hunter Dobbins, Texas Tech	2	0	1.35	6	0	20	17	5	25
Jake Carr, West Virginia	2	1	1.52	4	0	23.2	14	3	12
Ty Madden, Texas	3	0	1.80	4	0	25	18	4	26
Brett Standlee, Oklahoma State	1	0	1.83	7	1	19.2	19	4	17

BIG TEN CONFERENCE

	Conference		Overall	
	W	L	W	L
Iowa	0	0	10	5
Maryland	0	0	10	5
Penn State	0	0	10	5
Illinois	0	0	8	5
Indiana	0	0	9	6
Michigan State	0	0	9	6
Michigan	0	0	8	7
Purdue	0	0	7	7
Northwestern	0	0	6	6
Nebraska	0	0	7	8
Minnesota	0	0	8	10
Ohio State	0	0	6	8
Rutgers	0	0	6	9

INDIVIDUAL BATTING LEADERS
(Minimum 40 at-bats)

	AVG	OBP	SLG	AB	2B	3B	HR	RBI	SB
Zack Raabe, Minnesota	.463	.526	.612	67	7	0	1	10	0
Bailey Peterson, Michigan State	.441	.528	.542	59	4	1	0	15	8
Maxwell Costes, Maryland	.432	.620	.750	44	2	0	4	15	3
Branden Comia, Illinois	.426	.526	.702	47	3	2	2	10	1
Grant Richardson, Indiana	.424	.453	.797	59	3	2	5	17	1
Izaya Fullard, Iowa	.400	.449	.583	60	3	1	2	21	2
Bryce Kelley, Michigan State	.400	.486	.417	60	1	0	0	4	8
Gavin Homer, Penn State	.400	.500	.689	45	6	2	1	17	8
Elijah Dunham, Indiana	.390	.493	.559	59	7	0	1	11	1
Randy Bednar, Maryland	.387	.459	.581	62	9	0	1	16	5
Richie Schiekofer, Rutgers	.375	.478	.607	56	5	1	2	11	3
Jack Wassel, Minnesota	.364	.475	.591	66	7	1	2	16	2
Evan Albrecht, Purdue	.364	.442	.432	44	3	0	0	14	3
Jordan Nwogu, Michigan	.353	.389	.456	68	1	0	2	4	3
Leighton Banjoff, Nebraska	.341	.517	.636	44	4	0	3	13	3

INDIVIDUAL PITCHING LEADERS
(Minimum 15 innings pitched)

	W	L	ERA	G	SV	IP	H	BB	SO
Michael Doherty, Northwestern	1	0	0.86	4	0	21	17	5	20
Mason Erla, Michigan State	2	0	1.04	4	0	26	20	6	42
Adam Berghorst, Michigan State	0	1	1.17	6	1	15.1	14	6	6
Ty Weber, Illinois	2	0	1.31	4	0	20.2	17	2	15
Cole Kirschsieper, Illinois	3	0	1.35	4	0	20	18	5	12
Conor Larkin, Penn State	1	0	1.69	4	0	21.1	15	8	28
Bailey Dees, Penn State	1	2	1.88	5	0	28.2	14	11	27
Jett Jackson, Purdue	1	0	1.89	4	0	19	12	12	13
Max Meyer, Minnesota	3	1	1.95	4	0	27.2	15	8	46
Sean Burke, Maryland	2	0	1.99	4	0	22.2	15	11	35

BIG WEST CONFERENCE

	Conference		Overall	
	W	L	W	L
UC Santa Barbara	0	0	13	2
Cal State Northridge	0	0	10	5
Long Beach State	0	0	10	5
Hawaii	0	0	11	6
UC Davis	0	0	9	7
UC Riverside	0	0	9	7
UC Irvine	0	0	8	7
Cal Poly	0	0	5	11
Cal State Fullerton	0	0	4	12

INDIVIDUAL BATTING LEADERS
(Minimum 40 at-bats)

	AVG	OBP	SLG	AB	2B	3B	HR	RBI	SB
Spencer Gedestad, UC Davis	.417	.463	.517	60	6	0	0	8	2
Kole Kaler, Hawaii	.407	.486	.661	59	9	3	0	17	4
Denzel Clarke, Cal State North.	.400	.529	.775	40	4	1	3	9	5
Connor Kokx, Long Beach State	.400	.491	.511	45	5	0	0	5	3
Jake Palmer, UC Irvine	.368	.479	.456	57	5	0	0	8	4
Travis Bohall, UC Riverside	.344	.438	.459	61	4	0	1	7	7
Zach Lew, Cal State Fullerton	.339	.453	.419	62	3	1	0	9	2
Jayson Newman, Cal State North.	.333	.375	.529	51	4	0	2	13	0
Leonard Jones, Long Beach State	.327	.377	.509	55	2	1	2	9	2
Scotty Scott, Hawaii	.321	.433	.411	56	3	1	0	7	4

INDIVIDUAL PITCHING LEADERS
(Minimum 15 innings pitched)

	W	L	ERA	G	SV	IP	H	BB	SO
Zach Torra, UC Santa Barbara	3	0	0.36	4	0	25.1	11	9	39
Michael McGreevy, UCSB	2	0	0.99	4	0	27.1	19	7	26
Adam Seminaris, LBSU	1	0	1.23	4	0	22	9	3	36
Taylor Dollard, Cal Poly	1	0	1.67	4	0	27	20	4	36
J.D. Callahan, UC Santa Barbara	2	0	1.76	4	1	15.1	7	6	14
Alfredo Ruiz, Long Beach State	3	1	1.80	4	0	25	15	5	24
Conner Roberts, UCSB	4	1	2.04	7	0	17.2	9	5	24
Brett Erwin, UC Davis	2	0	2.14	4	0	21	20	14	9
Aaron Davenport, Hawaii	4	0	2.15	5	0	29.1	29	6	30
Trenton Denholm, UC Irvine	2	2	2.28	4	0	23.2	12	10	25

COLONIAL ATHLETIC ASSOCIATION

	Conference		Overall	
	W	L	W	L
College of Charleston	0	0	12	2
UNC Wilmington	0	0	11	5
Northeastern	0	0	10	5
James Madison	0	0	10	6
Delaware	0	0	8	7
William & Mary	0	0	8	9
Towson	0	0	7	8
Elon	0	0	7	10
Hofstra	0	0	4	10

INDIVIDUAL BATTING LEADERS
(Minimum 40 at-bats)

	AVG	OBP	SLG	AB	2B	3B	HR	RBI	SB
Austin Gauthier, Hofstra	.411	.515	.714	56	6	1	3	11	2
Anthony D'Onofrio, Hofstra	.407	.508	.519	54	4	1	0	15	5
Matt Arceo, Towson	.395	.490	.442	43	2	0	0	7	2
Chase DeLauter, James Madison	.382	.455	.559	68	7	1	1	14	7
Nick Zona, James Madison	.370	.433	.426	54	1	1	0	13	5
Ari Sechopoulos, Charleston	.360	.475	.680	50	6	2	2	20	2
Jared Dupree, Northeastern	.359	.394	.578	64	6	1	2	13	1
Harrison Hawkins, Charleston	.333	.365	.483	60	7	1	0	12	1
Jack Goan, Delaware	.333	.355	.596	57	3	0	4	15	1
Brandon Raquet, William & Mary	.328	.453	.705	61	3	4	4	11	1

INDIVIDUAL PITCHING LEADERS
(Minimum 15 innings pitched)

	W	L	ERA	G	SV	IP	H	BB	SO
Chris Farrell, William & Mary	2	0	0.42	4	0	21.1	14	16	19
Justin Showalter, James Madison	4	0	0.68	5	0	26.2	13	4	21
Caswell Smith, Charleston	3	0	1.35	4	0	20	14	8	20
Landen Roupp, UNC Wilmington	3	1	2.00	4	0	27	19	7	30
Zarion Sharpe, UNC Wilmington	2	1	2.18	4	0	20.2	17	8	20
Jack Cone, William & Mary	3	1	2.86	4	0	22	23	8	18
Austin Weber, Towson	2	0	2.93	7	0	15.1	13	2	12
Kyle Murphy, Northeastern	2	2	3.00	4	0	18	13	13	25
Nick Ramanjulu, Towson	1	3	3.22	4	0	22.1	17	12	18
Sam Jacobsak, Northeastern	2	1	3.28	4	0	24.2	19	5	25

CONFERENCE USA

	Conference		Overall	
	W	L	W	L
Old Dominion	0	0	12	4
Southern Mississippi	0	0	12	4
Florida International	0	0	10	5
Louisiana Tech	0	0	11	6
Western Kentucky	0	0	10	6
Florida Atlantic	0	0	10	6
Texas-San Antonio	0	0	10	7
Charlotte	0	0	9	8
Alabama-Birmingham	0	0	7	9
Middle Tennessee State	0	0	7	10
Marshall	0	0	4	10
Rice	0	0	2	14

INDIVIDUAL BATTING LEADERS
(Minimum 40 at-bats)

	AVG	OBP	SLG	AB	2B	3B	HR	RBI	SB
Juan Teixeira, FIU	.482	.508	.643	56	3	0	2	14	5
Parker Bates, Louisiana Tech	.422	.531	.891	64	4	1	8	28	2
Steele Netterville, Louisiana Tech	.407	.500	.797	59	5	0	6	22	1
Dominic Pilolli, Charlotte	.381	.458	.540	63	2	1	2	14	2
Alex Ray, Louisiana Tech	.380	.396	.500	50	1	1	1	9	2
Justin Farmer, FIU	.375	.435	.589	56	5	2	1	13	3
Matt Phipps, Western Ky.	.368	.463	.474	57	6	0	0	8	0
Kyle Battle, Old Dominion	.367	.487	.667	60	5	2	3	16	2
Derek Cartaya, FIU	.367	.472	.400	60	2	0	0	6	4
Dylan Rock, Texas-San Antonio	.365	.449	.508	63	6	0	1	10	10

INDIVIDUAL PITCHING LEADERS
(Minimum 15 innings pitched)

	W	L	ERA	G	SV	IP	H	BB	SO
Mike Entenza, Florida Atlantic	3	0	0.55	10	0	16.1	10	5	27
Jake Kates, Western Ky.	2	0	1.04	6	1	17.1	10	6	29
Will Saxton, FIU	1	1	1.17	4	0	15.1	14	8	13
Walker Powell, Southern Miss	3	0	1.24	4	0	29	22	2	22
Hunter Gregory, Old Dominion	2	0	1.69	4	0	21.1	20	7	28
Ryne Moore, Old Dominion	2	1	1.93	4	0	23.1	16	4	18
Andrew Roach, Charlotte	2	2	1.99	4	0	22.2	17	8	22
Ben Ethridge, Southern Miss	3	0	2.29	4	0	19.2	18	5	26
Logan Allen, FIU	2	1	2.46	4	0	25.2	17	6	41
Sean Bergeron, Western Ky.	2	0	2.59	4	0	24.1	24	9	14

Closer Burl Carraway locked down the end of games for Dallas Baptist.

COURTESY OF DALLAS BAPTIST

IVY LEAGUE

	Conference W	L	Overall W	L
Harvard	1	0	2	5
Dartmouth	1	1	3	6
Pennsylvania	0	0	3	4
Yale	0	0	4	7
Brown	0	0	3	9
Columbia	0	0	1	7
Cornell	0	0	1	8
Princeton	0	1	0	8

INDIVIDUAL BATTING LEADERS
(Minimum 40 at-bats)

	AVG	OBP	SLG	AB	2B	3B	HR	RBI	SB
Eduardo Malinowski, Penn	.471	.526	.735	34	1	1	2	10	0
Peter Matt, Penn	.457	.525	.543	35	3	0	0	9	4
Josh Nicoloff, Columbia	.394	.382	.485	33	0	0	1	4	2
Teddy Hague, Yale	.364	.404	.659	44	3	2	2	10	2
Tyler MacGregor, Yale	.364	.391	.455	22	2	0	0	2	1
Julian Bury, Columbia	.355	.429	.452	31	0	0	1	1	1
Carson Swank, Yale	.341	.429	.439	41	4	0	0	13	4
Rich Ciufo, Brown	.333	.385	.521	48	5	2	0	6	0
Blake Crossing, Dartmouth	.318	.375	.409	22	2	0	0	2	1
Alex Stiegler, Yale	.318	.400	.409	22	2	0	0	2	0

INDIVIDUAL PITCHING LEADERS
(Minimum 15 innings pitched)

	W	L	ERA	G	SV	IP	H	BB	SO
Christian Scafidi, Penn	2	0	0.00	2	0	15	9	5	13
John Natoli, Cornell	1	0	0.82	3	0	11	10	3	13
Justin Murray, Dartmouth	1	1	1.38	2	0	13	8	2	8
Ben Gibbs, Yale	0	1	2.70	3	0	16.2	12	10	15
Grant Kipp, Yale	1	0	3.18	3	0	11.1	7	4	13
Collin Garner, Brown	1	2	3.38	3	0	16	20	4	13
Mitchell Holcomb, Penn	1	1	3.46	2	0	13	10	6	14
Austen Michel, Dartmouth	0	2	4.22	2	0	10.2	15	3	8
Garett Delano, Brown	1	2	5.00	3	0	18	20	5	16
Colby Wyatt, Cornell	0	3	5.65	3	0	14.1	18	6	14

METRO ATLANTIC ATHLETIC CONFERENCE

	Conference W	L	Overall W	L
Rider	0	0	6	8
Niagara	0	0	6	10
Monmouth	0	0	5	9
Marist	0	0	3	9
Canisius	0	0	3	11
Manhattan	0	0	3	11
Quinnipiac	0	0	3	11
Iona	0	0	3	12
Fairfield	0	0	2	9
Saint Peter's	0	0	1	14
Siena	0	0	0	17

INDIVIDUAL BATTING LEADERS
(Minimum 40 at-bats)

	AVG	OBP	SLG	AB	2B	3B	HR	RBI	SB
Pat O'Hare, Siena	.367	.523	.612	49	4	1	2	8	0
Cole O'Connor, Niagara	.341	.400	.477	44	3	0	1	8	1
Matt Padre, Manhattan	.340	.379	.472	53	4	0	1	10	0
John Gavura, Saint Peter's	.333	.455	.519	54	5	1	1	3	0
Will Trochiano, Manhattan	.333	.441	.375	48	2	0	0	4	1
Johnny Zega, Monmouth	.327	.407	.346	52	1	0	0	5	1
Sam Franco, Manhattan	.321	.397	.500	56	3	2	1	5	1
Brian Picone, Iona	.314	.390	.490	51	3	0	2	10	2
Andy Leader, Canisius	.311	.354	.475	61	3	2	1	10	2
Peter Battaglia, Niagara	.297	.361	.469	64	5	0	2	15	0

HORIZON LEAGUE

	Conference W	L	Overall W	L
Youngstown State	0	0	7	7
Wright State	0	0	6	9
Illinois-Chicago	0	0	4	12
Oakland	0	0	2	8
Wisconsin-Milwaukee	0	0	1	14
Northern Kentucky	0	0	0	17

INDIVIDUAL BATTING LEADERS
(Minimum 40 at-bats)

	AVG	OBP	SLG	AB	2B	3B	HR	RBI	SB
Michael Stygles, Oakland	.395	.500	.526	38	2	0	1	8	1
Zach Nogalski, Wis.-Milwaukee	.377	.421	.509	53	5	1	0	9	0
Cam Post, Oakland	.364	.447	.424	33	2	0	0	2	1
Quincy Hamilton, Wright State	.357	.471	.452	42	1	0	1	7	3
Cameron Roundtree, Wright State	.351	.359	.459	37	4	0	0	6	1
Konner Piotto, Wright State	.333	.417	.452	42	5	0	0	3	3
Collin Luty, Northern Kentucky	.333	.439	.467	45	3	0	1	10	1
Andrew Bacon, Northern Kentucky	.318	.356	.530	66	2	0	4	9	2
Damon Dues, Wright State	.316	.426	.395	38	1	1	0	4	2
Blake Griffith, Oakland	.310	.396	.500	42	2	0	2	8	0

INDIVIDUAL PITCHING LEADERS
(Minimum 15 innings pitched)

	W	L	ERA	G	SV	IP	H	BB	SO
Jake Schrand, Wright State	1	0	1.26	6	1	14.1	8	6	15
Collin Floyd, Youngstown State	2	1	2.74	4	0	23	13	5	25
Fred Gosbeth, Illinois-Chicago	0	0	3.00	6	0	12	13	6	15
Colin Clark, Youngstown State	1	1	3.38	4	0	26.2	21	3	26
Cristian Lopez, Illinois-Chicago	1	0	3.46	3	0	13	15	4	12
Matt Vanek, Wis.-Milwaukee	0	2	3.75	4	0	12	10	11	10
Chad Coles, Youngstown State	1	0	4.09	8	0	11	4	9	9
Sam Wirsing, Wright State	0	0	4.50	4	0	12	12	5	8
Mark McCabe, Illinois-Chicago	2	2	4.58	5	0	19.2	19	9	13
Tristan Haught, Wright State	1	0	4.76	5	1	11.1	14	5	7

INDIVIDUAL PITCHING LEADERS
(Minimum 15 innings pitched)

	W	L	ERA	G	SV	IP	H	BB	SO
Christian Nicolosi, Quinnipiac	0	2	1.80	3	0	15	12	7	12
Pete Soporowski, Rider	1	2	2.13	4	0	25.1	28	6	11
Jacob Bruning, Niagara	1	1	2.35	5	0	23	19	9	28
Blake DeCarr, Quinnipiac	1	0	2.35	4	0	15.1	11	4	10
Dan Kiepchick, Monmouth	0	1	2.40	3	0	15	9	4	9
T.J. Stuart, Manhattan	1	1	2.42	5	0	26	19	8	27
Rob Hensey, Monmouth	2	1	2.42	4	0	26	17	3	21
Frank Doelling, Rider	2	0	2.53	4	0	21.1	14	13	24
Ryan Cardona, Marist	0	2	3.00	4	0	21	21	8	26
Will Frank, Canisius	0	0	3.22	5	0	22.1	22	12	18

INDIVIDUAL BATTING LEADERS
(Minimum 40 at-bats)

	AVG	OBP	SLG	AB	2B	3B	HR	RBI	SB
Brian Cordell, Md. Eastern Shore	.438	.578	.604	48	2	0	2	9	2
Luis DeLeon, NCCU	.393	.500	.689	61	6	0	4	24	6
Jared Weber, Florida A&M	.393	.439	.557	61	7	0	1	11	2
Marcos Castillo, Coppin State	.378	.491	.711	45	4	1	3	9	3
Ty Hanchey, Norfolk State	.368	.455	.404	57	2	0	0	8	3
Justin Banks, Coppin State	.348	.474	.578	46	5	0	2	8	0
Blake Coleman, Md. Eastern Shore	.347	.373	.551	49	2	1	2	8	3
Vinny Bailey, NCCU	.345	.446	.473	55	1	0	2	11	0
Justin Rodriguez, NC A&T	.341	.420	.432	44	2	1	0	5	4
Dillon Oxyer, Md. Eastern Shore	.339	.413	.429	56	3	1	0	5	6

MID-AMERICAN CONFERENCE

	Conference		Overall	
	W	L	W	L
Central Michigan	0	0	11	6
Western Michigan	0	0	9	6
Kent State	0	0	7	6
Miami	0	0	8	7
Ball State	0	0	7	9
Northern Illinois	0	0	7	10
Ohio	0	0	3	7
Toledo	0	0	3	13
Bowling Green	0	0	2	11
Eastern Michigan	0	0	2	12
Akron	0	0	1	11

INDIVIDUAL BATTING LEADERS
(Minimum 40 at-bats)

	AVG	OBP	SLG	AB	2B	3B	HR	RBI	SB
Darryn Davis, Toledo	.400	.532	.550	60	4	1	1	17	1
Charlie Harrigan, Miami	.388	.464	.531	49	3	2	0	7	0
Trenton Quartermaine, Ball State	.385	.441	.462	52	4	0	0	16	1
Ben Carew, Kent State	.377	.468	.528	53	8	0	0	8	4
Noah Navarro, Ball State	.368	.429	.544	57	5	1	1	4	7
Zach Lechnir, Central Michigan	.350	.451	.533	60	5	0	2	15	2
Brady Huebbe, Northern Illinois	.342	.410	.425	73	6	0	0	9	2
Will Vogelgesang, Miami	.340	.439	.660	53	3	1	4	16	4
Zavier Warren, Central Michigan	.328	.469	.406	64	2	0	1	9	0
John Servello, Toledo	.323	.378	.385	65	2	1	0	10	6

INDIVIDUAL PITCHING LEADERS
(Minimum 15 innings pitched)

	W	L	ERA	G	SV	IP	H	BB	SO
Jordan Patty, Central Michigan	3	0	0.72	4	0	25	12	13	17
Nate Thomas, Northern Illinois	2	2	1.42	6	1	19	12	11	24
Tyler Hays, Bowling Green	0	2	1.66	4	0	21.2	15	14	16
Zach Losey, Ball State	2	0	1.69	5	0	16	10	3	12
Collin Romel, Kent State	1	1	1.86	4	0	19.1	18	8	20
Luke Albright, Kent State	2	2	1.90	4	0	23.2	20	8	22
Ryan Lane, Kent State	2	1	2.31	4	0	23.1	28	2	19
John Baker, Ball State	1	2	2.42	4	0	22.1	22	9	27
Kyle Nicolas, Ball State	0	1	2.74	4	0	23	15	7	37
Easton Sikorski, Western Mich.	2	1	3.12	4	0	17.1	20	9	10

MID-EASTERN ATHLETIC CONFERENCE

Northern Division	Conference		Overall	
	W	L	W	L
North Carolina A&T	0	0	7	9
North Carolina Central	0	0	6	11
Bethune-Cookman	0	0	6	12
Maryland Eastern Shore	0	0	4	11
Coppin State	0	0	3	10
Delaware State	0	0	3	12
Norfolk State	0	0	3	13
Florida A&M	0	0	5	10

INDIVIDUAL PITCHING LEADERS
(Minimum 15 innings pitched)

	W	L	ERA	G	SV	IP	H	BB	SO
Nick Rogers, Bethune-Cookman	0	2	0.87	4	0	20.2	11	15	16
Alec Mendez, Bethune-Cookman	2	0	1.04	4	0	26	18	4	22
Shane Davis, NCCU	1	1	2.01	4	0	22.1	12	10	28
Evan Gates, NC A&T	1	1	2.40	8	2	15	8	5	25
Kelyn Fox, Florida A&M	0	1	2.41	6	1	18.2	16	6	17
Alex Sniffen, NCCU	0	1	2.45	5	0	18.1	14	5	20
Ethan Chavis, NC A&T	2	1	2.70	5	0	23.1	24	7	25
Michael Johnson, NC A&T	1	3	2.77	5	0	26	31	8	20
Marty Tolson, Md. Eastern Shore	1	1	2.84	4	0	19	18	4	9
Scott Meylan, NCCU	1	0	2.87	9	0	15.2	10	8	24

MISSOURI VALLEY CONFERENCE

Team	Conference		Overall	
	W	L	W	L
Dallas Baptist	0	0	12	4
Southern Illinois	0	0	12	6
Indiana State	0	0	8	6
Missouri State	0	0	9	8
Illinois State	0	0	7	9
Bradley	0	0	4	6
Evansville	0	0	5	11
Valparaiso	0	0	2	14

INDIVIDUAL BATTING LEADERS
(Minimum 40 at-bats)

	AVG	OBP	SLG	AB	2B	3B	HR	RBI	SB
Jimmy Glowenke, Dallas Baptist	.415	.458	.509	53	2	0	1	7	1
Ian Walters, Southern Illinois	.411	.516	.562	73	6	1	1	14	9
Austin Ulick, Southern Illinois	.362	.444	.468	47	2	0	1	6	0
Nick Neville, Southern Illinois	.361	.443	.542	72	5	1	2	16	4
Dan Bolt, Bradley	.357	.449	.881	42	1	0	7	15	1
Jeffrey David, Dallas Baptist	.351	.367	.526	57	4	0	2	15	2
Tanner Craig, Evansville	.345	.479	.759	58	3	0	7	19	0
Philip Archer, Southern Illinois	.344	.430	.500	64	5	1	1	18	3
Jordan Schaffer, Ind. State	.339	.406	.375	56	0	1	0	6	2
Aidan Huggins, Illinois State	.327	.404	.367	49	0	1	0	7	1

INDIVIDUAL PITCHING LEADERS
(Minimum 15 innings pitched)

	W	L	ERA	G	SV	IP	H	BB	SO
Matthew Steidl, Southern Illinois	1	0	1.71	10	0	21	21	3	12
Tristan Weaver, Ind. State	1	1	1.85	4	0	24.1	8	8	34
Cameron Edmonson, Ind. State	2	1	1.96	5	0	18.1	13	5	25
Mason Hiser, Southern Illinois	2	0	2.35	6	0	23	27	5	11
Forrest Barnes, Missouri State	3	0	2.37	6	0	19	9	4	17
Trey Ziegenbein, Missouri State	0	1	2.79	11	0	19.1	10	8	22
Trent Turzenski, Valparaiso	0	2	2.84	4	0	19	17	6	16
Brad Harrison, Southern Illinois	0	0	3.00	5	0	18	19	8	16
Logan Wiley, Missouri State	2	1	3.09	4	0	23.1	22	2	23
Connor Cline, Ind. State	1	1	3.18	4	0	17	10	10	15

MOUNTAIN WEST CONFERENCE

	Conference W L	Overall W L
New Mexico	0 0	14 4
Boise State	0 0	9 5
San Diego State	0 0	10 6
Fresno State	0 0	9 7
Air Force	0 0	7 12
Nevada- Las Vegas	0 0	6 11
San Jose State	0 0	5 12
Nevada	0 0	2 12

INDIVIDUAL BATTING LEADERS
(Minimum 40 at-bats)

	AVG	OBP	SLG	AB	2B	3B	HR	RBI	SB
Kyler Castillo, New Mexico	.417	.476	.500	72	6	0	0	12	9
Kyle Landers, New Mexico	.411	.533	.571	56	6	0	1	18	5
Eric Bigani, UNLV	.394	.431	.530	66	7	1	0	14	0
Michael Hicks, Boise State	.386	.453	.579	57	8	0	1	11	0
Harry Fullerton, New Mexico	.367	.486	.717	60	6	3	3	15	1
Cayden Zimmerman, Air Force	.357	.404	.429	42	3	0	0	6	6
Ryan Higgins, Fresno State	.350	.400	.600	60	7	1	2	12	0
Cole Blatchford, Air Force	.349	.414	.635	63	9	0	3	13	5
Jaden Fein, San Diego State	.348	.404	.435	46	1	0	1	7	0
Ruben Ibarra, San Jose State	.344	.474	.574	61	5	0	3	8	0

INDIVIDUAL PITCHING LEADERS
(Minimum 15 innings pitched)

	W	L	ERA	G	SV	IP	H	BB	SO
Will Armbruester, New Mexico	1	0	1.14	4	0	23.2	14	3	24
Jacob Flores, San Diego State	2	0	1.45	8	0	18.2	14	11	25
Wesley Harper, Boise State	0	0	1.76	6	2	15.1	11	9	14
Chase Maddux, UNLV	1	0	2.59	4	0	24.1	20	4	19
Jake Jackson, Nevada	1	3	3.00	4	0	24	26	7	16
Troy Melton, San Diego State	3	1	3.22	4	0	22.1	15	9	26
Jaime Arias, Fresno State	2	1	3.75	4	0	24	22	3	22
Michael Paredes, San Diego State	1	1	4.05	4	0	20	24	6	17
Josh Sharman, UNLV	2	1	4.13	4	0	24	21	11	23
Shane O'Malley, Nevada	1	2	4.29	4	0	21	24	10	12

NORTHEAST CONFERENCE

	Conference W L	Overall W L
Long Island	0 0	5 5
Sacred Heart	0 0	6 7
Wagner	0 0	6 8
Merrimack	0 0	6 9
Central Connecticut State	0 0	4 8
Fairleigh Dickinson	0 0	4 9
Bryant	0 0	4 11
Mount St. Mary's	0 0	2 10

INDIVIDUAL BATTING LEADERS
(Minimum 40 at-bats)

	AVG	OBP	SLG	AB	2B	3B	HR	RBI	SB
Nick Shumski, Merrimack	.443	.469	.508	61	4	0	0	12	3
Anthony Warneke, Long Island	.438	.491	.542	48	3	1	0	3	9
Tom Ruscitti, Fairleigh Dickinson	.364	.472	.773	44	3	0	5	11	2
Justin Jordan, Sacred Heart	.316	.375	.386	57	1	0	1	5	4
Nate Brodsky, Fairleigh Dickinson	.308	.357	.365	52	3	0	0	4	2
Kurtis Stadnicki, Merrimack	.302	.321	.358	53	1	1	0	10	0
Jake Gustin, Bryant	.294	.410	.471	51	6	0	1	6	8
Henry Martinez, Wagner	.292	.352	.333	48	2	0	0	3	1
Cody Bey, Wagner	.291	.400	.345	55	3	0	0	6	3
Shane Kelly, Bryant	.283	.333	.491	53	3	1	2	9	2

INDIVIDUAL PITCHING LEADERS
(Minimum 15 innings pitched)

	W	L	ERA	G	SV	IP	H	BB	SO
Joshua Loeschorn, Long Island	2	0	0.00	3	0	15	9	6	14
Brandon Fox, CCSU	1	2	0.43	3	0	21	16	2	14
Anthony Mozzicato, CCSU	1	1	1.50	3	0	18	10	4	11

Jackson Svete, Long Island	1	1	1.50	3	0	18	13	7	25
Alec Huertas, Long Island	1	1	1.50	3	0	18	14	6	13
Jake Thibault, Merrimack	1	2	1.59	7	1	17	15	2	11
Andrew Braun, CCSU	1	1	2.55	3	0	17.2	11	7	21
McCae Allen, Wagner	0	0	2.61	4	0	20.2	15	12	28
Mason Palmieri, Bryant	1	1	2.91	5	0	21.2	13	8	22
Luke Hansen, Sacred Heart	0	0	4.11	3	0	15.1	14	6	14

OHIO VALLEY CONFERENCE

	Conference W L	Overall W L
Belmont	3 0	14 3
Southern Illinois-Edwardsville	3 0	8 7
Murray State	2 1	10 7
Eastern Illinois	2 1	8 6
Southeast Missouri State	2 1	9 8
Jacksonville State	1 2	7 8
Austin Peay	1 2	7 10
Tennessee-Martin	1 2	5 11
Eastern Kentucky	0 0	12 2
Morehead State	0 3	5 10
Tennessee Tech	0 3	3 12

INDIVIDUAL BATTING LEADERS
(Minimum 40 at-bats)

	AVG	OBP	SLG	AB	2B	3B	HR	RBI	SB
Daniel Harris, IV, Eastern Kentucky	.460	.541	.680	50	3	1	2	16	5
A.J. Lewis, Eastern Kentucky	.451	.541	.843	51	7	2	3	21	3
Bryson Bloomer, Murray State	.429	.468	.554	56	4	0	1	10	1
Jordan Cozart, Murray State	.417	.486	.750	60	5	0	5	19	0
Justin Dirden, SE Missouri State	.414	.471	.900	70	3	2	9	26	9
Jason Hinchman, Tennessee Tech	.414	.485	.793	58	4	0	6	13	3
Tyler Wilber, SE Missouri State	.406	.494	.696	69	9	1	3	12	3
Andrew Keck, SE Missouri State	.400	.463	.500	70	4	0	1	19	7
Gino Avros, Austin Peay	.373	.457	.597	67	9	0	2	12	3
Danny Wright, SE Missouri State	.372	.424	.526	78	4	1	2	16	6

INDIVIDUAL PITCHING LEADERS
(Minimum 15 innings pitched)

	W	L	ERA	G	SV	IP	H	BB	SO
Trevor McMurray, Murray State	3	0	0.35	4	0	25.2	15	8	23
Corley Woods, Jacksonville State	1	2	1.06	7	1	17	13	3	10
Kenny Serwa, SI-Edwardsville	4	0	1.33	4	0	27	20	4	42
Kyle Brennan, Belmont	5	0	1.45	9	3	18.2	14	4	23
Sam Gardner, Murray State	3	0	1.47	4	0	18.1	16	4	18
Blake Malatestinic, Eastern Ill.	3	0	1.69	4	0	26.2	19	6	23
Jesse Wainscott, Eastern Illinois	1	1	2.08	4	0	17.1	15	11	9
Logan Bowen, Belmont	1	1	2.31	4	0	23.1	15	11	23
Joshua South, Belmont	2	0	2.42	4	0	26	22	7	26
Shane Burns, Murray State	1	2	2.60	4	0	17.1	12	13	24

PACIFIC-12 CONFERENCE

	Conference W L	Overall W L
UCLA	0 0	13 2
Arizona State	0 0	13 4
Arizona	0 0	10 5
Southern California	0 0	10 5
Washington	0 0	9 6
Washington State	0 0	9 7
Oregon	0 0	8 7
Utah	0 0	6 7
Oregon State	0 0	5 9
California	0 0	5 11
Stanford	0 0	5 11

INDIVIDUAL BATTING LEADERS
(Minimum 40 at-bats)

	AVG	OBP	SLG	AB	2B	3B	HR	RBI	SB
Kyler McMahan, Oregon State	.439	.492	.544	57	6	0	0	4	3
Kyle Manzardo, Washington State	.435	.500	.694	62	7	0	3	14	0
Kenyon Yovan, Oregon	.429	.566	.714	56	2	1	4	9	0

	AVG	OBP	SLG	AB	2B	3B	HR	RBI	SB
Aaron Zavala, Oregon	.418	.493	.491	55	1	0	1	22	2
Matt McLain, UCLA	.397	.422	.621	58	4	0	3	19	1
Jamal O'Guinn, Southern California	.378	.533	.511	45	6	0	0	7	2
Ryan Holgate, Arizona	.377	.459	.547	53	6	0	1	12	1
Noah Hsue, Washington	.375	.444	.417	48	0	1	0	3	2
Austin Wells, Arizona	.375	.527	.589	56	6	0	2	14	1
Trevor Hauver, Arizona State	.356	.508	.822	45	6	0	5	17	0
Rhylan Thomas, Southern California	.356	.412	.422	45	1	1	0	6	2
Garrett Mitchell, UCLA	.355	.425	.484	62	6	1	0	8	5
Donta Williams, Arizona	.348	.527	.500	46	3	2	0	14	2
Clay Owens, Southern California	.346	.400	.577	52	1	1	3	17	0
Kyle Cuellar, UCLA	.341	.451	.537	41	2	0	2	9	0

INDIVIDUAL PITCHING LEADERS
(Minimum 15 innings pitched)

	W	L	ERA	G	SV	IP	H	BB	SO
Alex Williams, Stanford	2	1	0.51	3	0	17.2	11	4	18
Stevie Emanuels, Washington	3	1	0.79	4	0	22.2	17	9	38
Christian Chamberlain, Oregon St	2	1	0.82	4	0	22	6	11	34
Brett Walker, Oregon	3	0	0.84	3	0	21.1	13	1	10
Boyd Vander Kooi, Arizona State	1	1	1.02	4	0	17.2	11	2	14
Zach Pettway, UCLA	3	0	1.05	4	0	25.2	13	1	29
John Beller, Southern Cal	3	0	1.13	4	1	24	10	6	25
Isaac Esqueda, Southern Cal	0	1	1.20	3	0	15	14	6	13
Jesse Bergin, UCLA	4	0	1.27	4	0	21.1	13	7	27
Zane Mills, Washington State	3	0	1.44	4	0	25	15	10	32

PATRIOT LEAGUE

	Conference		Overall	
	W	L	W	L
Navy	0	0	14	1
Army	0	0	6	9
Holy Cross	0	0	5	10
Lehigh	0	0	5	10
Lafayette	0	0	4	10
Bucknell	0	0	4	12

INDIVIDUAL BATTING LEADERS
(Minimum 40 at-bats)

	AVG	OBP	SLG	AB	2B	3B	HR	RBI	SB
Alex Smith, Navy	.368	.457	.526	38	4	1	0	9	0
Austin Masel, Holy Cross	.344	.414	.443	61	4	1	0	12	1
Evan Lowery, Navy	.341	.500	.477	44	6	0	0	8	0
Andre Walden, Army	.333	.387	.439	57	1	1	1	8	8
Chris Cannizzaro, Bucknell	.328	.403	.517	58	5	0	2	17	2
David Kale, Holy Cross	.326	.415	.413	46	4	0	0	5	3
Colin Hartey, Lafayette	.321	.387	.375	56	3	0	0	5	2
Chris Rinaldi, Holy Cross	.319	.373	.468	47	5	1	0	5	3
Anthony Giachin, Army	.308	.361	.338	65	2	0	0	5	1
Jacob Williamson, Navy	.308	.383	.462	52	0	1	2	12	0

INDIVIDUAL PITCHING LEADERS
(Minimum 15 innings pitched)

	W	L	ERA	G	SV	IP	H	BB	SO
Charlie Connolly, Navy	1	0	1.04	4	0	26	20	3	32
Luke Dawson, Holy Cross	1	1	1.11	4	0	24.1	25	8	20
Logan Smith, Army	2	1	1.61	4	0	28	15	6	24
Tommy Goodridge, Navy	2	0	2.25	4	0	20	14	11	18
Brett Kreyer, Lafayette	0	2	2.31	4	0	23.1	17	6	15
Anthony LoRicco, Army	1	1	2.70	4	0	20	17	11	24
Mark Anderson, Lafayette	1	0	3.00	5	1	15	13	8	7
Luke Rettig, Lehigh	0	2	3.52	4	0	23	21	7	27
Mason Black, Lehigh	1	2	3.68	4	0	22	17	8	29
Nate Grisius, Bucknell	2	2	4.99	4	0	21.2	13	13	21

SOUTHEASTERN CONFERENCE

	Conference		Overall	
East Division	W	L	W	L
Florida	0	0	16	1
Tennessee	0	0	15	2
Georgia	0	0	14	4
South Carolina	0	0	12	4
Vanderbilt	0	0	13	5
Missouri	0	0	11	5
Kentucky	0	0	11	6

	Conference		Overall	
West Division	W	L	W	L
Mississippi	0	0	16	1
Alabama	0	0	16	1
Texas A&M	0	0	15	3
Mississippi State	0	0	12	4
Auburn	0	0	13	5
Louisiana State	0	0	12	5
Arkansas	0	0	11	5

INDIVIDUAL BATTING LEADERS
(Minimum 40 at-bats)

	AVG	OBP	SLG	AB	2B	3B	HR	RBI	SB
Brandt Belk, Missouri	.457	.544	.652	46	3	0	2	9	4
Jacob Young, Florida	.450	.514	.517	60	4	0	0	9	6
Heston Kjerstad, Arkansas	.448	.513	.791	67	5	0	6	20	1
Tyler Gentry, Alabama	.429	.554	.750	56	6	0	4	21	2
John Rhodes, Kentucky	.426	.485	.672	61	10	1	1	19	1
Zach DeLoach, Texas A&M	.421	.547	.789	57	3	0	6	17	6
Ben Anderson, Georgia	.414	.544	.552	58	6	1	0	13	5
Matt Scheffler, Auburn	.412	.516	.549	51	4	0	1	14	1
Rankin Woley, Auburn	.412	.487	.618	68	8	0	2	22	0
Tyler Keenan, Mississippi	.403	.488	.791	67	5	0	7	33	1
Tucker Bradley, Georgia	.397	.513	.730	63	3	0	6	23	8
Austin Schultz, Kentucky	.393	.479	.754	61	5	1	5	20	5
Anthony Servideo, Mississippi	.390	.575	.695	59	3	0	5	17	9
Brett Auerbach, Alabama	.388	.506	.642	67	8	0	3	14	12
Christian Franklin, Arkansas	.381	.467	.619	63	4	1	3	11	3

INDIVIDUAL PITCHING LEADERS
(Minimum 15 innings pitched)

	W	L	ERA	G	SV	IP	H	BB	SO
Connor Prielipp, Alabama	3	0	0.00	4	0	21	5	6	35
Mason Hickman, Vanderbilt	2	0	0.48	3	0	18.2	8	3	26
Asa Lacy, Texas A&M	3	0	0.75	4	0	24	9	8	46
Christian MacLeod, Miss. State	4	0	0.86	4	0	21	9	6	35
Caleb Bolden, Arkansas	1	0	1.13	4	0	16	14	3	15
Gunnar Hoglund, Mississippi	3	0	1.16	4	0	23.1	18	4	37
Hunter Barco, Florida	2	0	1.40	5	0	19.1	11	6	26
Ethan Smith, Vanderbilt	3	0	1.42	5	0	19	12	9	23
Jackson Leath, Tennessee	4	0	1.45	5	0	18.2	11	5	29
Cole Wilcox, Georgia	3	0	1.57	4	0	23	18	2	32

SOUTHERN CONFERENCE

	Conference		Overall	
	W	L	W	L
Samford	0	0	13	2
Wofford	0	0	14	3
Mercer	0	0	13	3
East Tennessee State	0	0	12	3
UNC Greensboro	0	0	11	5
The Citadel	0	0	10	6
Western Carolina	0	0	8	8
Furman	0	0	8	9
VMI	0	0	4	13

INDIVIDUAL BATTING LEADERS
(Minimum 40 at-bats)

	AVG	OBP	SLG	AB	2B	3B	HR	RBI	SB
Brooks Carlson, Samford	.500	.644	.760	50	4	0	3	19	0
Will Knight, VMI	.431	.484	.586	58	7	1	0	6	1
Pres Cavenaugh, UNC Greensboro	.425	.479	.525	40	2	1	0	7	6
Daniel Walsh, Western Carolina	.386	.493	.439	57	3	0	0	9	3
Tilo Skole, The Citadel	.377	.492	.415	53	2	0	0	11	4
Hudson Byorick, Wofford	.373	.500	.542	59	7	0	1	8	3
Caleb Webster, UNC Greensboro	.369	.447	.631	65	7	2	2	13	4
Jake Lyle, East Tennessee State	.362	.464	.638	58	6	2	2	13	12
Jeffery Brown, The Citadel	.350	.461	.533	60	5	3	0	10	8
Tyler Corbitt, The Citadel	.349	.413	.524	63	1	2	2	10	4

INDIVIDUAL PITCHING LEADERS
(Minimum 15 innings pitched)

	W	L	ERA	G	SV	IP	H	BB	SO
Jackson Kelley, Mercer	3	0	0.70	4	0	25.2	22	2	20
Cameron Reeves, The Citadel	4	0	1.04	4	0	26	18	5	32
Austin Koehn, UNC Greensboro	1	0	1.04	4	0	17.1	15	4	19
Landon Knack, East Tenn State	4	0	1.08	4	0	25	12	1	51
Samuel Strickland, Samford	3	0	1.17	4	0	23	20	1	30
John Michael Bertrand, Furman	3	1	1.50	4	0	24	16	4	23
Garrett Mathes, Mercer	1	0	1.59	6	1	17	7	8	19
Hayes Heinecke, Wofford	3	1	1.75	4	0	25.2	22	3	36
Austin Parsley, UNC Greensboro	3	0	1.86	6	0	19.1	8	5	17
Matt Lazzaro, Furman	0	0	2.12	6	1	17	11	9	15

SOUTHLAND CONFERENCE

	Conference		Overall	
	W	L	W	L
Stephen F. Austin	3	0	6	10
Northwestern State	2	1	12	4
New Orleans	2	1	11	6
Central Arkansas	2	1	8	8
Texas A&M-Corpus Christi	2	1	8	10
Houston Baptist	2	1	6	11
Incarnate Word	1	2	9	7
Nicholls State	1	2	10	8
Sam Houston State	1	2	7	7
Abilene Christian	1	2	7	8
Southeastern Louisiana	1	2	6	10
McNeese State	0	0	10	7
Lamar	0	3	7	10

INDIVIDUAL BATTING LEADERS
(Minimum 40 at-bats)

	AVG	OBP	SLG	AB	2B	3B	HR	RBI	SB
Jake Dickerson, McNeese State	.415	.487	.662	65	4	0	4	18	3
Connor Emmet, Central Arkansas	.397	.449	.571	63	6	1	1	7	1
Jack Rogers, Sam Houston	.396	.450	.698	53	7	3	1	14	4
Beau Orlando, Central Arkansas	.392	.515	.431	51	2	0	0	7	2
Johnny Gonzales, Houston Baptist	.382	.447	.632	68	8	3	1	12	0
Luther Woullard, New Orleans	.367	.451	.533	60	3	2	1	12	2
Brayden Jobert, Nicholls State	.365	.459	.556	63	3	0	3	11	3
Payton Harden, McNeese State	.356	.388	.441	59	3	1	0	12	4
Lenni Kunert, Northwestern State	.351	.435	.404	57	3	0	0	14	3
Jared Martin, Stephen F. Austin	.347	.484	.449	49	2	0	1	7	1

INDIVIDUAL PITCHING LEADERS
(Minimum 15 innings pitched)

	W	L	ERA	G	SV	IP	H	BB	SO
Logan Hofmann, NW State	4	0	0.00	4	0	28	14	5	38
Lance Lusk, Sam Houston State	2	0	1.15	6	1	15.2	16	3	17
Dominic Robinson, Sam Houston	1	1	1.23	4	0	22	12	5	30
Trey Shaffer, SE Louisiana	3	1	1.23	4	0	22	8	12	32
Gavin Stone, Central Arkansas	3	1	1.30	4	0	27.2	15	6	31
Grant Upton, SE Louisiana	1	1	1.46	4	0	24.2	21	6	17
Cal Carver, NW State	1	1	1.50	4	0	18	11	6	22
Matt Dillard, Sam Houston	2	1	1.53	4	0	17.2	15	4	17
Will Warren, SE Louisiana	2	0	1.90	5	2	23.2	15	4	30
Austin Wagner, Abilene Christian	1	2	1.96	4	0	18.1	14	1	22

SOUTHWESTERN ATHLETIC CONFERENCE

	Conference		Overall	
East Division	W	L	W	L
Alabama State	2	0	13	4
Jackson State	2	0	9	7
Alcorn State	3	2	5	7
Alabama A&M	3	3	3	14
Mississippi Valley State	0	3	0	11

	Conference		Overall	
West Division	W	L	W	L
Southern	3	0	6	10
Texas Southern	4	2	7	12
Arkansas-Pine Bluff	3	3	6	12
Grambling State	1	2	5	10
Prairie View A&M	1	5	4	15

INDIVIDUAL BATTING LEADERS
(Minimum 40 at-bats)

	AVG	OBP	SLG	AB	2B	3B	HR	RBI	SB
Jaylyn Williams, Jackson State	.434	.508	.528	53	5	0	0	13	4
Equon Smith, Jackson State	.429	.500	.595	42	0	2	1	9	8
Chandler Dillard, Jackson State	.426	.486	.541	61	1	3	0	7	11
Roderick Coffee, Texas Southern	.383	.474	.830	47	0	0	7	15	2
CJ Newsome, Jackson State	.375	.438	.446	56	2	1	0	8	6
Oscar Ponce, Texas Southern	.370	.427	.479	73	5	0	1	24	0
Wesley Reyes, Jackson State	.333	.424	.544	57	6	0	2	14	1
Tristin Garcia, Alcorn State	.333	.413	.436	39	1	0	1	11	0
JanMikell Bastardo, Alabama A&M	.323	.348	.446	65	4	2	0	6	6
Chris Prentiss, Jackson State	.322	.388	.373	59	1	1	0	10	8

INDIVIDUAL PITCHING LEADERS
(Minimum 15 innings pitched)

	W	L	ERA	G	SV	IP	H	BB	SO
Jacknell Guzman, Alabama State	3	0	2.05	4	0	30.2	20	15	31
Ricardo Rivera, Alabama State	0	1	2.29	5	0	19.2	12	10	24
Kyle Smith, Prarie View A&M	2	2	2.37	4	0	30.1	27	6	30
Fernando Diaz Jr., Alabama A&M	1	2	2.95	7	2	21.1	22	5	28
Anthony Becerra, Jackson State	1	1	3.1	4	0	20.1	10	12	30
Austin King, Alabama State	2	0	3.32	4	0	21.2	18	7	25
Peyton Baker, Alabama A&M	1	1	3.46	6	0	26	19	12	22
Aaron Barkley, Miss Valley State	0	5	3.57	7	0	35.1	32	9	47
Steven Davila, Jackson State	2	0	3.64	7	1	17.1	13	11	23
Kerry Boykins Jr., Grambling	1	1	3.93	4	0	18.1	23	4	9

SUMMIT LEAGUE

	Conference		Overall	
	W	L	W	L
Nebraska-Omaha	0	0	10	4
North Dakota State	0	0	8	9
Oral Roberts	0	0	6	10
Purdue-Fort Wayne	0	0	5	10
South Dakota State	0	0	5	12
Western Illinois	0	0	0	13

INDIVIDUAL BATTING LEADERS
(Minimum 40 at-bats)

	AVG	OBP	SLG	AB	2B	3B	HR	RBI	SB
Aaron Chapman, PUFW	.382	.411	.500	68	4	2	0	11	3
Dylan Stewart, PUFW	.381	.509	.452	42	0	0	1	6	5
Keil Krumwiede, Neb.-Omaha	.360	.459	.600	50	6	0	2	10	0
Garrett Mohler, PUFW	.357	.400	.411	56	3	0	0	7	1
Garrett Lake, PUFW	.333	.422	.407	54	2	1	0	9	1
Gus Steiger, South Dakota State	.321	.433	.482	56	5	2	0	6	7
Brock Anderson, ND State	.317	.434	.444	63	5	0	1	12	3
Jordan Wiley, ND State	.317	.423	.600	60	5	0	4	9	0
Adam Oviedo, Oral Roberts	.302	.353	.556	63	1	0	5	13	1
Tucker Rohde, ND State	.297	.352	.422	64	5	0	1	11	0

INDIVIDUAL PITCHING LEADERS
(Minimum 15 innings pitched)

	W	L	ERA	G	SV	IP	H	BB	SO
Hunter Swift, Oral Roberts	2	0	1.13	3	0	16	10	3	18
Brett Mogen, South Dakota State	1	0	2.14	8	1	21	13	7	15
Richie Holetz, Neb.-Omaha	2	2	2.49	4	0	21.2	16	10	22
Easton Smith, Neb.-Omaha	2	1	2.65	4	0	17	11	10	9
Spencer Koelewyn, Neb.-Omaha	2	0	2.70	4	0	20	16	13	23
Max Loven, North Dakota State	2	1	3.13	4	0	23	20	5	19
James Notary, Oral Roberts	2	1	3.20	4	0	25.1	21	9	21
Joey Machado, Neb.-Omaha	2	1	3.72	4	0	19.1	19	7	17
Michael Madura, PUFW	0	0	4.60	4	0	15.2	21	5	10
Adam Mazur, North Dakota State	1	2	5.75	4	0	20.1	20	12	18

SUN BELT CONFERENCE

East Division	Conference W	L	Overall W	L
Coastal Carolina	0	0	11	5
Georgia Southern	0	0	11	5
Appalachian State	0	0	11	6
Georgia State	0	0	9	7
Troy	0	0	9	8
South Alabama	0	0	8	10

West Division	Conference W	L	Overall W	L
Texas State	0	0	14	4
Texas-Arlington	0	0	12	4
Louisiana-Monroe	0	0	12	5
Arkansas-Little Rock	0	0	9	8
Louisiana	0	0	8	9
Arkansas State	0	0	7	9

INDIVIDUAL BATTING LEADERS
(Minimum 40 at-bats)

	AVG	OBP	SLG	AB	2B	3B	HR	RBI	SB
Kale Emshoff, Arkansas-Little Rock	.417	.527	.800	60	2	0	7	12	0
Drew Frederic, Troy	.409	.500	.545	66	4	1	1	13	11
Elian Merejo, Georgia State	.407	.527	.763	59	6	0	5	13	5
Ryan Humeniuk, Louisiana-Monroe	.406	.481	.594	69	2	1	3	14	4
Andrew Beesley, Louisiana-Monroe	.400	.565	.600	45	4	1	1	15	5
William Sullivan, Troy	.396	.468	.547	53	6	1	0	12	0
Caleb Bartolero, Troy	.394	.423	.634	71	9	1	2	18	1
Connor Aube, Texas-Arlington	.375	.426	.464	56	5	0	0	5	0
Will Mize, Georgia State	.373	.448	.508	59	5	0	1	17	1
Cooper Weiss, CCU	.372	.473	.628	43	5	0	2	14	5

INDIVIDUAL PITCHING LEADERS
(Minimum 15 innings pitched)

	W	L	ERA	G	SV	IP	H	BB	SO
Wyatt Divis, Texas-Arlington	1	0	0.00	4	2	16	7	7	15
Levi Thomas, Troy	2	1	0.39	4	0	23	6	6	42
Tyler Owens, Ga. Southern	2	0	0.51	5	0	17.2	9	3	15
David Moffat, Texas-Arlington	1	0	0.67	4	0	27	13	4	16
Brandon Young, Louisiana	3	0	1.10	4	0	24.2	13	9	37
Carter Robinson, Louisiana	2	1	1.31	4	0	20.2	15	6	15
Jordan Jackson, Ga. Southern	3	1	1.57	4	0	23	12	9	24
Carlos Tavera, Texas-Arlington	3	1	1.71	4	0	21	11	14	31
Zach McCambley, CCU	3	1	1.80	4	0	25	20	7	32
Noah Hall, Appalachian State	2	0	1.80	10	1	20	13	10	21

WEST COAST CONFERENCE

	Conference W	L	Overall W	L
Pepperdine	0	0	12	3
San Diego	0	0	12	4
Portland	0	0	12	4
Santa Clara	0	0	12	5
San Francisco	0	0	9	8
Saint Mary's	0	0	8	8
Loyola Marymount	0	0	8	8
Pacific	0	0	8	9
Brigham Young	0	0	7	9
Gonzaga	0	0	6	10

INDIVIDUAL BATTING LEADERS
(Minimum 40 at-bats)

	AVG	OBP	SLG	AB	2B	3B	HR	RBI	SB
Jake Holcroft, Portland	.484	.522	.758	62	7	2	2	11	4
Aharon Modlin, Pepperdine	.413	.472	.571	63	5	1	1	11	3
Charles Middleton, Pacific	.403	.494	.657	67	5	0	4	20	1
Reese Alexiades, Pepperdine	.397	.458	.571	63	6	1	1	15	2
Gio Diaz, Saint Mary's	.396	.442	.417	48	1	0	0	2	3
Robert Emery, San Francisco	.381	.451	.540	63	4	0	2	9	0
Alex LeForestier, Pacific	.371	.467	.500	62	4	2	0	15	2
Cooper Uhl, Loyola Marymoung	.361	.487	.443	61	5	0	0	9	5
Thomas Luevano, San Diego	.356	.424	.593	59	8	0	2	14	1
Tyler Rando, Gonzaga	.352	.431	.389	54	2	0	0	6	1

INDIVIDUAL PITCHING LEADERS
(Minimum 15 innings pitched)

	W	L	ERA	G	SV	IP	H	BB	SO
Christian Peters, Portland	3	1	0.63	4	0	28.2	19	3	35
Carter Rustad, San Diego	4	0	0.84	4	0	21.1	5	8	24
Cooper Chandler, Pepperdine	3	0	1.00	3	0	18.0	14	5	20
Wil Jensen, Pepperdine	3	0	2.19	4	0	24.2	18	6	26
Hayden Pearce, Pacific	2	0	2.28	4	0	23.2	17	2	22
Dalton Ponce, Saint Mary's	2	1	2.46	4	0	22	18	2	16
Jake Miller, San Diego	1	1	2.49	5	1	21.2	10	10	29
Justin Sterner, Brigham Young	0	0	2.53	4	0	21.1	21	9	24
Mac Lardner, Gonzaga	0	2	2.55	4	0	24.2	17	8	33
Gunnar Groen, Pepperdine	2	1	2.57	5	1	21	14	6	135

WESTERN ATHLETIC CONFERENCE

	Conference W	L	Overall W	L
New Mexico State	0	0	12	4
Texas-Rio Grande Valley	0	0	11	7
Sacramento State	0	0	9	7
Grand Canyon	0	0	9	9
California Baptist	0	0	7	8
Seattle	0	0	7	9
Cal State Bakersfield	0	0	5	9
Utah Valley	0	0	5	14
Northern Colorado	0	0	4	13
Chicago State	0	0	2	16

INDIVIDUAL BATTING LEADERS
(Minimum 40 at-bats)

	AVG	OBP	SLG	AB	2B	3B	HR	RBI	SB
Nick Gonzales, New Mexico State	.448	.610	1.155	58	3	1	12	36	4
Julian Kodama, Seattle	.379	.422	.500	58	7	0	0	7	1
Juan Colato, Grand Canyon	.367	.419	.620	79	5	0	5	14	6
Chad Castillo, California Baptist	.350	.451	.500	60	3	0	2	9	5
Zerek Saenz, New Mexico State	.344	.429	.375	64	2	0	0	9	1
Ulises Caballero, California Baptist	.340	.404	.560	50	2	0	3	8	2
Mitch Moralez, Utah Valley	.329	.365	.418	79	7	0	0	9	1
Ryan Walstad, Sacramento State	.321	.463	.509	53	4	0	2	9	4
Damian Henderson, CSUB	.321	.446	.528	53	1	2	2	10	1
Nick Plaia, California Baptist	.321	.433	.429	56	4	1	0	8	3

INDIVIDUAL PITCHING LEADERS
(Minimum 15 innings pitched)

	W	L	ERA	G	SV	IP	H	BB	SO
Jesse Schmit, Utah Valley	2	0	1.08	4	0	25.0	13	7	27
Parker Brahms, Sacramento State	2	1	1.14	4	0	23.2	18	0	32
Travis Adams, Sacramento State	2	1	1.57	4	0	23.0	18	2	19
Matt Amrhein, California Baptist	3	0	1.72	9	0	15.2	14	8	21
Scott Randall, Sacramento State	2	1	1.75	4	0	25.2	20	1	23
Chris Jefferson, New Mexico St	2	1	2.05	4	0	22.0	19	6	17
Chris Barraza, New Mexico State	2	0	2.66	4	0	20.1	22	8	16
Alex Jemal, Seattle	0	0	2.81	8	0	16	17	5	17
Bryan Pope, California Baptist	3	1	2.84	4	0	25.1	19	2	23
Pierson Ohl, Grand Canyon	1	2	2.89	4	0	28	28	1	17

The San Diego League instituted new protocols, including a socially distanced national anthem.

COURTESY OF SAN DIEGO LEAGUE

Summer Ball Provides Sense Of Normalcy

BY TEDDY CAHILL

The summer ball season was unlike any other—the venerable Cape Cod League canceled its season for the first time since World War II and the summer became much more regionalized as many players opted to stay close to home—but baseball in some form continued in several leagues around the country.

Many leagues this spring joined the Cape in cancelling their seasons. But others continued, played out their seasons and crowned a champion.

For the conferences that continued, being able to provide players, who missed out on most of their seasons this spring, the opportunity to play this summer was a highlight.

"We had our own terminology—we created a bubble of normalcy," San Diego League vice president Mark Rogoff said. "Yeah, there were blue Xs all over the place, there was hand sanitizer in the dugouts and we took temperatures every day, but it was our bubble of normalcy. Kind of an escapism.

"To me, it seems like there's something about (the players) that they want to compete. We gave them that opportunity and it was fun to watch."

That chance was also appreciated by the players themselves. South Florida League commissioner Vince Farfaglia said the commitment level of the players impressed him the most this summer. He noticed it from Day 1, when the teams were just holding preseason training camp to help the players get back up to speed after a long layoff this spring.

"We had guys driving from two, three hours just to practice for the day," he said. "That commitment level and grind, you really appreciate it."

That kind of discipline and want was required this summer. Players had to adjust after their long spring layoff and then continue to follow safety protocols all summer. No league operated in a true bubble, meaning practicing social distancing, wearing a mask and making smart decisions were of vital importance to completing the season.

It didn't go smoothly everywhere. The Northwoods' Northern Michigan pod played just one weekend before an outbreak of the virus led to it shutting down for two weeks and two of the four teams being removed from play. Both the Coastal Plain League and Texas Collegiate League had a team forced to end its season early due to the virus, though both teams completed the majority of their schedules and the rest of the league continued.

Farfaglia said there were four positive tests in the South Florida League. After a positive test, the player needed a negative test to return to play and the whole team was quarantined. But they were able to avoid having to shut down for any period of time and their players did a good job sticking to strict guidelines.

The league's plan for playing this summer had to go all the way to the governor's office to be approved. No more than 50 people were allowed on the field, leading the league to limit game-day rosters to 20 players. Players staying at the condos the league rented had to maintain a curfew, which was enforced by room checks. Everyone had to wear a mask in the dugout and social distancing was a point of emphasis.

Farfaglia said the hardest part of the summer was building trust with everyone that needed to sign off on the protocols.

"The toughest thing was convincing the public and government officials that we were confident our plan was going to work and we would execute it properly," he said. "The biggest thing was putting the mitigation plans together and gaining trust that we needed. The baseball stuff falls in line and is pretty simple."

Overall, summer ball's experience with the virus wasn't that much different from any other sport playing this summer in the United States. MLB endured outbreaks early in its season before settling into a more stable schedule and Major League Soccer sent two teams home from its bubble in Orlando before its MLS Is Back Tournament began in July.

On the field, the game was a little different this summer. With USA Baseball's Collegiate National Team and the Cape canceled, many premium prospects chose not to play. Those that did typically stayed more local to their hometowns or schools, leading to a higher level of talent in many leagues than in a typical summer.

Florida State outfielder Robby Martin before the pandemic was slated to return to Cotuit with the Cape Cod League, where he played last summer. After the Cape's season was canceled, he wasn't sure what to do or if there would even be a summer season. Eventually, he made a late decision to play for the Orlando Scorpions in the Florida League, joining his Florida State outfield-mate Reese Albert on the roster.

"I'm getting more reps after not playing a whole season," he said. "I'm working on things I think I need to work on and showcase more of what I maybe haven't done during the season at school.

"I'm trying to showcase more of what I can do as well as get more reps."

College coaches said they mostly gave their players going into summer ball similar instructions to what they always do. Some players went to improve or refine specific things. Some simply needed the reps.

"It depends on who you are or where you are in your baseball life," Mississippi coach Mike Bianco said. "Some guys are playing summer ball that weren't playing much in the abbreviated season and some guys were everyday players. It's kind of an individual thing. I don't think there's that much different from a normal year in that respect."

While the mindset didn't change much for players this summer, the environment around them did. There were fewer premium players in summer leagues and they were much more spread out, instead of being concentrated on Team USA or the Cape. About 40 percent of the top 50 players in the 2021 draft class played in summer leagues. In a typical year, that number is around 80 or 90 percent.

In some ways, that changes the way players can be evaluated in the summer as they face more uneven competition. But coaches and scouts alike are not expecting players to return from a three-month shutdown in mid-season form.

"You're limited in what summer is," Bianco said. "You've got all these different leagues and kids are choosing to either play or not and get in the weight room and summer school. Now, we just want them doing something. If that's in the Northwoods League, great. If you're here locally in Jackson, Miss., and you're playing a couple times a week, that's awesome."

The long layoff this spring also had repercussions on the field. Early in the summer season there were reports across many leagues that the pitchers were ahead of the hitters. Eventually, the hitters caught up, but this summer saw many standout pitching performances.

No matter how different the summer may have felt a times, it was still baseball offering a chance to compete, develop and chase a trophy. Throughout the summer, at ballparks across the country, players responded to that opportunity.

"My No. 1 goal is to win—nothing beats winning," said Tate Samuelson, who played in the San Diego League. "Going out, creating relationship with these guys and winning is what will make that the best. For myself, continuing to get better at the plate and continue to get reps at third base.

"Just continue to get better."

"Championship day was great," Rogoff said. "The smiles were everywhere. There was a lot of happiness, excitement. You can call it cheesy, lovey dovey, but it was a special day.

"It was very cool to see kids doing what they should be doing, and that was playing ball this summer."

COLLEGE *SUMMER LEAGUES*

Outfielder Jud Fabian (Florida) starred in the Florida League this summer.

COASTAL PLAINS LEAGUE

Mid-Atlantic Division	W	L	PCT
Wilson Tobs	9	5	.643
High Point-Thomasville HiToms	9	7	.563
Peninsula Pilots	8	11	.421
Martinsville Mustangs	7	10	.412

Southern Division	W	L	Pct
Savannah Bananas	16	14	.533
Macon Bacon	13	13	.500
Lexington County Blowfish	8	10	.444

INDIVIDUAL BATTING LEADERS

	AVG	AB	R	H	2B	3B	HR	RBI	SB
Hogan Windish, 2B, HiToms	.447	94	28	42	13	4	6	37	1
Trey Sweeney, INF, Tobs	.397	68	19	27	7	0	4	16	3
Luke Spiva, 1B/OF, HiToms	.387	62	12	24	3	1	3	13	2
Damon Dues, INF, Tobs	.373	51	15	19	0	0	2	14	11
Jared Carr, OF, Tobs	.356	73	16	26	3	1	8	26	7
Michael Turconi, SS, HiToms	.344	96	32	33	7	1	4	27	7
Joe Simone, OF, Mustangs	.329	79	18	26	5	0	0	10	9
Chris Meyers, INF, Tobs	.318	66	20	21	3	0	3	15	0
Dusty Baker, OF, Tobs	.313	64	20	20	5	1	6	20	6
Christian Easley, OF, Mustangs	.286	77	21	22	2	0	3	16	

INDIVIDUAL PITCHING LEADERS

Player, Team	W	L	ERA	G	SV	IP	H	BB	SO
Kyle Ruehlman, Mustangs	2	1	0.95	6	0	19	16	1	17
Will Abbott, Blowfish	1	1	1.01	12	1	27	13	5	27
Ryan Cusick, HiToms	1	3	1.14	5	0	24	12	9	40
Avery Cain, HiToms	3	0	1.37	8	0	20	15	1	19
Eli Ellington, Bananas	1	0	1.62	8	0	17	4	9	23
Nolan Daniel, Bananas	4	0	1.77	9	0	20	15	10	26
Cade Povich, Bananas	2	2	2.05	7	0	26	16	7	34
Jack Dragum, Pilots	2	0	2.25	11	1	16	9	4	19
Shane Smith, HiToms	1	0	2.45	5	0	15	9	4	13
Ty Bothwell, Bacon	0	1	2.86	9	0	22	15	6	36
Luke Zimmerman, Pilots	2	1	2.86	10	0	22	19	6	29

FLORIDA COLLEGIATE SUMMER LEAGUE

	W	L	PCT
Leesburg Lightning	18	5	.783
Sanford River Rats	15	6	.714
Orlando Scorpions	13	5	.711
Winter Garden Squeeze	12	9	.568
Leesburg Storm	11	11	.500
Winter Park Diamond Dogs	11	11	.500
Seminole County Snappers	10	10	.500
Sanford Mavericks	5	14	.275
Seminole County Loggerheads	5	16	.250
DeLand Suns	5	18	.217

Outfielder Robby Martin (Florida State) stayed close to home for summer, playing for Orlando.

CHAMPIONSHIP: Sanford River Rats defeated Leesburg Lightning, 2-0, in best-of-three championship series.

INDIVIDUAL BATTING LEADERS

	AVG	AB	R	H	2B	3B	HR	RBI	SB
Jeffrey Mejia, OF, Storm	.451	51	13	23	2	0	0	9	9
Giovany Lorenzo, C, Snappers	.397	58	8	23	5	0	0	19	1
Alex Freeland, SS, Storm	.397	63	15	25	4	2	0	17	7
Cole Beeker, 1B, D. Dogs	.382	55	9	21	6	1	0	9	3
Joe Burke, 1B, Suns	.379	66	10	25	2	0	2	13	0
Collin Teegarden, SS, Lightning	.371	35	18	13	2	0	0	7	8
JD Urso, SS, Snappers	.371	62	11	23	2	0	0	4	2
Naphis Llanos, SS, Snappers	.370	27	6	10	0	0	1	3	3
Lucas Dunn, SS/OF, Squeeze	.365	63	15	23	6	0	4	11	2
Chenar Brown, 1B, D. Dogs	.364	55	11	20	3	0	1	16	

INDIVIDUAL PITCHING LEADERS

	W	L	ERA	G	SV	IP	H	BB	SO
Dalton Ross, Snappers	1	1	0.00	13	2	17	6	4	25
Parker Messick, Squeeze	3	0	0.49	5	0	18	5	3	27
Dylan Ross, Snappers	1	0	0.60	6	0	15	5	7	23
Bryce Hubbart, Squeeze	2	0	0.60	5	0	15	6	9	31
Rese Brown, Diamond Dogs	2	0	0.98	6	0	18	11	8	19
Keith Kutzler, Diamond Dogs	1	1	1.08	6	0	17	14	9	15
Zachary Henderson, Storm	1	0	1.19	13	1	23	15	4	12
Nick Vieira, Scorpions	1	0	1.29	7	0	14	10	9	9
Grayson Moore, River Rats	1	0	1.39	5	0	13	8	4	15
Jack Leftwich, Scorpions	4	0	1.39	4	0	13	4	5	18

FUTURES COLLEGIATE LEAGUE

	W	L	PCT
Worcester Bravehearts	23	15	.605
Nashua Silver Knights	23	16	.590
Brockton Rox	19	20	.487
North Shore Navigators	18	20	.474
Westfield Starfires	17	21	.447
New Britain Bees	15	23	.395

CHAMPIONSHIP: Nashua Silver Knights defeated Worcester Bravehearts, 2-1, in best-of-three championship series.

INDIVIDUAL BATTING LEADERS

	AVG	AB	R	H	2B	3B	HR	RBI	SB
Sal Frelick, OF, Navigators	.398	98	26	39	8	1	3	16	9
Ben Rice, C, Bravehearts	.350	123	23	43	6	1	11	27	0
John Mead, OF, S.K.	.345	113	23	39	9	0	3	15	3
Cody Morissette, INF, Navigators	.340	94	18	32	4	3	2	31	12
Ben Malgeri, OF, Navigators	.333	147	46	49	9	7	4	27	18
Logan Bravo, INF, Navigators	.328	137	20	45	6	2	2	20	1
Jared Dupere, OF, S.K.	.327	101	21	33	5	2	6	26	3
Noah Martinez, INF, Bees	.323	93	18	30	5	0	4	22	3
Dominic Keegan, 1B, S.K.	.317	120	28	38	9	2	8	38	1

INDIVIDUAL PITCHING LEADERS

	W	L	ERA	G	SV	IP	H	BB	SO
Joey Walsh, Rox	1	0	0.00	10	3	17	5	8	24
Nick Guarino, Silver Knights	4	0	1.12	8	0	24	17	7	24
Angelo Baez, Bravehearts	3	1	1.28	7	0	35	25	9	46
Jeff Taylor, Starfires	4	0	1.60	6	0	28	19	9	34
Nick Sinacola, Rox	3	1	1.61	7	0	39	25	13	55
Griffin Green, Navigators	2	0	1.62	10	0	17	17	7	14
Griffin Young, Silver Knights	3	2	1.75	11	1	26	10	10	31
Chase Jeter, Starfires	3	1	1.75	7	0	36	21	7	36
Chris Chaney, Silver Knights	0	0	1.84	12	4	15	13	5	17
Tim Noone, Rox	0	1	1.90	6	0	33	26	8	36

NORTHWOODS LEAGUE

Kenosha Division	W	L		PCT
Kenosha Kingfish	17	9		.654
K-Town Bobbers	9	17		.346
Michigan North Division	**W**	**L**		**PCT**
Traverse City Pit Spitters	33	8		.786
Northern Michigan Dune Bears	1	1		.500
Great Lakes Resorters	8	34		.186
Michigan South Division	**W**	**L**	**T**	**PCT**
Kalamazoo Growlers	40	25	6	.597
Kalamazoo Mac Daddies	32	40	4	.447
Battle Creek Bombers	31	39	4	.440
Minnesota-Iowa Division	**W**	**L**		**PCT**
Waterloo Bucks	28	13		.683
St. Cloud Rox	27	13		.675
Wilmar Stingers	22	20		.524
Mankato MoonDogs	17	25		.405
Rochester Honkers	7	30		.189
North Dakota Division	**W**	**L**		**PCT**
Bismarck Larks	33	15		.688
Mandan Flickertails	24	24		.490
Bismarck Bull Moose	14	33		.292
Wisconsin-Illinois East Division	**W**	**L**		**PCT**
Fond Du Lac Dock Spiders	31	17		.646
Green Bay Booyah	18	28		.391
Rockford Rivets	16	27		.372
Wisconsin-Illinois West Division	**W**	**L**		**PCT**
Wisconsin Rapids Rafters	35	11		.761
La Crosse Loggers	23	25		.479
Wisconsin Woodchucks	16	31		.340

INDIVIDUAL BATTING LEADERS

	AVG	AB	R	H	2B	3B	HR	RBI	SB
Jayson Newman, OF, Stingers	.405	111	23	45	9	1	5	37	2
Jalen Smith, 2B, Bucks	.390	136	44	53	9	0	4	27	11
Justice Bigbie, INF, Bobbers	.380	79	16	30	3	0	0	10	0
Wyatt Ulrich, OF, Larks	.375	104	35	39	4	3	1	14	17
Zach Gilles, OF, MoonDogs	.366	112	18	41	4	0	0	18	12
Brett Harris, INF, Bobbers	.356	73	16	26	2	2	2	10	2
Spencer Schwellenbach, SS, P.S.	.356	87	17	31	6	1	0	17	12
Tim Elko, INF, Dock Spiders	.351	131	28	46	2	1	8	32	0
Blake Dunn, OF, Growlers	.349	146	47	51	9	4	3	16	32
Parker Noland, 3B, Dock Spiders	.348	115	28	40	5	0	1	12	10

INDIVIDUAL PITCHING LEADERS

	W	L	ERA	G	SV	IP	H	BB	SO
Spencer Arrighetti, Rapids Rafters	4	0	0.00	7	0	24	5	10	37
John Wilson, Flickertails	2	1	0.00	5	1	22	13	2	19
Justin Kelly, Rox	1	1	0.41	7	1	22	19	5	12
Jordan Wicks, Rivets	2	0	0.45	4	0	20	12	5	29
Ben Thomas, Growlers	3	1	0.48	12	0	19	13	11	15
John Farley, Flickertails	2	0	0.51	9	0	18	13	2	14
Reed Butz, Larks	1	2	0.53	4	0	17	8	10	22
Eric Torres, Booyah	0	0	0.55	11	1	16	13	9	23
Pablo Arevalo, Bombers	2	4	0.58	9	0	31	30	7	31
Zane Mills, Rox	3	0	0.58	7	0	31	17	6	26

SAN DIEGO LEAGUE

Land Division	W	L	PCT
Brewers	14	6	.700
Warriors	13	9	.619
Wild	10	11	.476
Jets	8	11	.421
Sea Division	**W**	**L**	**PCT**
Hooks	12	10	.545
Waveriders	11	12	.478
Long Boarders	9	11	.450
Sharks	7	14	.333

CHAMPIONSHIP: Hooks defeated Brewers, 10-6, in championship game.

INDIVIDUAL BATTING LEADERS

	AVG	AB	R	H	2B	3B	HR	RBI	SB
Ruben Fontes, OF, Wild	.444	45	8	20	4	1	3	12	1
Matt Rudick, OF, Warriors	.419	62	22	26	4	3	3	18	9
Kyle Carr, OF/LHP, Brewers	.415	53	16	22	6	1	3	10	0
Davis Heller, 1B, Wild	.404	52	12	21	4	1	3	21	6
Gage Howard, OF, Waveriders	.385	39	11	15	3	0	3	12	9
Mike Jarvis, OF, Hooks	.366	71	21	26	3	1	1	8	19
Dayton Dooney, INF, Brewers	.361	61	13	22	4	0	3	19	3
Deron Johnson, C, Wild	.360	25	5	9	3	1	0	2	1
Sam Dinerman, INF, Jets	.350	60	17	21	2	1	0	5	1
Brian McClellin, INF, Warriors	.346	78	16	27	4	0	1	16	2

INDIVIDUAL PITCHING LEADERS

	W	L	ERA	G	SV	IP	H	BB	SO
Dylan Pottgieser, Hooks	0	0	0.00	5	0	17	19	7	19
Grady Miller, Jets	1	1	0.00	4	0	9	6	0	12
Grant Holman, Jets	0	0	0.00	5	0	8	0	1	15
Jack Hyde, Sharks	0	1	0.54	6	0	17	11	2	27
Conner Thurman, Warriors	1	0	0.69	5	0	13	3	4	24
Parker Askegreen, Brewers	2	0	0.74	11	1	24	17	1	22
Ethan Paulson, Waveriders	1	0	0.77	5	0	12	9	2	6
JJ Rytz, Brewers	3	0	0.89	11	1	20	8	10	25
Christian Lewis, Hooks	0	0	0.90	6	0	10	6	4	6
Garrett Nasif, Warriors	1	0	1.04	5	1	9	12	1	5

SOUTH FLORIDA COLLEGIATE LEAGUE

North Division	W	L	PCT
Palm Beach Diamond Ducks	25	13	.658
Delray Beach Lightning	25	16	.610
Boca Raton Blazers	17	20	.459
Boynton Beach Buccaneers	17	23	.425
Phipps Park Barracudas	12	24	.338
South Division	**W**	**L**	**PCT**
West Boca Snappers	27	12	.692
Florida Pokers	20	19	.513
Fort Lauderdale Knights	18	19	.487
Pompano Beach Clippers	17	20	.459
Palm Beach Xtreme	13	25	.342

CHAMPIONSHIP: West Boca Snappers defeated Florida Pokers, 9-3, in championship game.

INDIVIDUAL BATTING LEADERS

	AVG	AB	R	H	2B	3B	HR	RBI	SB
Zack Neto, INF/RHP, Lightning	.439	98	22	43	10	2	6	32	11
Daniel Labrador, C, Blazers	.437	71	21	31	8	1	2	14	1
Cade Doughty, INF, Blazers	.429	91	29	39	9	0	3	17	4
Cade Beloso, INF, Barracudas	.412	68	14	28	7	0	1	7	1
Andrew Martinez, OF, Ducks	.381	105	23	40	13	0	4	33	13
Connor Goodman, OF, Clippers	.363	80	15	29	2	0	0	11	2
Derek Cartaya, INF, Snappers	.360	89	21	32	3	0	0	9	7
Willie Escala, INF, Ducks	.352	88	30	31	1	1	1	11	19
Braden Forchic, INF, Lightning	.346	104	28	36	7	3	2	33	2
Marcos Sevillano, OF, Snappers	.341	85	24	29	3	0	0	12	10

INDIVIDUAL PITCHING LEADERS

	W	L	ERA	G	SV	IP	H	BB	SO
Mason Black, Blazers	3	0	0.64	7	0	28	10	10	42
Matt Svanson, Snappers	4	0	1.00	7	0	27	15	5	41
Hunter Kloke, Knights	2	1	1.30	5	1	21	11	10	10
Adrien Reese, Ducks	1	1	1.40	10	0	32	23	13	40
Justin Alintoff, Lightning	1	0	1.52	7	0	24	20	6	23
Mitch Hartigan, Knights	2	1	1.52	14	2	18	6	12	21
Nathan Cochran, Ducks	2	1	1.58	10	0	23	18	5	18
JT Larson, Pokers	2	1	1.60	6	0	28	22	6	30
Chuck Fishbaugh, Ducks	2	0	1.61	9	0	22	14	19	9
Ryan McLinskey, Barracudas	1	1	1.63	6	0	22	18	7	33

Righthander Mason Black (Lehigh) was one of the stars in the South Florida Collegiate League.

SUNFLOWER COLLEGIATE LEAGUE

	W	L	PCT
Cheney Diamond Dawgs	33	6	.846
Hutchinson Monarchs	26	6	.813
Rose Hill Sluggers	25	11	.694
Great Bend Bat Cats	16	16	.500
Derby Twins	16	18	.471
Newton Rebels	15	20	.429
Mulvane Patriots	12	22	.353
Sunflower Seeds	9	24	.273
Haysville Aviators	9	28	.243

INDIVIDUAL BATTING LEADERS

	AVG	AB	R	H	2B	3B	HR	RBI	SB
Lenny Ashby, OF, Dawgs	.403	72	14	29	6	1	3	22	1
Clayton Chadwick, OF, Monarchs	.400	80	25	32	9	3	6	11	8
Lincoln Andrews, 1B, Rebels	.398	123	24	49	13	1	7	35	0
Zach Baxley, C, Sluggers	.392	102	27	40	13	1	2	31	11
Bryce Zimmerer, OF, Patriots	.390	59	14	23	3	1	0	6	7
George Specht, INF, Dawgs	.383	120	27	46	7	3	7	22	6
Jackson Glenn, 3B, Dawgs	.378	98	34	37	7	2	7	21	6
Hunter Gibson, OF, Sluggers	.371	97	23	36	8	0	6	27	4
Dylan Nedved, INF, Monarchs	.368	125	28	46	11	1	4	21	9
Kyler Castillo, OF, Dawgs	.364	121	31	44	11	2	5	18	10

INDIVIDUAL PITCHING LEADERS

	W	L	ERA	G	SV	IP	H	BB	SO
Aaron Haase, Monarchs	2	0	1.08	9	2	17	7	3	31
Colby Peachin, Patriots	2	0	1.12	6	0	16	10	8	23
Grant Adler, Sluggers	1	0	1.28	7	0	21	14	6	17
Hunter O'Toole, Dawgs	2	0	1.43	9	0	31	26	15	35
Trevin Reynolds, Dawgs	4	1	1.48	8	0	36	27	14	44
Preston Snavely, Monarchs	3	0	1.50	6	0	30	16	14	39
Liam Eddy, Monarchs	4	1	1.68	7	0	32	24	5	23
Cody Bush, Seeds	2	0	1.77	4	0	20	18	7	17
Zach Moore, Sluggers	3	1	1.84	7	0	24	17	10	22
Nate Postlethwait, Dawgs	4	0	1.92	8	1	28	16	20	24

HIGH
SCHOOL

Prep Seniors Deal With Reality Of COVID-19

MIKE JANES/FOUR SEAM IMAGES

Senior Chase Davis played just three games this spring before his season was canceled.

BY CARLOS COLLAZO

Since his sons were just 3 and 4 years old, Tommy Davis was looking forward to this moment.

This year, his older son Chase was entering his senior baseball season at Franklin High in Elk Grove, Calif. For the first time, that meant Chase and his younger brother Jordan would play alongside each other on the same varsity team: the elder Davis in center field, the younger in right.

"Well it was a collection of ideas, thoughts, emotions," Tommy said, thinking back before the season began. "(Chase) put the work in. He did what he was supposed to do with what he was in control of. He was dedicated to what he was doing. He was actually living out his dream. We figured—like any of these draft parents—we figured he would chase it, go do what he does and everything would turn out well in June.

The novel coronavirus allowed Chase and Jordan just three games together before their season ended. The Elk Grove unified school district was one of the first in the country to cancel classes and athletic events because of the growing pandemic, first shutting things down from March 7-13.

On the opposite side of the country in New York City, things were similar. New York Governor Andrew Cuomo tightened restrictions on March 20 as COVID-19 cases in the state eclipsed 7,000.

New Yorkers were instructed to stay indoors and non-essential businesses mandated to keep workers home.

For righthander Alex Santos at Mount St. Michael Academy in the Bronx, his life became eerily similar to Chase's—and every other high school senior planning to graduate in 2020.

"Making memories for your senior year. . . . It's everything," said Santos' father Alex Santos Sr. "You're going to have kids, grandkids. You explain to them everything that you did for your senior year. That's the bad part that is getting taken away from him—just kind of finishing the year out with his friends, guys he's played with, three or four years already in high school.

Like high school seniors around the country, Santos and Davis missed out on moments that those who have already graduated might take for granted. Big things, like proms and graduations, won't take place. Small ones, like random, meaningless conversations in the hallways or the cafeteria with childhood friends—those won't happen either.

Both the Davis and Santos families understand that those losses were small compared to some of the difficulties that others around the country and world faced. But thinking of the small ways families are impacted around the country is not the same as diminishing larger concerns. It's just another example of how this far-reaching virus was affecting us all.

"We are concerned about the lives of people and the deaths for sure," Tommy Davis said. "People's lives are not going to be the same. Life as we knew it three weeks ago is no longer."

While Davis and Santos could both commiserate with all high school seniors who had their final prep season taken away—both were also in a position to look ahead.

This year's draft was vastly different than a typical draft, with a short amateur season to evaluate for many players and little or none for others.

Teams had been watching many of the high-level players for some time now, and that included both Santos and Davis, who were first- or second-round talents. Santos ranked as the No. 45 prospect on the final BA 500 and was the most prominent player in New York, while Davis ranked No. 55 with a loud package of tools that includes impressive raw power.

Both did enough over the summer and fall to give teams confidence in selecting them this June.

"Our process will be fine with those high school kids in my opinion," said one American League scouting director, "and I'm speaking for all 30 teams here, but primarily us. Our process will be fine."

The challenge for draft prospects, then, was to ways to stay in shape without games taking place and with increased restrictions on where you were allowed to go. Santos was set up nicely. His father runs a facility along with his partner, Melvin Perez, called Citius Prep.

Santos was able to continue throwing his routine bullpen sessions, because the facility controls the volume of players inside at any given time. After focusing on adding muscle mass and strength over the offseason, as well as refining his changeup, Santos continued his arm care routine and bullpen work despite high school baseball being shut down.

For a gym rat like Davis, it was frustrating but something he knew was out of his control.

"I understand that everything in life happens for a reason," he said. "And those balls I was hitting each and every single day, it was to honestly prepare for the season. But now we're most likely not going to have one.

"It's not something for me to be really mad about, because it's not really in my control. It would be a completely different story if it was something I did. But it's not."

COVID-19 created unexpected speed bumps for both Davis and Santos. Because of their talent, though, this won't be the end of their baseball careers. Santos was still selected in the five-round

draft, signing for $1,250,000 with the Astros in the supplemental second round. Davis went unselected but now ranks as the No. 3 college prospect in the 2023 draft and should provide an immediate impact at Arizona.

But for many other high school seniors in the country, this is it.

"What kind of makes me sad sometimes, kind of brings me close to tears is the fact that there are countless kids—at the junior college level, at the university level, who couldn't wait (for this season) and had done everything that they possibly could to prove themselves worthy of a higher draft pick," Tommy said. "Or kids who were doing the same thing and working hard for scholarships . . . So our hearts go out to them."

PRESEASON ALL-AMERICAN TEAMS

FIRST TEAM

Pos.	Player	State
C	Tyler Soderstrom	California
MIF	Ed Howard	Oklahoma
SS	Milan Tolentino	California
CIF	Jordan Walker	Georgia
CIF	Blaze Jordan	Mississippi
OF	Austin Hendrick	Pennsylvania
OF	Pete Crow-Armstrong	California
OF	Robert Hassell	Tennessee
SP	Jared Kelley	Texas
SP	Mick Abel	Oregon
SP	Alex Santos	New York
SP	Carson Montgomery	Florida
SP	Jared Jones	California

SECOND TEAM

Pos.	Player	State
C	Drew Romo	Texas
MIF	Masyn Winn	Texas
MIF	Colby Halter	Florida
CIF	Yohandy Morales	Florida
CIF	Drew Bowser	California
OF	Zac Veen	Florida
OF	Dylan Crews	Florida
OF	Chase Davis	California
SP	Alejandro Rosario	Florida
SP	Victor Mederos	Florida
SP	Masyn Winn	Texas
SP	Max Rajcic	California
SP	Daxton Fulton	Oklahoma

THIRD TEAM

Pos.	Player	State
C	Kyle Teel	New Jersey
MIF	Carson Tucker	Arizona
MIF	Steven Ondina	Puerto Rico
CIF	Coby Mayo	Florida
CIF	AJ Vukovich	Wisconsin
OF	Isaiah Greene	California
OF	Enrique Bradfield	Florida
OF	Petey Halpin	California
SP	Nick Bitsko	Pennsylvania
SP	Cam Brown	Texas
SP	Kyle Harrison	California
SP	Ben Hernandez	Illinois
SP	Cade Horton	Oklahoma

DRAFT

Torkelson Tops Shortest Draft Ever

BY CARLOS COLLAZO

Regardless of the quality of its players, the 2020 draft will be remembered for a long time. The coronavirus pandemic ground the season to a halt in mid-March and complicated the scouting process for both scouts and players, much the same way the virus had complicated life around the globe.

With Major League Baseball's decision to shorten the draft to just five rounds, it catered to owners looking to cut costs at the expense of amateur players and in opposition to front offices and scouting departments looking to add as much talent as possible during an exceptionally strong draft year. Fewer draft rounds guarantee that fewer future big leaguers will enter pro ball in 2020.

The 2020 class itself is one of the deeper groups in recent years and had the chance to be the best draft class since at least 2014.

"The industry entered the spring believing the 2020 class was strong, but the class looked even better than expected in the first four weeks of the college season," one front office executive of an American League club said before the draft. "The upper crust of college talent is excellent on both sides of the ball, and a number of pitchers really

Spencer Torkelson was no surprise as the first overall pick in the 2020 draft.

MARK CUNNINGHAM/MLB PHOTOS VIA GETTY IMAGES

elevated their stock early in the spring. We'll never really know what the spring would've held now. But it was shaping up to be a special spring."

After a historically weak pitching class in 2019, the 2020 class boasted a wealth of pitching depth

FIRST-ROUND BONUS PROGRESSION

MLB's negotiated deal with the MLB Players Association to cut the draft from 40 rounds to just five for the 2020 draft also came with an agreement to use the same draft slots as 2019. Typically slot values are tied with increasing revenues around the league and the last few years that increase has hovered around 4%. This year that number was static, though that didn't preclude teams from spending almost 8% more on first-round bonuses than in 2019. During the 2019 draft, teams spent an average of $3.79 million on first-round bonuses, while that nuber went up over the $4 million mark for the first time in draft history in 2020.

After the first draft in 1965, first-round bonuses rose by an average of just 0.6% annually for the rest of the 1960s and 5.2% per year in the 1970s. Bonus inflation picked up in the 1980s, averaging 10.2% annually, and soared to 26.9% per year in the 1990s.

Below are the annual averages for first-round bonuses since the draft started in 1965. The 1996 total does not include four players who became free agents through a loophole in the draft rules.

Year	Average	Change	Year	Average	Change	Year	Average	Change	Year	Average	Change
1965	$42,516	—	1979	$68,094	0.20%	1993	$613,037	27.20%	2007	$2,098,083	8.50%
1966	$44,430	4.50%	1980	$74,025	8.70%	1994	$790,357	28.90%	2008	$2,458,714	17.20%
1967	$42,898	-3.40%	1981	$78,573	6.10%	1995	$918,019	16.10%	2009	$2,434,800	-1.00%
1968	$43,850	2.20%	1982	$82,615	5.10%	1996*	$944,404	2.90%	2010	$2,220,966	-8.80%
1969	$43,504	-0.80%	1983	$87,236	5.60%	1997	$1,325,536	40.40%	2011	$2,653,375	19.50%
1970	$45,230	3.90%	1984	$105,391	20.80%	1998	$1,637,667	23.10%	2012	$2,475,167	-6.70%
1971	$45,197	-0.10%	1985	$118,115	12.10%	1999	$1,809,767	10.50%	2013	$2,641,538	6.70%
1972	$44,952	-0.50%	1986	$116,300	-1.60%	2000	$1,872,586	3.50%	2014	$2,612,109	-1.10%
1973	$48,832	8.60%	1987	$128,480	10.50%	2001	$2,154,280	15.00%	2015	$2,774,945	6.23%
1974	$53,333	9.20%	1988	$142,540	10.90%	2002	$2,106,793	-2.20%	2016	$2,897,557	4.42%
1975	$49.33	-7.50%	1989	$176,008	23.50%	2003	$1,765,667	-16.20%	2017	$3,880,723	25.4%
1976	$49,631	0.60%	1990	$252,577	43.50%	2004	$1,958,448	10.90%	2018	$3,754,123	-3.37%
1977	$48,813	-1.60%	1991	$365,396	44.70%	2005	$2,018,000	3.00%	2019	$3,791,729	1.01%
1978	$67,892	39.10%	1992	$481,893	31.90%	2006	$1,933,333	-4.20%	2020	$4,080,307	7.61%

DRAFT

at all levels, but particularly among collegians, headlined by first-rounders Max Meyer, Asa Lacy and Emerson Hancock and extended by the second and third tier of college arms who came out showing both stuff and performance during the shortened season.

The top of the class is college-heavy, led by impact bats Spencer Torkelson—whom the Tigers selected with the first overall pick—of Arizona State, Austin Martin of Vanderbilt and Nick Gonzales of New Mexico State.

Teams were happy with the strength of the college class and there was some thought that the 2020 draft would be the most college-heavy ever as teams flocked to the less-risky demographic in an extremely risky year. While it wasn't quite as college-heavy in the first round as 2019, it was still more college-heavy than every other draft this decade.

Many prep players in the South benefitted from more exposure than their Northern counterparts this spring, with players like Florida outfielder Zac Veen and Texas righthander Jared Kelley getting seen frequently while others like Pennsylvania products Austin Hendrick and Nick Bitsko and Oregon righthander Mick Abel barely got on the field. In the end, teams' confidence in evaluations from the previous summer for the premium high school prospects allowed teams to spend significant money with or without extensive spring evaluations.

However, the 2020 class winds up in the future, it'll be an unforgettable year given the circumstances and the changes that it signals for the future of the draft.

"It'll be a draft we talk about for a while," one National League scout said. "This draft will be a case study moving forward. We're going to be talking about this draft forever."

A Surprise At No. 2

We heard plenty of rumors about the Orioles exploring a non-Austin Martin selection with the second pick of the draft. Teams behind them were uncertain what Baltimore would do with its pick up until the moment it made it happen.

But the team liked Arkansas outfielder Heston Kjerstad and while the pick did save more than $2.5 million with a signifcantly underslot deal, it was still a risk.

While Kjerstad's power is significant, and his college performance in the Southeastern Conference and with Team USA is among the best in the class, we had him ranked as the No. 13 player on the BA 500.

The decision-making group with the Orioles

BONUS SPENDING BY TEAM

The draft was shortened to just five rounds in 2020 to cut costs, and that's exactly what happened. After spending a record $316.5 million on draft bonuses in 2019, total bonuses fell to just $238.1 million in 2020—about 33% less year-over-year.

The coronavirus pandemic essentially curtailed spending more effectively than anything has since the CBA of 2012 implemented bonus pools and harsh penalties for teams who exceeded those pools by more than five% . Prior to this year, bonus pool spending had increased year-over-year as MLB revenues and bonus slot values increased. With MLB losing a significant chunk of revenue during the shortened 2020 season, it is unsurprising that bonus money fell as well and 2020 spending fell to the lowest rate since 2014, when clubs spent$222.8 million total. That year, clubs averaged $7.4 million per team. In 2020, teams averaged $7.9 million per team.

The 2021 draft will almost surely surpass the 2020 draft in terms of bonuses, with the draft being at least 20 rounds long. Whether it gets back to 2017-2019 levels is the real question.

The Tigers and Orioles both spent more than any other team in 2020 and both surpassed $13 million in bonuses, while the Astros spent just $2.2 million with only four picks and their first not coming until the supplemental second round.

TEAM	2019	2018	2017
Tigers	$13,978,600	$11,980,800	$14,784,100
Orioles	$13,672,300	$15,168,600	$10,433,500
Royals	$12,520,000	$14,452,200	$14,768,200
Marlins	$12,004,700	$14,832,700	$10,415,200
Padres	$11,180,004	$13,010,900	$12,565,515
Pirates	$11,067,400	$12,111,400	$10,402,600
Rockies	$10,332,800	$8,073,300	$8,549,000
Blue Jays	$10,202,325	$10,677,000	$9,890,300
Mariners	$9,961,100	$8,927,500	$8,655,200
Giants	$9,457,500	$10,384,500	$13,935,000
Reds	$8,546,000	$11,273,400	$12,952,000
Cardinals	$8,290,000	$8,205,000	$9,534,100
White Sox	$7,757,500	$13,633,200	$12,284,400
Mets	$7,499,000	$9,497,000	$11,017,238
Rays	$7,474,200	$11,685,800	$13,786,100
Indians	$7,390,000	$8,010,505	$11,222,459
Rangers	$7,275,000	$12,858,300	$9,150,500
Diamondbacks	$7,184,900	$17,045,500	$5,769,400
Cubs	$6,866,800	$6,987,900	$9,218,950
Nationals	$6,647,000	$7,683,580	$6,908,000
Angels	$6,454,200	$9,751,300	$8,760,000
Dodgers	$6,224,000	$10,539,300	$5,139,540
Phillies	$5,700,000	$8,779,800	$11,342,900
Athletics	$5,447,400	$6,696,900	$10,888,200
Brewers	$5,417,900	$6,908,200	$7,747,400
Red Sox	$5,250,000	$6,369,200	$7,252,900
Twins	$4,330,000	$10,892,800	$6,876,700
Braves	$3,991,800	$14,338,000	$5,815,000
Yankees	$3,687,400	$9,327,300	$8,148,400
Astros	$2,283,000	$6,462,099	$6,440,800
Total	**$238,092,829**	**$316,563,984**	**$294,653,602**
Average	**$7,936,428**	**$10,552,133**	**$9,821,787**

has made moves like this before, back when Mike Elias was calling the shots for the Astros. The team moved away from the consensus top talent at the No. 1 spot (Byron Buxton) and instead signed shortstop Carlos Correa to a $4,800,000 bonus, sending money down their draft to get righthander Lance McCullers at pick No. 41 for $2,500,000—the highest bonus in the supplemental first round that year.

The Orioles were able to afford overslot deals

for each of their three final selections including shortstop Anthony Servideo ($105,800 over slot), prep third baseman Coby Mayo ($1,184,400 over slot) and prep righthander Carter Baumler ($1,077,700 over slot).

Two Day One Winners

If you told the Royals they would be able to pick between Martin and Texas A&M lefthander Asa Lacy with the fourth pick of the draft, they probably wouldn't have believed you. Most in the industry—including us at Baseball America—expected both players to be gone among the first three picks.

It would have seemed even crazier for the Blue Jays to be sitting at pick No. 5 with Martin, the second-ranked player in the class, sitting there waiting to be picked. Toronto scouting director Shane Farrell admitted as much.

"I think we were a little surprised. Obviously we're keeping an eye on the mock drafts as they come out throughout the week and we're aware of industry consensus, but I think it really started to shake up at picks two and three," Farrell said on a call with media members following the selection. "We were surprised a little bit, but certainly prepared to make that selection and we're ecstatic to have the chance to pick Austin."

JULIAN AVRAM/ICON SPORTSWIRE VIA GETTY IMAGES

The Blue Jays were pleasantly surprised when Austin Martin fell to them at No. 5.

HIGHEST BONUSES EVER

Four of the top five drafted players made the list of the highest bonuses ever this year, with No. 1 overall pick Spencer Torkelson taking the top spot. Only Torkelson, Austin Martin, Max Meyer and Asa Lacy signed for more than $6 million in the 2020 draft.

Player, Pos.	Team, Year (Pick)	Bonus
Spencer Torkelson, 3B	Tigers, 2020 (No. 1)	$8,416,300
Adley Rutschman, C	Orioles, 2019 (No. 1)	$8,100,000
Gerrit Cole, RHP	Pirates, 2011 (No. 1)	$8,000,000
Bobby Witt Jr., SS	Royals, 2019 (No. 2)	$7,787,400
Stephen Strasburg, RHP	Nationals, 2009 (No. 1)	*$7,500,000
Bubba Starling, OF	Royals, 2011 (No. 5)	+$7,500,000
Casey Mize, RHP	Tigers, 2018 (No. 1)	$7,500,000
Hunter Greene, RHP/SS	Reds, 2017 (No. 2)	$7,230,000
Andrew Vaughn, 1B	White Sox, 2019 (No. 3)	$7,221,200
Joey Bart, C	Giants, 2018 (No. 2)	$7,025,000
Brendan McKay, 1B/LHP	Rays, 2017 (No. 4)	$7,005,000
Austin Martin, SS	Blue Jays, 2020 (No. 5)	$7,000,825
Kyle Wright, RHP	Braves, 2017 (No. 5)	$7,000,000
Royce Lewis, SS	Twins, 2017 (No. 1)	$6,725,000
Kris Bryant, 3B	Cubs, 2013 (No. 2)	$6,708,400
MacKenzie Gore, LHP	Padres, 2017 (No. 3)	$6,700,000
Max Meyer, RHP	Marlins, 2020 (No. 3)	$6,700,000
JJ Bleday, OF	Marlins, 2019 (No. 4)	$6,670,000
Asa Lacy, LHP	Royals, 2020 (No. 4)	$6,670,000
Carlos Rodon, LHP	White Sox, 2014 (No. 3)	$6,582,000
Jameson Taillon, RHP	Pirates, 2010 (No. 2)	$6,500,000
Dansby Swanson, SS	D-backs, 2015 (No. 1)	$6,500,000
Nick Madrigal, SS	White Sox, 2018 (No. 4)	$6,411,000
Danny Hultzen, LHP	Marinters, 2011 (No. 2)	*$6,350,000
Mark Appel, RHP	Astros, 2013 (No. 1	$6,350,000
Donavan Tate, OF	Padres, 2009 (No. 3)	+$6,250,000
Bryce Harper, OF	Nationals, 2010 (No. 1)	*$6,250,000
Buster Posey, C	Giants, 2008 (No. 5)	$6,200,000
Nick Senzel, 3B	Reds, 2016 (No. 2)	$6,200,000

**Part of major league contract. +Bonus spread over multiple years under MLB two-sport provisions*

We believe the Royals and Blue Jays both stumbled into exceptional value because of the Orioles and Marlins going with Kjerstad and Minnesota righthander Max Meyer in front of them and it's difficult not to see them as winners of day one as a result.

The Royals continued to grab value with their compensation pick at No. 32, grabbing Baylor shortstop Nick Loftin, who was ranked No. 29 on the BA 500 and was thought to be a factor as high as the middle of the first round.

The Blue Jays may have gotten the best one-pick value in Martin at No. 5, but Royals fans should be ecstatic with the two college prospects added to their rapidly rising system.

Was Boston's 1st Rounder A Reach?

While the Orioles pick was a surprise, it wasn't the surprise of day one. That honor goes to the Red Sox and Archbishop Mitty (Calif.) High shortstop Nick Yorke.

According to the BA 500, Yorke was the biggest off-the-board pick on day one, as he ranked as the No. 96 prospect in the class. However, with no second-round pick due to penalties related to the team's sign-stealing scandal, the Red Sox had to get a bit aggressive with a bat they really liked.

"From 17 to 89 is a long way. It felt like an eternity. I think that our perception of the industry's interests didn't match the public perception," Red Sox scouting director Paul Toboni said.

But while the pick was surprising, and it is rare to see a high school second baseman drafted this high, the pick might not be as crazy as you think. Yorke's bat is legit, and in our scouting report we

NO. 1 OVERALL PICKS

Year Team: Player, Pos., School	Bonus
1965 Athletics: Rick Monday, OF, Arizona State	$100,000
1966 Mets: Steve Chilcott, C, Antelope Valley HS, Lancaster, Calif.	$75,000
1967 Yankees: Ron Blomberg, 1B, Druid Hills HS, Atlanta	$65,000
1968 Mets: Tim Foli, SS, Notre Dame HS, Sherman Oaks, Calif.	$74,000
1969 Senators: Jeff Burroughs, OF, Centennial HS, Long Beach	$88,000
1970 Padres: Mike Ivie, C, Walker HS, Atlanta	$75,000
1971 White Sox: Danny Goodwin, C, Peoria (Ill.) HS	Did Not Sign
1972 Padres: Dave Roberts, 3B, Oregon	$70,000
1973 Rangers: David Clyde, LHP, Westchester HS, Texas	*$65,000
1974 Padres: Bill Almon, SS, Brown	*$90,000
1975 Angels: Danny Goodwin, C, Southern	*$125,000
1976 Astros: Floyd Bannister, LHP, Arizona State	$100,000
1977 White Sox: Harold Baines, OF, St. Michaels (Md.) HS	$32,000
1978 Braves: Bob Horner, 3B, Arizona State	*$162,000
1979 Mariners: Al Chambers, 1B, Harris HS, Harrisburg, Pa.	$60,000
1980 Mets: Darryl Strawberry, OF, Crenshaw HS, Los Angeles	$152,500
1981 Mariners: Mike Moore, RHP, Oral Roberts	$100,000
1982 Cubs: Shawon Dunston, SS, Jefferson HS, New York	$135,000
1983 Twins: Tim Belcher, RHP, Mount Vernon Nazarene (Ohio)	Did Not Sign
1984 Mets: Shawn Abner, OF, Mechanicsburg (Pa.) HS	$150,500
1985 Brewers: B.J. Surhoff, C, North Carolina	$150,000
1986 Pirates: Jeff King, 3B, Arkansas	$180,000
1987 Mariners: Ken Griffey Jr., OF, Moeller HS, Cincinnati	$160,000
1988 Padres: Andy Benes, RHP, Evansville	$235,000
1989 Orioles: Ben McDonald, RHP, Louisiana State	*$350,000
1990 Braves: Chipper Jones, SS, The Bolles School, Jacksonville	$275,000
1991 Yankees: Brien Taylor, LHP, East Carteret HS, Beaufort, N.C.	$1,550,000
1992 Astros: Phil Nevin, 3B, Cal State Fullerton	$700,000
1993 Mariners: Alex Rodriguez, SS, Westminster Christian HS, Miami	*$1,000,000
1994 Mets: Paul Wilson, RHP, Florida State	$1,550,000
1995 Angels: Darin Erstad, OF, Nebraska	$1,575,000
1996 Pirates: Kris Benson, RHP, Clemson	$2,000,000
1997 Tigers: Matt Anderson, RHP, Tigers	$2,505,000
1998 Phillies: Pat Burrell, 3B, Miami	*$3,150,000
1999 Devil Rays: Josh Hamilton, OF, Athens Drive HS, Raleigh	$3,960,000
2000 Marlins: Adrian Gonzalez, 1B, Eastlake HS, Chula Vista, Calif.	$3,000,000
2001 Twins: Joe Mauer, C, Cretin-Derham Hall, St. Paul	$5,150,000
2002 Pirates: Bryan Bullington, RHP, Ball State	$4,000,000
2003 Devil Rays: Delmon Young, OF, Camarillo (Calif.) HS	*$3,700,000
2004 Padres: Matt Bush, SS, Mission Bay HS, San Diego	$3,150,000
2005 D-backs: Justin Upton, SS, Great Bridge HS, Chesapeake, Va.	$6,100,000
2006 Royals: Luke Hochevar, RHP, Fort Worth (American Assoc.)	*$3,500,000
2007 Devil Rays: David Price, LHP, Vanderbilt	*$5,600,000
2008 Rays: Tim Beckham, SS, Griffin (Ga.) HS	$6,150,000
2009 Nationals: Stephen Strasburg, RHP, San Diego State	*$7,500,000
2010 Nationals: Bryce Harper, OF, JC of Southern Nevada	*$6,250,000
2011 Pirates: Gerrit Cole, RHP, UCLA	$8,000,000
2012 Astros: Carlos Correa, SS, Puerto Rico Baseball Acad., Gurabo, P.R.	$4,800,000
2013 Astros: Mark Appel, RHP, Stanford	$6,350,000
2014 Astros: Brady Aiken, LHP, Cathedral Catholic, San Diego	Did Not Sign
2015 D-backs: Dansby Swanson, SS, Vanderbilt	$6,500,000
2016 Phillies: Mickey Moniak, OF, La Costa Canyon HS, Carlsbad, Calif.	$6,100,000
2017 Twins: Royce Lewis, SS, JSerra Catholic HS, San Juan Capistrano, Calif.	$6,750,000
2018 Tigers: Casey Mize, RHP, Auburn	$7,500,000
2019 Orioles: Adley Rutschman, C, Oregon State	$8,100,000
2020 Tigers: Spencer Torkelson, 3B, Arizona State	$8,416,300

Part of major league contract.

note that "some evaluators believe Yorke is the best pure hitter on the West Coast, among high schoolers."

That means there were at least some scouts who liked Yorke's bat better than other first-round West Coast preps like Pete Crow-Armstrong, Carson Tucker and Tyler Soderstrom. The Red Sox could certainly be one of those teams. Yorke is far from the biggest "reach" that teams have made on the first day of the draft in recent years.

The Cubs took RHP Ryan Jensen at pick No. 27 last year and Jensen was ranked outside of the top 100 in the 2019 class, at No. 109. A few picks later the Astros selected C Korey Lee at No. 32—Lee was rated as the No. 173 player in the class.

Go back to the 2018 draft and you see the Twins second-round pick of C Ryan Jeffers as a notable "reach." Jeffers ranked all the way down at No. 295 at the time. And to the Twins credit, the Jeffers selection has so far looked pretty good, with Jeffers playing a crucial role in 2020 and in the playoffs

So it isn't crazy to see the Red Sox jumping on a bat they liked in Yorke at No. 18. With no second-round pick there could have been a real shot he didn't make it to their next pick at 89. With a full season, who knows, Yorke could have hit enough to rise up boards and get more public attention, similar to Carson Tucker— another high school middle infielder who showed off a good bat this spring and got taken by the Indians at pick No. 23.

There's certainly some risk with Yorke, but we'll have to wait and see if it pays off.

Outside of Yorke, the first round was fairly chalky.

The lowest-ranked non-Yorke player to be selected among the first 37 picks was Tucker, who checked in at No. 61.

While we didn't hit for a great average in our final mock draft, all of the names that were taken on day one made sense in terms of talent and in regard to what we were hearing leading up to the draft.

Perhaps that's a function of the

shortened spring, which could have led many teams toward the consensus top talent and provided less time for some players to separate themselves between different scouting departments.

Putting The 2020 Draft Behind Us

The romantic notion about the draft is that it is all about dreams.

When Spencer Torkelson's phone rang just before commissioner Rob Manfred announced the Arizona State slugger as the first pick in the 2020 draft, he became the 56th player ever to fulfill a dream that fuels thousands of young kids playing on Little League fields.

It's also about fans' dreams. No matter how dire the state of one's favorite big league team, the draft provides hope for brighter days ahead, whether one cheers for the Tigers, Orioles, Marlins or Royals.

All of that was still true in the 2020 draft. Dreams turned into reality. Players became pros. Fanbases were given hope.

But in what has been a brutal year for the world and for baseball, the dreams that surround the draft ran into reality. In a year that will best be forgotten, at least from a baseball perspective, the abbreviated draft did not salve the wounds.

This draft was different from all others, slashed by nearly 1,000 picks so teams could save on bonus spending. With a mere 160 picks, everyone knew that there would be many draftable players and players with major league potential who would be left unpicked.

But when UC San Diego shortstop Shay Whitcomb was picked with the 160th and final selection of the 2020 draft, the scope of the difference became clear.

It was a fine year to be a top high school or college player. But for that next tier of prospects, especially college players with third- to seventh-round potential, it was brutal

"You had so many guys for those spots. They probably had 10-20 guys for their third-, fourth- or fifth-round pick," Louisville coach Dan McDonnell said. McDonnell's Cardinals had two pitchers (Reid Detmers and Bobby Miller) picked in the first round, but his team also had four players in the BA500 who went undrafted and are likely headed back to school.

As teams assessed signability for players in the fourth and fifth rounds, there were more draftable players with the willingness to sign than spots to take them, which meant that players who would receive $300,000 to $400,000 in a normal draft were having to decide if they were willing to sign for $100,000 or $150,000.

THE BONUS RECORD

Rick Monday, the No. 1 overall pick in baseball's first draft in 1965, signed with the Athletics for $100,000—a figure that no draftee bettered for a decade. The record has been broken many times since, including in 2019, when Adley Rutschman signed with the Orioles as the No. 1 overall pick for $8,100,000. Spencer Torkelson broke the record immediately, signing for $8,416,300 as the No. 1 pick in the 2020 draft with the Tigers.

The longest bonus record stretch dates back to Todd Demeter, whose $208,000 bonus in 1979 held the mark for nine years until 1988 when Andy Benes topped him with a $235,000 bonus.

The list below represents only cash bonuses and doesn't include guaranteed money from major league deals, college scholarship plans or incentives. It also considers only players who signed with the clubs that drafted them and doesn't include draft picks who signed after being granted free agency.

Year	Player, Pos. , Club (Round)	Bonus
1965	Rick Monday, OF, Athletics (1)	$100,000
1975	Danny Goodwin, C, Angels (1)	$125,000
1978	Kirk Gibson, OF, Tigers (1)	$150,000
	*Bob Horner, 3B, Braves (1)	$162,000
1979	Todd Demeter, 1B, Yankees (2)	$208,000
1988	Andy Benes, RHP, Padres (1)	$235,000
1989	Tyler Houston, C, Braves (1)	$241,500
	*Ben McDonald, RHP, Orioles (1)	$350,000
	*John Olerud, 1B, Blue Jays (3)	$575,000
1991	Mike Kelly, OF, Braves (1)	$575,000
	Brien Taylor, LHP, Yankees (1)	$1,550,000
1994	Paul Wilson, RHP, Mets (1)	$1,550,000
	Josh Booty, 3B, Marlins (1)	$1,600,000
1996	Kris Benson, RHP, Pirates (1)	$2,000,000
1997	Rick Ankiel, LHP, Cardinals (2)	$2,500,000
	Matt Anderson, RHP, Tigers (1)	$2,505,000
1998	*J.D. Drew, OF, Cardinals (1)	$3,000,000
	*Pat Burrell, 3B, Phillies (1)	$3,150,000
	Mark Mulder, LHP, Athletics (1)	$3,200,000
	Corey Patterson, OF, Cubs (1)	$3,700,000
1999	Josh Hamilton, OF, Devil Rays (1)	$3,960,000
2000	Joe Borchard, OF, White Sox (1)	$5,300,000
2005	Justin Upton, SS, D-backs (1)	$6,100,000
2008	Tim Beckham, SS, Rays (1)	$6,150,000
	Buster Posey, C, Giants (1)	$6,200,000
2009	Donavan Tate, OF, Padres (1)	$6,250,000
	*Stephen Strasburg, RHP, Nationals (1)	$7,500,000
2011	Gerrit Cole, RHP, Pirates (1)	$8,000,000
2019	Adley Rutschman, C, Orioles (1)	$8,100,000
2020	Spencer Torkelson, 3B, Tigers (1)	$8,416,300

Part of major league contract.

This year 12 college players who ranked among the top 150—including four who spent last summer with USA Baseball's Collegiate National Team—went unpicked. Last year, just two collegians in the top 150 went unpicked. One was an injured pitcher, the other a junior college lefty.

It was a wild draft, and one that left a number of scouts and front office officials apologizing to draftable players who weren't picked.

"That was so bad for baseball on so many levels," Arkansas-Little Rock coach Chris Curry said. "Nobody won on that draft. Not the kids, not the teams, not the coaches."

Curry himself was drafted four times as a catcher, eventually signing with the Cubs as a ninth-round pick in 1999 for $60,000. Curry's

BONUSES VS. PICK VALUES

Assigned slots for the 2019 draft increased by 3.9% from the 2018 draft, but in 2020 slot values remained the same as 2019 due to the coronavirus pandemic. Despite slot values being stagnant, the bonus record was still re-set, as Spencer Torkelson signed for a slightly overslot $8,416,300 that set a new record. Over the past several drafts, bonus values have generally increased around 4% every year.

The top-50 bonuses added up to $165,359,025 compared to a slot value of $160,077,200 for those picks. That signing bonus value is up 1.8% from the 2019 top-50 bonuses. Fourteen of the first-round bonuses were underslot deals compared to nine overshot deals. Six players signed for slot in the first round. By comparison, when MLB unilaterally determined slot recommendations in the last year of the previous Collective Bargaining Agreement (2011) but had no enforcement mechanism, the total of the first 50 bonuses ($120.5 million) dwarfed that of the top 50 slot values ($70 million).

Player, Pos., Team (Round/Overall Pick)	Bonus	Pick Value
1. Spencer Torkelson, 3B, Arizona State (1st round/No. 1)	$8,416,300	$8,415,300
2. Austin Martin, SS, Vanderbilt (1st round/No. 5)	$7,000,825	$6,180,700
3. Max Meyer, RHP, Minnesota (1st round/No. 3)	$6,700,000	$7,221,200
4. Asa Lacy, LHP, Texas A&M (1st round/No.4)	$6,670,000	$6,664,000
5. Emerson Hancock, RHP, Georgia (1st round/No. 6)	$5,700,000	$5,742,900
6. Nick Gonzales, SS, New Mexico State (1st round/No. 7)	$5,432,400	$5,432,400
7. Heston Kjerstad, OF, Arkansas (1st round/No. 2)	$5,200,000	$7,789,900
8. Zac Veen, OF, Spruce Creek HS, Port Orange, Fla. (1st round/No. 9)	$5,000,000	$4,949,100
9. Reid Detmers, LHP, Louisville (1st round/No. 10)	$4,670,000	$4,739,900
10. Garrett Crochet, LHP, Tennessee (1st round/No. 11)	$4,547,500	$4,547,500
11. Robert Hassell, OF, Independence HS, Thompson's Station, Tenn. (1st round/No. 8)	$4,300,000	$5,176,900
12. Mick Abel, RHP, Jesuit HS, Portland, Ore. (1st round/No. 15)	$4,075,000	$3,885,800
13. Austin Hendrick, OF, West Allegheny HS, Imperial, Pa. (1st round/No. 12)	$4,000,000	$4,366,400
14. Patrick Bailey, C, North Carolina State (1st round/No. 13)	$3,797,500	$4,197,300
15. Ed Howard, SS, Mount Carmel HS, Chicago (1st round/No. 16)	$3,745,500	$3,745,500
16. Pete Crow-Armstrong, OF, Harvard-Westlake HS, Studio City, Calif. (1st round/No. 19)	$3,359,000	$3,359,000
17. Tyler Soderstrom, C, Turlock (Calif.) HS (1st round/No. 26)	$3,300,000	$2,653,400
18. Cole Wilcox, RHP, Georgia (3rd round/No. 80)	$3,300,000	$755,300
19. Justin Foscue, 1B, Mississippi State (1st round/No. 14)	$3,250,000	$4,036,800
20. Garrett Mitchell, OF, UCLA (1st round/No. 20)	$3,242,900	$3,242,900
21. Cade Cavalli, RHP, Oklahoma (1st round/No. 22)	$3,027,000	$3,027,000
22. Nick Bitsko, RHP, Central Bucks East HS, Doylestown, Pa. (1st round/No. 24)	$3,000,000	$2,831,300
23. Nick Loftin, SS, Baylor (supp. 1st/No. 32)	$3,000,000	$2,257,300
24. Jared Kelley, RHP, Refugio (Texas) HS (2nd round/No. 47)	$3,000,000	$1,580,200
25. J.T. Ginn, RHP, Mississippi State (2nd round/No. 52)	$2,900,000	$1,370,400
26. Jordan Walker, 3B, Decatur (Ga.) HS (1st round/No. 21)	$2,900,000	$3,132,300
27. Aaron Sabato, 1B, North Carolina (1st round/No. 27)	$2,750,000	$2,570,100
28. Nick Yorke, 2B, Archbishop Mitth HS, San Jose (1st round/No. 17)	$2,700,000	$3,609,700
29. Bryce Jarvis, RHP, Duke (1st round/No. 18)	$2,650,000	$3,481,300
30. Austin Wells, C, Arizona (1st round/No. 28)	$2,500,000	$2,493,900
31. Kyle Harrison, LHP, De La Salle HS, Concord, Calif. (3rd round/No. 85)	$2,497,500	$699,700
32. Dax Fulton, LHP, Mustang (Okla.) HS (2nd round/No. 40)	$2,400,000	$1,856,700
33. Slade Cecconi, RHP, Miami (supp. 1st/No. 33)	$2,384,900	$2,202,200
34. Jordan Westburg, SS, Mississippi State (supp. 1st/No. 30)	$2,365,500	$2,365,500
35. Jared Jones, RHP, La Mirada (Calif.) HS (2nd round/No. 44)	$2,200,000	$1,689,500
36. Jared Shuster, LHP, Wake Forest (1st round/No. 25)	$2,197,500	$2,740,300
37. Bobby Miller, RHP, Louisville (1st round/No. 29)	$2,197,500	$2,424,600
38. Masyn Winn, SS/RHP, Kingwood (Texas) HS (2nd round/No. 54)	$2,100,000	$1,307,000
39. Drew Romo, C, The Woodlands (Texas) HS (supp. 1st/No. 35)	$2,095,800	$2,095,800
40. Carmen Mlodzinski, RHP, South Carolina (supp. 1st/No. 35)	$2,050,000	$2,312,000
41. Justin Lange, RHP, Llano (Texas) HS (supp. 1st/No. 34)	$2,000,000	$2,148,100
42. Carson Tucker, SS, Mountain Pointe HS, Phoenix (1st round/No. 23)	$2,000,000	$2,926,800
43. Cole Henry, RHP, Louisiana State (2nd round/No. 55)	$2,000,000	$1,276,400
44. Dillon Dingler, C, Ohio State (2nd round/No. 38)	$1,952,300	$1,952,300
45. Hudson Haskin, OF, Tulane (2nd round/No. 39)	$1,906,800	$1,906,800
46. Alika Williams, SS, Arizona State (supp. 1st/No. 37)	$1,850,000	$1,999,300
47. C.J. Van Eyk, RHP, Florida State (2nd round/No. 42)	$1,797,500	$1,771,100
48. Blaze Jordan, 3B, Desoto Central HS, Southaven, Miss. (3rd round/No. 89)	$1,750,000	$657,600
49. Coby Mayo, 3B, Stoneman Douglas HS, Parkland, Fla. (4th round/No. 103)	$1,750,000	$560,000
50. Zach DeLoach, OF, Texas A&M (2nd round/No. 43)	$1,729,800	$1,729,800
Total	**$165,359,025**	**$160,077,200**

catcher at Arkansas-Little Rock, Kale Emshoff, is a significantly better player than Curry was by Curry's own estimation. Emshoff didn't get drafted, but then had 25 teams call him interested in signing him after the draft. Emshoff ultimately signed with the Royals and received the maximum $20,000 bonus for an undrafted player.

Emshoff's story was not unique. Many in baseball expressed hope that the 2021 draft, which will likely be 20 rounds thanks to the March agreement between Major League Baseball and the players' union, will be a return to normalcy.

The 2020 draft is in the books. May there never be another draft like it.

Team, Player, Pos., School	Bonus
1. DET, Spencer Torkelson, 3B, Arizona State	$8416300
2. BAL, Heston Kjerstad, OF, Arkansas	$5200000
3. MIA, Max Meyer, RHP, Minnesota	$6700000
4. KCR, Asa Lacy, LHP, Texas A&M	$6670000
5. TOR, Austin Martin, SS, Vanderbilt	$7000825
6. SEA, Emerson Hancock, RHP, Georgia	$5700000
7. PIT, Nick Gonzales, SS, New Mexico State	$5432400
8. SDP, Robert Hassell III, OF, Independence HS, Thompson's Station, Tenn.	$4300000
9. COL, Zac Veen, OF, Spruce Creek HS, Port Orange, Fla	$5000000
10. LAA, Reid Detmers, LHP, Louisville	$4670000
11. CWS, Garrett Crochet, LHP, Tennessee	$4547500
12. CIN, Austin Hendrick, OF, West Allegheny HS, Imperial, Pa	$4000000
13. SFG, Patrick Bailey, C, North Carolina State	$3797500
14. TEX, Justin Foscue, 2B, Mississippi State	$3250000
15. PHI, Mick Abel, RHP, Jesuit HS, Portland, Ore	$4075000
16. CHC, Ed Howard IV, SS, Mount Carmel HS, Chicago	$3745500
17. BOS, Nick Yorke, 2B, Archbishop Mitty HS, San Jose	$2700000
18. ARI, Bryce Jarvis, RHP, Duke	$2650000
19. NYM, Pete Crow-Armstrong, OF, Harvard-Westlake HS, Studio City, Calif	$3359000
20. MIL, Garrett Mitchell, OF, UCLA	$3242900
21. STL, Jordan Walker, 3B, Decatur (Ga.) HS	$2900000
22. WAS, Cade Cavalli, RHP, Oklahoma	$3027000
23. CLE, Carson Tucker, SS, Mountain Pointe HS, Phoenix	$2000000
24. TBR, Nick Bitsko, RHP, Central Bucks East HS, Doylestown, Pa	$3000000
25. ATL, Jared Shuster, LHP, Wake Forest	$2197500
26. OAK, Tyler Soderstrom, C, Turlock (Calif.) HS	$3300000
27. MIN, Aaron Sabato, 1B, North Carolina	$2750000
28. NYY, Austin Wells, C, Arizona	$2500000
29. LAD, Bobby Miller, RHP, Louisville	$2197500
30. BAL, Jordan Westburg, SS, Mississippi State	$2365500
31. PIT, Carmen Mlodzinski, RHP, South Carolina	$2050000
32. KCR, Nick Loftin, SS, Baylor	$3000000
33. ARI, Slade Cecconi, RHP, Miami	$2384900
34. SDP, Justin Lange, RHP, Llano (Texas) HS	$2000000
35. COL, Drew Romo, C, The Woodlands (Texas) HS	$2095800
36. CLE, Tanner Burns, RHP, Auburn	$1600000
37. TBR, Alika Williams, SS, Arizona State	$1850000
38. DET, Dillon Dingler, C, Ohio State	$1952300
39. BAL, Hudson Haskin, OF, Tulane	$1906800
40. MIA, Dax Fulton, LHP, Mustang (Okla.) HS	$2400000
41. KCR, Ben Hernandez, RHP, De La Salle HS, Chicago	$1450000
42. TOR, C.J. Van Eyk, RHP, Florida State	$1797500
43. SEA, Zach DeLoach, OF, Texas A&M	$1729800
44. PIT, Jared Jones, RHP, La Mirada (Calif.) HS	$2200000
45. SDP, Owen Caissie, OF, Notre Dame Catholic SS, Brampton, Ont	$1200004
46. COL, Chris McMahon, RHP, Miami	$1637400
47. CWS, Jared Kelley, RHP, Refugio (Texas) HS	$3000000
48. CIN, Christian Roa, RHP, Texas A&M	$1543600
49. SFG, Casey Schmitt, 3B, San Diego State	$1147500
50. TEX, Evan Carter, OF, Elizabethton (Tenn.) HS	$1250000
51. CHC, Burl Carraway IV, LHP, Dallas Baptist	$1050000
52. NYM, J.T. Ginn, RHP, Mississippi State	$2900000
53. MIL, Freddy Zamora, SS, Miami	$1150000
54. STL, Masyn Winn, SS/RHP, Kingwood (Texas) HS	$2100000
55. WAS, Cole Henry, RHP, Louisiana State	$2000000
56. CLE, Logan Allen, LHP, Florida International	$1125000
57. TBR, Ian Seymour, LHP, Virginia Tech	$1243600
58. OAK, Jeff Criswell, RHP, Michigan	$1000000
59. MIN, Alerick Soularie, OF, Tennessee	$900000
60. LAD, Landon Knack, RHP, East Tennessee State	$712500
61. MIA, Kyle Nicolas, RHP, Ball State	$1129700
62. DET, Daniel Cabrera, OF, Louisiana State	$1210000
63. STL, Tink Hence, RHP, Watson Chapel HS, Pine Bluff, Ark	$1115000
64. SEA, Connor Phillips, RHP, McLennan (Texas) JC	$1050300
65. CIN, Jackson Miller, C, Mitchell HS, New Port Richey, Fla	$1290000
66. LAD, Clayton Beeter, RHP, Texas Tech	$1196500

Arkansas outfielder Heston Kjerstad was a surprise pick to the Orioles at No. 2. overall.

COURTESY OF ANDY ALTENBURGER/ICON SPORTSWIRE VIA GETTY

67. SFG, Nick Swiney, LHP, North Carolina State	$1197500
68. SFG, Jimmy Glowenke, SS, Dallas Baptist	$597500
69. NYM, Isaiah Greene, OF, Corona (Calif.) HS	$850000
70. STL, Alec Burleson, OF, East Carolina	$700000
71. WAS, Sammy Infante, SS, Monsignor Pace HS, Miami	$1000000
72. LAA, Alex Santos II, RHP, Mount St. Michael Academy, Bronx, N.Y.	$1250000
73. DET, Trei Cruz, SS, Rice	$900000
74. BAL, Anthony Servideo, SS, Mississippi	$950000
75. MIA, Zach McCambley, RHP, Coastal Carolina	$775000
76. KCR, Tyler Gentry, OF, Alabama	$750000
77. TOR, Trent Palmer, RHP, Jacksonville	$847500
78. SEA, Kaden Polcovich, 2B, Oklahoma State	$575000
79. PIT, Nick Garcia, RHP, Chapman (Calif.)	$1200000
80. SDP, Cole Wilcox, RHP, Georgia	$3300000
81. COL, Sam Weatherly, LHP, Clemson	$755300
82. LAA, David Calabrese, OF, St. Elizabeth Catholic HS, Vaughan, Ont	$744200
83. CWS, Adisyn Coffey, RHP, Wabash Valley (Ill.) JC	$50000
84. CIN, Bryce Bonnin, RHP, Texas Tech	$700000
85. SFG, Kyle Harrison, LHP, De La Salle HS, Concord, Calif	$2497500
86. TEX, Tekoah Roby, RHP, Pine Forest HS, Pensacola, Fla	$775000
87. PHI, Casey Martin, SS, Arkansas	$1300000
88. CHC, Jordan Nwogu, OF, Michigan	$678600
89. BOS, Blaze Jordan, 3B, Desoto Central HS, Southaven, Miss.	$1750000
90. ARI, Liam Norris, LHP, Green Hope HS, Cary, N.C.	$800000
91. NYM, Anthony Walters, SS, San Diego State	$20000
92. MIL, Zavier Warren, C, Central Michigan	$575000
93. STL, Levi Prater, LHP, Oklahoma	$575000
94. WAS, Holden Powell, RHP, UCLA	$500000
95. CLE, Petey Halpin, OF, Mira Costa HS, Manhattan Beach, Calif	$1525000
96. TBR, Hunter Barnhart, RHP, St. Joseph HS, Santa Maria, Calif	$585000
97. ATL, Jesse Franklin, OF, Michigan	$497500
98. OAK, Michael Guldberg, OF, Georgia Tech	$300000
99. NYY, Trevor Hauver, 2B, Arizona State	$587400
100. LAD, Jake Vogel, OF, Huntington Beach (Calif.) HS	$1622500

2020 CLUB-BY-CLUB SELECTIONS

ARIZONA DIAMONDBACKS (18)

1. Bryce Jarvis, RHP, Duke
1s. Slade Cecconi, RHP, Miami
3. Liam Norris, LHP, Green Hope HS, Cary, N.C.
4. AJ Vukovich, 3B, East Troy (Wis.) HS
5. Brandon Pfaadt, RHP, Bellarmine (Ky.)

ATLANTA BRAVES (25)

1. Jared Shuster, LHP, Wake Forest
3. Jesse Franklin, OF, Michigan
4. Spencer Strider, RHP, Clemson
5. Bryce Elder, RHP, Texas

BALTIMORE ORIOLES (2)

1. Heston Kjerstad, OF, Arkansas
1s. Jordan Westburg, SS, Mississippi State
2. Hudson Haskin, OF, Tulane
3. Anthony Servideo, SS, Mississippi
4. Coby Mayo, 3B, Stoneman Douglas HS, Parkland, Fla.
5. Carter Baumler, RHP, Dowling Catholic HS, West Des Moines

BOSTON RED SOX (17)

1. Nick Yorke, 2B, Archbishop Mitty HS, San Jose
3. Blaze Jordan, 3B, Desoto Central HS, Southaven, Miss.
4. Jeremy Wu-Yelland, LHP, Hawaii
5. Shane Drohan, LHP, Florida State

CHICAGO CUBS (16)

1. Ed Howard, SS, Mount Carmel HS, Chicago
2. Burl Carraway, LHP, Dallas Baptist
3. Jordan Nwogu, OF, Michigan
4. Luke Little, LHP, San Jacinto (Texas) JC
5. Koen Moreno, RHP, Panther Creek HS, Cary, N.C.

CHICAGO WHITE SOX (11)

1. Garrett Crochet, LHP, Tennessee
2. Jared Kelley, RHP, Refugio (Texas) HS
3. Adisyn Coffey, RHP, Wabash Valley (Ill.) JC
4. Kade Mechals, RHP, Grand Canyon
5. Bailey Horn, LHP, Auburn

CINCINNATI REDS (12)

1. Austin Hendrick, OF, West Allegheny HS, Imperial, Pa.
2. Christian Roa, RHP, Texas A&M
2s. Jackson Miller, C, Mitchell HS, New Port Richey, Fla.
3. Bryce Bonnin, RHP, Texas Tech
4. Mac Wainwright, OF, St. Edward HS, Lakewood, Ohio
5. Joe Boyle, RHP, Notre Dame

CLEVELAND INDIANS (23)

1. Carson Tucker, SS, Mountain Pointe HS, Phoenix
1s. Tanner Burns, RHP, Auburn
2. Logan Allen, LHP, Florida International
3. Petey Halpin, OF, Mira Costa HS, Manhattan Beach, Calif.
4. Milan Tolentino, SS, Santa Margarita HS, Rancho Santa Margarita, Calif.
5. Mason Hickman, RHP, Vanderbilt

COLORADO ROCKIES (9)

1. Zac Veen, OF, Spruce Creek HS, Port Orange, Fla.
1s. Drew Romo, C, The Woodlands (Texas) HS
2. Chris McMahon, RHP, Miami
3. Sam Weatherly, LHP, Clemson

4. Case Williams, RHP, Douglas County HS, Castle Rock, Colo.
5. Jack Blomgren, SS, Michigan

DETROIT TIGERS (1)

1. Spencer Torkelson, 3B, Arizona State
2. Dillon Dingler, C, Ohio State
2s. Daniel Cabrera, OF, Louisiana State
3. Trei Cruz, SS, Rice
4. Gage Workman, 3B, Arizona State
5. Colt Keith, 3B, Biloxi (Miss.) HS

HOUSTON ASTROS (30)

2s. Alex Santos, RHP, Mount St. Michael Academy, Bronx, N.Y.
3. Tyler Brown, RHP, Vanderbilt
4. Zach Daniels, OF, Tennessee
5. Shay Whitcomb, SS, UC San Diego

KANSAS CITY ROYALS (4)

1. Asa Lacy, LHP, Texas A&M
1s. Nick Loftin, SS, Baylor
2. Ben Hernandez, RHP, De La Salle HS, Chicago
3. Tyler Gentry, OF, Alabama
4. Christian Chamberlain, LHP, Oregon State
5. Will Klein, RHP, Eastern Illinois

LOS ANGELES ANGELS (10)

1. Reid Detmers, LHP, Louisville
3. David Calabrese, OF, St. Elizabeth Catholic HS, Vaughan, Ont.
4. Werner Blakely, SS, Detroit Edison Public School Academy
5. Adam Seminaris, LHP, Long Beach State

LOS ANGELES DODGERS (29)

1. Bobby Miller, RHP, Louisville
2. Landon Knack, RHP, East Tennessee State
2s. Clayton Beeter, RHP, Texas Tech
3. Jake Vogel, OF, Huntington Beach (Calif.) HS
4. Carson Taylor, C, Virginia Tech
5. Gavin Stone, RHP, Central Arkansas

MIAMI MARLINS (3)

1. Max Meyer, RHP, Minnesota
2. Dax Fulton, LHP, Mustang (Okla.) HS
2s. Kyle Nicolas, RHP, Ball State
3. Zach McCambley, RHP, Coastal Carolina
4. Jake Eder, LHP, Vanderbilt
5. Kyle Hurt, RHP, Southern California

MILWAUKEE BREWERS (20)

1. Garrett Mitchell, OF, UCLA
2. Freddy Zamora, SS, Miami
3. Zavier Warren, C, Central Michigan
4. Joey Wiemer, OF, Cincinnati
5. Hayden Cantrelle, SS, Louisiana-Lafayette

MINNESOTA TWINS (13)

1. Aaron Sabato, 1B, North Carolina
2. Alerick Soularie, OF, Tennessee
4. Marco Raya, RHP, United South HS, Laredo, Texas
5. Kalai Rosario, OF, Waiakea HS, Hilo, Hawaii

NEW YORK METS (19)

1. Pete Crow-Armstrong, OF, Harvard-Westlake HS, Studio City, Calif.
2. J.T. Ginn, RHP, Mississippi State
2s. Isaiah Greene, OF, Corona (Calif.) HS
3. Anthony Walters, SS, San Diego State
4. Matthew Dyer, C, Arizona
5. Eric Orze, RHP, New Orleans

NEW YORK YANKEES (28)

1. Austin Wells, C, Arizona
3. Trevor Hauver, 2B, Arizona State
4. Beck Way, RHP, Northwest Florida State JC

OAKLAND ATHLETICS (26)

1. Tyler Soderstrom, C, Turlock (Calif.) HS
2. Jeff Criswell, RHP, Michigan
3. Michael Guldberg, OF, Georgia Tech
4. Dane Acker, RHP, Oklahoma
5. Stevie Emanuels, RHP, Washington

PHILADELPHIA PHILLIES (15)

1. Mick Abel, RHP, Jesuit HS, Portland, Ore.
3. Casey Martin, SS, Arkansas
4. Carson Ragsdale, RHP, South Florida
5. Baron Radcliff, OF, Georgia Tech

PITTSBURGH PIRATES (7)

1. Nick Gonzales, SS, New Mexico State
1s. Carmen Mlodzinski, RHP, South Carolina
2. Jared Jones, RHP, La Mirada (Calif.) HS
3. Nick Garcia, RHP, Chapman (Calif.)
4. Jack Hartman, RHP, Appalachian State
5. Logan Hofmann, RHP, Northwestern State

SAN DIEGO PADRES (8)

1. Robert Hassell, OF, Independence HS, Thompson's Station, Tenn.
1s. Justin Lange, RHP, Llano (Texas) HS
2. Owen Caissie, OF, Notre Dame Catholic SS, Brampton, Ont.
3. Cole Wilcox, RHP, Georgia
4. Levi Thomas, RHP, Troy
5. Jagger Haynes, LHP, West Columbus HS, Cerro Gordo, N.C.

SAN FRANCISCO GIANTS (13)

1. Patrick Bailey, C, North Carolina State
2. Casey Schmitt, 3B, San Diego State
2s. Nick Swiney, LHP, North Carolina State
2s. Jimmy Glowenke, SS, Dallas Baptist
3. Kyle Harrison, LHP, De La Salle HS, Concord, Calif.
4. R.J. Dabovich, RHP, Arizona State
5. Ryan Murphy, RHP, Le Moyne (N.Y.)

SEATTLE MARINERS (20)

1. Emerson Hancock, RHP, Georgia
2. Zach DeLoach, OF, Texas A&M
2s. Connor Phillips, RHP, McLennan (Texas) JC
3. Kaden Polcovich, 2B, Oklahoma State
4. Tyler Keenan, 3B, Mississippi
5. Taylor Dollard, RHP, Cal Poly

ST. LOUIS CARDINALS (21)

1. Jordan Walker, 3B, Decatur (Ga.) HS
2. Masyn Winn, SS/RHP, Kingwood (Texas) HS
2s. Tink Hence, RHP, Watson Chapel HS, Pine Bluff, Ark.
2s. Alec Burleson, OF, East Carolina
3. Levi Prater, LHP, Oklahoma
4. Ian Bedell, RHP, Missouri
5. LJ Jones, OF, Long Beach State

TAMPA BAY RAYS (24)

1. Nick Bitsko, RHP, Central Bucks East HS, Doylestown, Pa.
1s. Alika Williams, SS, Arizona State
2. Ian Seymour, LHP, Virginia Tech
3. Hunter Barnhart, RHP, St. Joseph HS, Santa Maria, Calif.
4. Tanner Murray, SS, UC Davis
5. Jeffrey Hakanson, RHP, Central Florida

TEXAS RANGERS (14)

1. Justin Foscue, 2B, Mississippi State
2. Evan Carter, OF, Elizabethton (Tenn.) HS
3. Tekoah Roby, RHP, Pine Forest HS, Pensacola, Fla.
4. Dylan MacLean, LHP, Central Catholic HS, Portland, Ore.
5. Thomas Saggese, SS, Carlsbad (Calif.) HS

TORONTO BLUE JAYS (5)

1. Austin Martin, SS, Vanderbilt
2. C.J. Van Eyk, RHP, Florida State
3. Trent Palmer, RHP, Jacksonville
4. Nick Frasso, RHP, Loyola Marymount
5. Zach Britton, OF, Louisville

WASHINGTON NATIONALS (17)

1. Cade Cavalli, RHP, Oklahoma
2. Cole Henry, RHP, Louisiana State
2s. Sammy Infante, SS, Monsignor Pace HS, Miami
3. Holden Powell, RHP, UCLA
4. Brady Lindsly, C, Oklahoma
5. Mitchell Parker, LHP, San Jacinto (Texas) JC

APPENDIX

■ **EDWARD ADAMCZYK,** a righthander who served in the U.S. Marine Corps in World War II before pitching for the Indians and Reds organizations in 1947 and '48, died Sept. 24 in Orchard Park, N.Y. He was 96.

■ **JOHN ADAMS,** a lefthander who played in the minor leagues in 1952 and '53, died July 12. He was 88.

■ **KENNETH ADAMS,** who played in the minor leagues in 1951, died July 10. He was 87.

■ **DAVID ALBRIGHT,** a lefthander who pitched in the minor leagues for the Royals organization from 1979-1982, died March 7 in Liberty, Mo. He was 63.

■ **DAVE ALEXANDER,** who served as head baseball coach at Purdue from 1978-1991 and later worked as a scout for the Mariners, died Feb. 26 in Lafayette, Ind. He was 79.
Alexander guided the Boilermakers to a 407-378-7 record in 14 seasons and led the team to its first NCAA Tournament apperance in 1987.

■ **JOHN ALTOBELLI,** an outfielder who played for the Marlins in the Florida State League in 1985, died Jan. 26 in the helicopter crash that killed former NBA superstar Kobe Bryant and seven others in Calabasas, Calif. He was 56.
Altobelli served as head coach for Orange Coast (Calif.) JC for 27 seasons, winning more than 700 games and capturing five California state junior college championships.

■ **NORM ANGELINI,** a lefthanded reliever who played for the Royals in 1972 and '73, died Dec. 21. He was 72.
Angelini appeared in 28 games during his major league career, going 2-1, 2.75. He struck out 19 batters in 19.2 innings across two seasons.

■ **MIKE ANTONE,** a first baseman who played in the minor leagues in1975 and '76, died Sept. 11. He was 65.

■ **JOHNNY ANTONELLI,** a lefthander who pitched 12 years in the major leagues, including seven seasons with the Giants, died Feb. 28 in Rochester, N.Y. He was 89.
Antonelli amassed a 126-110, 3.34 career record during his big league career, made six all-star teams and helped the Giants win the 1954

World Series. His best season came in 1954 when he led the league in ERA (2.30) and was named the Sporting News Pitcher of the Year.

■ **CHARLES ARCHAMBAULT,** who played in the minor leagues in 1953, died July 11 in North Grosvenor Dale, Conn. He was 87.

■ **GEORGE ARNOTT,** who was drafted by the Pirates in the 23rd round in 1967 but did not play professional baseball, died Nov. 5 in Paradise, Calif. He was 70.

■ **RAMON AVILES,** a second baseman and shortstop who played four seasons for the Phillies and Red Sox, died Jan. 27 in Manati, Puerto Rico. He was 68.
Aviles appeared in 117 games and hit two regular season home runs in 1980 for the Phillies' World Series championship team. He appeared in one game in the National League Championship Series against the Astros during the 1980 playoffs and scored a run. Aviles finished his career with two home runs and 24 RBIs.

■ **BRAD BABCOCK,** who served as head baseball coach at James Madison from 1971-89 and led the Dukes to the College World Series in 1983, died June 2. He was 81.
Babcock retired with a 558-251-4 record and four NCAA Tournament appearances under his belt.

■ **CAL BAILEY,** a righthander and first baseman who played in the minor leagues for the Pirates organization from 1966-71 and the Padres organization in 1970, died April 19. He was 77.
After his playing career ended, Bailey was named head coach at West Virginia State, his alma mater, in 1978. He amassed a 1,063-521-4 record between 1978 and his retirement in 2014 and won 19 conference championships. Bailey was inducted into the West Virginia Sports Hall of Fame in 2018.

■ **DONALD BAKKELUND,** a righthander who pitched in the Cardinals organization from 1939 to '42 and again in 1946 and '47 after serving in the U.S. Army in World War II, died Jan. 29 in Rockford, Ill. He was 99.

■ **JAMES BANKS,** a righthander who pitched in the Nebraska State and Midwest leagues for the Kansas City Athletics organization in in 1956 and '57, died Nov. 14 in Macon, Ga. He was 82.

■ **JERRY BANKS,** a relief pitcher who played in the minor leagues in 1954, died July 23 in Shakopee, Minn. He was 85.

■ **LARRY BARTON JR.,** a catcher and first baseman who played in the Dodgers organization in 1963 and '64, died Feb. 6 in Louisville. He was 80.

After his playing career ended, Barton served as an amateur scout for 38 years with the Reds. In 2004, Barton was named West Coast scout of the year. He later scouted for the Rangers and Dodgers before returning to the Reds in 2015.

■ **SHAWN BARTON,** a shortstop and second baseman who played in the minor leagues from 1981-1987 and from 1989-1990, died Aug. 11 in Citrus Heights, Calif. He was 58.

■ **KIM BATISTE,** a third baseman and short-stop who played in the major leagues for five seasons from 1991-94 and in '96, died Oct. 7 in Louisiana. He was 52.

Batiste hit .234/.250/.318 with 10 home runs, 64 RBIs and four stolen bases in 251 career games for the Phillies and Giants.

■ **GLENN BECKERT,** a second baseman who played in the major leagues from 1965-75, includ-ing from 1965-73 with the Cubs and from 1974-75 with the Padres, died April 12. He was 79.

During his successful big league career, Beckert made four consecutive all-star teams with the Cubs from 1969-72 and won a Gold Glove in 1968. He retired with a career line of .283/.318/.345.

■ **BERNARD BELAN,** a righthanded reliever who played for the Phillies organization from 1960-1964, died Dec. 25 in Jefferson Hills, Pa. He was 81.

Belan played alongside future Hall of Fame righthander Ferguson Jenkins and first base-man Dick Allen, who went on to win the 1972 American League MVP, for the Arkansas Travelers in 1963.

■ **BOB BENNETT,** who coached Fresno State from 1970-2002 and amassed a 1,302-759-4 record during his tenure, died May 31. He was 86.

Bennett led the Bulldogs to 17 conference titles during his tenure. Fresno State made the College World Series in 1988 and 1991 with Bennett at the helm.

■ **JOHN BEVIL,** a lefthander who pitched in the New York-Penn, Carolina and Florida State leagues for the Tigers organization from 1968-70, died Nov. 14 in New Braunfels, Texas. He was 73.

■ **EDWIN BINDER,** a righthander who pitched for the Red Sox organization from 1958-1962, died on Dec. 26. He was 93.

■ **WILLARD BISHOP,** who played in the minor leagues for the Kansas City Athletics orga-nization in 1959 and '60, died Dec. 27. He was 79.

■ **RICHARD BOKELMANN,** a righthander who pitched for the Cardinals organization from 1951-1953, died Dec. 27. He was 93.

Bokelmann pitched in 34 games during his big league career, posting a 3-4, 4.90 record over three seasons. He pitched 68 innings and struck out 27 batters, while finishing his career with three saves. His best season came in 1951 as a rookie, when Bokelmann earned three saves, struck out 22 batters, pitched 52.1 innings and finished with a 3.78 ERA.

■ **FRANK BOLLING,** a second baseman who played in the major leagues in 1954 and from 1956-66 for the Tigers and Braves, died July 11 in Mobile, Ala. He was 88.

Bolling, who hit 106 home runs and hit .254/.313/.366 for his career, made two all-star teams and won a Gold Glove in 1958.

■ **LOUIS "LOU" BOSSIE,** an outfielder who played in the minor leagues for the Orioles orga-nization in 1955, died Jan. 3 in Westminster, Md. He was 85.

■ **DOC BOWDEN,** a second baseman who played in the minor leagues from 1950-1954, died Aug. 11. He was 91.

■ **WELDON "HOSS" BOWLIN,** a third base-man who played in the minor leagues for the Cardinals, Athletics and Twins from 1959-1971, and appeared in two major league games for the Kansas City Athletics in 1967, singling once in five at-bats, died Dec. 8. He was 78.

Bowlin collected 1,387 hits in 1.466 games

over his career and finished with a .260 average. After his playing career ended, Bowlin coached the West Alabama baseball team and led the program to a 311-327-2 record. He led the Tigers to two Gulf South Conference Eastern Division titles in 1978 and '79, and two Division II NCAA Tournament appearances in 1976 and '79. The program also made the D-II World Series in 1976. In 2002, he was inducted into the West Alabama Hall of Fame.

■ **OLLIE BRANTLEY,** a righthander who pitched in the minor leagues from 1953-69, including in 1953 and '54 and from 1958-60 in the White Sox organization, in 1956 with the Braves organization, in 1961 with the Reds organization and from 1962-69 with the Twins organization, died April 5 in Dallas. He was 87.

Although Brantley never appeared in a big league game, he made 640 minor league appearances and posted a 155-117 career record in 2,082.1 innings.

■ **BART BRAUN,** a righthander who played in the minor leagues from 1976-82 before serving as a scout and most recently as a Phillies special assistant, died July 17 in Vallejo, Calif. He was 64.

Braun famously identified 16-year-old righthander Sixto Sanchez on a 2014 scouting trip to the Dominican Republic. The Phillies had sent him to scout another player.

■ **BOB BROCK,** who played in the minor leagues in 1953, died Aug. 16. He was 92.

■ **LOU BROCK,** a Hall of Fame outfielder who spent 19 years in the major leagues for the Cubs and Cardinals and who shattered Maury Wills' single-season stolen base record in 1974 with 118 stolen bases, died Sept. 6. He was 81.

Brock finished his career with a .293/.343/.410 slash line, 149 home runs, 900 RBIs, 1,610 runs scored, 3,023 hits and 938 stolen bases. He made six all-star teams and won two World Series titles in 1964 and 1967.

■ **BEARL BROOKS,** a shortstop who played in the Evangeline, South Atlantic and Kentucky-Illinois-Tennessee leagues from 1949-52 and returned as a player-coach after serving in the Navy in World War II in Japan, died Nov. 10, in Jonesboro, Ark. He was 93.

■ **VIRGIL "VIRG" BROUGHTON,** who

umpired from 1969-71 in the Florida State, Carolina and Southern leagues, died Jan. 19 in Elkins, W.Va. He was 81.

■ **OSCAR BROWN,** an outfielder who played in the major leagues for the Braves from 1969-73, died June 3 in Carson, Calif. He was 74.

Brown hit .244/.284/.339 in 337 career plate appearances to go along with four home runs and 28 RBIs. Brown is the brother of former major league outfielder Ollie Brown and NFL Hall of Fame defensive back Willie Brown.

■ **WILL BRUNSON,** a lefthander who pitched parts of three seasons with the Dodgers and Tigers, died Nov. 23 in Big Bend National Park, Texas.

Brunson appeared in 27 games, ending his career with a 1-1, 5.71 record and 11 strikeouts in 17.1 innings. He joined the Phillies' amateur scouting department in October 2016, covering South Texas. He was 49.

■ **GENE BUDIG,** who served as co-owner for the Charleston RiverDogs for 14 years and was the last president of the American League from 1994-1999, died Sept. 8. He was 81.

Budig, whose various job titles included president at Illinois State, Kansas and West Virginia, later worked as a senior advisor to Major League Baseball.

■ **MICHAEL BURKHART,** who worked for the Cubs organization for 34 years, including working as the Wrigley Field visiting clubhouse manager from 2004-19, died April 7. He was 63.

■ **BETTY CONGOUR CAYWOOD BUSHMAN,** who was the first female MLB announcer, hired by the Kansas City Athletics in 1964, died on Sept. 3. She was 89.

Bushman's first game as a broadcaster came on Sept. 16, 1964. She called 15 games for the club alongside Monte Moore and George Bryson.

■ **MARK BUTLER,** who owned the Double-A Harrisburg Senators of the Eastern League since 2015, died Dec. 1. He was 61.

In addition to serving as a managing partner of the Senators since Feb. 25, 2015, Butler helped install a baseball field at the Boys and Girls club in Harrisburg, Pa., in 2013 through the Cal Ripken Sr. Foundation.

CHARLES BYRD, an outfielder who played in the minor leagues from 1963-66, died July 7. He was 76.

TED BYRNE, who was a longtime play-by-play broadcastor for the College of Charleston, Georgia Southern, the Charleston Rainbows and Charleston RiverDogs, died Nov. 30 in Mount Pleasant, S.C. He was 71.

Byrne was inducted into the Charleston Baseball Hall of Fame in 2016.

TERRY CANNON, the founder of the baseball museum, Baseball Reliquary, and the Institute of Baseball Studies at Whittier College, died Aug. 1. He was 66.

HAYES CARGILL, who served as an umpire for 33 years, including in the Cotton State and Kitty leagues in the 1950s, died Jan. 12 in Grand Rapids, Mich. He was 93.

MARGARET CARROLL, who signed with the Rockford Peaches of the All-American Girls Professional Baseball League at the age of 16 and pitched for the team in 1951, died June 26. She was 85.

Carroll pitched to a 1-1 mark in 26 innings as a rookie in 1951 in her only season in the AAGPBL.

JOHN WILLIAM CARTER, who played in the minor leagues in the 1940s, died June 22 in Gulf Breeze, Fla. He was 92.

NICHOLAS CASALETTO, who played in the minor leagues in 1947 and '48, died April 9. He was 94.

EUGENE CASTIGLIONE, a second baseman who played in the minor leagues for five seasons, including four with the Dodgers organization from 1948-50 and in 1953, died Jan. 7 in Springfield, Ill. He was 91.

JACK CASTRO, who played in the minor leagues for four seasons from 1948-49 and again from 1952-53, including a three-year stint with the Indians, died Jan. 26. He was 92.

CHARLES CAUDILL, a catcher who played for the Senators organization in 1959, died Jan. 16 in Urbana, Ohio. He was 82.

PETE CAVA, who was a longtime member of The Society of American Baseball Research and wrote at least three books, including "Indiana-Born Major League Baseball Players: A Biographical Dictionary, 1871-2014," died Dec. 18 in Indianapolis. He was 73.

JOSEPH "JOE" CHEZ, an All-American righthander at Stanford who pitched in the Eastern League for the Tigers organization in 1952 and the Pacific Coast League in 1953, died Oct. 27 in Sacramento. He was 88.

BOBBY CLARK, a shortstop who played in the minor leagues from 1949-1950 and from 1953-1956, died Aug. 23 in Columbus, Ga. He was 91.

HORACE CLARKE, a second baseman and shortstop who spent 10 years in the major leagues from 1965-74 including parts of 10 seasons with the Yankees and part of a season with the Padres, died Aug. 5 in Laurel, Md. He was 81.

Clarke hit .256/.308/.313 with 27 home runs and 304 RBIs and led the league in at-bats in 1969 and '70.

ERNEST CLIFFORD, a righthander who pitched for the Pirates organization for the Thomasville Tomcats in the Georgia-Florida League in 1952, died Dec. 21 in Silver Spring, Md. He was 87.

GIL COAN, a left fielder who played 11 seasons in the major leagues for the Washington Senators, Orioles, White Sox and Giants from 1946-56, died Feb. 5 in Hendersonville, N.C. He was 97.

In 1954, Coan collected the first major league hit in Orioles franchise history. He finished his career with 731 hits in 918 games. His best season came in 1951 for the Senators when he hit seven triples, nine home runs and knocked in 62 RBIs to go with a .303/.357/.426 batting line.

JIM COATES, a two-time all-star and two-time World Series champion who pitched for the Yankees, Washington Senators, Reds and Los Angeles Angels from 1956-67, died Nov. 15 in Lancaster, Va. He was 87.

In nine major league seasons, the righthander pitched to a 43-22, 4.00 record with 396 strikeouts in 683.1 innings. Both of Coates' all-star selections came with the Yankees, in 1960 and 1962. While with the Yankees, Coates appeared in three straight World Series, in 1960, '61 and '62. He finished his career with an 0-1, 4.15 record in six postseason appearances. After his playing career, Coates was inducted into the Virginia Hall of Fame in 1994.

■ **NIELSEN COCHRAN,** a third baseman and shortstop who played in the Orioles organization from 1959-1965 and was the brother of U.S. Senator Thad Cochran, died Dec. 2 in Jackson, Miss. He was 78.

■ **CHRIS COMBS,** a first baseman and right-hander who played in the minor leagues from 1997-1999, died Sept. 3. He was 45.

■ **RICHARD "DICK" CONRAD,** a lefthander who pitched in the Northern and Midwest leagues for the White Sox and Tigers organizations in 1957 and '60, died Nov. 13 in South Bend, Ind. He was 84.

■ **DON CORELLA,** a lefthander who pitched in the minor leagues from 1953-1956 and from 1959-1962, died Aug. 19. He was 86.

■ **RYAN COSTELLO,** an corner infielder who played in the Mariners and Twins organizations from 2017-19, died Nov. 18, in Auckland, New Zealand. He was 23.

After hitting 15 home runs across two levels in the minors this season, Costello signed to play winter ball with the Auckland Tuatara of the Australian Baseball League. Costello was drafted by Seattle in the 31st round in 2017 out of Central Connecticut State and had reached Double-A for the first time in 2019.

■ **FRANK CREWS,** a pitcher who played in the minor leagues in 1952, died Aug. 22 in Boonville, Ind. He was 86.

■ **MAURICE CRON,** a righthander who pitched in the minor leagues in 1957 and '58, died July 24 in Dayton, Ohio. He was 84.

■ **HAL CRUTHERS,** a second baseman who played in the minor leagues for the Cubs organization in 1938 and the Dodgers organization in 1939, died April 3 in Chesapeake, Va. He was 102.

Cruthers was not the only member of his family who played professional baseball. His father Charles Preston "Press" Cruthers was a second baseman for the Athletics in 1913 and '14, and

his brother Charles Preston Cruthers Jr. was a minor league shortstop in 1939 and '40.

■ **ELENO CUEN,** a righthander who pitched in the minor leagues for the Astros from 1972-76 and Pirates from 1981-82, died Oct. 25 in Esperanza, Mexico. He was 67.

■ **JIM CUNEO,** who served as a replacement umpire during the umpires' strike in 1979, died June 27. He was 87.

■ **RONALD DADALT,** who umpired in the minor leagues in the 1950s, died May 24 in Stafford Springs, Conn. He was 93.

■ **GLENN "BUD" DANIEL,** who was the head coach of the University of Wyoming from 1951-71, with a one-year break in 1962, died Nov. 1 in Tucson. He was 95.

Daniel took his 1956 team to the College World Series. He won four Mountain States Conference championships and retired with 295 victories. Daniel was inducted into the College Baseball Hall of Fame in 1996.

In addition to his successful career in baseball, Daniel served in the Marines during World War II.

■ **JAMES DELANEY,** who umpired in the minor leagues in the 1950s after serving in the Marines during World War II and the Korean War, died Nov. 13 in Brick, N.J. He was 90.

■ **JOSEPH DESPIRITO,** a minor leaguer who played in the Georgia-Florida League for the Philadelphia Athletics organization in 1953, died Nov. 11 in Providence, R.I. He was 84.

■ **BILL DEZERNE,** a pitcher who played in the minor leagues in 1942 and after serving in World War II in 1947, died Aug. 1. He was 99.

■ **CHESTER "CHET" DiEMIDIO,** who played in the minor leagues in 1952 and '54 for the Phillies, Cardinals and Washington Senators organizations, died Oct. 12 in Philadelphia. He was 89.

In addition to playing in the minor leagues, DiEmidio served as a coach in the White Sox organization in 1988 and '90.

■ **FRANK DIGREGORIO,** a second baseman who played in the minor leagues from 1946-

1951, died Aug. 18. He was 96.

■ **JOHN DOLDOORIAN,** who served as a scout for the Cardinals and White Sox, died July 10. He was 90.

■ **TOM DULMAGE,** who played for the Kinston Eagles of the Coastal Plain League in 1951, died Jan. 26 in Henrietta, N.Y. He was 92.

■ **ANGEL ECHEVARRIA,** an outfielder and first baseman who played seven seasons in the major leagues for the Rockies, Brewers and Cubs, died Feb. 7 in Bridgeport, Conn. He was 48.

Echevarria appeared in 328 games over his career and hit 21 home runs. His best season came in 1999 with the Rockies when he hit 11 home runs and posted a .293/.360/.503 line. Echevarria ran his own business "Simply Baseball" after he retired and gave free clinics to children in Bridgeport.

■ **JOSEPH "JOE" ELBLE SR.,** who played in the Mississippi-Ohio Valley and Kansas-Oklahoma-Missouri leagues in 1951, died on Jan. 18 in Bloomington, Ill. He was 87.

■ **NARCISO ELVIRA,** a lefthander who pitched in four games for the Brewers in 1990, died Jan. 28 in Medellin de Bravo, Mexico. He was 52.

■ **FRANCISCO "PAQUIN" ESTRADA,** who played in the minor leagues for the Cubs, Orioles, Angels and Mets while also appearing in a game for the Mets during the 1971 major league season, died Dec. 9 in Mexico. He was 71.

Estrada also played in the Mexican League and managed there for 30 seasons after his playing career.

■ **ED FARMER,** a righthander who pitched in the major leagues from 1971-74 and from 1977-83 for eight different teams and was a 1980 American League all-star with the White Sox, died April 1 in Los Angeles. He was 70.

Farmer posted a 30-43, 4.30 career mark and recorded 75 saves. After his playing career ended, Farmer served as a broadcaster for the White Sox beginning in 1991, a role he continued every year since.

In his all-star season, Farmer made 64 relief appearances, logged 30 saves and recorded a 3.34 ERA with 54 strikeouts in 99.2 innings.

■ **JOHN FERENCHICK,** a righthander who pitched for the Tigers and Orioles in 1963 and '64, died Aug. 12 in Flying Hills, Pa. He was 76.

Ferenchick suited up with Hall of Famer Jim Palmer during 1964 spring training with the Stockton Ports.

■ **TONY FERNANDEZ,** a shortstop who played for the Blue Jays, Padres, Mets, Indians, Reds, Yankees and Brewers from 1983-1999 and again in 2001, died Feb. 16 in Weston, Fla. He was 57.

Fernandez won four Gold Gloves and made five all-star appearances during his decorated career. He finished with 2,276 career hits, 94 home runs and a .288/.347/.399 batting line and won a World Series in 1993 with the Blue Jays. Fernandez still holds the record for most career hits in Blue Jays history (1,583).

For the Blue Jays in 1987, Fernandez hit .322/.379/.426, scored 90 runs, stole 32 bases, collected eight triples and five home runs and knocked in 67 runs. He finished eighth in MVP voting, won his second Gold Glove and made the American League all-star team.

■ **CARMEN FERULLO,** a righthander who pitched in the minor leagues from 1947-1951 after serving in the U.S. Navy in World War II, died Aug. 15. He was 93.

■ **WHITEY FORD,** a Hall of Fame lefthander who spent all 16 seasons with the Yankees and won six World Series, a Cy Young Award and a World Series MVP, died Oct. 8 in New York. He was 91.

Ford pitched to a 236-106, 2.75 record and holds the highest winning percentage (.690) of any pitcher with 150 or more victories. In addition to holding the Yankees franchise mark for wins, Ford's 10 World Series victories are the most in history. In 1961, he won the American League Cy Young Award and finished fifth in MVP voting with a 25-4, 3.21 record and 209 strikeouts in a league-high 283 innings.

■ **ROBERT "BOB" FREEMAN,** who played in the minor leagues for the Cubs organization in 1946 and '47 and the Giants organization in 1948, died Dec. 4 in Henderson, Nev. He was 97.

■ **LYLE FRITSCH,** a righthander who pitched in the minor leagues in 1941, died Aug. 18 in Sandwich, Ill. He was 100.

■ **GEORGE FUCHS,** a righthander who pitched for the Phillies organization in 1954 and '55, died Dec. 24 in Mantua, N.J. He was 86.

■ **DUNCAN FUTRELLE,** who played in the minor leagues from 1947-1949, died March 3 in Rock Hill, S.C. He was 91.

■ **DAMASO GARCIA,** a second baseman who played in the major leagues from 1978-87 and from 1988-89, including with the Yankees in 1978 and '79, the Blue Jays from 1980-86, the Braves in 1988 and the Montreal Expos in 1989, died April 15 in the Dominican Republic. He was 63.

Garcia made back-to-back all-star teams with the Blue Jays in 1984 and '85 and won a Silver Slugger award in 1982. He finished his career with a .283/.309/.371 line and 203 stolen bases.

■ **HUMBERTO GARCIA,** a first baseman/third baseman and righthander who played in the Mexican League in 1965 and from 1967-81, died July 16 in McAllen, Texas. He was 73.

■ **BOB GARVEY,** who signed a contract to play for the Cardinals organization for the 1951 season, died Jan. 21 in Millsboro, Del. He was 87.

■ **ROBERT GATES,** a lefthander who pitched in the minor leagues in 1947 and in 1949 and '50 after serving in the Navy in World War II, died Dec. 11 in Fairport, N.Y. He was 94.

■ **MICHAEL GAZELLA,** a pitcher who played in the minor leagues from 1951-1957, died Aug. 26. He was 93.

KENT GEISLER, a righthander who pitched in the minor leagues in 1956 and '57, died Sept. 29 in Idaho Falls. He was 84.

■ **RAY GERARD,** a pitcher who played in the minor leagues in 1955, died July 8. He was 86.

■ **GERRET GERRETSEN,** a minor leaguer who played in the New England League for the Boston Braves organization in 1948 and the Colonial League in 1949 after serving in the Navy during World War II, died on Oct. 31 in Queens, N.Y. He was 94.

■ **BILL GILBRETH,** a lefthander who pitched in the major leagues for the Tigers in 1971 and '72 and for the Angels in '74 before serving as head baseball coach at Abilene Christian (Texas), his alma mater, from 1991-95, died July 12. He was 72. Gilbreth posted a career 2-1, 6.69 mark in 36.1 innings.

■ **MIKE GILLESPIE,** who won a College World Series both as a player and coach at Southern California, died July 29. He was 80.

Gillespie's coaching career, which included stints at College of the Canyons (Calif.), USC and UC Irvine, lasted 47 seasons. He won more than 1,500 games, led USC to a national title in 1998, reached Omaha four other times, including with UC Irvine in 2014, and retired after the 2018 season as a legend in the college coaching world.

■ **BILL GLADSTONE,** who served as a part owner for the short-season Tri-City ValleyCats franchise since 1992, died April 30. He was 88.

■ **DAVID GLASS,** who served as chief executive office of the Royals beginning in 1993 and became the owner in 2000 before selling the team in November 2019, died Jan. 9. He was 84.

During Glass' ownership, the Royals reached the World Series in back-to-back years in 2014 and 2015. In 2015, the Royals won the organization's second title and first since 1985.

■ **JOHN GOETZ,** a catcher who played in the minor leagues in 1975, died Sept. 6 in Conway, S.C. He was 67.

■ **JOHN GOODELL,** a first baseman and third baseman who played in the minor leagues from 1953-1958, died March 4 in Amarillo, Texas. He was 89.

■ **BRADLEY GOODWIN,** an outfielder who spent one season in the Pioneer League in 1985, died Dec. 29 in Fall Creek, Ore. He was 56.

■ **LEE GREENE,** who authored "The Baseball Life of Willie Mays" and "The Johnny Unitas Story," died Dec. 19 in Fairfax, Va. He was 91.

■ **NELSON GRIEBEL,** a righthander who pitched in the minor leagues in 1972, died July 29. Griebel went on to twice run for governor in the state of Connecticut.

■ **JOE GRILLO,** a lefthander who pitched in the minor leagues in 1973, died Oct. 6. He was 69.

■ **RAYMOND GRUND,** a righthander who pitched for the Cubs organization in 1951, '52 and '55 after serving in the Korean War, died Dec. 24 in West Bend, Wis. He was 87.

■ **JAMES "TONY" GWINN,** a catcher who played in the New York-Penn, Carolina, Florida State and Eastern leagues for the Yankees organization from 1987-89, died Nov. 8 in Oklahoma City. He was 55.

■ **JOE HABERL,** a righthander who pitched in the minor leagues from 1956-1957, died July 29. He was 87.

■ **BEN HADDIX,** a catcher who played in the minor leagues in 1942 in the Cardinals organization and in the Giants organization from 1947-1950 after serving in the US Merchant Marines in World War II, died Feb. 23 in Springfield, Ohio. He was 96.

■ **DONALD HALL,** who signed a contract with the Orioles to play for the organization's minor league Class A farm team in Stockton, Calif., but did not appear in a game, died Jan. 14 in Windsor Mill, Md. He was 74.

■ **SHERRILL HALL,** a righthander who played in the minor leagues from 1955-1956, died Aug. 30. He was 86.

■ **ARNIE HALLGREN,** a right fielder who played for the Braves, Tigers and Cubs organizations during 10 minor league seasons from 1952-61, died Jan. 14 in Vancouver, B.C. He was 86.

Hallgren was inducted into the British Columbia Hall of Fame in 2005.

■ **CHRIS HALLIDAY,** who was drafted twice by the Yankees in 1993 and '94 but never played in a professional game, died Sept. 18. He was 46.

■ **BRAD HAMES,** a starting pitcher who played in the independent North Central League in 1994, died Aug. 17 in Ackley, Iowa. He was 48.

■ **FRANKLIN HAMILTON,** who played in the minor leagues in 1946 and '47 after serving in World War II, died Dec. 28. He was 95.

■ **LOU HAMMER,** who pitched for Kansas in the 1940s and was on the 1948 Topeka Owls roster, died Sept. 11. He was 96.

■ **JAY HANKINS,** an outfielder who played in the major leagues for the Royals in 1961 and '63, died Jan. 20 in Greenwood, Mo. He was 84.

Hankins appeared in 86 major league games over two seasons, hit four home runs and collected 38 hits. After his playing career ended, he continued to stay involved with the game, scouting for the Indians (1967-68), Royals (1969-74), Phillies (1994) and Angels and managing the Kingsport Royals in 1972. Hankins served as the Phillies' scouting director from 1989-1992.

■ **GENE HARP,** a righthander who pitched in the minor leagues for two seasons in 1955 and '56, died Oct. 2. He was 84.

■ **DONALD HARRIS,** a righthander who pitched in the minor leagues from 1948-51, died Sept. 18. He was 92.

■ **DONALD RUDOLPH HARRIS,** a shortstop who played for the Cubs organization in the Mississippi-Ohio Valley League in 1955, died Jan. 21 in Hobart, Ind. He was 84.

■ **DON HASENMAYER,** a second and third baseman who played two seasons for the Phillies in 1945 and '46 after serving in the U.S. Navy during World War II, died Jan. 28 in Warrington, Pa. He was 92.

In 30 at-bats over 11 games, Hasenmayer collected three hits and drove in one run. He served as manager of Portsmouth of the Piedmont League in 1951.

■ **ANDREW HASSLER,** a lefthander who pitched for the Angels, Royals, Red Sox, Mets, Pirates and Cardinals from 1971-1985, died Dec. 25 in Wickenburg, Ariz. He was 68.

Hassler went 44-71, 3.83 during his 14 years in the big leagues. He appeared in 387 games (112 starts) and struck out 630 batters in 1,123.1 innings while finishing with 29 career saves. In 1974, Hassler sported a 7-11, 2.61 mark for the Angels and pitched 10 complete games.

■ **WILLIAM HAYDEN,** a shortstop who played in the minor leagues in 1950 and 1953, died Feb. 27 in Navarre, Ohio. He was 91.

■ **VAL HEIM,** an outfielder who appeared in 13 games for the White Sox in 1942, died Nov. 21 in Superior, Neb. He was 99.

In 45 major league at-bats, Heim totaled

nine hits, including a double and a triple. Heim was the oldest surviving former major leaguer, succeeding Tom Jordan who passed away in August.

■ **JAKE HELMUTH,** who played in the Cardinals organization from 1949-51 and in the Giants organization in 1958, died Nov. 26 in Arlington Heights, Ill. He was 90.

■ **BRUCE HENDERSON,** a first baseman who played in the minor leagues in 1972, died July 20 in Richmond, Texas. He was 70.

■ **BENTLEY J. HERBERT SR.,** a righthander who pitched in the Georgia-Florida League in 1952 before serving in both the Korean War and Vietnam War, died Feb. 28 in Lawrence, Mass. He was 88.

■ **HARRY HICKMAN,** who was a scout for the Cubs organization in the 1950s, died Dec. 31 in Hattiesburg, Miss. He was 92.

■ **SAM HINDS,** a righthander who pitched for the Brewers in 1977 and pitched in the minor leagues in the Brewers organization from 1974-1979, died Sept. 19, 2019, in Hanford, Cali. He was 66. In 29 career appearances, Hinds pitched to a 0-3, 4.73 record and struck out 46 batters in 72.1 innings.

■ **STEVEN HODGES,** a lefthander who pitched in the minor leagues for the Braves organization in 1990, died Dec. 27 in Victoria, B.C. He was 53.

In addition to playing one season in the minors, Hodges represented Team Canada in the Intercontinental Cup tournament in Havana, Cuba, in 1987. His son Jesse was a third baseman in the Cubs organization prior to his release in July 2019.

■ **JIM HOELSCHER,** who played in the minor leagues in 1951 and 1956, died Sept. 11. He was 88.

■ **TUFFY HORNE,** who served as head baseball coach at Kentucky from 1973-78 and posted a 127-126-1 career record, died May 11. He was 77.

■ **ROGER HOWARD,** a righthander who pitched in the minor leagues for the White Sox

organization from 1953-1954 and in 1957, died March 6. He was 88.

■ **BUTCH HUGHES,** who played in the minor leagues from 1962-64 before serving as a coach and manager in the minor leagues and head baseball coach at Merced (Calif.) from 1972-81, died July 21. He was 79. Hughes retired from his post at Merced with a 307-73 career record.

■ **GARY HUGHES,** a longtime scout who worked for multiple organizations during a distinguished 54-year career in the game, died Sept. 19. He was 79.

A member of the Professional Baseball Scouts Hall of Fame, Hughes most recently worked for the Red Sox and Diamondbacks. He also spent time with the Giants, Mariners, Mets, Yankees, Expos, Marlins, Rockies, Reds and Cubs over the course of his career.

■ **DICK HYDE,** a righthander who pitched in the major leagues for the Senators in 1955 and from 1957-60 and for the Orioles in 1961, died April 15 in Champaign, Ill. He was 91.

Hyde retired from baseball with a career record of 17-14, 3.56 in six seasons. In 1957, he pitched to a 10-3, 1.75 mark for the Senators, appearing in 44 games and converting 19 saves. He finished 12th in the American League MVP voting that season.

■ **CHARLES JACKSON,** who served as a big league umpire in one American League game during the umpire strike of 1979, died Aug. 8. He was 97.

■ **JACK JACOBS,** who played in the minor leagues for the Giants in 1952, died Dec. 25. He was 87.

Jacobs was a third generation baseball player. In 1952 while in spring training camp with the Giants in Phoenix, he struck out Hall of Famer Willie Mays.

■ **MIKE JACOBS,** who played at South Alabama in the 1970s and coached the University of Mobile for 30 years, died Dec. 3 in Mobile, Ala. He was 61.

Jacobs founded the Mobile baseball program in 1990. During his 30 seasons, he won 993 games, seven conference championships and appeared in the NAIA World Series in 2001.

Jacobs was elected to the Alabama Baseball

Coaches Association Hall of Fame in 2018.

■ **ROBERT JACOBS,** a second baseman who played for the Braves organization for six seasons from 1956-61, died Dec. 23 in St. Louis. He was 82.

■ **RICHARD JANACONE,** who played in the minor leagues for the Washington Senators organization in 1949 and '50 and the Cubs organization in 1953 after serving in the Army in the Korean War, died Dec. 20 in New Castle, Pa. He was 91.

■ **NOEL JENKE,** a 1969 first-round pick of the Red Sox who played in the minor leagues from 1969-72, died July 23 in Milwaukee. He was 73.

■ **REN JENKINS,** a righthander who pitched in the minor leagues in 1958 and '59, died July 7 in Orwigsburg, Pa. He was 81.

■ **BOB JINGLING,** a shortstop and second baseman who played in the minor leagues in 1955 and '60, died May 29. He was 86.

Jingling played college ball at Wyoming, where he was named All-America, and represented the United States in the 1955 Pan American Games.

■ **BOB JOHNSON,** a middle infielder for the Athletics, Senators, Orioles, Mets, Reds, Braves and Cardinals from 1960-70, died Nov. 9 in St. Paul, Minn. He was 83.

Johnson's career spanned across 11 seasons. He played in 874 games and ended his career with a .272/.320/.377 slash line to go along with 44 home runs and 230 RBIs.

Johnson served primarily as a reserve infielder, spending only the 1962 season as a regular. Batting 504 times for the Senators that season he hit .288 with 12 home runs and 43 RBIs.

■ **LOU JOHNSON,** who played in the major leagues for eight seasons from 1960-62 and from 1965-69 for the Dodgers, Angels, Cubs, Indians and Braves, died Sept. 30. He was 86.

Johnson hit .258/.311/.389 with 48 home runs, 50 stolen bases and 232 RBIs and won a World Series with the 1965 Dodgers.

■ **RAY JOHNSON,** an outfielder who played in the Cardinals organization in 1941 and '42 and served in the Army during World War II, died Nov. 21. He was 95.

■ **REX JOHNSTON,** a left fielder who played for the Pirates in 1964 and played as a halfback for the Pittsburgh Steelers of the National Football League in 1960, died Dec. 15 in Los Angeles. He was 82.

In 14 games for the Pirates, Johnston scored one run and walked three times in 10 plate appearances.

Johnston, who played for Southern California, scored the winning run in the 12th inning of the 1958 College World Series championship game. He hit .374 during that memorable season.

■ **JAY JOHNSTONE,** an outfielder who played in the major leagues for 20 seasons from 1966-85 with eight different clubs, died Sept. 26 in Granada Hills, Calif. He was 74.

Johnstone won two World Series with the Yankees in 1978 and Dodgers in 1981. He hit .267/.329/.394 over 4,703 at-bats to go with 102 home runs and 50 stolen bases.

■ **HOWIE JUDSON,** a righthander who pitched in the major leagues with the White Sox and Reds from 1948-1954, died Aug. 18 in Winter Haven, Fla. He was 95.

Judson posted a career 17-37, 4.29 mark in 615 innings while striking out 204 batters. He also converted 14 saves.

■ **GREG JURGENSON,** a lefthander who pitched in the minor leagues in 1974, died July 11. He was 67.

■ **AL KALINE,** a Hall of Fame right fielder who played for the Tigers for 22 seasons from 1953-74, made 18 all-star teams, won 10 Gold Gloves, captured the 1955 American League batting title and won a World Series in 1968, died April 6 in Bloomfield Hills, Mich. He was 85.

Kaline finished in the top five in MVP voting four times in his accomplished career. He posted a .297/.376/.480 line to go along with 399 home runs and 1,582 runs batted in and is one of 32 players in major league history to collect 3,000 hits. Kaline was enshrined in Cooperstown in 1980, his first year on the ballot.

■ **EDDIE KASKO,** a middle infielder who played in the major leagues for the Cardinals, Reds, Astros and Red Sox from 1957-66 and later served as manager for the Red Sox from 1970-73, died June 24. He was 88.

Kasko finished his career with a .264/.317/.331

slash line, 22 home runs and 261 RBIs in 10 seasons and made an all-star team in 1961. He managed the Red Sox to a 345-295 mark in four seasons.

■ **ROBERT KENDRICK,** an outfielder who spent three seasons in the minor leagues and played for the Boston Braves organization in 1952, died Dec. 25 in South Yarmouth, Mass. He was 87.

■ **MATT KEOUGH,** a righthander who pitched in the major leagues from 1977-83 and from 1985-86, including from 1977-83 with the Athletics, died May 1 in California. He was 64.

Keough pitched in 215 career games, making 175 starts, and posted a 58-84, 4.17 record with 590 strikeouts in 1,190 innings. Keough made the American League all-star team in 1978, when he went 8-15, 3.24 in 197.1 innings and led the league in home run rate.

■ **RUDY KINARD,** a second baseman, shortstop and third baseman who played in the minor leagues from 1972-79, died Sept. 12 in Omaha. He was 70.

■ **LEWIS KLEIN,** who played in the minor leagues in 1952 and '53, died July 26. He was 93.

■ **BILL KLENK,** who served as head baseball coach at his alma mater, Alma (Mich.), from 1973-1995, died Aug. 1 in The Villages, Fla. He was 83.

Klenk retired with a record of 283-288-2 and was inducted into Alma's hall of fame as a player in 1975 and as a coach in 2015.

In addition to serving as head baseball coach, Klenk coached the men's and women's basketball teams at the university.

■ **WILL KOPS,** a righthander who pitched in the Blue Ridge, Georgia State and Evangeline leagues from 1948-50 after serving in the Army in World War II, died Nov. 18 in Edgewood, Ky. He was 92.

■ **JAMES KOVARIK,** a righthander who pitched four seasons in the Giants organization from 1950-53, died Jan. 5 in Kirkwood, Mo. He was 87.

■ **ROBERT KREMENS SR.,** an infielder who played in the minor leagues for the Athletics organization in 1947 and the Dodgers organiza-

tion in 1948, died Feb. 6, in Lakewood, N.J. He was 92.

■ **RAYMON LACY,** who played in segregated leagues including the Negro National League for the Homestead Grays in 1947, died at 97.

After his playing career ended, Lacy and his wife combined to teach for 110 years in the Texas public school system.

■ **VICTOR "VIC" LAPINER,** a righthander who pitched in the Eastern and Northwest leagues for the Indians and Kansas City Athletics organizations in 1956 and '59, died Nov. 16 in Tarzana, Calif. He was 85.

Lapiner was a standout pitcher for Southern California and he led the Trojans to their fourth College World Series appearance in 1955.

■ **EUGENE LEACH,** a righthander who pitched in the minor leagues in 1949 and '50, including a stint with the Braves organization in 1950, died Feb. 2 in Shady Spring, W.Va. He was 92.

■ **AL LEBEL,** a third baseman who played in the minor leagues in 1952, died Aug. 14 in Waterbury, Conn. He was 87.

■ **BOB LEE,** a righthander who pitched in the major leagues for five years from 1964-68, including three seasons spent with the Angels, died March 25 in Lake Havasu City, Ariz. He was 82.

Lee posted a 25-23, 2.71 record in 269 career appearances. In 1965, he made the American League all-star team and finished the year 9-7, 1.92 with 23 saves in 131.1 innings.

■ **TED LEPCIO,** a second baseman who played for 10 seasons in the major leagues for the Red Sox, Tigers, Phillies, White Sox and Twins, died Dec. 11 in Dedham, Mass. He was 90.

Lepcio hit .245/.318/.398 over 10 years in the big leagues to go along with 69 home runs. In 1956, he hit 15 home runs, drove in 51 runs and hit .261/.335/.454 for the Red Sox.

■ **CLIFFORD LINDLOFF,** who played in the minor leagues in 1950 after a distinguished collegiate career at Texas A&M, died July 5 in Waco, Texas. He was 93.

■ **GEORGE LOTT,** a first baseman and catcher who played for the Pirates and Dodgers organizations for 10 seasons from 1963-72, died Jan. 23 in Summit, Miss. He was 76.

■ **AL MACKOWIAK,** who played in the minor leagues in 1948, died July 11. He was 94.

■ **LARRY MANTLE,** the youngest brother of Mickey Mantle who had a long career as a high school football coach in Oklahoma and Texas, died Aug. 10 in Fresno, Calif. He was 79.

■ **SYLVIO MASTROIANNI,** a righthander who pitched in the minor leagues for three seasons from 1949-1950 and '54, including with the Tigers and Giants organizations, died Jan. 24 in Stony Point, N.Y. He was 89.

■ **JAKE MAUER,** the grandfather of Twins all-star catcher Joe Mauer who signed with the White Sox in 1954 but never appeared in a minor league game, died Aug. 11. He was 89.

■ **JOHAN MAYA,** a second baseman, short-stop and third baseman who played in the minor leagues in 1999 and 2000 and who recently joined the D-backs organization as a scout after 15 years with the Astros, died July 23 in the Dominican Republic. He was 40.

■ **GEORGE MCBEE,** who played for Ozark in the Alabama State League in 1950 and served in the Army, died Dec 12. He was 90.

■ **DICK MCCALLUM,** a righthander who pitched in the Pirates organization from 1948-50, died Nov. 24 in Monongahela, Pa. He was 90.

■ **JOHN MCKINSTRY,** who played in the Wisconsin State, Alabama-Florida and Georgia-Florida leagues for the Milwaukee Braves organization from 1953-55, died Nov. 12 in Grover Beach, Calif. He was 84.

■ **JOHN MCNAMARA,** who played in the minor leagues from 1951 to '67 and later won the 1986 American League Manager of the Year award while guiding the Red Sox to within one out of the World Series title, died July 28 in Brentwood, Tenn. He was 88.

McNamara went 1,160-1,233 in his 19 years managing in the big leagues for the Athletics, Padres, Reds, Red Sox, Indians and Angels. McNamara guided the Reds to the National League West title in 1979 in addition to helping the Red Sox win the AL pennant in 1986.

■ **FRANK McNULTY,** who was the model for the Cubs' batboy in Norman Rockwell's painting "The Dugout," died Jan. 9 in Bloomfield, Conn. He was 88.

■ **MIKE MCCORMICK,** a lefthander who pitched in the major leagues for 16 seasons from 1956-71 for the Giants, Orioles, Senators, Yankees and Royals, died June 13 in Cornelius, N.C. He was 81.

McCormick made two all-star teams while pitching for the Giants in 1960 and '61. He won the 1967 National League Cy Young Award in his return to the Giants after spending four seasons with the Orioles and Senators. That year he pitched to a 22-10, 2.85 mark while throwing 14 complete games and pitching 262.1 innings.

McCormick retired in 1971 with a 134-128, 3.73 record, 2,380.1 innings and 91 complete games.

■ **ANDREW PAUL MELE,** the author of several books about the Brooklyn Dodgers, died Aug. 8 in Staten Island, N.Y. He was 81.

■ **JOHN MILLER,** a righthander who pitched in the major leagues for five seasons with the Orioles from 1962-63 and from 1965-67, died June 5 in Westminster, Md. He was 79.

Miller posted a 12-14, 3.89 mark in five seasons, striking out 178 batters in 227 innings.

■ **DARWIN MINNIS,** who served in the Marine Corps in the Korean War and started and coached the Missouri Western State College baseball program, died Dec. 26. He was 90.

Minnis served as head baseball coach of the Missouri Western program from 1969-1999, winning almost 700 games. During his coaching career, he was selected to coach the U.S. National Team.

Following his retirement, Minnis was elected to nine different halls of fame, including the American Baseball Coaches Association, the NAIA and the Missouri Sports Hall of Fame.

■ **ROBERT MONTGOMERY,** a righthander who pitched in the minor leagues in 1949 and '50, died Nov. 25 in Shawsville, Va. He was 87.

■ **JASON MOORE,** who served as an umpire in the minor leagues in the 2000s, died July 9 in

San Bernardino, Calif. He was 46.

■ **JOE MORGAN,** a Hall of Fame second baseman who won five Gold Gloves and two World Series over a 22-year career, died Oct. 11. He was 77.

Morgan was a 10-time all-star and won back-t0-back MVPs in 1975 and 1976, leading the majors in OPS in both years and combining to hit a .324/.456/.541 slash line with 44 home runs and 205 RBIs. Morgan finished his career with 268 home runs, a .271/.392/.427 slash line, 1,865 walks (fifth most all time) and 689 stolen bases (11th most all time).

■ **CHARLES CARROLL MOULDEN,** who played in the minor leagues from 1964-71, died July 17. He was 75.

■ **BILL MURPHY,** a righthander who pitched in the minor leagues in 1958, '59 and '61, died July 31 in Knoxville, Tenn. He was 82.

■ **ED NAPOLEON,** an outfielder who played in the minor leagues from 1956-58 and from 1960-70 before serving as a minor league manager and a major league coach for the Yankees, Athletics and Rangers, died April 28 in Florida. He was 82.

■ **ROLLIN "OLE" NATER,** who umpired in the Mississippi-Ohio Valley League in the 1950s, died Nov. 25 in Janesville, Wis. He was 90.

■ **MARK NEWMAN,** a pitcher who helped take Southern Illinois to the 1969 College World Series championship game before serving as the school's pitching coach for nine seasons, Old Dominion's head coach for nine seasons and an executive for the Yankees who helped oversee five World Series titles, died Sept. 12. He was 71.

Newman was inducted into the Old Dominion Hall of Fame in 1997 and the Southern Illinois Hall of Fame in 2000, posted a 321-167-3 record as a collegiate head coach and later held a variety of roles with the Yankees including coordinator of minor league instruction, player development/ scouting director, vice president of player development and scouting and senior VP of baseball operations.

■ **KATSUYA NOMURA,** a Japanese baseball Hall of Famer who played in the Pacific League for 26 seasons, died Feb. 11 in Tokyo.

Nomura was one of the greatest offensive catchers in Japanese history and finished his career with 657 home runs and 1,988 RBIs to go along with 2,901 hits. In 1965, he won the Pacific League triple crown and hit .320 with 42 home runs and 110 RBIs. He finished his career with five MVP awards.

Nomura also served as a manager for 24 seasons, some of which overlapped with his playing career. He posted a 1,565-1,563 career record with four different teams and won three Japan Series championships for the Yakult Swallows in the 1990s before retiring after the 2009 season.

■ **IRV NOREN,** an outfielder who played in the major leagues from 1950-60 for the Washington Senators, Yankees, Kansas City Athletics, Cardinals, Cubs and Dodgers died Nov. 15 in Oceanside, Calif. He was 94.

Noren was named to the 1954 all-star team and was a five-time World Series champion, twice as a player. He won two titles with the Yankees as a player in 1952 and '53 and thee with the Athletics where he served on the coaching staff from 1971-74.

In Noren's all-star season of '54, he hit .319 with 12 home runs and 66 RBIs while serving as a regular corner outfielder for the 103-win Yankees. Noren played in 1,093 games and ended his career with a .275/.348/.410 slash line.

■ **BOB OLIVER,** a first baseman, right fielder and third baseman who played in the major leagues for eight seasons with the Pirates, Royals, Angels, Orioles and Yankees in 1965 and from 1969-1975, died April 19 in Rio Linda, Calif. He was 77.

Oliver posted a .256/.295/.400 slash line with 94 home runs, 419 RBIs and 17 stolen bases in 847 games. In 1970 he hit 27 home runs for the Royals.

■ **BILL O'NEIL,** a catcher who played in the Red Sox organization from 1966-67, died Nov. 24 in Windsor Locks, Conn. He was 71.

■ **BILL OSTER,** a lefthander who pitched in the major leagues for the Athletics in 1954, died June 6. He was 87.

Oster pitched in eight games and 15.2 innings in his sole major league season, posting an 0-1, 6.32 record and striking out five batters.

■ **GEORGE PALATI,** who served in the U.S. Army Air Corps during World War II before playing in the minor leagues from 1946-49 and suiting up for the Cubs and Giants organizations, died Jan. 14 in Bridgewater, Mass. He was 98.

■ **LILLIAN PATTERSON,** who worked in Major League Baseball's Umpire Development program from 1992-97 before working for Minor League Baseball's Professional Baseball Umpire Corp from 1998-2017, died July 27. She was 71.

■ **PAUL PAVELKO,** an outfielder who played nine seasons in the minor leagues for the Tigers and Twins organization from 1962-70, died Feb. 5 in Bethlehem, Pa. He was 76.

■ **DON PAVLETICH,** a catcher and first baseman who played 12 seasons in the major leagues with the Reds, White Sox and Red Sox in 1957, 1959 and 1962-1971 after serving in the US Army, died March 5 in Brookfield, Wis. He was 81.

Pavletich played in 536 career games in the big leagues. He batted .254/.328/.420 to go along with 46 home runs and 193 RBI.

■ **REX PEARCE,** a multi-sport athlete at Mississippi and the Central Arkansas who played in the Southern Association for the White Sox organization in 1946 and the Longhorn League after service in World War II, died Nov. 12 in Nashville. He was 71.

■ **JOSE PERAZA,** who played in the California League for the Boston Braves as well as the Arizona-Texas, Gulf Coast and Mexican leagues from the 1940s to the '60s, died Nov. 4 in Mexico. He was 91.

■ **DAN PETERS,** who played in the Braves organization in 1956, died Aug. 22 in West Branch, Iowa. He was 82.

■ **CHARLES PETERSON,** a 1993 first-round pick who played in the minor leagues for six seasons, the Mexican League for two seasons and independent leagues for eight seasons before serving as a scout for the Cardinals since 2012, died Sept. 13. He was 46. Peterson signed Georgia high school third baseman Jordan Walker, the Cardinals' 2020 first-round pick.

■ **STEVE PETERSON,** a former catcher for Columbia State and Jacksonville State who later served as a head coach in college baseball for 31 years and posted a 944-733-3 record, died March 11 in Murfreesboro, Tenn. He was 68.

Peterson began his head coaching career at Roane State Community College in 1979, a post he occupied until the end of the 1984 season.

Peterson was named the head coach of Middle Tennessee St in 1987 and retired following the

2012 year. He posted a 791-637-3 record during that time, winning 11 regular-season conference titles, nine conference tournament titles and making nine NCAA Regional appearances. Peterson was inducted into the American Baseball Coaches Association Hall of Fame in 2016.

■ **EDWIN "ED" PETRAZZOLO,** who played in the Pennsylvania-Ontario-New York, Middle Atlantic and Eastern Shore leagues for the Yankees organization in 1943 and after service in the Army in World War II from 1946-47, died Nov. 20 in Staten Island, N.Y. He was 94.

■ **BIFF POCOROBA,** a catcher who played for the Braves from 1975-84 and made one all-star team in 1978, died May 24. He was 66. Pocoroba finished his career playing in 576 games, hitting 21 home runs and driving in 172 runs. He finished with a .257/.339/.351 slash line. In 1978 he hit .242/.312/.332 with six home runs and 34 RBIs.

■ **JOSEPH P. "JOE" POLAHA,** who played in the Central Association for the St. Louis Browns organization in 1948, died on Nov. 21 in Allentown, Pa. He was 91.

■ **DENNY POLAND,** a righthander who played in the minor leagues in 1961, died March 25 in Florida. He was 77.

■ **MARY PRATT,** who played in the All-American Girls Professional Baseball League from 1943-47, died May 6 in Bridgeport, Conn. She was 101. Pratt was the last known living member of the original Rockford Peaches team that she joined in 1943.

■ **DENNIS PUGH,** who served as head baseball coach at Cal State San Marcos from the program's birth in 2007 until 2016, died May 15 in Pacific Beach, Calif. He was 73.

■ **ROBERT QUINN,** a lefthander who pitched in the Athletics organization in 1955 and '56, died Aug. 12 in Doylestown, Pa. He was 87.

■ **RANDY QUINTRELL,** who was drafted by the Braves in the eighth round in 1973 but chose to play at Clemson, died July 23. He was 65.

■ **BOBBY LAMONTTE RAMSEY,** who played for the Yankees organization in 1949 and '50 and served in the Air Force, died Dec. 14 in Franklin, Tenn. He was 88.

■ **JOHN RECCO,** a first baseman who played in the minor leagues from 1944-1945 and from 1947-1951, died Sept. 1. He was 93.

■ **BOB REDDING,** who played in the minor leagues in 1949, died July 19 in Hedgesville, W.Va. He was 90.

■ **RICK REED,** who umpired in the major leagues from 1979-2009, died in July. He was 70.
Reed's long career included calling two All-Star Games and a World Series.

■ **KEN RETZER,** a catcher who played in the major leagues for the Washington Senators from 1961-64 and appeared in 237 games, died May 17 in Sun City, Ariz. He was 86.
Retzer hit .264/.316/.367 during his career and finished with 14 home runs and 72 RBIs.

■ **EDWARD EARL "ED" RICHARDSON,** who played in the minor leagues for the Dodgers, Orioles and Astros organizations from 1958 to '62, missing two seasons for military service, died Nov. 11 in Jasper, Ala. He was 86.

■ **PHIL RIZZO,** who played in the minor leagues from 1951-56 before becoming a successful scout, died Feb. 1. He was 90.
Rizzo served his son, Nationals general manager Mike Rizzo, as a senior advisor beginning in the 2009 season.

■ **JOE ROBERSON,** a righthander who pitched in the minor leagues for the Dodgers organization from 1954-56, died Jan. 13 in Grand Blanc, Mich. He was 84.
Roberson served as the athletic director for Michigan from 1994-97 and resided over the school's national championships in hockey, swimming and diving and football.

■ **ARTHUR EUGENE ROBINSON,** a righthander who played in the minor leagues in 1977 and '78, died Sept. 3 in New Orleans. He was 65.
Robinson was a member of the 1978 Visalia Oaks championship squad in the California League that finished with a 97-42 record. He led the circuit in multiple categories including average, home runs and runs.

■ **KELLY RODMAN,** a longtime scout for the Yankees, died March 4. She was 44.
After playing college softball at Eastern Connecticut State University, she joined the New England Women's Baseball League. Rodman, who

was hired by the Yankees in 2017, was one of three female scouts in major league baseball.

■ **BOB ROFFERS,** a lefthander who pitched in the minor leagues in 1961, died July 25 in Green Bay, Wis. He was 78.

■ **JEFFREY RUDOLPH,** a catcher, shortstop and righthanded reliever who played in the Yankees organization from 1979-1981, died Dec. 7 in Cocoa Beach, Fla. He was 62.

■ **EDWARD RULLMAN,** a catcher who served in World War II before playing in the minor leagues for four seasons from 1946-49, including stints with the Phillies, Indians and Braves organizations, died Jan. 3 in Clarksville, Tenn. He was 94.

■ **RICHARD "RICH" RUNDLES,** a lefthander who pitched for the Indians in 2008 and '09, died Dec. 16, in Livingston, Ala. He was 38.
Rundles appeared in nine games over two seasons with the Indians, striking out seven batters in six innings and finishing his career with a 1.50 ERA.
After his playing career ended, the son of West Alabama head baseball coach Gary Rundles joined the program as operations manager and pitching coach in the fall of 2017. Rundles was getting ready to begin his third season as pitching coach for the program.

■ **MIKE RYAN,** who played in the major leagues from 1964-74 with the Phillies, Red Sox and Pirates before serving as a major league coach and minor league manager, died July 7 in Wolfeboro, N.H. He was 78.
Ryan played in 636 games, hitting 28 home runs, driving in 161 and hitting .193/.252/.280.

■ **ELDRED "SALTY" SALTWELL,** who spent 50 years in professional baseball and 30 years with the Cubs organization including serving as the Cubs' general manager in 1976, died May 3. He was 96.

■ **WILLIAM "BILL" SAMS,** a righthander who played in the Reds organization in 1941 and with the Dodgers organization in '46 after serving in the U.S. Army Air Corps in World War II, died Jan. 8 in York, Pa. He was 96.

■ **WILLIAM SAAR,** who played in the minor leagues for the Dodgers organization in 1951 and in 1954 and '55 after serving in the Coast Guard in the Korean War, died Dec. 24. He was 87.

After his playing career ended, Saar served as a referee in the National Basketball Association for 22 years.

■ **ALVIN DWANE "AL" SANDERS,** who played in the Alabama-Florida, Georgia-Florida, Midwest and Carolina leagues for the Cardinals organization in 1953-and '54 and again from 1956-58 after serving in the Army during the Korean War, died on Nov. 8 in Lincoln, Ark. He was 85.

■ **LOU SCHWECHHEIMER,** the majority owner of the Pacific Coast League's Wichita Wind Surge who helped move the team from New Orleans before the 2020 season, died July 29. He was 62.

Schwechheimer spent the majority of his career with the Pawtucket Red Sox before helping bring the Marlins' Triple-A affiliate to Wichita.

■ **RICHARD SCOTT,** a lefthander who pitched for the Dodgers in 1963 and the Cubs in 1964, died Feb. 10 in Carrollton, Ga. He was 86.

Scott converted two saves in his big league career and pitched 16.1 innings across two seasons.

■ **TOM SEAVER,** a Hall of Fame righthander who won more than 300 games in his 20-year career, led the Mets to the 1969 World Series title and was a three-time Cy Young Award winner, died Aug. 31. He was 75.

Seaver is widely recognized as one of the greatest pitchers in history, having posted a 311-205, 2.86 mark with 3,640 strikeouts in 4,783 innings.

Seaver's other accolades include three ERA titles, 12 all-star appearances and being named the 1967 National League Rookie of the Year. Seaver ranks 18th on the all-time wins list, seventh in wins above replacement for pitchers at 106, 19th in innings and sixth in strikeouts.

Seaver appeared on 98.84% of Hall of Fame ballots in 1992, which stood as the record for 24 years.

■ **BOB SEBRA,** a righthander who pitched for six seasons in the major leagues for the Phillies, Expos, Rangers, Reds and Brewers, died July 22 in Miami. He was 58.

Sebra had a career 15-29, 4.71 mark in 94 appearances with one save. The righthander's best year was in 1986 for the Expos, when he went 5-5, 3.55 in 17 appearances (13 starts).

■ **DAN SEVERINO,** a righthander who pitched in the minor leagues in 1956 and '57, died July 24 in Centerville, Mass. He was 86.

■ **GEORGE SMITH,** who played in the Cardinals organization in 1950 and '51 and from 1954-56 and served in the Marine Corps, died April 15 in Mesa, Ariz. He was 88.

■ **JOHN IVORY SMITH,** a righthander who pitched for the Reds organization from 1954-1960, died Nov. 27 in Columbia, S.C. He was 85.

In 1955, Smith went 19-14, 3.66 in 253 innings for the Daytona Beach Islanders of the Florida State League.

■ **KEITH VIRGIL SPECK,** who played in the Yankees organization in 1949 and '50 and again from 1953-55 after serving in the Korean War, died Nov.12 in Fort Collins, Colo. He was 91.

According to Kansas-Oklahoma-Missouri League expert John Hall, Speck was the winning pitcher in Mickey Mantle's first game in Organized Baseball. They were teammates for the Yankees' Independence, Kan., affiliate in the KOML in 1949.

■ **GENE CLINE "CHEE CHEE" STATON,** who played in the Indians organization in 1952, died Nov. 3 in Hickory, N.C. He was 85.

■ **JOHN THOMAS STEFANIK,** who played in the Colonial, Carolina and Florida International leagues from 1948-52 after service in World War II, died Nov. 14 in Webster, Mass. He was 95.

■ **DONALD STEGER,** who played in the minor leagues from 1948-1950, died Aug. 26 in Horner, N.Y. He was 96.

■ **HANK STEINBRENNER,** who served as the Yankees' general partner for 13 years and co-chairperson of the team for 11 years, died April 14 in Clearwater, Fla. He was 63.

■ **DEAN STEINKOENIG,** who played in the minor leagues in 1957, died July 27 in Bloomington, Ill. He was 83.

■ **DEMPSEY STERLING,** a lefthander who pitched in the minor leagues from 1947-1951, died Dec. 27 in Nacogdoches, Texas. He was 92.

■ **HARRY STILLE,** who served as head baseball coach at Erskine College in South Carolina from 1959-88, died Jan 6. He was 90.

While serving as head coach at Erskine, Stille won more than 400 games and was inducted into the NAIA Hall of Fame.

He also served for many years as mayor of Due West, the town where Erskine is located and some of his time as mayor of the town overlapped with the years he served as coach.

After Stille retired from coaching, he served in the South Carolina General Assembly for 12 years.

■ **BOB STOVER,** who umpired in the minor leagues from 1978-81, died July 13 in Perrysburg, Ohio. He was 73.

■ **JOHN STROHMAYER,** a righthander who pitched for the Montreal Expos from 1970-73 and the Mets in 1973 and '74, died Nov. 28 in Redding, Calif. He was 73. Strohmayer finished his five-year career with an 11-9, 4.47 record and 200 strikeouts in 312.1 innings. He made 124 of his 142 career appearances in relief.

■ **BARRY SULLIVAN,** who played for the Pompano Beach Cubs of the Florida State League in 1977, died Dec. 22 in Providence. He was 65.

After his playing career ended, Sullivan served as head coach for the Bristol (Mass.) Community College baseball program in 1979.

■ **ED SZADO,** a lefthander who pitched in the minor leagues from 1970-75, died Aug. 8 in Springfield, Mass. He was 71.

■ **MATT SZYKOWNY,** a third baseman and second baseman who played in the minor leagues in 1963 and '64, died July 27. He was 79.

■ **DANNY TALBOTT,** a third baseman who played in the Orioles organization in 1967 and spent another season in the minor leagues in 1973, died Jan. 19 in Rocky Mount, N.C. He was 75. Talbott was a two-sport star in baseball and football at North Carolina and won the 1965 Atlantic Coast Conference player of the year as a quarterback. In 1966, he won ACC athlete of the year and was inducted into the North Carolina Sports Hall of Fame in 2003. In addition to playing baseball, he was selected in the 17th round of the 1967 NFL draft and played on the Washington Redskins' taxi squad.

■ **TONY TAYLOR,** a second baseman, third baseman and first baseman who played in the major leagues from 1958-76, including 15 years with the Phillies, three with the Cubs and three with the Tigers, died July 16 in Miami Lakes, Fla.

He was 84.

Taylor made the 1960 National League all-star team as a 24-year-old second baseman when he hit .287/.330/.370 with 24 stolen bases.

For his 19-year career, Taylor hit .261/.321/.352 with 2,007 hits, 86 triples, 75 home runs and 234 stolen bases.

■ **PAUL TESLA,** who played in the minor leagues in 1951, died Aug. 23. He was 93.

■ **BERT THIEL,** a righthander who appeared in four games for the Braves in 1952, pitched in the minor leagues from 1947-59 and in '61 and later managed in the minor leagues, died July 31 in Pella, Wis. He was 94.

■ **WALTER TOWNS,** who played for the Victoria Tyees of the Winter International League in 1952 and served in the Korean War, died Nov. 2 in Los Angeles. He was 87.

■ **JEFF VAN HOUTEN,** an outfielder, second baseman and third baseman who played in the minor leagues in 2005 and '06 and in independent leagues in 2008, died July 3. He was 37.

■ **CLAUDELL WASHINGTON,** an outfielder who played 17 seasons in the major leagues for the Braves, Yankees, White Sox, Athletics, Rangers, Angels and Mets from 1974-90, died June 10 in San Francisco. He was 65.

Washington debuted with Oakland at age 19 and made two all-star teams during a 17-year career. He signed a five-year, $3.5 million deal with Atlanta for 1981 that sent shockwaves through the industry at the time.

Washington hit .278/.325/.420 with 1,884 hits, 164 home runs, 824 RBIs and 312 stolen bases.

■ **JULIUS WATLINGTON,** who played for the Athletics in 1953 and played in the minor leagues in 1941 and from 1947-58, died Dec. 29, in Yanceyville, N.C. He was 97.

Watlington left professional baseball to serve in the Army in World War II and received a Purple Heart and the French Legion of Honor Award for combat veterans for his service.

Watlington finished his big league career with three RBIs and seven hits in 44 at-bats.

■ **BOB WATSON,** who played in the major leagues for 19 seasons from 1966-1984, including for the Astros from 1966-1979, before later serving as general manager of the Astros and Yankees, died May 14 in Houston. He was 74.

Watson finished his career with a .295/.364/.447 slash line, 184 home runs and 1,826 hits. Watson made two all-star teams, in 1973 and 1975, and finished 11th in National League MVP voting in 1976, when he hit .313/.377/.458 with 16 home runs, 102 RBIs and 183 hits.

After serving as hitting coach for the Athletics in 1988 during the team's run to the World Series, Watson became the Astros' GM in 1993. He was hired by the Yankees for the same position in 1995 and won a World Series a year later, becoming the first black GM to accomplish the feat. He also served as a vice president with Major League Baseball from 2002-2010, focusing on rules and on-field operations.

■ **SAMUEL WATTLES,** an outfielder who played in the minor leagues in 1950 and '51, died July 3 in Meridian, Idaho. He was 93.

■ **RAY WEBSTER,** who played in 47 major league games in 1959 and '60 with the Indians and Red Sox, died June 3. He was 82.

Webster never appeared in the big leagues after his age-22 season, but hit two home runs and drove in 11 in 47 games.

Webster hit .195/.250/.325 for his career.

■ **JAMES WELLS,** a lefthander who pitched in the minor leagues from 1972-76, died July 21 in Cordele, Ga. He was 67.

■ **JOHN WHATCOTT,** a catcher who played in the minor leagues in 1957, died Sept. 5. He was 87.

■ **A.J. WHITE,** a righthander who pitched in the minor leagues in 1956 and from 1959-64, died July 26 in Carrollton, Ga. He was 86.

■ **CHARLES WILLARD WHITE,** who played in the minor leagues in 1963, died Nov. 25, in Aurora Fla. He was 78.

■ **DELORES BRUMFIELD WHITE,** a first baseman who played in the All-American Girls Professional Baseball League from 1947-52, died May 29 in Prescott, Ark. She was 88.

White was traded to the Fort Wayne Daisies in 1952, where she played for Hall of Fame first baseman Jimmie Foxx in her final season. She finished second on the team with a .332 average to conclude her career.

■ **RICHARD WILLIAMS,** an outfielder who played in the minor leagues in 1957 and '58, died Aug. 4 in Kingsport, Tenn. He was 81.

■ **WARD WILSON,** a righthander who pitched in the minor leagues from 1953-59, including seasons spent with the Tigers, Reds, Pirates and Washington Senators organizations, died Nov. 28 in Georgia. He was 84.

Wilson's son Ward Jr., a catcher and third baseman, played in the minor leagues in the Mets organization from 1975-78.

■ **BOBBY WINKLES,** whose lengthy coaching career at Arizona State included leading the Sun Devils to three College World Series championships, died April 17. He was 90.

Winkles coached at Arizona State from 1959-71, amassing a 524-173 record at the school and winning three CWS titles as ASU established itself as a national power. He was named NCAA coach of the year three times. Winkles went on to become a big league manager for the Angels in 1973 and '74 and the Athletics in 1977 and '78, finishing with a big league managing record of 170-213.

Prior to his coaching career, Winkles was a minor league shortstop from 1951-58 in the White Sox, Cubs and Phillies organizations..

■ **JIM WYNN,** an outfielder who played in the major leagues from 1963-77, including for the Astros from 1963-73 and also for the Dodgers, Braves, Yankees and Brewers, died March 26 in Houston. He was 78.

Wynn made three National League all-star teams during his 15-year career, in 1967, '74 and '75. He finished fifth in the 1974 MVP race, while playing for the Dodgers, after hitting 32 home runs, knocking in 108 runs and batting .271/.387/.497.

For his career, Wynn batted .250/.366/.436 with 291 home runs, 223 of which were hit for Houston. That total still ranks fourth in Astros franchise history behind Jeff Bagwell, Lance Berkman and Craig Biggio.

■ **EUGENE ZUBRINSKI,** a third baseman who played in the minor leagues from 1946-51 after serving in the navy during World War II, died July 8 in Framingham, Mass. He was 94.

■ **GEORGE ZURAW,** who played in the minor leagues from 1949-1951 and in 1954 and later served as a scout for the Reds, Pirates and Rays and as the assistant general manager for the Mariners, died April 24. He was 89. ■

MAJOR LEAGUES